THE APOSTLE OF THE FLESH

A CRITICAL LIFE OF CHARLES KINGSLEY

BRILL'S STUDIES IN INTELLECTUAL HISTORY

VOLUME 140

Charles Kingsley

THE APOSTLE OF THE FLESH
A CRITICAL LIFE OF
CHARLES KINGSLEY

BY

J.M.I. KLAVER

BRILL
LEIDEN · BOSTON
2006

Cover illustration: Drawing by Linley Sambourne
(*The Water-Babies*, Macmillan, 1886).

This book is printed on acid-free paper.

Library of Congress Cataloging-in-Publication Data

Klaver, J. M. I.
    The apostle of the flesh : a critical life of Charles Kingsley / by J.M.I. Klaver.
      p. cm. — (Brill's studies in intellectual history, ISSN 0920-8607 ; v. 140)
    Includes bibliographical references and index.
    ISBN 90-04-15128-1 (alk. paper)
    1. Kingsley, Charles, 1819-1875. 2. Authors, English—19th century—Biography. I.
Title. II. Series.

PR4843K57 2006
823'.8—dc22
[B]
                                      2005058235

ISSN   0920-8607
ISBN-13: 978-90-04-15128-4
ISBN-10: 90-04-15128-1

PRINTED IN THE NETHERLANDS

For Anna

CONTENTS

MUSCULAR CHRISTIANITY

SANITARY REFORM

ENEMIES

OLD AND NEW WORLDS

ACKNOWLEDGEMENTS

In writing this book I have incurred many debts. First of all I wish to acknowledge my indebtedness to the biographers who preceded me. Their research on Kingsley was, especially in its initial stages, very valuable to me. I would like to thank Ceil Brem of the Penrose Public Library, Colorado Springs, Sharon Peters of the Salt Lake City Public Library, Eleanor M. Gehres and Philip Panum of the Denver Public Library, Leah Davis Witherow, archivist at the Colorado Springs Pioneers Museum, and the staff of the London Library for their help in research for material. Timothy Gouldstone of the Diocese of Truro, Jeanine Klaver, Piero Toffano, Anthony Rew of Livermead House, Dan Kubick of the Omaha Public Library, and Jeff Korman of the Pratt Library Baltimore, all provided me with photocopies of rare publications. I wish also to express my thanks to Don Skemer, curator of manuscripts at the Princeton University Library, for giving me permission to microfilm their unpublished Kingsley manuscripts, to the staff at the British Library for providing me with microfilms of their collections of Kingsley papers, to Anne Barrett of Special Collections at Imperial College, London, for kindly arranging for photocopying from their Huxley papers, and to Mieke IJzermans for giving me access to the manuscript collections of the International Institute of Social History of the University of Amsterdam.

Over the years many people have given me advice and criticism on the manuscript. Special thanks are due to Alastair Hamilton, Roberta Mullini, William Rivière, and David Selbourne. I am very grateful for their valuable suggestions. I would also like to express my gratitude to the numerous people who have shared their knowledge of Kingsley with me. They include the members of the electronic discussion forum Victoria for 19th-century British culture and society hosted by Indiana University: Michelle Allen, Timothy Carens, Robert A. Colby, Sheldon Goldfarb, Thomas W. Goodhue, Jill Grey, Christopher Keirstead, Paul Lewis, Hugh MacDougall, Sally Mitchell, Penny Richards, Peter O'Neill, Jennifer Phegley, Patrick Scott, Amber Vogel, Stephen White, Ed Wiltse, Don Ulin; and the speakers at the Kingsley Study Day held in March 2002 at Liverpool John Moores University: Elaine Hartnell, Clare Horrocks, Nickianne Moody,

Tony Pinkney, Caroline Rose, Mike Sanders, Caroline Sumpter, Steve Woolfall. I would also like to thank all those with whom I discussed the various related matters that came up during the years that I did research for this biography: Robin Freeman, Michele Gelardi, Pietro Gattari, Paul Tucker, and Gioia Zaganelli.

Parts of chapter eight have appeared in a slightly different form in *Linguae &* 3 (2003) and parts of chapter nine in the *Dutch Review of Church History* 81 (2001). I wish to thank the publishers for granting me permission to re-use part of this material in this biography. I am also very grateful to Peter A.K. Covey-Crump and Anne Covey-Crump, who have generously given me permission to quote from the unpublished Kingsley correspondence.

Finally I would like to thank my editors Hendrik van Leusen, Brill's senior acquisitions editor, and Arjo Vanderjagt, editor of *Brill's Studies in Intellectual History*, for believing in my project the very moment they heard of it.

LIST OF ABBREVIATIONS

1) Manuscripts

The following manuscript collections have been used and are abbreviated as follows:

BL-62552–7	British Library Add. 62552–7: Correspondence, etc., of Charles Kingsley with his wife and family 1840–1874
BL-41297	British Library Add. 41297: Correspondence with F.D. Maurice
BL-41298	British Library Add. 41298: Correspondence and papers
BL-54911	British Library Add. 54911: Correspondence with Macmillan
MP-C0171	Morris L. Parrish Collection of Victorian Novelists, Princeton University Library C 0171: Miscellaneous Correspondence of Charles Kingsley
L-BC	Brotherton Collection at Leeds University Library: Gosse Correspondence
IC	Imperial College: T.H. Huxley Papers
IISH	International Institute for Social History, Amsterdam University Library: Letters from Thomas Cooper to Charles Kingsley

Correspondents

AS	Augustus Stapleton
CB	Charles Bunbury
CK	Charles Kingsley
FDM	Frederick Denison Maurice
FK	Fanny Kingsley (née Grenfell)
JB	John Bullar
JL	John Ludlow
JM	John Martineau
MK	Mary Kingsley (née Lucas)
PHG	Philip Henry Gosse
RP	Richard Powles

TH   Thomas Hughes
THH   Thomas Henry Huxley
WC   William Cope

2) Printed sources

Works

The standard edition of the Kingsley's works is the 28 volumes of Macmillan's *The Works of Charles Kingsley* (1879–1885). For references which are not to this uniform edition further bibliographic information has been provided between parentheses. The following abbreviations have been used:

AL	*Alton Locke*
AL¹	*Alton Locke 1st edn.* (repr. in *Oxford World Classics*, ed. Elizabeth Cripps, Oxford, Oxford University Press, 1983).
AtL	*At Last*
D	*Discipline*
G	*Glaucus* (5th edn.)
G¹,³,⁴	*Glaucus* 1st edn. (Macmillan 1855); 3rd edn (Macmillan 1856); 4th edn. (Macmillan 1859).
GNOG	*The Good News of God*
GPD	*The Gospel of the Pentateuch and David*
H	*Hypatia*
Herm	*The Hermits*
Heroes	*The Heroes*
HLE	*Historical Lectures and Essays*
HW	*Hereward the Wake*
LGLE	*Literary and General Lectures and Essays*
LML i,ii	*Charles Kingsley: His Letters and Memories of his Life*, ed. by Frances Kingsley, 2 vols. (Henry King: London 1877)
LMLM	*Charles Kingsley: His Letters and Memories of his Life*, ed. by Frances Kingsley (Macmillan: London 1895)
LMLM i.ii	*Charles Kingsley: His Letters and Memories of his Life*, ed. by Frances Kingsley, 2 vols. (Macmillan: London 1901)
MHLW	*Madam How and Lady Why*
P	*Poems*
P^{PE}	*Poems* (Macmillan Pocket Edition, London, (1889) 1907)

PI	*Prose Idylls*
PP	*Plays and Puritans*
RT	*The Roman and the Teuton*
SFT	*Sermons for the Times*
SLE	*Scientific Lectures and Essays*
SONS	*Sermons on National Subjects*
SSE	*Sanitary and Social Essays*
TS	*The Tutor's Story* (New York: Dodd, Mead, 1916)
TW	*True Words for Brave Men* (London: Kegan Paul, Trench, London, 1886)
TYA	*Two Years Ago*
VSTCS	*Village Sermons And Town and Country Sermons*
WB	*The Water-Babies*
WH	*Westward Ho!*
WOL	*The Water of Life*
WS	*Westminster Sermons*
WTDNM?	*What, Then, Does Dr, Newman Mean?* in John Henry Newman, *Apologia pro vita sua*, ed. by William Oddie (London: J.M. Dent, 1993)
Y	*Yeast*
Y^F	*Yeast; or, The Thoughts, Sayings, and Doings of Lancelot Smith, Gentleman* (*Fraser's Magazine*: July–Dec. 1848)

Journals

ChSoc	*The Christian Socialist: A Journal of Association*
PolP	*Politics for the People*

LIST OF ILLUSTRATIONS

INTRODUCTION

Charles Kingsley was born almost two centuries ago. Today his is a much-forgotten name in Victorian Literature and he is very rarely read out of the academic circle. This was not so when Kingsley died in 1875 after an energetic career lasting 35 years as one of England's leading voices as poet, novelist, social reformer, churchman and historian. *The Times* in its obituary lamented that "perhaps he will be none the less regretted that he had accomplished so much of the task he set himself; that he has left the stamp of a vigorous individuality on English society and English literature"and that his works "were invaluable as a protest against sickly sentimentality and morbid sensationalism, which were the snares and vices of some of his most popular contemporaries."[1]

Kingsley's fame remained high for another forty years until the First World War. His books went through numerous reprints and Macmillan issued a 28-volume complete works. Frances Kingsley's huge *Life* of her husband was a popular Victorian biography, which appeared on both sides of the Atlantic in various abridged forms. Expensively bound editions of *The Water-Babies* were popular as prize gifts at schools, and it has captured the imagination of a host of professional illustrators. The book, by now a classic, has never been out of print. It was with the advent of Modernism, however, that Kingsley's Victorian sermonizing and masculinity fell out of fashion. Some of his books were denigrated, a few were relegated to the status of children's literature. Although numerous editions of his novels have continued to come out, until recently Kingsley was hardly taken seriously. Now, however, critics and historians increasingly begin to see Kingsley as an eminent thinker and reformer of his time, and his complex struggle to work out the relationship between sexuality, Christianity, and society has commanded respect. But if a reappraisal of Kingsley's literary work is in full swing, a complete reassessment of his life has not been undertaken.

---

[1] "Death of Charles Kingsley," *The Times* 25 January, p. 9e.

Kingsley's life was an eventful one. His evangelical upbringing made it difficult for him to accept his sexual urges, which resulted, while at university, in a period marked by dissipation and religious doubt till he met his future wife, Fanny. Their courtship was romantic, erotic, and religious at the same time. In marriage Kingsley reconciled his sexuality with his spirituality in a way which he thought was acceptable to Christianity. To sublimate the marriage bond, he also decided to become a man of the cloth. Kingsley settled in the parish where he would stay for the rest of his life, and it was here that he wrote his first literary work, *The Saint's Tragedy*. With this closet play Kingsley produced a powerful plea against celibacy.

By 1848 a profound awareness of the social evils of his time had emerged in Kingsley's thinking. He became involved in the Chartist movement, and was active in social reform with a group of ardent young men led by the Anglican divine Frederick Denison Maurice. They would be known as the Christian Socialists. Kingsley's direct knowledge of the working classes in London stimulated the writing of his propaganda novel *Alton Locke*, in which he addressed his views of individual freedom for the Christian believer, and gave an answer to Thomas Carlyle's prophetic warnings. His liberal attitude to sex and religion on the one hand, and his socialist ideas on the other, had made him numerous enemies both in the church and among the "respectable" middle classes. Ferocious attacks against him appeared in the press, and under this pressure the Christian Socialist Movement disintegrated.

Kingsley had never abandoned his crusade against celibacy, but in the years 1852–55 it assumed a new dimension. Kingsley made the *body* the central theme, first in his poetry, and then in his fiction. In his famous novels *Hypatia* and *Westward Ho!* Kingsley presented his views in such vigorous and startling language that critics started calling him "the apostle of the flesh," while the physical violence in his poems and novels drew attention to the "muscular" element of his Christianity.

After the success of *Westward Ho!* Kingsley suffered a period of depression which paralysed his creative powers. It is significant that at this stage he turned to children's literature with *The Heroes*. These tales, however, can also be read against Kingsley's stand on celibacy. When he became a literary lion and started to withdraw from controversial social activities, his friends of the Christian Socialist years distrusted him increasingly. His next novel, *Two Years Ago*, in which he concentrated on sanitary reform, did little to reverse this tendency. Especially his justification of the British reprisals following the Indian Mutiny in 1857 found little sympathy with his old friends John Ludlow and Thomas Hughes. The end of the decade saw Kingsley involved in *The Origin of Species* debate. He exchanged numerous letters with Thomas Henry Huxley on the subject and became a champion of evolution.

The early 1860s were a period in Kingsley's life which is marked by the great number of enemies he made. He was further estranged from the Christian Socialists during the American Civil War, because he sustained the Southern States. His appointment as Professor of Modern History at the University of Cambridge was much derided, and when he joined the Eyre Defence Committee in 1865, he lost the respect of such eminent thinkers as John Stuart Mill and Thomas Henry Huxley. But his reputation suffered most of all in the disastrous dispute with John Henry Newman. Notwithstanding the exuberant quality of *The Water-Babies*, which he wrote during this period, the early sixties were dark years for Kingsley.

Kingsley's ecclesiastical preferment came late. His last years were divided between his duties as Dean of Chester and Dean of Westminster and his travels to the Americas. His travel book *At Last* was based on his experiences in the Carribean. His lecture tour in the United States in 1874 was followed step by step by the local press, and testifies to the extent of his fame in America. In 1875 Kingsley died prematurely at the age of 55.

Kingsley's life has long held the interest of readers. He was a public figure who was listened to. And there were very few issues of Victorian society on which he did not pronounce himself. His energetic and courageous reactions to important questions such as emancipation, sexuality, religion, evolution, slavery, patriotism, socialism, and hygiene make him a Victorian of great interest. At times he may seem predictable, at times exasperating in his contradictions. But, even for a modern reader, he is never disappointing.

In 1877 Mrs Kingsley published a lengthy two-volume biography of her late husband. It no doubt catered to the late Victorian demand for memorial biographies of eminent figures, and like so many late Victorian lives it was inevitably subjective. At the same time, notwithstanding Mrs. Kingsley's discretion, the biography described such an intense relationship between Kingsley and his wife that contemporary readers were struck by it. Numerous passages in the quoted letters revealed with a startling frankness the nature of Kingsley's inner feelings, both sexual and religious. They were enough to create a lasting interest in Kingsley's persona.

Five biographies appeared in the one hundred years following Mrs Kingsley's memorial volumes. In 1931, after the death of Kingsley's youngest daughter, the Kingsley family papers, on which Mrs Kingsley's biography had been based, were made available to Margaret Thorp. Working from these in 1937 she published her *Charles Kingsley 1819–1875*. Her biography corrected many of Mrs Kingsley's distortions. Ten years later, Una Pope-Hennessy saw much new material, which helped her to add more psychological depth to Kingsley's character than Thorp had managed to do. The inclusion of some of Kingsley's drawings in her *Canon Charles Kingsley* (1948) caused something of a sensation. However, the growing collections of letters that continued to come to light soon made a new biography necessary. In the early 1950s Robert Bernard Martin started working on an edition of Kingsley's correspondence, which he compiled up to 1856, but never published. His extended knowledge of Kingsley resulted in 1959 in his *The Dust of Combat*, a fine biography which remained the final word on Kingsley till the mid 1970s. In the occasion of the centenary of Kingsley death, two new biographies of Kingsley came out. Brenda Colloms' *Charles Kingsley: The Lion of Eversley* was an attempt to re-appraise the influence of Kingsley's ideas and actions on the social and political movements of his day, something she did well. What Colloms did not know, however, was that in 1974 about three hundred previously unknown letters between Kingsley and his wife had been made privately available to Susan Chitty. These letters were mainly love-letters which filled in many of the gaps that earlier biographers had left in the description of Kingsley's private character. For this reason, Chitty's account of Kingsley's life in *The Beast and the Monk* (antedating Colloms's by only a few months) has been seen by many historians and critics as the definitive biography.

Chitty's biography was a fine representation of Kingsley and deserves praise. Still, although Chitty was able to draw upon an unprecedented wealth of letters, serious scholarly objections can be brought against her work. The annotations and notes that reveal her sources are very imperfect. They make it extremely difficult to verify the facts she presents, and nobody seems to have done so on a significant scale. Checking her quotations against the originals one can find, for example, that at times she joins quotations which are years apart without informing the reader. Moreover, she often misquotes, and she rewords whole passages (while presenting them as Kingsley's) so as to make them more fluent. Because most of the letters Chitty used were then in private hands, the quotations from Kingsley's letters have been accepted rather uncritically by academics as they stand in her book, and corrupt passages have been reproduced in many studies. Moreover, the illustrious historian of the Victorian church Owen Chadwick had serious reservations about the way Chitty represented her subject. Although helpful in contributing to a fuller understanding of Kingsley, it remained to him a "one-sided biography about home and family and passion." "To understand Kingsley," Chadwick stressed, "you must take him as a whole."[2] It was this assessment of Chitty's work which originally convinced me of the need for a new Kingsley biography.

In this book I have tried to write a detailed intellectual biography which is at the same time a critical and contextual study. All Kingsley's literary and religious works are taken into account, especially as these are exceptionally closely related to his personal ideas and experiences. Generally working from the original manuscript letters, I have throughout placed the events of Kingsley's life against a social-historical-religious background. Analyses of Kingsley's relationships with important contemporaries such as James Anthony Froude, Frederick Denison Maurice, Thomas Hughes, George Henry Lewes, Philip Gosse, Thomas Huxley, John Colenso, Robert Chambers, Thomas Carlyle, John Stuart Mill, and many others are given ample space. Much attention has been paid to how Kingsley was affected by such main mid-nineteenth-century themes as geological discoveries, the Oxford Movement, biblical Higher Criticism, Chartism, sanitary reform, the Crimean War, the Indian Mutiny, Darwinism, the American Civil War, and the anti-slavery campaigns. Extensive use has been made of previously unexplored material, such as Kingsley's sermons, essays, *Glaucus*, *The Hermits* and *At Last*, as well as texts not included in the Complete Works, such as the serial *Yeast*, and his writings for *Politics for the People* and *The Christian Socialist*. New influences

---

[2] *The Historical Journal*, 1975, p. 320.

on Kingsley's more famous works are explored, and special emphasis has been given to themes on which previous biographies have
remained relatively silent, such as, for example, Darwinism and the
Newman controversy. Kingsley's famous encounter with Newman in
1863 is recast as the final outcome of a life-long discussion on celibacy
on Kingsley's part, explaining why Kingsley reacted in the way he did.

THE DEVIL AND THE FLESH

CHAPTER ONE

SEMI-SENSUAL DELIGHTS OF EAR AND EYE
(1819–1838)

In the spring and early summer of 1819 a young woman could be seen daily walking on the verge of Dartmoor around Holne, taking in the scenery of the moors towards the west, and of the chase to the River Dart towards the east. High up on the moor she delighted in the windy walks leading up to Leigh Tor, while down in the valley she marvelled at the river which foamed over its rocky bed between steep banks covered by lofty woods of gnarled trees, and her imaginative and poetic mind would dwell on the Barbados where she had been raised, on the child she was bearing, and on the life she had before her.

Mrs Kingsley reports in the *Letters and Memories* of her late husband that his mother walked the verge of Dartmoor "keenly alive to the charms of scenery" because "she believed that impressions made on her own mind, before the birth of her child for whose coming she longed, by the romantic surroundings of her Devonshire home, would be transmitted to him." She "gave herself up to the enjoyment of every sight and sound which she hoped would be dear to her child in after life."[1] It is a natural starting point for a biography of Charles Kingsley. Later in life he stated that he "firmly believe[d] in the magnetic effect of the place where one has been bred [...] The thought of the West Country will make me burst into tears at any moment."[2] The soft climate of south Devon and the ragged cliffs of its north coast would often be a refuge for an embattled spirit and a haven of peace for an overworked mind to which to retire from a far too energetic public life.

---

[1] *LML* i.4.
[2] *LMLM* i.3.

II

Charles Kingsley was born on 12 June 1819, in Holne, a small parish three and a half miles west of Ashburton in south Devon. The Kingsleys claimed to be descendants of the ancient Kingsleys of Kingsley near Delamere Forest. When in later life he became Canon of Chester, Charles Kingsley said at a meeting of the Archeological Society there that his "feeling in coming to Chester was that he was coming home, for although he was landless, his ancestors had not been." Proud here, as in other instances, of the Kingsley pedigree, Kingsley quoted from an old Tarporley hunting song:

> In right of his bugle and greyhounds to sieze
> Waif, pannage, agistment, and wind-fallen trees;
> His knaves through our forest Ralph Kingsley dispersed,
> Bow-bearer-in-chief to Earl Randall the First.[3]

The vigour expressed in this song appealed to Kingsley. He equally gloried "in the *morale*, the God-fearing valour and earnestness of the old heroes" who were his ancestors and who fought with Cromwell and then left as Pilgrim Fathers for America:

> My forefathers [. . .] fought by Cromwell's side at Naseby and Marston Moor; and what is more, lost broad acres for their Puritanism. The younger brother of an ancestor of mine was one of the original Pilgrim fathers.[4]

More recently the Kingsley family had still possessed considerable property. Judging from the wills, Charles's great-grandfather, Charles Kingsley of London, was able to dispose of a farm in York, an estate, Kingsley House near Canterbury, and other unspecified property, including two farms in Kent. Charles's paternal grandfather, Charles Kingsley of Canterbury, had considerably less to leave to his heirs. His will merely mentions one house and further some china, plate, jewels, pictures and printed books, and linen worked by his mother.[5] He died in 1786 when his son, Charles, was only five years old. When this son, the novelist's father, became an orphan at this early age, he was still reported to be of independent means, "brought up

---

[3] *LML* ii.320.
[4] CK to unnamed correspondent, 17/2/1857, *LML* ii.24.
[5] Pink (1914) 93–4.

with fair expectations as a country gentleman," keenly alive to field sports and natural history. He was educated at Harrow and Oxford, but his guardians mismanaged the funds, and what remained when he came of age was steadily spent. Thus at the age of thirty the novelist's father had to look for a profession, and, because he felt too old for the army, opted for the church. He entered his name to read for holy orders at Trinity College, Cambridge.

When Charles was born the family lived in the rectory at Holne where Charles's father officiated in its thirteenth-century church with a stunted tower. Within six weeks, however, the family moved first to Burton-on-Trent, then to Clifton in Nottinghamshire and later in 1824 to Barnack. It was in Barnack, with its proximity to the Fen country, that Kingsley got his first impressions of nature, which, as is apparent from the opening passages of "The Fens," stimulated a sense of mysterious awe in him: "And yet the fancy may linger, without blame, over the shining meres, the gold reed-beds, the countless water-fowl, the strange and gaudy insects, the wild nature, the mystery, the majesty—for mystery and majesty there were."[6] Although Kingsley always saw Devon as his home county, it was not until 1830 that the family returned there.

Kingsley's father was an "old type of English clergyman."[7] His son described him as "a magnificent man in body and mind" with a passion for knowledge. He had a special interest in languages, and possessed a well-stocked library. "[He] was said to possess every talent," Charles qualified, "except that of using his talents." Before reading for orders he spent most of his time painting and hunting, but even after entering the church he remained a keen sportsman who took his sons with him on shooting days and thus stimulated their "fighting blood."[8] He also inspired a profound love of nature in Charles, who fifty years later vividly remembered a scene which by then had long since disappeared, a landscape where "dark-green alders, and pale green reeds, stretched for miles round the broad lagoon, where the coot clanked, and the bittern boomed, and the sedge-bird, not content with its sweet song, mocked the notes of all the birds around; while high overhead hung, motionless, hawk beyond

---

[6] "Chalk-Stream Studies" *PI* 89.
[7] *LMLM* i.7.
[8] *LML* i.5.

hawk, buzzard beyond buzzard, kite beyond kite, as far as eye could see."[9] Notwithstanding these influential characteristics which the father handed on to the son, it was mainly his mother's temperament that Kingsley saw as "the most important hereditary peculiarity in his character." She was descended from a family of planters in the West Indies, and Charles felt her colonial blood run in his veins: he once mentioned "that he revelled in the Tropics, as in a climate congenial to his nature."[10] He also believed that his mother formed his sense of poetry and his sense of humour, and that she conveyed a practical view of life to him. Indeed, she was much more businesslike than her husband, and, apart from the pulpit, ran all the parish work for him.[11]

His maternal grandfather, Nathan Lucas, also spent a lot of time with the boy, and stimulated his imaginative powers. He was a good story-teller and had many wonderful stories to tell, in which Charles delighted. Lucas had been a great traveller and was intimate with Sir Joseph Banks and other scientific men of his time. He had been a judge in Barbados, and possessed estates in Demerara. His stories of the West Indies instilled a sense of the exotic in the boy which was to re-emerge in his novels in later life. His stories of tropical scenes are recalled in Kingsley's travel book *At Last* in 1871: "I had heard and read much, from boyhood, about these 'Lesser Antilles'. I had pictured them to myself a thousand times."[12] Lucas's presence in "the land of waters" coincided with the Napoleonic Wars when the British occupied what was then Dutch territory. He was on board *HMS Formidable* when his friend Lord Rodney destroyed seven French ships of war in 1782 in the battle off St Lucia. Accounts of such feats were greedily listened to by the young Charles, who might have had them in mind when he described the sea battles in *Westward Ho!*. As an estate owner, moreover, Lucas was directly confronted with slavery. Although the slave trade was abolished in Guyana in 1807, it took more than thirty years before its 100,000 slaves were fully emancipated. Later, Kingsley's views of Rajah Brooke's interventions in Sarawak and his sympathy for the Southern States dur-

---

[9] "The Fens" *PI* 96.
[10] Francis Galton to FK, 24/12/1875, *LML* i.6.
[11] Ludlow (1981) 132.
[12] *AtL* 26.

ing the American Civil War, were directly influenced by what his grandfather had told him about slavery.

Kingsley's first religious experiences took place at Barnack. Mrs Kingsley has recorded how the four-year-old Charles would create a pulpit in his nursery, arrange the chairs as an imaginary congregation, put on his pinafore as a surplice, and hold forth as a preacher. Such a game, by no means uncommon in those days,[13] was of course inspired by his father's sermons, and a specimen written down by his mother reveals a series of commonplaces of the evangelical pulpit with its emphasis on righteous behaviour and punishment for sin, of which the final passage runs as follows:

> Religion is reading good books, doing good actions, and not telling lies and speaking evil, and not calling their brother Fool and Raca. And if we rebel against God, He will certainly cast us into hell. And one day, when a great generation of people came to Christ in the Wilderness, he said, Yea ye generation of vipers![14]

As he grew up, much time was spent in the nursery at Barnack, playing with his younger brothers Herbert and Gerald, who were one and two years younger respectively. They got on well together, although, of course, quarrels occasionally arose. On one such occasion his mother intervened and took Herbert and Gerald's part. Charles greatly resented this and expressed his wish that she were not his mother. Remorse quickly followed, and he burst out crying. A certain religious consciousness had been instilled in the boy which at times bordered on the morbid. Thus, when the housemaid tried to convince him that his mother would surely forgive him, he exclaimed: "She *has* forgiven me, but don't *cant*, Elizabeth [. . .] It isn't mamma's forgiveness I want but God's."[15]

As a child Charles was delicate and tense. He suffered much from dangerous attacks of croup, a children's disease caused by an infection of the area of the vocal cords and characterized by coughing, hoarseness, and difficult breathing. Calomel (mercury chloride) was administered in those cases, and in later life Charles attributed to the frequent taking of this medicine a reclining lower jaw on which

---

[13] F.A. Iremonger calls it "a commonplace of ecclesiastical biography," in Paul Ferris, *The Church of England* (Harmondsworth: Penguin, 1964) 49.

[14] *LML* i.9.

[15] *LML* i.11.

he blamed his life-long stammer. It is more likely that the affliction of croup initially contributed to Charles's developing a habit of stammering, and that his parents, who would tactlessly remark upon it whenever it occurred, made the boy unnecessarily self-conscious of his expressions of speech. As a result, the boy worried about vexing his parents and became increasingly tense, which, of course, aggravated the stammer and made it impossible to conquer the defect in the long run.[16]

The curacy at Barnack was only temporary, and had been given to Charles's father by the Bishop of Peterborough, a man whom he had met during his studies at Cambridge, upon the understanding that it had to be vacated when the latter's son was ordained. Thus when that time arrived in 1830, the family had to move again. Charles's father had lately been suffering from ague and was advised to move to a warmer and drier climate. While staying at Ilfracombe on the north Devon coast, Sir James Hamlyn Williams happened to be looking for a curate for the living of Clovelly, a small fishing community west of Bideford. Charles's father accepted the curacy and when the rector died the following year, he was appointed to the post himself. Much of Charles's years of adolescence was thus spent on rough north-Devon cliffs.

III

Clovelly is situated opposite Ilfracombe on the south cliffs of Bideford Bay, and, as by land travellers had to go round the whole Taw estuary, the easiest way to get from one place to the other in those days was by crossing the Bay. The Kingsleys, therefore, moved to Clovelly by boat. As they approached, they had a good view of the village as it lay against the cliffs in an irregular row of white houses with grey slated roofs along one narrow street, or rather, a "paved stairs inaccessible to cart or carriage." Crawling up "Clovelly-street" to the Rectory, they saw behind them "a sheer descent, roof below roof, at an angle of 45°, to the pier and the bay, 200 feet below, and in front, another hundred feet above, a green amphitheatre of oak and

---

[16] CK to JB, 27/1/1857, *LML* ii.18.

ash, and larch, shutting out all but a narrow slip of sky."[17] The Rectory was a spacious eighteenth-century building on three floors with a surrounding lawn. It had a coach house and stables, and the 'semi-exotic' woods beyond were paradise for the children to play in. Charles and his brothers had their own ponies to explore the wooded cliffs, with beneath on their left the "wooded valleys, lawns spotted with deer" and on their right, from their "very feet, the sea spread out to the horizon."[18] Charles's sister Charlotte (who was five years younger than Charles and who in later life would return to Clovelly as the wife of its incumbent, John Mill Chanter) records, in a novel which otherwise does not contain much autobiographical information or local colour, how as a child she "would crawl on her hands and knees, to the edge of the most precipitous part of the cliff, and, dropping a stone over, send the wild sea-birds screaming from the nest they had built in the little chinks and crannies of the rock, making the black cormorant, who had been standing on some jagged rock in the sea, take wing, and sail past with his long neck out-stretched, looking like some messenger from a darker world."[19]

The country around Clovelly was full of ancient ruins that testified to a long and varied history. The furze-grown ruins of a Roman camp made Charles dream of its 10,000 stalwart men and of the Roman tribune in his house on the edge of Hartland Cliffs, which in the 1830s was "tumbling into the sea, tesselated pavement, baths and all."[20] Then there were the stunted oaks on White Cliff, which seemed like two huge cannons, and its "ring of turf-covered stones," allegedly the remains of an old watchtower where a Norman squire kept his fair lady.[21] In Clovelly church there were tablets which told the tale of those glorious Tudor days whose heroes were to feature twenty-five years later in Kingsley's bestselling novel *Westward Ho!*—and which enticed visitors from all over the world to come to Clovelly and "linger fondly over [the] one" to the memory of a Cary who died in 1652. An American visitor records in 1884 how, as he was looking at Carey's tomb, a "thoroughly incapable" old man, who

---

[17] "North Devon" *PI* 276–77.
[18] "North Devon" *PI* 287–88.
[19] Charlotte Chanter, *Over the Cliffs*, 2 vols, London: Smith, Elder, 1860, i.33.
[20] "North Devon" *PI* 278.
[21] "North Devon" *PI* 279.

had been cutting the daisied grass, came up to him and suddenly
became communicative: "Aye! That's him in Westward Ho! Will
Cary, he were called!"[22]

The new rector of Clovelly was much appreciated by the villagers,
as they saw in him essentially "a man, who, physically their equal,
feared no danger; and could steer a boat, hoist and lower a sail,
'shoot' a herring net, and haul a seine as one of themselves."[23]
Although the rough fishing life of Clovelly suited the rector's energetic nature, the daily life of the stalwart fishermen of the village
and their continuous struggle with the sea were also full of tragedy.
The constant presence of death had an enormous impact on Charles's
sensitive nature. Many a time, when a storm blew up, the rector
and his family would rush down to the pier to pray with the women
and children for their husbands and fathers out at sea. He witnessed
many shipwrecks, and many an old schoolfellow drowned. Vivid
memories of "shrieking women and old men casting themselves on
the pebbles in fruitless agonies of prayer, as corpse after corpse swept
up at the[ir] feet"[24] would often come back to Charles in later life,
memories of his "especial pet and bird-nesting companion [. . .] cold
and stiff, the little soul beaten out of him by the cruel waves,"[25] and
memories of ships of which "every plank and joint strained and
screamed with the dreadful tension" till "a dull, thunderous groan,
as if a mountain collapsed, rose above the roar of the tempest."[26] It
is this that formed the background to one of his most famous lyrics,
"The Three Fishers."

The stunning coastal scenery of Devon was very different from
the flat Fen Country. The sea itself was at once inspiring and awful
as "at every rush of the long ground-swell, mysterious mutterings,
solemn sights, sudden thunders, as of a pent-up earthquake, boom
out of them across the glassy swell."[27] The new fauna and flora of
the West country fascinated all the Kingsleys. The children would
venture out on the bay with their own boat. Conchology was taken

---

[22] L.H.M. Soulsby, "Charles Kingsley's Clovelly", *Overland Monthly and Out West*,
4(20), 1884, pp. 195–99 (p. 198).
[23] *LML* i.17.
[24] "North Devon" *PI* 297.
[25] "North Devon" *PI* 298.
[26] "North Devon" *PI* 296.
[27] "North Devon" *PI* 237.

up, and with their father they trawled for shells, which were ardently collected and classified. Finds and information were exchanged with Dr Turton of Bideford, a physician who had edited Linnaeus' *Systema naturae* and who was working on a manual of the shells of Britain at the time when the Kingsleys moved to North Devon.

The typically Victorian urge to collect and to classify revealed a perfect system of creation in which everything had its fixed place and function. The early nineteenth-century saw nature in the light of natural theology as the *vox dei in rebus revelata*, and as such it was proper for a clergyman (and his family) to investigate nature in a scientific sense. Many of the great scientists of the period were, in fact, men of the cloth. That the Kingsleys were often engaged in collecting scientific specimens becomes clear from various references to scientific details in contexts where they are least expected. A famous and much quoted instance is when, as a boy having a Latin lesson from his father, Kingsley, whose eyes had wandered to the fire, exclaimed: "I do declare, papa, there is pyrites in the coal."[28]

IV

In Clovelly the children did not initially go to school. They had their own private tutor at home, but in 1831 the rector thought it would be a good idea to send Charles and Herbert, twelve and eleven years of age, to a preparatory school before entering their names at Eton or Rugby the following year. The Rev. William Knight's school at Clifton on the outskirts of Bristol seemed just right, and the boys changed their wild outdoor-life for the city. Charles felt shy in the company of the other boys, and often took refuge with Knight's daughters and their governess. Knight remembered him as an affectionate and gentle boy who was "fond of quiet."[29] The change of life did not seem to have agreed with Charles, and may even have been traumatic. Out of the protected family circle Charles had to measure himself against his peers, who teased him about his speech defect. By this time it had become "so sore a trial to him that he seldom entered a room, or spoke in private or

---

[28] *LML* i.11.
[29] *LML* i.20.

public without a feeling, at moments amounting to terror, when he said he could have wished the earth would open and swallow him up there and then."[30] Nature became ever more a sanctuary, and he carefully treasured everything he found during his walks on the Downs, till most of his collection was one day thrown away as rubbish by the handmaid.

Other records of this brief period at Clifton are extremely scarce, except for one event which left an indelible mark on Kingsley's young mind. Earlier in 1831, Lord John Russell had introduced a far-reaching bill of reform to redistribute the electoral districts. Although the bill initially led to a fall of government, Russell's Whigs, who, after a general election with a larger majority in Parliament, brought forward a second bill, managed to get it passed in the Commons in September. The people had been stirred up by future prospects of an enlarged franchise and better representation in Parliament, and the excitement around the elections had been great. But when the Lords rejected the bill, riots broke out in Nottingham and Derby against those who had obstructed it, amongst them the bishops. Kingsley heard of all this at Clifton, but did not pay much attention to the riots "of which I understood nothing, and for which I cared nothing." But unrest was brewing in Bristol as well, and three weeks after the decision in the Lords, on 30 October, on a Sunday afternoon of sullen autumn rain, he saw glaring through "the fog [which] hung thick over the docks and lowlands [. . .] a bright mass of flame." He was told that the prison was on fire and all its inmates set free. When the recorder of Bristol, the much-hated Sir Charles Wetherel, who had voted against the bill, had come the previous day to the city for the gaol delivery, a mob had besieged the Mansion House. The following day the situation got out of hand: the crowd marched on the Bishop's palace and the prison, and set fire to these and other public buildings. When the fog dispersed, a blazing horizon revealed itself to the boys at Clifton. "Right behind Brandon Hill [. . .] rose the central mass of fire [. . .] and dull explosions down below mingled with the roar of the mob, and the infernal hiss and crackle of the flame."[31] The scenario of destruction witnessed from a distance aroused excitement and wonder in Charles, and he slipped away from the school premises to have a closer look. He soon reached

---

[30] *LML* i.22.
[31] *SSE* "Great Cities, and their Influence for Good and Evil" 188.

the scenes of tumult and saw soldiers with blood streaming from their faces waiting for orders to charge, while the mob plundered, destroyed and burned everything they found on their way. When casks of spirits were broken open and their contents flowed down the street, he saw people drinking on their knees from the gutters till the liquid caught fire and turned the prostrate drunkards into a row of blackened "corpse fragments."[32] Slipping out again two days later, he saw other scenes of horror, which were never forgotten:

> Along the north side of Queen's Square, in front of ruins which had been three days before noble buildings, lay a ghastly row, not of corpses. But of corpse-fragments. I have no more wish than you to dilate upon that sight. But there was one charred fragment—with a scrap of old red petticoat adhering to it, which I never forgot—which, I trust in God, I shall never forget.

These riots seriously alarmed men of property, and the monster meetings that followed suit in London roused fears of a revolution. Although the peace was ultimately kept and the Reform Bill passed the following year, Kingsley maintained that the insurrection in Bristol made him for years the "veriest aristocrat, full of contempt of those dangerous classes, whose existence I had for the first time discovered,"[33] while at a later stage, when more mature thought had convinced him of social wrongs, he confessed it made him a Radical.[34] No doubt memories of the horror that he had witnessed as a boy during the Bristol Riots re-awakened his fear of crowds when he was confronted with the Chartist rising of 1848.

V

After a year at Knight's preparatory school at Clifton, Charles and Herbert were sent to Helston Grammar School in the west of Cornwall, a small private school which was then run by Derwent Coleridge, the poet's son. It is not clear why the Rev. Kingsley's choice of a school no longer fell on Eton or Rugby. The famous public schools might have been too expensive, and Dr Arnold's Broad

---

[32] JM to FK, 24/12/1875, *LML* i.307–8.
[33] *SSE* "Great Cities, and their Influence for Good and Evil" 190.
[34] JM to FK, 24/12/1875, *LML* i.308.

Church principles at Rugby might not have agreed with the Rev.
Kingsley's more conservative outlook.

Life at Helston was not easy at the beginning. Charles made few
friends and was not popular with the other boys, who found him
condescending. He knew too much and unconsciously snubbed those
who knew less. Moreover, he did not like games, and never exerted
himself in them. He preferred more solitary feats and activities, such
as bird-nesting or tramping the Cornwall cliffs for plants and minerals. In later life he remembered well how he tried to impress the
other boys by jumping from the play-ground wall to the brick wall
of the field on the other side of a deep road, which was a trial of
considerable "nerve and muscle [as] the walls, which were not quite
on a level, were rounded at the top, and a fall into the deep lane
must have involved broken bones."[35] But apparently this was not
enough to become popular. Charles was keenly sensitive to ridicule,
and his stammer made him feel shy in company. A fellow pupil
remembered how he had again and again "seen him chafed to intens-
est exasperation by [the other] boys."[36] He was tender hearted and
easily irritated when others did not understand him. His attitude
called for reaction and "he had often excessive provocation from
those who could not enter in his feelings." As a result he would
often withdraw to Coleridge's well-stocked library, where he was
found one day reading up on the Neoplatonist Greek philosophers
Porphyry and Iamblichus. Generally, it was outdoor life that inspired
him. He would come back to school radiantly happy after having
run after some pigs, and with blood trickling down his face torn by
brambles. On another occasion he climbed a tall tree to take eggs
from a hawk's nest, not knowing the bird was in it. The hawk
attacked the outstretched hand with ferocity, and the boy came down
with a wounded hand streaming with blood.

During the first months at Helston Charles depended much on
the company of his brother, a cheerful and extrovert boy. Although
Helston was only about 80 miles from Clovelly, the two boys stayed
in Cornwall for their Christmas holidays. Most of their schoolfellows
had gone home, and the two brothers spent most of the time together
on boyish exploits. When a new boy, Richard Cowley Powles, was

---

[35] RP to FK, 30/10/1875, *LML* i.25.
[36] RP to FK, 30/10/1875, *LML* i.26.

introduced to them early in January before the other boys had returned, they were found sitting at the far end of a table in a long dimly-lit room, engaged in a series of experiments with gunpowder. Powles immediately took to Charles, and they became friends. The second-master under Coleridge, the 22-year-old Charles Alexander Johns, was a keen botanist who would take boys out on walks. He soon noted Charles's deep-rooted passion for nature, and before long Charles would go on regular expeditions with his tutor, "hammer in hand and his botanical tin slung round his neck".

These friendships helped Charles to get through a most dramatic event. In the spring of 1834 his brother Herbert died suddenly. He had fallen ill with rheumatic fever, a streptococcal infection which can lead to inflammation of the heart muscle and consequent cardiac failure. It is now a rare disease, but it was still fairly common and often lethal a century and a half ago. The impression on the fifteen-year-old Charles can easily be imagined when he was called out of his class by Coleridge. The pupils heard a "cry of anguish" which they never forgot.

There is a curious silence about Herbert's death and nothing can be gleaned about the boy from Kingsley's writings or private letters, and even the grave in Helston only bears his initials. Susan Chitty reports that in 1975 a rumour still persisted in Helston that Herbert drowned himself in Loe Pool, an estuary south of Helston.[37] Strange things had evidently been going on in the boy in the months prior to his death. He had run away from school, having stolen a silver spoon which he sold and, after having spent a night in the open, was arrested by a bailiff who led him handcuffed back to school, where he was locked up in a room on bread and water. It was soon after this event that he fell ill with rheumatic fever. Although Chitty does not pronounce on Herbert's death, the suicide hypothesis seems supported by the absolute silence about Herbert from that moment on. Frequent death in the family was an everyday experience in the early nineteenth century and though painful was less of a taboo than it is today. Seeing how frankly Kingsley later confronted death and its grief, it does seem strange that this terrible moment was never referred to again. Still, if the rumour about Herbert's death is based on any real event, it might provide a striking key to the rather

---

[37] Chitty (1974) 45.

unsatisfactory and ambiguous drowning of Tom in the opening pages
of the *Water-Babies*. Tom's journey of regeneration starts when he is
thought to have come to Harthover House to rob and is chased
over the Yorkshire moors, sleeps out for a night, and falls into a
river in the valley and drowns. If such a reading is pertinent, the
language in which all this is described becomes revealing and dramatic: as the boy stumbles downhill "very footsore, and tired, and
hungry, and thirsty" church bells starts ringing out loud, as if they
were in his head, and the river chimes in:

> Strong and free, strong and free,
> The floodgates are open, away to the sea,
> Free and strong, free and strong,
> Cleansing my streams as I hurry along,
> To the golden sands, and the leaping bar,
> And the taintless tide that awaits me afar.
> As I lose myself in the infinite main,
> *Like a soul that has sinned and is pardoned again.*[38]

As he gets to the river, the ambiguity increases. It never becomes
clear whether Tom jumps or falls. To the people of Harthover who
chased him, there is no mistake about it—"and there, upon an alder
stump, they saw Tom's clothes lying. And then they knew as much
about it all as there was any need to know"[39]—and later "they found
a black thing in the water, and said it was Tom's body, and that
he had been drowned."[40] Still, the narrator never wants to endorse
such a view. For him it was because Tom was simply hot and thirsty,
and "longed so to be clean for once," that he went to bathe in the
clear cool stream. But, "he had not been in it two minutes before
he fell asleep, into the quietest, sunniest, cosiest sleep that ever he
had in his life."[41] Notwithstanding the light-hearted use of language
in the passage and the humour with which the pursuers are described,
the reader should not let such narrative deceive him. Uneasiness of
feeling is present, though well-hidden, in Sir John's words the next
morning when he admits that "he [Tom] lies very heavily on my
conscience."[42] The whole community had cried when Tom was dis-

---

[38] *WB* 48–9, my italics.
[39] *WB* 76.
[40] *WB* 88.
[41] *WB* 66.
[42] *WB* 71.

covered, and had put "a pretty tombstone over Tom's shell in the little churchyard,"[43] presumably without name and dates, as nothing could be discovered about Tom's parents.[44]

Life must have been bleak after Herbert's death, but Charles was to stay on at Helston. His friendship for Powles grew and soon they would become inseparable. Also the passion for natural history he shared with the second master was of lasting importance and they would continue to tramp the moors and the irregular coast line looking for plants, shells and minerals. Charles's enthusiasm for nature was duly reported in his letters home to his parents, samples of which in 1835 abound with descriptions of special finds at Helston and enquiries about species around Clovelly. This is to be found in the following passage from a letter to his mother, which shows that, even from a distance, he tried to involve all his family in his pursuits.

> I have just received your letter about the plants & I wish to tell you—that you must not send the new plant away without either finding me some more, or keeping one piece. I intreat you, get me a bit.—It can hardly be a arum & they ought to be able to find out whether it is an orchis or not. [. . .] Dry me as much spurge as you can—as much bird's-nest orchis, & plenty of tway blade, of wh. there are quantities in the long walk—all the Arabis to be found— Woodpuff—Marsh Marigold & cockle. What do mean by this last. Give my love to Emily, & ask her to dry me some Adoxa—the plant in the moors is in flower *now*. Menyasthes trifoliata is its' name—& we found it here long ago—I question whether that is really "Arabis stricta"; "hirsuta", is very likely to be—if it is 'stricta', it is a most noble prize.[45]

His friendship with his master, who was only eight years his senior, had become such that they planned a walking holiday around Plymouth in the summer of 1835.

But life at Helston was not only rambling on the moors and coasts in search of flowers and minerals. Other "aching joys" and "dizzy raptures" made their entry. Charles wrote poetry and cultivated his interest in painting, which he saw as identical to poetry, as "the one is the figures, the other the names of beauty and feeling of every kind." He was very much impressed by the poetic qualities of Van Dyck and Murillo, and he thought Rubens was "magnificent, but

[43] *WB* 90.
[44] *WB* 90.
[45] CK to MK 16/5/1835, BL 41298 f.4.

dreadful. His "Day of Judgment" is the most *awful* picture I ever
saw. It rapt me in awe and horror, and I stood rivetted for many
minutes in astonishment."[46] It is difficult to say what Charles found
so dreadful in the picture. Admittedly, Rubens' throng of naked men
and women struggling to get to a broad-shouldered Christ in
Michelangelo-style at the top-centre is most impressive, but very few
of the faces of those to be judged show terror. It is more likely that
the sensuous and muscular forms of the men and women attracted
the boy's admiration. His early liking for Rubens prefigures what in
later life would earn him the epithet 'Apostle of the Flesh' and was
already latent in the boy of sixteen. The pictures he drew twelve
years later for *The Saint's Tragedy* have Rubens-like qualities, while
the broad-shouldered Christ in "The Day of Judgment" well represents the ideal of "Christ the man" in his first novel *Yeast*.

Charles's interest in Rubens also coincides with his falling in love.
Not much is known about this first love, but a few tantalizing references still exist. For example, in May 1835 an incident took place,
which shows that Charles and Johns had indeed become very intimate. During the walking holiday with Johns that summer they would
join the Coleridges at Plymouth. When Mrs Coleridge playfully
announced that "the Cosserats are going up to Plymouth with us,
so we shall be a good party & plenty of time for [. . . Charles] to
make love to them," Johns chimed in and added "there will be an
excellent opportunity for your suit Kingsley." Charles proudly wrote
home how he dealt with his master on this occasion by replying "I
leave that to you Sir," to which Johns "turned as red as fire." Johns
never meddled with Charles's loves again.[47] It would seem Johns's
affections concerned the Cosserats and Coleridges just as much as
Charles's love, who might well have been Coleridge's daughter.

Charles's views of love at this time were high-flowing and idealistic. To Powles, who had fallen in love too, Charles recommended:
"Teach her a love of nature. Stir her imagination, and excite her
awe and delight by your example. Point out to her the sublime and
terrible, the lovely and joyous, and let her look on them both with
the same over-ruling feeling, with a reference to their Maker. Teach
her to love God, teach her to love Nature. God is love; and the

---

[46] RP to FK, 30/10/1875, *LML* i.27.
[47] CK to MK, May 1835, BL 41298 f.5.

more we love Him, the more we love all around us."[48] This lofty view of love crystallized in two poems and a prose 'rhapsody'. They all feature a fairy woman who, in celestial light, comes to stand for a general idea of love which is closely linked to nature and mingles with a mystical sensuality and a morbid longing for afterlife. The platonic conception of the fairer sex in these three early writings can almost be seen as the sequence of images in a triptych. In "Trehill Well" (1835) Charles describes (in lines which in their detailed observation of "the low and ivied roof," "filmy fens," and "the basin's gnarled lip" are reminiscent of Tennyson's "Mariana") the appearance of a fairy maiden while, full of melancholy, the poet meditates on the well:

> When last I saw that little stream,
> A form of light there stood,
> That seemed like a precious gem,
> Beneath that archway rude:
>
> And as I gazed with love and awe
> Upon that sylph-like thing,
> Methought that fairy form must be
> The fairy of the spring.

The same maiden features in the prose tale "Psyche, a Rhapsody," written at the beginning of the following year. Here the maiden feels "that there was more in her soul than could be satisfied with such pleasures as earth gave; and she longed for things holier and purer, and for a love that should never satiate, a peace that should never be broken." In her desperate search for such love in nature she is dismayed by the hawk striking the dove in the heather, and the fox seizing the hare among the brakes. Looking elsewhere, she becomes aware of society's curses and strife, and its moans of anguish and shrieks of despair, while the monarch is troubled by fear and remorse, the old man in his sleep by the murmur of an evil conscience, and the young family by fear for what future days might bring. "Then she gazed upon two fond ones, as they lay with their fair limbs wreathed round each other, and their lips mingled in sleep [. . .] while their white breasts heaved together in mutual throbs." But she realized that such love might not last for ever, and she turned away.

---

[48] RP to FK, 30/10/1875, *LML* i.27.

She finally finds love in God, and "the birds missed her at even-tide, and she was seen by her blue well no more!"[49]

In "Hypotheses Hypochondriacae" (1835) the mystical maiden is imagined in her grave. The same morbid sensuousness is present:

> There should be no tall stone, no marbled tomb
> Above her gentle corse;—the ponderous pile
> Would press too rudely on those fairy limbs.

Her death is linked to unfulfilled love and joy—"In life she loved to see/Happiness in all things"—and the poet imagines that he would come

> And watch by her, in silent loneliness [. . .]
> All that gave life and love to one fond heart!

"Hypotheses Hypochondriacae" was probably a most accurate description of Charles's own state of mind, which alternated between moments of depression and joy. In the poem, he mentions that despite occasional adolescent senses of misgiving his mind often strangely turned to mirth and hope. Similar passages from his letters bear out such sentiments. To his mother, for example, he writes: "I am now quite settled, & very happy. I read my bible every night & try to profit by what I read—& I am sure I do. I am more happy now than I have been for a long time."[50]

After Herbert's death, Charles and Powles had become inseparable, and in 1836, as the oldest boys, they enjoyed certain privileges. Coleridge, for example, would allow them to study apart from the "noise & bustle of the school, which is past all endurance" as long as they had their lessons "ready at his hours."[51] But Charles was no systematic student. Although he loved reading, he had no interest in the Greek and Latin languages and no turn for mathematics. He studied intermittently as exams approached, by "fits and starts," and although Coleridge found his pupil remarkable, he added that he was "original to the verge of eccentricity."[52]

His parents were less satisfied with their son's progress, and when in 1836 the Rev. Kingsley was given the London living of Chelsea,

---

[49] *LML* i.33–36.
[50] CK to MK, January 1836, BL-41298 f.8.
[51] CK to MK, January 1836, BL-41298 f.8.
[52] D. Coleridge to FK, 7/19/1875, *LML* i.23.

a good opportunity offered itself to take Charles away from Coleridge's school. Biographers have tried to explain this sudden move by pointing out that the distance between London and Helston was too big to be practical. But as Charles only returned home for the longer holidays, this cannot have carried much weight in the decision. The few rare letters that survive from this period also show that Charles's parents thought that Coleridge's didactical ideas were wanting. Apparently he did not believe in (or was not interested in) providing his pupils with lessons in mathematics, but concentrated mainly on classics, as "one is not supposed to know any mathematics before one goes [to college], whereas one is expected to have obtained all requisite classical knowledge at school." This might have been part of the reason. But there might also have been a more serious objection to Helston. As the French critic Marc Reboul has suggested, it is not unlikely that his parents were seriously worried about Charles's growing pantheistic and neo-platonic idealism. His letters home abounded in scientific enquiry and Shelleyan pantheistic poetic expressions, of which some specimens were quoted above. To Reboul the boy's adolescence at Helston was marked by a growing loss of personal faith which induced a profound sense of guilt towards his mother and the low church religion she espoused.[53] The repeated assurances in his letters to his mother that he is reading his Bible do indeed seem to indicate that he had been admonished by his mother for neglecting his religion and his God. His (probably imposed) reading of Paley's *Evidences of Christianity* after leaving Helston supports this thesis.

That Charles experienced such an adolescent crisis, where pantheistic feelings of rapture and elation soared high one moment only to plummet immediately after into a profound sense of guilt, is borne out by a significant early autobiographical passage in Lancelot's "soul-almanac" in *Yeast*:

> Felt my heart expanded towards the universe. Organs of veneration and benevolence pleasingly excited [. . .]. An inexpressible joy bounded through every vein, and the soft air breathed purity and self-sacrifice through my soul. As I watched the beetles, those children of the sun, who, as divine Shelley says, 'laden with light and odour, pass over the gleam of the living grass,' I gained an Eden-glimpse of the pleasures

---

[53] Reboul 103–8.

of virtue. [. . .]—Barometer rapidly falling. Heavy clouds in the south-
east. My heart sank into gloomy forebodings. Read *Manfred*, and doubted
whether I should live long. The leaden weight of destiny seemed to
crush down my aching forehead, till the thunder-storm burst, and peace
was restored to my troubled soul.[54]

It is moreover tempting to see in the estrangement between Alton
Locke and his mother caused by her narrow puritan views a fiction-
alized reflection of Kingsley's own relationship with his mother:

> Was I so very wrong? What was there in the idea of religion which
> was presented to me at home to captivate me? What was the use of
> a child's hearing of "God's great love manifested in the scheme of
> redemption" [. . .] And this to a generation to whom God's love shines
> out in every tree and flower and hedge-side bird; to whom the daily
> discoveries of science are revealing that love in every microscopic ani-
> malcule which peoples the stagnant pool![55]

The fact that Alton has no father might be equally significant.
Charles's father, who had good sporting taste and was only interested in natural history and painting, seems to have been as absent
from the boy's life as Alton's in the novel. Indeed, all surviving correspondence of this period comes from Charles's mother, even those
letters containing decisions which, in Victorian times, one would have
expected a father to communicate to his son. In a letter after his
father's death Kingsley admitted that the narrow-minded evangelical views of the Low Church with which he had been brought up
had been crippling both to him as a child and to his father: "I was
brought up in the heart of the old Low Church school [. . .] and
saw my noble father's vain struggles against the traditions of the
elders."[56]

Thus it was Charles's mother who wrote to him with plans to
move him from Helston to London. She must have made her objections to Coleridge's teaching and morals clear. The criticism of
Coleridge's views must have been scorching and Charles, probably
upon request, burnt the letter. He clearly felt uneasy about his parents' decision and warned his mother "to let Mr C. know of your
intention immediately; for in the first place it will be rather uncomfortable to me, & therefore I wish it may be over as soon as possi-

---

[54] *Y* 2–3.
[55] *AL* 9.
[56] CK to J. Earnshaw, 7/9/1869, *LML* ii.108.

ble and besides, as you say, I hardly think it would be respectful to him." Still, however much he appreciated his parents' looking after his academic career—a private tutor was to prepare him in London for college—his foremost feeling was one of regret: "I cannot but be sorry at leaving Helleston, where I am already very happy."[57]

VI

St Luke's parish in Chelsea was in all respects different from Clovelly. It was one of the best parishes in the London area, had over 15,000 parishioners and a large Gothic church. The church was the earliest London commissioner church in the Gothic Revival style, with spectacular vaults over the nave and flying buttresses spanning the aisles. But Chelsea and St Luke's had no attractions for Charles. He grieved about leaving Devon and his friends. London meant no more botanizing and geologizing with Johns, no companionship of Powles, no stimulating intercourse with the Coleridges. St Luke's meant hard parish work for the Rev. Kingsley, who, with his wife, was busy from morning to night with district visitors and parish committees. London soon got Charles down and he started to hate the suburban narrow middle-class conventionality of the Chelsea churchgoers. He must have very much resented his parents' complete immersion in their parish work at the cost of family life, and in later life with a family of his own he made it a rule never to discuss parish matters before his children.

With his move to London his boyhood had abruptly come to an end. As an adult, wistfully looking back, he summed up his Devon years as "the dreamy days of boyhood, when I knew and worshipped nothing but the physical; when my enjoyment was drawn [. . .] from the semi-sensual delights of ear and eye, from sun and stars, wood and wave, the *beautiful inanimate* in all its forms. On the unexpressed and incomprehensible emotions which these raised, on strange dilation and excitement, and often strange tenderness and tears without object, was my boyhood fed."[58] When he mused on his boyhood impressions of the Fen country or the North Devon sea, he often

[57] CK to MK, 24/3/36, BL-41298 f.6.
[58] CK to FK, undated, *LML* i.36.

resorted to the word 'mystery'. The sentiment is as elusive as Wordsworth's, to whom Kingsley explicitly refers in the following description of his boyhood attitude to nature:

> Once this constituted my whole happiness; in the 'shadowy recollec-tions' and vague emotions which were called up by the inanimate cre-ation, I found a mine of mysterious wealth, in which I revelled while I knew not its value. The vast and the sublime, or the excitement of violent motion, affected me almost to madness; I have shed strange tears, I know not why, at the sight of the most luscious and sunny prospects.[59]

At this time, nature triggered inexplicable emotions. Such a response to nature was mainly physical and void of any moral, spiritual or religious importance.

This state of physical pleasure in which "nature was all in all" could not last. Although Kingsley often lamented a loss of emotion in his interaction with nature, he realized that his boyhood feelings themselves were far too shallow in a spiritual sense. The passage above about the "dreamy days of boyhood" finishes with the affirmation that "moral sense I had not so strongly as men of great minds have."[60] Like Wordsworth, Kingsley needed to have his moral being defined in a social context. Thus it is the interaction with man, and not nature itself, which Kingsley saw as leading to the creation of his (religiously) moral sense. The transition is clear from the follow-ing passage:

> But 'there has passed away a glory from the earth.' Though I feel the beauty more exquisitely than ever, I do not feel the emotions it pro-duced. I do not shun society as when a boy, because man and his coarseness and his folly seemed only to disarrange my world of woods and hills, and stream and sea, peopled not with actual existences, but with abstract emotions which were neither seen nor heard, while their presence was felt.[61]

The last year at Helston had already worked a change in Charles, in which the "beauty and the human began to attract me." The contemplation of art started to feed him with the "elements of beauty" and "the Ideal began to expand, dim but glorious, before my boy-ish eyes."[62] Although Kingsley himself defined this as a development

---

[59] CK to FK, undated, *LML* i.50.
[60] CK to FK, 15/1/1841, *LMLM* 15.
[61] CK to FK, undated, *LML* i.50.
[62] CK to FK, undated, *LML* i.36–37.

which stopped short of the perception that "beyond there lay another Ideal," it actually indicated the beginning of religious doubt which would result in a crisis a few years later as a student at Cambridge University.

VII

Chelsea in the 1830s belonged to the healthier parts of the metropolis. From the seventeenth century it had catered for the London fruit and vegetable markets, and had resembled an agricultural town with its orchards, gardens, and three-storey brick houses. Although this trade still flourished at the beginning of the nineteenth century, by the time the Kingsleys moved there it had grown so much with its 30,000 inhabitants that the rural atmosphere had all but vanished. In 1824 St Luke's, the new parish church, was completed, and the borough had been absorbed by London. Although Thomas Carlyle, who moved to Chelsea in 1834, still liked the air and quiet of "mere leafy regions with here and there a red high-peaked old roof," to Charles it was not a happy place. He kept up his correspondence with Johns, but there was little possibility to botanize in Chelsea. The large garden of the eighteenth-century rectory and the banks of the Thames offered poor recompense for the excitement he had known rambling the cliffs and moors in Devon. And Chelsea had little of the "beauty and the human" to offer the seventeen-year-old boy either. In a late unpublished novel set in the 1830s, *The Tutor's Story*, he describes Chelsea in terms which are a far cry from Carlyle's idyllic views: "Once you left the fashionable districts and main thoroughfares, [it] was frankly malodorous, not to say filthy." Half-way along King's Road "festering, foul smelling byways" branched to the backs of rows of mean two-storied houses interspersed by yards, one of which he describes as "strewn with all manner of unsightly rubbish, a dead cat included, [. . .] opposite a long stretch of much-defiled drab brick wall, pierced by a green-painted door, and furnished with a fringe of broken bottle glass along the top, above which showed the upper branches of a plane tree and the roof and chimney-pots of an otherwise invisible dwelling."[63]

---

[63] *TS* 319–20.

Religious life in the new parish, moreover, was stifling and unsettling. Charles thoroughly disliked his parents' visitors who talked of
nothing but "parochial schools, and duties, and vestries, and curates."
There were no sensible and intelligent women like Mrs Coleridge
(and her daughter) to talk to, and the girls all had "their heads
crammed full of schools, and district visiting, and baby-linen, and
penny clubs". "Confound!!!" he exclaimed to Powles, to whom he
unleashed all his spleen, all that these "ugly splay-footed" girls were
interested in was "going about among the most abominable scenes
of filth, wretchedness, and indecency, to visit the poor and read the
Bible." Three quarters of them could not sing, and the other quarter
sang "miles out of tune, with voices like love-sick parrots. Confound!!!"[64] To Powles he did not hide his feeling of disgust with, and
hatred for, these "dapper young-ladies-preachers" who made him
regret his departure from Helston most bitterly.

Notwithstanding Charles's contempt for the prim evangelical Chelsea
girls, he himself created the impression on Thomas Carlyle of being
a rather serious boy when one day he joined his mother on a visit
to the author. "I have a very vivid remembrance," Carlyle later
recalled, "of Charles coming with his mother to see me. A lovely
woman she was, with large clear eyes, a somewhat pathetic expression of countenance, sincerely interested in all religious questions.
The delicate boy she brought with her had much the same expression,
and sat listening with intense and silent interest to all that was said."[65]

Plans for Charles's education had changed again and he was not
to have a private tutor. Instead he enrolled at the General Literature
Department of King's College as a preparation for Cambridge. This
change indicates that there had been no precise arrangements which
made leaving Helston necessary for Charles and it reinforces the thesis that they decided on removal because his parents were no longer
satisfied with Coleridge's school. Early every morning he would set
out past the big and endless unimaginative rows of Georgian houses
of Chelsea and South Kensington towards the centre of the city.
The courses he pursued provided him with a liberal education of
mathematics, languages and physical science. Although he studied

---

[64] CK to RP, undated, *LML* i.38.
[65] M.D. Conway, "Thomas Carlyle", *Harper's New Monthly Magazine* 62 (372),
1881, pp. 888–912, (p. 903).

with "zeal, taste, and industry," he was a shy student, "gentle and diffident even to timidity,"[66] his stammer no doubt contributing to his feeling of uneasiness. Most of his time was spent cramming classics and mathematics for admission to Cambridge, and he would come home in the late afternoon to find his parents busy with their parish work. He took part in the activities of the debating society of King's College, and, after leaving the college, could often be seen with Herbert Edwardes and others pacing "arm in arm, up the Strand, and eagerly carry on the debate in which they had just been publicly engaged."[67] But at eighteen, life was decisively dreary, with no real friends, and estranged from the family-house. He could not share in the play of his younger brothers Henry and George in the big rectory garden, which looked paltry compared to the magnificent scenery of Cornwall, and Gerald had left for the Navy. The bustle of the city held little attraction for the boy, and his only interest seems to have been devouring any interesting book he could lay his hands on in the old-book stalls during his walks from Chelsea to the West End, reading on the way and in the stalls, not unlike Alton Locke's early reading habits. He had a great interest in tales of ancient days, and Spenser's *Faerie Queene* and Malory's *Morte d'Arthur* became favourites. He soon had Coleridge, Shelley and Southey by heart.

Charles's depression had further physical consequences. Early in 1837 he became easily irritable, suffered from nervous excitability, had spectral illusions and started to lose weight, while his skin grew spotty. The family doctor finally diagnosed a seriously congested left lung which threatened future disability. After all cures in London had failed, his parents decided to send him to Clovelly for the summer. The holiday in Devon was like coming home: "The dear old place looks quite natural—& yet somehow—it is like a dream when I think of the total revulsion that two day's journey has made in me—& how I seem like some spirit in the metempsychosis, wh. has suddenly passed back, out of a new life, into one wh. it bore long ago, & has recovered in one moment, all its old ties, its old feelings."[68] The effect on Charles's health of roving the country-side on

---

[66] T.G. Hall to FK, undated, *LML* i.40.

[67] Herbert Edwardes, [—], *Littell's Living Age* 179 (2317) Nov. 1888, 486–95 (p. 487).

[68] CK to MK, 24/8/37, BL-41298 f.11.

a black pony and the use of a boat on Bideford Bay was almost immediate, although his lungs would trouble him in damp weather for the rest of his life. After a week he reported: "I am exceedingly well here—and have grown fat already—I bathed the other day, & Papa saw me, & said he had no idea I was so fat—my skin has become quite fresh & clear." But the return to London loomed at the back of his mind. Even during the holidays he was steadily reading Paley and worked hard on mathematics; and, notwithstanding the pleasure of being back in Devon, he added more quietly: "my only fear is, that I shall not stay long enough."[69] Still, after the summer, life in London became more bearable when Powles joined him for his last year at King's College before he was entered as an undergraduate at Magdalene College, Cambridge.

[69] CK to MK, 24/8/37, BL-41298 f.10.

CHAPTER TWO

NOBLE COURTS AND CLOISTERS AND BOLD, BEDIZENED WOMEN (1838–1842)

University life in the early half of the nineteenth century was open to all the "temptations of youth and the dangers of wasteful extravagance."[1] D.A. Winstanley, the historian of Cambridge University, mentions cases of wild brawls with heavy drinking, smoking and gambling. Disorderly conduct during the university ceremonies was a recurrent feature, and 'town and gown' fights were notorious. The chief fighting men, it is reported, were at Magdalene "and their opponents were powerful bargees, with whom they often had a desperate fight, so that the bargees affectionately dubbed Magdalene 'our college'."[2]

Magdalene College, Cambridge, was a great change for one whom his tutor T.G. Hall would recall as a youth at King's College, London as "gentle and diffident even to timidity."[3] Kingsley's first impression upon entering the university town in 1838 seems to have been its "noble courts and cloisters, swarming with gay young men, whose jaunty air and dress seemed strangely out of keeping with the stern antique solemnity of the Gothic buildings around."[4] The shy, earnest, stammering student must have felt very much out of place in such a world, and the set of rooms he inhabited on the top floor of the front quadrangle was as much a refuge as an exclusion from it. However, Samuel Waud, the mathematics tutor often invited his students to come to his rooms to "have a problem or two and an oyster and cigar,"[5] and it was through such encounters that Kingsley became integrated in the world of the fashionable "gay young men."

---

[1] Quoted from the Report of the Graham Commission 1852, p. 16, in Sheldon Rothblatt, *The Revolution and the Dons; Cambridge and Society in Victorian England*, (New York: Basic Books, 1968) 183.

[2] D.A. Winstanley, *Early Victorian Cambridge* (Cambridge: Cambridge University Press, 1940) 372–423; diary of F.H. Bowring quoted in Winstanley, *op. cit.*, 418.

[3] T.G. Hall to FK, undated, *LML* i.40.

[4] *AL* 140.

[5] Martin (1959) 37.

One of these, Frank Penrose, a son of Mr Kingsley's curate at Clifton and with whom Kingsley must have played as a boy back in 1823, made him join the Magdalene Boat Club and the social life around it, although financially he could ill afford such a flashy life.

As Kingsley had become a good and active athlete, he soon got to be well-known by the inmates of his college. Most remembered him in later life as a nervous, but generally popular fellow who "mixed freely with all [. . .], a most agreeable companion, full of information of all kinds, and abounding in conversation."[6] There was a strange attraction in his excited and animated talk which to some was "so full of poetry and beauty,"[7] while it made outsiders think him "a little odd and cracky."[8] Encouraged by Waud, he took to smoking clay pipes to ease his agitation, a habit he would retain for the rest of his life. He also kept a dog called Muzzy, a grey Scotch terrier of whom he was very fond. Although Mrs Kingsley glosses over his defect of speech, and represents her husband as a brilliant talker, the memory he left on the College cook was his stammering to the animal: "You con—founded beast, why can't you earn your own living, and not oblige me to pay for you?"[9]

During the first winter as a freshman Kingsley formed one of the most important friendships of his life. Charles Blachford Mansfield was, like Kingsley, born in 1819 at a country parsonage. He was "graceful, active and daring" and this initially drew Kingsley to him. In his rooms at Clare Hall he "used to do strange feats" on a gymnastic pole, and "was more like an antelope than a man," Kingsley wrote in his obituary. The singularly good-looking athlete was also eccentric, with a sensitive nature of intense conscientiousness. He was haunted by having once killed a seal, an action he deplored as a sin, and he had "adopted the notion that it was wrong to take away animal life." He would scold Kingsley for his hunting instinct and told him that "the seal appeared to him in his dreams, and stood by his bed, bleeding, and making him wretched." In due course Mansfield became a vegetarian and would often subsist on dates, bread and lentils and give his savings to the poor. At Cambridge he fascinated all who knew him by his penetrating intellect, his pro-

---

[6] E. Pitcairn Campbell to FK, November 1875, *LML* i.46.
[7] E. Pitcairn Campbell to FK, November 1875, *LML* i.47.
[8] James Montagu to FK, undated, *LML* i.54.
[9] Mynors Bright to FK, undated, *LML* i.44.

found and earnest caring for truth, and his generosity of mind in countering opinions different from his own. He had an unwavering faith in what was good and true, and held that there existed "an ideal righteous polity, to which the world ought to be, and some day would be, conformed." Kingsley maintained that he owed to Mansfield his capacity in later life not to be afraid of truth. Although the latter was "what would be called a materialist," Kingsley "felt that his materialism was more spiritual than other men's spiritualism." When he wrote that Mansfield "left a trail of light wherever he went," he expressed what most of those who knew him felt.[10] Dr Stubbs maintained that "while Kingsley was at university, Mansfield was to him what Hallam had been to Tennyson."[11]

Although Kingsley intermittently read hard for his exams and managed to pass his May examinations at the end of the first year with a first in classics and mathematics, for which he was awarded the college freshman prize, his time seems to have been increasingly idled away. After Kingsley's death in 1875, his tutor during the first three terms, Dr Bateson, wrote, in tactful understatement that "from various causes he made but indifferent use of the opportunities which his residence in Cambridge afforded him [. . .] My own relations with Charles Kingsley in those early days were always agreeable, although I was unable to induce him to apply himself with any energy to his classical work."[12] Memories from fellow-students are less oblique. One of them remembers that they were all very idle, but that Kingsley was even idler, and that he often asked other students to finish his papers for him so that he might have something to show his tutor.[13] And Kingsley himself later admitted that "I was very idle—& sinful."[14]

Cambridge offered Kingsley the freedom to rove the countryside, which London had denied him. Here were possibilities to go hunting, duck-shooting and fishing. E. Pitcairn Campbell records how he was asked to join Kingsley on one of his "haunts up the Granta and the Cam." One night of pouring rain he had to climb over the wall of Magdalene College to call him. At three both climbed back

---

[10] *LML* i.441–3.
[11] Chitty (1974) 52.
[12] Bateson to FK, December 1875, *LML* i.58.
[13] J. Barstow to FK, undated, *LML* i.55.
[14] CK to FK, February 1841, BL-62552 f.7r.

into the adjacent stonemason's yard and tramped off a full nine miles
to Duxford, which they reached at 6.30. At other times they would
take the Times Coach to Shelford early in the morning, and after
a day's fishing walk back to Cambridge in the evening. Kingsley also
attended Adam Sedgwick's "glorious" geology lectures and followed
on horseback the "gaunt and grim" professor "on a bony giant"
galloping through the fields "in his adventurous rides, which the liv-
ery stable-keepers called jolly-gizing."[15] He was a great walker, and
managed on one occasion to walk the fifty-two miles to London in
one day.

Sports also took up a great deal of the undergraduate's time.
Fencing was a favourite pastime and Kingsley took boxing lessons
from a negro in order to learn what he called the "gentle art of
self-defence." That such boxing lessons were at the root of much of
the disorderly behaviour of Cambridge students and encouraged town
and gown riots is clear from the Vice-Chancellor's decree in 1842
that "if any person *in statu pupillari* should thereafter be found resort-
ing to, or having any communication whatever with, any professed
teacher of the art of boxing, or be found attending any prize-fight,
he should be liable to punishment of suspension, rustication or expulsion."[16] But in 1838–39 Kingsley still went about with the occasional
black eye. The crown of all sports, however, was the "all-absorbing
boating." He regularly rowed in the college's second boat and a
fellow-oarsman maintained that the joviality that used to exist at the
club had owed much to his presence.[17]

Although Cambridge in those days clearly opened the door to a
life of distinction, Kingsley did not respect it very much as a citadel
of learning. In a letter of 1841 he complained of the drudgery "at
the acquirement of confessedly obsolete and useless knowledge, of
worn-out philosophies, and scientific theories long exploded" and he
wished he "were free from this university system."[18] More scathing
were his comments in his first published novel almost ten years later
about the humbug of the university, observations which Kingsley
admitted "were drawn from my own recollections of 1838–1842."[19]

---

[15] E. Pitcairn Campbell to FK, November 1875, *LML* i.47.
[16] Winstanley, *op. cit.*, 421.
[17] Frank Penrose to FK, undated, *LML* i.55.
[18] CK to FK, January 1841, *LML* i.51.
[19] *AL* lxxxix.

Alton Locke speaks in no uncertain terms of the undergraduate's "contempt and unbelief with which they seemed to regard everything beyond mere animal enjoyment, and here and there the selfish advantage of a good degree":

> They seemed, if one could judge from appearances, to despise and disbelieve everything generous, enthusiastic, enlarged. Thoughtfulness was a 'bore';—earnestness, 'romance'. Above all, they seemed to despise the university itself. The 'Dons' were 'idle, fat old humbugs'; chapel, 'a humbug, too'; tutors, 'humbugs' too, who played into the trades-men's hands, and charged men high fees for lectures not worth attend-ing—so that any man who wanted to get on, was forced to have a private tutor, besides his college one. The university-studies were 'a humbug'—no use to man in after-life. The masters of arts were 'hum-bugs' too; for 'they knew all the evils, and clamoured for reform till they became Dons themselves; and then, as soon as they found the old system pay, they settled down on their lees, and grew fat on port wine, like those before them.' They seemed to consider themselves in an atmosphere of humbug—living in a lie—out of which lie-element those who chose were very right in making the most, for the gaining of fame or money. And the tone which they took about everything—the coarseness, hollowness, Gil Blas selfishness—was just what might have been expected.[20]

This is the notorious passage which Kingsley excised from the 1862 edition of the novel, the first to be published after he had become Professor of Modern History at his Alma Mater.

There is not much explicit information extant about Kingsley's first year at Cambridge, but the accounts of his second year hint clearly at the course his life had taken. Although he probably did not do worse than many a fellow-student at his college in pursuing a reckless life of idleness and dissipation, he had a growing sense of guilt that made him feel disgusted with himself. The bacchanalian Boat Club dinners often ended in total drunkenness, and Kingsley participated in some of the hard drinking. He played cards and incurred slight debts. There was nothing addictive in these dissipa-tions, but they did not help his self-esteem.

Similarly disturbing for his inner peace was his loss of religion while at university. His religious faith, never very strong after his romantic and pantheistic yearnings at Helston, now turned into a

---

[20] *AL¹* 155–6.

kind of gnostic disbelief, and much soul-searching ensued. Of course, Kingsley's spiritual crisis was by no means unique. The 1840s were a decade of bold and persistent questioning of official religion and of Biblical authority as the fount of truth. Within the Church of England the Tractarians at Oxford disturbed hitherto generally accepted views of Anglican orthodoxy, while new discoveries in science brought the veracity of the Biblical account of Creation under severe attack. Many who seriously contemplated these issues soon found themselves groping in the dark with, at best, religious uncertainty and doubt, and at its worst, with downright denial.

Kingsley's endless discussions with Mansfield about truth would certainly have concerned such religious questions. But whereas Mansfield found a strength in his spiritual materialism, Kingsley felt utterly bewildered by it all. It is likely that Kingsley felt some of the attraction of Tractarianism—in later life he would admit that he fully understood its lure—but the religious young men of that stamp Kingsley met at Cambridge either deemed "chastity and sobriety quite unnecessary" in their religion of crucifixes and Gothic architecture, or were "narrow, bitter, flippant, and un-earnest" ascetics.[21] Mansfield's earnest materialism seemed far superior to all this.

Part of his doubt also seemed to have stemmed from a perplexity of how to deal with his own sexuality, and how to relate it to his religious feeling. At Helston, as an adolescent, Kingsley seems to have responded to his instinctive sensuous nature with some kind of pantheistic rhapsody. At university the freedom from parental restraint and from the narrow evangelical "splay-footed girls" of Chelsea gave him further space to indulge more fully in such sentiments. The fact that Mrs Kingsley's over-respectable biography of her husband drops numerous hints about this period of dissipation and idleness indicates that it is difficult to be wrong about this. Moreover, the many references to and comments on similar situations in his novels have such a startling intensity that it is almost impossible not to read some personal experience into them. Even without Mrs Kingsley's word for it that Kingsley in those years "was just like his own Lancelot,"[22] the early passages of his novel *Yeast* match many an element that comes out in the few letters of this period that have survived. We

---

[21] *AL¹* 155.
[22] *LML* i.44.

have a fair picture of Kingsley himself during his first year at university, when, for example, he writes of his protagonist Lancelot Smith that the latter had gone to college with a large stock of general information, and with a keen interest in dried plants, fossils, butterflies, and sketching, believing that he was very clever, ought to make his fortune, that it was a fine thing to be 'superior,' gentleman-like, generous, and courageous, and finally that a man ought to be religious. What lies more or less concealed between the lines of the letters, however, is the passage with which Kingsley rounds up the description of Lancelot's studies:

> And left college with a good smattering of classics and mathematics, picked up in the intervals of boat-racing and hunting, and much the same creed as he brought with him, except in regard to the last article. [. . .] He had discovered a new natural object, including in itself all—more than all—yet found beauties and wonders—woman!

The female body that had forcefully and romantically presented itself through Rubens when Kingsley was at Helston with Mrs Coleridge and her daughter, was now offered in Cambridge as a real sexual experience. In the short description of the Cambridge sporting scene in *Alton Locke* he thought it necessary to fill in the scene by drawing the reader's attention to "a towing-path swarming with bold, bedizened women, who jested with the rowers," and he adds that "of their profession, alas, there could be no doubt."[23] And the passage in *Yeast* continues:

> What was to be expected? Pleasant things were pleasant—there was no doubt of that, whatever else might be doubtful. He had read Byron by stealth [. . .] All conversation on the subject of love had been prudishly avoided, as usual, by his parents and teacher. The parts of the Bible which spoke of it had been always kept out of his sight. Love had been to him, practically, ground tabooed and 'carnal.' What was to be expected? Just what happened—if woman's beauty had nothing holy in it, why should his fondness for it? Just what happens every day—that he had to sow his wild oats for himself, and eat the fruit thereof, and the dirt thereof also.
>
> O fathers! fathers! and you, clergymen, who monopolise education! either tell boys the truth about love, or do not put into their hands, without note or comment, the foul devil's lies about it, which make up the mass of the Latin poets![24]

---

[23] *AL¹* 130.
[24] *Y* 4.

One might infer from the vehemence of such comments eight years later that the cause was more than a mere expedient in creating a fictional character for his novel. Moreover, his confession to his future wife that he did not bring a virgin body to his marriage seems to indicate that some brothel visiting at Cambridge took place, possibly together with Mansfield. Although the experience resulted in a profound sense of disgust, it did not solve for him the problem of how to cope with his sexuality.

Mrs Kingsley, in her attempt to point to her own edifying influence on her future husband and to support her claim that it was she who finally turned him to a clerical career, discloses far more than she probably intended in the letters she quotes. Many revealing passages include a mention of his "unsatisfied hungering look,"[25] his "moments of self-abasement and self-shame"[26] and of "sensuality and dissipation,"[27] as well as his enjoyment of "the excitement of animal exercise,"[28] an unequivocal state of excitability which he does not want to destroy but "direct [. . .] into the proper channel."[29] A proper channel offered itself in the summer vacation of 1839.

II

For two months during the summer of 1839 Mr Kingsley exchanged his Chelsea parish work with that of the rector of Checkendon. So the Kingsleys moved with their daughter and two schoolboys to Oxfordshire in June. Charles came down from Cambridge to join them, and his brother Gerald, who had enrolled in the Royal Navy, happened to be on leave. The family was thus reunited for the summer.

The wooded chalk-lands of the Chiltern Hills around Checkendon, about six miles north of Reading, and in three directions of the compass encircled by the Thames, which is never more than five miles away, was excellent for riding and walking, and is still famed for it today. To Charles, as well as for the rest of the family, it was a

---

[25] *LML* i.44.
[26] CK to FK, December 1840, *LML* i.49.
[27] CK to FK, undated, *LML* i.53.
[28] CK to FK, February 1841, *LML* i.51.
[29] CK to FK, February 1841, *LML* i.52.

welcome change from the stuffy Chelsea parish in London, which could not have been very attractive after he had enjoyed the freedom of Cambridge. The frenetical physical activity that had started to characterize Charles's life at university continued here as well. The elder boys spent the days riding and fishing, while the Rev. Kingsley fulfilled his parochial duties in the parish of St Peter and St Paul and celebrated holy communion in the attractive little twelfth-century Romanesque church of the village.

On 4 July, Mrs Kingsley entertained four ladies at the rectory. They had come to pay a visit to the temporary rector of Checkendon and his family. As they were sitting and chatting in chairs outside on the lawn, Charles returned from a ride and was introduced to them. One of them, a buxom young woman with glossy brown hair and beautiful eyes, caught his attention immediately. What was said on the occasion has not been recorded, but she did make a profound impression on him: "That face and figure, and the spirit which spoke through them entered his heart at once, never again to leave it. Her features were aquiline and grand, without a shade of harshness; her eyes shone out like twin lakes of still azure, beneath a broad marble cliff of polished forehead; her rich chestnut hair rippled downward round the towering neck." While the young woman seemed to have said to herself: "What a horribly ugly face! [. . .] but so clever, and so unhappy!"[30]

The young woman was Miss Frances Eliza Grenfell who, with three elder sisters, had made Braziers Park their residence. The four unmarried sisters had been left comfortably off after the death the previous year of their father, Pascoe Grenfell. The Grenfell family had made a fortune in the smelting and trading of copper, doing business in London, Liverpool and Swansea, employing some eight hundred men, and having their own line of ships sailing between South Wales and Liverpool. When Grenfell had made his fortune, he successfully stood as member of parliament for Great Marlow, and bought the aristocratic Taplow House, where he lived till his death with his four unmarried daughters. They moved to Braziers Park a few miles away after the property was divided among his heirs in 1838.

---

[30] *Y* 15.

The Grenfell daughters at Braziers Park were very earnest about religion and eager to discuss Tractarian concerns with a higher standard of worship as well as the interest in reviving monastic orders and religious community life. As they had "no intention or hope of marrying," they had followed Dr Pusey's ideas about this to such an extent that they had decided to form a kind of religious sisterhood. Indeed, Georgiana, Charlotte, and Henrietta seemed past hope of finding marriage partners, and there was probably little sacrifice in their resolution to embrace voluntary virginity in the cause of a higher form of worship. Frances Eliza was much younger, and being "brought up [by her elder sisters] from childhood in a nunnery,"[31] she naturally followed in their wake. Still, she was different from her sisters, and immediately formed a lively interest in Charles's wild troubled look that day, "as if you lived such a *lone* life, and I felt, from our conversation, that I alone could understand you, that I alone had the key to your spiritual being and could raise you to your proper height."[32] Kingsley, too, felt he had found someone to whom he could talk. Although he had difficulties in following her in her admiration of the Oxford Tracts and the ascetic qualities they encouraged, he felt enticed by her unwavering Christian faith. Seeing that she felt a mission to save him, and that she possessed qualities he himself was longing for, it is not surprising that their acquaintance was not limited to this first visit. During the two months that the Kingsleys stayed at Checkendon, they met several times. She was five years his senior, but he felt "he could speak with perfect freedom" of "every doubt, every thought, every failing, every sin," while she increasingly 'feasted' on his conversation, in which he was "at one moment brilliant and impassioned; the next reserved and unapproachable; by turns attracting and repelling."[33]

Of course, Charles had fallen head over heels in love with Frances Eliza, and he had to argue hard to conquer the pride of her Tractarian mysticism in which she "fancied herself above so commonplace a passion as love," a state merely to be "investigate[d] and analyse[d] harmlessly as a cold scientific spectator [...] in metaphysical disquisitions about love and beauty."[34] But towards the end of the two

---

[31] Chitty (1974) 54.
[32] Chitty (1974) 55.
[33] *LML* i.44–5.
[34] *Y* 145–6.

months, they admitted to each other that they were in love. The future seemed bitterly bleak, however. With his return to university they could no longer prolong their intimacy, and, above all, it was clear that the rich Grenfells would never consent to Fanny, as her family and friends called her, tying herself to a poor Cambridge student with few prospects in life. As a consequence Charles went back to Cambridge after the summer vacation in a state of even greater confusion, and grew even more reckless in everything he did. Studies were neglected, and physical exertion had become his sole stimulus. He now "went in for excitement of every kind,"[35] and as a result was to feel "the bitterest self-abasement."

One of the few anecdotes that survives of Kingsley's undergraduate years is characteristic of Kingsley's dissolute life, which was always succeeded by feelings of remorse. In 1850 he told a pupil of his how after one day's geologizing in the Fens, he and his friends decided to stay overnight at a small country inn. The night was spent playing cards for money and drinking "rather more than enough wine." Kingsley had a winning hand and soon he did not know where to put the money any more, his pockets being full. In his drunkenness he started to fill his hat with the spoils, completely forgetting them when he stumbled into bed. The hat with the money was found by the maid next morning. She asked him what to do with it. Claiming the hat as his, and realizing how he had come by the money, he flung the hat and its contents out of the window "with an intense sense of self-disgust and loathing."[36]

Fanny remained a firm point of reference in such moments of profound despondency. To her he wrote for spiritual advice and confessed his "remorse and shame and agitation."[37] He seemed increasingly motivated to change his life for her sake: "I begin to love good for your sake." In November 1840 he wrote to her to say that, although he felt it was insulting to address her "reeking with the fumes of the world's frivolities and vices," he still wanted to reassure her that he had "struggled to alter lately and this alteration has been remarked with pleasure by some and with sneers by others. 'Kingsley,' they say, 'is not half so reckless as he used to be'."[38] Such

---

[35] *LML* i.45–6.
[36] Martineau 15–16.
[37] CK to FK, December 1840, *LML* i.49.
[38] CK to FK, November 1840, BL-62552 f.1.

seriousness of purpose was not easy, and self-examination revealed his own person in such a negative light that he only felt yet more "self-abasement and self-shame." One feeling led to another. He was torn between "hopes and fears for the future, and between faith and unbelief." In such a spiral of darkness and recklessness he felt increasingly unworthy of the woman who alone seemed to provide hope:

> The contact of her stainless innocence, the growing certainty that the destiny of that innocence was irrevocably bound up with his own, made him shrink from her whenever he remembered his own guilty career. To remember that there were passages in it which she must never know—that she would cast him from her with abhorrence if she once really understood their vileness? To think that, amid all the closest bonds of love, there must for ever be an awful, silent gulf in the past, of which they must never speak! That she would bring to him what he could never, never bring to her!—The thought was unbearable. And as hideous recollections used to rise before him, devilish caricatures of his former self, mopping and mowing at him in his dreams, he would start from his lonely bed, and pace the room for hours, or saddle his horse, and ride all night long aimlessly through the awful woods, vainly trying to escape himself. How gladly, at those moments, he would have welcomed centuries of a material hell, to escape from the more awful spiritual hell within him,—to buy back that peal of innocence which he had cast recklessly to be trampled under the feet of his own swinish passions! But, no: that which was done could never be undone,—never, to all eternity.[39]

This passage from *Yeast* unmistakably hints that the spectre of a previous sexual experience distressed him as he was trying to channel his own sexuality into his love for Fanny. In December his spirits were singularly low. The main character in *Yeast* at this point contemplates suicide, a stage that Kingsley himself might well have reached in his despair:

> And more than once, as he wandered restlessly from one room to another, the barrels of his pistols seemed to glitter with a cold, devilish smile, and call to him,—
>
> "Come to us! and with one touch of your finger, send that bursting spirit which throbs against your brow to flit forth free, and never more to defile her purity by your presence!"[40]

---

[39] *Y* 146.
[40] *Y* 147.

Such musing also resounds ominously in sentiments he expressed in a letter written in December in which he lamented his deficiency in faith and inability to find a true spiritual guide: "I, alas! have no stay for my weary steps, but that same abused and stupefied reason which has stumbled and wandered, and betrayed me a thousand times ere now, and is every moment ready to faint and to give up the unequal struggle."[41]

The despair had become so intense that Kingsley started forming plans to leave Cambridge, dismiss all religion, leave all English civilization behind, and become a prairie hunter in the Far West. This was not just a passing fancy. When he visited Council Bluffs at Omaha in 1874, which was once "the palavering ground of trappers & Indians," and thought of how near he was in 1840 to throwing himself "into the wild life, to sink or swim," he cried with "thankfulness & repentance."[42]

III

As Fanny's powerful influence on his moral character was clearly taking effect at the end of 1840, his past sins appeared ever more enormous. This was partly caused by the new dimension of his relationship with Fanny which began at the beginning of the new year. On 11 January 1841 she came over to London to see him, and on that occasion they kissed for the first time. This was stimulus to change! Afraid of having "mistaken the emotions of a few passionate moments,"[43] he set himself at hard reading and chapel attendance twice a day. This was difficult enough, as his heart was "in very different studies."[44] But the emotions were not to be mistaken. After meeting once more on 28 March, Fanny admitted her love for Charles. This put an end to all his doubts, and he wrote:

> Saved—saved from the wild pride and darkling tempests of scepticism, and from the sensuality and dissipation into which my own rashness and vanity had hurried me before I knew you. Saved from a hunter's life on the Prairies, from becoming a savage, and perhaps worse.[45]

[41] CK to FK, December 1840, *LML* i.49.
[42] CK to FK, 11/5/1874, MP-C0171–36915.
[43] CK to FK, January 1841, BL-62552 f.5.
[44] CK to FK, February 1841, *LML* i.52.
[45] CK to FK, undated, *LML* i.53.

What still baffled him, however, was how to connect his feelings of
love with spirituality. There was an unequivocal sexual longing for
Fanny's alluring body, and this desire, in his evangelical upbringing,
was associated with carnal sin. But he soon started to rebel against
such notions, with important effects on his understanding of Christianity.

Kingsley's religious faith was torn between his parents' evangelical views and Mansfield's materialism. The latter was sustained by
his own powerful worldly sensations, which he could not and would
not deny. "You cannot understand the excitement of animal exercise from the mere act of cutting wood or playing cricket to the
manias of hunting or shooting or fishing," he explained to Fanny:
"On these things more or less most men live. Every moment which
is taken from them for duty or for reading is felt to be lost—to be
so much time sacrificed to hard circumstance."[46] He had long felt
dismayed at how sterile religion seemed in this respect. A poem he
wrote in 1839 expresses a silent protest against such a notion of religion. The poem's lines are supposedly composed by a monk, who,
in an attempt to consecrate his worldly longings, writes them in an
illuminated missal:

> I would have loved: there are no mates in heaven;
> I would be great: there is no pride in heaven;
> [. . .]
> Lord, in this tome to thee I sanctify
> The sinful fruits of worldly fantasy.
> ("In an Illuminated Missal")

The poem might well be the result of his early discussions of religion with Fanny during the summer months of 1839. In the corresponding passage in *Yeast*, Kingsley describes his protagonist's reaction
when he had "dropped all faith in anything but Nature" and is asked
what exactly he believes in:

> "In this!" he said, stamping his foot on the ground. "In the earth I
> stand on, and the things I see walking and growing on it. There may
> be something beside it—what you call a spiritual world. But if He
> who made me intended me to think of spirit first, He would have let
> me see it first. But as He has given me material senses, and put me
> in a material world, I take it as a fair hint that I am meant to use
> those senses first, whatever may come after. I may be intended to

---

[46] CK to FK, February 1841, *LML* i.51–2.

understand the unseen world, but if so it must be, as I suspect, by understanding the visible one; and there are enough wonders there to occupy me for some time to come."[47]

An atheist he never was in those days.[48] If he proposed to follow the material senses first, he also hankered after the spiritual, and tried to unite both in a universal religious scheme of deism. When he admitted the importance of the instinctive "excitement of animal exercise" for man, he added that he did not "wish to destroy excitability, but to direct it into the proper channel, and to bring it under subjection."[49] Much of his struggle with religion in 1840 is just that, an attempt to see his animal nature as having a legitimate place in Christianity itself.

IV

Early in 1841 his religious conversion was beginning to take place. On a spiritual level he objected with all his soul to the Athanasian creed. Its preface and conclusion that belief in the truths it asserts is a prerequisite for salvation, and its so-called "damnatory clauses" made him define it as "bigotry, cruelty, and quibbling."[50] Of course, this was discussed with Fanny, who sent him parcels of books to read which included Thomas Carlyle's works and Coleridge's *Aids to Reflection*. These texts convinced him that God's government of the world was righteous after all, and he started to relax. Carlyle was just the spiritual amphetamine that his embattled faith needed. *Sartor Resartus* would have taught him that "here, in this poor, miserable, hampered, despicable Actual, wherein thou even now standest, here or nowhere is thy Ideal."[51] Carlyle was to Kingsley "that old Hebrew prophet [. . .] who goes to prince and beggar and says, 'if you do this or that, you shall go to Hell'—not the hell that priests talk of, but a hell on this earth."[52]

---

[47] *Y* 148.
[48] *LMLM* 14.
[49] CK to FK, February 1841, *LML* i.52.
[50] CK to FK, undated, *LML* i.48.
[51] *Sartor Resartus* Book II, Chapter IX.
[52] *LMLM* 17.

Although in January he still felt puzzled about his own conversion and afraid that he had been talking himself "into a fancied conversion,"[53] in May, after Fanny had confessed her love for him, the conversion had so far advanced that he started thinking of entering the church, and abandoning his original intention to read for the bar. Day after day there had been a "small involuntary still small voice" directing him to a calling in the church "as the only rest for my troubled spirit in this world or the next."[54] When at Sully near Cardiff for part of the summer vacation that year, he went out alone on the night of his birthday, "thinking deeply and strongly," and on the sea-shore formed "determinations which are to affect my destiny through time and through eternity. Before the sleeping earth and the sleepless sea and stars I have devoted myself to God; a vow never (if He gives me the faith I pray for) to be recalled."[55] It is significant that this vow was made before the earth, stars and sea. The retraction of his former student life is not only seen as conversion to Christianity but also as a return to the elements of nature, not alone, but together with Fanny. For this purpose he wrote an ode in 1841 to celebrate this moment:

> Mountains, and winds, and waves, take back your child!
> Upon thy balmy bosom, Mother Nature,
> Where my young spirit dreamt its years away,
> Give me once more to nestle: I have strayed
> Far through another world, which is not thine.
> Through sunless cities, and the weary haunts
> Of smoke-grimed labour, and foul revelry
> My nagging wing has swept. A mateless bird's
> My pilgrimage has been; through sin and doubt,
> And darkness, seeking love. Oh hear me, Nature!
> Receive me once again: but not alone;
> No more alone, Great Mother! I have brought
> One who has wandered, yet not sinned, like me.
> Upon thy lap, twin children, let us lie;
> And in the light of thine immortal eyes
> Let our souls mingle, till The Father calls
> To some eternal home the charge He gives thee.
>   ("Palinodia")

---

[53] CK to FK, January 1841, BL-62552 f.5.
[54] CK to FK, undated, *LMLM*.17.
[55] CK to FK, 12/6/1841, *LML* i.53.

As a result of his growing determination Kingsley had started read-ing steadily for his degree. This resolution was mainly connected with the possibility a degree offered "to enter the world with a *pres-tige* which may get me a living sooner."[56] Prestige and a living were necessary if he were to claim Fanny as his wife. Personally he also felt that "a clergyman's life is the one for which both my *physique* and *morale* were intended."[57] In it he felt he could channel his ani-mal excitement and sanctify his sexuality, as he admitted in a letter to Fanny: "the profession will check and guide the faulty parts of my mind, while it gives full room for my energy."[58] The married life of a clergyman seemed to offer him a perfect future life in which religious and sexual urges could be fearlessly combined.

V

The attachment Fanny had formed with the Cambridge student was not looked upon with favour by her sisters, who had been most alarmed at the constant flow of letters between the two lovers. They thought that a change of country might wean her from what they saw as a dangerous infatuation, and they decreed that the letters between them must stop. An opportunity offered itself in Lady Gainsborough, who was going for the summer months to the German spas and would gladly have Fanny for a travelling companion. Thus Fanny left for the continent, where she scribbled endless unsent notes to her lover, while Charles took rooms at Shelford to study hard for the exams that were coming up in January. He felt quite comfort-able at Shelford, his new lodgings "very clean, & large, with good furniture, & the people very civil." Moreover, being near Sir Charles Wale, an old family friend and keen angler, offered the necessary diversion from too much study. Complete separation from Fanny, however, was hard, but to his mother, to whom he had confided his deepest feelings for Fanny, he wrote: "Do not, dearest mother, make yourself unhappy about [Fanny] and me. I am young and strong."[59] Mrs Kingsley was a willing accomplice, and Fanny and Charles managed to correspond through her.

---

[56] CK to FK, May 1841, *LML* i.52.
[57] CK to FK, May 1841, *LML* i.53.
[58] CK to FK, May 1841, *LML* i.53.
[59] CK to MK, undated, *LML* i.56.

While Fanny was on the continent, a picture of her was exhibited at the Royal Academy. Charles came down to London to see it but found its likeness dismal: "He has given her a pair of little staring glassy eyes stuck close together, a huge heavy red round jaw and an expression of amazed ill-temper." "How horribly ugly they have made her," he complained to his mother, "If I meet the artist I think I *must* duck him."[60] But, apart from his trip to London, he allowed himself little or no diversion that summer, an exception being made for hooking a trout during an occasional three-quarters of an hour. Although he tried hard not to be distracted from his studies, the publication and notoriety of *Tract 90* touched chords in his heart on matters on which all his future bliss depended.

In *Tract 90* John Henry Newman proposed to analyse the catholicity of the Thirty-nine Articles with which the Anglican Church defined its position in 1536–1571 in relation to the Roman Catholic Church, and to which a clergyman of the Church of England was bound to subscribe upon ordination. Arguing that although the articles were formulated at uncatholic times, Newman found that intrinsically they were not uncatholic and could be taken to heart by any Catholic. Although Newman used the word 'catholic', most Anglicans read 'Roman Catholic' for it, concluding that Newman maintained the articles to be no obstruction to holding Roman Catholic dogmas within the Anglican Church. When it appeared on 27 February, *Tract 90* created a storm of protest at Oxford which then spread to the whole established Church.

As one who had decided to enter the Church after his degree, Kingsley was outraged with *Tract 90* when it came to his notice during the summer of 1841. He wished he could discuss it with Fanny. Although he had once felt the attraction of Tractarianism himself, he now saw it as rankest Jesuitry, and Newman the worst representative of it: "Whether wilful or self-deceived," he wrote to his mother, "these men are Jesuits, taking the oath to the Articles with moral reservations wh. allow them to explain them away in senses utterly different from those of their authors. All the worst *doctrinal* features of Popery Mr Newman professes to believe in."[61] Part of

---

[60] CK to MFK, 23/6/1841, BL-41298 f.15r.
[61] CK to MK, 23/6/1841, BL-41298 f.14v.

this backlash against the Tractarians was also due to the movement's approval of the reintroduction of monastic orders in the Anglican Church. Moreover, rumour got abroad that Newman was building a monastery. In 1840 he had, in fact, bought property in his Parish at Littlemore, and had started changing a barn into a large theological library while an adjacent row of small cottages was renovated as accommodation for himself, his curate and whoever else wanted to retire from the world to study theology. Kingsley himself at an early stage of his conversion "once formed a strange project," that "I went to France this year, going far away into the country, disguising myself, confessing to a Popish priest, performing some severe & public penance & receiving my absolution from him.—I would have gone to a monastery, & if they would have allowed me, and all had been safe, gone barefoot & in sackcloth into the chapel at mattins (midnight) & there confessed *every sin* of my whole life, before all the world, & offered my naked body to be there & then scourged by them!"[62] But now that he had won Fanny's love, celibacy was to be despised and denigrated as unmanly and unwomanly. Moreover, it had become important to him to take away whatever remnant of Fanny's desire for unmarried life in a sisterhood still remained. He, therefore, implored his mother to "talk & write to her" to "wean her from this pernicious superstition."[63] Not surprisingly Newman had become the bugbear of unmarried life, which he determined to fight for the rest of his life. But at the end of 1841 he had neither time nor energy to spare to confront questions of celibacy philosophically, although he did find time to pen reasons why celibacy would not do for him personally. However, this document, which he kept all his life in a leather deed box with other precious writings, has not survived.

VI

Fanny returned from Germany in October, and Charles tried to convince his mother to invite her and arrange a secret meeting between the lovers at Chelsea "as a spur to me towards the winter's

---

[62] CK to FK, undated, BL-62552 f.188.
[63] CK to MK, 23/6/1841, BL-41298 f.14v.

reading." As guests were staying at the rectory, such a meeting was not deemed opportune by Mrs Kingsley. The disappointment was great, and the long separation started to create the apprehension of losing her: "are we not *eternally* engaged now, Fanny?" he hastened to write to her when it became clear they could not meet after her return to England.

As the examinations neared, the heavy overwork started to tell. In November he wrote to his mother with a full but rather lonely heart that "that degree hangs over my thoughts like a vast incubus."[64] Rather ominously, he added that "I shall be an old man before I am forty," quoting the lines in Byron's *Manfred* about mortals who become "old in their youth, and die ere middle age" after a frenetic youth of pleasure, toil, or broken hearts. The sensation must have been powerful enough, as the passage was remembered and used to describe his main character in *Yeast*.

The six-months' hard toiling started to break down his health. After taking his degree in February he hoped to read divinity at his birthplace on Dartmoor, and he asked his mother to "send down to Holne & make all requisite enquiries."[65] The mathematics examinations came up in January, and to his great astonishment, and that of his tutor, he managed to get out "a tolerable second-class." The tremendous exertion of the mathematical tripos, however, left him with fearful headaches. His physician prescribed the application of leeches to his head and ordered him to shut up all books till his classical examination was over, "just when I ought to have been straining every nerve" to get a first. Holne with its "hard beds and dimity curtains, morning bathes and evening trout fishing, mountain mutton and Devonshire cream" was now becoming a necessity "to recover my health,"[66] as it would so often in his later life. Although his doctor's orders fretted him at first, he gradually managed to observe them. He found that one way not to think of the impending last examinations was to sleep "in an arm-chair dead tired," after a day's walking ten miles to a place on the Cam for pike-fishing, and then back again. "My panacea for stupidity and over-'mentation' is a day in a roaring fen wind," he wrote in a long letter to his old

---

[64] CK to MK, November 1841, BL-41298 f.16r.
[65] CK to MK, November 1841, BL-41298 f.16r.
[66] CK to RP, 13/2/1842, *LML* i.61.

schoolfriend Cowley Powles, who himself was preparing for his examinations at Oxford.[67]

Notwithstanding the last-minute interruption of his reading for his examinations, he did do well and came out with a first in classics. His tutor much admired the papers he sent up, but admitted that their excellence and power was "due far more to native talent than to industry or study."[68] It brought his student years to a close, and he wanted to hurry westward to his birthplace as if to be born again after an initial Sabbath "of the mind, when the intellect is stilled, and the emotions alone perform their gentle and involuntary functions."[69]

[67] CK to RP, 13/2/1842, *LML* i.62.
[68] Bateson to FK, December 1875, *LML* i.58.
[69] CK to RP, 13/2/1842, *LML* i.61–2.

CHAPTER THREE

MAKING OF THE DEBAUCHEE A PREACHER OF
PURITY AND HOLINESS (1842–1843)

Nothing came of the summer fishing plans with Powles at Holne. In April 1842 offers of two curacies in Hampshire were made. The choice fell on Eversley, which was situated "in the midst of lovely scenery—rich—but not exciting."[1]

Plans for taking Deacon's orders were fixed for July, and this meant studying hard at divinity. Now that Kingsley had got his degree and was preparing for the church, most of his doubts and feelings of unworthiness were firmly put behind him, and he assumed an increasingly confident attitude towards Fanny and their future together. In April, for example, he wrote from Chelsea that all his time had now to be confined to studying for the ministry, while she "may still range freely among the meadows of the beautiful, [. . .] I am mining in the deep mountains of the true." He saw this as a necessary preparation for their future union in marriage, in which "the woman's part should be to cultivate the affections and the imagination; the man's the intellect of their common soul. She must teach him how to apply his knowledge to men's hearts. He must teach her how to apply his knowledge into practical and theoretical forms. In this the woman has the nobler task."[2] In Kingsley's affirmation that he would be the guardian of "their common soul," a growing paternalistic (as well as maternalistic) attitude to Fanny is apparent, which was fast becoming a recurrent backdrop to their relationship.

The more decisive and confident attitude in Kingsley did not go unnoticed by the Grenfell sisters. If they had disapproved of him from the first, they now began to be seriously worried that the dissolute 'boy' was showing himself a 'man', with very modest but precise prospects in the world and who would ensnare Fanny into marriage. Ever since Kingsley had left Cambridge with success and

---

[1] CK to FK, April 1842, *LML* i.65.
[2] CK to FK, April 1842, *LML* i.65–6.

had definite plans of soon being in deacon's orders, Fanny had disclosed to her family her intentions of marrying him. This brought the wrath of the whole family down on her. Her half-brother Pascoe said he would never countenance such a union. The eldest sister Georgiana tried to exert her 'motherly' power over her and forbade the engagement. Charlotte joined in condemnation, and the good family name was appealed to. They all disapproved of what they saw as mere fortune-hunting on the part of Kingsley, and they pointed at the incompatibility in age.[3] Fanny was twenty-nine by now, her beauty would soon fade, they argued, and the youthful stammerer would soon look for younger beauty elsewhere. They thus put pressure on their younger sister, who went through a period of uncertainties and dilemmas. In the second week of May she received a "grievous" letter from her sister Henrietta, representing the 'family' opinion, which Charles told her to ignore. He further advised her to "notice them as little as possible." "As long as your sister thinks," he added, "that she can recover her improper ascendancy over you by complaints, she will continue them; [. . .] Give them no opportunity of exercising their power *against* you."[4] Understandably, Fanny more than ever before suffered the absence of a mother to guide her in her decisions against her sisters, and she unburdened her heart to her far from impartial lover, who promptly assured her that "you shall not when you are entwined in my arms, regret the want of a mother's love. And *she* will look down upon you from heaven, & thank her God more than ever, without jealousy at seeing *her* place supplied by a man."[5] The change in their relationship is well analysed by Kingsley himself in *Yeast*:

> Providence had found for Argemone a better guide than *her mother* could have done, and her new pupil was rapidly becoming her teacher. She was matched, for the first time, with a man who was her own equal in intellect and knowledge; and she felt how real was that sexual inferiority which she had been accustomed to consider as an insolent calumny against woman. Proudly and indignantly she struggled against the conviction, but in vain. [. . .] Argemone began to suspect that he was right,—at least to see that her opinions were mere hearsays, picked up at her own will and fancy; while his were living, daily-growing

---

[3] Pope-Hennessy 31.
[4] CK to FK, 15/5/1842, BL-62552 f.23v.
[5] CK to FK, 15/5/1842, BL-62552 f.24r.

ideas. Her mind was beside his as the vase of cut flowers by the side of the rugged tree, whose roots are feeding deep in the mother earth. In him she first learnt how one great truth received into the depths of the soul germinates there, and bears fruit a thousand-fold; explaining, and connecting, and glorifying innumerable things, apparently the most unlike and insignificant; and daily she became a more reverent listener, and gave herself up, half against her will and conscience, to the guidance of a man whom she knew to be her inferior in morals and in orthodoxy.[6]

Such a delineation of role-patterns was not uncommon in Victorian society. It brings out a series of presuppositions about women and their religious faculty, and about men and their reasoning power. Nineteenth-century art representing religious piety often concentrates on figures of women and children, reflecting that women retain a child-like naivety in their unquestioning devotion. As Schopenhauer crudely put it, they were seen as mentally inferior to their male counterparts. But in Kingsley's analysis the role-pattern assumes a more ambivalent endorsement of the different mental faculties in man and woman which, rather, follows Immanuel Kant's view that male and female understanding are equal in capacity, but different in type. His distinction between a female 'beautiful understanding' and a male 'deep understanding' finds resonance in the above passage from *Yeast*, which explicitly begins by mentioning the lovers' equality in intellect and knowledge, while at the same time reasserting male intellectual superiority in the dominion of truth, and the female in intuition. Thus the mother-child relationship can just as easily be reversed for Kingsley, as the following passage about Lancelot and Argemone indicates:

Lancelot's humility was even more irresistible than his eloquence. He assumed no superiority. He demanded her assent to truths, not because they were his opinions, but simply for the truth's sake; and on all points which touched the heart he looked up to her as infallible and inspired. In questions of morality, of taste, of feeling, he listened not as a lover to his mistress, but rather *as a baby to its mother*; and thus, half unconsciously to himself, he taught her where her true kingdom lay,—that the heart, and not the brain, enshrines the priceless pearl of womanhood, the oracular jewel, the "Urim and Thummim," before which gross man can only inquire and adore.[7]

---

[6] *Y* 143–4.
[7] *Y* 145, my italics.

There is in this a powerful sense that Kingsley was not yet willing to trust his own knowledge of the heart, let alone that of the soul, for both of which he trusted Fanny, while his degree had given him confidence in his own power of logical reasoning. Thus, the union with Fanny was seen as part of a task "more noble still," in which the male 'superior' prerogative to command assent to "truth [. . .] for truth's sake" was much lessened in quality as it was only the different capacities of understanding in man and woman that finally unite in order

> to find out from the notices of the universe, and the revelation of God, and the *uninspired* truth which He has made his creatures to declare even in heathen lands, to find out from all these the pure mind of God, and the eternal laws whereby He made us and governs us. This is true science; and this, as we discover it, will replace phantoms of reality, and that darkling taper of 'common sense,' by the glorious light of certainty.[8]

But such idealizing and sublimation of their love did not hide the fact that much of the attraction the two lovers felt for each other was purely physical, and the woman who had once been ready to embrace chastity as a béguine, still torn by religious doubt and sisterly reproof on this account, analysed her passions closely. Her love had become "not so rapturous as it was," she admitted. "Yet that is no proof of its having decreased," Charles reassured her. It is only that the initial exaltation of the mind has become a "continuous element in wh. we live, & then we are not startled by the presence of enjoyment, because we never feel the void of its absence," he argued, and to make his own "rapturous & ecstatic" (physical) love for her worthy of acceptance, he adds, "A woman who had not had your mind, I might have loved, as I now love you *independently* of your mind, but I could not have been happy with her."[9]

In soothing Fanny's doubts, Kingsley increasingly found himself fighting the asceticism of the Tractarians at Oxford. Keble's, Newman's and Pusey's open approval of monastic life in the Anglican Church and their reintroduction of private confession (and its implicit associations with bodily sin) continued to form a threatening obstacle to Charles's courtship. This conditioned the shape Kingsley's religious

---

[8] CK to FK, April 1842, *LML* i.65.
[9] CK to FK, 15/5/1842, BL-62552 f.25.

views were taking as he was studying divinity. He thus wrote to
Fanny that he started to like "more and more the experimental religion of the Low Church School." This was because he found their
knowledge of the human heart astonishingly deep and subtle. It was
definitely "refreshing after the cold dogmatism of the High Church."
Still, he did not want to discard dogmatism in his religion, but rather
seek to combine it with the 'experimental' religion of the Low Church,
and avoid at all costs any partial views such as those held by the
Dissenters at one extreme and those of the Tractarians at the other.
In the first he rejected their "modes of exciting self-worship," in the
latter their "outward formularies."[10] As the Grenfells tended to High
Church doctrine, Charles vented his suspicion that the Tractarians
were "not only disingenuous and cowardly, but false." Having read
some of the tracts and some of their poems and "nouvellettes," he
pressed Fanny to give her opinions of the Oxford Tracts, because
he feared that "these men" had bewildered her "with their sophistries
and their artful appeals to your veneration, imagination, and perception of the beautiful."[11] Fanny at times felt dismayed that Charles
called the Tractarians insincere,[12] and he conceded that some of it
"sometimes [is] very beautiful" but that it still seemed very wrong
to him. His tone is generally firm but gentle in such expositions, but
when Fanny inadvertently spoke in one of her letters about a father-
confessor, he sharply retorted: "What do you mean by a 'father-confessor?' Do not, pray, use such words. I am sure that it is unwomanly
for woman, and unmanly for man to make any man his *father*-con-
fessor." By allowing a priest the intrusive power to hear the private
confession of wives, and thus to arouse an obsessive awareness of
the sinfulness of human nature (and in particular of sex) in the penitent, many liberal churchmen saw the virility of the husband, and
by extension of the family and the nation at large, directly threatened. "All that another should know of our hearts should be told
in the almost involuntary overflowing of love, not in the midst of
blushes and trembling to a man who dares to arrogate *moral* superiority over us,"[13] Kingsley explained. Although the controversy around

---

[10] CK to FK, 8/6/1842, *LML* i.70.
[11] CK to FK, 5/6/1842, *LML* i.68.
[12] CK to FK, 5/6/1842, *LML* i.69.
[13] CK to FK, undated, *LMLM* 24.

private confession would sharpen considerably after Pusey's public endorsement of it in a sermon of 1846, Kingsley found himself already battling with the idea in 1842. It is not surprising that, after such attacks on Pusey and Newman, Kingsley started to veer ever more towards the liberal movement in the Church of England which these High-church men tried to counter in their tracts.

The publication of Newman's *Tract 90*, in which the thirty-nine articles of the Anglican Church were interpreted in such a way as to be compatible with the decrees of the Council of Trent (and thus with Roman-Catholicism), and which caused upon its publication in 1841 a violent controversy in the Church of England, convinced Kingsley (who said he read it "scientifically") that the Tractarians were mistaken. It was the religion of Frederick Denison Maurice and Thomas Carlyle, and his passionate love for Fanny, that would ultimately prevail.

II

Through May and June 1842 the two lovers managed to meet, as they had the year before, at the rectory in Chelsea. But sharpened surveillance of Fanny's movements made it increasingly difficult, and the uncertainty of when they would meet made Charles miserable with vain expectation and "pining about the house" till she would "be once more in my arms."[14] At the beginning of June the Kingsleys went to north Wales, and Charles went with them, trying to put some of the tiring theological argument about Tractarianism out of his mind through physical exhaustion by, in his "own wild way, [. . .] climbing 1000 feet to the top of a mountain" and fishing trout in a "delicious alder-fringed stream, with its clear shallows, and deep boiling pools."[15]

Before Charles left for ordination by Bishop Sumner at Farnham, Fanny came over to stay for a few days at the Chelsea rectory. Although Charles was suffering from a toothache, the days were later remembered as blissful, and a tender embrace and a long kiss would sustain both lovers during the oncoming separation.[16]

---

[14] CK to FK, 30/6/1842, BL-62552 f.28.
[15] CK to FK, 5/6/1842, *LML* i.70.
[16] Chitty (1974) 66.

On Thursday 7 July Charles set off for Farnham, promising to
write to Fanny on Friday night immediately after the two days of
examinations. On Sunday morning, after a day's fasting and meditation, he wrote home to his mother to say he was safely through
and to be ordained that very morning and he directed her to forward to Eversley his frock-coat, writing materials and a pair of dumb-
bells.[17] His letters to Fanny are more revealing of his emotional state
during these days at Farnham. The first examination day he was so
nervous that he could hardly stand. This nervousness was caused by
his sense of standing before God, doubting his own worthiness. He
suspected that his true motives for entering the Church were mainly
based on his desire to further his marriage plans. He prayed to God
that the bishop might reject ("repulse") him if there was any foundation for such doubts. But as he was duly ordained by the bishop,
he concluded: "After this what can I consider my acceptance but as
a proof that I have not sinned too deeply for escape!"[18] From this
moment their union in marriage was divinely ordained for them and
it seemed to have taken Fanny's lasts doubts about celibacy away
too. It also explains the connections they made in later life between
love, marriage and eros on the one hand and with religion on the
other.

The journey from Farnham to Eversley was only about ten miles.
The newly ordained deacon must have travelled the road with mixed
feelings: feelings of relief that an important step in his life had been
taken, feelings of uncertainty (though full of hope) as to his marriage
to Fanny, feelings of fatigue after the examinations, and feelings of
eager anticipation at the beginning of his duties in the new parish.

Eversley parish, five miles to the south-west of Wokingham, then
consisted of three hamlets running parallel to a stream called the
Blackwater, which made up the Berkshire-Hampshire border. Although
Kingsley defined the parish initially as "not exciting," it had much
to offer to a sporting naturalist. His daughter Rose recorded in later
life that a family acquaintance observed that "when the Almighty
made the world, all the rubbish was shot in the parish of Eversley."[19]

---

[17] CK to FK, [10/7/1842], BL-41298 f.22v.
[18] CK to FK, 10/7/1842, *LML* i.72–3.
[19] Rose Kingsley, *Eversley Gardens and Others* (London: George Allen, 1907) 24.

There were indeed many alternations of gravel and sand, sour marshy land with streaks of marl, little patches of primæval oak, deep peat bogs running in heather-clad stretches, fir woods, and lowland pastures of turfy loam. Most of the moorland around Eversley was still common land where geese and donkeys fed—"a maze of little pathways among the Furze bushes [. . .] where the Camomiles gave forth their pungent scent as the foot crushed them, and the boys [. . .] hunted for stone-chats' nests."[20] Warren Heath just south of the village was fine riding ground, and the Blackwater and Hart rivers that circumscribed the parish north and south were excellent streams for trout fishing.

The parish was in the gift of the Cope family and most of the land around was owned by them. The family resided at Bramshill, a sumptuous Jacobean country house standing on a promontory of the magnificent grounds with lake and deer park. It was originally built by James I as a hunting lodge for Prince Henry in 1603, but was sold after the prince's untimely death in 1616, and passed in 1695 into the hands of the Copes. Although Bramshill Park could boast a glorious history of noble inhabitants, the parish, apart from a small group of red brick cottages around Eversley Cross, remained mainly neglected and poor. In 1842 it had a scattered population of tall, ruddy and dark-haired heath croppers who had been poachers from time immemorial. At worst, "the clod of these parts," at least once in his life, "'hits the keeper into the river,' and re-considers himself for a while over a crank in Winchester goal"; at best he is "a thorough good fellow [. . .] Civil, contented, industrious, and often very handsome."[21] Religion was at a low pitch; the rector, John Toovey-Hawley, often decided at the very last moment on Sundays that he felt unwell and sent the clerk to announce to those few parishioners who had not yet resorted to the ale-house that there would be no service that day, while Sir John Cope seemed to be altogether rather indifferent to the spiritual welfare of the parish. The parish church too was in a state of sad neglect. Mrs Kingsley describes, for example, how sheep grazed around the unkempt graves in the church-yard. Inside the church things were hardly better. The altar was supported at one end by a broken old chair and was

---

[20] Rose Kingsley, *op. cit.*, 1–2.
[21] "My Winter Garden" *PI* 171–2.

covered by an old moth-eaten cloth. Mrs Kingsley also recalls that alms were collected in an old wooden saucer, and that a cracked kitchen basin inside the font was used to hold the water for Holy Baptism.[22]

When Kingsley arrived in Eversley, Hawley was about to absent himself for six weeks, leaving the rectory and the parish to his young and inexperienced curate. He started immediately fulfilling the ideal priestly duties he had so often discussed with Fanny. He wrote to her about how he went to the school every day to teach a group of about forty children as long as he could "stand the heat & smell" in the small room, and how he went after dinner to read to an old woman of 87. "So you see I have begun," he added. He also paid a visit to the "Seigneur de pays" at Bramshill, but what impressed him especially was seeing the very tree where Archbishop Abbot, Kingsley's ancestor, as a guest at Bramshill, accidentally shot the keeper and consequently never smiled again. It brought vividly to Kingsley's mind the solemn portrait hanging in the dining room at Chelsea whose austere frown had haunted and spoken to him all his childhood. Now he read in the very fact that "*that* is almost the only portrait saved in the wreck of our family" a personal admonition "not to stain my priestly robes with the bloody sports of the field."[23] The thought of Chelsea also created a sense of loneliness. Describing his room at the rectory at Eversley, notwithstanding the view from his window of the sloping ground which rose in a furze hill "perfectly beautiful in light and shade, and colour," he ends his letter looking at the "drab curtains" of the bow window "where I sit— plenty of furniture, & poor *me* solitary in one corner [. . .] like a kitten in the wash-house copper with the lid on!!"[24] To keep him company, his younger brother Henry came to stay with him for the summer holidays.

On 17 July Kingsley first preached in Eversley Church, and much time was devoted to composing the sermon. Through careful preparation he thought he would be able to conceal his stammer, and he proved right. Although he reported afterwards that he was not nervous on the occasion, "for I had prayed before going into the desk

---

[22] *LML* i.123.
[23] CK to FK, [14/7/1842], MP-C0171–36913.
[24] CK to FK, [14/7/1842], MP-C0171–36913.

that I might remember that I was not speaking on my own authority, but on God's,"[25] the fact that the congregation was very small would also have helped to keep his nerves in control. But as time passed he noticed that he was attracting people who had never gone to church before. Apparently the parishioners started to like the active curate who could just as easily talk with one parishioner about "the points of a horse" as with another about "the mercy of God to sinners." He felt that the people respected him for this, and he thanked God for turning "all the strength and hardihood I gained in snipe shooting and hunting, and rowing and jack-fishing in those magnificent fens to His work! While I was following my own fancies, He was preparing me for His work!" He boasted about making "my sermons while I am cutting wood," and when Fanny expressed her fears that he was overworking, he answered: "There has always seemed to me something impious in the neglect of personal health, strength, and beauty, which the religious, and sometimes clergy-men of this day affect." This is an early indication of how the sporting joys of his wild student days would later be channelled into the new, and more acceptable, necessary premises for a clergyman's life. "I could not do half the little good I do here, if it were not for that strength and activity which some consider coarse and degrading," he asserted.[26] Archbishop Abbot would have smiled at this.

After the initial six weeks, when Hawley returned, Kingsley took lodgings in a small thatched cottage called "The Brewery." From its position in the corner of Cross Green at Eversley Cross, one of the three hamlets that made up the parish, one could see, according to Mrs Kingsley who visited her son at this time, "dogs, and pigs, and geese, some running frolic races, and others swimming in triumph in a glassy pond [. . .] Every object around is either picturesque or happy." There was in her son's situation "independence in every good sense of the word, and yet no loneliness," she thought. Moreover, the people at the Brewery were truly "devoted to Charles, and think they cannot do enough for him."[27] Kingsley's own view of Eversley was often far less idyllic. To Peter A.L.H. Wood, an old friend of his Cambridge days, he wrote that although he was not discontented with his situation, he still implored a visit:

---

[25] CK to FK, undated, *LML* i.78.
[26] CK to FK, undated, *LML* i.83–4.
[27] MK to [her husband], undated, *LML* i.93.

Peter! I am alone! Around me are the everlasting hills, and the ever-lasting bores of the country! My parish is peculiar for nothing but want of houses and abundance of peat bogs; my parishioners remark-able only for aversion to education and a predilection for fat bacon. I am wasting my sweetness on the desert air.[28]

With some humour Kingsley signed this letter with the name "Boanerges Roar-at-the-Clods".

He also asked Wood whether he had any trout-fishing friends around Eversley who would be willing to do some angling with him, "for my hand is getting out of practice."[29] Angling was evidently seen by Kingsley, as by so many of his contemporaries, as the per-fectly permissible, if not truly edifying, field sport for a clergyman, and an exercise, moreover, which helped to control one's excitability.

Although friends came to visit Kingsley in his lodgings from time to time, his parish life was hardly stimulating. Hawley, good-natured enough though he was with his young curate, was not interested in what Kingsley did for the parish. Apart from some Cambridge friends, and some friends from the nearby military college at Sandhurst who would stroll into Eversley and pay him a visit, he made no real friendships in the parish. Only with one of the churchwardens, Augustus Granville Stapleton, did Kingsley establish some true under-standing. He was frequently invited to Warbrook, Stapleton's house in the woodlands between the rectory and Eversley Common, where he met many of the county families, and where he delighted in dis-cussing politics. But Kingsley was much in awe of the aristocratic Stapleton, who had been George Canning's private secretary and who had written the statesman's three-volume biography after his death in 1827.

III

In his loneliness, Kingsley frenetically corresponded with Fanny about points of dogma, as, for example, the meaning of baptism. Baptismal purity as preached by the Roman Catholic Church was to him hereti-cal "Oxford clap-trap" for schoolboys, while the Calvinist view that

---

[28] CK to Peter Wood, 5/8/1842, *LML* i.94.
[29] CK to Peter Wood, 5/8/1842, *LML* i.94

man should wait for grace and live "as a heathen" till the age of eighteen and then be converted was equally unacceptable to him. Grace, rather, is given in baptism and "you have nothing to do, but to rise and walk, and if you do not, so much the greater will be your condemnation." And he announces: "Dangerous or not as it may appear, I will preach it."[30] Such ideas about sin were now to be reinforced by Frederick Denison Maurice's *Kingdom of Christ* which he was just then starting to read. But as he was etching out his future theology, Fanny still tried to channel it towards the High Church tone of the Tractarians and kept sending him sermons to read. About these sermons he answered Fanny:

> Talking of the Tractators—so you still like their tone! And so do I. There is a solemn and gentleman-like, and gentle earnestness which is most beautiful, and which I wish I may ever attain. But you have just as much reason for following them, or even reading them on that account, as the moth has for fluttering round the candle because it is bright.[31]

One of the sermons Fanny sent him was Newman's "Christian Reverence," in whose "moaning piety" Charles found something "very dark and dismal," especially in the view that the clergy should not "solicitously press the truth on those who do not profit by what they already possess."[32] It is an early impression of Newman which was to last with Kingsley, and would be vented in the disastrous controversy with Newman over truth in 1864.

Still, Fanny's letters to him were not so much attempts to convert him as to participate actively in Charles's theological study for the essay he was writing. Although the publications of the Oxford Movement had undoubtedly influenced her religious thinking, she was equally impressed by Maurice's theology, and it was she who brought him initially to Charles's attention. In her daily letters from Woodford Bridge, where she stayed with one of her married sisters, she delighted in discussing with Charles all her theological reading, which was by no means slight. She suggested and sent him books to read and eagerly awaited his opinions. Although the spiritual was of importance to Fanny in her relationship with Charles, she also

---

[30] CK to FK, 17/7/1842, *LML* i.79.
[31] CK to FK, August 1842, *LML* i.81.
[32] CK to FK, August 1842, *LML* i.81.

felt physically much attracted to the ardent young man. Half a year after the embrace at the Chelsea Rectory at the beginning of July the memory of it still made her blood "boil and bound."[33] The two lovers had become so intimate in their daily correspondence that all the letters by this time were duly signed 'dear husband' and 'dear wife'.

A kind of peaceful satisfaction with his new life at times seemed to descend on Kingsley. On one hot morning in August he wandered out into the fields around Eversley and had a woodland bathe in a little stream trickling off the moors. The beauty of nature, religion and love all seemed to come together. While "drinking in all the forms of beauty which lie in the leaves and pebbles" and "possessed with the feeling that all had a meaning [. . .] the intellect was not dreaming asleep, but alternately investigating my essay-subject, and then wandering to you [Fanny]." The scene brought him a "delicious sense of childhood" which he associated with Wordsworthian "back glimpses into the former ages, when we wandered—beside the ocean of eternal love!" and it brought "thoughts of Paradise."[34] But such foretastes of bliss were constantly frustrated by the hostile attitude of Fanny's family to the young curate. Seeing no other way to prove to the Grenfells their true love and dedication, Charles now decided, as a final test of the integrity of their love, to interrupt any communication between him and Fanny for a year. Fanny was aghast at the prospect. Lately the psychological aggression of her family, and the knowledge that they could not touch her private income, had made her more independent and turned her hopes on Charles. Writing letters to him seemed to have become the centre of her happiness, and that was now going to be sacrificed, and with no future certainties. Charles was more sanguine. "All will be well," he reassured her, "I shall have a living soon, & your family will be pleased."[35] "Consider the next year or two as a season of *solemn preparation*," he added.[36] But although Fanny had initially approved of the plan of separation, her mind increasingly filled with foreboding as the idea of total separation for a year sank in and she now told Charles that

---

[33] Chitty (1974) 66.
[34] CK to FK, August 1842, *LML* i.80.
[35] CK to FK, [11/8/1842], BL-62552 f.35r.
[36] CK to FK, 9/9/1842, BL-62552 f.36r.

she had started to have second thoughts. But there was no way of retracting at this stage, as Charles reminded her:

> When you have done a thing, leave it alone. [. . .] Second thoughts may be best before acting; they are folly after action, unless we find that we have sinned. The consistent believer should have no second thoughts but do good by the first impulse![37]

Moreover, he advised her to "avoid this morbidity of mind:"[38]

> Cure yourself of this *habitually*, before we meet again, or believe me, *marriage will not make you happy*. When [deletion]. you will still picture a *dark picture if you have once permitted the habit to grow on you*. Take warning before it is too late! When married, you will dread the possibility of dying in childbed. When the child is born, you will always be expecting it to die—& so on through a miserable life, rejecting the blessings w. God had given you in answer to your prayers![39]

When she asked him how to occupy her mind during a year of silence, Charles proposed in a long letter a series of 'rules' as guidelines as to what to read and study. Keeping oneself busy through constant work would make the year pass quickly and fruitfully. "God is the noblest study of man,"[40] he told her, and He could be studied in three ways: (1) from his dealings in history, (2) from his image as developed in Christ and in all good men, (3) from his works. To do the first he recommended her to read the lectures on modern history by Thomas Arnold of Rugby, who had died suddenly in June that year—"Oh why did that noblest of men die! God have mercy upon England! He takes the shining lights from us, for our national sins!";[41] for the second he thought Maurice and Carlyle most pertinent; and to study nature he told her to "[r]ead geology—Buckland's Bridgewater treatise is the best—you will rise up awe-struck, & cling to God!"[42] Charles also asked Fanny to draw and to practise music, and, more playfully, but still seriously, to study medicine: "You cannot conceive the delight with wh, half sitting on my knee & half supported in my arms, in K.'s Room, you told me you were 'such

---

[37] CK to FK, 9/9/1842, BL-62552 f.44v.
[38] CK to FK, 9/9/1842, BL-62552 f.36v.
[39] CK to FK, 9/9/1842, BL-62552 f.36r,43r.
[40] CK to FK, 9/9/1842, BL-62552 f.45v,37r.
[41] CK to FK, 9/9/1842, BL-62552 f.37r.
[42] CK to FK, 9/9/1842, BL-62552 f.38r.

a good doctress'."[43] But above all he commanded her "*Never give way to reveries. Have always some employment in your hands!*"[44]

The self-imposed separation also had elements of ritual, which seem to reflect the outcome of a continued repression of their erotic feelings. Although Kingsley had found in 1839 a "proper channel" for his "excitability" in his love for Fanny, the long expectation and suspension over the years had resulted in a mounting psycho-sexual tension for which there was no release. Both were constantly, it seems, haunted by the idea of each other's naked bodies. Fanny at night imagined herself in his arms in "delicious nightery,"[45] and Charles represented their union in marriage as "feed[ing] our Love in delicious embraces all nights."[46] But although to them such passion had elements of the sacred, it also at times seemed dangerously near mere animal excitement. Therefore, as in their separation they would imagine lying in each other's arms every Thursday night at eleven, on Friday nights at ten Charles would scourge his body in monkish fashion to punish himself for impure thoughts. The constant employment recommended by the 'rules' also served the purpose of not giving way to erotic reveries:

> *Never give way to reveries. Have always some employment in your hands! I charge you! When you are in bed & doing nothing else, kiss me! & pray & praise!*
>
> See how much a day can do! I have since 9 this morning, cut wood for an hour; spent an hour and more in prayer & humiliation, & thereby established a chastened, but happy tone w. lasts till now— written 6 or 7 pages of a difficult part of my essay. Taught in the school. Thought over you & your mind while walking. Gone round 2/3rd of the parish visiting & doctoring & written all this for my own head! Such days are *lives* & happy ones.[47]

A recurrent word of reassurance in Charles's letters to Fanny at this time is that he felt perfectly "calm". Maureen Duffy did not make anything of the wording of "employment in your hands" in this letter. She could perhaps have used it in sustaining her thesis that the fear of masturbation is a (maybe unconscious) master-theme in the *Water-Babies*.[48]

---

[43] CK to FK, 9/9/1842, BL-62552 f.39v.
[44] CK to FK, 9/9/1842, BL-62552 f.41r.
[45] Chitty (1974) 74.
[46] CK to FK, [11/8/1842], BL-62552 f.35r.
[47] CK to FK, 9/9/1842, BL-62552 f.41.
[48] Maureen Duffy, *The Erotic World of Faery* (London: Hodder and Stoughton, 1972) 283–4.

IV

Fanny's family must have received the proposal of separation favourably. One year without communication would undoubtedly bring the lost sheep back to her senses and restore in her a true appreciation of her noble family name. To spur this on they decided that a long trip abroad would advance their object, and an elderly female companion was found for her. At the end of October they left England for France, reaching Nice in mid-November, where they would stay for almost a year. But Fanny felt broken-hearted. Her spirits fell while she sat longing for her lover, and her health was affected. At times she stayed in bed in a dark room all day. But in the end she braved the separation. She studied as Charles had recommended in his rules, and she did a bit of painting in watercolour, mainly of flowers. Her deepest feelings of unhappiness were confided to a diary, and she did not mix much in society. The beautiful surroundings did not inspire her either, and she was terrified by everything that reminded her of celibate priesthood.[49]

Meanwhile in the first months of separation Charles struggled fiercely with his 'reveries'. The intensity of his struggle emerged in his fasting, sleeping on the floor, and meagre dressing, and on 1 November the strain of pent-up erotic desires had become almost unbearable, as he reported afterwards to Fanny:

> I went into the woods at night & lay naked upon thorns & when I came home my body was torn from head to foot. I never suffered so much. I began to understand Popish raptures and visions that night, and their connection with self-torture. I saw such glorious things.[50]

The passage is striking in the admission of how near Kingsley was at this time, notwithstanding his constant attacks on the Tractarians, to the Roman Catholic Church and a monastic life of deprivation of the flesh.

However, as time passed and with the prospect of meeting Fanny again, Kingsley started to express his ambivalent sexual feelings in writing a life of St Elizabeth of Thuringia, which he intended as a wedding gift to Fanny. It was inscribed on vellum and it was illustrated

---

[49] Chitty (1974) 74–5.
[50] CK to FK, undated, BL-62552 f.113v.

by his gifted hand. St Elizabeth was to him a perfect example of
what the "popish" system of celibacy did to a healthy mind, "[f]or
her affections had free vent, and did not ulcerate to the surface in
brutal self-torture, or lazy mysticism, or unthankful melancholy, or
blasphemous raptures. And because, too, she was no 'hot-bed saint,'
laid on a sick bed, or pent up in a cloister, but abroad and at work."
The *Life* was meant to shed light on whether human love was inconsistent with perfect worship and therefore marriage less honourable
than virginity, or, more generally, whether "nature [was] a holy type
or a foul prison to our spirits." Settling such "heart questions" would
either mean that Charles and Fanny were 'safe' or it would send
them to "Popery and celibacy." The proposition had been rejected
a priori, but with it Kingsley admitted the attraction he himself had
once felt for the ideals of the Oxford Movement:

> You know what first turned my attention to the Oxford Tracts; but
> you do *not* know that my own heart strangely yearned towards them
> from the first; that if they had not struck at the root of wedded hap-
> piness, I too had been ensnared![51]

Of the work on St Elizabeth only a first chapter and an introduction were written, and many of the pencil-drawings (some of them
merely ornamental arabesques, others full-page illustrations) were left
unfinished. These drawings, which tell us even more about Kingsley's
state of mind than the text itself, have become notorious ever since
they were first described and reproduced by Una Pope-Hennessy in
her 1948 biography. The drawings are mainly representations of
naked women undergoing agony either by torture or by penance.
There is a detailed drawing of the crude and obscene murder of
Elizabeth's mother, which has elicited much scandalous comment,
and crucified naked female figures with long dishevelled dark hair
abound. In two of these there is a rather nightmarish presence of
devilish and bestial forms with a prominent monkey jeering, in one
picture, at Elizabeth carrying a huge cross uphill, and, in another,
at an elevated crucified Elizabeth on an anchor-shaped cross. Fanny's
likeness can easily be discerned in many of the female figures. Of
this Kingsley made no secret. When their correspondence was resumed
in September 1843, he admitted as much to Fanny, and even asked

---

[51] *LMLM* 22.

if "my baby will be model I will be able to draw such lovely pictures for her."[52]

V

In July 1843, Kingsley was ordained priest by the same bishop who
had ordained him deacon a year before. Just back from Farnham
"'a priest ordained' and very happy," he wrote to his mother that
Sumner "seemed well contented" with him.[53] In the same breath he
mentions that he had met the perpetual curate of St Saviour's in
Chelsea who felt "agreably" surprised that the newly ordained deacon
was no "puseyite", which reflects the influence Pusey had over the
young clergy during the early 1840s. Charles added triumphantly
that he had "a little anti-tractarian pamphlet, in hand."[54] More quietly he asked her to inform Fanny of his ordination. Fanny had
returned from Nice in May, but the silence between the lovers had
not yet been broken, and Fanny's health had declined visibly. Staying
with her married sister Caroline in London, she started taking doses
of morphine to alleviate the pains in and around her heart, of which
she had been complaining since her return. Fanny's two married sisters became convinced that she was pining away in love and that
communication between the two had better be resumed, even though
the outcome would probably be marriage. That it was Fanny's family who decreed that the silence might be broken, and not the simple expiring of a year, is clear from Kingsley's first letter when, in
September, correspondence was reopened, although they still did not
meet. In a rather confused tone, caused by the overpowering joy
felt at the decision—"Men have gone mad at such moments"—he
put aside for a moment any trace of rancour at his "twelve month's
sorrow:"

> God bless them all! Riversdale Pascoe, your sisters—God bless them—
> they are noble hearts. I felt they could not be the children of your
> mother, & not be noble. I understand them all now. Gradually I began,
> during this last penance-year, to understand them, to love them better
> & better.

[52] CK to FK, undated, BL-62552 f.113r.
[53] CK to MK, 10/7/1843, BL-41298 f.24r.
[54] CK to MK, 10/7/1843, BL-41298 f.24v.

Fanny, however, specified that consent to their correspondence did
not mean that her family had changed "opinion." But this "would
not go down with [him]," as he explained rather tactlessly: "If they
can see us corresponding & not be angry, all opposition of the head
will die—the heart rules the head, even with merchants!" But there
were various other reasons to rejoice and be thankful. Since his ordination as priest he had felt honour, reputation and friends coming
from ever quarter. Financially, the future looked less sombre. His
father managed to get him a clerkship at Chelsea which would render him £120 a year for life, and just three days before Fanny's letter his mother had received a legacy, from which she gave her son
"a hundred pounds to pay my debts & be free!" These debts, incurred
during his Cambridge days, had been a distressing weight on his
mind ever since. "Lord there too thou didst answer my prayers," he
wrote when he heard of the legacy. "And then comes this letter!"
Fanny's letter. All in all there were plenty of reasons to be in an
exultant and forgiving mood. "The universe has shifted—and the
future is present."

There was much to tell Fanny in this first long letter. Both had
"grown very old" and he found Fanny's letter "so different from the
old ones. So calm & sober." But the twelve months had been to
him too as twelve years of experience: "The ages have spoken to
me since I kissed you last, & I know mighty secrets, gained by mighty
study & prayer & fasting, & all bitter, & delicious struggles with the
mystery of life, within me & without me!" But Fanny worried about
his mortifications, and feared that he was injuring his health. He
confessed that "they have been what self-indulgent persons would
call severe, & that I found them very trying," but he added, in an
afterthought scribbled in between the lines, that he had learnt "to
consider physical pain as the least of evils!" And he further protested
that he owed his health so much to these mortifications and that
has been "getting so strong & stout, & you would have hardly known
me."[55] Still Fanny insisted, and prevailed, so that the scourging part
of Charles's mortifications was stopped. "Coward darling baby," he
scolded her gently, "to be afraid of a little cord touching your husband—he has stood worse pain, for folly's sake."[56] Fanny, on the

---

[55] CK to FK, undated, BL-62552 f.49–52.
[56] CK to FK, 23/9/1843, BL-62552 f.57v.

other hand, repented that she had "not use[d] much voluntary mortification" herself[57] and now repeatedly expressed her desire to be scourged by her lover, but he firmly refused to do so:

> And so you would let me scourge you! dear *woman*! No! No! If you find hereafter that such severities are good for your education, your own hands, or your maid's, not *mine* must give the stripes! I will kneel outside & pray that God may bless it to you, in making you strong to bear *all* things for *His sake*! *I* will only bring kisses, & sweets to the sweet![58]

Notwithstanding the joy at being allowed to correspond again and the near prospects of marriage, the letters of early October make oppressive reading in their over-earnest quest for religious purity through physical self-torture. Moreover, elaborate plans were drawn up in prospect of an austere married life, specifying duties and prayers from hour to hour, steering clear of anything that might savour of self-indulgence or 'fineries':

> Do not my darling fancy that I intend to impose on you when married, any severe mortifications.—We must do enough to *keep us sober*, without destroying a single bliss.—All the fasts of the calendar we will keep.—I think the *healthiest* & most mortifying fasts will be to eat nothing but plain *gruel* or bread & water, *once* in the day, & dine at 6 eating no meat, except in Lent, when we may eat a little—Only 2 meals a day.[59]

He was also to promise he would give up smoking—it had become "slavery! [. . .] very heavy bondage!"[60]—and "not hunt or shoot, *of course*, or fish, but *very very* seldom, when we want a dish for a friend."[61] In all this mortification and deprivation of life's luxuries there was, in the event, more idealism than realism. Kingsley never gave up his pipe smoking, would fish regularly, and hunt or shoot often in later life, and he always enjoyed a good meal with a bottle of claret or beer. Undoubtedly, the austere life-style Kingsley proposed before his marriage was partly dictated by necessity, while from a different angle it was also clearly a reaction to spite the rich Grenfell family

[57] CK to FK, [1/10/1843], BL-62552 f.62v.
[58] CK to FK, 4/10/1843, BL-62552 f.70v.
[59] CK to FK, [1/10/1843], BL-62552 f.64r.
[60] CK to FK, undated, BL-62552 f.176r.
[61] CK to FK, undated, BL-62552 f.205r.

who had repeatedly made clear that they rejected him on grounds of his poverty. Thus, when Fanny enquired about furnishing a house, Charles hoped that she "did not mean all those pretty artificial knick-knacks with wh. you darling & Charlotte & others have made her rooms look so lady-like." And with a touch of unintended humour he concluded with a statement that could have been found in *The Water-Babies*: "we must be *above* artificial refinements, you know. All I want is plenty of baths & soap, & clean linen."[62]

VI

A year of separation with its attendant sorrow was ultimately seen by the two lovers as a process of spiritual and physical purification, which was finally reached through constant prayer. It is perhaps only natural that their renewed happiness in October 1843 was seen as God's answer to their daily prayers, but, although prayer was important to Kingsley throughout his life, the enthusiastic emphasis it gets in the letters of 1843 at times trivialises its spiritual meaning. Mrs Kingsley in her biography, for example, quotes from one of her husband's letters to show his devout view of prayer. Starting with "What an awful weapon prayer is! With the prayer of faith we can do anything," she builds up an example of her husband's interpretation of Mark xi.24, i.e. that one should expect much from God to receive much, "also [to] expect the least things, for the greater faith, I often find, is shown about the least matters."[63] The letter from which these quotations are taken, however, is not an exercise in Biblical hermeneutics, as Mrs Kingsley seems to suggest. Instead, Kingsley's letter has to do with an important document belonging to Stapleton that Kingsley thought he had lost, and which occasioned Kingsley's assertion of belief in the power of prayer:

> I had an important document of Stapleton in my keeping, w. he asked me for back again yesterday. I said (as I paled) that it was in my desk, & he should have it immediately. Conceive my terror when I could find it nowhere. I laid awake & prayed about it. I got up at 2 o'clock this morning & searched. Then prayed again, then I searched the

---

[62] CK to FK, October 1843, BL-62552 f.88r.
[63] CK to FK, October 1843, *LML* i.97.

whole morning—no paper! & yet I *had faith*! I believed that God would hear my prayers. At last I wrote up to Chelsea to see if it was there, & then set out sorrowfully to Stapleton's in a pouring rain still believing *against hope!* As I got to his gate, praying all the way, I remembered *one* pocket book where I had not looked & I felt sure it was there. The feeling was so strong on me that I walked back from his gate a mile & half, without going in, went up to my desk, opened then this pocket book, & found the document! Conceive my thankfulness! What an awful weapon prayer is!—Darling Darling! With the prayer of *faith we can do anything*![64]

The year of separation and the sudden concessions of Fanny's family were, understandably, emotionally difficult to handle. The lovers had not seen each other for a year, and though they swore their unchanged love, much had changed. The early letters of the resumed correspondence are in fact often about *change*. In Kingsley's first answer to Fanny in September, he writes for example that "I am so changed! Yet so unchanged,"[65] while she fretted that her beauty "should be a little diminished by this sorrow."[66] There is a strange, almost tense, holding back from seeing each other again. While he explained this initially with expressions such as "I am glad I am not with you. I should *die of joy*,"[67] a few days, and a few letters, later the reasoning becomes more articulate: "But we must not expect things too soon. The sun has risen on us but it will take him a few minutes at least to disperse the night clouds [. . .] A twelvemonth's torture is not recovered in a day."[68]

At the same time, the year of separation was cast in terms of necessary spiritual preparation for marriage. Fanny's "morbid Manichean Popish fancies" had been staved off in the process, and she was now as convinced as he that marriage was the right thing for their love:

> Do I believe in marriage? Why else did God separate us, but that we might think over the glorious mystery till we had learnt how to use it! Why has he joined us now, without marrying us, but that we may now pour to each other the mysterious knowledge w. we gained apart [. . .] But oh the bliss to find *you* too believe in marriage! that suffering

---

[64] CK to FK, [31/10/1843], BL-62552 f.106.
[65] CK to FK, 25/9/1843, BL-62552 f.52v.
[66] CK to FK, 28/9/1843, BL-62552 f.57r.
[67] CK to FK, 28/9/1843, BL-62552 f.59r.
[68] CK to FK, [1/19/1843], BL-62552 f.63v.

has not brought back morbid Manichean Popish fancies! That alone,
is enough to shew me that God had been good to you! that this
suffering has been for good.[69]

The twelvemonth's separation had been a trial in self-knowledge and
constancy that was not to be underrated: "I would not have married you as I was twelve months ago for millions. Not for *you*! This
12 months has been our salvation, humanly speaking,"[70] because

> What might have been the consequence, if we had come to each
> other's arms with faults of w. we were ignorant? What, but that as in
> so many couples those hidden failings would have begun to shew them-
> selves when *it was too late*, & we should have been disappointed in each
> other.[71]

It was out of the effort of making sense of the year of separation
that both lovers invested their "mortifications" with so much spiritual meaning, both on a spiritual and on a physical plane. The
theme recurred with obsessive frequency in their resumed correspondence. Spiritual torment went hand in hand with self-inflicted
bodily pain and a voluntary deprivation of comfort in their exegesis of the relationship between spirit and body. Physical mortification,
of course, had much to do with an awareness of the body that could
be seen as a larger attempt to endow it with a sacred significance
in a Christian context, refusing to suppress it in opposition to the
spiritual. Thus while meeting each other was postponed, the correspondence almost immediately resumed an intimacy which is striking for the presence of the physical body. Feet, limbs and bosoms
were often evoked, and a sensuous vein came out when Charles
urged Fanny to have done with secrecy and tell the whole world of
their love, "[t]ear off your garments, walk naked through the world
& say—I am clothed! for I am his & he is God's. And all then will
bow down to your exceeding beauty!"[72] Much of the mysterious
knowledge Kingsley had discovered during the year of separation
was "too deep for words," he wrote, but he promised he would teach
her "some day with every limb & atom of my loving body."[73] And,

---

[69] CK to FK, 28/9/1843, BL-62552 f.57r.
[70] CK to FK, 25/9/1843, BL-62552 f.52r.
[71] CK to FK, [1/10/1843], BL-62552 f.62r.
[72] CK to FK, 28/9/1843, BL-62552 f.60r.
[73] CK to FK, 28/9/1843, BL-62552 f.57v.

when Fanny wanted to open her heart and tell him of all her doubts and misgivings during their year of separation, he stipulated that she should come one morning "a penitent barefoot with dishevelled hair, wearing one garment only [. . .] & you shall confess *all*,"[74] a scene of which he also made a drawing in ink. More explicit yet is his writing to Fanny on 5 October how he woke up early that morning "& as I lay, white limbs gleamed before me, & soft touches pressed me, & a wanton tongue—yet chaste & holy!, stole between my lips!" Distinguishing this piece of eroticism from mere sensuality, he added: "What is sensuality! Not the *enjoyment* of *holy glorious matter*, but blindness to its spiritual meaning!"[75] This view was taken seriously by both lovers in defining and circumscribing their erotic longings and desires, and provides the key to the open enjoyment of sexual experience throughout Kingsley's life.

VII

While the renewed correspondence was going on, Kingsley left for Helston where he visited C.A. Johns, his former schoolteacher at Helston Grammar School, who had now succeeded Coleridge as headmaster. The present happiness was combined with Wordsworthian memories of childhood once more:

> I have been wandering all day through ancient haunts, with Johns and his sweet wife, and all heaven, and earth has flashed up into my face inspired with spirits' meaning, and my joy has burst out in words, wh. have startled me with their inspiration! I am not the same man! I can once more hold communion with all nature.[76]

Johns and his wife exerted themselves to reconcile Kingsley to Fanny's relatives in Cornwell by "giving (exaggerated I am afraid) praise of poor me to your family." He also discovered that their long years of courtship, including the final year of self-imposed separation, were "known among your Cornish relations here; and that I am *a lion* on that account & the kindness of all (of Frederick Hill too, who knows

---

[74] CK to FK, 28/9/1843, BL-62552 f.58r.
[75] CK to FK, 4/10/1843, BL-62552 f.73r.
[76] CK to FK, 28/9/1843, BL-62552 f.57r.

all), is excessive."[77] Frederick Hill and his wife, one of Fanny's married sisters, invited Kingsley over to their house, and were particularly kind to him. Fanny's brother Riversdale Pascoe, too, seemed to relent somewhat, and he asked Kingsley to see one of the family's copper mines at Tresavean. Having descended 272 fathoms in a shaft, Kingsley insisted on doing some work with a pickaxe, a scene he vividly drew for Fanny at the bottom of his letter the following day, although his hand still shook "from the exertion & perspiration consequent on going down."[78]

Being in Cornwall again after all those years also made Kingsley uncomfortably aware of his own accent. If poverty had been a major barrier to acceptance by the Grenfells, Kingsley's West Country accent was a minor one, but one that, with his stammer, contributed to the unfavourable image they had conceived of him from the beginning. Even Fanny, while admitting she liked the simple-heartedness of Cornish men, did not like their accent. Kingsley regretted this: "But you must not despise their accent—for it is the remains of a purer & nobler dialect than our own!" And he added about his own Devonshire accent: "And you will be surprised to hear *me* when I am merry, burst out *intentionally* into *pure* & unintelligible Devonshire!— When I am very *childish*, my own country's language comes to me like a dream of old days!"[79]

But family obstacles to their marriage were collapsing in quick succession. The couple had firmly decided on marriage now, Fanny even having declared that poverty had charms for her, no doubt in the face of her family's warnings. Charles urged Fanny to have no more secrets from her family—"let your brothers all be told *instantly*! no more concealment!"[80] but, at a loss how to tackle the question, she asked him what to tell them. "Do what God teaches you [. .] I will write to E. & S.G.O. tomorrow,"[81] he answered. Sympathy, they thought, was most likely to come from Sydney Godolphin Osborne, Fanny's brother-in-law and clergyman. They were not mistaken. As Fanny was staying at Durweston, near Blandford in Dorset—for her health had not improved during the first half of October—her brother-

---

[77] CK to FK, 28/9/1843, BL-62552 f.58r.
[78] CK to FK, 3/10/1843, BL-62552 f.66v.
[79] CK to FK, 4/10/1843, BL-62552 f.71r.
[80] CK to FK, 28/9/1843, BL-62552 f.60r.
[81] CK to FK, 4/10/1843, BL-62552 f.73r.

in-law exerted himself with his patron Lord Portman to get a curacy for Kingsley. The curacy of the parish of Pimperne, a mere three miles from Durweston, happened to fall vacant, and it was duly offered to Kingsley with further promises of the first vacant living that Lord Portman, who was patron of most of the livings in the area, would have in his gift. As the rector of Pimperne was an absentee, the curate-in-charge lived in the rectory. Although Kingsley regretted leaving Eversley—"I want to do a great deal to poor Eversley before I leave"[82]—the offer of the curacy at Pimperne could not be refused. With a house and a promise of a future living, it all meant that marriage plans became more realistic. Moreover, as Fanny was now constantly suffering from neuralgia and 'spasms', the Osbornes thought that it was high time the two lovers met again, and Kingsley was invited to the rectory at Durweston. That decision was momentous, and as a sign of gratitude Charles even proposed to Fanny to give their copy of Maurice's *Kingdom of Christ* to Osborne "as the *noblest present* we can give."[83]

Notwithstanding the pent-up feelings and anxieties of months, the meeting was all the lovers could have hoped for. There were no reservations or obstacles to their mutual love and attraction, and they had three delicious days together. Kingsley went for walks with Fanny in the country around Durweston, "lifting her over stiles,"[84] feeling much at ease with the Osbornes, and loving their children. The Hon. Sydney Godolphin Osborne was a younger son of Lord Godolphin and, like so many second sons of the nobility, decided on a clerical career out of expediency rather than vocation. Although not a bad clergyman, Osborne was principally interested in medicine, surgery, and microscopic investigation. When he was appointed rector of Durweston he became intimately acquainted with the deplorable living conditions of the poor in Dorset. He decided to devote much of his time to helping them improve their situation, and he became a life-long campaigner in the columns of *The Times* where, between 1844 and 1888, he published a series of letters on the ills of the agricultural south. Although Kingsley told Fanny in the autumn of 1843 "not to fear those accursed "Associations"

---

[82] CK to FK, October 1843, BL-62552 f.86r.
[83] CK to FK, October 1843, BL-62552 f.87r.
[84] CK to FK, October 1843, BL-62552 f.102v.

Chartism & socialism," and stick to the Bible as "our only guide,"[85] Osborne's activities were soon to have much influence on him.

The lovers managed to have some intimate moments together at Durweston. The day after leaving, for example, Kingsley wrote that his "hands are all perfumed with her delicious limbs & I cannot wash off the scent," and that he was unable not to think constantly of "those mysterious recesses of beauty where my hands have been wandering."[86] As a result of the success of the reunion, the previous oppressive tone of many of their letters now gave way to a more light-hearted and joking vein, and the morbid sexual attraction of doing penance turned into even more explicit, but more joyful, erotic fancies. When he left Durweston to see the absentee rector of Pimperne, Dr Wyndham, about his curacy, Kingsley, who had travelled all the way in vain to Hinton, near Christchurch, found a letter from Fanny on his return to Eversley. He answered that he thought her letter

> A very solemn old-maidish attack upon a poor lonely country curate, or no curate, for I am like to be turned out of this next week by a new curate, & have not heard a word of the other yet! There are your consolations to me for travelling 20 miles on a wildgoose chace after Dr Wyndham to Hinton, & finding him gone to Salisbury, & coming back & writing to him & getting no answer yet!—These are my sorrows, and then you write, heaping rooms of paper, ages of punctuality-lectures, on my head![. . .] There I have done with joking, and now I want—what? why to coax some ministering angel to carry you here, & put you down in my little room, & lock the door, & lay you on my bed, & undress you with my own hands from head to foot & cover you all over with burning kisses, till you were tired of blushing & struggling, if you did struggle, wh. I fancy you would not! & then when you could do nothing but kiss me in return, I would tell you, that you were the most loving, wise, simpleminded baby in the whole world.[87]

The day after leaving Durweston Kingsley also communicated that although his fasts were not abandoned, they were lightened to "as much as I can without tiring myself," and above all that they were no longer a "sorrowful fast" but were necessary to "acquire self-

[85] CK to FK, [26/11/1843], BL-62552 f.151r.
[86] CK to FK, 24/10/1843, BL-62552 f.97r.
[87] CK to FK, October 1843, BL-62552 f.99.

control, & to keep under the happy body, to w. God has permitted of late such exceeding liberty & bliss!"[88]

VIII

Marriage was not far off after the meeting at Durweston. When Kingsley was back at Eversley one of the officers from Sandhurst happened to pay him a visit and "found him almost beside himself, stamping things into a portmanteau." Asking what the matter was, he got the reply: "I am engaged. I am going to see her *now—to-day*."[89] Relations with Fanny's family remained difficult, however, and when she upbraided him in a letter for not trying hard enough to like them, he protested: "I do love your sisters—but as yet I can have no communion with them (in the popular sense of the word) because their love for you makes them cautious as to expressing content in me. When they trust me all will be well!"[90] But that trust was not given. Although the Grenfells had acquiesced in what had become inevitable, much of the sudden gratitude Kingsley had felt for them earlier that autumn evaporated just as quickly when they requested him to settle £100 on Fanny. By doing so they seriously hurt his honour and made him feel that, after the proof of their unchangeable love through a year of separation, they still saw him as potentially being after Fanny's fortune. He made up his mind immediately and wrote to Fanny "that no farthing of your money shall pass through my hands." He felt truly heated about the settlement and for his own peace of mind, to ease the "feeling of soreness" their treatment had caused, found it imperative "to prove that I am more trustworthy than they think me by never touching a farthing of your money."[91] This noble resolution might have put all marriage plans in jeopardy if Kingsley's father had not decided to help out at this stage with £150 per year and if his mother had not settled "£1500 more on you at her death (w. God avert) wh. last will bring you in £75 per annum."[92] He concluded that, according

---

[88] CK to FK, 24/10/1843, BL-62552 98r.
[89] Unidentified correspondent to FK, undated, *LML* i.96.
[90] CK to FK, [26/11/1843], BL-62552 f.151r.
[91] CK to FK, undated, BL-62552 f.172v.
[92] CK to FK, undated, BL-62552 f.201r.

to his calculations, their income would thus come to £700 a year
"from w. deducting £90 for insurance & £100 for alms, leaves us
£510 to live on!—And my parents have been calculating that house-
keeping, servants, taxes, & our house, ought not to cost us £250!
So we shall be rich.—Cowley Powles has promised me a handsome
horse to ride or drive, as his marriage present. And I have other
presents promised from other places! So that your family need not
fear our comfort."[93] But disgusted with all the money talk, a resolution was made for their married life that they "must look over our
books together the first Monday morning in every month. And there
must be an appointed hour, (between breakfast & 10 o'clock) during wh. household matters may be mentioned and at no other time,
especially not at meals—& thus, my darling baby, we shall escape
seeing the skeleton of domestic life glaring through at every turn, as
it does in the house here."[94]

The marriage ceremony was fixed for 10 January the following
year, after which they would go on their honeymoon to Cheddar
for five weeks, and then wait till they could take possession of the
rectory at Pimperne. Although some uncertainty about when Kingsley
was to start his curacy in Pimperne remained as late as November,
a reply finally came from Dr Wyndham, after repeated unanswered
letters, that the present curate meant to leave on 6 April, and he
was therefore asked "to take possession of Pimperne on that day."[95]
Kingsley had given Hawley notice in September, and was initially
to leave Eversley by mid-November, but problems in substituting
him at Eversley delayed his departure there until 18 December. And
notwithstanding the prospect of married bliss in the new year in
Dorset, parting from his first parish remained a melancholy affair.
In the midst of discussing Pimperne plans, he burst out:

> I must go out and see my school, and strike a last blow for God, now
> I am parting from this beloved place, hallowed to me by my prayers,
> my tears, my hopes, my first vows to God—my pæan of pardoned sin
> and answered prayers.[96]

[93] CK to FK, undated, BL-62552 f.204v.
[94] CK to FK, undated, BL-62552 f.175v.
[95] CK to FK, November 1843, *LML* i.105.
[96] CK to FK, 27/10/1843, *LML* i.107.

CHAPTER FOUR

WHO CAN TELL WHITHER THE WIND MAY WAFT ITS
SEEDS WHEN THE CROP IS RIPE? (1844–1845)

The wedding took place on Wednesday 10 January, and the ceremony was celebrated in Bath by Fanny's brother-in-law Sydney Godophin Osborne. The Rev. Kingsley had gracefully waived any claims to officiating at his son's wedding ceremony in Chelsea, and Bath proved rather convenient a place to make the day something of a family reunion for Kingsley's "W. India relations" who happened to be staying there.[1] Although the rectory of Pimperne would not be vacant before April, the families had been busy looking for things to furnish the house. Gifts such as a good-value sofa, a rose-wood drawing-room table, a library table, and "a beautiful inlaid wood French clock, such a lady like thing" all dwindled into insignificance when Kingsley's parents decided to give them the big double bed from the Chelsea rectory:

> The dear bed wh. we both have slept in! Strange that that should be our marriage bed! Our altar! that *there*, where we have moaned & languished for each other alone, you should be the victim & I the priest, in the life of full communion! and our children will be born in it! & perhaps unless God reserves us for *higher honours*, we may die in it, & go to *perfect bliss*, to our blessed, loving, merciful Lord & God![2]

The impending marriage of his eldest son not only made the Rev. Kingsley most generous in terms of money, but it also made him more confidential than usual with his son. One day he said to him that he was convinced "that no two young creatures can enter life with brighter prospects or greater chances of self-perfection & happiness, if [. . . they] will but go on [. . . and] not forget to be lovers when we get older, but carry out our love-dream into every little circumstance of married life!" He mentioned a popular manual of family counselling, "Family cares & joys," which he himself too

---

[1] CK to FK, undated, BL-62552 f.203v.
[2] CK to FK, undated, BL-62552 f.201v–202r.

decided to buy and read. Aware that his mother had "never been able to *rest* upon a husband's love,"[3] Kingsley sighed "With God's blessing it may do much good here. Pray that it may."[4]

The wedding was followed by a five-week honeymoon at Cheddar where the newly-wed couple was offered the use of the country house of Fanny's sister Caroline. Although being together alone for the first time as husband and wife was all they had desired, the honeymoon was not entirely successful, as Fanny still felt weak and indisposed. Kingsley too had complained of ill-health since the end of the previous year, and one day had dolefully written to Fanny how he "was trying some of my old athletic feats last night, & could do none of them! I am so weakened by care & sickness."[5] The decision to stop smoking at such a psychologically tiring moment was most untimely. A gastric reaction ensued.[6] Regular physical exercise seemed to help somewhat—"I am getting strong again & walked 10 miles yesterday without being tired. I could once walk *50!*"—but the strain of the last half year was starting to tell. He felt worn out with "a very jaded brain." The doctor who was consulted confirmed that stopping smoking had something to do with it, but added "moreover that every body is ill just before they are married. And he cannot find out the reasons but that it always happens!"[7] With the wedding a week away Kingsley reported "I have been very low-spirited & worn" and was unable to face the bliss of consummating the marriage: "Strange to say I rejoice more & more in the thought of our month's abstinence! I am too worn for my *mind* to bear such bliss! I must have calm of heart, & nerves must be recruited in both of us, before we can *worthily enjoy* our bliss!"[8] The fear of disappointment made Kingsley hold back now, just as in October 1843 he was unwilling to meet Fanny after a year's separation. It all seemed too much like a dream: "I *cannot* cannot realize it! better not—imagination indulged beforehand might perhaps *dull reality*, when it came!"[9] In the end, however, they fully enjoyed their marital bliss when they

---

[3] CK to FK, 17/4/1844, BL-62553 f.38r.
[4] CK to FK, [17/1/1844], BL-62553 f.11v.
[5] CK to FK, undated, BL-62552 f.205r.
[6] CK to FK, undated, BL-62553 f.3–4.
[7] CK to FK, [6/1/1844], BL-62553 f.8r.
[8] CK to FK, [2/1/1844], BL-62553 f.1v.
[9] CK to FK, [7/1/1844], BL-62553 f.11r.

returned from their honeymoon in February and went to live with Kingsley's parents at Chelsea, where they were allotted the spare bedroom until the rectory at Pimperne was ready. "Oh, those naked nights at Chelsea," he sighed years later when abroad alone and desperately longing for Fanny.

The desire to have children was also fulfilled, as Fanny immediately became pregnant. However, the psychological strain on the couple had not been eased yet, and when in the early stages of her pregnancy Fanny could not resist the temptation to take morphine to alleviate her feelings of morning-sickness, Kingsley lost his temper with her for the first time, and they quarrelled. He sorely repented when towards the end of March he moved to Dorset alone, in order to prepare for taking office at Pimperne the next month, while Fanny remained behind with relatives.

Kingsley set out for Salisbury once more trying to get hold of the absentee rector of Pimperne, but again found him elusive. This time Dr Wyndham had been kept at Christchurch. After having sent off an urgent letter to the incumbent of his new parish, there was nothing left to do but visit the city's cathedral, whose spire Kingsley thought a

> fit emblem of the result of curbing systems. The moment the tower escapes above the level of the roof, it bursts into the wildest luxuriance[,] retaining the general character of the building below, but disguising it in a thousand fantastic excrescences—like the mind of man, crushed by human systems, & then suddenly asserting its own will in some burst of extravagance, yet unconsciously retaining the harsh & severe lineaments of the school in wh. it has been bred. And then its self-willed fancies exhaust themselves & it makes one final struggle upward, in a vast simple pyramid like that spire, emblem of the return, the revulsion rather to "pure" & naked spirituality. And when even that has dwindled to a point—it must end—if it would have either safety, or permanence, or shelter, or beauty—as that spire ends—*in the Cross*! Oh that cathedral is an emblem, unconscious to its builders of the whole history of Popery from the 12th century to the days when Luther preached once more Christ crucified for us!—for ever above us, yet for ever among us.[10]

But Kingsley's thoughts were not confined to the spiritual in church architecture. He had brought his fishing tackle with him for some

---

[10] CK to FK, 23/3/1844, BL-62553 f.17–8.

angling with his brother-in-law Osborne, and even before moving to Pimperne he had a delightful time fishing, which he expressed in a passage which compares well with the description of Salisbury Cathedral:

> Conceive my pleasure at finding myself in Bemerton, George Herbert's parish, and seeing his house and church, and fishing in the very meadows where he, and Dr Donne, and Izaak Walton, may have fished before me. I killed several trout and a brace of grayling, about three quarters of a pound each—a fish quite new to me, smelling just like cucumbers. The dazzling chalk-wolds sleeping in the sun, the clear river rushing and boiling down in one ever-sliding sheet of transparent silver, the birds bursting into song, and mating and toying in every hedge-row.[11]

It is a relief to pass from the gloomy and zealously self-conscious "mortification" letters of 1843 to such fine expressions of poetic perception of nature. Kingsley had reason to be in high spirits. News had come from Eversley that the rector, Mr Hawley, had become involved in an amorous scandal with one of his female parishioners. Stapleton, as churchwarden, investigated the question, interviewed the woman, and informed the ecclesiastical authorities. The bishop answered that in the mean time "a formal charge of the most revolting nature has been laid before me by the husband of the female whom you saw in the parish of Eversley, against the Rector of the Parish." Hawley had wisely decided not to await further developments and fled the country, taking the parish funds with him, and the bishop declared his benefice void after the period prescribed by law. The parishioners, and especially Stapleton, now pressed Sir John Cope to present the living to Kingsley. It was with such prospects that Kingsley set out to do his duty at Pimperne.

From Salisbury Kingsley had written to Osborne and asked him to arrange "pro tempore" lodgings at the Pimperne inn or at some farmhouse, but much hoping that Fanny's brother-in-law would accommodate him at Durweston Rectory, as he could easily walk the few miles of beautiful chalk downs to his new parish every day. Osborne did not hesitate to invite him to his house, and on 1 April Kingsley reached the dear place where he had met Fanny again after their long separation, "where we wandered & kissed, & did all

---

[11] CK to FK, 31/3/1844, *LML* i.118.

we could *before* we were one!"[12] He also fully responded to the beauty of the landscape, which was "of the most beautiful turf & natural woodlands" and which he liked for a moment even better than Devon moorland. "It is more *simple*, & yet not so *severe*," he explained, "more tender in its soft *greys* & *greens*." His elated spirits at the beauty around him seemed to know no bounds, and he expressed his wish "to preach a sermon on chalk downs, & another on chalk streams."[13]

Kingsley also delighted in the Osbornes' company. Although he thought Fanny's sister Emily very kind and "very warmhearted & good," he initially felt rather afraid of her touchiness and "could never feel *safe* with her, bright as she is."[14] After a few days, however, he had a "delightful drive" with her to Blandford and reported that they seemed "very good friends" by then.[15] But it was Sidney Osborne who was just to Kingsley's liking. Osborne, who was eleven years older than Kingsley, was a brilliant and informed talker, and the two got on admirably, especially in their common love of fishing. Fanny, however, looked at these developments with mixed feelings. She felt wary of her brother-in-law's clerical mind and habits. Osborne was a keen sporting man who had earned the name "Galloping Osborne" at Oxford. His biographer mentions that he "was in the Church of England rather than of it," and tells how he quietly accepted the church without either inclination or repugnance when his future career was communicated to him by his father during a shooting party.[16] Not surprisingly, Fanny could hardly hide her misgivings when her husband enthusiastically wrote to her about his fishing sprees with Osborne. All this was rather different from the ideal spiritual life they had stipulated to each other, and she feared a loosening of sober standards in her husband. Maybe the fact that he was thoroughly enjoying himself also irked her as she was still feeling rather sick during the early stages of her pregnancy. So she protested, and he, rather unconvincingly, promised not to fish overmuch "if I can help it without seeming odd to Sidney Osborne," and added that he had thought about it himself before she pointed

---

[12] CK to FK, 1/4/1844, BL-62553 f.29r.
[13] CK to FK, 1/4/1844, BL-62553 f.30v.
[14] CK to FK, 1/4/1844, BL-62553 f.28v.
[15] CK to FK, undated, BL-62553 f.34v.
[16] *Letters of S.G.O.*, ed. by Arnold White, (London: Griffiths, Farrar, Okeden & Walsh, n.d.) x.

out the incongruities of his behaviour in her letter, "but [that] I could not get off going out for a couple of hours yesterday afternoon with him." To reassure her he concluded: "However it is not as if I was in *the habit* of fishing."[17]

Kingsley was particularly impressed by the good Osborne was doing in his parish amongst the poor, and hoped that he himself might "at the same time that I avoid his faults, be half as useful in my generation as he is!"[18] Osborne had just started his S.G.O. letters in *The Times*, which would remain his platform for almost half a century. At the outset he started to campaign against the foul dwellings provided for the agricultural labourers around Durweston, and contrasted the extravagance and luxury of the upper classes with the squalor and suffering of the submerged in society. It brought him enemies on all fronts. The labourers did not understand what he was after and thought his efforts an intrusion into their lives, and the landlords saw it as pestilential interference in their affairs. But Kingsley was won over almost immediately. Soon both were "deep in statistics & abuses," probably along the lines of Edwin Chadwick's influential parliamentary paper, *Report on the Sanitary Condition of the Labouring Population of Gt. Britain* (1842), and Kingsley agreed to collect similar statistics at Eversley for Osborne's letters in *The Times*. To Fanny he explained that he would "never believe that any man has a *real* love for the good & beautiful, except he, who attacks the evil & the disgusting the moment he sees it!"—and he declared to her that henceforth

> you must make up your mind to see me, with God's help a hunter out of abuses, *till the abuses cease*. Only till then.—It is very easy to turn our eyes away from ugly sights, & so consider ourselves *refined*. The *refined* man to me is he, who cannot rest in peace with a coal-mine, or a factory, or a Dorsetshire peasant's house near him, in the state in wh. they are.[19]

What he himself saw of some of the cottages confirmed the findings of Chadwick's report, in which the Dorsetshire cottages were described as "mere mud hovels, and situated in low damp places with cesspools or accumulations of filth close to the doors" and its inhabitants as

---

[17] CK to FK, undated, BL-62553 f.33r.
[18] CK to FK, 1/4/1844, BL-62553 f.28v.
[19] CK to FK, undated, BL-62553 f.34r.

"generally very, very poor, very dirty, and usually in rags, living almost wholly on bread and potatoes." Chadwick's Dorset correspondent, a physician, also voiced his conviction that if good cottages could be provided "it would not only improve the health of the poor by removing a most prolific source of disease, [. . .] but I am convinced it would also tend most materially to raise the moral character of the poor man, and render him less susceptible to the allurements of the idle and the wicked."[20] Kingsley reached similar conclusions about the paupers in his parish and asked himself what good the priesthood could do in such a situation. "What is the use of talking to hungry paupers about heaven?" he desperately asked Fanny in one letter, "they care for no hope & no change, for they know they can be no worse off than they are."[21] It was in such moments that Kingsley formed his life-long conviction that spiritual welfare could only come after the basic necessities of life had been supplied.

The paupers Kingsley saw in Dorset, and helped Osborne to help, were entitled to very limited relief under the New Poor Law of 1834. Kingsley saw this as taking away all hope from the poor. The Poor Laws, which had provided relief for the poor since the sixteenth-century, had become an increasing burden on parishes, and were therefore revised in 1834. The New Poor Law, in its essence, considered pauperism among the able-bodied as a failure of initiative. No relief was therefore provided for such poor other than employment in the workhouse. It was thought that this approach would stimulate workers to seek employment rather than just ask for charity. Of course, where there was no employment, such a measure was futile, and for the resulting hopeless situation of the poor Kingsley blamed, in general, "the craft & subtlety of the Devil & man, & all the misrule & ignorance of this miserable, rotten age,"[22] and more specifically, the ignorance of those who supported the Poor Law:

> Those who lounge upon Down Beds, & throw away thousands at Crockford's and Almack's, *they*, the refined of this earth, have *crushed it* out of them! I have been very sad lately seeing this, & seeing the

---

[20] Edwin Chadwick, *Report on the Sanitary Condition of the Labouring Population of Gt. Britian* (Edinburgh: Edinburgh University Press, 1965), 82–4.
[21] CK to FK, undated, BL-62553 f.45v–46r.
[22] CK to FK, undated, BL-62553 f.49r.

horrid effects of that Devil-invented new Poor Law. You must be behind the scenes to see the truth—in places wh. the Martineaus & Malthuses & Gladstones know nothing of.[23]

Osborne's influence is very clear in this condemnation of the idle luxury of the rich, and shows how much Kingsley's earlier Tory attitude had changed.

Kingsley at times felt the hopelessness of the cause. He was firm in his decision, however, that his lot would be "trying in my way to do good." We will be, he reminds Fanny, "more than conquerors, again, if we not only overcome the world, but *improve* the world! Our field may be small but it *is* a field—there tillage is possible. *Who can tell whither the wind may waft its seed, when the crop is ripe?*"[24]

II

Kingsley might indeed have wondered whither the wind might waft him. Whether he was going to get the Eversley living or not remained uncertain because of procrastination in making decisions. Dr Wyndham's letter to release him from his curacy did not arrive. Nor had Sir John Cope relieved Kingsley's growing anxiety—"what is to be, I know not," he said in May. Moreover, loneliness in Dorset caused by being once more separated from Fanny lowered his spirits. He also felt alarmed that Fanny still felt rather sick and he was irritated that she had again started taking morphine and salvolatile. He repeatedly asked her to leave off, try some wine and brandy, and be strong while waiting for their impending reunion at Eversley, where he would nurse her day and night. Eversley air would surely do her good, and he proposed to "get a horse & carriage immediately."[25]

The good news finally arrived and Kingsley was summoned to London for an interview with Sir John Cope, who decided that he was to be presented with the living forthwith. Apart from the excellent impression Kingsley had made on the churchwardens, Sir John had seen the active curate following the hounds on foot. He had heard of Kingsley's Cambridge reputation as a "hard and fearless

---

[23] CK to FK, undated, BL-62553 f.46v.
[24] CK to FK, undated, BL-62553 f.50r.
[25] CK to FK, undated, BL-62553 f.35r.

rider," and hoped he would make "a boon companion."[26] Kingsley himself was more modest and maintained that the "recital" of Fanny's "beauty & virtue &c. &c. &c. had great influence (so I heard from good authority) on Sir John."[27]

Kingsley rushed straight to Eversley to bring the good news to Stapleton, and to start organizing the move to his new living. He wrote to Fanny that he was packing the van with all the conveniences they needed in order to move in at Eversley immediately, "except blacking brushes, wh. I must buy." Overjoyed with Eversley Rectory he concluded his letter that the "place looks like a paradise!"[28]

In reality, the place was far from paradise. Hawley had severely neglected the rectory. No repairs had been carried out for more than a hundred years, and the dampness created by the series of unwholesome ponds around the house, which overflowed after heavy rains and left all the rooms of the ground floor under water, made the air far from healthy. Before the rectory was inhabitable, much work on the house itself had to be done, and the ponds had gradually to be drained. This incurred large expenses, which all had to be paid by Kingsley. No dilapidation money could be counted upon because of Hawley's disappearance. As the new rector, Kingsley was also held responsible for the arrears of the poor rates and for the pay of the new curate. All the necessary money had to be borrowed, and Kingsley once more found himself in debt. For years to come, the living, although it brought in £600 a year, would remain unremunerative.

Although Kingsley had already officiated for almost a year and a half at Eversley as curate, the direct responsibilities of the neglected parish that the status of Rector brought with it were manifold. Many of the parishioners had never been confirmed. Hawley left confirmation entirely to the initiatives of the candidates, who had to present themselves for the occasion at some distant church to meet the bishop. Not surprisingly, very few in the parish took the trouble. Kingsley now instituted classes and accompanied the catachumens himself to neighbouring Heckfield for confirmation. He also wanted to introduce monthly holy communion at Eversley, which had been celebrated hitherto only three times a year. But this, like all the changes

---

[26] Ludlow (1893) 497.
[27] CK to FK, undated, BL-62553 f.62v.
[28] CK to FK, undated, BL-62553 f.65v.

he wanted to introduce, met with reserve from the parish authorities, and it was only accepted when he promised to supply the wine for the celebration himself. Illiteracy ran high in the parish and religious instruction had never been provided for. Too much up-hill work needed to be done with the limited means in Kingsley's hands. The cobbler of the parish, who also acted as clerk, would keep his pupils in the small stifling room "where cobbling shoes, teaching and caning went on together." Kingsley decided to use the available space at the rectory itself as a Sunday school, and as an adult school three evenings a week. He established cottage lectures in the more outlying parts of the parish. These were to be mostly on English history, by which he hoped to make "the agricultural eyes open once or twice, by showing that they did not grow out of the earth originally, like beetles, but came from somewhere else; and might probably have to go somewhere else, and make room for their betters, if they continued so like beetles, human manure-carriers, and hole-grubbers, much longer."[29]

It took years of hard work before a regular school-building and school-master could be introduced. The desire to know all his parishioners intimately meant incessant visiting whenever his other duties allowed it. Eversley clearly offered enough space for his intention of "trying in my way to do good." This work fell personally to the new rector, as all the incurred expenses made it impossible to retain Hawley's last curate. Mrs Kingsley writes that her husband's only relaxation was "a few hours' fishing in some stream close by" but that he abstained from shooting or hunting as he thought it "might bring him into unpleasant collision" with the poaching tastes of the people, although he did not refrain from becoming intimate with the Bramshill huntsmen and whips.[30] This activity and interest in the welfare of the parish gradually gained the new rector respect from most of his parishioners. But not from his patron, Sir John, who had discovered that Kingsley was not in the least disposed "to stop and soak with him after dinner." Instead the rector seemed interested only in his parochial duties, and also had the presumption not only to ask him for money to improve instruction but to point out to him that some of his cottages were unfit to live in.[31]

---

[29] CL to William Lees, 4/12/1850, *LML* i.245.
[30] *LML* i.123–5.
[31] Ludlow (1893) 497.

Kingsley's interest in the welfare of the Dorset poor was now duly shifted to the poor in his own parish in Eversley. At Durweston he had been reading Samuel Richard Bosanquet's *The Rights of the Poor and Christian Almsgiving Vindicated; or the State and Character of the Poor and the Conduct and Duties of the Rich Exhibited and Illustrated* (1841)[32] and Thomas Carlyle's *Miscellanies* and *Past and Present*, the second of which had appeared the previous year in 1843. Carlyle had been shocked into writing after witnessing in the workhouse of St Yves (Huntingdonshire) the waste of the potential of working men. When he subsequently visited the ruins of the abbey at Bury St Edmunds, he thought of medieval monastic society and how the poor were then treated. He lamented the stasis caused by England's nineteenth-century productive and social system, which caused "tall robust figures, young mostly or of middle age" to sit in a kind of enchanted torpor in front of their workhouses ("Bastilles") while "the Sun shines and the Earth calls; and, by the governing Powers and Impotences of this England, we are forbidden to obey. It is impossible, they tell us!" "Rich and Poor, when once the naked facts of their condition have come into collision, cannot long subsist together on a mere Poor-law," Carlyle prophesied.[33] Kingsley was struck by Carlyle's effective rhetoric and his intense moral fervour, not least because it expressed in powerful language what he himself had seen of the poor in Dorset. What no doubt appealed to Kingsley was Carlyle's conviction in *Past and Present*, that moral force, guided by Divine justice, would triumph: "When Mammon-worshippers here and there begin to be God-worshippers, and bipeds-of-prey become men, and there is a Soul felt once more in the huge-pulsing elephantine mechanic Animalism of the Earth, it will be again a blessed Earth."[34] Such writing moved Kingsley profoundly. "More & more I find that these writings of Carlyle's do not lead to gloomy discontent—that theirs is *not* a dark, but a *bright* view of life," he commented, and added that he thought that

---

[32] Mrs Kingsley identifies the book her husband mentions as follows: "This book of Bosanquet's ('Perils of the Nations')" (*LML* i.110). She most likely confused Samuel Richard Bosanquet's *The Rights of the Poor and Christian Almsgiving Vindicated* with Robert Benton Seeley's *Remedies for the Perils of the Nation: An Appeal* (1843). It is likely that Kingsley read both books at this time. Apparently, Mrs Kingsley realized her mistake, and the reference to Bosanquet is not reproduced in any subsequent edition of her biography (see: *LMLM* 44; *LMLM* i.80).

[33] *Past and Present* Book I, Chapter I.

[34] *Past and Present* Book IV, Chapter VIII.

> In reality, more evil-speaking against the age & its inhabitants is thun-
> dered from the pulpit daily by both Evangelical and Tractarian, than
> Carlyle has been guilty of in all his works but he finds fault in real,
> tangible, original language. *They* speak evil of every one except their
> own party, but in such conventional language, that no ear is shocked
> by the old oft repeated formulae of "original sin" & "unconverted
> hearts" & so on, and the man who would be furious if Carlyle had
> classed him among the "valets", bears with perfect equanimity the
> information of [. . .] Dr Pusey that he has put himself beyond the pale
> of Xt's atonement by sin after baptism.[35]

Carlyle's writings exerted such an influence on the young Kingsley
that it would culminate in his use six years later of a Carlylean
mouthpiece in his condition-of-England novel *Alton Locke*.

A different kind of prophet, who was to influence Kingsley even
more deeply, and in a more lasting way, was Frederick Denison
Maurice. Maurice's theological ideas were based on the view that
humanity is created and constituted in Christ. It is Christ, and not
Adam, who represents humanity, and the redemption of Christ is
seen as the revelation of the full glory of humanity. Similarly, baptism is a celebration of an already existing link with God, and not
the initial unity between man and God. Maurice thus places more
emphasis on man's unity with God than did most current theolo-
gies, both evangelical and Roman Catholic, which stressed man's
alienation from his creator through the Fall. It all meant that the
kingdom of Christ was here and now. Such premises entailed various other views, such as a profound dislike of Church parties ("systems") and an emphasis on the importance of the family and nation
as symbols of unity and relationship, as well as a fervent interest in
the condition of the poor and a defence of social reform.

This kind of thing had been attractive to Kingsley ever since Fanny
had recommended the *Kingdom of Christ* (1838, 1842) in the time of
their courtship. He appreciated Maurice's work because it was also
grounded on a sound theological basis. It became for him "the foundation of any coherent view of the word of God, the meaning of
the Church of England, and the spiritual phenomena of the present
and past ages."[36] Although much of the attraction of the *Kingdom of
Christ* lay in the fact that it was originally written as an answer to

---

[35] CK to FK, 17/4/1844, BL-62553 f.39r.
[36] CK to FDM, undated, *LML* i.127.

the Tractarians, and, in particular, to Pusey's views on baptism, Maurice's emphasis on the here and now of the divine scheme helped Kingsley to integrate both the physical and spiritual in one Christian scheme. He had long wanted to write to the author of the *Kingdom of Christ*, and when Maurice, then chaplain at Guy's hospital, took the rectory at Chelsea off the Rev. Kingsley's hands during the summer months of 1844, an opportunity presented itself.[37] Doubting how to read the Scriptures "without seeing in them merely proofs of human systems," and feeling himself unable to cope with the ultra-Calvinism of the great prevalence of "the Baptist form of dissent" in his parish, Kingsley asked "the elder prophet" whether he could come over to Chelsea for an interview, feeling "that much may be said that would not be written." Although he was most willing to meet Kingsley, Maurice decided that it was easier to piece his thoughts together on such questions "in writing than in speaking," and wrote Kingsley a long answer that signalled the beginning of an influential and life-long friendship.[38] The two men met soon after this exchange of letters, and Maurice immediately developed a profound affection for the young clergyman. John Ludlow writes in his autobiography that "Mr Maurice's affection for him was unspeakable; in fact, with all his kindness and friendly benevolence, I have often doubted whether he ever really loved anyone except Kingsley of all the young men who from this period began to gather round him."[39]

There was no doubt a sincere wish to get to know Maurice, as Kingsley's perplexities about how to tackle the Calvinism of dissent were real enough. Hawley had severely neglected his pastoral duties, and "the hungry sheep meanwhile [were] looking up, foodless to the respective dunghills of particular and general Baptist communions, whereon their respective hirelings sit muck enthroned," he wrote with a Carlylean twang to Powles at about the same time he wrote to Maurice.[40] Dissent in the parish was strong, but his passionate and hard parish work slowly started to bring a change. "I have never seen a country church so well attended as that of Eversley in Kingsley's days," Ludlow remembered in after years.[41]

---

[37] Florence Higham, *Frederick Denison Maurice* (London: SCM Press, 1947) 51.
[38] FDM to CK, 22/7/1844, *LML* i.127.
[39] Ludlow (1981)127.
[40] CK to RP, July 1844, *LML* i.133.
[41] Ludlow (1893) 497.

III

At the beginning of November 1844 a daughter was born, and she was given the name Rose Georgiana. With little Cocky, as Kingsley called her, family bliss was now complete. Fanny felt well and attributed her health and comfort to the fostering care of "the best of husbands,"[42] and Kingsley enjoyed the "*gaudia ruris*, thick shoes, and a wood axe."[43] But the felicity that Kingsley felt at the birth of his daughter was soon dampened by tragedy. On 24 February 1845 *The Times* carried the news that a leaking and dismasted *H.M.S. Royalist* had reached Singapore the autumn before. Many a man had died, including all the officers of the ship, and the rest had been reduced to a most pitiable state. The Rev. Kingsley, who happened to hear the news in a library, fainted on the spot, as this was the ship in which his son Gerald had sailed for the Far East as second-in-command. Kingsley hurried to Chelsea when the rumour reached him, and found out that the sad news about *H.M.S. Royalist* was true:

> As far as externals go, it has been very sad. The sailors say commonly that there is but a sheet of paper between Torres Straits and Hell. And there he lay, and the wretched crew, in the little brig, roasting and pining, day after day-never heard of, or hearing of living soul for a year and a half. The commander died—half the crew died—and so they died and died on, till in May no officer was left but Gerald, and on the 17th of September he died too, and so faded away, and we shall never see him more—forever?

In writing thus to Fanny, Kingsley also added something about the "internals" of his brother's fate which give us perhaps the only surviving comment on Gerald's character in early adulthood. He seemed to have grown into a somewhat reckless adventurer:

> O God, Thou alone knowest the long bitter withering baptism of fire, wherewith the poor boy was baptized, day and night alone with his own soul. And yet Thou wert right—as ever—perhaps there was no way but that to bring him to look himself in the face, and know that life was a reality, and not a game! And who dare say that in those weary, weary months of hope deferred, the heart eating at itself, did not gnaw through the crust of vanities (not of so very long growth

---

[42] CK to AS, undated, MP-C0171–36919.
[43] CK to RP, July 1844, *LML* i.133.

either) and the living water which he did drink in his childhood find vent and bubble up![44]

The death of Gerald must have been a great blow. Indeed, the recollection of Gerald's early childhood was in the forefront of Kingsley's mind as he commented on the tragedy that had befallen the *Royalist*. With the death of Gerald, he had lost the only remaining brother who had been the playmate of his happy childhood in Clovelly, Herbert having died ten years before in mysterious circumstances while at school at Helston. The difference in age between Charles, Herbert, and Gerald had been small, one and two years respectively, and they had shared many of the "semi-sensual delights of ear and eye" that the north Devon coast offered. The remaining siblings, Charlotte, George, and Henry, were much younger, and had spent their childhood mainly in Chelsea.

Parish matters towards the end of 1844 were also far from reassuring. Following a change in the rates of payment of tithes from April and October to January and July, Kingsley feared he would have to wait for his tithes till January, losing half a year's money, something he could ill afford right then. He also feared that wages in general would go down, with "gloomy forebodings as to the want of work this winter," all of which meant that many of the poor in his parish would starve. The inadequate political reaction brought the possibility of a revolution for a moment to his mind, something he had discussed with Osborne. The latter had warned in one of his first S.G.O. letters in *The Times* that the evils caused by the social condition of the labourers "will at last be the utter destruction of all that makes landed property desirable [. . .] it needs not the spirit of prophecy to foretell the curse they will become to the country."[45] Kingsley was even more pessimistic than this:

A revolution now-adays would be more terrible & ferocious than such things used to be—from the sham-decent restraint of one large part of the discontented—and the dreadful immorality of another party, I

---

[44] CK to FK, 26/2/1845, *LML* i.134. It is possible that a few lines inserted in the 1851 edition of *Yeast* also refer to Gerald: "I had a brother once—affectionate, simple, generous, full of noble aspirations—but without, alas! A thought of God; yielding in a hundred little points, and some great ones too, to the infernal temptations of a public school . . . He died at seventeen. Where is he now?" *Y* 117.

[45] *The Times*, 31/3/1844, 3–4.

mean the town-dwellers, of wh. I am afraid, the go-a-head party have very little *real* knowledge.[46]

Religious controversy in the Anglican Church about the Tractarians was also blazing up once more. On the last day of the year rumours reached Eversley that Newman had seceded to Rome. He "rises immeasurably in my opinion," Kingsley wrote to Powles, "as every man must do, who, however, wrong, yet feeling himself not of us, goes out from us." He especially hoped that, for the Church of England, the "disease has reached its crisis" with Newman.[47] Although the rumour was wrong—Newman would not officially break away from the Anglican Church to be received into the Roman Catholic Church till the autumn of the next year—William George Ward's secession was fully in the making. Ward, fellow of Balliol and an ardent follower of Newman, had published in June 1844 a book which hastened a head-on confrontation between Tractarians and anti-Tractarians. In *The Ideal of the Christian Church* Ward had pushed Tractarian ideals to the extreme by glorifying the Roman Catholic sense of absolute authority in its teaching. He repudiated the critical approach of the Reformation wholesale by insisting on the necessity to free the Church of Lutheranism and evangelicalism. He concluded that the Anglican Church would do well to take the Roman Catholic Church as its example in its moral, ascetic and mystical theology. Many at Oxford were outraged, and in order to emphasize the importance of the Thirty-nine articles, asked the University for the official censure of *The Ideal of the Christian Church* and of *Tract 90*. This linked Ward's name even more closely to Newman's. The profound religious divisions at Oxford became clear when Ward's book was condemned by 777 votes to 386 and its author stripped of his degrees by only 569 votes to 511. The minority which voted for Ward was a consistent minority. When the results were announced, deep silence ensued. No cheers or angry shouting. A worried Kingsley, who followed the controversy from a distance and who was duly updated by Powles, commented: "The plot is thickening with the poor Church of England. All parties are in confused and angry murmur at they know not what—every one is frightened."[48] Kingsley must have rejoiced at the unexpected aftermath of

---

[46] CK to AS, undated, MP-C0171–36919.
[47] CK to RP, 31/12/1844, *LML* i.133.
[48] CK to FK, 26/2/1845, *LML* i.134.

an affair which had considerably weakened the image of the Tractarians. After the vote Ward no longer dared to conceal that he was engaged to be married, maintaining that he found celibacy the higher form of life for a priest but that he himself never contemplated such a "high and ascetic" vocation. Kingsley remained restless and wanted to do something himself against the Oxford Movement: "God help us all & save our country—not so much from the fate of France, as from the fate of Rome, internal decay & falling to pieces by its own weight."[49] He toyed with the idea of a periodical, and went up to Oxford to talk it over with Powles and other anti-Tractarians. He analysed the situation in the Church as "Nobody trusts nobody. The clergy are split up into innumerable parties, principally nomadic. Every one afraid to speak," and had thoughts of a periodical where young men like himself could speak out freely. What irked Kingsley was that in religious debate "Popery and Puritanism seem to be fighting their battle over again in England, on the foul middle ground of mammonite infidelity."[50] Maurice was consulted, but, with his fear of parties and systems, declined to join any such project. Kingsley also wondered whether the *Oxford and Cambridge Review*, which was going through a crisis, might not be used as their vehicle, and asked Powles to forward a letter to Anthony Froude, who he knew was interested in the review's welfare. Froude, however, answered that he did "not like 'fresh starts'," because "if there are many people laugh."[51] Nothing came of Kingsley's project.

IV

The emerging interest in national social questions in 1844, and the desire to speak out on religious questions on a national level the following year, mark the beginning of a new phase in Kingsley's life. After obtaining a living, some further clerical recognition was conferred upon him when he received an honorary canon's stall at Middleham in Yorkshire. Although the canonry was presented to him by the father of his old college friend Peter Wood, who received a stall

---

[49] CK to FK, undated, BL-62553 f.89v.
[50] CK to RP, 11/12/1845, *LML* i.137–8.
[51] JAF to CK, 8/12/1845, Dunn i.102.

himself, the title was useful and was proudly reproduced on the titlepage of his first published volume of sermons in 1849, or, as Mrs Kingsley put it in her biography, the canonry "being of historic interest, he accepted it gladly."[52] The conferment of the canonry was an attractive pretext in May 1845 for a first visit to Yorkshire, and he wrote enthusiastically to Fanny of the high hills, the deep gorges, and the rising terraces of rock called scars that would feature in his future novels *The Water-Babies* and *The Tutor's Story*. The crystal clear rivers in Yorkshire were a new experience, and he concluded that "as for fishing, I am a clod—never did I see or hear of such tackle as these men use—finer than our finest." A local squire remarked that Kingsley's fishing tackle was "only fit to hold carthorses."[53] Although he missed Fanny and 'Cocky' sorely, the trip was an unconditional success and the "jollifications seem[ed] perpetual."[54] "Really everyone's kindness here is extreme after the stiff South. The mere meeting one, is sufficient to cause an invitation to stay; parties of pleasure, gifts of flies and tackle (everyone fishes and hunts), and dinners and teas and cigars inexhaustible."[55]

Yorkshire offered welcome relief, as Eversley made him feel rather isolated after the Stapletons had moved to London in April and had let Warbrook to a Dr Hawkins, who with his "taciturn & retiring" habits was but a "very poor substitute" for Stapleton's intellectual company.[56] Stapleton's absence was keenly felt. Already on 1 May Kingsley wrote to him that it seemed "an age since any communication has past between us [. . .] how many things would I ask you, were you but here." Relations with Bramshill remained awkward. Sir John felt too ill to intervene in person with the estate, and delegated everything to his overseer Mr Clacy, while Mrs Clacy ruled as his housekeeper at Bramshill. The Clacys did not appreciate the initiatives of the new rector of the parish, and having attempted with "ineffectual efforts first to quarrel," remained coldly civil in an "armed neutrality" towards Kingsley. "Clacy is almost unbearable," Kingsley found, and he was shocked as he saw Clacy let his sheep die by dozens of starvation and rot that winter, combining "bad farming

[52] *LMLM* 54.
[53] CK to FK, undated, BL-62553 f.77v.
[54] CK to FK, 18/5/1845, BL-62553 f.73r.
[55] CK to FK, 22/5/1845, *LML* i.136.
[56] CK to AS, October 1845, MP-C0171–36919.

& oppression." He finally confided to Stapleton that he could see only one event that could bring change to Eversley, and that was the death of Sir John Cope.[57]

After the summer the parish went on in its own "primaeval fashion." A new gallery was added to the church, which would greatly enhance its comfort. Kingsley wondered about the question whether the Irish training college at Maynooth for Roman Catholic priests should receive additional grants, a question which absorbed the political debate in England for some time in 1845, and upon which Kingsley did not see his way clearly. If justice needs to be done to Ireland, Kingsley thought, then there is little doubt what needs to be done.[58] He had no tender feelings for the protestant Church of Ireland, which he thought had "established itself there [. . .] as a state-sect, by an act of invasion & robbery as gross as ever polluted the annals of a Christian church." Although he admitted that perhaps he did not properly understand the question, he concluded that he would rather have Popery, which he could not consider "as evil *in the abstract*—though accursed, as it stands," until some pure movement should reawaken the true faith and common humanity "among the deluded slaves of Ireland."[59]

There was no uncertainty in Kingsley's attitude to another event that had held many intellectual minds captivated since October 1844, when an anonymous book entitled *Vestiges of Creation* was brought out. Its author presented the whole of scientific discovery, from astronomy to phrenology, as confirming an underlying law of cosmic progress which reduced God to a mere series of principles ruling existence: "The Eternal One has arranged for everything beforehand, and trusted all to the operation of the laws of his appointment, himself being ever present in all things," he argued. Even moral affairs he considered under the presidency of law. The book, which was written with great journalistic skill and which was an immediate best-seller—it went through four editions in about six months— was scientifically rather unsound. But it was mainly the moral implications of the kind of godless materialism which the book seemed to advocate that shocked and enraged readers in the mid-40s. Not

---

[57] CK to AS, 1/5/1845, MP-C0171–36919.
[58] CK to AS, 1/5/1845, MP-C0171–36919.
[59] CK to AS, October 1845, MP-C0171–36919.

surprisingly, Kingsley was amongst those who deprecated the book. *The Edinburgh Review* carried a thundering article against it in 1845, which Kingsley thought "a most masterly review [. . .] of the much bespattered vestiges of creation," which he was "inclined to attribute to the wise Professor Forbes." It truly was "as splendid an exposure of materialism, in a condensed form, as I ever met."[60] Kingsley failed to recognize in the review the hand of his own geology professor at Cambridge, Adam Sedgwick, who overreacted to *Vestiges of Creation* because he did "from my soul abhor the sentiments and I believe I could have crushed the book by proving it base, vulgar in spirit, [. . .] false, shallow, worthless." To Kingsley the book would henceforth be damned along with all manifestations of materialism and atheism.

The dangers and suffering caused by materialism were close at hand. During 1845 Kingsley saw much of his old university friend Charles Mansfield, who started medical studies after his Cambridge degree. But after mastering its elements he decided that medicine did not convince him, and abandoned it to specialize in chemistry and dynamics. In the first he was recognized "as one of the most promising young chemists in England," while ornithology, geology and mesmerism were enthusiastically pursued in his free time. He had gradually estranged himself from members of his family through his eccentric social conduct, and they broke with him when he lost his religious faith and declared himself a confirmed materialist. During the second half of 1845, however, Mansfield was going through a profound crisis of re-conversion to Christianity, and, on one of his visits to him in London, Kingsley "found him undergoing all the horrors of a deep & I do think healthy baptism of fire—not only a conversion, but a discovery that God & the Devil are living realities fighting for his body & soul."[61] Mansfield entreated Kingsley not to leave him alone, and they walked the London streets together, meeting Maurice at Temple Bar, and after Kingsley briefly visited Stapleton at Clapham, they dined together. Late at night Mansfield accompanied Kingsley back to Chelsea. It was clear that, as "a man of vast thought & feelings," Mansfield was having a very hard time.

---

[60] CK to AS, 7/8/1845, MP-C0171–36919.
[61] CK to FK, undated, BL-62553 f.87v–88r.

When Mansfield subsequently visited Eversley, he became one of the very few of Kingsley's former friends who immediately gained Mrs Kingsley's trust and liking.

V

In the spring of 1845 Kingsley had started on a small agricultural project called "our little industrial field of two acres," which created employment in the parish for four men for a month. Although the result was positive, he realized that it was "but a stop gap." Still it made clear to him that "we are bound either to render the labourer independent of our wages or to give him work to support himself."[62]

The year 1845 closed with dark prospects of a winter of famine. In August it had become clear that the potato crop would fail. Blight appeared on the Isle of Wight and in Kent, and the Irish crop was feared for. As the potato was the vegetable that yielded the greatest return per acre, small farmers and cottagers concentrated almost entirely on this crop, while the prosperous farmers grew potatoes for home consumption and grain for export. A potato crop failure, therefore, would mean nothing less than starvation. The situation was bleak, especially as it was discovered that the seed would be unfit for the following year as well, thus raising the prospect of a further famine in 1846.

By October it was also clear that the two acres of potatoes in the "industrial field" were blighted, this constituting a heavy financial loss to Kingsley. The general potato failure made him think about crops, and when frost and snow arrived at the end of November, Kingsley, in "The Poetry of a Root Crop," phrased his impression of the "eider-robe[d]" fields, where swedes, globes and carrots were treasure houses burrowed in a charmed sleep, while the "Toiling town [. . .] will not heed/ God His voice for rage and greed." In the poem Kingsley draws a picture of a frozen field which powerfully evokes Carlyle's enchanted fruit that the workers cannot touch in *Past and Present*:

---

[62] CK to AS, 1/5/1845, MP-C0171–36919.

Like some marble carven nun,
With folded hands when work is done,
Who mute upon her tomb doth pray.
Till the resurrection day.

The poem is not of outstanding quality, but it shows that Kingsley had the time and the inspiration to take up writing poetry again. Much more was to follow over the following two years.

CHAPTER FIVE

WHAT RIGHT HAVE I TO ARROGATE CHRIST'S BRIDE-BED? (1846–1847)

In one of the editions of her husband's *Letters and Memories*, Mrs Kingsley remarked that "1846 passed uneventfully in the routine of parish work, and domestic happiness."[1] Subsequent biographers have felt hampered by the same lack of material confronted by Mrs Kingsley when she collected information for her husband's biography. If they did not head directly for the tumultuous beginning of 1848, they hurried hastily over the sparse events of 1846 and 1847. Few letters have survived from 1846, and hardly any family letters, which seems to indicate that the year did indeed pass in domestic happiness and without significant events.

At the beginning of May the monotony of Eversley was broken for a few days when the Stapletons came to stay at the Rectory. It was during the same month that Mrs Kingsley was laid up with a bad form of influenza, which the climate of Eversley made difficult to get rid of. Although the rectory had been made habitable when the Kingsleys moved in, and notwithstanding fires burning in most rooms, the dampness of the house made Kingsley anxious about the health of his infant daughter and wife, who was in the early stages of another pregnancy. He therefore decided to send them on a holiday to Shanklin on the Isle of Wight for a change of air, while he himself would join them as soon as his parish duties permitted.

At Eversley, loneliness made itself felt immediately, and the hiving of a swarm of bees was about the only event that fully caught Kingsley's imagination. He had never seen a hiving before, and, standing "in the middle of the flying army," he meditated on the courage of the bees in protecting their sister-queen: "I hate to think that it is vile self-interest—much less mere brutal magnetism (called by the ignorant 'instinct'), which takes with them the form of loyalty, prudence, order, self-sacrifice." It even made him wonder whether

---

[1] *LMLM* 59.

animals had souls as well as man. The wonders of nature and dreams of Fanny "& Baby romping in bed in the morning" filled his time till duty was over. When he finally left Eversley, he was unwilling to prolong the separation more than was necessary by waiting for coaches at Ryde, and decided to cover the ten miles to Shanklin on foot.

When the Kingsleys returned from the Isle of Wight, summer was near and the rectory at Eversley comfortable enough. But the problem of damp returned when autumn arrived, and it was decided to redo parts of the house and to drain the glebe in front of it. In December works started with bricklayers and carpenters all over the house, and Kingsley lamented that he was "seven times too rich, and therefore I'm as poor as Job" since most of their money was needed to repair far too big a house: "Had I been Will Barker there in the drain, I should never have found out that it was cold, and damp, and shabby."[2] The "sum and substance" of this complaint was that an invitation from Powles in Oxford had to be declined with a heavy heart; Kingsley very much wanted to discuss the future of religion with his friends at Oxford. "Young men of this day must get faith," he wrote to Powles, "I am more and more painfully awake to the fact that the curse of our generation is that so few of us deeply believe anything."[3] The urge to assume a more public role in national religion was still part of Kingsley's reaction against the Oxford Movement and its ideal of medieval monastic life. He explained that there was no looking back for him at any ideal age, no "retrogression, outward or inward," but progression only.

Kingsley's presentiment of an approaching political and social crisis owed much to Carlyle's dire prophecies in *Past and Present*. Like Carlyle, he thought that society's inability to deal with its ills would in the end lead to a struggle in which religion would be brushed aside as a superfluous institution. "I speak with fear and trembling," he confided in a particularly outspoken letter to Powles,

> I cannot stave off the conviction of present danger and radical disease in our national religion. And though I laugh at myself sometimes for conceit and uncharitableness—tamen usque recurrit—that hand-writing on the wall; that 'mene, mene' against Anglicanism and Evangelicalism

[2] CK to RP, December 1846, i.140.
[3] CK to RP, December 1846, i.140–1.

at once—both of which more and more daily prove to me their utter impotence to meet our social evils. Six months in a country parish is enough to prove it. What is to be done I do not see. A crisis, political and social, seems approaching, and religion, like a rootless plant, may be brushed away in the struggle. Maurice is full of fear—I had almost said despondence—and he, as you know, has said in his last book, that "The real struggle of the day will be, not between Popery and Protestantism, but between Atheism and Christ." And here we are daubing walls with untempered mortar—quarrelling about how we shall patch the superstructure, forgetting that the foundation is gone—Faith in anything.[4]

Kingsley had thus started to look beyond a personal anti-Tractarianism in his quest for elements of spiritual good in his own age. His connection with Sydney Osborne and "six months in a country parish" had brought out a new social and political outlook that was rapidly maturing (or 'yeasting', as he himself would call it) his religious convictions. As a result of his sympathy with the plight of the poor, he had begun to see that "democracy, in Church and State" would be the inevitable outcome of the present social struggle, and that the church had better appropriate it positively. And, he asked himself, was democracy not the very essence of Christ's message?

Waiving the question of its evil or its good, we cannot stop it. Let us Christianize it instead; and if you fear that you are therein doing evil that good may come, oh! consider, consider carefully, whether democracy (I do not mean foul licence, or pedantic constitution-mongering, but the rights of man as man—his individual and direct responsibility to God and the State, on the score of mere manhood and Christian grace) be not the very pith and marrow of the New Testament.[5]

The future of England lay with democracy if only religious leaders knew how to channel it in the right direction, and how "in the widest and divinest sense, [to] make friends of the Mammon of unrighteousness." "It is the new commercial aristocracy; it is the scientific go-ahead-ism of the day which must save us, and which we must save. We have licked the feet of the feudal aristocrats for centuries, and see whither they have brought us." Now more then ever there was need for action in the spirit of true Christianity, as Kingsley saw it embodied in the middle-class ideals of the late Thomas Arnold:

---

[4] CK to RP, December 1846, i.142–3.
[5] CK to RP, December 1846, i.141–2.

In plain truth, the English clergy must Arnold-ise, if they do not wish
to go either to Rome or to the workhouse, before fifty years are out.
There is, I do believe, an Arnoldite spirit rising; but most 'laudant,
non sequuntur.' Decent Anglicanism, decent Evangelical Conservatism
(or Evangelicalism) having become the majority, is now quite Conservative, and each party playing Canute and the tide, as it can scramble
in turn into the chair of authority.[6]

"I would devote soul and body to get together an Arnoldite party
of young men," Kingsley sighed in his frustrated longing to be doing
something active in church reform. And looking back at the Middle
Ages, he added in Carlylean style, "If we could but start anything
daring and earnest as a 'coroccio,' or flag of misery, round which,
as David in the mountains, the spiritual rag-tags might rally, and
howl harmonious the wrongs of the clergy and of literary men, it
were a great thing gained."[7]

II

Although Kingsley's ideals were not set on the 'medieval retrogression' of the Tractarians, he was deep in the Middle Ages himself.
Publishing a journal to give voice to a reforming movement was still
his dearest wish. Notwithstanding his constant sounding in 1845 and
1846 among Powles's Oxford friends for an opening, nothing came
of such a plan, so he decided to take up his pen himself. Thus early
in 1846 his work on the life of his exemplary 'healthy' St Elizabeth
was resumed. The prose tale, however, was now substituted for verse
as it slowly grew into a long play in the style of the late romantic
dramatic poems, meant for private (closet) reading rather than for
the stage. Its subject matter also shifted, from a preoccupation with
the religious meaning of celibacy that reflected his own early marital uncertainties to a whole range of social questions. Although many
personal views of marriage, masculinity, and penance remained pivotal, the drama embraced critiques of the corn-laws, the poor laws,
free-trade, self-help, emigration, Malthusian principles, and the attitude of the aristocracy towards social problems.

---

[6] CK to RP, December 1846, i.143.
[7] CK to RP, December 1846, i.143.

Kingsley worked on St Elizabeth throughout 1846 and till the beginning of May 1847, when, according to Mrs Kingsley, it "crossed his mind" to publish it. It seems more likely, however, that the idea of publication was the stimulus behind the project from the first. Kingsley's ardent hopes since the end of 1845 of setting up a journal, and the recasting of the prose tale (which was originally written as a private wedding present to his wife) into a book-length verse-drama, points to a more ambitious goal. Moreover, his friends at Oxford had asked for something from his pen for the 'Review', and it seems likely that he was initially willing to comply, although he realized as early as May 1846 that "dear St. Elizabeth is now becoming too far developed to cut her in pieces, and serve her up in a magazine." It was decided that "she shall appear as a poem."[8] For a year Kingsley worked from what he saw as the only "entire and unbiassed" original biography of St Elizabeth, written by her near contemporary, Dietrich of Apolda, and printed in *Lectionis antiquae* compiled by Henricus Canisius (1605). To show how strictly he adhered to the historical truth given there, Kingsley started to add to his dramatic text a series of elaborate notes and cross-references that made comparison with Dietrich's text possible. One thinly veiled reason why Kingsley chose to follow only the first account of Elizabeth's life, and ignore all later sources, was that in Dietrich's version he found a remarkable "omission of Mariolatry," which he made it his business to copy.[9]

The manuscript was shown at an early stage to Fanny, but by the middle of April 1847, when the play was finished, he went up to London to see how he could get it published. As there were various other things to do and arrange in London, Kingsley reluctantly left Fanny behind at Eversley; he felt "at once very happy & very lonely & very anxious"[10] as she had been delivered of a son early in the year. The child was given the name Maurice, his clerical namesake and Powles both serving at his baptism as godfathers. There were plans for a long holiday on the coast to give Mrs Kingsley a much needed "change of air & sea bathing," but someone had first to be found to take over his duties at Eversley. That was easily

---

[8] CK to RP, May 1846, i.139.
[9] "Introduction to *The Saint's Tragedy*" *P* 5.
[10] CK to FK, [17/4/1847], BL-62553 f.97r.

arranged with his father, who decided to come over himself with his wife and "all their family."[11] However, finding a publisher for St Elizabeth proved more difficult.

In London Kingsley showed the manuscript to his parents and to F.D. Maurice. "E's success with my father & mother is quite glorious. They are astonished at it," he wrote home, but "I find my father & mother agree in your dislike of some of the coarser passages, & I have resolutely scratched them out."[12] The play also served to strengthen the already affectionate ties with his mother: "My mother has been reading me a quantity of beautiful poetry of her own, w. I never heard of before. We had a delightful evening of peace & intellect alone together."[13] Maurice too was enthusiastic about Kingsley's play and they went over many a passage together and discussed his representations of medieval Christianity. In Kingsley's hands Elizabeth's story had become above all an outspoken condemnation of "the Manichean contempt with which a celibate clergy would have all men regard the names of husband, wife, and parent."[14] This was clearly aimed at the High Church party. Maurice expressed his doubts whether the homely scene in Elizabeth's bedroom after her wedding night was appropriate or not, but having read it to an approving Powles, who happened to breakfast with him one day, he decided that there was nothing offensive in it at all. Still, as the play represented the Middle Ages in a generally unflattering way—"in the gross, a coarse, barbarous, and profligate age"[15]— Maurice thought the play "certainly a dangerous one" and in points "a little too bold for the taste and temper of this age."[16] To put those who cannot take its message in at ease, he thought the work would benefit from a preface, which he himself volunteered to write. Kingsley was overjoyed at this, as he wrote home to Fanny: "he will help me to one, by writing me something which, if I like, I can prefix. What more would you have!"[17] The preface was written, and Maurice publicly agreed that after all it was right that Kingsley

[11] CK to AS, 20/5/1847, MP-C0171–36919.
[12] CK to FK, [15/4/1847], BL-62553 f.99r.
[13] CK to FK, [15/4/1847], 62553 f.101r.
[14] "Introduction to *The Saint's Tragedy*" P 4.
[15] "Introduction to *The Saint's Tragedy*" P 6–7.
[16] "Preface to *The Saint's Tragedy*" P^PE xviii–xx.
[17] CK to FK, 15/4/1847, BL-62553 f.97r.

"retained what I should from cowardice have wished him to exclude."[18]

Notwithstanding Maurice's preface, finding a publisher remained hard. Moxon and Murray were approached but neither was willing to hazard his name. Moxon, however, suggested that Kingsley try Pickering. Maurice had proposed to show the manuscript of St Elizabeth to Alexander Scott, Alfred Tennyson and Sara Coleridge. Although, for unknown reasons, the manuscript was apparently not given to the first two, Henry Coleridge answered for his wife that he was enthusiastic about it and wrote a "highly recommendatory" note of introduction for Kingsley to the Pickering publishing house. Contrary to all biographical accounts, Pickering was willing to publish. He proposed an edition of 500 copies, but on condition that Kingsley would be liable for any loss incurred if there were copies unsold after a period of one year. In a gentlemanly way he left Kingsley free to look for a better deal elsewhere, but said that he could always "fall back on him" if that failed.[19] It was a victory, and one not dampened by a visit to the dentist, who, to put his mouth "in better order than it has been for several years," had to torture him "in divers ways [. . .], for w. have to pay him £2.2."[20] But before accepting Pickering's offer, Kingsley tried Parker in The Strand, and met with success. As it turned out, Pickering missed out on a future successful author through "the heroic magnificence" of John Parker, "who, though a burnt child, does not dread the fire."[21]

Kingsley thus had reason to return to Eversley in high spirits and prepare for a six-week holiday in June and July on the south coast near Lymington, which, after his first literary success and renewed family bliss, was to prove a happy one. The family stayed at Milford on Sea on the southern edge of the New Forest, where Kingsley's father had spent his early manhood. After years of self-imposed deprivation, Kingsley now had a horse at his disposal and enjoyed himself riding in the New Forest, taking in, as he recorded years later, the "softness of rolling lawns, feathery heath, and rounded oak and beech woods," reining in his mare for an occasional chat with the keeper with his "noble bloodhound eying him "from between his

---

[18] "Preface to *The Saint's Tragedy*" *P*[PE] xx.
[19] CK to FK, [17/4/1847], BL-62553 f.100v.
[20] CK to FK, [21/4/1847], BL-62553 f.102r.
[21] CK to RP, undated, *LML* i.147.

master's legs."[22] He was carrying out some minimal duties at nearby
Pennington on Sundays to pay for his holidays, but on other days
"in the saddle once more, or alone with his beloved ones, with leisure
to watch his babies, his heart's spring bubbled up into song:"[23]

> So I'm aff and away to the muirs, mither, to hunt the deer,
> Ranging far frae frowning faces, and the douce folk here;
> Crawling up through burn and bracken, louping down the screes,
> Looking out frae craig and headland, drinking up the simmer breeze.
>
> Oh, the wafts o' heather honey, and the music o' the brae,
> As I watch the great harts feeding, nearer, nearer a' the day.
> Oh, to hark the eagle screaming, sweeping, ringing round the sky-
> That's a bonnier life than stumbling ower the muck to colt and kye.
>   (from "The Outlaw")

Kingsley's poetic imagination, which had lain barren during the last
few years, flared up again in 1847. A children's hymn in the style
of Wesley's "Gentle Jesus, Meek and Mild," undoubtedly inspired
by the birth of a son, was followed by a series of short lyrical poems
and ballads of which "Airly Beacon" has become the most famous.
Kingsley caught the melodious oral nature as well as the dramatic
but impersonal tragedy of the ballad genre in these pieces, which
are among his best poetic efforts. Many of the poems were inspired
by the New Forest's atmosphere and featured deserted lovers, desperate knights, wicked landowners, poachers and game-keepers.
Hunting took up his full fancy, from the lover of the game-keeper's
daughter shooting "a mighty hart" in "A New Forest Ballad," the
besotted monarch who is killed during a hunt in "The Red King"
and the bonny hunting life of "The Outlaw," to the more socially
outspoken "The Bad Squire" which would later feature in his first
novel *Yeast*. The freshness of these poems owes much to Kingsley's
own elevated spirits in 1847.

Susan Chitty remarks that with the birth of their second child,
Fanny abandoned any programme of religious chastisement and
humiliation.[24] Much the same could be said for Kingsley himself,
who now returned increasingly to being an active sporting gentleman. Family bliss and a sense of having accomplished something

---

[22] "North Devon" *PI* 284.
[23] *LML* i.148.
[24] Chitty (1974) 99.

had much to do with this, and it is almost as if with *The Saint's Tragedy*, which reflects so much of his early married years, he was able to put one stage of his life behind him.

III

During the last months of 1847, his work was in the press, coming out immediately after Christmas (but dated 1848) as *The Saint's Tragedy; or, the True Story of Elizabeth of Hungary, Landgravine of Thuringia, Saint of the Romish Calendar.*

The story of St Elizabeth (1207–1231), as it stands in Kingsley's play, is as follows. Elizabeth, daughter of King Andrew II of Hungary, grew up at the magnificent court of Thuringia in Germany, where she was taken as a child to be the future bride to the Landgrave's son. As the years passed, the girl showed a propensity for pious conduct combined with acts of self-mortification, conduct which was mocked by stepmother and courtiers alike. She marries Lewis at the age of fourteen, and bears him three children. The marriage was a happy one, between a devoted husband and wife. Lewis, moreover, is as devout as Elizabeth, and, as he had in the meantime succeeded his father, Elizabeth is free to put into action her yearnings to dedicate her life to charity. She is untiring in assisting the poor, and freely distributes alms, food and clothes. But because she still feels unsure about her religious devotion, she appoints Conrad of Marburg, an ascetic priest and inquisitor, as her spiritual director. When Lewis goes on a crusade to Palestine, but dies of a fever at Otranto, Elizabeth retires from public life and gives herself up to Conrad's guidance. He firmly steers her towards sainthood, insisting that she renounce the world (and her family), and enter a religious order. The constant labouring for the poor damages her fragile health and she dies at the age of twenty-four. Conrad does much for her canonization, and she is declared a saint just before an angry crowd assassinates him.

Kingsley gathered most of these facts from Dietrich's account, although there are small deviations in this story from the historical Elizabeth, who came to Thuringia as a future bride for the Landgrave's eldest son Hermann, but was betrothed to the second son Ludwig (Lewis) when Hermann died in 1216. There is no mention either of the fact that the marriage was part of a strategy to consolidate the

political alliance against the German emperor Otto IV. Both facts
would have diminished the idea that they were divinely destined for
each other. Following Dietrich, Kingsley blackens the role of Elizabeth's
stepmother (who in reality was a religious and loving influence on
her) in order to emphasize the fairy-tale motif of the story. The only
major anachronism is that Kingsley postpones Conrad's assassina-
tion until after Elizabeth's canonization, since by following the exact
dates he felt he "must either lose sight of the final triumph, which
connects my heroine for ever with Germany and all Romish Christen-
dom, and is the very culmination of the whole story, or relinquish
my only opportunity of doing Conrad justice, by exhibiting the
remaining side of his character."[25] Kingsley also admitted being intentionally anachronistic in his language, since he had made it a rule
to follow "the Shakespearian method of bringing the past up to my
readers, and not the modern one of bringing my readers down to
the past."[26] It was a rule he would stick to in his later historical
fiction and one which helps make such fiction of interest to the student of the Victorian age.

The play was clearly written in imitation of Shakespeare. Its blank
verse is interspersed with occasional prose scenes, attempts are made
at a pithy turn of phrase, and there are characters such as a court-
fool, peasants for low-life scenes, and fickle and ungrateful com-
moners, as well as a character like Walter of Varila, who, in the
manner of Shakespeare's Kent, functions as a kind of moral ideal
in the action of the play. The tragic element of the story lay for
Kingsley in the misguided notion with which thirteenth-century
churchmen held ideas of celibacy, and "the miserable consequences,
when [they are] received into a heart of insight and determination
sufficient to follow out all belief to its ultimate practice."[27] The play
also has moments of autobiographical interest which were less clear
to the contemporary reader.

Kingsley chose to introduce Elizabeth as a devout young woman,
who, in praising Christ, sings of him in terms that define a mother-
child relationship. Emphasis on her womanly as opposed to her
saintly qualities is developed in his further representation of her.

---

[25] "Notes to *The Saint's Tragedy*" *P* 174.
[26] CK to J. Conington, 15/1/1848, *LML* i.153.
[27] "Introduction to The Saint's Tragedy" *P* 4.

When Lewis (Ludwig), who is in love with her beauty, admits the hopelessness and immorality of wooing a saint—

> What! shall my selfish longings drag thee down
> From maid to wife? degrade the soul I worship?
> That were a caitiff deed![28]

—he is promptly put right by Walter of Varila who asserts for Kingsley that "if she looks an angel now, you will be better mated than you expected, when you find her—a woman. For flesh and blood she is, and that young blood."[29] This convinces Lewis to propose to Elizabeth, who responds in the gladness of the moment that "I am a woman,/ And all things bid me love!" and that it is "my dignity/ [. . .] thus to cast my virgin pride away."[30] But at the bridal feast, while a minstrel sings of blissful married life, in the background a group of monks chant "A carnis illectamentis/ Domine libera nos [. . .] A vanitatibus saeculi/ Domine libera nos" and Elizabeth feels "The spectre of my duties and my dangers" crowding in her "heart with terror."[31]

The next act opens with the night-scene in Elizabeth's bower to which Maurice originally objected. The scene has a certain erotic quality with a naked Elizabeth doing penance on the cold floor in the foreground, presumably after having made love, and her husband sleeping in an alcove at the back, while "the fragrant lips of night even now are kissing [. . .] many many brows of happy lovers." Elizabeth is torn between her sense of duty and love for her husband and her love for Christ, having sworn to love her earthly husband but feeling at the same time spiritually "widowed from mine Eden." The theme had already been introduced in a cursory way when, in Act I, scene 2, Lewis wondered: "Is wedlock treason to that purity,/ Which is the jewel and the soul of wedlock?" But it now becomes obsessive. The scene, of course, owed much to Kingsley's own experience. The Christian dilemma of how to accept both sexual and spiritual love that had disturbed him in his early days of courtship surfaces for a moment in Elizabeth's question whether the

---

[28] I.2, *P* 28.
[29] I.2, *P* 29.
[30] I.3, *P* 34.
[31] I.4, *P* 36–6.

"base emotions picture Christ's embrace." The picture of Elizabeth being flagellated is a familiar one too:

> Alas! what's this? These shoulders' cushioned ice,
> And thin soft flanks, with purple lashes all,
> And weeping furrows traced! Ah! precious life-blood

as is her apologia for it:

> I know the use of pain: bar not the leech
> Because his cure is bitter—'Tis such medicine
> Which breeds that paltry strength, that weal devotion,
> For which you say you love me.—Ay, which brings
> Even when most sharp, a sharp, a stern and awful joy
> As its attendant angel[32]—

The language and the sentiment it expresses is close to the many exhortations to penance during the years of Kingsley's courtship. Even closer to his own experience is the passage when Lewis breaks the news to Elizabeth of his intention to set out on a crusade. She reacts to the imminent separation by saying that she will

> [. . .] *nerve myself with stripes* to meet the weary day,
>   And labour for thy sake.
> Until *by vigils, fasts*, and tears,
> The flesh was grown so sparse and light,
> That I could slip its mesh, *and flit by night*
> O'er sleeping sea and land *to thee*—or Christ till morning light.[33]

Elizabeth's struggle in choosing between her husband and Christ thus has autobiographical origins. Unable herself to settle the question of her duties, she asks her husband to entrust her spiritual guidance to Master Conrad of Marburg, to make him the "Director of my conscience and my actions" so that "I could live for thee and thine." The error of judgment in this decision is at the core of the tragedy that follows, in which Kingsley seeks to depict the matrimonial (and national) misery that ensues when wives chose to rely on father-confessors rather than on their husbands. The contemporary reader of *The Saint's Tragedy* could not have failed to notice the allusions to Tractarianism and, in particular, to John Keble's wish to re-introduce regular confession in the Anglican Church.

---

[32] II.1, *P* 40, 41.
[33] II.9, *P* 80, my italics.

The tragic flaw in Lewis and Elizabeth's marriage grows out of this misguided decision. Lewis is not man enough to contradict his pious wife's desire for a father-confessor. All he can do is give this feeble answer to her request:

> I own thee guide
> Of my devotions, mine ambition's lodestar,
> The Saint whose shrine I serve with lance and lute;
> If thou wilt have a ruler, let him be,
> Through thee, the ruler of thy slave.[34]

It is evident from these lines that Lewis still sees his wife as a saint rather than as a woman. He acquiesces without further remonstrance and Conrad becomes her father-confessor. He asks Walter what he thinks of Conrad, but takes no notice of the opinion of Kingsley's mouthpiece that he is one of those "sleek, passionless men, who are too refined to be *manly*, and measure their grace by their effeminacy."[35]

Conrad's presence as a spiritual guide does not reduce Elizabeth's qualms about earthly love, however. Happy moments, when she feels that "this wedlock seems/ A second infancy's baptismal robe," are immediately followed by thoughts of having irremediably fallen, and that "whatsoe'er is not of faith is sin."[36] When Lewis leaves on a crusade never to return, it seems as if Elizabeth's early misgivings about her marriage have come true:

> What if mine heavenly Spouse in jealous ire
> Should smite mine earthly spouse? Have I two husbands?
> The words are horror—yet they are orthodox![37]

Conrad certainly sees it that way. Bent on guiding her through a sure process of sanctification, he convinces the young widow to enter a religious order and renounce her children by emphasizing that "Nature's corrupt throughout":

> Our nature, even in Eden gross and vile,
> And by miraculous grace alone upheld,
> Is now itself, and foul, and damned, must die
> Ere we can live[38]

---

[34] II.2, *P* 46–7.
[35] II.2, *P* 48, my italics.
[36] II.9, *P* 78.
[37] II.1, *P* 38.
[38] IV.1, *P* 115.

Before acquiescing in Conrad's commands, however, Elizabeth wonders what right she has thus "to arrogate Christ's bride-bed;" and Kingsley at the last turns her demise into a triumph for marriage. In her death-bed confession, Elizabeth refrains from any expression of "self-abhorrence/ For the vile pleasures of her carnal wedlock," while her final words assert the purity and dignity of matrimony. Marriage is ultimately perceived not as the carnal infirmity of fallen man, but as the true glory of Protestant Christianity:

> *Eliz.* I must begone upon a long, long journey
>   To him I love.
> *Con.*   She means her heavenly Bridegroom—
>   The Spouse of souls.
> *Eliz.*   I said, to him I love.[39]

There is no ambiguity in this affirmation. Kingsley's defeat of celibacy in Elizabeth's instance celebrates what he saw as "the distinctive superiority of Protestant over Popish nations."[40]

Notwithstanding, or because of, her virtues, Elizabeth is not an attractive character; the description of her enjoyment of suffering being almost as hard to bear for the reader as the sublimation of desire by means of penance was in Kingsley's letters to Fanny in 1844–5. The moral and social worth of Walter of Varila often comes as much as a relief as Kingsley's own budding social consciousness did after he had settled into matrimony. More than any other character in the play, Walter was Kingsley's *alter ego*, and it is clear that he delighted in creating the plain-spoken (and prose-speaking) knight whom he describes as representing "the 'healthy animalism' of the Teutonic mind, with its mixture of deep earnestness and hearty merriment."[41] He is the direct antithesis of the effeminate Master Conrad, whom he charges with deception of the faithful when the play reaches its climax:

> I have watched you and your crew, how you preach up selfish ambition for divine charity and call prurient longings celestial love, while you blaspheme that very marriage from whose mysteries you borrow all your cant. The day will come when every husband and father will hunt you down like vermin.[42]

---

[39] IV.4, *P* 142.
[40] "Introduction to *The Saint's Tragedy*" *P* 8.
[41] "Introduction to *The Saint's Tragedy*" *P* 6.
[42] IV.2, *P* 123–4.

Walter was to Kingsley the 'manly' counterpart to Lewis, the type of husband whose woman-worship was based on "a semi-sensual dream of female-saint-worship," and which left their wives an easy prey to the subtleties of an effeminate priesthood. In the end, Walter was meant to stand for an arising "lay-religion" founded on faith in the divine and in the universal qualities of humanity and nature, a faith that would find freedom in the Lutheran reformation. To the reader of Kingsley's works he is the first representative of what came to be called his Muscular Christianity, and as such he is the prototype of Lancelot in *Yeast* and Amyas in *Westward Ho!*.

The villain of the piece, Conrad of Marburg, is a more challenging and more complex character than either Elizabeth or Walter. The anachronism in making Conrad survive Elizabeth's canonization indicates that Kingsley felt fascinated by the psychological depth of this character. His guidance of Elizabeth towards sainthood is done in good faith, but not blindly or merely from ambition. When Elizabeth begs for his spiritual direction, he shrinks at first from the responsibility in a revealing soliloquy:

> Obedience to my will! An awful charge!
> But yet, to have the training of her sainthood;
> To watch her rise above this wild world's waves
> Like floating water-lily, towards heaven's light
> Opening its virgin snows, with golden eye
> Mirroring the golden sun; to be her champion,
> And war with fiends for her; that were a 'quest';
> That were true chivalry; to bring my Judge
> This jewel for His crown; this noble soul,
> Worth thousand prudish clods of barren clay[.]

There is a suppressed feeling of erotic desire for the beautiful Elizabeth—"she is most fair!/Pooh! I know nought of fairness"—which finds expression in an unconscious, but unmistakably sadistic, delight in her physical suffering:

>   't will cost her pain—
> But what of that? there are worse things than pain—[43]

When he looks at the still image of Elizabeth shortly before her death, Conrad comes near to realizing that such distorted feelings derive from a mistaken view of love and beauty:

---

[43] II.3, *P* 50.

> O happy Lewis! Had I been knight—
> A man at all—What's this? I must be brutal,
> Or I shall love her: and yet that's no safeguard:
> I have marked it oft: ay—with that devilish triumph
> Which eyes its victim's writhings, still will mingle
> A sympathetic thrill of lust—[44]

Elizabeth's deathbed hopes that she will be reunited with her late husband shatter Conrad's faith. His "inner voice is sad and dull,/ Even at the crown and shout of victory," and he asks himself whether there had been no "gentler way" to lead her to sainthood:

> We [priests] make, and moil, like children in their gardens,
> And spoil with dabbled hands, our flowers i' the planting

Looking his mistakes steadfastly in the face "with the pregnant terror/Of life unseen," some of his last expressions before he is lynched by a mob of furious husbands and fathers are those of a muted repentance:

> Oh! to have prayed, and toiled—and lied—for this!
> For this to have crushed out the heart of youth,
> And sat by calm, while living bodies burned![45]

Kingsley finally judges Conrad to have possessed a "noble nature warped and blinded by its unnatural exclusions from those family ties through which we first discern or describe God and our relations to Him,"[46] a victim of the "phantoms which Popery substitutes for the living Christ."[47]

IV

Although set in the Middle Ages, *The Saint's Tragedy* is truly nineteenth-century in spirit, especially when it discusses the plight of the poor. Elizabeth describes a dismal social situation, a weltering "black fermenting heap of life,"[48] which closely resembles the misery and suffering that Kingsley had witnessed around Eversley and Durweston,

---

[44] IV.3, *P* 134.
[45] V.2, *P* 152–3.
[46] "Introduction to *The Saint's Tragedy*" *P* 6.
[47] "Introduction to *The Saint's Tragedy*" *P* 9.
[48] II.4, *P* 53.

while her vocabulary closely resembles that which Kingsley himself was to use in his social-problem novels. Thus to Elizabeth the comparison of the degraded human beings with swine presents itself naturally, an image that was to be re-used with insistency in Kingsley's descriptions of the labourers in *Yeast*, while the woeful housing conditions of the poor prefigure the gruesome scenes on Jacob's Island in *Alton Locke*:

> The light of heaven,
> The common air, was narrow, gross, and dun;
> The tiles did drop from the eaves; the unhinged doors
> Tottered o'er inky pools, where reeked and curdled
> The offal of a life; the gaunt-haunched swine
> Growled at their christened playmates o'er the scraps.
> Shrill mothers cursed; wan children wailed; sharp coughs
> Rang through the crazy chambers; hungry eyes
> Glared dumb reproach, and old perplexity,
> Too stale for words;[49]

And Elizabeth's resolution to lead an active life in combating these evils is representative of Kingsley's own life-long restlessness:

> I do not love that contemplative life:
> No! I must headlong into seas of toil,
> [. . .]
> Oh! contemplation palls upon the spirit,
> Like the chill silence of an autumn sun:
> While action, like the roaring south-west wind,
> Sweeps laden with elixers, with rich draughts
> Quickening the wombed earth.[50]

There is an echo of Carlylean diatribe in *The Saint's Tragedy* on the Condition-of-England-Question. In a sequence of three scenes towards the end of the second act, Kingsley introduces two low-life characters—a peasant and a woodcutter—who discuss the "true division of labour," i.e. that there are people who work and earn, and people who merely spend. Before enlarging on the principles underlying the nineteenth-century market-situation, Kingsley wants to drive home to the reader what the economic situation of England amounts to for the poor. In the next scene the attention shifts to Elizabeth,

---

[49] II.4, *P* 55.
[50] II.2, *P* 44.

who is unable to satisfy the demands of a mob of starving com-
moners imploring her for bread, the wheat which she has ordered
having failed to arrive. Count Walter then enters with a merchant
who is unwilling to part with his goods unless he is paid three times
their value,

> Not a penny less—
> I bought it on speculation—I must live—
> I get my bread by buying corn that's cheap,
> And selling where it's dearest.
> [. . .]
> The trade['s] protected. Why, I kept the corn
> Three months on venture.[51]

Elizabeth pledges the amount the merchant asks, but Walter begins
distributing the corn for market-price, threatening to set the mob on
the merchant if he dare protest, a hint at Carlyle's warning that
popular revolution might be at hand if the rights of the poor are
further denied.

Kingsley oscillated considerably in his opinions on free-trade and
protectionism in the years preceding his publications on the subject.
If in the autumn of 1845 Kingsley seemed to approve the imminent
abrogation of the corn-laws, a letter from Stapleton reporting on
Lord Ashburton's speech in the House of Lords at the beginning of
1846 made Kingsley "tremble a little."[52] Ashburton pointed out that
the colonial and commercial interests of the nation would be greatly
endangered if the corn-laws were abolished. As a result, in *The Saint's
Tragedy* Kingsley condemned both the corn-laws that kept prices of
bread artificially high and the moral implications of free-trade. When
he brings together a group of noblemen in the eighth scene to discuss the situation of the poor, he addresses a number of contemporary attitudes to poor relief. For example, he makes one nobleman
analyse the social situation by maintaining that the root of all evil
is that "[t]here are too many of us," and that charity keeps too
many from emigrating. This makes the Abbot contend, in a Malthusian
fashion that it would therefore be better to leave providence undisturbed and let "this dispensation [. . .] work itself out." Count Hugo,
a practical champion of laissez-faire, argues that "the sharper the

---

[51] II.7, *P* 65–6.
[52] CK to AS, 5/6/1846, MP-C0171.

famine, the higher are prices, and the higher I sell, the more I can spend; so the money circulates," and he concludes that the real friends of the farmers are a "bloody war and a wet harvest." Another nobleman declares that "every alms is a fresh badge of slavery," to which the Abbot agrees by insisting that they "Leave the poor alone. Let want teach them the need of self-exertion." Walter's disapproval of all such policies stands for Kingsley's own: "No, Sir, to make men of them, put them not out of reach, but out of the need, of charity." How this is to be done is not clear, but Kingsley warns that, if revolution is to be avoided, church and nobility can no longer afford to be the idle onlookers that free-trade makes them.

V

Notwithstanding the fact that many themes and the character-typology of *The Saint's Tragedy* were to become Kingsley's trade-marks throughout a thirty-year-long career as a writer, the play has kept a remarkably low profile in critical studies of Kingsley's works. Although it cannot be called a masterpiece, it is still a remarkable work for a beginner. Admittedly, the poetic quality of the work as a whole is uneven, but at times a striking aptitude for imaginative verse becomes apparent, as in the following example:

> Is that angel-world
> A gaudy window, which we paint ourselves
> To hide the dead void night beyond?[53]

On the strength of such passages, John Ludlow would maintain till the end of his life that Kingsley's real literary genius lay in poetry, and that he firmly believed that "in some of his poetry he rises higher than in all his prose, ay, to the level of his greatest contemporaries" and that, "since Shakespeare, there has been no such Shakespearean promise as that of the 'Saint's Tragedy'."[54] The Prussian ambassador, Chevalier Bunsen, echoed this sentiment years later in a letter to the Oxford philologist and linguist Max Müller: "I have for several years made no secret of it, that Kingsley seems to me

---

[53] IV.1, *P* 117.
[54] Ludlow (1893) 498.

the genius of our country called to place by the side of that sublime dramatic series from King John to Henry VIII., another series
from Edward VI. to the landing of William of Orange."[55] Such comparisons say probably more for the critical faculties of Ludlow and
Chevalier Bunsen than they do about Kingsley's poetical qualities.
Still, despite the many faults discerned by the critics (coarseness of
expression, exaggeration of its subject, lack of coherence in action,
scenes out of keeping with the spirit of the times, lifeless imitation
of other poets), *The Saint's Tragedy* was hailed as the debut of a
promising talent, and this was also brought out by the handful of
reviews which appeared. An early review in *The Spectator* of 22 January
1848 praised the work's style as possessing a "genuine poetic spirit."[56]
A more elaborate appraisal in *Fraser's Magazine* followed in March.
Kingsley's play was written with "great brilliancy and vigour" and
the reviewer, John Conington, maintained that the story it told might
be devoured by the reader "without stopping to appreciate the intense
poetical beauty of its parts."[57] Realizing that Wordsworth's reign was
"nearly over," Conington looked wistfully at a list of possible suc-
cessors. The most likely candidate for the next poet laureateship was
Tennyson, but he was thought to be sadly lacking in "those qualities which depend on education and mental training." Of the other
poets of the day Conington thought that John Keble's "contempla-
tive tranquillity disqualifies him from doing justice to the more stirring elements of our time," that Robert Browning's abstruseness
"soars far beyond the sphere of common men," that Henry Taylor
was unlikely to produce anything new—"art being in his case more
than usually long, while life must be comparatively short"—and that
Monckton Milnes's sketches of Mahometan faith were not "the most
tangible object for the sympathies of his railway-speculating, opera-
crowding, game-preserving, bishop-baiting fellows."[58] These shortcomings in other poets show where Conington thought the promise
of Kingsley's verse lay. *The Saint's Tragedy* seemed to him "an indication of a worthier state of things"[59] if only Kingsley would let other
poets alone: "The author can write so well when he trusts simply

[55] C.C.J. Bunsen to Max Müller, undated, *LML* i.151.
[56] *The Spectator*, 21 (22 January 1848), 87–8.
[57] [Conington], 331, 330.
[58] [Conington], 238.
[59] [Conington], 329.

to his own force of language, that we are less inclined to excuse him when he puts us off with the echo of another."[60] Even the generally hostile assessment in the *English Review* of Kingsley's exaggerated stand on the asceticism of the Tractarians had to admit that, artistically, the play had "merits of a high order."[61]

The play, however, was never to become a favourite with the reading public, although the composer John Hullah found inspiration in the melancholy song "Oh that we two were Maying" given to Elizabeth in the second act, and made it one of Kingsley's most celebrated lyrics to be played in the Victorian drawing room. At Oxford, *The Saint's Tragedy* was much discussed. While visiting Powles in March 1848, Kingsley wrote home that "I am here undergoing the new process of being made a lion of [. . .] They got up a meeting for me, and the club was crowded with men merely to see poor me."[62] The interest at Oxford, ironically, had much to do with Newman's secession to Rome just two years before. With the departure of its dominant thinker, the Oxford Movement had lost its influential grip on the University and its religious core was left in an intellectual void. In groping for new ideals, liberalism found an opening at the University, and it is therefore not surprising that Kingsley's outspoken religious play attracted much attention there. Otherwise, the play went unnoticed, except for the impression it made on two readers who would prove to be influential in Kingsley's later life: one of these two enthusiastic readers of *The Saint's Tragedy* was the Prince Consort, the other was Daniel Macmillan, his future publisher.

---

[60] [Conington], 332.
[61] *The English Review*, 12 (December 1849), 378–94.
[62] CK to FK, 30/3/1848, *LML* i.153.

CHRISTIAN SOCIALISM

CHAPTER SIX

THE FLAG AND THE HORNS (1848)

The social unrest of the early months of 1848 convinced Kingsley more than ever before that democracy could not be stopped and that it needed to be adopted by the Church if religion was to survive in the process of social transition. The 1848-revolution of the proletariat in France stirred up new hope in the English Chartists. If Chartism had had a mainly national character in the previous uprisings of 1839 and 1842, by the mid 1840s it had become decisively more European in collocation. Indicative of this is perhaps the stay in England of Friedrich Engels, the son of a German factory owner, who studied the condition of the workers in Manchester, and discussed socialist issues with English Chartist leaders such as Feargus O'Connor and Ernest Jones. When he left England in 1844 to study the condition of the workers in France (where he met Karl Marx), he formed a symbolic link between the pioneers of socialism in three countries.

European socialist movements had become of greater importance in England. The abolition of the monarchy in France, and the subsequent creation of a radical Republic with inclinations to socialist principles, made workers all over Europe aware that they were fighting for a common cause. A revival of Chartist ideas in England in1848 was thus hardly surprising. The workers' newspaper *The Northern Star* proclaimed that the time had come for the English Charter, which, however, would only be achieved by something more drastic than mass meetings and petitions. As a result riots started breaking out all over the country in March. In Glasgow shops were looted and slogans like "Vive la République" were heard. Five men were shot by soldiers in encounters with the authorities. In Manchester a mob besieged a workhouse to set its inmates free. These and other incidents were not official Chartist initiatives. In London, however, a protest against income tax was turned into an official Chartist demonstration which offered an opportunity to declare sympathy with the French Republic. Other demonstrations and meetings in London followed.[1] By the Convention of 3 April, the Chartists decided to present their third petition of reform to Parliament on 10 April, for which purpose a mass meeting was organized on Kennington Common from where a procession was to proceed to Westminster. The prospect of such a mass-demonstration in the capital and the threat of revolution if Parliament refused the Petition led to the creation of an impressive police force of 170,000 constables, led by the Duke of Wellington. Two such enormous forces in London boded ill.

The security measures stimulated Kingsley's love of action, and, eager to escape the monotony of Eversley for a few days, he longed to be on the scene himself. John Parker, the son of his publisher, and an old University friend, happened to be staying at Eversley on Sunday 9 April and the Petition was discussed. Parker told Kingsley of his fears of rioting the following day and the possible damage to private property, his own included. Kingsley decided to go up to London with him the next day and see what could be done to convince the demonstrators to keep the peace. When they left early in the morning on the day of the Petition, Parker nervously told Mrs Kingsley that "she might expect to hear of his shop having been broken into, and himself thrown into the Trafalgar Square fountains by the mob."[2]

Upon reaching London they went to Parker's business in The Strand, and finding everything quiet walked on to Maurice, whom they found in bed with a bad cold. By midday Kingsley wrote home reassuringly that "all is right as yet. Large crowds, but no one expects any row."[3] But Kingsley's restless nature called for some kind of action on this legendary April day, and Maurice's confinement to his rooms was highly frustrating to him. Somebody had to guide the guileless Chartists, to show them that their cause was right but that violent means would not bring them to success. Handbills, he enthusiastically told Maurice, were needed to communicate with the masses. Maurice, unable to restrain Kingsley, thought of John Malcolm Ludlow and scribbled a note of introduction to him.

Ludlow, an idealistic intellectual who had grown up in France, was looking for a synthesis of religion and democracy and dreamed of some form of social fraternity. Although his heart was with the

---

[1] See also Nowell-Smith 288–90.
[2] LML i.155.
[3] CK to FK, 10/4/1848, BL-62553 f.105r.

socialist endeavours in France, he had enrolled at Lincoln's Inn to study for the bar. It was here in 1846 that he went to listen to Maurice's preaching and thought he had found a person to lead a movement which would embody his ideals of religious democracy. He searched the chaplain out in private and talked about his ideas, but was disappointed with Maurice's shy and unenterprising character. Two years later Ludlow contacted Maurice again, because the latter had been preaching on the truth of man's brotherhood, a truth which Maurice felt was mocked by the existing social systems of the time. Ludlow now wrote to Maurice about Louis Blanc and his co-operative workshops, by which he had been impressed when on a visit to Paris earlier that year.[4]

At about midday on 10 April Kingsley tramped with his note through a London drizzle to seek Ludlow out at his chambers at 69 Chancery Lane. Ludlow, as much against violence as Kingsley, was at home, and found at his door "a tall young clergyman with strongly marked features," "very thin and gaunt, lanthorn-jawed", who stuttered something about Maurice, and who handed him a letter of introduction: "Will you let me introduce you to my friend Mr Kingsley. He is deeply in earnest and seems obsessed with the idea of doing something with handbills. I think there is hope in this. Will you talk to him about it? He was exceedingly interested in your plans."[5] A single glance at the man convinced Ludlow that he had "no ordinary man before [him]"[6] and he listened patiently as words first came stuttering out, and, once the initial impediment was conquered, to all that Kingsley then told him with a certain "raciness" in his voice. Ludlow took to the young clergyman when the latter explained that he felt apprehensive about the lot of the "misguided fellows" on Kennington Common if they were "goaded on until a collision took place."[7] Ludlow, however, tried to calm Kingsley and told him he did not see any reason to worry. He must have explained to Kingsley that he had seen two revolutions in France and that he felt perfectly satisfied that there were no signs of one that day. "Revolutions do not come off at fixed dates," he added.[8] Moreover,

---

[4] Letter lost, but see answer FDM to JL, 16/3/1848, Maurice i.458.
[5] Masterman 66.
[6] Ludlow (1981) 123.
[7] Masterman 67.
[8] Ludlow (1981) 121.

the safety precautions which had been taken were overwhelming. But Kingsley was not appeased and meant to go to the Common all the same, and Ludlow decided to accompany him through London. Ludlow was right. Even before reaching Waterloo Bridge they found out from people coming from the south bank that most of the crowd on Kennington Common had dispersed and that all danger of collision had been averted. The Chartists had assembled on the Common, but the drizzle which had turned into pouring rain had not helped to make the demonstration a success. And many people stayed away out of fear of what might happen if forces started clashing. Although O'Connor, one of the leaders, boasted half a million souls, 20,000 is probably a safer estimate. There was still fear of some "marauding in the suburbs at night," Kingsley gathered from talking to a militia man. As it was, the following day he could write home that "the storm is blown over till to-morrow." Actually, the uprising of 1848 was a defeat for the national movement of Chartism from which it never really recovered, especially after much of the Petition turned out to be a joke. Although it contained almost two million signatures, upon examination by Parliament it was found that it had been signed by such unlikely persons as Queen Victorian and Prince Albert. And the Duke of Wellington had signed seventeen times.

However, Kingsley did not waste the opportunity of the walk. Ludlow recorded years later that "we had talked all the way from Chancery Lane. We talked all the way to Queen Square, and by the time we were there we were friends."[9] They talked about co-operative workshops and newspapers. Ludlow expressed his conviction that England needed an organ "of a broad outspoken Christianity, ready to meet all social and political questions."[10] He had already intimated to Maurice in March that he had thought of going to Paris to "set up a paper to be called *La Fraternité Chrétienne*," but such ideas were thwarted when funds had not been forthcoming. Still, Maurice liked the idea and put Ludlow's letter in circulation amongst his friends, hoping that something might be done to realize such a paper in England. At first Charles Knight wanted to offer some pages to Ludlow in the *Voice of the People*, a radical middle-class

---

[9] Florence Higham, *Frederick Denison Maurice* (London: SCM Press, 1947) 58.
[10] Masterman 67.

journal he edited with Harriet Martineau, but he retracted after speaking to him personally.[11]

The idea of setting up a paper, of course, made Kingsley, who could not wait to use his pen in the cause of Christianity and socialism, enthusiastic. In this Ludlow had found a fervent collaborator. They went to 21 Queen's Square to discuss the project again with Maurice, who this time "determined to make a decisive move." Kingsley wrote home that "Maurice has given me a highest proof of confidence. He has taken me & Ludlow to counsel, & we are to have meetings for prayer & study, when I come to London, & we are to bring out a new set of real 'Tracts for the Times,' addressed to the higher orders."[12] Although the prospect of *Tracts* was most satisfactory to Kingsley, it was still unbearable to think of the time which would be required to set the publication up and write the tracts. Before returning to Eversley, he wanted to do something immediate, "to help these poor wretches to the truest alms [. . .] to words, texts from the psalms, anything wh. may keep even one man from cutting his brother's throat."[13] He proposed the idea of handbills again. Maurice again approved, and Kingsley sat down to write ("under Maurice's auspices") till four in the morning, tired but satisfied. So ended that much feared 10 April for Kingsley. He glowingly added in his letter to Fanny: "Maurice is à la hauteur des circonstances, determined to make a decisive move. He says, if the Oxford Tracts did wonders, why should not we? [. . .] A glorious future is opening, and both Maurice and Ludlow seem to have driven away all my doubts and sorrows, and I see the blue sky again and my Father's face!"[14]

Ludlow was equally enthusiastic about the outcome of 10 April. Kingsley invited him to Eversley, and he came over to stay from 25 to 27 April. "Kingsley was a delightful host, nor was his wife less delightful as a hostess."[15] Moreover, it was during this brief stay in Eversley that he met Charles Blanchfield Mansfield, who was to become one of Ludlow's dearest friends. As an old man, he looked

---

[11] Maurice i.458–60.
[12] CK to FK, 11/4/1848, BL-62553 f.109.
[13] CK to FK, 11/4/1848, BL-62553 f.109r.
[14] CK to FK, 10/4/1848, BL-62553 f.109v.
[15] Ludlow (1981) 127.

back at this spring of 1848: "Four or five months had made a vast
change in my life. At the beginning of March 1848 I had not one
intimate friend in England; at the close of July I was one of a group
bound together by their common veneration for one of their number,"[16]
and "foremost amongst these stands, unquestionably, Charles
Kingsley."[17] If he had not been in his chambers that day "the whole
current of my life might have been changed. I should not have met
Charles Kingsley under circumstances which made us intimate from
the first."[18]

II

On the morning of 12 April one of Kingsley's pamphlets was plac-
arded on walls in London, and when Maurice's brother-in-law Julius
Hare, Archdeacon of Lewes, came up to Queen's Square that day,
he found Kingsley and A.J. Scott with Maurice. Very likely Hare
was one of those to whom Maurice had forwarded Ludlow's project of a newspaper for the people, and he now came to Maurice
to propose a penny journal, which Parker was to be cajoled into
publishing. Although Maurice's main interest lay in theology, he sustained his brother-in-law's proposal. Kingsley accompanied Hare to
Parker's in the afternoon, and the idea came off. A weekly penny
paper for the people was decided upon and given the title *Politics
for the People*.

Kingsley's excitement was such that he rushed off to brief Ludlow
about these new developments, but he must have stammered frightfully and confused Ludlow. Maurice was obliged to explain everything to Ludlow by letter the following day: "I am afraid from your
not being used to Kingsley's infirmity, that you have got a wrong
impression from his words." Their plans had not been changed by
Hare without consultation, he hastened to point out. Hare had proposed the penny paper without knowing of the tracts. All Maurice
had said to Kingsley, when Parker accepted to publish for them,
was that he "hoped this plan would not interfere with our own; and
that I thought it need not; for that the paper could be an address

---

[16] Ludlow (1981) 134.
[17] Ludlow (1893) 494.
[18] Ludlow (1981) 121.

to middle or working classes expressly and emphatically about suffrage, &c., and that we might direct our tracts rather more to the religious people and clergy, pointing out to them the necessity of their meeting the questions of the day."[19] Although Ludlow was appeased, Maurice here had a slight foretaste of the misunderstanding which could ensue when Kingsley's vehement spirit, his stammering and unbounded enthusiasm were combined.

On 13 April, Kingsley returned to Eversley in high spirits. His visit to London to do something for the Chartists had been successful beyond expectation. It was the beginning of a movement which marked a new episode in his life. Although little came of the tracts in the end, *Politics of the People* started to come out in weekly instalments from 6 May onwards. Maurice and Ludlow, who functioned as its editors, were its real thinkers, but it was Kingsley's incandescent language which did much to communicate with the people they wanted to reach. As such, the placard Kingsley posted in London on 12 April could be seen as a prelude to *Politics for the People*. In the end, his contribution to the movement of democratic reform in a Christian context, and the lasting image he created of it, were real and compelling. Still, the victory of 10 April had gone to England's middle-classes, and unwittingly Kingsley affirms this when he closes his last letter home the following day with "Parker begs to remark that he has not been thrown into the Trafalgar fountain."[20]

III

Kingsley's pamphlet to the workmen of England is a powerful expression of sympathy, criticism and encouragement in his noble and direct way of addressing the wrongs of his time. It hinges on three points: first, it states that the workers are right to complain about their material conditions:

> WORKMEN OF ENGLAND! You say that you are wronged. Many of you are wronged; and many besides yourselves know it. Almost all men who have heads and hearts know it—above all, the working clergy

[19] FDM to JL,13/4/1848, Maurice i.461.
[20] CK to FK, 12/4/1848, BL-62553 f.112v.

know it. They go into your houses, they see the shameful filth and darkness in which you are forced to live crowded together; they see your children growing up in ignorance and temptation, for want of fit education.

Such a prospective alliance of sympathy and support for the Chartist cause by "a working parson" sounded promising for those fighting for their rights, but, Kingsley hastens to warn then, the workers should not be misled into believing that the Charter can appease their griefs. There is no solution in a mere representation in Parliament—"Friends, you want more than Acts of Parliament can give"—the Charter alone will never make free men:

> Will it free you from slavery to ten-pound bribes? Slavery to beer and gin? [...] That, I guess, is real slavery; to be a slave to one's own stomach, one's own pocket, one's own temper.

Freedom, therefore, is not found on "the precipice of riot, which ends in the gulf of universal distrust, stagnation, starvation," because riot thwarts the way to progress, which is the only hope of the future. He warns the Chartists not to "humbug yourselves into meaning 'licence,' when you cry for 'liberty'." Real freedom is based on quite different things: "A nobler day is dawning for England, a day of freedom, science, industry! But there will be no true freedom without virtue, no true science without religion, no true industry without the fear of God, and love to your fellow-citizens." This third point is inspired by Christianity and manifested by the progress of science itself, which at the same time inspires and is inspired by a sense of true brotherhood.

Few critics have failed to remark on the presence in the pamphlet of both radical and conservative sentiments, but what is most characteristic of Kingsley has mainly been ignored. The emphasis which is given to the relation between freedom and science at the end of this short handbill of less than 300 words is most perceptive, and shows how important his scientific outlook was even in politics. It was a theme he was to amplify later in life, and which carried so much conviction with those nearest to him that his daughter in a novel of hers lays it down in 1901 as an axiom that natural science is "the great leveller."[21] Moreover, most practically, Kingsley realized

---

[21] Lucas Malet, *Sir Richard Calmady* (New York: A.L. Burt, 1901) 20.

that man's spiritual perfection would never be reached as long as his physical conditions were ignored: "They who will not take care of their own house, how should they care for the house of God?"[22] The means of dealing with the "filth and darkness" mentioned at the beginning of the pamphlet are to be found in the practical application of what man has discovered through science about the laws of nature. Only thorough knowledge of these laws will lead to real freedom. That Kingsley believed true science to be religiously inspiring or revealing is part of his a priori reasoning but is less salient here. Hope for the working man is founded as much on science as on Christ, or, on science which will be reached through the realization of a Christian brotherhood.

Charles E. Raven, the historian of Christian Socialism, has called Kingsley's placard epoch-making, "the first manifesto of the Church of England, her first public act of atonement for a half-century of apostasy, of class-prejudice and political sycophancy."[23] Although there is a great amount of exaggeration in this remark—and Raven has been criticized for it—it is true that, if non-conformist sects were often closely involved in the Chartist cause, the Church of England had largely kept aloof. David Jones describes how a vicar in Norwich who quoted St Paul's "I have learned, in whatever station of life, therewith to be content" was shouted down by his working-class congregation with "You get £200 a year!"[24] Such keeping of the established order was not acceptable to the Chartists, and the Anglican Church more often than not embodied the establishment. No doubt Raven's remark refers to this. But Kingsley's dramatic outpourings in this first pamphlet and in his later contributions to *Politics for the People* should not be seen as providing an opening for involvement of the Anglican Church in the Chartist movement. In the first place, Kingsley's pamphlet came after the defeat of Chartism as a *national* movement, and although throughout the summer of 1848 minor uprisings occurred, often of a violent kind, the Charter itself was all but dead after the humiliation which followed the scrutiny of the Petition in Parliament. Notwithstanding Ludlow's attempts, the Christian Socialist movement was never to become an integral part

---

[22] CK to AS, 7/11/48, MP-C0171.
[23] Raven 107–8.
[24] David Jones, *Chartism and the Chartists* (London: Allen Lane, 1975) 52.

of Chartism, and, though sympathizing with the cause of the workers, it was more of a critical and alternative sideline to democracy
which took off when the general enthusiasm for Chartism had started
to wane in England. Therefore, Kingsley's placard was of little importance in Chartist politics and is very rarely mentioned in its histories. Still, Raven's evaluation of the pamphlet does indicate its
importance as the first public proclamation of what was to become
the Christian Socialist movement, in which Kingsley was to play
such a representative role, and which the historian of the Victorian
Church Owen Chadwick, with his usual gift of presenting history in
a few memorable words, describes as follows: "In this unusual crew
Ludlow stood at the helm, Kingsley flew the flags and sounded the
horns, Maurice poked round the engine-room to see that the engines
were of authentic Christian manufacture."[25]

Politics for the People ran from 6 May to 29 July before Maurice
and Ludlow decided to suspend its publication. Somehow the journal never had the success they had anticipated. Chadwick comments
that "if more of the contributors had resembled Kingsley, more of
the workers might have read the paper."[26] This may be true. Most
of the writing was well-thought out, but its sophisticated reasoning
was either far over the average worker's head or sounded patronizing to the better educated Chartists. Moreover, although Kingsley
in his writing appealed directly to his readers' feelings, he did not
always keep up the radical tone he had used in his handbill. In addition, his contribution to the journal remained rather modest. Of the
approximately 270 published pages of *Politics for the People* Kingsley
wrote 22, of which probably only half was of the kind of writing
which was most needed to make the journal a success.

For his articles in *Politics for the People* Kingsley assumed the pseudonym Parson Lot, a name he would often use until 1852. It was
during one of the gatherings of Maurice's friends that in a theological discussion Kingsley found everybody against him, and jokingly
said, referring to Genesis 19:14, that "he felt much as Lot must have
felt in the Cities of the Plain, when he seemed as one that mocked
to his sons-in-law."[27] The name Parson Lot was thus suggested.

---

[25] Chadwick (1987) i.351.
[26] Chadwick (1987) i.353.
[27] Hughes (1876) xii.

Unfortunately nobody reported what the friends had been discussing, but it must have been about the iniquity of London, as Lot had been forewarned by angels of the brimstone and fire which was to rain down upon Sodom and Gomorrah. A certain apocalyptic vein runs through Kingsley's socialist thinking in this period, as is seen most clearly in "The Day of the Lord," a poem he published two years later in *The Christian Socialist*:

> Gather you, gather you, angels of God—
> Freedom, and Mercy, and Truth;
> Come! for the Earth is grown coward and old,
> Come down, and renew us her youth.
> Wisdom, Self-Sacrifice, Daring, and Love,
> Haste to the battle-field, stoop from above,
> To the Day of the Lord at hand.

Parson Lot's first article for *Politics* is a short exposition of the benefits a working man might feel in contemplating the pictures in the National Gallery after a hard day of toil. It is difficult not to feel disappointed with this early piece when its author exalts the beautiful in art to the worker of "the world of stone and iron." Instead of attaching a reflection on the misery and ugliness of the present, he seems to reduce it to a mere longing for a better hereafter: "Believe it, toil-worn worker, in spite of thy foul alley, thy crowded lodging, thy grimed clothing, thy ill-fed children, thy thin, pale wife— believe it, thou, too, and thine, will some day have *your* share in beauty."[28] This sits awkwardly between Maurice's article on holding "converse with our readers of all classes, as fellow-men and fellow-workers, by labouring strenuously in God's strength, that we may realize the true Fraternity of which this age has dreamed, and without which we believe it cannot be satisfied," which immediately preceded it, and Dumoulin's motto that "it is the fundamental rule of all great reformations, that the things to be amended must be brought back to their beginnings," which is printed beneath Kingsley's article. One might question the effectiveness of such writing for the first issue of *Politics for the People*. Yet, Kingsley's idea of freedom was based on cultivating the tastes of the individual to make him aware that he "has a fellow-feeling with noble men and noble deeds." It is a point which he makes more clearly in a later contribution, where

---

[28] "The National Gallery—No. I," 6/5/1848, *PolP* 6.

he asserts that it is places like the National Gallery and the British
Museum which are "truly equalizing," places "where the poor and
the rich may meet together" and where the poor man can say
"Whatever my coat or my purse, I am an Englishman, and therefore I have a right here."[29]

At first sight the "Letters to Chartists" for *Politics for the People* are
more inflammatory contributions than his first article. "My only quarrel with the Charter is, that it does not go far enough in reform,"
he writes in his first letter. But he qualifies this statement by saying
that Chartism disappoints him as being only "poor, bald, constitution-mongering," which is not even worth a thousandth of the French
idea of "organization of labour," while not even that goes "to the
bottom of the matter by many a mile."[30] Next follows a condemnation of the reading habits of the workers, of such "French dirt
such as Thomas Paine and Voltaire, "'Flash Songsters,' and 'Swell's
Guide', and 'Tales of Horror,' and dirty milk-sop French novels."
True and honest action could never spring from such reading, Kingsley
complains, and the more he has read of Chartist publications the
more he is convinced that too many of them "are trying to do God's
work with the devil's tools."[31] Instead, the Chartist should learn to
see the Bible as "The Poor Man's Book," the "Radical Reformer's
Guide," the book which is "from beginning to end, written *to keep
the rich in order*."[32] Such a severe scolding of both the Chartists' aims
and their reading habits was similar to much of the criticism that
Chartists had received from the middle-class press, and could be
held to demonstrate the same dissociation from and condemnation
of the Anglican Church that the Chartists had received all along.
But there was one essential difference: if the poor do not read the
Bible, Kingsley adds, it is the clergy who are to blame for this: "We
have used the Bible as if it was a mere special constable's hand-
book—an opium-dose for keeping beasts of burden patient while
they were being overloaded [. . .] I have been as bad as any one,
but I am sick of it."[33] Such writing was bound to create enemies on
both fronts.

---

[29] "The British Museum," 1/7/1848, *PolP* 183.
[30] "Letters to the Chartists—No. I," 13/5/1848, *PolP* 28.
[31] "Letters to the Chartists—No. I," 13/5/1848, *PolP* 29.
[32] "Letters to the Chartists—No. II," 27/5/1848, *PolP* 59.
[33] "Letters to the Chartists—No. II," 27/5/1848, *PolP* 58.

One of the readers reacted to Kingsley's harangue in the third issue of *Politics for the People* by saying that, much as he appreciated the emphasis on "social regeneration," to the Chartists "social reforms are the ultimatum; political reforms the means." As such the proceedings of the Chartists were lawful and their claim to political life genuine. The letter, which was well-argued and written with dignity, and which was signed "One of the Wicked Chartists of Kennington Common,"[34] made Kingsley realize that his middle-class attitude might lead to opposition rather than understanding. "We must thus gain their sympathy, before we begin scolding" he writes to Ludlow, and admits that "that was my great fault in my first letter to the Chartists—I learnt a great deal from that letter *by* a Chartist."[35] This feedback also shows some of the ambiguity that underlay the project of the Christian Socialists. *Politics for the People* was not written by the workers and at times seemed to deny all that Chartism stood for: political rights. Kingsley's first letter to the Chartists is symptomatic of that and might have made many a worker feel impatient with it. Although Kingsley sympathized with the plight of the workers, he did not want to see a drastic change in society's hierarchical structure. "I respect vested rights—but will have no *vested wrongs*," he explained to Ludlow, "I make no scruple of bullying the sins of the lower classes [...] but do not suppose that I do not wish to bully the higher all the more daringly."[36] Such an approach created enemies rather than friends, and Parker received many letters attacking Parson Lot. "I am afraid my utterances have had a great deal to do with the Politics' unpopularity—I have got worse-handed than any of you, by both poor & rich."[37] But Kingsley's battling spirit did not regret this so much as enjoy it, and he announced that his "future explosions are likely to become more & more obnoxious."

Still, at times, criticism of his writings and views hurt him more than he was willing to admit to Ludlow or Maurice. When the Chartist organ *The Commonwealth* dismissed Parson Lot as an aristocrat advocating "mediæval tyranny," he sat down to write a most humble letter to Thomas Cooper. Cooper, a self-taught Leicestershire

---

[34] "Letter from a Chartist," 20/5/1848, *PolP* 45; Christensen 98 attributes the letter to Joseph Millbank.
[35] CK to JL, May 1848, BL-41298 f.193r.
[36] CK to JL, 22/5/1848, Martin (1950) 85.
[37] CK to JL, 1/7/1848, Martin (1950) 88.

shoemaker who had turned schoolmaster and Methodist preacher, worked for various Chartist papers in the early 1840s and became the leader of a Chartist association in Leicester that claimed 2,500 members. His efforts to sustain a general strike in the pottery district led to a conviction for seditious behaviour and he was sentenced to two year's imprisonment. In jail he wrote *The Purgatory of Suicides*, a long political poem in which he expounded Chartist principles. Kingsley thought *Purgatory* "brilliant" and had meant to write to its author ever since its publication in 1845, but had "held back—from shame—a false shame, perhaps, lest you should fancy me a hypocrite." The accusations in *The Commonwealth* however, made it "intolerable [to Kingsley] to be so misunderstood [. . .] to be regarded as an object of distrust and aversion by thousands of my countrymen [. . .] just because I was a clergyman." He was therefore writing to a person "intimately acquainted with the mind of the working classes" to help him "consecrate my powers effectually to their service," because, he explains, "I would shed the last drop of my life blood for the social and political emancipation of the people of England.[38] Cooper was enchanted by Kingsley's letter, and it was the beginning a correspondence which would last till the late 1850s.

By the end of June *Politics for the People* was on its last legs, and in the issue of 1 July Maurice announced that, although the contributors to the journal submitted their work without remuneration, the sales did not cover the costs of publication, and that therefore "a month hence [. . .] we shall probably bid our readers farewell." But Kingsley's words to Ludlow about "future explosions" were not without purpose. Something had been on his mind from the beginning of their joint project for working men. In a letter written to Ludlow in the first half of May, he tells of his intention of contributing to their penny journal with "*'What is the matter with the parish?'* An exposé of things as they are." Of this plan only a tantalizing fragment survives, which runs: "How to mend the parish, continued till the Nun pool does flow up to Ashy Down, & the curse is taken off the Lords of Whitford."[39] Actually, for the May supplement of *Politics*, a "tale of the country" about a squire and his neglected estate was written, in which Kingsley promised to be "very

---

[38] CK to Thomas Cooper, 19/6/1848, LML i.183–4.
[39] CK to JL, May 1848, BL-41298 f.193r.

hard on the landlords—they deserve it [. . .] to shew the accursed sloth & folly & tyranny, of the common, respectable, average working of landlordism."[40] The story—"The Nun's Pool"—was set up in print, but at the very last moment Maurice decided to suppress the supplement.[41] Kingsley's tale, Maurice thought, "ran counter to those earnest and deliberate convictions of other men, upon the preservation and enlightening of which all our hope of doing them good depends."[42]

Maurice's decision did not come unexpectedly. Kingsley's writing had increasingly provoked the criticism of the theologian's older friends. Hare in particular was horrified when he saw the second letter to the Chartists and its slogan that the Bible was a book written to "keep the rich in order," and appealed to Maurice to suppress the article. He sensed conceit and arrogance in the affirmation that it was much the "fault of us parsons" that the poor man ignored the Bible. The case was embarrassing, but Maurice was unwilling to sacrifice pure and free thoughts to words pleasing to bishops. Hare was altogether wrong about Kingsley: "Kingsley spoke from his heart, I am sure, without the least of that conceit which you impute to him. He felt he was confessing his own sin, not taking honour to himself for discovering it in others."[43] On the contrary, it was people like Kingsley who seemed to Maurice the best possible mediators between "young England of the middle and upper classes, and the working people."[44] Maurice's answer to Hare was a brave one, but it was a sign that there were amongst its contributors conflicting opinions as to what *Politics for the People* should be. In a sense Maurice had to back Kingsley, because the younger man was executing a programme he had laid out himself, so that the subjects were mainly his. What Hare did not know was that Maurice had written in April to Kingsley saying: "We want poetry very much, and something on pictures (what you like), and could you not write a working country parson's letter about the right and wrong use of the Bible—I mean,

---

[40] CK to JL, 22/5/1848, Martin (1950) 84.

[41] The first June issue, which was ready at the same time, carried the next consecutive number (five) in the series, but left a gap of 17 pages in the page numbering of the journal.

[42] FDM to JL, 10/6/1848, Maurice i.479.

[43] FDM to Julius Hare, 28/5/1848, Maurice i.476–7.

[44] FDM to Julius Hare, 28/5/1848, Maurice i.477–8.

protesting against the notion of turning it into a book for keeping the poor in order."[45] No wonder that Maurice almost seems to put Hare in his place when he defends Kingsley for offending the bishops: "I believe we must offend them and a great many more," he concluded.[46] Anyway, Hare was offended, and so were "a great many more," as Kingsley was soon to find out to his own cost.

IV

Maurice had, since 1840, been associated with King's College, London, where he held professorships in English Literature and History and in Theology. He hoped to procure a post for Kingsley too, which would mean some badly needed extra income. When a possible vacancy was discussed in the early spring of 1848, Kingsley's name was put forward to R.W. Jelf, the College's Principal. He received him "very kindly" when Maurice introduced him on 11 April, and "expressed himself very anxious to get me the professorship."[47] The appointment was pending for some time, but in the second half of May a final decision came through. Jelf had had second thoughts in the meantime and realized that Kingsley's views in *Politics for the People* were most unorthodox. In order to avoid having him, it was decided not to fill the post at all. "I have rarely met with a more reckless and dangerous writer," Jelf confessed three years later.[48] Maurice, for whom trouble was brewing at King's as well, concluded: "Their refusal of him is intended as an admonition to me to set my house in order, and as such I shall take it."[49] Thus, to prevent further harm to Kingsley's career, as well as to his own precarious reputation, Maurice had decided at the very last moment that "The Nun's Pool" should not appear in print.

Although Maurice was firm in defending Kingsley's "Letter to Chartists" in *Politics for the People* to Julius Hare in May 1848, a letter to Ludlow on the same subject two weeks later shows that he had felt it necessary to caution Kingsley on his burning language about

[45] FDM to CK, 22/4/1848, Maurice i.463.
[46] FDM to Julius Hare, 28/5/1848, Maurice i.478.
[47] CK to FK, 11/4/1848, BL-62553 f.112.
[48] R.W. Jelf to FDM, 7/11/1851, Maurice ii.79.
[49] FDM to Julius Hare, 28/5/1848, Maurice i.478.

the misuse of the Bible by clergymen. Maurice clearly felt responsible for having asked Kingsley to write about the right and wrong use of the Bible. "So far as we wound the conscience of any man, we do a positive injury to him and to ourselves," Maurice had answered in response to Ludlow's pleas for the necessity of "different opinions" in *Politics for the People* when "The Nun's Pool" had been suppressed. "We do that which cannot be undone or neutralised by ever so many articles which will soothe or conciliate him [. . .] On this principle it is that I stopped Kingsley's tale, on this principle I urged him to reconsider his letter to the Chartists."[50] But Maurice did not like having to interfere in such a way:

> Of course it is much pleasanter for me to offend all the bishops and 15,000 clergy and both Houses of Parliament, of whom I know nothing, than to take the responsibility to reject an article of Hare's or Kingsley's—men whom I love heartily and am seeing continually. But the question is, what is right for our purpose? [. . .] I was somewhat comforted about Kingsley, because I thought I was doing him good, as well as the paper, though I would sooner have lost two or three teeth.

And there were beginning to be clear signs of misgivings about his involvement in publishing *Politics for the People*:

> the effort of interference and the consciousness of missing my aim continually and of never saying or doing what I intend, and the weariness of different and lesser occupations and of neglecting home duties, often make me think I must have been a mere madman to have entered upon such an enterprise.[51]

Kingsley acquiesced in Maurice's decision to suppress "The Nun's Pool", but the idea was not abandoned. "This is a puling quill-driving soft-handed age" in which man needs to be knocked down by a pickaxe rather than be pricked to death with a pin, he confided to Ludlow.[52] The "pickaxe" was the novel "for the cause of the Labourer" that he had started writing, and of which the first instalment was to come out in *Fraser's Magazine* that same month with the title *Yeast; or, The Thoughts, Sayings, and Doings of Lancelot Smith, Gentleman.* But although this writing took a heavy toll on his time and intellectual resources, Kingsley embarked on another enterprise.

---

[50] FDM to JL 10/6/1848, Maurice i.478.
[51] FDM to JL 10/6/1848, Maurice i.478–9.
[52] CK to JL, 1/7/1848, Martin (1950) 89.

V

Governesses in the first half of the nineteenth century often did
badly-paid and unrewarding jobs. F.D. Maurice's sister Mary, who
had run a school herself, had become interested in the fate of retired
governesses and found that the work was so badly paid that many
were unable to save and in old age ended up in the workhouse. She
consulted the Committee of the Governesses' Benevolent Institution,
and asked her brother to become a member of that organisation.
The Committee agreed that the professional status of governesses
had to be raised, and although examinations for girls by professors
of King's College were instituted, it soon became clear that tests
without training were useless. Therefore, in 1848, Queen's College
was founded by Maurice at 66 Harley Street, as a school providing
higher education (on the payment of a moderate fee of 9*l.* 9*s.* per
term) for girls from sixteen to about twenty years of age, while it
offered at the same time courses for younger girls. Professors of
King's College were invited to give lectures and set essays for cor-
rection on various branches of female education, including mathematics. Amongst its professors were Maurice himself for Ecclesiastical
History, Arthur Stanley for Theology, John Hullah for Music; and
Kingsley was asked for English Literature. Although the post might
have opened up future prospects in the academic world, it was far
from lucrative. No doubt Kingsley also accepted because he believed
in the need for female emancipation. As a true admirer of progress—
"I know no century which the world has yet seen so well worth
living in"[53]—he saw an opportunity in his lectures "to vindicate
women's rights to an education in all points equal to that of men,
to demolish the difference between sexes based on a "fancied infe-
riority of mind."[54] Woman will "never get a hearing" in "this nineteenth century" he announced in his inaugural lecture, "till her
knowledge of the past becomes more organised and methodic"[55] and
her use of language enables her to portion out "thoughts distinctly
and authentically."[56]

---

[53] "On English Literature," *LGLE* 254.
[54] "On Composition," *LGLE* 240.
[55] "On English Literature," *LGLE*.259.
[56] "On Composition," *LGLE* 237.

Although the project for the college was successful—towards the end of the first term, it could boast about 200 pupils—and the institution as such met with praise, Maurice's insistence on seeing religion in everything was less appreciated by critics. Maurice expressly drew attention to the fact that the linking sentiment in all classes at Queen's was that all subjects were considered from a religious standpoint, "all as concerned with the life and acts of a spiritual creature; not to be contemplated out of their relation to such a creature."[57] The *Quarterly Review* warned that, although this was a noble principle, "it only remains to ascertain whether the views [of the professors] are, or are not, those we would wish implanted in the youthful mind, of those especially who are hereafter to be teachers of others," and with "deep regret" the author could not fail to detect "traces of a school of so-called *theology* which seems to be gaining ground among us—a sort of modified pantheism and latitudinarianism—a system not of bringing religion into everything, but of considering everything as more or less inherently religious" which results in "abnegating the proper idea of religion."[58] Such practices were not acceptable in a public institution which had no supervisory board whatsoever, the *Quarterly* complained.

After such preliminary warnings it was not surprising that Kingsley's lectures on English Literature should get more than their share of the criticism directed at the teachers of Queen's College. Kingsley of course agreed with Maurice's idea of religion underlying all teaching. His approach to literature was based on his view that a country's literature is its true autobiography, that literature is true history, "not of one class of offices or events, but of the living human souls of English men and English women. And therefore one most adapted to the mind of woman; one which will call into fullest exercise her blessed faculty of sympathy, that pure and tender heart of flesh, which teaches her always to find her highest interest in mankind, simply as mankind; to see the Divine most completely in the human; to prefer the incarnate to the disembodied, the personal to the abstract, the pathetic to the intellectual; to see, and truly, in the most common tale of village love or sorrow, a mystery deeper and more divine than lies in all the theories of politicians or the fixed

---

[57] *Introductory Lectures Delivered at Queen's College* (1849) 24.
[58] *QR* 86 (1850) 373.

ideas of the sage." He adds that his teaching will not be "sexless, heartless abstraction," as the purpose of Queen's College was not reached by women renouncing "their sex, but by fulfilling it; by becoming true women, and not bad imitations of men."[59] This much he expounded publicly during his first lecture, but more specifically he wrote to his colleague Strettell that such scope amounted to the following: "Your business and that of all teachers is, not to cram them with things, but to teach them to read for themselves [...] We want to train—not cupboards full of 'information' (vile misnomer)—but real informed women." He also told Strettell that, in expounding Chaucer, one should not be "afraid of talking about marriage. We must be real and daring at Queen's College or nowhere. The 'clear stage and no favour' which we have got there is so blessed and wonderful an opening, that we must make the most of it to utter things there which prudery and fanaticism have banished from pulpit and colleges."[60] The social dangers of such premises to teaching got a devastating critique in the *Quarterly*: "How would our readers like to receive into their families as a governess, one who had been taught to feel such an interest in 'tales of village love' [...] to offer them her 'sympathy,' not as events properly and naturally call it forth, but as her chief vocation and highest duty."[61] The religious didacticism in Kingsley's voice, moreover, profoundly alarmed and disgusted the critic. He hit hard at Kingsley's use and exegesis of Scripture, describing it a "portentous specimen of audacity in trampling on the plainest rules of criticism and common sense. No High-Dutch pedagogue ever vented more pompous smoke."[62]

Although Maurice was delighted to have Kingsley as professor with him at Queen's, his presence was beginning to taint the reputation of the college. Kingsley's lectures started just when *Yeast* had begun to come out in instalments in *Fraser's Magazine*, much of which was regarded by its middle-class readers with a wary eye. In delineating the divine function of the poet in society Kingsley was very much describing what he saw as the "priestly calling" of the craft; and in defending the inclusion of modern authors in his course of

---

[59] "On English Literature," *LGLE*.258,265.
[60] Grylls 28; the last part of this letter was expunged by Mrs Kingsley in her biography.
[61] *QR* 86 (1850) 381.
[62] *QR* 86 (1850) 377.

lectures, his apologetics are based on the view that wholesale dis-approbation of living authors merely injures the reverence for author-ity when the young find out that "the author who was said to be dangerous and unchristian, somehow makes them more dutiful, more earnest, more industrious, more loving to the poor." The conclusion to this passage has an autobiographical ring when he adds: "I speak of actual cases."[63]

At the end of term Kingsley interrupted his lectures at Queen's. The strain of writing and his demanding parish work had led to ill-health and profound depression, and made it necessary for him to give up his weekly visits to London for the time being. But Kingsley's connection with the college led to further grumbling, and when his second novel, *Alton Locke*, came out in 1850 and was immediately seen as a scandalous and dangerous work, he decided in November to sever any link with Queen's. "I have done this because I do not wish my name to be used as a handle against [it]," he announced publicly in the *Record* on 7 November 1850. One of Kingsley's col-leagues, Mr Nicholay, thought it necessary to clear the name of the College by emphasizing in an announcement in the same paper that Kingsley had withdrawn from the committee.[64] The post had not led, as both he and Maurice had hoped, to promotion to a chair at King's College, Nicholay rather slyly explained. Kingsley's col-laboration at Queen's College is more benevolently commemorated in Rosalie Glynn Grylls's history of the College's first 100 years as a contribution of "the muscular Christian who put cleanliness very close to godliness and made right principles of plumbing the main plank in his public platform as social reformer, [and] the girls at Queen's owed instruction much before its time in physiology and hygiene."[65]

VI

Although in July *Politics for the People* was coming to the end of its brief life, Kingsley still had lots of ideas. At the beginning of the month he forwarded an article on the game laws to Ludlow, and

[63] "On English Literature," *LGLE* 256.
[64] Maurice ii.54.
[65] Grylls 27.

asked for space for a second article on the same "& for one on over-population & another on the poor laws [. . . and] another on the duties of property."[66] Only two of these subjects were turned into articles; they were published in the last numbers of the paper as "Letters to Landlords." The rest found their way into *Yeast*.

The first Letter to Landlords marks an interesting shift of attention from the working man to the landowner, "as this paper," Kingsley admits, "is hardly at all read by the working-classes."[67] If in one of the May issues he still grudgingly wrote of the landlords as a necessary evil in the national economy—

> [. . .] call them tyrants, or idlers, or asses,
> Still, however sorely against their will,
> Scantily, clumsily, slowly, and ill,
> Must day by day, lay the golden eggs,
> Which keep your artisans all on four legs,
> Namely, *wages and occupation*.[68]

—he now tried to prevail on the moral sense of the members of such higher classes. Kingsley's rhetoric here is as effective as when addressing the workers. He assures his imaginary landlord-reader that in the working class "hearty old fashioned feudal affection" is struggling with "dull discontent, almost contempt." It is the landlords' fault that they will not allow themselves to be loved, but, Kingsley prophesies glowingly, if the landed classes just try to play the role they are expected to in society, "the labourers will worship him, obey him, die for him." They are "all but the kings of England at this moment." Like two other contemporary writers on the condition of England, Benjamin Disraeli and Elizabeth Gaskell, Kingsley was clearly not disposed to question the vested rights of what he calls the "captains of industry," the born leaders whose divine calling it is to be the "honoured and beloved champions of civilization and art, freedom, and religion," especially as "the agricultural population is not yet fit for self-government or associate labour."[69] Such affirmations make clear that Kingsley never was a truly socialist thinker the way Ludlow was. Still, his seemingly conservative over-

---

[66] CK to JL, [3July 1848], Martin (1950) 91.
[67] "Letters to Landlords," 22/7/1848, *PolP*.228.
[68] "The Golden Goose," 27/5/1848, *PolP* 64.
[69] "Letters to Landlords," 22/7/1848, *PolP*.228.

ture in praise of landlords then turns to their moral obligations to "undo many things, and first of all, undo these accursed Game-Laws." The keeping and preservation of game, Kingsley argues, is directly responsible for the degradation of the working classes, not only in the agricultural districts but in the whole of England, as pheasants are most damaging to the crops which are necessary to feed the mouths of the English. "While thousands are all but starving in these very days, what right have you to lessen the produce of England, for your own amusement, by a single grain?" Kingsley's grasp of problems of demography and subsistence is based here on an understanding of the food chain, and still sounds as a dilemma to us today. In a simple line: "A pheasant, in a single winter's meal, consumes that which would have by next harvest sufficed for a whole human family!"[70]

This would have been a grand theme for the novel he had started writing by this time. He chose, however, to concentrate on yet another objection to the game laws, which he made the subject of his last article for *Politics for the People*. Game-laws, he warns, have a harmful effect on the poor "hapless field-drudge," unable to "exist without the demoralizing degradation of alms,"[71] who cannot but be tempted to poach that to which the landlords' monopoly of game has given an "unnatural" value on the market of fashionable London. Moreover, the game-laws are smeared with blood, as many a man dies in the ferocious encounters between keepers and poachers, and all this because the gentlemen want to keep up a sport. "How will it sound in the ears of posterity," Kingsley asks in bewilderment, "how does it sound in the ears of Almighty God?"[72]

The close of *Politics for the People* was by no means the end of Kingsley's diatribe against the wrongs of the times. He steadily pumped everything he still wanted to say into *Yeast*, but this time without the censorship of a Maurice or Ludlow, although both were asked to read drafts of it. Material from the rejected tale about the Nun's Pool, the duties of property, the moral consequences of the Game-laws, and, later in the book edition, his views on the Roman Catholic Church—all found their way into the novel. *Yeast* is a strange

---

[70] "Letters to Landlords," 22/7/1848, *PolP*.231.
[71] "Letters to Landlords—No. II," 29/7/1848, *PolP*.246.
[72] "Letters to Landlords—No. II," 29/7/1848, *PolP*.247.

mixture of the ideas and convictions of an animated and hasty mind which fails to concentrate steadily on one theme and, though thus vitiating its artistic form, produces an interesting picture of the times and of its writer. Kingsley did not consider the novel only as a work of art. True art revealed divine truths, and writing was to him a preaching instrument and part of his calling: "He [God] has taught me things about the heart of fast sporting men, & about the condition of the poor, & our duty to them [...] Did he, too, let me become a strong daring, sporting wild-man-of-the-woods for nothing? Surely the education w. he has gn. me so difft. from that w. we authors generally receive, points out to me a peculiar calling to preach on these points."[73]

VII

The manuscript of what had been written of *Yeast* thus far was given to Ludlow to read. Ludlow's comment was critical and encouraging at the same time. He gently reproached Kingsley for trying to say too much, anticipating what a reader today might feel about the novel: "There is a little awkwardness now & then in the putting together." Remembering that Ludlow had only seen the first chapters as yet, his praise of Kingsley's skills is equally interesting: "for depth, & breadth, & wit, & fun, and thought, & feeling, & interest, it holds as much of all this as a first-rate three volume novel of the day. It is easy for you to become the greatest novelist of the age."[74] Kingsley undoubtedly had literary talent, but often spoilt it by never missing an occasion to preach. Even the hostile reviewer for *The Guardian* had to interrupt a devastating harangue to "frankly admit the great artistic power of the writer."[75] George Eliot, a much better literary critic than Ludlow, also took Kingsley's artistic gift seriously, although she could not stomach many of his ideas. In a letter to a friend she assessed the first five years of Kingsley's literary career in ambiguous terms: "perhaps you may not be as much in love with Kingsley's genius, and as 'riled' by his faults, as I am."[76] However,

---

[73] CK to JL, 17/7/1848, Martin (1950) 94–5.
[74] JL to CK, 15/7/1848, Martin (1950) 96.
[75] [Coleridge], 332.
[76] George Eliot to Mrs Peter Alfred Taylor, 1/2/1853, Haight ii.86.

despite its shortcomings, modern critics have seen *Yeast* as the "'essen-tial' Kingsley,"[77] the novel which is "seminal for all [his novels]."[78]

The opening chapter of *Yeast* is fine writing indeed. It paints with ease a hunting scene, drawn from life and with passion. Mrs Kingsley says that this first chapter made Sir Francis Astley, "one of the proud-est old Tory Baronets in England," offer Kingsley the run of his hunting stables, while an officer in the Crimea who read the scene as he lay wounded at Scutari resolved to visit such a vigorous preacher if he ever came out of it alive. He did, and when he returned to England became a regular attendant at the Sunday services at Eversley Church. The description and action are captivating, but the chapter promised more. The main character, Lancelot Smith, who, on "a soulless, skyless, catarrhal day," sulks in waiting for the fox to break cover and who then loses control over his horse till he is thrown off, is a symbol of the failure of the land-owning classes in England to lead the nation. The description of the country, on a day which the author describes as "truly national," suggests futility rather than purpose:

> A silent, dim, distanceless, steaming, rotting day in March. The last brown oak-leaf which had stood out the winter's frost, spun and quiv-ered plump down, and then lay as if ashamed to have broken for a moment the ghastly stillness, like an awkward guest at a great dumb dinner-party. A cold suck of wind just proved its existence, by toothaches on the north side of all faces. The spiders having been weather-bewitched the night before, had unanimously agreed to cover every brake and briar with gossamer-cradles, and never a fly to be caught in them.[79]

And even the moment of expectation, the spotting of the fox, is ephemeral and dies away as quickly as it is born: "the sweet hub-bub suddenly crashed out into one jubilant shriek, and then swept away fainter and fainter among the trees."[80] Lancelot's mood is con-templative that day, and he senses that there is something wrong in his being there:

---

[77] Uffelman (1979) 48.
[78] Hartley 61.
[79] *Y*[F] 104.
[80] *Y*[F] 105.

> There were the everlasting hills around, even as they had grown and grown for countless ages, beneath the still depths of the primeval chalk ocean, in the milky youth of this great English land. And here was he, the insect of a day, fox-hunting upon *them!* He felt ashamed, and more ashamed when the inner voice whispered,—'Fox-hunting is not the shame—thou art the shame. If thou art the insect of a day, it is thy sin that thou art one.'[81]

And when the hounds are finally on the fox's trail and, half berserk, leap the rails of a churchyard, Lancelot pulls up his horse and shudders: " 'it was no one's fault,' but there was a ghastly discord in it. Peace and strife, time and eternity—the mad, noisy flesh, and the silent, immortal spirit—the frivolous game of life's outside show, and the terrible earnest of its inward abysses, jarred together without and within him."[82] At this crucial moment, the door of the churchyard chapel opens and Argemone, the woman who will lead to his spiritual salvation later in the novel, appears.

The more socially engaged subject of the "Letters to Landlords" is picked up in the events surrounding the Carlylean gamekeeper Tregarva, whose ballad on the fate of a poacher had not minced words in accusing the landowning classes of having blood on their hands. Squire Lavington finds the poem, and Tregarva is dismissed. The ballad sets much of the tone of *Yeast* and explains why in later years it was condemned as a radical piece of work which was to taint Kingsley's reputation in some eyes for the rest of his life. It describes a widow sighing in the dark at the sight of hares:

> Leaping late and early,
> Till under their bite and their tread
> The swedes, and the wheat, and the barley,
> Lay cankered, and trampled, and dead.
>
> [. . .]
>
> She watched a long tuft of clover,
> Where rabbit or hare never ran;
> For its black sour haulm covered over
> The blood of a murdered man.

The social criticism becomes more pointed, as Kingsley voices, in much harsher language than he had dared to use in *Politics for the People*, his objections to the game laws:

---

[81] Y^F 107.
[82] Y^F 107.

A labourer in Christian England,
Where they cant of a Saviour's name,
And yet waste men's lives like the vermin's
For a few more brace of game.

There's blood on your new foreign shrubs, squire;
There's blood on your pointer's feet;
There's blood on the game you sell, squire,
And there's blood on the game you eat!

You made him a poacher yourself squire,
When you'd give neither work nor meat;
And your barley-fed hares robbed the garden
At our starving children's feet;

When we lay in the burning fever
On the mud of the cold clay floor,
Till you parted us all for three months, squire,
At the cursed workhouse door.

When packed in one reeking hovel,
Man, maid, mother, and sucklings lay;
While the rain pattered in on the rotting bride-bed,
And the walls let in the day;

We quarrelled like brutes, and who wonders?
What self-respect could we keep,
Worse housed than your hacks and your pointers,
Worse fed than your hogs and your sheep?

Our daughters with base-born babies
Have wandered away in their shame;
If your misses had slept, squire, where they slept,
Your misses would do the same.

Although Lancelot points out to the squire that he should not suppose that the poem applied to him or his family, the latter shrewdly retorts: "If it don't, it applies to half the gentlemen in the vale, and that's just as bad."[83] Of course, most of the readers of *Fraser's Magazine* belonging to the squirearchy did not like this, and the stanza on the clergy did not much endear the author to his brethren of the cloth either:

When your youngest, the mealy-mouthed rector,
Lets your soul rot asleep to the grave,
You will find in your God the protector
Of the freeman you fancied your slave.

---

[83] *YF* 458.

Such outspoken condemnation serves as prelude to a visit to a village revel, where the agricultural workers are described as seeming "rather sunk too low in body and mind,—too stupefied and spiritless, to follow the example of the manufacturing districts; above all, they were too ill-informed."[84] When Lancelot listened to the conversation around him he "hardly understood a word of it. It was made up almost entirely of vowels, half articulate, nasal, guttural, like the speech of savages."[85]

The core of Kingsley's social protest is in these scenes, and it worked well. In a review which was generally speaking far from encouraging, the critic for *The Guardian* felt it nevertheless necessary to praise the sincerity of Kingsley's attempt to have "taken pains to master the causes of our social evils" and that moreover he had succeeded well in understanding "the poor, and feels for them as a manly and right-minded person should. He is in earnest in all that pertains to this subject; and [. . .] he sees clearly many evils of which most people have but dim and vague conceptions."[86]

Unfortunately Kingsley could not maintain this standard in later parts. The weekly experience of writing for *Politics for the People* seems to have had its influence on writing a novel in instalments for *Fraser's*. The style of the short tract is all but too evident in *Yeast* and leads to a fragmentary plot and scarcely developed characters. But Kingsley tried to forestall criticism on this head when he affixed a note for the reader before the story starts:

> N.B.—This work is composed according to no rules of art whatsoever, except the cardinal one,—That the artist knowing best what he wants to say, is also likely to know best how to say it. Readers are commanded to believe that it has a spiritual sequence and method, invisible, like other spiritual matters, to all but 'the eye of faith,' and to be discovered only in its fruits; which, again, depend mainly on the sort of soil with which it may meet in the brain-gardens of a reading public.[87]

This marks *Yeast* out as a tale of conversion, in which Kingsley joined those writers who had used the novel as a medium by which to discuss controversial religious questions of the day. Published more or

---

[84] Y^F 540.
[85] Y^F 539.
[86] Y^F 332.
[87] Y^F 102.

less contemporarily with *Yeast* were titles such as *Loss and Gain* (1848), *The Nemesis of Faith* (1849), *From Oxford to Rome* (1847), or *Rest in the Church* (1848). The religious novel had become so common by the late 1840s that a reviewer in the *Athenaeum* grumbled that "We are weary of pro- and anti-Pusey novels."[88]

The conversion which stands centrally in *Yeast* is that of Paul Tregarva, the gamekeeper whom Lancelot becomes acquainted with when, after his fall from his horse, he is nursed at Squire Lavington's house. The course of this conversion is thus described:

> as if you put a soul into a hog, and told him that he was a gentle-man's son; and, if every time he remembered that, he got spirit enough to conquer his hoggishness, and behave like a man, till the hoggish-ness died out of him, and the manliness grew up and bore fruit in him, more and more each day.[89]

When Lancelot heard Tregarva's words he was already on his way to conversion himself, though he only "half understood him." Lancelot is an interesting case of a young man with independent means and no aim in life. His spiritual longings have been awakened by read-ing St Francis de Sales, but he finds that such longings cannot be catered for by any established church. As yet he only believes in

> the earth I stand on, and the things I see walking and growing on it. There may be something beside it—what you call a spiritual world. But if he who made me intended me to think of spirit first, He would have let me see it first. But as He has given me material senses, and put me in a material world, I take it as a fair hint that I am meant to use those senses first, whatever may come after. I may be intended to understand the unseen world, but if so, it must be, as I suspect, by understanding the visible one; and there are enough wonders there to occupy me for some time to come.[90]

Kingsley himself had known the attractions of pantheism in his stu-dent days. Although in the novel Kingsley repeatedly mentions Shelley, who could "commune with no deity but the all-pervading spirit of beauty,"[91] in reality the following is aimed at the American poet-philosopher Ralph Waldo Emerson:

---

[88] Tillotson 128.
[89] Y^F 544.
[90] Y^F 449.
[91] Y^F 201.

> In these Pantheist days especially [. . .] authors talk as if Christians
> were cabbages, and a man's soul as well as his lungs might be saved
> by sea-breezes and sunshine, or his character developed by wearing
> guano in his shoes, and training himself against a south wall.[92]

To Kingsley, Emerson had come to stand for those thoughtless 'any-
thingarian' days he himself had shrugged off with pain; and when
he was preparing the first instalment of *Yeast* for the press, he felt
alarmed that Emerson was drawing large audiences in London for
his lectures on nature.

VIII

No doubt, Lancelot owes much to Kingsley's own early days, and
many critics saw Fanny in Argemone. Lancelot's process of religious
regeneration starts when he meets Argemone, as Kingsley's did when
he met Fanny, the moment which he referred to in later life as his
true wedding day. Similarly in *Yeast* Kingsley writes of Lancelot and
Argemone's moment of "eye-wedlock". Mrs Kingsley in her personal
copy of the novel annotated that she wanted it to be buried with
her (although she later changed her mind and gave the copy to her
son), underlining many passages which referred with all probability
to their own courtship.[93] It is plausible to see Lancelot's religious
struggle as Kingsley's own. Lancelot is an amateur geologist, who
proudly prefers Bacon to the Bible and insists that "if that Hebrew
Bible is to be believed by me, it must agree with what I know already
from science." It takes time before Lancelot realizes that the mere
study of nature makes him "hear nothing in her but the grinding
of the iron wheels of mechanical necessity," and that something is
needed in addition to it. This something else is found in Christianity.
Here Lancelot's struggle with his knowledge of science is similar to
the struggle Tennyson was to analyse in *In Memoriam* (1850). Indeed
it is a struggle characteristic of the early Victorian period, and it
was this struggle that gave novel its title: "these papers have been,
from beginning to end, as in name, so in nature, Yeast—an honest
sample of the questions which, good or bad, are fermenting in the

---

[92] *Y*^{F} 102.
[93] Thorpe 53.

minds of the young of this day, and are rapidly leavening the minds of the rising generation."[94]

As in most stories of conversion, Lancelot has to plunge deep into misery and deprivation before he can start on his journey of spiritual regeneration. First he falls head over heels in love with Argemone, and the plot promises him a happy future. This, however, is thwarted when Lancelot loses all his property in a bank failure. Material loss is followed by personal loss when Argemone, who in her process of regeneration had caught typhus when visiting some workers' cottages, dies. There is something Bunyanesque about Kingsley's first novel, which goes back to both the autobiographical tradition of *Grace Abounding* and Christian's journey in *The Pilgrim's Progress*. Not surprisingly, Lancelot starts reading *The Pilgrim's Progress* shortly after meeting Argemone,[95] and the novel concludes that "it was a true vision that John Bunyan saw," that the way to salvation, "as this year 1848 is preaching to us, lies past the mouth of Hell, and through the Valley of the Shadow of Death."[96]

Argemone's death is the outcome of interweaving the original idea of a story about the Nun's Pool with Lancelot's process of purification. Her father, Squire Lavington, is one of those landlords whom Kingsley held responsible for the miserable conditions of the workers on their lands, and his irascible and immoral character seems to have been based on Kingsley's own patron, Sir John Cope. In the novel Kingsley invents a curse on the Lavington family to justify Argemone's death as part of the process of purification. The reader is told that during the dissolution of monasteries in the reign of Henry VIII, when the nuns at the priory of Whitford were ousted and insulted, a curse was laid on the family which would be lifted when they helped the poor and the Nun's Pool ran up to Ashy-Down. The story seems to owe something to an alleged curse on the Orme family of Lavington, and on which Samuel Wilberforce based his poem "The Hall" (1833). Kingsley knew Wilberforce, and might have heard the story firsthand from him.[97] That he was impressed by it is shown by his preoccupation with the curse, first in the tale for *Politics for the People*, and then in *Yeast*. Kingsley saw a powerful means in it by which to

---

[94] *Y*[F] 690.
[95] *Y*[F] 207.
[96] *Y*[F] 711.
[97] Chapman 91.

give the theme of reform a symbolic and supernatural dimension. And having used it in *Yeast* he came back to it in 1851, publishing it as a short-story in *The Christian Socialist*. Moreover, the fascination with the curse was handed on in later years to his younger daughter, who, in her turn, used it more than half a century afterwards as an underlying motif in her novel *Sir Richard Calmady*, a modest best-seller in 1901.

It is in the fulfilment of the curse that Kingsley introduces a theme that was to feature in many of his works, and most prominently in *The Water-Babies*: his well-known obsession with cleanliness. On her death-bed Argemone exclaims to Lancelot:

> The Nunpool! Take all the water, every drop, and wash Ashy clean again! Make a great fountain in it—beautiful marble—to gurgle, and trickle, and foam, for ever and ever, and wash away the sins of the Lavingtons, that the little rosy children may play round it, and the poor toil-bent woman may wash—and wash—and drink—Water! water![98]

Washing is seen at the same time as a means to improve the housing conditions of the workers (and as such as an earnest part of his campaign for sanitary reform), and symbolically as the Christian rite of regeneration through baptism. Thus, just as Tom's drowning in *The Water-Babies* can be seen as a re-birth, so Argemone's death makes a new beginning possible for Lancelot. But whereas Tom's regeneration is the theme of the later book, Lancelot's was cut short by Parker's wish to conclude the novel. Kingsley had no space to convey more than the mere direction of Lancelot's spiritual regeneration. A mysterious prophet is suddenly introduced who leads a still not completely converted Lancelot into St Paul's Cathedral. But the place only "breathed imbecility, and unreality, and sleepy life-in-death, while the whole nineteenth century went roaring on its way outside."[99] The Prophet points out to Lancelot that there remains "a germ of Eternal Truth" in such institutions and that there is hope in an age "in which the condition of the poor, and the rights and duties of man, are becoming the rallying-point for all thought and all organisation."[100] But the time is not ripe yet, and Lancelot leaves old England with the Prophet to go to "the youngest continent,—

---

[98] *Y*^F 704.
[99] *Y*^F 707.
[100] *Y*^F 708.

to our volcanic mountain ranges, where her bosom still heaves with the creative energy of youth, around the primeval cradle of the most ancient race of men."[101] This is where the reader leaves Lancelot—"he followed his guide through the cathedral door"—and the novel finishes with this vague utopian prospect and a few other remarks a posteriori on the fate of the other characters.

The Prophet Kingsley introduces at the end of the novel is undoubtedly based on F.D. Maurice, who was known by this name among his friends. In looking back to the origins of Christianity Maurice found inspiration for a theology of a universal church of the future. In this, his friends thought, he differed radically from the Tractarians, whom they saw only as looking sadly back to the past, wanting to turn the clock back by annihilating the progress of Protestantism towards such a Church Universal. So, what better a guide for Lancelot than Maurice? The enigmatic character of the Prophet also owes something to the mysterious Sidonia in Benjamin Disraeli's *Coningsby* (1844). He is the main character's lodestar—a man who "had exhausted all the sources of human knowledge [. . . and] pursued the speculations of science to their last term,"[102] and whose family adhered to "a belief in the unity of the God of Sinai, and the rights and observances of the laws of Moses."[103] To Kingsley Judaism was not a satisfactory basis for a quest for unity and, in giving Christian meaning to it, he creates a prophet who will lead Lancelot to the "mysterious Christian empire" of Prester John. This 'empire' was a utopian civilization which, according to medieval legend, was created by a king-priest "in the Far East beyond Persia and Armenia," although late fourteenth-century tradition also located it in Ethiopia. Kingsley saw a powerful archetype of Christian society in it which could serve as an example to modern English society. The Abyssinian location of Prester John's empire was not acceptable, as Lancelot hurries to specify, referring to Colonel Harris's account of his journey into Africa in *Highlands of Æthiopia* (1844), a book Kingsley had been reading. Harris writes that although the Christian court of Shoa might once have been a terrestrial paradise it was now the scene of utmost depravity:

---

[101] *Y*ᴲ 709.
[102] Disraeli, *Coningsby* (Oxford University Press) 189.
[103] Disraeli 183.

Morality is thus at the very lowest ebb; for there is neither custom
nor inducement to be chaste, and beads, more precious than fine gold,
bear down every barrier of restraint. Honesty and modesty both yield
to the force of temptation [. . .] The soft savage requires but little
inducement to follow the bent of her passions according to the dictates of unenlightened nature; and neither scruples of conscience nor
the rules of the loose society form any obstacle whatever to their entire
gratification.[104]

Imperialist writing of this kind convinced Kingsley that Asia, and
not Africa, was to be scoured for Prester John's Christian utopia.
The similarity between the English agricultural poor and Harris's
Ethiopians with "the dirty appearance of their unwashed faces. Water
[. . .] being studiously avoided,"[105] and their deplorable housing conditions must also have drawn Kingsley attention: "The absence of
drains or sewers compels the population of the towns and villages
to live like swine in the filth of their own styes, inhaling all the
odours of decomposing matter and stagnant water."[106] The comparison with swine, or hogs, is indeed so frequent in *Yeast* that a
cartoonist for *Punch* picked on this theme to represent the message
of the novel. The cartoon, entitled "The Rivals", shows a lean English
labourer and a fat English pig for sale, for respectively £2.2.0 and
£3.3.0.

In 1851 a critic of *The Guardian* was quick to sense the similarities
between Kingsley's Prophet and Disraeli's character: "This gentleman, who is either Prester John, or Sidonia, or the wandering Jew,"
holds forth a great deal about " 'the great Asian mystery,' in short,
on which Mr. Disraeli is so lucid."[107] By 1848, when *Yeast* was coming out in instalments, John Conington, a friend and fellow-con-
tributor to *Politics for the People* with a handful of poems, had already
remarked to Kingsley that his Prophet seemed to be taken from
Disraeli's book, and Kingsley was forced to reply. In an answer to
Conington, dated 19 December 1848, he answered firmly that at
the time the Prophet was created he had not read *Coningsby*. Although
Kingsley's answer has been taken for granted by his biographers,[108]

---

[104] W. Cornwallis Harris, *The Highlands of Aethiopia*, vols 3 (London: Longman,
Brown, Green, and Longmans, 1844) iii.167–8.
[105] *Ibid.* iii.160.
[106] *Ibid.* iii.163.
[107] [John Duke Coleridge], *The Guardian* 7/5/1851, 332.
[108] All critics seem to follow Cazamian (1903) 467: "Rien ne nous autorise mettre
en doute sa parole."

it is difficult to believe he had not read Disraeli's novel, since much of *Yeast* seems to be a direct reply to the elder novelist's views of reform. Moreover, in describing Lord Vieuxbois' policy towards his workers in the instalment for November ("He fats prize-labourers, sir, just as Lord Minchampstead fats prize-oxen and pigs") Kingsley does not hide his contempt for a similar reformer in Disraeli's famous novel:

> Lancelot could not help thinking of that amusingly inconsistent scene in *Coningsby*, in which Mr. Lyle is represented as trying to restore "the independent order of peasantry," by making them the receivers of public alms at his own gate, as if they had been middle-age serfs or vagabonds, and not citizens of modern England.
>
> "It may suit the Mr. Lyles of this age," thought Lancelot, "to make the people constantly and visibly comprehend that property is their protector and their friend, but I question whether it will suit the people themselves, unless they can make property understand that it owes them something more definite than protection."[109]

As the Prophet is introduced in a successive chapter, and published in the following instalment (December), Kingsley's explanation to Conington does not appear very credible. It seems then that Kingsley found much in the elder novelist's thought that was worth emulation, although it also needed adjusting. Rather than invalidating *Yeast* as plagiarism, this makes Kingsley's first novel more important in that genre which literary critics nowadays recognize as the "social problem novel." *Yeast* becomes a direct reaction to Disraeli's views of the solutions for the ills of the nation.

There are other interesting elements which Kingsley's novel possesses in common with Disraeli's. At the beginning of the second instalment Lancelot announces: "I have been for years laughing at Young England, and yet its little finger is thicker than my whole body, for it is trying to do something."[110] Moreover, the influence which both Disraeli and Kingsley attribute to women in reform is striking. Disraeli's statement that "It is the Spirit of Man that says, 'I will be great;' but it is the Sympathy of Woman that usually makes him so"[111] finds echo in Lancelot's drawing representing the "Triumph of Woman." The two writers also seemed to share certain ideas

---

[109] *Y*^{F} 538.
[110] *Y*^{F} 286.
[111] Disraeli 135.

about the benefits of a true feudal system. Although Kingsley felt disdain for Mr. Lyle's patronizing attempts to protect labour, he still asserted, as he had done in his "Letters to Landlords," that the workers expected to be led.

IX

Although *Yeast* contains many attractive episodes, the hurry in which it was written harmed the representation of many of the characters and their interrelationships. Most of them are not thought out well and, once introduced, are not turned into realistic characters. After the brilliant opening chapter, the meetings between Lancelot and Argemone seem contrived and psychological development is wanting. The dissection of the mind of the Romish vicar, on whom so much of the plot depends, is absurd and Colonel Bracebridge's fate borders on the melodramatic. At the novel's end the Prophet provides only a misty denouement.

This ultimate failure of *Yeast* can be attributed in part to Kingsley's intrusive voice and his innate tendency to preach, and in part to the ill-health which started to trouble him in the second half of 1848. His work for *Politics for the People*, his appointment at Queen's College, and his parish work in Eversley made it nearly impossible for him to keep up with his work. In the summer he had taken a short trip in the Fen country with F.D. Maurice. They had started off from Duxford near Cambridge, sailed down the river to Ely, from there went to Peterborough, and before returning to Cambridge, went by dogcart to Crowland. Time was spent visiting cathedrals and churches, seeing the pictures at the Fitzwilliam Museum, admiring butterfly collections, and trout-fishing on the Cam. The reiterated assurance in his letters to his four-year-old daughter Rose that "Daddy was so happy" seems to indicate his highly-strung emotions. Depression (and despair) was never far off and at Crowland he broke down and cried when he visited the ruins of a church. Maurice had to console him with a divine promise. Still, the trip offered a much-needed distraction. A four-pound trout was caught at Duxford, and he came back home with a "real live stork [. . . to put] in the kitchen garden to run about."[112]

---

[112] CK to Rose Kingsley, Summer 1848, Martin (1950) 97–8.

This spell of happiness was of short duration. Back in Eversley, writing *Yeast* "at night when the day's work was over, and the house still" soon became an additional burden.[113] The excitement of spring and the hard work which followed drained his creative energy, and led to a nervous breakdown in the autumn. It was a symptom that would recur in the following years. His doctor ordered immediate rest at Bournemouth, where he stayed for a month. But whether at Eversley or Bournemouth, *Yeast* was coming out in monthly instalments which could not be interrupted. The ill-success of the novel did not help. Parker grumbled and wanted Kingsley to finish it. In November he was back again in Eversley, struggling with the last instalment (to oblige Parker), and not feeling much better.

Notwithstanding ill-health and Parker's desire to bring the publication of *Yeast* to an end, Kingsley kept thinking about his story and the philosophy he wanted to transmit in it. He himself did not feel satisfied with the work, especially as "it was finished, or rather cut short, to please Fraser."[114] In a letter to Ludlow, written after he had finished the last instalment for *Fraser's*,[115] he tried to "consolidate" his own notions on the novel. "It is not going to die, but reappear under a difft. name & form, & in fresh scenes,"[116] he explains. In a five-year project—probably much influenced again by the trilogy-form Disraeli had adopted for *Coningsby, Sybil* and *Tancred*—*Yeast* was going to be followed by two further volumes. The next would be called *The Artists*, in which Lancelot would try to become a painter of historical scenes only to discover that there was nothing to paint except "landscapes & animals." This part would mainly consist of conversations on art, "connected as they will be necessarily with the deepest questions of Science, Anthropology, & Social life, & Christianity." Even Argemone's death in *Fraser's* seems only to have been dictated by Parker's wish to cut the novel short. She was to reappear in the second volume as Lancelot's "complementum, & consider on the ground of the affections, the same questions wh. he is examining on the ground of the intellect," and, as heiress of the estate, would try in vain to improve the social condition of the workers of Whitford. She would fail because her methods were "unconnected with the

---

[113] *LML* i.184.
[114] CK to John Conington, 30/12/1848, *LMLM* i.156.
[115] Martin (1950) 110–11.
[116] CK to JL, 16/11/48, Martin (1950) 108.

great principles w. God is manifesting in this age." Success would follow only when the lovers were united and formed "an ideal pair of pioneers toward the society of the future." This ideal society, which Kingsley calls the στοιχεια (basic principles), was going to be the theme of the third volume.

What is striking in this sketchy project is that the importance of the Prophet seems much reduced (if not entirely removed) and that Lancelot's process of regeneration was to be brought to perfection mainly through art as the "truest symbol of faith" and as a "vast means for further education." But, although *Yeast* was rewritten for volume publication in later years, this large project never material- ized. However, two characters created for *Yeast*, the irresponsible artist Claude Mellot (pagan and Fourierist) and his pretty wife Sabine were to feature in *Two Years Ago* and in *Prose Idylls*. They seem to have enchanted their creator and show the more playful side of Kingsley's character.

The winter of 1848–49 was hardly a good time to embark on such a five-year project. Kingsley was still in need of a rest. The stay in Bournemouth had not had the desired effect. Fanny blamed his brother Henry, who joined them at the seaside resort. It is no longer possible to discover why Mrs Kingsley felt such a strong dis- like for Henry, which remained with her for the rest of her life and which is reflected in the silence about him in *Letters and Memories*. But Mansfield, who was also staying with the Kingsleys in Bourne- mouth, cautioned Ludlow that "Mrs Kingsley is scarcely aware of the terrible effect which overwork has had on his intellect."[117] That *Yeast* was written with his "heart's blood," as Mrs Kingsley com- mented,[118] was almost literally true; overwork from this point in his life onward undermined his health. Upon his return to Eversley he was advised to look for a milder climate for the winter. Curates could not be found, but when his father offered to take his parish work off his hands until a curate could be found, the Kingsleys left for Ilfracombe on the north coast of Devon.

---

[117] Charles Mansfield to JL, 2/11/48, Martin (1950) 105.
[118] *LMLM* 77.

CHAPTER SEVEN

ADDLE BRAIN, HOGGISH LIFE, AND THE WILD
LONGING TO DO SOMETHING (1849)

On the North Devon coast, just five miles from Barnstaple, Ilfracombe "with its rock-walled harbour, its little wood of masts within, its white terraces, rambling up the hills, and its capstone sea-walk" provided a pleasant and cheap place of cure "if you are sea-sick, or heart-sick, or pocket-sick."[1] In the past it had been a market town and seaport, originally built along a steep road from the summit of the cliffs down to the sea-front. In the 1820s it was discovered by tourists and by the late 1840s, when the Kingsleys moved there, it had become a resort of about 4,000 inhabitants. The town had grown rapidly once the fine white beaches had been opened up by digging tunnels through the rocky cliffs, and many handsome marine villas on terraces, public rooms, and baths were erected. It was, like Bournemouth, a place to Fanny's taste. First a house in town was taken on trial, but she went out "nesting" and found Runnamede Villa more appropriate for her family. One of the fashionable new houses, it was, in Mansfield's eyes, "the most perfect bijou of a place; having every thing that could be wished for except a view of the sea."[2] Kingsley must have loved the place too. Although Susan Chitty[3] has suggested that because he never referred to Ilfracombe in his books, he did not feel any special affection for the place, this is contradicted by a 100-page article he wrote that year for *Fraser's Magazine*. In "North Devon" he expresses his admiration for Ilfracombe's "finest 'marine parade', as Cockneydom terms it, in all England" and for its "quiet nature and its quiet luxury, its rock fairy-land and its sea-walks, its downs and combes, its kind people, and, if possible, its still kinder climate." To Claude Mellot, his imaginary walking companion, he recommends: "Believe me, Claude, you will not stir

---

[1] "North Devon" *PI* 255.
[2] Charles Mansfield to JL, 30/11/48, Martin (1950) 113.
[3] Chitty (1976) 28.

from the place for a month at least."[4] In 1849 Ilfracombe promised the much-looked-for rest, and the Kingsleys rented Runnamede for a term.

When another overworked invalid, George Henry Lewes, visited Ilfracombe a couple of years later he hoped to find "sands whereon to loll or stroll [. . .] to wander nourishing one's middle age sublime with fairy tales of science and the long results of time."[5] There were few things on which the two men agreed. But the exhaustion of writing *Yeast* and the Chartist activities of 1848 had left Kingsley prostrate and "hardly up to much work" while Lewes, when he fled the stress of London life in 1856, found relief in wandering on the same sea-shore, collecting shells and zoophytes. Rest would have done Kingsley good—he complained about his "poor addle brain, which feels, after an hour's reading, as if some one had stirred it with a spoon"—but a review which he had promised for *Fraser's* represented a source of income, however small, that could not be refused. His stay at Ilfracombe thus commenced with literary activity. Notwithstanding his 'addle brain,' he managed to get together "something light and quaint by way of a review."[6] Anna Jameson's two-volume *Sacred and Legendary Art* provided Kingsley with an opportunity to write a long article on Roman Catholic figurative art and the importance it had for Protestantism. He thus adumbrated what he had had in mind for the effect of art on the minds of Lancelot and his cousin Luke in the projected (but never written) second part of *Yeast*. The review also indicates why art was to play such an important part in the progress toward the ideal (Protestant) society in the contemplated final part of the novel.

The "quaint" element of the review lay in his proposition that the Roman Catholic Church would "vanish away" when it had no more truths to teach the Protestant Church. To acknowledge the fact that in its art the Roman Catholic Church was able to express true religious sentiment was of supreme importance if the Anglican Church was to have a sound basis. Therefore, as long as Protestantism indiscriminately vilified Roman Catholic art, it committed a capital error by leaving "the deepest cravings of the human heart [. . .] utterly

---

[4] "North Devon" *PI* 255.
[5] George Lewes, *Sea-side Studies*, (Edinburgh: William Blackwood, 1858) 10.
[6] CK to John Conington, 19/12/48, *LML* i.191.

unsatisfied."[7] In crying "No Popery!", Kingsley warns, "we have very nearly burnt the Church of England over our heads, in our hurry to make a bonfire of the Pope."[8] Although Roman Catholicism was undeniably erroneous as a creed, it was absurd that virtue and noble feelings were such only when given Anglican form.

Kingsley had no patience with the puritan view that all art was either pagan or Popish, and he strongly repudiated the idea that "Protestantism had nothing to do with the imagination,"or that the devil was "the original maker of that troublesome faculty in man, woman, and child." There is a moment in each person, he argued, when a person wakes up to the beauty and truth of many a medieval legend and picture. But if "little or no proper care has been taken of the love for all which is romantic, marvellous, heroic, which exists in every ingenious child,"[9] English Protestants should not be surprised that their educated and pious young men joined the Church of Rome, since truly earnest people sooner or later wanted to associate their deep spiritual need for the beautiful with religion. Warnings against Rome produce no effect here and the Protestant Church is at fault when all it "can do is, like quacks, increase the dose" of anti-popery slogans.[10] Instead, they should be taught that "these legends, these pictures, are beautiful just in as far as they contain in them the germs of those eternal truths about man, nature, and God [. . . and] that unless you do remain Protestants, you will never enter into their full beauty and significance."[11] Thus, the time "for calling Popery ill names is past," Kingsley states, "though to abstain is certainly sometimes a sore restraint for English spirits." An apt warning, which he himself repeatedly disregarded when caught up in controversy.[12]

II

In Devon, at the beginning of December 1848, and with the stress of parish work taken off his hands, Kingsley felt he was leading "a

---

[7] *LGLE* 191.
[8] *LGLE* 189.
[9] *LGLE* 191.
[10] *LGLE* 190.
[11] *LGLE* 193.
[12] *LGLE* 189.

hoggish life" which had restored his overworked mind. There was time to read some recent books, such as Bulwer-Lytton's *Harold, the Last of the Saxon Kings* and Arthur Clough's *Bothie of Tober-na-vuolich*. The first he thought "a pedantic & unhealthy but very amusing book," but he was much impressed by the hexameters of the latter. He recommended it to Ludlow, even asking him to review it, because he thought it "a hopeful sign for 'Young Oxford'."[13] Ludlow did not like it and declined to review it, explaining in mock hexameters to Kingsley: "I have work enough & to spare, without vying with others."[14]

But the 'hoggish' pleasures and their restorative powers were short-lived. During the second week of December the weather was poor and Kingsley's nerves started to deteriorate. Initially, company was intended to help him ease his strained mind, and Charles Mansfield had gone with the Kingsleys out to Devon. Mansfield tried hypnosis on Kingsley to see if he could help him to relax, but rather than assisting the patient it drained the practitioner's energy. Company began to weigh on Kingsley, and Mansfield, himself exhausted and 'used up', left on 14 December. There also seem to have been arrangements for Henry Kingsley to join them, but by the middle of the month he was no longer welcome. "I heartily wish I were equal to the exertion of taking him in—but I am equal to no exertion at all," he apologized to his mother, "I can not think, I cannot even read—all I do almost is to stare at the sea & pick shells."[15] His spirits were low, his mind "broken-winded." Doctors advised sedatives, which he thought were a fashion rather than a serious medication. Still, he started taking them but felt humiliated by the stultifying effect they had on his thought and action.

His neglected parish duties had also started to add to his worries. His leave from Eversley was coming to an end, and if a curate were not found, he would have to return home, the prospect of which he "literally could not face."[16] But a curate was found, a Mr J. Knox, who started to officiate in the new year. However, as soon as this worry had been taken off his shoulders, others presented themselves. Although Ilfracombe was ideal for the "pocket-sick," the rent of

---

[13] CK to JL, 4/12/48, Martin (1950) 112.
[14] JL to CK, 25/12/48, Martin (1950) 116.
[15] CK to MK, 16/12/48, BL-41298 f.33v.
[16] CK to MK, 16/12/1848, BL-41298 f.32v.

Runnamede Villa had added to the family expenses, and now the cost of maintaining a curate at Eversley increased Kingsley's money worries. A year before he had borrowed a substantial sum from the Clerical Insurance Office, and now had difficulty paying off the first instalment of £140. The "crushing weight of unavoidable debt" came to torture Kingsley at a delicate moment. He went out riding to Morte where "old starved mother Earth's bare-worn ribs and joints [were] peeping out through every field and down," a most proper place for "some 'gloom-pampered man' to sit and misanthropize."[17] And descending the steep cliffs to Morte Sands the early fine weather found no echo of either joy or promise in Kingsley:

> let the sad quiet winter hang o'er me—
> What were the spring to a soul laden with sorrow and shame?
> Gary rock, bough, surge, cloud, waken no yearning within.
> Sing not, thou sky-lark above! even angels pass hushed by the weeper.
> Scream on, ye sea-fowl! my heart echoes your desolate cry.
>
> ("Elegiacs")

The "desolate cry" no doubt had much to do with his financial straits as he wandered along the coast ransacking his weary mind for solutions. Where could he look for money? Failing to meet the first instalment would bring disgrace. His father would certainly have helped him out, but Kingsley knew that he did not then have the means, and therefore did not ask. Fanny might have suggested her prosperous parents, but pride excluded such recourse to his parents-in-law; he "would rather die than ask them, who tried to prevent my marriage because forsooth I was poor." He thought of writing a second novel which "may by God's blessing bring us in honourably earned money." But writing a novel would take time, and the £140 were due in February. Therefore, at the end of January—"as a dernier ressort, & God knows where I shall turn next"—he decided, following Fanny's advice, to unburden himself to Ludlow and ask him if he, as a lawyer, could tell him of any means of borrowing £500 for five years at reasonable interest.[18] By return of post Ludlow asked for a statement of incomings and outgoings, letting it be understood that he knew of someone who might be willing to lend the money. Within a couple of days Ludlow was able to report that

---

[17] "North Devon" *PI* 260.
[18] CK to JL, 30/1/1849, Martin (1950) 120.

£140 were immediately forthcoming from a colleague of his, a Mr H.B. Turnstiles, and that the rest of the requested sum could be asked for later. Fanny replied to Ludlow full of gratitude: "I believe you have saved my husband fm. going out of his mind" and when Kingsley added his gratitude and remarked that "it really seems magical,"[19] he was not far wrong. Money was not easily borrowed at five percent interest. The money was not in fact coming from a money-lender, but from Mansfield's own purse. Ludlow had shown the letter to him, and Mansfield's first impulse was to put the needed banknotes in an envelope and send them anonymously to Ilfracombe. Ludlow dissuaded Mansfield and instead proposed that a sham contract be drawn up. The humbug was discovered months later by Mrs Kingsley, and, upon being asked, Ludlow let the cat out of the bag and a 'grand' scene followed. Still, the money came at the right moment, and it restored Kingsley's peace of mind. Indeed, he was no longer in the mood to complete the elegy from which the lines quoted above are taken, having discovered that "out of winter *must* come spring."[20]

When Kingsley had first appealed to Ludlow for money, he had added in his letter that he needed a few more years respite as in due time "my books may be selling well." When he wrote this in the midst of his despair he had already embarked on his second novel, and by 5 February had written the first two chapters. It was not going to be the promised second part of his trilogy, but an autobiography of a Chartist poet, and, once the money troubles were out of the way, the novel got on "swimmingly." His walks on the coast also started to bear fruit in the form of an article on North Devon which he started preparing for *Fraser's Magazine*, and in which Claude Mellot was called back to life.

III

Although Mrs Kingsley felt relieved when financial ruin and shame were averted, her peace of mind was not restored. She had felt alarmed about her sister Charlotte's decision to embrace the Roman Catholic creed, but when, at the beginning of February, Charlotte

---

[19] CK to JL, 5/2/1849, Martin (1950) 124,125.
[20] CK to JL, February 1949, Martin (1950) 132.

made up her mind to join a Roman Catholic convent, she despaired of her. Fanny and her other sisters argued with Charlotte, but she stood her ground and explained that her Jesuit confessor Father Brownhill had convinced her that she had a vocation for retirement and self-denial. Still, to indulge her sisters, she was willing to wait for another six months before joining the sisterhood. Although Mrs Kingsley entertained little hope of changing her mind, Charlotte was invited to come and stay with them in Ilfracombe.

Almost at the same time another visitor was invited to take refuge at Runnamede Villa. James Anthony Froude had got himself in an awkward position by writing *Nemesis of Faith* (1849), a novel about the destructive power of doubt in a young clergyman, in which the author advances the view that ultimately faith is so incompatible with reason that it can exist only in Roman Catholic incredulity. Kingsley's impulse to help a man who had literally nowhere to go was as generous as it was injudicious. Froude had been for some time a most controversial and suspect presence at Oxford, friendship with whom could damage Kingsley's reputation.

Froude was a Fellow of Exeter College, where he was known as Poor Froude. As the younger brother of Hurrell Froude, an inspiring member of the Oxford Movement who had died in 1836, he was received in Oxford by John Henry Newman. Tractarianism both attracted and repelled him. It was associated with his brother and reminded him of an unhappy childhood when his authoritarian father had whipped him, and his brother bullied him. Having escaped his family and the sadistic usages at Westminster, he became an extravagant and irresponsible undergraduate who plunged into debt. Nervous and self-conscious, he felt disgusted with himself, but, incapable of reform, laboured under a heavy weight of guilt. Although Oxford helped him to trust his intellectual powers, he never overcame his resentment at the Christian orthodoxy of his father and brother. At thirty-one, still a deacon and unlikely to take priest's orders, he wrote an autobiographical account of his religious problems in a story which was published in a volume entitled *Shadows of the Clouds*. Writing such autobiographical fiction was to Froude a liberating confessional, but his contemporaries were disconcerted by a tendency in the book to excuse both doubt itself and the wickedness that was believed to have caused it.

Much has been made of Kingsley's impulsive invitation to a man he allegedly hardly knew, and the generosity of the gesture has been remarked upon. However, it is not true that the two men were unacquainted, and the invitation to stay with the Kingsleys preceded the protests against him which broke out at Exeter College in 1849. The beginning of their acquaintance went back to the end of 1845, when Kingsley, worried about the conflicting partisanship in the Church, was looking for a platform from which to make his views known. Through Powles, Froude was approached. Froude could not help with Kingsley's magazine project, but he was much taken with Kingsley's interest and asked for their correspondence to continue. Although they remained in touch, there is not enough material surviving to gauge the intensity of their correspondence over the following two years. At one stage Froude came over to stay at Eversley, attended one of the Sunday services and was most impressed: he thought Kingsley "in his pulpit the best preacher to a country congregation" that he had ever listened to. This occasion was vividly remembered by Froude when he wrote to Kingsley during his trouble in 1849.[21]

Initially Kingsley seems to have found Froude's cold and polished manners disappointing and they made him feel uneasy. But this changed during Kingsley's brief visit to Oxford in March 1848. Kingsley wrote to Fanny: "Froude gets more and more interesting. We had such a conversation this morning—the crust is breaking, and the *man* coming through that cold polished shell."[22] To Froude the meeting was successful too, "one of those little watered spots in the life desert."[23] They had indeed become intimate by 1848, and all through the following spring, while Kingsley was hot with revolution, Froude unburdened his heart. One dramatic passage in a letter runs as follows:

> There goes twelve o'clock striking, and the Earth's shadow has cleared off the creatures up in the sky. I feel as if it had gone off me, too, but my lucid intervals are commonly of brief duration, and experience teaches me not to be sanguine. This day week I may be ready to cut my throat again.[24]

---

[21] "Autobiographical Notes" Dunn i.97; JAF to CK 27/2/1849 Dunn i.134.
[22] CK to FK, 30/3/1848, *LML* i.153.
[23] JAF to CK, 19/3/1848, Dunn i.117. There is a problem with dates here: Kingsley writes to Fanny from Oxford on 30/3/48, while Froude writes to Kingsley on 19/3/48 when the visit had already taken place. Either Mrs Kingsley or Dunn is wrong.
[24] JAF to CK, 19/3/1848, Dunn i.116.

"What a beast one is to be fretting and bothering with one's little pitiful individuality when young Europe is waking in its cradle and strangling serpents," he apologized, but "one can't help it".

Froude had by this time started contemplating *The Nemesis of Faith*, and when he withdrew to Ireland during the summer to write it, he knew that things were coming to a head at Exeter College. In the autumn he decided to leave England, and asked Powles to consult his father about possibilities in the colonies. In December a post as schoolmaster in Hobart Town in Tasmania came up and he applied for it. On New Year's Day 1849 he informed Kingsley about his forth-coming book and his intention to resign from his college. "There are many matters I wish to talk over with you," he wrote, "I wish to give up my fellowship. I hate the Articles. I have said I hate chapel to the Rector himself; and then I must live somehow, and England is not hospitable."[25] They did not meet to talk things over, partly because of Kingsley's poor health at the beginning of that year, but mainly because Froude hung back, afraid of Kingsley's condemnation.

When in February 1849 *The Nemesis of Faith* came out, the outcry against Froude was amazing in its violence. The author's overtly sympathetic view of the process of dissolution of faith was heretical to many of his colleagues. They started cutting him, and he was publicly denounced during a sermon in chapel. His father stopped his allowance, disinherited him, and declined to have anything further to do with him. When on 27 February the senior tutor William Sewell caught a student reading Froude's book during a lecture, he tore it to pieces and threw it in the fire. Froude resigned his fellowship.

Froude now received a kind letter from Kingsley, a copy of *Village Sermons* as a farewell present, and an invitation to come to stay with him before leaving for Tasmania. Touched by it, Froude wrote back the very day that Sewell burnt *Nemesis*, admitting his shame in not having trusted the sincerity of Kingsley's friendship:

> I believed my way of thought was radically different from yours, and that when you came to know what I really was you might be sorry perhaps you had been betrayed into a regard for me. I was in labour with the book. I felt I must write, and then I wished to see you, and

---

[25] JAF to CK, 1/1/1849, Dunn i.131.

then I feared to see you, and I have hung on and off waiting till you
had read it.

Now how much must I thank you for almost the only kind hearty
words I have heard about it? [. . .] Now I *will* come, and pray thank
Mrs. Kingsley most deeply from me for *her* kind note too.[26]

Thus, Kingsley's invitation came before Sewell's demonstrative gesture in the college hall.

After such correspondence it was difficult for Kingsley to go back
on his words, but Froude did not want to take advantage of this.
When he communicated his promised visit at the beginning of March
he added: "It shall be Tuesday—if it may—and you will have time
to say No, if you wish to say No."[27] Kingsley did not change his
mind. Froude's honest decision to resign his fellowship meant giving
up the security in life that a fellowship offered. And, although not
agreeing much with Froude's religious scruples, Kingsley immediately
sympathized with his plight when the whole world attacked him.

IV

Froude arrived on 6 March, and became a regular inmate of
Runnamede Villa until his appointment in Tasmania came through.
This hospitality was courageous on Kingsley's part and did not help
his own public image. Still, Kingsley remained loyal when a week
later the board for the post in Tasmania, frightened by the stream
of criticism in the press which followed the publication of *Nemesis*,
rejected Froude's candidacy. Letters of protest started to arrive at
Kingsley's address too, but they were kept secret from Froude. His
"intensely sensitive mind is utterly abattu by the misconception &
persecution to w. his book has given rise, & and the cruelty of his
own family," Kingsley wrote to Ludlow.[28]

Kingsley and Froude spent much time together: "We talked, we
wandered and fished on the moors, discussing all subjects from *The
Vestiges of Creation* to the Athanasian creed," Froude recollected in
after years.[29] They discovered that they did not agree on a good

---

[26] JAF to CK, 27/2/1849, Dunn i.133.
[27] JAF to CK, 4/3/1849, Dunn i.136.
[28] CK to JL, 19/3/1849, Martin (1950) 136.
[29] "Autobiographical Notes" Dunn i.148.

many points in religion and politics. Froude could not believe in the incarnation and therefore had doubts about the catholicity of Anglican faith, and he felt impatient with Kingsley's socialist sympathies. On 10 April, exactly one year after the Chartist uprising, Froude wrote to Powles: "Kingsley is such a fine fellow—I almost wish, though, he wouldn't write and talk Chartism, and be always in such a stringent excitement about it all. He dreams of nothing but barricades and provisional Governments and grand Smithfield bonfires, where the landlords are all roasting in the fat of their own prize oxen."[30] Notwithstanding such differences, Froude was grateful, and told Kingsley that he had done him much good and "perhaps saved him fm. suicide."[31]

Mansfield and Ludlow's curiosity about Froude had been aroused. Both were probably led to expect that the writer of *The Nemesis of Faith* would be a man deeply in earnest upon spiritual questions. Mansfield came over to meet him, and felt abashed by Froude's condescending manners. Ludlow started a short-lived correspondence with Froude, but he too was disappointed when he invited him to London for a couple of days. There was something about Froude that Ludlow did not like, a certain kind of femininity about his person. It was partly "that horribly false laugh, which chills the blood in one's veins to hear; that foul sensual mouth & eyes, that horrid made up voice of common talk," he told Kingsley in a most outspoken letter.[32] Apart from the "laugh & voice" there was a want of spiritual depth in the man. Froude had a bad influence on Kingsley, or so Ludlow maintained to the end of his life.

Kingsley did his best to get his friends to like Froude: "I do not think that you wd. be afraid of Froude if you knew him. There is an under-current of deep earnest reverence & tenderness," he wrote to Ludlow towards the end of the month.[33] Most people, he added, had fallen into the error of thinking that *The Nemesis of Faith* was autobiographical. In *The Standard* of 9 March, Froude protested against identifying a character in a novel with its author. Kingsley hurried to his defence: although Froude admitted that "I cut a hole in my

---

[30] JAF to RP, 10/4/1849, Paul 437.
[31] CK to JL, April 1849, Martin (1950) 145.
[32] JL to CK, 26/5/1849, Martin (1950) 157.
[33] CK to JL, 27/3/1849, Martin (1959) 138.

heart, and wrote it with my blood,"[34] the book, Kingsley argued, should be seen as expressing only the negative side of his belief, not the whole. However, to Maurice, who was one of the few who thought *Nemesis* a "very awful" but "very profitable" book, Kingsley confessed that there were many passages in Froude's book that "tormented and upset" him.[35]

When the Kingsleys moved in April to Lynmouth, a small fishing village ten miles east of Ilfracombe on the edge of Exmoor, Froude followed them. But although Kingsley intended to stand by his decision to help a man who had been unfairly treated, Froude's stay was becoming a bit of an ordeal: "I have been dreadfully worried lately," he admits to Ludlow, "People seem to think that my companionship with Froude is dangerous to my orthodoxy."[36] It was easy to set aside the letters of protest that reached Runnamede, but when Kingsley's parents too started raising objections to Froude's presence in their son's household, Kingsley expressed his perplexity but humbly responded "pray for me that I may be kept unspotted." Although he firmly maintained that Froude was no atheist, he acknowledged that it was his duty to honour his parents and to promise "either to get rid of Froude, or leave Lynmouth immediately and not remain in his company one day longer than the common courtesies of life require."[37] By this time other friends came forward. Chevalier Bunsen and Monckton Milnes made a generous offer to subsidize Froude for two years at a German university in order that he might study theology "scientifically," while Samuel Dukinfield Darbishire, a wealthy Manchester man, offered Froude a post as tutor to his son. When Froude left Lynmouth and the Kingsleys in April, he decided to go to Manchester before going to Germany.

Mrs Kingsley must have viewed the storm around Froude's book with dismay. And when Froude became interested in Charlotte's case, she wrote to Ludlow: "Strange strange to say Mr. Froude has taken the matter in hand." She was keenly aware of the absurdity of a resigned Oxford fellow who had lost faith in the Articles of the Anglican Church trying to minister to a convinced Roman Catholic who was to enter a nunnery. And when Charlotte seemed charmed

---

[34] JAF to CK, (Paul's date of 1/1/1849 is dubious), Paul 47.
[35] FDM to CK, 9/3/1849, Maurice i.517.
[36] FDM to CK, 9/3/1849, Maurice i.517.
[37] CK to MK, April 1849, BL-41298 f.59v.

by Froude's presence, she added in bewilderment: "I *hope* I wd. rather see her in her convent even, clinging to any positive faith in our Blessed Saviour however much error was tacked onto such a faith, then belonging to me again with poor dr. Mr. F's views."[38] Nevertheless, the Kingsleys did not discourage the growing attachment between Froude and Charlotte, and although Froude's prospects were anything but reassuring, marriage soon seemed inevitable—"You cannot go back now, Mrs. Kingsley," he wrote.[39] The biggest obstacle was Charlotte's family, who objected to the match, but they eventually gave way and the wedding took place in London on 3 October. In consequence, Froude did no go to Germany to study but became a professional historian, while Charlotte did not enter a convent but re-converted to the Anglican Church. As brothers-in-law Kingsley and Froude would often be thrown together thereafter.

Despite Froude's presence, Kingsley was now convinced that life had become truly 'hoggish'. At the beginning of April he reported that eighteen hours of his day were spent sleeping, four eating, and two walking. With Mansfield he went geologizing and gathering shells. "Old childish recollections" of the well-known places came back to him, and he discovered that these recollections had painted the "grandeur of the scenery" much smaller than it actually was in the attempt to bring "away only as much of it as I could hold." The glorious country had put new life in him and brought him to tears at times: "What a mysterious transcendental curse-blessing is this same 'heim-weh', this intense love of one's own country, wh. makes it seem pleasanter to lie down here & die, than to live any where else on earth."[40] A visit to Clovelly by boat, described in "North Devon,"[41] also made him feel "a little boy again" with "the same dear old smells, the dear old handsome loving faces."[42] This insistence on his leisurely life is telling. As in reality he was far from inactive, it indicates that he felt buoyant again and ready for battle. In April, he had a review of recent poetry ready in which he praised Matthew Arnold's *The Strayed Traveller*, while his article on North Devon was going to have a sequel. He kept working at his

---

[38] FK to JL, May 1849, Martin (1950) 131.
[39] JAF to FK, undated, Kegan Paul 53.
[40] CK to his parents, April 1849, BL-41298 f.38v.
[41] "North Devon" *PI* 246–52.
[42] CK to FK, undated, *LML* i.202.

Chartist autobiography, and sought information about the London
tailoring business. He was also longing to plunge back into the socialist cause, writing a poem for his Chartist poet novel in the excited
language which Froude disapproved. An interesting shift had taken
place in Kingsley's representation of the cause of the people. The
cautious approach towards a Christian idea of true freedom which
he had adopted in his 1848 activities now gave way to a more apocalyptic and radical vein:

> Weep, weep, weep and weep,
> For pauper, dolt, and slave!
> Hark! from wasted moor and fen,
> Feverous alley, stifling den,
> Swells the wail of Saxon men—
> Work! or the grave!
>
> Down, down, down and down
> With idler, knave, and tyrant!
> Why for sluggards cark and moil?
> He that will not live by toil
> Has no right on English soil!
> God's word's our warrant!
>
> Up, up, up and up!
> Face your game and play it!
> The night is past, behold the sun!
> The idols fall, the lie is done!
> The Judge is set, the doom begun!
> Who shall stay it?

V

During the first half of 1849 Kingsley's first volume of sermons
appeared. Although the instalments of *Yeast* in *Fraser's Magazine* had
not fared well, Parker thought that bringing out a volume of Kingsley's
sermons was innocuous enough. *Twenty-five Village Sermons* contained
material mainly written during the previous year, and they give the
reader a vivid picture of Kingsley preaching from his Eversley pulpit on Sundays. The style of the sermons is generally fluent, at times
colloquial, and they possess a freshness and energy even for the
reader today. This is particularly true of the volume's first sermons,
mainly based on texts from the Hebrew Bible, which emphasize that
God "gives life, not only to us who have immortal souls, but to

everything on the face of the earth [. . .] beasts, fishes, trees, and rivers, and rocks, sun and moon," and that "there is a sort of life in everything, even to the stones under our feet."[43] As an authority for such views, Kingsley often refers to Psalm 104. It is a recurring theme in these early sermons and at times approaches an animated idea of "mother earth,"[44] or Gaia, where "nothing that dies perishes to nothing."[45] Examples abound, from the vegetative cycle of wheat to the erosion of rock and soil. Volcanic powers are evoked, and other worlds stretching away into boundless space are not forgotten.

The sermons are also an affirmation of Kingsley's personal conviction that "God gave us bodies"[46] which in themselves are not corrupt. "The flesh is not evil," it is only our sinful souls that make it so, he argues,[47] and he is not afraid to admit to his congregation how he himself had "abused" the "spring-time of youth."[48] Maurice's influence on Kingsley's theology is apparent in the embedded notions of family and nation, which again incorporate the principle of association, and he scorns that kind of religion which means "the art of getting to heaven when we die, and saving our own miserable souls from hell."[49]

Kingsley's notion of true Christianity in *Twenty-five Village Sermons* is consistently phrased in terms of 'manliness,' by which he meant that "wickedness consists in *unmanliness*, in being unlike a man, in becoming like an evil spirit or a beast. Holiness consists in becoming a *true man*, in becoming more and more like the likeness of Jesus Christ."[50] In one sermon he even puts those qualities before godliness when he asks his congregation whether they have grown and progressed in their Christianity during the past year: "Am I more manly, or more womanly—more godly?"[51] he begins. Admittedly, Kingsley argues, Christian courage is not that of the bull-dog who "thrusts his head into a fight [. . .] because he likes it, because he is angry; and then every blow and every wound makes him more

---

[43] "Life and Death" *VTCS* 19.
[44] "The Resurrection" *VTCS* 133.
[45] "Life and Death" *VTCS* 22.
[46] "Faith" *VTCS* 35.
[47] "The Spirit and the Flesh" *VTCS* 48.
[48] "The Work of God's Spirit" *VTCS* 33.
[49] "Heaven on Earth" *VTCS* 156.
[50] "Faith" *VTCS* 41.
[51] "Lenten Thoughts" *VTCS* 170.

angry, and he fights on, forgetting his pain from blind rage."[52] Still, "that is not altogether bad; men ought to be courageous [. . .] There are times when a man must fight—for his country, for just laws, for his family, but for himself it is seldom that he must fight."[53] The overall impression of these sermons is one of straightforward honesty phrased in energetic language, which no doubt captured the attention of his congregation.

VI

While in North Devon Kingsley was briefed by Ludlow and Mansfield about developments on the Chartist front, and his restless spirit was longing for London again. In 1848, after the failure of *Politics for the People*, Ludlow had wished to establish relations with working people, and was directed to a tailor in Fetter Street, Walter Cooper, "a professed chartist and infidel." They had a good talk and Ludlow told him about Maurice. Cooper's curiosity was roused, and in the following year he came to Lincoln's Inn to listen to the master. Although there was much that puzzled him in what Maurice said, he resolved to become a regular attender, at least till he had understood more. In April Ludlow wrote proudly to Kingsley that Cooper "was rapidly becoming a devoted Maurician."[54]

In March, Cooper had suggested holding meetings at which Maurice's followers could debate with working men, and the first of a series of such meetings took place at the Cranbourne Inn near Leicester Square. In April, Kingsley, who had begun work on a new novel, asked Ludlow—at a time when he was in need of source material—to pass on a letter to Cooper, seeking information about a paper called *The Tailor's Advocate*. By the end of May Kingsley went to London to stay with his parents at the Chelsea rectory for the remainder of his absence from Eversley.

After six months' idleness, the London Chartist climate was a stimulus. Kingsley attended a meeting with the Chartists at the Cranbourne Coffee Tavern on 3 June. Maurice presided but bitter speeches followed the president's address, and when the Anglican clergy was

---

[52] "The Courage of the Saviour" *VTCS* 185.
[53] "The Courage of the Saviour" *VTCS* 185,189.
[54] Ludlow (1981) 145.

attacked Kingsley got up "folded his arms across his chest, threw his head back, and began—with a stammer which always came at first when he was much moved, but which fixed every one's attention at once—'I am a Church of England parson'—a long pause—'and a Chartist'." In an eloquent speech he proclaimed that he sympathized with the Chartist cause, that he denounced the injustice of the legal system, that he would help them to set it right, but that he equally disapproved of the Chartists' methods." Thomas Hughes, looking back in 1879, testified to the impression made that day: "The most violent speaker on that occasion was one of the staff of the leading Chartist newspaper. I lost sight of him entirely for more than twenty years, and saw him again, a little grey shrivelled man, by Kingsley's side, at the grave of Mr. Maurice."[55]

Ludlow had a different recollection of the event. In his autobiography he records that Kingsley had come in late and sat down a few seats from Archie Campbell who had brought his young friend David Masson. In Ludlow's version, Kingsley got up and stammered that he was a p-p-parson and a ch-ch-chartist, and whispered "church of England, I mean." Kingsley's utterance caused Campbell to stuff his pocket handkerchief into his mouth, "evidently writhing with all but uncontrollable laughter." After the meeting Campbell described how Masson leant over to him when Kingsley had begun to speak and declared full of concern, "The man is drunk!"[56]

But Kingsley did not feel intimidated and went heart and soul into the socialist cause. He liked encountering working people, attended another workman's meeting on the question of Land Colonization, and felt satisfied when he heard that Walter Cooper was unable to retrieve his copy of Kingsley's *Village Sermons* as it was being "lent from man to man, among the South London Chartists" and that Manchester workers had stolen his copy of *The Saint's Tragedy*.[57] Kingsley also met his London friends of Lincoln's Inn, and found Maurice's preaching more impressive than ever. "Last night will never be forgotten by many many men," he wrote home, "Chartists told me this morning that many were affected even to tears. The man was inspired—gigantic."[58] Kingsley's twenty-three year-old brother

[55] Hughes (1876) xix.
[56] Ludlow (1981) 149–50.
[57] CK to FK, undated, *LML* i.205–6.
[58] CK to FK, 12/6/1849, BL-62553 f.132r.

George felt "quite in a new world"[59] when he was introduced to his
elder brother's friends at one of Parker's soirees. He enjoyed, too,
the company of those such as Charles Robert Walsh, a doctor who
had shared rooms with Mansfield and who was much in earnest
about sanitary reform, who came to see Kingsley one evening at the
parental house in Chelsea. George was also introduced to the Chartist
Thomas Shorter, and Mansfield's cousin Archie Campbell, by profession an architect.

Walsh gave an account of the dire living conditions of the London
poor. A follower of Maurice, Walsh was one of those who had been
"stirred to a different train of thought and action by seeing or hearing
of the sufferings of their fellow-men, and forced to rise, as if spellbound, with bristling hair and creeping flesh, to follow the appari-
tion which beckons" all who "have felt that they could no longer
live in comfort while others lived in hopeless and ever-increasing dis-
comfort."[60] His activities as a sanitary reformer were to have a profound (and forgotten) influence on Kingsley, and gave a new impulse
to his projected novel.

Kingsley met other people while he was in London. He sought
out Carlyle, and breakfasted once with the Prussian ambassador
Bunsen, and once with Frank Newman, John Henry Newman's free-
thinking brother who had just published a book entitled *The Soul;
Her Sorrows and Aspirations*. One evening at Ludlow's chambers he
also met Jules le Chevalier, a French socialist who had taken refuge
in England when he was no longer welcome in his own country
after the insurrection of 13 June. Ludlow, who had known Lechevalier
(as he spelled his name in England) for some time, thought him
much improved and introduced him to his friends, with whom he
became popular. Maurice and his friends welcomed the Frenchman's
belief that "nothing but Christianity can save France or the world."
Kingsley too was greatly struck by his conversation. In a sense the
two reformers were similar in character. Intellectually both were restless, and with their wit, knowledge and resources charming com-
panions. That evening at Ludlow's chambers the talk became "intensely
interesting"[61] to Kingsley when Lechevalier elaborated on his views

---

[59] CK to FK, undated, BL-62553 f.138r.
[60] Jacob [Charles Walsh], "[Review of] *Lectures on Social Sciences and the Organization
of Labour*. By James Hole," 22/2/51, *ChSoc* i.135.
[61] CK to FK, undated, BL-62553 f.137v.

that although co-operation was the essence of socialism, it was Christianity which proclaimed such principles.

With his new novel in mind on the sanitary condition of the workers in London, Kingsley continued to collect information. Walsh had told him of the wretched conditions of the poor in London; Kingsley now went out to gauge their medical condition. He breakfasted with William Guy, Dean of the Medical Faculty at King's College and an early contributor to *Politics for the People*, and afterwards went "tailor hunting." One afternoon he was with Richard Owen at the College of Surgeons and "saw unspeakable things."[62] He picked up the thread where he had left off the previous summer. The days passed quickly and he found himself postponing his departure for Eversley. When he returned, hard work awaited him.

VII

That summer cholera struck England, and at Eversley a low fever broke out. Although a curate had been appointed to help Kingsley, the period for Kingsley was one of almost unceasing anxiety and toil. The fear of cholera made it difficult to find people who were willing to nurse the sick, and the rector was constantly visiting. As high as his restless spirits had soared in London, they now fell low, and after sitting up a night with a labourer's wife, he broke down. Doctors recommended sea air, and a trip to America was considered, but he could not face the long separation from Fanny and his parents were against it. Instead, a month of Devon air was decided upon, and in August he was back in Clovelly, leaving Fanny and the children at home. Once on his way he improved, and from Appledore, where he remained stranded for a night because there were no trawlers to Clovelly, he wrote: "This rich hot balmy air, wh. comes in now through the open window, off Braunton Burrows, & the beautiful tide river, a mile wide, is like an 'Elixer of life' to me."[63] In Clovelly he took lodgings at the top of the street, and from his twelve-feet square room he could see "the tops of the nearest houses, & the narrow paved cranny of a street, vanishing downwards,

[62] CK to FK, undated, BL-62553 f.178r.
[63] CK to FK, 10/8/1849, BL-62553 f.142v.

stair below stair & then above all, [. . .] the glorious blue bay, with
its red & purple cliffs."[64] For the first week he rested, reporting to
Ludlow: "I lie in the window, & smoke & watch the glorious cloud-
phantasmagoria, infinite in colour & form, crawling across the vast
bay & deep woods below, & draw little sketches of figures."[65] Strength
soon returned and time was spent fishing for trout on the Torridge,
and riding on the moors. If there was wind he would sail in the
bay; if not, he would go butterfly hunting in the hills. The scenery
inspired poetry, and a visit to Lundy provided material for a chapter
of "North Devon." He read Rabelais, whom, "were he seven times
as unspeakably filthy as he is; I consider as priceless in wisdom, and
often in true evangelic godliness"; and Ruskin's *Seven Lamps of Architecture*,
which he thought a noble and godly book.

Notwithstanding repeated affirmations that life seemed truly idyllic, even Devon reminded him of overpopulation, bad housing and
grinding poverty: "Clovelly is in a bad state—the houses tumbling
down, population increased, houses not—people pigged together like
cattle," he wrote to his parents. In his prophetic vein he added:
"What can one say, except 'Lord, *thy* kingdom come!'"[66] Ludlow
had recommended Pierre Leroux' socialist writings to him and from
the beginning of his stay in Devon he had occupied his mind with
questions of cooperation. He thought Leroux's egalitarian ideas the
sign of a "blessed dawn," but this 'blessed dawn' of socialism was
accompanied by the same apocalyptic sentiments of change he had
been nursing in late spring. Now, however, such sentiments were
jubilant and inflammatory rather than gloomy and fatalistic.

VIII

Kingsley finished his Devon holiday tramping on Dartmoor. Although
he drank in all the magnificent beauty around him, his mind kept
returning to the things Walsh had told him about the plight of the
people, feelings which found expression in a poem with the significant
title "The Day of the Lord," showing that in the year following
Politics for the People Kingsley had become more revolutionary than

---

[64] CK to FK, undated, BL-62553 f.150v–151r.
[65] CK to JL, 17/8/1849, Martin (1950) 164..
[66] CK to MK, 27/9/1849, BL-41298 f.51v.

otherwise. The poem, reminiscent of Shelley's calls for insurrection, did not find its way into *Alton Locke*, but was published under Kingsley's pseudonym Parson Lot in *Fraser's Magazine*, and reprinted the following year in the first issue of *The Christian Socialist*. Other poetry was written in 1849, mostly minor poems around the recurrent idea of a "blessed dawn," a belief of the imminent rebirth of the social state. This theme had occupied Kingsley's mind during the revolutionary year of 1848, and obviously continued to do so in 1849 as he was writing his Chartist novel. When compared with the bleak "Elegiacs" earlier that year, these poems indicate that Kingsley was finally rallying after his period of despondency. Thus the theme of a process which is coming to maturity with the promise to bear fruit, becomes a homely image of marriage and birth of children: in the short lyric "Dartside" the "Sweet Earth is faithful, and young,/ And her bridal day shall come ere long." Similarly, in "The Watchman," he defies the darkness of the present as a most "fruitful time" when "to many a pair are born children fair,/ To be christened at morning chime." On the other hand, expressions of a vigorous struggle leading to freedom (both physical and spiritual) are brought in, a reflection of Kingsley's steadfast belief in heroic (English) progress. Such a Whiggish conception of progress comes out clearly in "The World's Age," where Kingsley describes how "the race of Hero-spirits/ Pass the lamp from hand to hand," or when he emphasizes his own heroic duty in such an endeavour: "Forward! Hark forward's the cry!/ One more fence and we're out on the open" ("My Hunting Song"). It could be said that these poems are not of particular literary interest in themselves. But they express Kingsley's moods and hopes in 1849 and give some indication of the ideas which were shortly to be attributed by Kingsley to his creation, Alton Locke. Although contemporary criticism appreciated the powerful expression of "The Day of the Lord," most reviewers remained perplexed at the quality of the other poems; they "are very good; but not good enough," declared one critic.[67] There was one exception: "The Sands of Dee." This fine poem, inserted in *Alton Locke* as one of the main character's poetic efforts (for which insertion Alton apologizes), was to become Kingsley's most celebrated lyric. The reviewer for *Fraser's Magazine* went so far as to say that it was "characterized by a

---

[67] Shirley 742.

perfection and completeness of form which is not found except in the greatest poets—Burns, Keats, Tennyson."[68] Another reviewer, W.C. Roscoe, praised the poem's sweetness and mournful cadence and explained: "It owes its charm to pathos, embodied in an utterance of exquisite simplicity; it moves us more deeply by the very absence of any appeal to the feelings."[69] It is on such premises, however, that he regrets Kingsley's choice of attributing cruelty and hunger to foam, a poetic choice which John Ruskin, on the other hand found most felicitous: "Now so long as we see that the *feeling* is true, we pardon, or are even pleased by, the confessed fallacy of sight which it induces." Kingsley's lines are good "not because they fallaciously describe foam, but because they faithfully describe sorrow."[70] Whatever the final verdict, "The Sands of Dee" is one of the few poems by Kingsley which are still anthologized today.

IX

Visiting Holne, his birthplace, Kingsley heard of the increased sickness in his parish, and hurried home when Rose was reported to be ill.[71] Rose recovered, but news of cholera came from all parts of England. Hundreds of people lay dying around Plymouth, and the crowded parts of London were desperate scenes of illness and death. Alarm bordered on religious hysteria and proposals were made to proclaim a fast. Kingsley felt he had to answer from his pulpit. "We have just been praying to God to remove us from the cholera, which we call a judgment from God, a chastisement," he opened his sermon on the last Sunday of September, adding that it was right to do so for sins committed. But it was mere cant and hypocrisy, he continued, to repent while ignoring "*which* sin God is punishing us for." Instead, people needed to repent of "the covetousness, the tyranny, the carelessness, which in most great towns, and in too many villages also, forces the poor to lodge in undrained stifling hovels, unfit for hogs, amid vapours and smells which send forth on every breath the seeds of rickets and consumption, typhus and scarlet

---

[68] Shirley 743.
[69] [Roscoe] 129.
[70] John Ruskin, *Modern Painters* iii 12.11.
[71] CK to Charles Kingsley sr., 12/9/1849, BL-41298 f.52.

fever, and worse and last of all, the cholera." There was nothing new in all this, he emphasized, sanitary commissioners having long since stated these truths. But because it was the poor rather than the rich who suffered these diseases, little was done about it. "So the filth of our great cities was left to ferment in poisonous cesspools, foul ditches and marshes and muds."[72] Idleness, neglect, and ignorance had brought on the outbreak of cholera; it was the breaking of God's laws of nature which had led to pestilence.

The following week, while cholera raged, he returned to the subject. The second sermon, based on "visiting the sins of the fathers upon the children," was more aggressive in tone and illustrated the application of the verse to the current epidemic. If parents, landlords and politicians neglected their common duty of cleanliness, then children, tenants, and the nation would be visited by the consequences: "We have had God's judgment about our cleanliness; His plain spoken opinion about the sanitary state of this parish. We deserve the fever, I am afraid; not a house in which it has appeared but has had some glaring neglect of common cleanliness about it."[73] Readers today should not be surprised at Kingsley's preoccupation with cleanliness. He literally saw people dying, year by year, because they were ignorant of basic rules of hygiene. As he made clear in a third sermon, prosperity and progress rested upon such rules: "every house kept really clean, every family brought up in habits of neatness and order, every acre of foul land drained [. . .] is a clear call to mankind, a good example set which is sure sooner or later to find followers, perhaps among generations yet unborn."[74] This invocation of cleanliness is thus both spiritual and utilitarian. The laws of nature are the expression of God's existence, and observation of them both a moral and a practical necessity. Thus, he concludes in his Thanksgiving sermon of 15 November: "For every case of cholera could be traced to some breaking of these laws—foul air—foul food—foul water, or careless and dirty contact with infected persons; so that by this God showed that He and not chance ruled the world."[75]

It seems that Kingsley wrote at least the first sermon before becoming acquainted with Henry Mayhew's account in the *Morning Chronicle*

---

[72] "First Sermon on the Cholera" *NS* 134–6.
[73] "Second Sermon on the Cholera" *NS* 151.
[74] "Third Sermon on the Cholera" *NS* 163.
[75] "On the Day of Thanksgiving" *NS* 172.

of 24 September of the cholera districts of Bermondsey. In it the author describes the conditions in which people lived in an area called Jacob's Island, a patch of ground cut off by stagnant sewer canals, where the air had "literally the smell of a graveyard." Kingsley recognized in the report conditions he had himself witnessed in a few streets of upper Chelsea, but the scale of dirt and pestilence of Bermondsey appalled him. He was angry and bewildered when he read that the water which served for cooking, drinking and washing was "covered with a scum almost like a cobweb, and prismatic grease." Mayhew's article on Jacob's Island was not the first in the series published in the *Morning Chronicle* to draw attention to the poor sanitary conditions in the London slum area, but his description of a girl dangling a tin cup into the stream in which a neighbour emptied a bucket of night-soil at the same moment and in which "floated large masses of green rotting weed, and against the posts of the bridges are swollen carcasses of dead animals, almost bursting with the gases of putrefaction" was as distressing to Kingsley as it was emblematic.

Charles Robert Walsh had long wanted to put his ideals of reform into practice and when cholera broke out in London that summer, he accepted an appointment as Superintending Inspector to Southwark and Bermondsey for the General Board of Health, thus losing the favour of his wealthy patients. He asked the friends who had gathered around Maurice to see the situation for themselves, and when he showed them over Jacob's Island during the month of October, all were aghast that local people had no other water to drink than that of the sewer floating with "dead fish, cats and dogs." Immediate action was necessary.

Kingsley visited Jacob's Island on October 23 with Walsh and Mansfield, and immediately joined Ludlow in making the conditions known to a wider public. He wrote to his wife, who at the time was staying with her relative Mr Warre, member of Parliament for Ripon, asking her to show the latter the accounts in the *Morning Chronicle* and see what he could do. There was no time to wait for "committee meetings and investigations" he explained, because, "while they will be maundering about 'vested interests', and such like, the people are dying."[76] People needed to be aware of the atrocious

---

[76] CK to FK, 24/10/1849, *LML* i.217.

living conditions, and he hurried to Bishop Wilberforce of Oxford, who had a reputation for taking an interest in humanitarian matters, to inform him of the calamity that was going on. Although Kingsley mentioned in a letter to Fanny that the interview with Wilberforce was satisfactory, to Ludlow he was more explicit about the general attitude in Oxford to the condition of the poor: "Oxford turns one sick. Nobody believes anything, or wish to believe."[77] Frustrated at the little he had achieved, he suggested Ludlow ask Maurice to exercise his influence in Oxford, while he himself would try, upon Wilberforce's advice, to get interviews with Lord Carlisle and Lord John Russell.

Ludlow came up with the idea of reprinting Kingsley's "dirt-sermons" in a farthing edition, and a pamphlet was written and distributed as the start of a series of tracts on sanitary reform. Ludlow had also contacted the editor of *The Morning Chronicle*, who promised to report their activities. Other friends spoke to the responsible local authorities and to the landlords of the hovels. Walsh suggested evening lectures, while Mansfield was analysing water and studying the Public Health Act. Kingsley had written to his brother-in-law Osborne asking him to write a letter to *The Times*, but told Ludlow he had low hopes in this direction as "he is so conceited & contrary that he will perhaps not do it, just because the dirt is not of his own finding."[78] He also prompted Ludlow to find out if his friend Tom Taylor could help in *Punch*. The only result of this campaigning was a cartoon in *Punch* of an alderman complacently observing the dirty reflection of his own person in the Thames. "The City Narcissus, Or, The Alderman Enamoured of his Dirty Appearance," ran the caption.

Kingsley was especially outraged that a month after Mayhew's article appeared in *The Morning Chronicle*, the authorities had still done nothing about the situation in Bermondsey. But Kingsley and his friends had started to help the population of Jacob's Island with fresh drinking water. They had raised money for a water-cart, which Kingsley, Ludlow, Mansfield and the Campbells offered to operate. To Kingsley this strategy of helping the population in practical ways and of having their campaign covered in the press was constructive and effective, but he saw the diplomacy required in discussions with

---

[77] CK to JL, 30/10/1849, Martin (1950) 179.
[78] CK to JL, 1/11/1849, Martin (1950) 181.

the landlords as fruitless and a waste of precious time. "Why are you so confoundedly merciful and tender-hearted? Do you actually fancy that you can talk those landlords into repentance?" he wrote to Ludlow, scolding him for neglecting the more effectual form of help: "Why tarry the wheels of your water-carts, why are your stand-pipes truly stand still pipes?"[79]

The voluntary field-work was not always easy. The population eyed the group of enthusiasts with suspicion. They were a bad lot and heavy drinkers, Ludlow reported. The brass-cocks of the water-butts were almost immediately stolen and when questioned by an old man as to their motives, the latter concluded it was patriotism. He added "Well, I also joined the Volunteers for six months when I was a young man!"[80]

It is not surprising that sanitary reform provided Ludlow's friends with a motive for social action, and when he proposed a national Health League, all were in favour. With Walsh and Mansfield he drafted a plan "for uniting all classes of society in the promotion of the Public Health, and the removal of all causes of disease which unnecessarily abridge man's right to live." They stated that their main objects were collecting and diffusing information, the execu-tion and amendment of the law, and prompting private and public bodies to do their duty.[81] Kingsley was enthusiastic: "it will act as a wedge," he prophesied. He was therefore disappointed when Maurice, always suspicious of clubs and parties, refused to support the league. Kingsley fumed, and wanted to go ahead without Maurice: "His imagination is defective," he protested, "may it not be the way in w. *He* is teaching you, & me too, to "call no man master"?" The Health League had to go ahead, "it must *agitate*, & *shout*, & by "coarse unscrupulous" means—everything w. a gentleman & a Christian dare do, *bully* existing authorities & interests into reason."[82] "Are you game?" he asked Ludlow. But Ludlow restrained him. Maurice had emphasized the importance of the "duties of neighbourhood" and that they should not waste their energy in all-absorbing national movements. "It is a very great principle," Ludlow uneasily explained to Kingsley, "to establish this of the right of a number of persons

[79] CK to FK, 24/10/1849, *LML* i.217.
[80] Ludlow (1981) 155.
[81] Ludlow (1894) 30.
[82] CK to JL, 27/11/1849, Martin (1950) 186.

not connected with a parish to go in and help to remove a certain number of parochial nuisances because they are also national crimes, and if we begin with too coarse a wedge, we shall never get the small end in, without which the block cannot be split."[83] Finally all the friends obeyed, and returned to their work of immediate relief in Bermondsey, of which Maurice did approve. But the wrangle had taken the edge off their enthusiasm. Moreover, with the hostile attitude of the population of Bermondsey and the greatest dangers of the cholera epidemic over, enthusiasm ebbed until in December another series of articles by Mayhew in the *Morning Chronicle* changed the focus of their attention.

On December 14 Ludlow read accounts of the dependence of journeymen tailors upon the sellers of ready-made clothes (slop sellers), and wrote immediately to Kingsley: "Have you or have you not read the letters in the *Morning Chronicle* [. . .] If you have not, read them forthwith; if you have, tell me whether I am not right in saying that operative associations or partnerships such as they have in Paris *must* be set up forthwith."[84] Ludlow had agreed with Mansfield, Hughes and Campbell that money was needed to set up such cooperative workshops, which then had to be provided with custom. But as a first step, people needed to be informed of the abuses to which the tailors who made the clothes they wore were subjected. Here Kingsley's powerful pen could be counted upon. Ludlow had a high regard for Kingsley's powers as a propagandist and the two collaborated closely. While they were trying to publicize the problems of the Bermondsey sewers in October, Ludlow had written to Fanny that he relied "upon Charles to make us a good stirring placard or two for the purpose."[85] Suggesting to Kingsley that he read Mayhew's articles, Ludlow was confident of spurring him to action. Kingsley had not seen the articles, but wrote by return of post to ask for them and promised to come up to London around Christmas to help. Mayhew's work provided him with information for his novel, but, at Ludlow's suggestion, he also started on a pamphlet, part of which was written on 28 December at Eversley Rectory while outside in a freezing tempest snow fell thick from a "pitiless mocking blue sky."

---

[83] Ludlow (1981) 156.
[84] Ludlow (1981) 158.
[85] Martin (1950) 180.

Ludlow himself had not been idle and had prepared a long essay, "Labour and the Poor," for *Fraser's Magazine*. To his delight, it drew attention by being the first article in the 1850 volume. In the essay he exposed a barbarous system of competition in the tailoring trade which forced prostitution on women dressmakers as the only option for their families to survive. Government was held guilty by him for "accepting contracts at the lowest tender, without inquiring into the morality of each contract"[86] and should be ashamed of making money out of "the prostitution-wages of the female slop-workers."[87] Ludlow concluded with a powerful appeal for the principle of association.

When Kingsley read Ludlow's essay he felt "stunned & sickened," as well as humbled by its powerful insistence on the need for cooperation, about which he felt he did not know enough. Discouraged, Kingsley offered his own uncompleted pamphlet to Ludlow, suggesting he "make something" of it "by doctoring" it.[88] Ludlow would not hear of it, and Kingsley completed his tract. It was published at the end of January. Ludlow recognized it as an important "blow" and Maurice liked it "exceedingly." As in Ludlow's case, Kingsley borrowed much from the *Morning Chronicle*, and added little that was new. However, the most impressive parts of Kingsley's account were the descriptions of how tailors were trapped by sweaters—middlemen who oppressively overworked and underpaid workers—with six men in "a room that was a little better than a bedstead long. It was as much as one could do to move between the wall and the bedstead when it was down. There were two bedsteads in this room, and they nearly filled the place when they were down. The ceiling was so low, that I couldn't stand upright in the room. There was no ventilation in the place."[89] When, as a last resort, the underpaid workers pawned their clothes to the 'sweater,' and temporarily lost their freedom to leave the premises, they would keep warm in the small overcrowded rooms by donning parts of the clothes on which they were working. It is here that the pamphlet becomes most effective, when Kingsley warns his reader of the consequence of buying cheap:

---

[86] [Ludlow] (1850) 14.
[87] [Ludlow] (1850) 15.
[88] CK to JL, 30/12/1849, Martin (1950) 195.
[89] *Cheap Clothes and Nasty AL* lxx.

The Rev. D—finds himself suddenly unpresentable from a cutaneous disease, which it is not polite to mention on the south of Tweed, little dreaming that the shivering dirty being who made his coat has been sitting with his arms in the sleeves for warmth while he stitched at the tails. The charming Miss C—is swept off by typhus or scarlatina, and her parents talk about "God's heavy judgment and visitation"—had they tracked the girl's new riding-.habit back to the stifling undrained hovel where it served as a blanket to the fever-stricken slopworker, they would have seen why God had visited them.[90]

Although the language used by Kingsley—"let no man enter [a slop-shop . . .]—they are the temples of Moloch—their thresholds are rank with human blood"—is more effective in its prophetic quality than Ludlow's, it was above all Kingsley's title *Cheap Clothes and Nasty* that helped it to be remembered by posterity, while Ludlow's article soon fell into the shadow of Mayhew's revelations.

Kingsley was to be more outspoken still in the novel he was writing. The things he had seen on Jacob's Island would be integrated in a picture of the workers' London, while the sweating system gained dramatic saliency in its plot. Much of the novel had been written by the end of 1849, almost certainly the initial chapters, the Jacob's Island pieces, and the final conversion scenes. At the beginning of December he had asked Thomas Cooper about the history of Chartism, and this also found its way into the novel. At the beginning of 1850 he was able to start filling in the gaps that were still left in the narrative.

X

Notwithstanding their common humanitarian battle against contemporary social conditions, towards the end of 1849 a difference of opinion between Kingsley and Ludlow indicated a fundamental divergence of moral outlook between the two. Although Ludlow later emphasized that it did not affect their friendship, it would lead in the following years to differences over which their fellowship would eventually founder. Their disagreements unexpectedly concerned the military feats of the white Rajah Brooke in Sarawak.

---

[90] *Cheap Clothes and Nasty AL* lxxix.

Brooke, an adventurer with means who had set out with a schooner
to explore the Far East, had become famous—and to some notorious—for his sanguinary exploits in Borneo. The Sultan of Brunei
had proclaimed him governor of Sarawak for his decisive help in
the defeat of parties of rebels who for some time had made the territory unstable. With the publication of his diaries in 1846, Rajah
Brooke had become known to the English, and public opinion saw
in him a national hero. When he landed at Southampton on the
2 October 1847, he was invited to Windsor Castle and soon after
received a knighthood. But not all people admired Brooke. In humanitarian quarters protesters declared him to be a blood-thirsty and
self-seeking man.

Kingsley was uncritically attracted to a man who had sailed to
the Far East in a ship named *Royalist*, upon a heroic enterprise which
he saw as part of the English duty to civilize the coastal populations
of Borneo. It also evoked the image of his brother Gerald, who had
also sailed the Indonesian archipelago in a ship with a nearly identical name *(HMS Royalist)* and who was the last officer to die on
board in the Gulf of Carpenteria. Moreover, Kingsley admired
Brooke's daring spirit, which was expressed in the journals in vigorous and impetuous language not unlike Kingsley's own, as for
example in: "Am I really fond of War?—I ask this question of myself,
and I answer—Certainly—for what man is not."[91]

Joseph Hume, a Liberal member of Parliament, had objected to
the expenditure in the colonial administration in 1848 while others
pointed out that the Royal Navy had engaged in massacres in Borneo.
Although nothing came of Hume's motion at the time, towards the
end of 1849 two developments inflamed the controversy in England
over Brooke's methods of suppressing piracy. The first was the account
of the Battle of Batang Maru on 31 July, in which Brooke put an
end to the confederacy of pirates with the help of the English Navy
and of the coastal tribes of Sarawak. Gunfire, the revenge of long-
persecuted tribes and the sharp paddle-wheels of the steamers caused
heavy casualties among the pirates in their canoes. About 500 died
in the battle, while another 500 died from the wounds and injuries
they suffered. The news reached England in the autumn and coincided more or less with the re-publication of Brooke's diaries, which

[91] Steven Runciman, *The White Rajahs; A History of Sarawak from 1841 to 1946*
(Cambridge: Cambridge University Press, 1960) 97.

included some of the sanguinary passages that had been omitted from previous editions. Hume consulted his colleague Richard Cobden, and both were convinced that Brooke had used the English Navy to slaughter innocent aborigines in order to take possession of their lands. They decided to bring the matter before Parliament once more.

Repeated attacks in the newspapers on the methods pursued in Sarawak led Kingsley to write about his "hero Rajah Brooke" to Ludlow, who had also expressed his condemnation of the sacrifice of so much human life. Ludlow held that such bloodshed could not but be repudiated by a person who called himself a Christian. It was a proposition Kingsley was not prepared to embrace. "Prove that it is *human* life," he replied, "It is beast-life". The sentence, isolated from its context, suggests racism in Kingsley, as some critics have argued. But whatever one's feelings about Brooke's methods, it is fair to Kingsley to relate the statement to the pirates and not to indigenous people in general. A refusal to do so distorts the image of a man who was essentially humane and generous by nature. Ludlow did not question Kingsley's humanity. What seems to be wanting in Kingsley's view is a critical distance between his idea of rightfulness and the inflicted violence itself. Kingsley insisted: "you who have been warned, reasoned with—who have seen in the case of the surrounding nations the strength & happiness w. peace gives, & will not repent but remain still murderers & beasts of prey—You are the enemies of [. . .] peace," and added "Honour to a man, who amid all the floods of sentimental coward cant [. . .] dares act manfully on the broad sense of *right*."[92] Kingsley made it sound like the destruction of the Canaanites.

Indeed, Kingsley's Christ was close to a Moses, Joshua or David, while Ludlow's remained one of "neighbourly love." To the latter the Government prize money for killing pirates was nothing less than "blood-money," to which Kingsley again replied: "I think the preserving that great line of coast from horrible outrage by destroying the Pirate fleet—*was* loving his neighbour as himself & taking the blood-money—*not* to spend on himself—for he spends nothing on himself, but to use in civilizing the wretched people whom these pirates have been butchering for centuries—was *right*."[93]

[92] CK to JL, December 1849, *LML* i.222–3.
[93] CK to JL, December 1849, *LML* i.223–4.

Notwithstanding the self-confident tone of this, at the end of 1849 Kingsley seemed in something of a moral quandary. At Christmas, the contradiction between human want near to home and the happy Christian message appeared a sharply one:

> Still in cellar, and in garret, and on moorland dreary
> The orphans moan, and widows weep, and poor men toil in vain,
> Till earth is sick of hope deferred, though Christmas bells be cheery.
> ("A Christmas Carol")

"I have no confidence in myself, "he explained to Ludlow. Still, admission of the defeat of Christianity was far off: "Thou wilt heed no less the wailing, yet hear through it angels singing," the "Christmas Carol" concluded. And to Ludlow Kingsley wrote that there was in him a "wild longing to do *something*," to which he added "I think he that believeth *must* make haste, or get damned with the rest."[94]

---

[94] CK to JL, 30/12/1849, Martin (1950) 195.

CHAPTER EIGHT

RED-HOT SHOT AGAINST THE
DEVIL'S DUNG-HEAP (1850)

"Mr. Kingsley is rather grave, and, like me, never laughs," was John Martineau's initial impression when he came as a shy fifteen-year-old boy to Eversley in January 1850 to become the rector's first full-time pupil. "But," he added "he is very kind, and I like him very much." Martineau was to stay with the Kingsleys for the next year and a half until he was ready to go to university. His boyish accounts of Kingsley's family in his letters provide a vivid picture of every-day life at the rectory. The timetable of the day was unfolded in the first letter to his mother. They had prayers with all the servants present at a quarter to nine, during which Kingsley first read a chapter from the Bible and then prayers. After a substantial meat break-fast they worked until lunch at one. They went walking early in the afternoon until about five, which was dinner time, and work was resumed from seven to nine. At half past nine Kingsley read three or four verses from the Bible, after which the boy was sent up to his bedroom.

Martineau, who had had a miserable time at school before he was entrusted to Kingsley's care, seemed to have felt almost at once at home in the rectory. Mrs Kingsley was "particularly kind and delicately attentive." She insisted on having a fire lit in his room before he went to sleep and when he woke up in the morning. Even the dog Dandy became fond of him and followed him "coolly" into the drawing room or into church. He also met Kingsley's friends who often came to visit. In March, for example, first Mansfield and then Parker came to stay, the first "altogether a very nice fellow indeed," and Little John Parker, "a funny little, clever man" who was "very little indeed." With his curate, Kingsley seemed very "dor-mousish" at dinner, Martineau thought, until they all were "just thinking about going to bed, when he becomes suddenly quite lively, and brings out his atrocious puns by the dozens." The boy liked the unrestrained life at the rectory and became entirely devoted to his tutor, although he found it difficult to get used to his stammer, which "is very unpleasant to listen to; it seems to be worse some days than others."[1]

At the beginning of 1850, life looked more promising to Kingsley than it had been at the beginning of the previous year. His financial situation had improved somewhat and although another instalment had to be paid back on the money he had borrowed from the Clerical Insurance Office, the near completion of his novel and the arrival of a pupil made it possible to give up being Clerk in Orders in Chelsea. He had also recovered his health. Although February meant hard work on the last parts of his novel, getting up at five in the morning to write until breakfast, he did not overwork himself this time. He had finished it at the beginning of March and while it was going through the press, he compensated by "being idle as a dog, & fishing & gardening & basking in the glorious sun."[2]

Work on the social-question front continued into 1850. Although Maurice had been firm in his decision against the Health League, he unexpectedly approved of a scheme for founding cooperative workshops which was set up during a meeting at Ludlow's house and to which Maurice invited himself. In January the meetings with the Chartists started to bear fruit and the Working Tailors' Association was founded in Castle Street East with Walter Cooper as manager. A Needlewomen's association was also decided on. These examples made other associations follow suit. Notwithstanding so much tangible influence of their work, the group of friends around Maurice remained active in their literary expressions of the evils of the times, which helped to keep the reformers together as a movement. Most important in the strengthening of the ties within the brotherhood was the decision to write a series of tracts, an idea already much cherished by Maurice in the days of *Politics for the People*, and he proposed the name *Tracts on Christian Socialism*. It was with this that Maurice's friends for the first time got a name and a definition. The first tract was by Maurice and came out on 19 February. Of the seven tracts that were published during 1850, all were written by Maurice and Ludlow, with one contribution by Hughes. Kingsley did not write for the series, although his "Cheap Clothes and Nasty" was in 1851 reprinted in it. At the end of the year Ludlow could

---

[1] Martineau 5–6.
[2] CK to TH, 31/5/1850, Martin (1950) 202.

feel satisfied that the tracts had even been "favourably noticed in the most unforeseen quarters by men perhaps whose candour their authors were presumptuous enough to distrust."[3]

But association was not without problems. It became clear that the associative activities which the small brotherhood of men around Maurice had set up needed better organisation if they were to remain successful in the face of bitter competition. Charles Sully, a bookbinder who had lived and worked for several years in Paris and had taken part in the February Revolution of 1848, had been engaged by Ludlow to help out in the organisation of the associations. He expressed his conviction that a "Central Board" was needed to supervise the individual associations. Maurice was approached for its chair, but he refused. It would mean setting up an organisation which would allow the working associations to participate in the competition against others and would therefore be "a fatal desertion of the principles upon which I have for years striven to act," he wrote to Ludlow, "above all of that principle of fellowship and brotherhood in work which I have felt called to assert with greater loudness of late."[4] As tension between Maurice and his followers rose once more, it was again Ludlow who insisted on a compromise. While a board with the representatives was eventually left to the associations themselves, Sully was asked to set up a Society for Promoting Working Men's Associations which would concentrate on the spiritual and ethical aspects of association. To this Maurice was willing to assent. Sully became secretary and drafted a project which was published with Ludlow as Tract V of their series.

II

Kingsley was worrying about different things. When in February he received from Thomas Cooper the first number of *Cooper's Journal*, a new Chartist paper which carried the subtitle *Unfettered Thinker and Plain Speaker for Truth, Freedom and Progress*, he felt alarmed. Much as he admired its editor's eloquence, he found in its contents something which weighed dreadfully on his mind: "Here is a man," he explained

---

[3] "History of this Journal" 4/1/1851 *ChSoc* i.74.
[4] FDM to JL, Maurice ii.42.

to Ludlow, "of immense influence, openly preaching Straussism to the workmen, and in a fair, honest, manly way, which must tell." David Friedrich Strauss's *Das Leben Jesu* had been anonymously translated for the English reader by George Eliot in 1846. Cooper read this translation when he was released from prison and had become a fervent enthusiast of the controversial German theologian and biblical historian who refused to accept the historical value of the Gospels and discarded their supernatural ingredients as the mythology of the primitive Christian community of the second century. To Kingsley such affirmations were absurd, but Cooper's powers of rhetoric might induce too many workers to believe in such claims. "Who will answer him? Who will answer Strauss?" he exclaimed to Ludlow, "Who will denounce Strauss as a vile aristocrat, robbing the poor of his saviour—of the ground of all democracy, all freedom, all association—of the Charter itself? [. . .] If the priests of the Lord are wanting to the cause now!—woe to us!"[5]

Ludlow was not an unwilling listener. Like Kingsley he regretted the premature end of *Politics for the People*, and it needed little to attract him to the idea of a new journal as a follow-up. He was still meditating on his *Fraternité Chrétienne* project which had not been fulfilled in the pages of *Politics* and he outlined by return of post his ideal of a journal of association, all of which Kingsley whole-heartedly embraced. "As for the subjects. It seems to me that, to spread the paper, you must touch the workman at all his points of interest," Kingsley added, furnishing a long list of priorities: "First and foremost at Association; but also at political rights as grounded both on the Christian ideal of the Church and on the historic facts of the Anglo-Saxon race; then National Education, Sanitary and Dwelling-house Reform, the Free Sale of land, and corresponding Reform of the Land-Laws, moral improvement of the Family relation, public places of Recreation."[6]

But calling a new paper into being was more problematic than it had been in the spring of 1848 when they managed to bring out the first issue of *Politics* within a month of 10 April. Much had to be discussed in order to avoid the ill-fated life of *Politics*. This time, Ludlow insisted, the journal was "to be mainly a channel of com-

---

[5] CK to JL, undated, *LML* i.234.
[6] CK to JL, 13/2/1850, *LML* i.235.

munication for the associated workmen with the Promoters and the public" and not a middle-class organ addressed to the working classes.[7] A large number of contributors was needed to make the new paper a success. Those who had written for *Politics* were entreated to participate, but, as Ludlow bitterly noted, some important contributors defected: "no Archbishop, Bishop or Dean [. . .] no Arthur Helps, no James Spedding, no Bellenden Kerr."[8] Then there was a lot of literary talent lying waste in the working classes which needed to be channelled into the right direction. It was also difficult to decide whether the weekly appearance of *Politics* had been a wise strategy or whether there was need of a daily newspaper this time. Ludlow, Jones and Lechevalier warmed towards the idea of a newspaper, but Maurice refused and was seconded by Mansfield, Walsh and Furnivall. Moreover, finding a publisher held up the enterprise, as Parker was unwilling to hazard anything similar to *Politics for the People*, which with *Yeast* had, he maintained, considerably damaged the reputation of his firm.

These problems delayed the publication of the journal beyond Kingsley's endurance. Although early in July Ludlow had written that a two-penny journal called *Brotherhood, a Journal of Association* was about to appear and that it was going to be edited by him, and subedited by Furnivall, Kingsley had to urge Ludlow again in a letter written in August. To him the moment seemed just right for a journal of association, that "the young men are thirsting for something of the kind." He also told Ludlow not to bother too much beforehand about contributors, as those would turn up in due time. "If we can count on six hacks to write every week, we can keep up a team," he reassured Ludlow. As for contributions of his own: "You tell me what you want weekly, and you shall have it." Uncertainty about the journal's title had also surfaced by this time. Do not call it *The Workshop*, he warned, people "will think it merely a mechanic's trade thing." "Now—quick—present—fire. Can you and Walsh talk all over with the Master, and run down here for three or four hours, and let us organise this paper?"[9]

---

[7] JL to CK, 6/7/1850, Ludlow (1981) 188.
[8] Ludlow (1981) 190.
[9] CK to JL, August 1850, *LML* i.240.

All this shows a high-spirited Kingsley who seemed to have recovered from the overwork of the previous two years. A heavy thunderstorm in June which threatened to flood his garden and house gave him occasion to enjoy the pure physical exercise which he had not enjoyed to the full for some time:

> Up till one this morning, keeping a great flood out—amid such light-ing and rain as think I never saw before; up to my knees in water, working with a pickaxe by candle-light to break holes in the wall, to prevent all being washed away. Luckily my garden is saved. But it all goes with me under the head of 'fun'. Something to do—and light-ning is my highest physical enjoyment. I should like to have my thun-derstorm daily, as one has one's dinner.[10]

It was such energy that made the delay and inactivity of publishing frustrating. But it was not only the delayed publication of the jour-nal which worried Kingsley. His novel, too, which had been finished in March, did not come out until the end of the summer of that year. It was offered to Parker, but was declined. Carlyle, who was then consulted as to a publisher, was "right glad [. . .] to hear of a new explosion, or salvo of red-hot shot against the Devil's Dung-heap" and wrote to Chapman and convinced them to publish it. But the printers were slow, and as the book was written with prospects of extra income, this delay also created financial problems, and towards the end of May Kingsley was forced to write apologetically to his new publisher: "I know not whether I am transgressing liter-ary etiquette, while I do know that I am taking a great liberty: but you would be doing me a greater convenience than I like to describe, if you could oblige me by paying in the sums agreed on for this edition of Alton Locke, *before Saturday next*."[11] Chapman was obliging and the sum was immediately paid, but it would take another two months before the book was out.

June and July passed with only one interesting event. Ludlow felt he had no choice but to dismiss Sully on moral grounds as secre-tary of the Promoting Society and pack him off to America. Not much can be gleaned from the comments on the original circum-stances, but the "domestic tragedy in his life" which Ludlow refers

---

[10] CK to JL, June 1850, *LML* i.235.
[11] CK to Chapman, 20/5/1850, Martin (1950) 197.

to in 1894[12] had something to do with Sully leaving his adulterous wife to go and live with another woman. Ludlow felt uneasy about his decision, but Kingsley, although he was aware that Sully was "the victim of the villainous marriage laws," approved of Ludlow's firmness, lest prosecution for a case of bigamy should stain the reputation of socialism: "the great dread of socialism is that it undermines the marriage tie," he reminded Ludlow, but that "now here we have in our hands a case, which proves that we so strictly respect the marriage tie, that even in its most tyrannous form, our Socialists must obey it, or quit us."

So much for policy. Although Kingsley had never trusted Sully's intellectual capacities—"'Il a tête de fanatique' [. . .] that eye should end in a madhouse"—he did not blame him and felt sincerely for his plight. He therefore gladly subscribed to help him on in America and decided that "this scandalous impossibility of divorce for the poor shall exist no longer, & I will work at it till I get a cheap-divorce bill—for cases of adultery."[13] When, years later, Sully returned to England, he started a correspondence with Kingsley in which he questioned his unbelief until he gradually became a Christian. The correspondence unfortunately does not survive. Ludlow regretted until the end of his life that he had to expel Sully when he described him as "a man upon whom one could more thoroughly rely for carrying out, with as much discretion as resolution, any duty which he might undertake."[14]

III

The summer was quiet, with little work in the parish and a bit of teaching his two pupils, John Martineau and William Lees, a young man of ample means whom Kingsley was preparing for ordination. But the quiet routine of gardening, and 'idling' around the house was interrupted in August when, because of a general depression in the south-east of England, bands of unemployed workers, rather than

---

[12] Ludlow (1894) 37.
[13] CK to JL, 18/7/1850, Martin (1950) 206–7.
[14] Ludlow (1894) 37.

face the workhouse, started raiding property in the area. This new economic plight and its consequences made Kingsley despair for the future of England. "I feel," he confided to Maurice, "we are all going on in the dark,"[15]

> Property is frightfully insecure. Houses almost in hundreds, in the neighbouring counties, have been either robbed or attacked. No one in his senses goes to bed without looking at his pistols, and expecting to have to use them sooner or later. Men travel armed on the high roads after dark. Thousands of "tramps," far more degraded, and generally more destitute in body, mind, and morals, than the Red Indian or the Esquimaux, roam from parish to parish, begging, pilfering, extorting money by threats out of women, now and then stripping a child, now and then firing a rick, now and then breaking into a house— a pleasant and rational state of things for the neighbourhood of England's metropolis, in this "glorious nineteenth century."[16]

On 1 September Mr Hollest, the rector of the nearby parish of Frimley, was killed in his garden by robbers when he gave chase to some of the housebreakers, at whom he managed to shoot before he died. The clergyman's death was the emblematic outcome of a desperate situation, and as clergymen's houses were common targets it contributed to the mounting alarm at Eversley Rectory. Moreover, as a suspicious figure was reported lurking one night in the garden, and another night in the adjacent churchyard, and yet another night in the oaks outside the gate. Kingsley had an extra bolt put on the backdoor and a system of wires and bells was installed so that anyone trying to force the door would set the alarm off. Moreover, a metal shutter was bought to be pulled over the glass door of the side study.[17] Footprints were spotted in the garden, and both Kingsley and Lees slept with loaded pistols and rifle by their bedsides. John Martineau's boyish excitement was roused by the affair and he wrote home about the night the bells started ringing at half past two. "Mr Kingsley jumped up and ran with pistols straight down to the back door." But the burglars too had heard the bells and had fled before Kingsley reached the garden. With Lees, who had come out of his room with "a cocked pistol in each hand," he tried to give chase while the boy stood guard with a rifle in the hall and passage. The

---

[15] CK to FDM, October 1850, *LML* i.242.
[16] "Thoughts on the Frimley Murder" 2/11/1850 *ChSoc* i.3.
[17] Colloms 125.

next day again revealed footprints and the marks of a crowbar on the door.

The burglars had not been discouraged by the bells. A man was again seen prowling around the premises and one night the latch of the yard gate was heard being lifted and dropped. During afternoon church on 6 September Mrs Kingsley stayed at home with John Martineau. However, Kingsley could hardly get through the reading of the prayers and suddenly hurried home, leaving the sermon to his curate Smith. When Mrs Kingsley went to Maidenhead to visit the Froudes and their new-born child, she was escorted home from Reading by her husband and Lees, both armed to the teeth. When for the fourth time in five days, someone was seen lurking around the house, Kingsley wrote to Odiham for a 'blue bottle' (policeman) to protect the rectory. The same night, when they were about to station someone in the stable, the dog Dandy growled suddenly and set upon a man who was heard running away. Although unprepared, Kingsley managed to fire a shot over the dog's head. "Unfortunately," Martineau commented, "Mr. K. had one of the short little pistols loaded with three slugs and not a bullet." The man escaped. A policeman from Odiham arrived the next day and remained until the situation had calmed down. Eversley Rectory did not suffer any further attacks. The same week a man was apprehended as Mr Hollest's murderer when he went to a surgeon in London to take "a charge of shot" out of his back.[18]

The biography of John Martineau mentions that "Mr. Hollest's widow eventually married the detective who investigated the burglary," as if to indicate that with that the matter ended. But it was not so for Kingsley. When in November the first issue of *The Christian Socialist*, Ludlow's new journal, appeared, he contributed with an article in which he declared the science of political economy to be inadequate if it could not pronounce on the moral behaviour of the labour force. "The hop-picking," he explains, "creates a sudden and enormous demand for hands, in response to which, according to the laws of nature, rascaldom by thousands pours into the hop-districts, and there lives, generally in a state of filth, drunkenness, promiscuous concubinage, and brutal heathendom."[19]

---

[18] Martineau 6–10.
[19] "Thoughts on the Frimley Murder" 2/11/1850 *ChSoc* i.3.

IV

In the middle of August Kingsley received six author's copies of *Alton Locke* from Chapman, but he had to wait another two months for the first review. Ludlow, who was one of the novel's first readers wrote to say that much as he admired the first part of the novel, he could not but feel perplexed about the second. He sensed that Kingsley had not fulfilled the promises with which he set out and, as he had done with *Yeast*, had again invented a mystical denouement to get the work off his hands.

In the first volume Kingsley produces a dramatic narrative of Alton's boyhood dreams and his early working experiences in London as he grows up and is apprenticed to a tailor. But the story is not merely personal: the narrator steadily becomes critical of the social predicaments of the poor and increasingly blames the rich, government and the church for turning people into Chartists. The indignation with these classes is probably expressed best in the Cambridge boating episode in the first volume. When Alton, having left the sweating system of the tailor trade, goes to the university town to find patronage as an author, the following scene stirs up his admiration:

> It was a noble sport—a sight such as could only be seen in England—some hundred of young men, who might, if they had chosen, been lounging effeminately about the streets, subjecting themselves voluntarily to that intense exertion, for the mere pleasure of toil. The true English stuff came out there; I felt that, in spite of all my prejudices—the stuff which has held Gibraltar and conquered at Waterloo—which has created a Birmingham and a Manchester, and colonised every quarter of the globe—that grim, earnest, stubborn energy, which, since the days of the old Romans, the English possess alone of all the nations of the earth. I was as proud of the gallant young fellows, as if they had been my brothers—of their courage and endurance [...], their strength and activity, so fierce and yet so cultivated, smooth, harmonious, as oar kept time with oar, and every back rose and fell in concert

The sentiment is one of identification with another social class in which complete brotherhood is realized in a strong sense of nationalistic pride. The expression is Kingsleyan in its celebration of muscularity and masculinity:

> my soul stirred up to a sort of sweet madness, not merely by the shouts and cheers of the mob around me, but by the loud, fierce pulse of the rowlocks, the swift whispering rush of the long, snake-like eight

oars, the swirl and gurgle of the water in their wake, the grim, breath-less silence of the straining rowers. My blood boiled over, and fierce tears swelled into my eyes; for I, too, was a man, and an Englishman;

As Alton comes to life in these lines—and he very rarely comes to life in the novel—and the "fierce pulse of the rowlocks" pulses through his veins and the "swift whispering rush" breathes through his being, his hatred of upper-class life is almost forgotten. The illusory bond is soon severed: "I ran and shouted among the maddest and the foremost. But I soon tired, and, footsore as I was, began to find my strength fail me." Alton cannot become part of a class to which he does not belong, and the moment of identification will only crush him down further:

I tried to drop behind, but found it impossible in the press. At last, quite out of breath, I stopped; and instantly received a heavy blow from behind, which threw me on my face. I looked up, and saw a huge long-legged grey horse, with his knees upon my back, in the act of falling over me. His rider, a little ferret-visaged boy, dressed in sporting style, threw himself back in the saddle, and recovered the horse in an instant, with a curse at me, as I rolled down the steep bank into the river, among the laughter and shouts of the women, who seemed to think it quite a grand act on the part of the horseman.

'Well saved, upon my word, my lord!' shouted out a rider beside him.

'Confound the snob! I'm glad he got his ducking. What do the fel-lows want here, getting in a gentleman's way?'

'For shame, Swindon! the man is hurt,' said another rider, a very tall and handsome man, who pulled up his horse, and, letting the crowd pass, sprang off to my assistance.

'Leave him alone, Lord Lynedale,' said one of the women; 'let him go home and ask his mammy to hang him out to dry.'

'Why do you bother yourself with such muffs?' &c. &c. &c.

But I had scrambled out, and stood there dripping, and shaking with rage and pain.

'I hope you are not much hurt, my man?' asked the nobleman, in a truly gentlemanlike, because truly gentle, voice, and he pulled out half-a-crown, and offered it to me, saying, 'I am quite ashamed to see one of my own rank behave in a way so unworthy of it.'

But I, in my shame and passion, thrust back at once the coin and the civility.

'I want neither you nor your money,' said I, limping off down the bank. 'It serves me right, for getting among you cursed aristocrats.'[20]

---

[20] AL^1 131–3.

The climax of this scene—reminiscent of Lancelot crashing from his horse into the flint road—represents the unbridgeable gap between the social classes and the crushing effect free competition between classes had on the poor. Disraeli might have envied Kingsley for his symbolic representation of his 'two nations'. Ludlow too sensed in it the premises for a true social problem novel, especially as the novel steadily works towards the conclusion of the first volume in the introduction of a sweater's den in which Mike Kelly, a poor Irish tailor ("unwashed, unshaven, shrunken to a skeleton"), presents the lowest possible state of slavery: man stripped of everything physical and spiritual that makes him human. The description is meant to be emblematic of the predicament of the London working class:

> And as he clutched my arm, with his long skinny, trembling fingers, I saw that his hands and feet were all chapped and bleeding. Neither shoe nor stocking did he possess; his only garments were a ragged shirt and trousers; and—and, in horrible mockery of his own misery, a grand new flowered satin vest, which to-morrow was to figure in some gorgeous shop-window!
> 'Och! Mother of Heaven!' he went on, wildly, 'when will I get out to the fresh air? For five months I haven't seen the blessed light of sun, nor spoken to the praste. . . .'[21]

As his "Labour and the Poor" had made clear earlier that year, Ludlow saw the principle of association as "the only effectual remedy against this fearful beating down of wages below 'living prices,' against this fearful realizing of capitalists' imaginary profits out of the starvation and degradation of the workman."[22] Seeing that this article was the outcome of his thinking about the London workers which he had shared with Kingsley, it is not surprising that he felt disappointed with the second volume of *Alton Locke*. Rather than steadily pursuing association as a solution, Kingsley swerves into unexpected directions. After unadvisedly inciting country labourers to violent rioting (in which description Kingsley seemed to have recalled the Bristol riots he had witnessed himself as a boy), Alton is arrested and imprisoned. This event isolates Alton from society, and the story becomes increasingly inward looking. Out of prison, three years later, the narrative hurries to the 10 April 1848. On its

---

[21] *AL¹* 201.
[22] [Ludlow] (1850) 16–7.

eve Mackaye, Alton's Carlylean mentor, who had condemned the petition, dies. The following description of the legendary day is brief and as low-key as possible—"the meeting broke up pitiably piece-meal, drenched and cowed, body and soul, by pouring rain on its way home."[23] In his misery, Alton breaks down, has terrible and fantastic dreams, and is converted to Christianity on waking up. The novel ends with Alton leaving England for America with the money he had inherited from Mackaye.

Ludlow saw this denouement as the result of Kingsley's desire to get the novel finished because he was hard pressed for money. Although Ludlow's criticism is not altogether without foundation—one might question, for example, the artistry of Alton's conversion as an adequate solution to the social problems raised in the novel—the accusation of haste was probably unjust. In fact, *Alton Locke* was one of Kingsley's few works which was written and rewritten with care, and he defended himself: "I assure you I did not get tired of my work but laboured as earnestly at the end as I did at the begin-ning." And, slightly offended, he added: "How do you know that the historic & human interest of the book was not intended to end with Mackaye's death, in whom *old* radicalism dies [...] to make room for the radicalism of the future? How do you know that the book from that point was not intended to take a mythic & prophetic form; that those dreams come in for the very purpose of taking the story off the ground of the actual into the deeper, & wider one of the ideal."[24]

Ludlow was not the only one to have reservations about the novel. The book did not fare better in the reviews that came out in the autumn of 1850 and which Kingsley must have read with mixed feelings. On 18 October a reviewer in *The Times* rose from a perusal of the novel indignant and disappointed. "The unreality of the novel is fearful," he explained, "[it] is not the labour of a working man with a smattering of learning, but of a scholar with an inkling of Chartism [...] It displays Chartism contemplated by an enthusiast from some country nook, not the flesh and blood business with which 10 April brought us into bodily acquaintance." What the reviewer objected to was Alton's "incessant invective against the institutions

---

[23] *AL¹* 324.
[24] CK to JL, undated, Martin (1950) 214.

and well-to-do people of the country" while he has more than his share in being offered help to rise in the world. The reviewer's insistence on the honourable respectability of Alton's uncle and cousin culminate in playing the cousin's "manly and commendable" behaviour off against the "journeyman tailor, this ninth part of a man, this stunted sickly piece of irritable humanity." The message of *Alton Locke* is dismissed as wild levelling anarchy. The novel would, moreover, play no role (either negative or positive) in the process of solving the condition of the poor which just then seemed more successful than ever before.

W.E. Aytoun in *Blackwood's* felt less sanguine about imminent solutions to the condition of the poor in England and was consequently more sympathetic to Kingsley's novel. Although he too wrote that it was "palpably absurd" in its details and that most situations were "ludicrously incongruous," he yet felt impelled to "honour and respect the feeling which has dictated it [the novel]."[25] This reviewer too sensed a fraud in the autobiography but rather than attack the Chartist side of Alton, he attacked the tailor in him: it is "but a barefaced and impudent assumption of a specific character and profession by a person who never handled a goose in his life, and who knows no more about tailoring or slop-selling than he has learned from certain letters which lately appeared in the columns of the *Morning Chronicle*."[26] But the reviewer did not so much object to the fraud as to the tendency in the novel to obscure its main issues. To make clear that the novel discusses real problems, a pamphlet is extensively quoted as to leave no doubt in the reader's mind that *Alton Locke* is really about shocking conditions. The pamphlet turns out to be Kingsley's own *Cheap Clothes and Nasty*. If the reviewer for *The Times* could only feel contempt for the cause advocated in the novel, his colleague in *Blackwood's* approved of the attention given to the condition of the poor, but, he warns, "what sympathy we do feel is not with Alton."[27] A reviewer in *Fraser's Magazine* reacted in a similar way to Alton's "perverse" character and generally found the social comment in the novel weak. He concluded that "he who adopts this book as his manual is bound by the naked force of its

---

[25] [Aytoun] (1850) 594–5.
[26] [Aytoun] (1850) 593.
[27] [Aytoun] (1850) 608.

results to renounce Chartism for ever"[28] and he complains that the book does not contain any clear moral message.

Although criticism of the contents was predominant in these early reviews, the reviewers could not hide their admiration for the remarkable powers of the novelist who must have been "a man of no common acquirements, zeal, energy, and purity of purpose."[29] The "author's eloquence and masculine energy" impressed the reviewer for *Fraser's*,[30] while even the acerbic commentator in *The Times* has to "confess that great power, strong feeling, and masculine language are visible throughout the work."[31]

Modern criticism has been much kinder to the contents and themes of Kingsley's novel and has felt it to be "a work of surprising complication and emotional force."[32] Indeed, many of those undercurrents that contemporary reviewers found so irritating in the narrative, and in the character of Alton, have proved the novel to be much richer in psychology than those critics initially suspected. Thus the discussion of free will, the search for a self, the discourse of the body, and the representation of evolutionary principles in the novel have taken a central place. The Dulwich Gallery episode, for example, described as "deliciously absurd" in *Blackwood's*,[33] has led modern gender studies to comment on the sexual implications of Alton's case. Such readings provide fascinating approaches to the novel that lay bare some of the ambiguities and tensions latent in Kingsley's character.

It is risky to attribute opinions and feelings expressed in a novel to its author, especially when the novel is not implicitly or explicitly autobiographical. It is easy to see the seventeen-year-old Kingsley in the descriptions of Alton's emotions and dreams: "every cabbage and rhubarb-plant in Battersea-fields was wonderful and beautiful to me. Clouds and water I learnt to delight in, from my occasional lingerings on Battersea-bridge, and yearning westwards looks toward the sun setting above rich meadows and wooded gardens."[34] But,

---

[28] [-], "A Triad of Novels" *Fraser's Magazine* 42 (1850) 583.
[29] [Aytoun] (1850) 597.
[30] [-], "A Triad of Novels" *Fraser's Magazine* 42 (1850) 578.
[31] "The Autobiography of a Chartist", *The Times*, 18/10/1850, 3.
[32] Kaye 284.
[33] [Aytoun] (1850) 601.
[34] *AL¹* 9.

although for Alton Locke's childhood Kingsley drew on his own boy-hood years in Chelsea, Locke clearly has not the autobiographical depth of Lancelot in *Yeast*. On the other hand, *Alton Locke* was con-ceived as a propaganda novel, and as such Alton represents in fiction the author's own ideas and values.

V

Kingsley drew heavily on Thomas Cooper's life for Alton's. In November 1849 he had prevailed upon Cooper to write for him an account of the history of Chartism. "I deeply feel this proof of confidence, and you will not find me unworthy of it," he wrote to Cooper. Although Cooper's account has not survived, it is likely that the history was a very personal one. As Cooper's Autobiography, published in 1872, shows, the course of Alton's fictional life runs parallel with many circumstances in Cooper's eventful life. Cooper, like Alton, grew up with his widowed mother, pined to know "the names of flowers, which none could tell,"[35] was apprenticed to a shoemaker, started writing poetry, met a mentor who counselled him in his reading, taught himself Latin with the help of a grammar, felt his health failing him, started to be troubled by religious doubt, became a professional writer for newspapers. A Chartist speaker made him embrace the people's cause. He became embroiled in a meeting and unintentionally incited his listeners to strike, and ended up in prison. However, Kingsley decided to make Alton a tailor rather than a cobbler, because that profession enabled him to play on a series of themes and references that were central to his story.

Alton Locke is in many senses Kingsley's treatise on the meaning of freedom. The full title of the novel, *Alton Locke, Tailor and Poet; An Autobiography*, raises multiple expectations in the reader. The combination Locke-tailor-poet denotes philosopher-worker-poet, or perception-work-imagination. The protagonist's name also creates the assumption that, in a Lockian sense, personal identity depends on self-consciousness. Moreover, the combination tailor-autobiography also glances at the metaphor in Carlyle's *Sartor Resartus*, in which its author, in a semi-autobiographical account, speaks of the necessity to embody "the

---

[35] *The Life of Thomas Cooper* (Leicester University Press, 1971) 19.

Divine Spirit of religion in a new Mythus, in a new vehicle and vesture."[36]

The Carlylean influence in the novel is evident. Carlyle is a constant presence to most characters in the novel and it is well-known that Carlyle stood model for Mackaye, but few critics have realized how powerful Carlyle's influence was on the book as a whole. There are various tensions in the novel which Kingsley tries, if not to solve, at least to analyse in a complex interplay of notions gleaned from Locke, Carlyle and Maurice.

In his pamphlet "To the Workmen of England" Kingsley had warned the Chartists not to pursue a perverse ideal of freedom, but now he had a much broader canvas to explore this issue. One of the recurrent themes of the novel is the questioning of the validity, or even the possibility, of individual freedom in the face of deterministic necessity: "Our Life is compassed round with Necessity; yet is the meaning of Life itself no other than Freedom, than Voluntary Force: thus have we a warfare," Carlyle wrote in *Sartor Resartus*.[37] This can be used to sum up the clashing versions of freedom in Kingsley's novel. In a letter to an unnamed friend and correspondent Kingsley wrote in 1848: "Christ, in every age of the Church for the sake of enabling our piecemeal and partial minds to bring out one particular truth, seems to permit of our pushing it into error, by not binding it with its correlative; *e.g.*, state authority *v.* ecclesiastical authority, and Free Will *v.* Predestination [. . .] In this day only can we reconcile the contradiction by which both Scripture and common sense talk of our bodies as at once not us, and yet us."[38] Alton's namesake provided Kingsley with a set of philosophical presuppositions about freedom that were a good starting point for a much needed examination of these forces in the nineteenth-century industrial context.

John Locke's political idea that ultimately sovereignty lay with the people who had the right to overthrow government when it no longer enjoys their trust made the philosopher "well known to reading artisans."[39] It explains why Alton bears his name. No less important in Locke's philosophy is the emphasis that nothing is innate to the

---

[36] *Sartor Resartus* bk II, ch. 9.
[37] *Sartor Resartus* bk II, ch. 9.
[38] CK to unidentified correspondent, undated, *LML* i.187–8.
[39] *AL¹* 165.

human mind but that it is gradually formed by experience, thus, with its stress on education, suggesting a firm idea of possible improvement of the individual. Such ideas nurture Alton's ideal of freedom. But Alton soon finds out that society obstructs the quest for individual improvement. After the first dreamy stages of Alton's boyhood reading and early apprenticeship as a tailor, "the burning thought arose in my heart, that I was unjustly used; that society had not given me my rights,"[40] and he curses God for having made him an "untutored working man." It is from this moment that the narrator initiates a long journey towards an ideal of freedom. "Yes, it was true," Kingsley-Alton dramatically signals at the end of the chapter, "Society had not given me my rights. And woe unto the man on whom that idea, true or false, rises lurid, filling all his thoughts with stifling glare, as of the pit itself. Be it true or false, it is equally a woe to believe it; to have to live on a negation."[41] It is with this warning that Kingsley invites us to see freedom thus claimed in the light of Carlyle's "Everlasting No": "it is ever the bitterest aggravation of his wretchedness that he is not conscious of Virtue, that he feels himself the victim not of suffering only, but of injustice."[42] But as he persists in his Lockian quest for improvement and freedom, Alton still has a long way to go before he realizes the depth of negation.

Alton's first step towards his ideal is to break with his Calvinist mother. He quarrels with her about religion, saying that "nobody believes in it," that the rich fill "their churches up with pews, and shut the poor out," but Alton's anger is as much phrased in the language of social protest as it is in the discourse of individual freedom: "have I not slaved for you," he reprimands her for not trusting him, "Have I not run to and fro for you like a slave"? This moment sets the tone of a long and tortuous process of emancipation in the novel: "I'm old enough to think for myself, and a free-thinker I will be."[43] Although Kingsley cannot accept the mother's deterministic Calvinist view of life, it is more difficult to reject the socially deterministic impediments Alton finds on his way. Thus the critique in Carlylean terms of Locke's mechanic empiricism is maintained.

---

[40] *AL¹* 50.
[41] *AL¹* 51–2.
[42] *Sartor Resartus* bk II, ch. 7.
[43] *AL¹* 55–56.

However, in the quest for freedom, the physical and intellectual soon clash. Alton's manual labour is difficult to reconcile with his intellectual ambitions, as they constitute two irreconcilable worlds to him. He begins to lead two separate lives, one as a worker, one as an imaginative writer: "to escape from my own thoughts, I could not help writing something."[44] If to Carlyle "he that must toil outwardly for the lowest of man's wants, [but who] is also toiling inwardly for the highest"[45] constitutes the sublimest combination of man, Kingsley starts to express some of the reservations he felt for Carlyle's idealist vision of the labourer. There was, for example, little Kingsley could recognize in the following extracts after having witnessed the horrible conditions of the poor:

> Venerable to me is the hard Hand; crooked, coarse; wherein notwithstanding lies a cunning virtue, indefeasibly royal, as of the Sceptre of this Planet. Venerable too is the rugged face, all weather-tanned, besoiled, with its rude intelligence; for it is the face of a Man living manlike. Oh, but the more venerable for thy rudeness, and even because we must pity as well as love thee! Hardly-entreated Brother! For us was thy back so bent, for us were thy straight limbs and fingers so deformed: thou wert our Conscript, on whom the lot fell, and fighting our battles wert so marred. For in thee too lay a god-created Form, but it was not to be unfolded; encrusted must it stand with the thick adhesions and defacements of Labour: and thy body, like thy soul, was not to know freedom. Yet toil on, toil on: *thou* art in thy duty, be out of it who may; thou toilest for the altogether indispensable, for daily bread[46]

and

> It is not because of his toils that I lament for the poor: we must all toil [. . .]; no faithful workman finds his task a pastime. The poor is hungry and athirst; but for him also there is food and drink: he is heavy-laden and weary; but for him also the Heavens send Sleep, and of the deepest; in his smoky cribs, a clear dewy heaven of Rest envelops him; and fitful glitterings of cloud-skirted Dreams.[47]

Such sentiments could not be reconciled with what Kingsley had seen of the London poor, of the devastating effects of the sweating system, of the physical suffering he had witnessed in Bermondsey.

---

[44] *AL¹* 84.
[45] *Sartor Resartus* bk. III, ch. 4.
[46] *Sartor Resartus* bk. III, ch. 4.
[47] *Sartor Resartus* bk. III, ch. 4.

Carlyle's, like Locke's, idea of freedom, it would seem, presented severe limitations in confronting the Chartist problem. But while this sentiment is gradually fostered in the background, Alton's quest for freedom and emancipation continues.

When the establishment where Alton works turns to the sweating system, that "all work would in future be given out, to be made up at the men's own homes," Alton leaves his place because he realised that "it was a real sin against my class to make myself a party in the system by which they were allowing themselves [. . .] to be enslaved."[48] That evening he goes to a Chartist meeting and becomes a Chartist "heart and soul". He "began to look on man [. . .] as the creature and puppet of circumstances."[49] In an attempt to find patronage for his poetry, Alton starts on a trip to Cambridge, where his cousin studies at the university. The day is described as "a glorious morning [. . .] when I escaped from the pall of smoke which hung over the city."[50] As before, his quest for independence and freedom is phrased in terms of an escape from his social environment. The impossibility of such escape comes home to Alton in the boating episode which is quoted in full above. But before this climax, it occurs to Alton that there might be perversity in his quest for individual freedom: "if there was an accursed artificial gulf between their class and mine, had I any right to complain of it, as long as I helped to keep it up by my false pride and surly reserve?"[51] He still, however, has a long way to go when he asserts that "A man-servant, a soldier, and a Jesuit, are to me the great wonders of humanity— three forms of moral suicide,"[52] a remark which elicited the ire of the reviewer in *The Times*. But after Cambridge Alton has to return to London and write for Mr O'Flynn's paper (a caricature of demagogue O'Connor's *Northern Star*) and Kingsley entitles his chapter "Pegasus in Harness". Necessity has now established itself as a true deterministic reality, and the tension between John Locke's idea of the right of improvement and Carlyle's prophetic but impractical warnings grows. Alton starts expressing his doubts about Mackaye's wisdom, but still adheres to Carlyle's refutation of "The Everlasting

---

[48] *AL¹* 105.
[49] *AL¹* 110.
[50] *AL¹* 115.
[51] *AL¹* 120.
[52] *AL¹* 159–60.

No." He longs to know whether "all this misery and misrule around us [was] His will—His stern and necessary law—His lazy connivance? And were to free ourselves from it by any frantic means that came to hand? Or had He ever interfered himself?"[53] and he finds answers in a lecture by a Mr Windrush, a thinly veiled personification of Ralph Waldo Emerson (but at the same time Carlyle carried to the extreme) who reinforces Alton's sensation that man cannot break God's law, whatever he does, as "God is circumstance, and thou His creature! Be content! Fear not, strive not, change not, repent not! Thou art nothing! Be nothing, and thou becomest a part of all things [. . .] the happy puppet of universal impulse."[54] And Alton enthusiastically retorts: "is not complete freedom of thought a glorious aim—to emancipate man's noblest part—the intellect—from the trammels of custom and ignorance?"[55] Such freedom of thought, however, Alton denies himself when he emasculates his poetry to please the aristocratic patrons he had found in Cambridge, and he is punished for this by exposure in O'Flynn's newspaper. Alton's feelings are significant: "It is good—anything is good, however bitter, which shows us that there is such a law as retribution; that we are not the sport of blind chance or a triumphant fiend, but that there is a God who judges the earth—righteous to repay every man according to his works."[56] But such thoughts are in retrospect. Alton, to show his heart is with the people, goes out into the country for the Chartist cause, and unwittingly stirs up a riot that lands him in gaol for the next three years. Such a verdict on Alton's ideal of freedom could not be clearer. But Alton has not learned his lesson yet, and reads up on radical literature, and out of prison, plunges into the preparations for the Chartist rising of 10 April 1848, still insisting on his old idea of freedom: "Liberty? And is that word a dream, a lie, the watchword only of rebellious fiends, as bigots say even now? [. . .] Had not freedom, progressive, expanding, descending, been the glory and the strength of England?"[57]

It is on the eve of the Petition that Alton's mentor, Mackaye dies. As Mackaye was modelled on Carlyle, this indicates that Carlylean

---

[53] *AL¹* 193.
[54] *AL¹* 211.
[55] *AL¹* 213.
[56] *AL¹* 244.
[57] *AL¹* 296.

philosophy could offer no further help in the process of Alton's emancipation, or even that it had utterly failed to procure freedom. Alton
now plunges into physical-force Chartism—"in our imagination a
wild possible future of tumult, and flame, and blood"[58]—which called
forth that extraordinary force of constables in London. But that day
"the people would not rise", "O'Conner's courage failed him after
all," and "the meeting broke up pitiably piecemeal."[59] Philosophical
resources (Locke's and Carlyle's) having come to nothing, Alton, in
despair, contemplates jumping from Waterloo Bridge, where, however, he prevents a former fellow-worker from taking his life.
Accompanying the man home, the reader is given one of the most
terrible scenes of the novel. Kingsley drew fully on the horrors he
had seen on Jacob's Island in 1849:

> He stopped at the end of a miserable blind alley, where a dirty gas-
> lamp just served to make darkness visible, and show the patched win-
> dows and rickety doorways of the crazy houses, whose upper stories
> were lost in a brooding cloud of fog; and the pools of stagnant water
> at our feet; and the huge heap of cinders which filled up the alley—
> a dreary black formless mound, on which two or three spectral dogs
> prowled up and down after the offal, appearing and vanishing like
> dark imps in and out of the black misty chaos beyond.[60]

And entering the house further desolation becomes visible:

> What a room! A low lean-to with wooden walls, without a single article
> of furniture [. . .] The stench was frightful—the air heavy with pesti-
> lence. The first breath I drew made my heart sink, and my stomach
> turn. But I forgot everything in the object which lay before me, as
> Downes tore a half-finished coat off three corpses laid side by side on
> the bare floor.
> There was his little Irish wife;—dead—and naked—the wasted white
> limbs gleamed in the lurid light; the unclosed eyes stared, as if reproach-
> fully, at the husband whose drunkenness had brought her there to kill
> her with the pestilence; and on each side of her a little, shrivelled,
> impish, child-corpse.[61]

Overmastered by the scene before his eyes, the husband jumps from
the window into "bubbles of poisonous gas, and bloated carcases of
dogs, and lumps of offal, floating on the stagnant olive-green hell-

---

[58] *AL¹* 304.
[59] *AL¹* 324.
[60] *AL¹* 330.
[61] *AL¹* 331.

broth."[62] Alton breaks down at this point, and at home sinks into illness, wavering on the brink of death, having the strangest dreams, which constitute some of the most extraordinary parts of the novel.

VI

In the Wordsworthian tradition the adult has to go back to his childhood to find the sources for spiritual growth and rebirth, but Kingsley goes one step further and has Alton tracing his past in terms of a greater 'evolutionary' process in which "the longing of my life to behold that cradle of mankind was satisfied."[63] Moving through "the lowest point of created life" he starts as a madrepore, then becomes in succession a soft crab, a remora, an ostrich, a mylodon, a baby-ape in Bornean forests, and, finally, "a child upon a woman's bosom." At each stage Alton is aware of his own self and the state he is in, so much so that he exclaims in retrospect: "Where I had picked up the sensation which my dreams realized for me, I know not; my waking life, alas! had never given me experience of it. Had the mind power of creating sensations for itself? Surely it does so, [. . .] which would seem to give my namesake's philosophy the lie."[64] It is in Alton's dreamland that Kingsley diverges once more, and this time more explicitly, from John Locke.

Kingsley's impressive use of successive stages of animal creation on earth has elicited numerous brief reactions that range from confusion to admiration, but very little in terms of analysis. Still, the dream is conceived of along regular ideas and concepts. Starting as a polyp without any distinct individuality—"I grew and grew, and the more I grew the more I divided, and multiplied thousand and ten thousand-fold"[65]—Alton moves through the different stages of low animal life to mammal life and eventually to man, each stage adding to his individuality and human qualities. During each reincarnation, Alton is judged and refused by Lillian and exterminated by his cousin. The following passage, which reflects Kingsley's own inner sense of insecurity, frustration and shame, is an effective and uncomfortable example:

[62] *AL¹* 333.
[63] *AL¹* 335.
[64] *AL¹* 338.
[65] *AL¹* 336.

And I was a soft crab, under a stone on the seashore. With infinite starvation, and struggling, and kicking, I had got rid of my armour, shield by shield, and joint by joint, and cowered, naked and pitiable, in the dark, among dead shells and ooze. Suddenly the stone was turned up; and there was my cousin's hated face laughing at me, and pointing me out to Lillian. She laughed too, as I looked up, sneaking, ashamed, and defenceless, and squared up at him with my soft useless claws. Why should she not laugh? Are not crabs, and toads, and monkeys, and a hundred other strange forms of animal life, jests of nature—embodiments of a divine humour, at which men are meant to laugh and be merry? But alas! my cousin, as he turned away, thrust the stone back with his foot, and squelched me flat.[66]

When Alton reaches the mammal state as a South American sloth, the tension between the animal and the human comes out for the first time. Although Alton (as a mylodon) "had never before suspected the delight of mere physical exertion,"[67] a "spark of humanity [. . .] was slowly rekindling" in him, a humanity which initially articulates itself in a spark of altruistic feeling when mylodon-Alton brings on his own death when trying to save his cousin's. And Alton is reborn as a baby-ape and "felt stirring in me germs of a new and higher consciousness," he was able to define a "yearning of love towards the mother ape" but finally "the animal faculties in me were swallowing up the intellectual."[68] Lillian once more recoils from Alton—"[s]he pointed up to me in terror and disgust"—and the cousin appears and shoots Alton. But Alton has learned the basic qualities of altruism and love, and is now ready to be reincarnated as a social human being. The following stages Alton has to go through in the second part of the dream are spiritual rather than physical.

In producing a sequence of states of organic existence from the madrepore to ape to man, Kingsley conveys what Tennyson expressed in *In Memoriam* in the very same year:

> A soul shall draw from out the vast
> And strike his being into bounds,
>
> And moved through life of lower phase,
> Result in man, be born and think,
> And act and love, a closer link
> Betwixt us and the crowning race

---

[66] *AL¹* 337.
[67] *AL¹* 338.
[68] *AL¹* 341.

Both are fascinating instances of how educated Victorians pondered the development theory which reached them from (Lyell's representation of) Lamarck through to Chambers's *Vestiges of Creation*, and both are emotional searches for the self in the stunning and imbecile vastness of what increasingly seemed an indifferent universe. More important than the idea that these early dreams anticipate Darwinian evolution (which strictly speaking they do not), is the representation of instinctive physical strength and a struggling consciousness of moral purpose in man. Kingsley felt fascinated by the idea of successive creations on a perfect (divine) plan, and tried to link the animal and spiritual in an even more comprehensive theory of successive development in which a notion of improvement stands central. Thus, Alton's dreams show why Kingsley thought Darwinism so attractive when he, and the world, became acquainted with it ten years later.

The dream chapter clearly perplexed the first reviewers. Whereas *Fraser*'s and *The Times* kept silent about Alton's delirious dreams, *Blackwood*'s reviewer W.E. Aytoun admitted that these "visions of delirium [were] ambitiously written, but without either myth or meaning, so far as we can discover," that they were "decidedly of a tawdry and uninterpretable description." Moreover, he adds that the dreams "bear internal evidence of having been copied at second-hand from Richter."[69] The reviewer made an interesting point here, which, however, has not been followed up by later critics, not even in the recent renewed interest in Kingsley's novel. The German Romantic author Johann Paul Friedrich Richter, commonly known under the pseudonym Jean Paul, made frequent use in his works of mystical dreams—short independent visionary pieces in dream form called 'Traumdichtungen'—which display an obsession with conflicting polarities such as thought and feeling, temporal and eternal, despair and hope, and which are generally ways to overcome a tendency to atheism in the dreamer.[70] Kingsley, who always showed interest in German literature, had most likely read Richter's works or knew about them through Carlyle who wrote two essays on the German author in the 1830s, including a translation of one of his dreams. In Carlyle's

---

[69] [Aytoun] 596.
[70] Cf. J.W. Smeed, *Jean Paul's "Dreams"* (London, Oxford University Press, 1966) p. 6, p. 69.

works he is mentioned regularly and he did not hesitate to evoke Richterian language and imagery to convey Teufelsdröckh's religious despair and his subsequent sensation of rebirth and faith in *Sartor Resartus*. In the "Rede des todten Christus" in *Siebenkäs*, the dream Carlyle translated for his 1830 essay on Jean Paul, Christ "schauete in den Abgrund," or, in Carlyle's translation, "looked down into the Abyss," which in *Sartor Resartus* becomes "through the ruins as of a shivered Universe was he falling, falling, toward the abyss." Kingsley's hero, too, "looked down the abysses" and "fell and fell for ages." But although Kingsley seems to have picked up many elements of the "Rede des todten Christus" distilled in *Sartor Resartus*, Alton's dream also owes much to Jean Paul directly. It is difficult to pinpoint one clear example for Alton's dream, and ingredients of at least three other Traumdichtungen are present. In *Siebenkäs* a character is, like Alton, laid up with a fever and the delirious visions of his illness turn into a nightmarish dream of destruction and annihilation, a state also evoked by Kingsley at the beginning of his dream chapter. The river Alton is doomed to climb up is reminiscent of Albano's second dream in *Titan*, and the final dream of *Flegeljahre* is presented in the form of a creation myth which traces the genesis of the earth out of the "Welt-ei" in a watery chaos through a series of brutal images of animal earthly desire ("Heisshunger und Blutdurst"). In general, the cosmological vastness of its settings, and the religious and mystical sensations of Jean Paul's dreamers, are present in Alton's dream, and the rhythmical language of the Traumdichtungen is reproduced by Kingsley.

These examples seem to indicate that Kingsley was indeed influenced by Richter's Traumdichtungen, as the reviewer in *Blackwood's Magazine* maintained, but to say that these dream passages were "copied at second-hand" from the German writer is excessive and unfair to Kingsley's genius. Although there are a few signs of verbal parallels, which most likely crept in through Kingsley's knowledge of *Sartor Resartus*, the other parallels mentioned here do not bear traces of copying or rewriting Jean Paul, but rather show a wish to write in the tradition of the German Traumdichtungen. Moreover, the theme which is at the base of most of Jean Paul's dreams—the existence of a "zweite Welt"—is not uncommon in Kingsley's works generally. Alton's journey into the unconscious past of mankind is, in fact, not unlike the baptismal rebirth of Tom that Kingsley created thirteen years later in *The Water-Babies*. For example, Alton's initiation in dreamland is described as his soul being carried "to a cavern by the sea-side, and [being] dropped [in]" and he "fell and fell for ages," until he has, like Tom, to start his process of regeneration from the very bottom of creation. Kingsley clearly felt fascinated with the idea by falling from a height or precipice into another world. Thus Tregarva in *Yeast* is converted on the brink of a Cornish mine-shaft where he "saw through the ground all the water in the shafts glaring like blood, and all the sides of the shafts fierce red-hot. As if hell was coming up."[71] A turning point in the unpublished novel *The Tutor's Story* is also created, though less skilfully managed, when Mr Brownlow falls in a wide black fissure in the Yorkshire countryside and wavers on the brink of death for a dark and cold night before being rescued.[72] But Alton's fall stands out from all these in its spellbound tracing of the biological and spiritual origins of man. From the creation of the earth to the final boring of the mountain, which is developed along the lines of Moses leading the people into the Holy Land, the whole episode is Mosaic in scope.

With Alton's dream Kingsley returned to the structure of *Sartor Resartus* by signalling the passage from the 'Everlasting No' to the 'Everlasting Yea', from utter negation to acceptance of the "poor, miserable, hampered, despicable Actual" as the Ideal.[73] It is therefore natural that Kingsley would emphasize in it the Carlylean idea of duty and work which made the acceptance of the Actual possible and which reveals Kingsley's answer to Chartism:

> But I went out, and quarried steadfastly at the mountain.
>
> And when I came back the next morning, the poor had risen against the rich, one and all, crying, 'As you have done to us, so will we do to you'; and they hunted them down like wild beasts, and slew many of them, and threw their carcases on the dunghill, and took possession of their land and houses, and cried, 'We will be all free and equal as our forefathers were, and live here, and eat and drink, and take our pleasure.'
>
> Then I ran out, and cried to them, 'Fools! will you do as these rich did, and neglect the work of God! If you do to them as they have done to you, you will sin as they sinned, and devour each other at the last, as they devoured you. The old paths are best. Let each man, rich or poor, have his equal share of the land, as it was at first, and

---

[71] *Y* 217.
[72] *TS* ch. 14.
[73] *Sartor Resartus* bk. II, ch. 9.

go up and dig through the mountain, and possess the good land beyond, where no man need jostle his neighbour, or rob him, when the land becomes too small for you. Were the rich only in fault? Did not you, too, neglect the work which the All-Father had given you, and run every man after his own comfort? So you entered into a lie, and by your own sin raised up the rich men to be your punishment. For the last time, who will go up with me to the mountain?'

Then they all cried with one voice, 'We have sinned! We will go up and pierce the mountain, and fulfil the work which God set to our forefathers.'

We went up, and the first stroke that I struck, a crag fell out; and behold, the light of day! and far below us the good land and large, stretching away boundless towards the western sun.[74]

At this point Alton is ready to wake up. It is out of such dreams that the dreamer in the Romantic tradition awakes cured and reborn. After a "healing sleep, the heavy dreams rolled gradually away, and I awoke to a new Heaven and a new Earth," Carlyle has Teufelsdröckh say in *Sartor Resartus*,[75] and Alton too, "passed, like one who recovers from drowning through the painful gate of birth into another life."[76] But Alton's reconciliation with the Actual, with necessity and freewill, is not simply Teufelsdröckh's. It had been made clear earlier on in the novel that such conclusions might lead to the meaningless, because outdated, pantheism of a Mr Windrush-Emerson. Moreover, nature as a healing force was not available to the urban worker in early Victorian society. Therefore, waking up, Alton is reconverted to Christianity and is made aware of the fallacy of his ideal, with the Charter "dead, and liberty further off than ever", that "You are free; God has made you free. You are equals—you are brothers."[77]

It is in the final chapters that Alton embraces what Maurice's theology taught, and as with the introduction of the Prophet in *Yeast*, turns *Alton Locke* into a celebration of his ideals of a Christian brotherhood. The ex-aristocrat Eleanor, who nurses Alton through his illness, also turns out to be his spiritual nurse. She tells him how she herself had "succeeded [in projects of association]—as others will succeed, long after my name, my small endeavours, are forgotten amid the great new world—*new church* I should have said—of enfran-

---

[74] *AL¹* 347–8.
[75] *Sartor Resartus* bk. II, ch. 9.
[76] *AL¹* 359.
[77] *AL¹* 361.

chised and fraternal labour."[78] It is the clergy (of the Church of England) who are to lead the people to association: "Without the priesthood there is no freedom for the people."[79] The final turn of the novel is thus away from Locke, away even from Carlyle, in a complete embrace of Maurice's teaching of the kingdom of Christ. As such, *Alton Locke* was a perfect expression of the Christian Socialist movement, out of which it grew. The novel gained it the fame the brotherhood around Maurice and Ludlow craved for.

VII

The influence of Carlyle's thinking in *Alton Locke* has often been pointed out, and the presence of the Scottish prophet in the novel, as a real-life writer and in the fictional guise of Mackaye, has led many critics to use the novel as evidence for the influence he had on Kingsley. It is often asserted that the Carlylean Mackaye is Alton's mentor and as such the leading light for the problems the novel raises. Although most characters in the novel have been judged flat, Mackaye has had full praise. Carlyle himself, not realizing (or pretending he did not realize) that Kingsley had portrayed him in Mackaye, wrote to thank the author for the copy he sent him and added:

> Apart from your treatment of my poor self (on which subject let me not venture to speak at all), I found plenty to like [...] my invaluable countryman [Mackaye] in this book, is nearly perfect; indeed I greatly wonder how you did contrive to manage him—his very dialect is as if a native had done it, and the whole existence of the rugged old hero is a wonderfully splendid and coherent piece of Scotch bravura.[80]

Jane Welsh Carlyle was less enthusiastic about Kingsley's novel, although she too liked the character Mackaye, as she wrote to her husband:

> To-morrow I shall lay out two sixpences in forwarding Alton Locke (The Devil among the Tailors would have been the best name for it).

---

[78] *AL¹* 376; italics mine.
[79] *AL¹* 380.
[80] Thomas Carlyle to CK, 31/10/1850, *LML* i.244.

It will surely be gratifying to you, the sight of your own name in almost every second page! But for that, I am ashamed to say I should have broken down in it a great way this side of the end! It seems to me [. . .] a mere—not very well-boiled—broth of Morning-chronicle-ism, in which you play the part of the tasting-bone of Poverty Row. An oppressive, painful Book! [. . .] And then, all the indignation against existing things strikes somehow so numbly! like your Father whipping the bad children under the bedclothes! But the old Scotchman is capital,—only that there never was nor ever will be such an old Scotchman. I wonder what will come of Kingsley—go mad, perhaps.[81]

The fact that Mackaye is the most lively character of the novel— Catherine Gallagher has pointed out that his language, in order to be comprehended, needs to be spoken out loud, so that he really has a voice[82]—has tended to obfuscate what Kingsley was really trying to examine. Kingsley often acknowledged the great influence Carlyle had on him during the early 1840s, but, although he had been an assiduous reader of his works and admired his original and vigorous language and his moral standpoints, by the end of the decade he felt increasingly disenchanted with Carlyle's views. Something changed in Kingsley's attitude to him during the second half of 1849 while he was writing *Alton Locke*. In April he could still write to Carlyle:

At a time when I was drowned in sloth and wickedness, your works awoke in me the idea of Duty; the belief in a living righteous God, who is revealing Himself in the daily events of History; the knowledge that all strength and righteousness, under whatever creed it may appear, comes from Him alone; and last, but not least, the belief in the Perfect Harmony of the Physical with the Spiritual."[83]

But "the belief in a living righteous God" was wavering every time he was confronted with the desperate suffering of the poor, which contributed to his many depressions during this period. He broke down, for example, "after sitting up a whole night with one bad case" in Eversley. As we have seen, this breakdown followed a very active period in London where he was desperately looking for solutions for the condition of the poor. He talked to Bunsen, who was

---

[81] *New Letters and Memorials of Jane Welsh Carlyle*, ed. by Alexander Carlyle (London and New York: John Lane, The Bodley Head, 1893) ii.21–2.
[82] Gallagher 104.
[83] CK to Thomas Carlyle, 26/4/1849, Thorp 22.

"divine-looking," to Froude ("interesting"), Maurice was "inspired—gigantic," the evening with the Campbells, Shorter and Walsh was "glorious," and his talk to Lechevalier was "intensely interesting." Adjectives abound in all these accounts, but there is no praise of Carlyle as he merely reports: "I have just been to see Carlyle."[84] During these encounters Kingsley was trying to find *practical* solutions to the problems of the poor, and it is possible that Carlyle disappointed him here. The Scottish prophet had got to a gloomy stage in his life. He sensed that all his warnings in writings like *Chartism* and *Past and Present* had come to nothing and that soon it would be too late for England. He vented his frustration at not being listened to in moments of unbridled rage. His ferocity was like a child's, full of cursing and swearing, Erasmus Darwin remarked.[85] It has not been recorded for posterity how Carlyle behaved when Kingsley visited him in May 1849, but when Kingsley in his novel has Alton affirm that "Mackaye had nothing positive, after all, to advise or propound. His wisdom was one of apophthegms and maxims, utterly impractical, too often merely negative, as was his creed,"[86] a sense of disillusionment with Carlyle seems to have been transferred from the author to his fictional character. And, after these words, Mackaye dies and disappears from the novel. This leaves Alton and Crossthwaite on the eve of 10 April with "just what we had the right to do; and therefore, according to the formula on which we were to act, that mights are rights."[87] The formula is Carlyle's. In *Chartism* he argues that "might and right, so frightfully discrepant at first, are ever in the long-run one and the same."[88] The futility of such doctrine is made clear by the outcome of Petition day, and Kingsley's conclusion works itself free of Carlylean ideas:

> If, henceforth, you claim political enfranchisement, claim it not as mere men, who may be villains, savages, animals, slaves of their own prejudices and passions; but as members of Christ, children of God, inheritors of the kingdom of heaven, and therefore bound to realise it on earth. All other rights are mere mights.[89]

---

[84] CK to FK, undated, *LML* i.205–6.
[85] Cited in Fred Kaplan, *Thomas Carlyle: A Biography* (Ithaca, New York: Cornell University Press, 1983), p. 326.
[86] *AL¹* 193.
[87] *AL¹* 319
[88] *Chartism* ch. 5.
[89] *AL¹* 364.

Although Alton's sudden verdict on Mackaye is bewildering in its peremptory directness, the rejection is by no means complete. Mackaye's warnings and philosophies do have value for the moral point of the novel—he, for example, dissociates himself from the Chartist uprising—but in the end he has to make way for Eleanor and her Maurician message of Christianity. Allen John Hartley has argued that this final shift of loyalty from Carlyle to Maurice makes the novel faulty in conception. Although the novel signals Kingsley's disenchantment with Carlyle, who "grew daily more and more cynical"[90] and increasingly seemed to prophesy merely from his ivory tower (like Teufelsdröckh from his room over the city), it is questionable whether the repudiation was already as clear-cut in 1850 as Hartley maintains. It is only in 1856 that Kingsley could write of Carlyle: "never heard I a more foolish outpouring of Devils' doctrines—Raving Cynicism w. made me sick. I kept my temper with him but when I got out I am afraid I swore with wrath & disgust—at least I left no doubt on my 2 friends' minds [Froude and Parker] of my opinion of such stuff—all the ferocity of the old Pharisee without Isaiah's prophecy of mercy & restoration—the notion of sympathy with sinners denounced as a sign of innate scoundrelism."[91] But that was six years hence. While writing *Alton Locke* Kingsley had begun to feel uncomfortable about Carlyle for himself and for the nation. Still, Hartley's conclusion is helpful in understanding Kingsley's state of mind while thinking about social questions in 1849–1850: "*Alton Locke* was the battlefield of his conflict and the writing of the novel itself the therapy that clarified his own thinking."[92] The scenes Kingsley had witnessed in London, "frightful scenes of hopeless misery [. . .] the ever widening pit of pauperism and slavery,"[93] had brought on a spiritual crisis about questions of divine intervention and predetermination, and he discovered that ultimately there was no hope in Carlyle. Alton says: "poor Mackaye could give no comfort there: 'God was great—the wicked would be turned into hell.' Ay—the few wilful, triumphant wicked; but the millions of suffering, starving wicked, the victims of society and circumstance—what hope for them?"[94]

---

[90] *AL¹* 193.
[91] CK to FDM, undated, BL-41297 f.99v.
[92] Hartley 80.
[93] *AL¹* 195.
[94] *AL¹* 193.

CHAPTER NINE

WHAT ARE WE TO DO WITH THE CHRISTIAN SOCIALISTS? (JANUARY–JUNE 1851)

I

The end of the old and the beginning of a new year meant assessing the family's financial situation. Prospects were not cheerful at the beginning of 1851 and Kingsley wrote to Maurice for council on a number of questions. He started to wonder how to pay off the loan for the expenses of repairing and refurnishing the rectory. It was true that his conscience was more at ease now that he had given up the clerkship at Chelsea, but it meant a considerable cut in income. Moreover, agricultural distress in the parish had forced him to return ten percent of the tithes, so that all in all he thought he had to reckon with £200 less for the coming year. The school at Eversley that Kingsley had helped to set up was something he felt proud of, but part of its success rested on his own financial support. His only private pupil, John Martineau, was going to leave in June, and, as saving on other expenses was impossible ("I cannot reduce my charities"), this left him an income of less than £400. The frightening prospect of having to give up his curate loomed large on the horizon. "If I do not use my pen to the uttermost in earning my daily bread, I shall not get through this year," he writes dolefully. But without a curate, and with "lectures or night school every night in the week, & 3 services a Sunday" little time would remain for writing.[1] New pupils might come now that Martineau was going. Much as he liked the boy, Kingsley suspected that the lack of other pupils had to do with his presence at Eversley rectory, many Anglican families having been frightened away by the idea of placing their boys in the same house with one whose family counted a non-conformist Unitarian theologian (James Martineau) as well as a confessed atheist (Harriet Martineau). Most likely, however, Kingsley's own growing controversial publications had more to do with a lack of students.

[1] CK to FDM, 16/1/1851, BL-41297 f.13v.

The new year started with a scathing article on the Christian Socialists in the *Edinburgh Review* in which Christian Socialism was called communism and in which the author, while discussing *Cheap Clothes and Nasty*, wondered how "any Christian minister, a thinker, a gentleman, and a scholar, [could] permit himself to pour forth such rant as this." This hit hard at Kingsley's reputation, especially as he was mentioned by name in the article. Kingsley responded immediately with a letter in the *Morning Chronicle*, but two months later still felt hostility to William Rathbone Greg, the writer of the anonymous *Edinburgh* article: "the man has grossly insulted me, in language wh. he dared not have made use of to my face,"[2] "*My Socialism prevents my getting pupils*—I am a martyr to my opinions!!!" Kingsley concluded in a letter to Hughes.[3]

Another way for Kingsley to earn extra money was to try to get *Yeast* re-published in book form, "for wh. purpose I wd. alter & improve it, & finish it off."[4] But after repeated solicitations, Parker, "shilly shallying, still letting I dare not wait upon I would," remained unwilling to commit himself to bringing out a book which, he maintained, had damaged his sales. Kingsley therefore asked Maurice's legal advice: "Am I bound if he still hangs off & on, to publish it with him, because he publishes the magazine, or in the event of his refusing it, or refusing to refuse, w. is as bad, can I take it to whom I like?"[5] Brooding on a subject for a new novel, he also asked the Master what to read for information "about those later Alexandrian Platonists." Maurice's answer arrived by return of post, but apart from a series of useful instructions on fourth-century Alexandria, it also contained an alarming postscript which read: "Holyoake has declared war [. . .] You young men must fight, if it is necessary."[6]

II

George Jacob Holyoake was one of those militant freethinkers whom Kingsley thought detrimental to the socialist cause, because he robbed

[2] CK to JL, 25/3/1851, Martin (1950) 239.
[3] CK to TH, 20/2/1851, Martin (1950) 231.
[4] CK to FDM, 13/1/51, Martin (1950) 223.
[5] CK to FDM, 13/1/51, Martin (1950) 223.
[6] FDM to CK, 15/1/51, Maurice ii.57.

"the poor of his saviour." Holyoake grew up in Birmingham and, like Alton Locke, was mainly self-educated. Though originally a Christian, he turned in adulthood to Owenite socialism, and at the age of twenty-five had started lecturing on co-operation and on the importance of the environment for human and social improvement. He joined Charles Southwell in editing the *Oracle of Reason*, an atheist's paper addressed to working men and which carried a motto that declared that it waged war "not with the forms of Christianity but with Christianity itself." In 1842 he was arrested on charges of atheism and was sentenced to six-months jail. As during his term in Gloucester Goal he was not able to maintain his family, his eight-year-old daughter died of malnutrition. In 1846 he edited another freethinking weekly, *The Reasoner and Theological Examiner*, which, like its predecessors, had a special interest in the principle of cooperation. *The Christian Socialist*, as a journal of association, had attracted his attention when it started to appear in November 1850, but there was much in its columns that he could not stomach. On 15 January he therefore launched an attack in his paper on Parson Lot's "Bible Politics."

The first two instalments of "Bible Politics" were the embodiment of the direct reasons of Kingsley's insistence that Ludlow start a second paper for Chartists: an answer to Cooper's manly and influential teaching of Straussism to working men. The series, which would run unevenly for 24 weeks from 9 November 1850 to 26 April 1851, was meant as a continuation of the main subject of "Letters to Chartists" for *Politics for the People*, and which Maurice had originally suggested to Kingsley, namely that the Bible is not "a book for keeping the poor in order,"[7] the notion that had displeased Julius Hare so much back in 1848.

As Kingsley mainly targets his free-thinking readers, he first begs a "fair and patient hearing" from them—"If any of you consider yourselves enlightened and rational, you cannot show your reason and enlightenment better than by fairly weighing both sides of a question"—and then spoils for a manly stand-up fight: "There are other 'bigots' in the world besides 'priests,' and other 'superstitions' beside Christian ones. It is just as easy to be a bigoted and superstitious Infidel as to be a bigoted and superstitious Churchman [. . .]

---

[7] FDM to CK, 22/4/1848, Maurice i.463.

You have, many of you, been told, and told till you believe it, that the Bible is a book which, above all others, supports priestcraft, superstition, and tyranny. I say this is a lie." This was spirited language which Ludlow thought worthy of the front-page of the second issue of *The Christian Socialist*. It was the courage of the man who had published *Alton Locke*. "If," Kingsley continues, "as you say, Christian ministers are humbugs in everything, why may they not have been humbugging you when they have told you that the Bible makes against the People's cause?" Such reasoning might serve the Bible, but not the Church. We can again imagine a displeased Julius Hare reading this passage and find confirmation of Kingsley's (and Ludlow's) arrogance in the following qualifying statement: "Mind— I do not say they are humbugs. I say they are frail, inconsistent, prejudiced men." The final addition "just like you and me" could not mitigate the accusation. Kingsley is still where he was when he wrote in the heat of action for *Politics for the People*, but having become a public figure in the meantime by having published two controversial novels, it corroded an already dubious reputation, so that advancement in the Church was becoming ever more difficult. Whereas Hare was ultimately sympathetic to Kingsley's cause, many influential churchmen of the establishment were not.

Although Kingsley was not unwilling to criticize the use to which the clergy had put the Scriptures, the Bible itself was free of blame. The mistake of "such men as Strauss" was that they had never looked at the general purpose of the Bible and in their haste "to prove their private notions" had seized upon particular texts to wrench "a few apparent arguments for bigots and tyrants" out of them. "Allow me," he therefore pleaded, "to point out to you what I believe to be the general idea of the Bible with regard to national and social life," as it was the Bible that first "made me a Radical and Socialist. Before I learned to love and appreciate the Bible, I cared not a jot for the People, or the People's cause."[8]

Kingsley argues in the second instalment of 23 November that "the Bible throughout is the history of the People's Cause." Kingsley's notion is Maurician in maintaining that Christianity is inclusive, not exclusive, and that its values rest in notions of family and brotherhood. This implied that the assertion of the individuality of the self

---

[8] "Bible Politics: or God Justified to the People No. I" 9/11/1850 *ChSoc* i.9.

is a willful expression against God which accounts for the existence of evil in the world. In true Christianity alone can man claim membership in a brotherhood of humanity. "The Bible first taught me," Kingsley writes, "that from the beginning men had had a Father Who loved the people, a King Who was labouring to deliver the people, and will labour till He has put down all authority and power, and put all His enemies and yours, beneath his feet." This is clear in the story of the Exodus, which is "the first account which we have of the enfranchisement of the masses," and which shows that God actively guides the people's cause against tyranny, that "God loves so well the just liberty of men that He has interfered Himself, again and again, to procure it for them."

As the Bible asserts universal principles or ideas, the Exodus must therefore be seen as the biblical precursor of recent social ferment, such as the French Revolution. Undeniably, such a notion of God, Kingsley concludes, will be preferred by the working man over that of "the philosopher who, sitting serenely in his easy chair, preaches to you like Strauss about a dead, lazy, wooden pedant of a God, who can look on unmoved at Austrian butcheries and St. Giles cellars, and cares for nothing, provided his world-machine spins to his own satisfaction, though its pitiless wheels should be bedewed with your tears and the blood of millions? [. . .] such a God may suit Professor Strauss, but I will have none of him."[9]

III

Thus far Kingsley had proceeded with "Bible Politics" before Holyoake reacted to the *Christian Socialist* on the front page of the *Reasoner* of 15 January 1851 with "An Appeal to the Good Sense of its Promoters." From various parts of the country the inquiry "What are we to do with the Christian Socialists?" had come, Holyoake reported. His advice to his readers was of the moderate kind that was alien to Kingsley: "Open your halls to them whenever asked; give them the hand of generous fellowship, till time furnishes the proper opportunity of remonstrating without damaging the efforts after practical good which they are making." Holyoake did not hide his approval

[9] "Bible Politics: or God Justified to the People No. II" 23/11/1850 *ChSoc* i.25.

and admiration of the Christian Socialists' "excellent practice [. . .]
in the Co-operative exertions" and hoped that, although their position
was both "illogical and ungracious," they would improve in time.
Their error, he affirmed, is merely doctrinal, their work unquestionably
good. However, he wanted to say a few words about the errors, as it
seemed to him that "the teachings of the *Christian Socialist* are neither
satisfactory to us, nor, I perceive, to Christians. Such a title as 'God
Justified to the People' must always sound blasphemously in the ears
of a man of religious nature. Were I a Christian, nothing would
induce me to use so immodest or so presumptuous a phrase." But
although Holyoake singled out Kingsley's "Bible Politics" for criticism
of the movement's 'Christian' point of view, he also objected to the
proselytising nature of many of the other contributors and the controversial matter that filled their writings: "These publications contain
so much which those who at present retail them have shown to be
false, that they must put a restraint upon themselves greater than
they were wont [. . .] not to do battle for their own truth and con-
fute the articles they sell." They were "carrying us back to the Valley
of Death, through which we have bitterly passed." Although the
Christian Socialist ideal was based on Maurice's abhorrence of any
form of party spirit or religious sectarianism, to Holyoake Christianity
was an obstacle itself, not because of a personal aversion to it, but
because "a co-operative coat need not be a *Christian* coat, any more
than it need be an Atheistic one." The time had passed when
Owenites had to resort to proselytising atheism because Christianity
was hostile to their progress, he explained, no doubt referring to
Kingsley's articles on Owen's socialism. But this was not the case
now: most freethinkers were of the same opinion as "these new
Socialists" about co-operation. Therefore, he concluded, "let Socialism
be the *neutral* ground on which all men can work for the common
good."[10] Of course, this went against everything that socialism stood
for in Maurice's understanding of social reform, and the article could
not be passed over silently. That is why he wrote to Kingsley
"Holyoake has declared war [. . .] You young men must fight, if it
is necessary," misrepresenting Holyoake's moderating words, but
knowing that if one of the brotherhood would fight, Kingsley would.
And Kingsley's battling spirit was probably the least suitable for a
constructive dialogue with Holyoake and the freethinkers.

---

[10] Holyoake 265–6.

In a second appeal to the good sense of the Christian Socialists, Holyoake, who admitted he had been forced to be brief because of a lack of sleep, added to his charges not only that Kingsley's method was irreverent to God but also that the Bible-accounts themselves were "unworthy of God's character." To illustrate his argument, he quoted Sir William Drummond's facetious remarks on Exodus 31:1–9 of God's "condescending to superintend the patterns of spoons and dishes for Moses." He brought forward more serious objections, however, in the case of the extermination of the Canaanites in the Book of Joshua as "unjust and unmerciful."[11] It is not clear whether Kingsley had seen Holyoake's accusations when he hesitantly wrote to Maurice about the dilemma of continuing with the "Bible Politics" series or not: "I dare not go on with them, for the next subject wh. I shall have to face are those exterminations of the Canaanites." But it was a point freethinkers generally made use of in their argument to reject a God who had ordered the Jews to exterminate all the men, women and children of the Canaan, "until they left them none remaining" (Joshua 11:8), and Kingsley had from the beginning planned it as an integral part of "Bible Politics" to answer those who objected to the Bible that there are stories in it "of the Jews being commanded by God to do cruel deeds, deeds quite contrary to His love and mercy."[12]

All except the last of these allegations were easy to answer, and Kingsley did so on 8 February. If the correspondent for the *Reasoner* professed to deny the existence of God, Kingsley wrote, he could not logically "know what the dignity of God is," and therefore had no title to attack "Bible Politics." Holyoake and Drummond might sneer at the divine in handicraft, he continued, but to him design, both industrial and artisan, was as much part of divine inspiration as Shakespeare's art: "If you cannot see the message they bring to the engine-turner, and the weaver, and the painter; if you cannot see the divine dignity they claim for man's labour, and man's inventions, all I can say is, that I hope all my working readers will not be as blind to their own dignity." And he concluded: "Which has the higher notion of the 'dignity of labour'—you or the Bible?"[13]

---

[11] "Bible Politics: or God Justified to the People No. IV" 22/2/1851 *ChSoc* i.130.
[12] "Bible Politics: or God Justified to the People No. II" 23/11/1850 *ChSoc* i.25.
[13] "Bible Politics: or God Justified to the People No. III" 8/2/1851 *ChSoc* i.113–4.

But there was not a word on the destruction of the Canaanites
in all this. Kingsley was aware that defence of these acts of atrocity in the Hebrew Bible might lead him to shallow waters, and he
therefore felt uneasy about committing his explanations to print. He
expressed his misgivings about the reception of his interpretation.
However, as for him "Bible Politics," and indeed *The Christian Socialist*
itself, was born out of his need to answer Strauss's higher criticism,
the violence in Joshua needed to be justified as true acts ordered by
a universal loving God. There was no possibility other than demon-
strating that even "this slaughter of the Canaanites must have been
in itself just and right, and merciful and loving, or it has no business in the Bible."[14] It had to be done, he decided. But he still held
back and decided to consult Maurice on the orthodoxy of his
hermeneutics of the Canaan passage.

It is interesting how during these Christian Socialist years Kingsley
swerved from siding with Ludlow when Maurice seemed to obstruct
the course of pure action, and back to Maurice when Ludlow became
critical of his ideas. It shows where the attraction of these men lay
for Kingsley. He never doubted Maurice's spiritual leadership but
found in Ludlow a more willing ally for his inner urge to *do* something. Thus, the mutual understanding between Ludlow and Kingsley
was essential in setting up both *Politics for the People* and *The Christian
Socialist*, and Kingsley shared Ludlow's frustration with Maurice's
"system-phobia." Still, Kingsley repeatedly turned to Maurice to seek
advice for his writings. As Maurice had accepted to read *The Saint's
Tragedy* and write a preface for it in 1847, at the beginning of 1851
he was checking the re-written chapters of *Yeast* which Kingsley forwarded to him as soon as he finished them. "I will obey *your* orders.
Other mens' [*sic.*] I will not," he wrote to Maurice. Ludlow's criticism, however well-meant, had a paralysing effect on Kingsley's creative imagination. He had felt this ever since Ludlow expressed his
dislike of the later developments of *Yeast*, which Kingsley regarded
as the very bone and marrow of the novel. "Not that there is the
least unpleasantness," he admitted to Maurice, "but he has renewed
about the last letter [on the "Frimley Thoughts"] the old theory w.
he started about the latter part of Yeast that it was written when I
was ill & tired, & therefore unworthy of me . . . And though I am

---

[14] "Bible Politics: or God Justified to the People No. IV" 22/2/1851 *ChSoc* i.130.

not thinskinned & nervous, after the manner of poets, yet such a notion does utterly paralyze my pen, when I cannot alter my opinions, & must go on in the same strain or none."[15]

But it was not only uneasiness at the prospect of incurring further literary criticism from Ludlow that made Kingsley hold back. He feared Ludlow's opinion of his thoughts on the nature of humanity: "I must say things wh. will horrify him, & he will have to protest against them."[16] As we have seen, he had already differed with Ludlow over his defence of James Brooke's measures against the pirates in Sarawak, which he had compared to the extermination of the Canaanites in the Book of Joshua: "Oh, Ludlow," he had exclaimed in 1849, "read history; look at the world, and see whether God values mere physical existence [. . .] Do you believe in the Old Testament? Surely, then, say, what does that destruction of the Canaanites mean? If it was right, Rajah Brooke was right. If he be wrong, then Moses, Joshua, David, were wrong."[17]

To Ludlow, however, it savoured of justifying human crime in the name of God. As this was a matter of hermeneutics, the verdict of Maurice was necessary. The Master's answer brought relief. "I approve of your letter," he reassured Kingsley, "and think Ludlow will: you have managed it so skilfully and in a way so much to conciliate his prejudices." Moreover, "You have told me more than I ever knew, and have cleared up the whole subject to me marvellously." He admitted that he himself had felt perplexed when his late brother-in-law, John Sterling, had laid the question before him and objected to the Jewish wars. "I asked myself why? [. . .] and if it was an end for humanity, and a higher end than the other, was it wrong to say God was the author of it? Could it be any one else?" "But this," he wrote to Kingsley, "you have worked out more clearly than I did then, or have done since." This was more than Kingsley could have hoped for and it took away all further fears. "The only thing I should wish you to bring out more distinctly in these letters," Maurice added, "is that God, according to the scripture view of His character and dealings, *cannot* make men right by any exercise of omnipotence."[18]

---

[15] CK to FDM, 16/1/1851, BL-41297 f.11.
[16] CK to FDM, 16/1/1851, BL-41297 f.11.
[17] CK to JL, December 1849, *LML* i.223.
[18] FDM to Ck, 30/1/51, Maurice ii.58.

What Maurice had seen and read was the fourth instalment of "Bible Politics"[19] in which Kingsley elaborated on the dangerous tendencies of free-thinking, of every attempt to "separate morality and religion, and make every man his own God, by making the spirit of man the only rule of right and wrong." The Bible bore witness that such thinking had, at various points in history, resulted in "the grossest idolatry,"

> And that is what it would come to again, if the every-man-his-own-God-gospel according to Strauss and Emerson, and their followers, got the upper-hand here, and still faster if the-every-man-his-own-God-destroyer-gospel of the *Reasoner* got the upper-hand . . .[20]

Right and wrong were not man-made ideas. Neither was right made by God. But, "Right is God." He therefore warned not to judge rashly the acts of destruction in the Hebrew Bible. Judging God's commands incurred the risk of doing exactly that for which the Canaanites were punished. As the Bible professed to be a book that reveals God to the People, the destruction of the Canaanites "cannot, I think, have been an unique case; that is one like which nothing ever happened or is to be expected to happen again," or, as he explained in the following instalment of 8 March:

> We talk of barbarous and ignorant ages . . . are we so very clear that the men of this generation, with their drunkenness, and their improvidence, and their covetousness, and their competition, and their wars, and their revolutions, are very fit judges of what God ought to do?[21]

And to illustrate that such cruel destruction as that of the Canaanites is by no means unique in the history of mankind, he pointed out that in earthquakes as much human life perishes as in the whole of Canaan. "Now, did God command these earthquakes, or did he not?" To Kingsley there is no doubt about it:

> I congratulate those [. . .] who can read all the awful tragedies which make up the pages of history, and believe that they have no purpose, no method, no justice, no mercy in them. I congratulate them; not on the wisdom of their belief, but on the strength of their minds, which enables them to face such a record of, in their eyes, useless and chaotic horrors, without madness or suicide.[22]

---

[19] Not the 3rd instalment, as Frederick Maurice maintains, Maurice ii.57.
[20] "Bible Politics: or God Justified to the People No. IV" 22/2/1851 *ChSoc* i.131.
[21] "Bible Politics: or God Justified to the People No. V" 8/3/1851 *ChSoc* i.146.
[22] "Bible Politics: or God Justified to the People No. VI" 15/3/1851 *ChSoc* i.153.

If Kingsley believed that with these points he had left Holyoake defeated—"Let us hope that we have left him behind, and that [. . .] he will not follow us, and interfere with arguments, of which by his own confession, he cannot possibly comprehend a word"[23]—he was mistaken. He was soon confronted with objections that were phrased in language much harsher than Holyoake's. Correspondence from angry readers started to reach Ludlow, which convinced him that Kingsley's "Bible Politics" was leading them to dangerous subjects.

IV

James Benny, who would later become manager of the Tailors' Association which the Christian Socialists had helped to set up, used the columns for "Free Correspondence" in *The Christian Socialist* to object to Kingsley's "Bible Politics." On the whole, the series irritated Benny as "Parson Lot assumes a power which does not say much for the meekness of his Christianity or the equality of his Socialism."[24] The Bible is the least representative of all books for the people's cause, Benny wrote: "what narrow views of the People's Cause has Parson Lot, when here is an instance given, where, under the orders of the God of Abram, ten communities of peoples are to be sacrificed to the seed of one man." The whole history of the Chosen People, which Kingsley traced to modern English times, was most dubious to Benny:

> Was this an effort in the sacred cause of the People? Was this any advance in the glorious idea of universal brotherhood, where the destruction of men, women, children, and property, is accompanied by the horrible brutality of afterwards setting fire to the city, and burning their mangled corpses?

And he concluded: "In a few words, the Bible is anything but a People's Book; it merely advocates the cause of a class or sect, while all other men are left to perish."[25]

By 28 February, Benny's objections to Parson Lot had reached Ludlow, who held them back so that he could first ask Kingsley what he proposed to do about them. Kingsley now asked Ludlow

---

[23] "Bible Politics: or God Justified to the People No. V" 8/3/1851 *ChSoc* i.146.
[24] "Parson Lot and Bible Politics" 15/3/1851 *ChSoc* i.158.
[25] "Parson Lot and Bible Politics" 15/3/1851 *ChSoc* i.159.

to send the already written "Bible Politics VI" back to him "for improvement" and forwarded a rejoinder to Benny's letter. Ludlow announced in the issue of 8 March of *The Christian Socialist* that Benny's letter would be published the following week. On 15 March "Bible Politics VI" appeared on the front page, while Benny's letter and Kingsley's answer to it followed four pages later. While "Bible Politics" traced a providential course of progressive history in which "righteous work [at times] was done by unrighteous men," the rejoinder to Benny was weak and mainly promised that most of his points would be refuted in the following instalments of "Bible Politics." To Ludlow, Kingsley tried to defend his spineless rejoinder to Benny. "You will see that I have tried to answer Mr. B. ex cathedrâ & and yet meekly, & and have taken no notice whatsoever of his impertinence. One has no time for flicking at flies. Either *squash* them, or let them buzz & walk on."[26] But Kingsley was beginning to get tired of the Canaanite question. "I want to get over it & onward," he told Ludlow.[27] The kind of diplomacy necessary to tackle it was not to Kingsley's impulsive taste. After four instalments of rambling he had hinted at his thoughts but had not fully unfolded them. Notwithstanding Maurice's encouragement, he had restrained himself for fear of incurring Ludlow's displeasure. But he could no longer fight Holyoake or Benny without laying bare the core of his notions on the Canaanites. He started to do so with "Bible Politics VII."

If in the sixth instalment he had vindicated the conquest of peoples as part of God's progressive plan towards an ideal form of civilization in which "God has given the English England," he now added that the Canaanites "had been for many generations, indulging in unnatural crimes too horrible to name," and that "we know as a fact that such crimes create hereditary disease, cripple and brutalize, in body and mind, the races which indulge in them; their blood becomes tainted; their brain becomes, generation by generation weaker, and addicted to brutal animalism."[28] The progress of civilization was based on the survival of the morally fittest, and the moral state of an individual was reflected in the outward form of the physical body. Such development could be seen as a natural course of positive progress of the species, but it could work just as

[26] CK to JL, 3/3/1851, Martin (1950) 233.
[27] CK to JL, 3/3/1851, Martin (1950) 233.
[28] "Bible Politics: or God Justified to the People No. VII" 22/3/1851 *ChSoc* i.162.

well the other way round through degradation to the point that human life ceases to be human life. Of course, this is why he replied when Ludlow regretted the sacrifice of so much human life in Sarawak in 1849: "Prove that it is *human* life. It is beast-life."[29] Likewise in the case of the Canaanites: "I read nowhere in the Old Testament of any destruction of *human* life. By the Jewish swords *animal* life in plenty was destroyed." The extermination of the Canaanites, far from being a sign of cruelty, had to be seen as an act of providential mercy. They inevitably "fall to a point from which they cannot rise again," losing "the power of increasing their species," and finally be "exterminated by slow interior decay, by famine produced by laziness or by pestilential disorders."[30] They were "literally 'put out of their misery',," just as

> thousands of children who die yearly miserable and lingering deaths—worse than any Canaan slaughter, in our great towns, of diseases which are the fruit of their parents' neglect and intemperance, and of the foul air, foul food, foul dwellings, caused by neglect of proper sanitary reform—a thought which ought to drive one mad, if one was not able to say of them, as of those poor Canaanite innocents, "Their Father has taken them away from the evil to come."[31]

This pietistic notion suggests that Kingsley struggled with the existence of suffering in the world, and his meandering towards this final pronouncement suggests that the Canaan passage *was* an irksome one to him to which he had given much thought. It needed justification. If Kingsley could have embraced the findings of the Higher Critics, he would have found a way around it as purely historical or mythical. But that way was not open to him. "The Bible is written to tell you how all that happens really happens—what all things really are," he wrote in one of his *Village Sermons*.[32] Kingsley set out with his articles in *The Christian Socialist* to stem the flow of atheism that resulted from the Straussism in the writings of socialists like Cooper and Holyoake. It is therefore difficult to see how Kingsley could have reached different conclusions from such premises.

But, although this part of Kingsley's position on the Canaanite question shows a rather rigid adherence to the literal truth of the

---

[29] CK to JL, December 1849, *LML* i.222.
[30] "Bible Politics: or God Justified to the People No. VII" 22/3/1851 *ChSoc* i.162.
[31] "Bible Politics: or God Justified to the People No. VII" 22/3/1851 *ChSoc* i.162.
[32] "The Work of God's Spirit" *VSTCS* 28.

246   CHAPTER NINE

Bible, the rest is coupled with a more imaginative quality of Kingsley's philosophy. If in *Alton Locke*'s "Dreamland" he had given his contemporaries a daring and poetic vision of some kind of evolutionary principle, it is in "Bible Politics" that he sees the dynamics of population as the expression of such a principle. He moves effortlessly from an idea of a universal struggle, which had been well-known since the latter half of the eighteenth century, to a startling interpretation of it as conducive to the perfection of the race, using terminology similar to that used by Herbert Spencer in 1864 in his description of "survival of the fittest":

> He is taking away those who might be harmful, or at least useless, and leaving room for others, who are, though no better than those destroyed, more fitted to carry on the great work of increasing and civilising, and raising the human race [. . . and He] sends those evils on the fallen few for the ultimate good of the many.[33]

That Kingsley meant such notions to be read as underlying organic change as well is clear from the dream passages in *Alton Locke*. The step from here to Darwin's concept of "natural selection" is a small one. No wonder Kingsley would embrace Darwin's findings barely ten years later as confirming his own convictions, even if he would never accept that such selection occurred randomly.

A general idea of a leading nation in the advance of Christian civilization can be traced in other authors of the early Victorian period, and the destruction of innocent life in the Book of Joshua, as conducive to the advancement of civilization, could easily be assimilated in an approach to progressive world history. Thomas Arnold held such a view of Christianity, and the specific justification of the massacre of the Canaanites emerges powerfully in one of his sermons:

> It is better that the wicked should be destroyed a hundred times over than that they should tempt those who are as yet innocent to join their company. Let us but think what might have been our fate, and the fate of every other nation under heaven at this hour, had the sword of the Israelites done its work more sparingly. [. . . H]ad the heathen lived in the land in equal numbers, and, still more, had they intermarried largely with the Israelites, how was it possible, humanly speaking, that any sparks of the light of God's truth should have survived to the coming of Christ? [. . .] The Israelite's sword, in its bloodiest executions, wrought a work of mercy for all the countries of the earth

---

"Bible Politics: or God Justified to the People No. VII" 22/3/1851 *ChSoc* i.163.

to the very end of the world. They seem of very small importance to us now, those perpetual contests with the Canaanites [...] We may half wonder that God should have interfered in such quarrels, or have changed the course of nature, in order to give one of the nations of Palestine the victory over another. But in these contests, on the fate of one of these nations of Palestine the happiness of the human race depended.[34]

Kingsley, with his admiration for the late headmaster of Rugby, seems to have read and adopted this stance in "Bible Politics," and explained it in terms of the "survival of the fittest."

V

Seeing how far Kingsley got in his reasoning about the struggle for survival, consequent change, and the benefit for the perfection of the race, it is not surprising that he would also want to air his views on Malthus' theory on population. On 15 February he started a series of articles called "The Church *versus* Malthus" which were simultaneously published with the rest of "Bible Politics" for a month to come. Initially Kingsley simply insisted that humans are "sexual being[s]" who "are able, *if fairly treated*, to produce more than they consume," and that preventive measures to contain the growth of the population are consequently to be deplored, especially as it would mean taking away from man that "which he has always, in proportion as he has risen above mere brutality, considered as among his noblest, most mysterious, holiest [fulfilment]."[35] Darwin would claim in his "Introduction" to the first edition of *The Origin of Species* in 1859 that Malthus' *Essay on the Principle of Population* had inspired him to understand the process of un-providential "natural selection." "Many more individuals of each species," he wrote, "are born than can possibly survive; and [...] consequently, there is a frequently recurring struggle for existence."[36] Kingsley, who seemed to have reached such conclusions as well, however, remained disappointingly unimaginative on this point. There are no signs or promises of further delineation of his idea when he finished his article of 15 February.

---

[34] *Arnold's Sermons*, vi.35–7, as quoted in Arthur Penrhyn Stanley, *Lectures on the History of the Jewish Church*, 3 vols. (New York 1893), i.227–8.
[35] "The Church *versus* Malthus" 15/2/1851 *ChSoc* i.121.
[36] Charles Darwin, *The Origin of Species* (Harmondsworth: Penguin 1985) 68.

But when a reader who identified himself as F. (finally one who did not "revile and misrepresent, and denounce me, as some have done") reacted, Kingsley laid bare another aspect of his thinking on population that is of interest in the present context.

Kingsley did not refute Malthus' basic principles that war, famine and disease were a countercheck to the tendency that population growth might outstrip food production. But, although "the fact which Malthus proclaimed stands strictly true," it remained a matter of interpretation whether death, famine and disease check the excessive growth of the population, or whether the fecundity of women is increased to make up for the loss of life caused by these three factors. Kingsley opted for the second. Once the checks were no longer results but causes, it meant that misery should be combatted. That is why Kingsley advocated sanitary reform, and how in "Bible Politics" he could claim in the same breath the ultimate goodness of calamities and bestow "honour and blessings on Sanitary Reformers, Peace Societies, Scientific discoveries; on every man who labours, in any way whatsoever, to lessen the amount of pain and death in the world; to save a single ache to any human being." Although it is ultimately comforting to know that nothing perishes without purpose, "the aches are still there," and therefore,

> [s]o far from making us less eager for sanitary reform, less eager to prevent war and cruelty of every kind, it will, I think, make us all the more eager; because all the more hopeful; because we shall believe that in trying to lessen human suffering, we are not fighting against a blind brute destiny, but working in concert with a loving and just God.[37]

Thus, although Kingsley's hermeneutics of the extermination of the Canaanites brought out a mixture of belief in divinely ordained progress and a Spencerian conception of "survival of the fittest" for society, he did not share the pessimistic Malthusian representation of creation which was grounded on the idea that the checks secured an inviolable equilibrium of population, and which, through the Paley school of Natural Theology of the Bridgewater Treatises, had come to underlie the defence some political economists applied to a politics of *laissez faire*. In the 1830s, Thomas Chalmers had employed the argument of design in his Bridgewater Treatise on political economy,

---

[37] "Bible Politics: or God Justified to the People No. VII" 22/3/1851 *ChSoc* i.163.

maintaining that human intervention in the social problems of the time risked disturbing the clock-like perfection of such a system. But to Kingsley it was man who was out of tune, and war, famine and disease were the *results* of

> man's ignorance, man's laziness, man's selfishness, man's brutality [. . .] man's social iniquities which render increased production of food, as in England now, an 'unprofitable investment' while fertile land is crying out for tillage, and the poor for labour and for food.[38]

When Chalmers published his views on political economy, he was ferociously attacked in the *Quarterly Review* by George Poulett Scrope. It has been argued by historians[39] that Scrope was contemptuous of Chalmers's market politics and his apathy to the material condition of the poor because the two men had a different understanding of time. Scrope, an able geologist who, with his *Memoir on the Geology of Central France* (1827), had instilled in Charles Lyell the idea that what is "echoed from every part of her [nature's] works, is—Time!—Time!—Time!", did not feel the urgency of the Malthusian warnings that Chalmers felt. Chalmers was unable to think in terms of infinite time and therefore could not "distinguish between a present and an ultimate threat, for judgement was here and now, ubiquitous and continual."[40] To Kingsley, man-made solutions to social problems did not breach a divinely ordained equilibrium, but proved rather that such an equilibrium was still in the making. And this is where a disapproval of Malthusian measures is added to his intricate discussion of the cause of the people.

If Scrope argued unconsciously from his understanding of time in judging political measures to alleviate the suffering of the poor, Kingsley, as a keen amateur geologist who had imbibed ideas of deep time, might have instinctively argued along similar lines. Scrope did not deny Malthus' principles but did not see the urgency of them. Kingsley's social outlook is similarly a realization that the present was not the measure of all times, and not unlike Scrope in his

---

[38] "The Church *versus* Malthus III" 5/4/1851 *ChSoc* 179.

[39] See, for example, Martin J.S. Rudwick, "Poulett Scrope on the Volcanoes of Auverne: Lyellian Time and Political Economy," *British Journal for the History of Science*, 7 (1974); Boyd Hilton, "Politics of Anatomy and an Anatomy of Politics, *c.* 1825–50," in *History, Religion and Culture: British Intellectual History 1750–1950*, ed. by Stefan Collini, Richard Whatmore, and Brian Young (Cambridge: Cambridge University Press, 2000), pp. 179–97.

[40] Boyd Hilton (see previous note) 196.

attack on Chalmers, he emphasized that "as long as vast sheets of English land are lying waste, and the average of cultivated land is not producing more than three fourths of what it might do, men have not a right to demand of a society which could not exist without their labour, that it shall [. . .] compel them to celibacy, and selfish monopoly of land which it cannot cultivate for itself, and will let no one cultivate for it."[41] It is a notion which would engage Kingsley further in *Westward Ho!*.

In this digression on population, Kingsley, of course, did not dwell on Malthus in the sense Darwin was to do when he traced part of his inspiration for "natural selection." He rather refuted the negative conclusions of his theory of population by making it part of Maurician evidence of human aberration from a divine plan yet to be unfolded— i.e. man's failure to obey God's command to "replenish the earth and subdue it." Still, his linking of Malthus with ideas of survival of the fittest for the benefit of the race did provide him with the premises for evolutionary thinking later in the decade.

Notwithstanding an ultimately benign view of the potential and necessity to lessen human suffering, Kingsley's reasoning about the destruction of human life invited further angry reactions from readers. A ferocious letter from a George Smith of Salford now reached Ludlow after the sixth instalment of "Bible Politics." Smith's tone was savage: Parson Lot's concept of violence, he argued, is a "monstrous belief," born from a brain "bemuddled by priestly teachings." "I am at a loss to conceive its *necessity impelling* an OMNIPOTENT GOD to govern his creatures by the *unmeasured use of the same instrument of destruction*, or KILLING THEM TO CHASTISE THEM, by earthquakes, shipwrecks, or explosions." "If I had not previously had a thorough contempt for the world's notions of a God, your description of his character and exposition of his cruel and impotent government of the universe, would have made me an Atheist."[42] Receipt of Smith's letter was acknowledged by Ludlow in *The Christian Socialist* of 29 March, but with the addition that "it cannot be yet inserted"[43] and the epistle was held back from Kingsley, as Ludlow probably wanted him to finish the series without adding yet more fuel to an already embarrassing public dispute with his readers. Moreover, he must

---

[41] "The Church *versus* Malthus" 12/4/1851 *ChSoc* i.186.
[42] "Against Parson Lot's Bible Politics" 26/4/1851 *ChSoc* i.206.
[43] "Notices to Correspondents" 29/3/1851 *ChSoc* i.174.

have seen some of what Kingsley had already written for following instalments, and probably thought they answered some of the charges made against him. But other angry letters continued to arrive, and Ludlow felt obliged to print in his "Notices to Correspondents" that "the free expression of opinion which we court is something quite different from attacks upon individuals, and we beg leave to say, once for all, that personalities of this description will not be noticed."[44]

Ludlow, of course, knew where Kingsley's heart lay. Notwithstanding his belief in a kind of "natural-selection principle" for society, he could not, and did not, sit still in the face of misery. Moreover, the note of brotherhood and cooperation that transpires from Kingsley's passages is central. He made it clear, for example, that nothing is more detrimental to true civilization than the existence of slavery. Part of his argument in justifying the Canaanite slaughter of innocent life is based on this premise. The natural course of history would have turned the conquered Canaanite population into slaves, and

> [t]hey, like every nation in the world which lives by slave-labour, would have gradually been corrupted down to the moral and intellectual level of their own slaves, and have fallen by them, as Athens fell, as Rome fell; as the Spaniards in America have fallen, as the Southern United States will surely fall, unless they cast away, as an accursed and destroying sin, their present madness of treating their brother-men like beasts that perish.[45]

In the end, Mosaic law against slavery set an example, which if followed would have helped to make Palestine a free nation "under laws of equal justice between man and man:"

> The Jews [. . .] were forbidden to take any male captives; the most hideous form of slave-breeding was impossible; for even a temporary concubine could not be sold, much less the children by her; the runaway slave was in case to be given up to his master (as is now the law in the Christian United States), but allowed to dwell as a free man wherever he took refuge. And in a word, not only all the infernal indecencies and iniquities of the neighbouring nations towards their captives, but even all the cruelties which are now legalized in the Slave States of North America, were made impossible.[46]

---

[44] "Notices to Correspondents" 5/4/1851 *ChSoc* i.181.
[45] "Bible Politics: or God Justified to the People No. VIII" 19/4/1851 *ChSoc* i.193.
[46] "Bible Politics: or God Justified to the People No. VIII" 19/4/1851 *ChSoc* i.194.

With this plea against slavery Kingsley concluded his hermeneutics of the violence in the Book of Joshua.

Although the violence in the Old Testament had been answered for, "Bible Politics" continued, and the following week, on 26 April, the ninth instalment appeared in which the notion of priestcraft, another favourite subject of freethinkers, was addressed, "for there is a great deal of disgusting priestcraft afloat in England now."[47] There was a promise of further quarrels in these premises, but this time with fellow brethren of the cloth. Before going into the question, Kingsley wrote, it was essential first to define what the words 'priest' and 'priestcraft' mean, and he therefore invites his readers write down their definitions and forward them to *The Christian Socialist*. At this point, however, the series is interrupted. Ludlow seems to have thought that with the part on priestcraft Kingsley had "answered at least a large portion" of the protests against Parson Lot,[48] and that George Smith's letter could now be published. This delay seems to indicate that Ludlow did not want Kingsley to answer Smith's letter, an impression enforced by the fact that Ludlow himself wrote a rejoinder to it, asking Smith: "Do you take us for liars, when we say we have a Father in heaven whom we love? Supposing we were mistaken in saying so, do you think it is kindly, manly, brotherly, to pour forth such unrestrained abuse of a Being whom we treat as such?"[49] He also confronted the question of the Canaanite slaughters himself, ignoring the fact that Kingsley had already done so, and asserted in a few words that God's government of the earth should be seen as "the education of the human race," that evil is invariably the result of "some act of human negligence or cupidity, or some violation, ignorant or perverse, of the laws of nature." And he concluded: "It is because we do not yet understand or value man, that we are so quick to cast our puny insults in the face of God."[50]

Notwithstanding the promise "To be continued" at the end of "Bible Politics IX", and notwithstanding the fact that letters with definitions of priestcraft were received and sent on to Parson Lot,[51] Kingsley's contributions to *The Christian Socialist* stopped and were

---

[47] "Bible Politics: or God Justified to the People No. IX" 26/4/1851 *ChSoc* i.202.
[48] "Bible Politics: or God Justified to the People No. IX" 26/4/1851 *ChSoc* i.206.
[49] "Bible Politics: or God Justified to the People No. IX" 26/4/1851 *ChSoc* i.206.
[50] "Bible Politics: or God Justified to the People No. IX" 26/4/1851 *ChSoc* i.207.
[51] "Priestcraft and Craft in General" 10/5/1851 *ChSoc* i.220.

not resumed till the beginning of July when his only short-story "The Nun's Pool" was published.

VI

Although Kingsley's writing for *The Christian Socialist* during February and March 1851 took up much of his time, there were other things that demanded attention. Maurice had written about a possible new pupil. Julius Hare was trying to place one of his brother's sons, who had provoked a scandal with a girl, with a private tutor, and thought Kingsley just the right person. Although Kingsley had reservations about such a difficult pupil, he would not refuse Hare, to whom he "owe[d] too much," nor could he refuse an honest means to add to his income. In his answer, Kingsley responded with words that were characteristic of his own temperamental make-up:

> I do not mind a lad's having been a scapegrace about girls, or even having tried to lie himself out of a scrape, if there is any tolerable substratum of tenderness & chivalry, to w. one can appeal. The selfish, silent, sly animal is the only one for w. I see nothing but "jackass's medicine". If you think there is a soul in the lad wh. will wash, I will try to wash it. I shd. make no secret of knowing his faults, & try to put it to his honour not to corrupt Martineau, & to wean him from low pleasure by a Stoic, as well chivalrous teaching. I have some half-laid wind-eggs on this matter on my brain [. . .][52]

The matter of the "half-laid wind-eggs" was only hatched years later in the form of *The Water-Babies*.

In the end, however, the young Hare was not placed under Kingsley's guidance, which probably saved him some trouble, but also eliminated a much-needed possibility of adding to his income. The ever-growing financial problems were now laid before Thomas Hughes. Kingsley explained that repairs on "this old lanthorn of a house" had exhausted all his reserves and that previous loans had to be repaid. He inquired after a 'party' willing to receive 5 per cent for £500 for seven to ten years, offering as security his policy of insurance and, jokingly, his "title deeds of my estates in Prester John's country," which he feared were no good. But failure to obtain

---

[52] CK to FDM, 19/6/1851, BL-41297 f.16.

such a loan would constrain him to "write up G.T.T. [Gone To Texas] on the door & go to another & abetter."[53] Hughes proposed Lees, but that was too much for Kingsley's pride, who would rather "smash, than borrow money of a pupil."[54]

Notwithstanding his financial straights and uncertain prospects, Kingsley felt remarkably high-spirited at the time, as he himself explained: "I am joking about it, because there are things in the world wh. *are too bad to trust oneself to be sad over*." But things were turning out all right. As Lees would not do, Hughes now came up with a friend of his, a Mr James Crowdy, who was willing to lend the money if Kingsley could provide a security, which was soon found in his old schoolfriend Richard Cowley Powles. "I feel as if a mountain was taken off my breast—I can work now with a good will & free," he wrote when thanking Hughes.[55] And work there was. Kingsley's literary fame was spreading fast. *Alton Locke* was beginning to create quite a reputation for its author, and Parker had become convinced that it was an opportune moment to re-publish *Yeast* in book-form.

Kingsley realized that the Fraser version of *Yeast* was far from suitable for republishing as it stood, and he had started to rewrite the novel completely, aspiring to make its religious meaning clearer. Chapter after chapter was sent off to Maurice for approval, who then sent them on to Parker, who in turn printed them as he received them. On 20 February, Kingsley reported with satisfaction to Hughes that "Yeast is in the course of republication, with additions."[56] It came out within a month. Numerous variations with the original serial version can be noted. Many minor corrections were made, words substituted, and titles of chapters changed. But there were substantial changes as well. Kingsley tried to be more outspoken on religion itself. Froude thought the novel version a great improvement on the serial version: "I have been reading all the evening," he wrote to his brother-in-law, "with a more complete understanding than I could get out of it when it dropt in upon me intermittently. On the whole it is *stronger* than *Alton Locke*, and is more real to me in many ways, even though it has not Sandy [MacKaye]."[57]

---

[53] CK to TH, 20/2/1851, Martin (1950) 230.
[54] CK to TH, 5/3/1851, Martin (1950) 234.
[55] CK to TH, March 1851, Martin (1950) 236.
[56] CK to TH, 20/2/1851, Martin (1950) 230.
[57] JAF to CK, 19/3/1851, Dunn i.181.

VII

John Henry Newman's novel *Loss and Gain* might well have influenced Kingsley in writing *Yeast*, as Allen John Hartley has argued. Although both novels belong to 1848, Newman's was out before Kingsley started on his. But such influence went no further than that both novels were tales of religious conversion. Luke, Lancelot's Tractarian cousin, is presented as the main character's alter-ego, and Kingsley uses him as an example of the uncertain intellectual and religious atmosphere of the times. No doubt, Luke represented the attraction Kingsley himself had felt for Tractarianism at one stage of his life, and as such he got a fair amount of sympathetic treatment from his creator. But in the new 1851 edition the contrast between Lancelot and Luke is more pronounced. A long correspondence between the two cousins now shows that the two are opposites rather than complements. Luke's decision to go over to Rome and become a Catholic is hinted at in an early addition,[58] and as the correspondence between the two unfolds, Kingsley's condemnation of a Newmanite conversion to Roman Catholicism turns into a conspicuous new theme. Although Luke seems to be in search of "a great idea" in the Romish Church, Lancelot's language is clear enough to make us suspect a "selfish and superstitious terror" to be Luke's driving force: "it is a new and very important thought to me, that Rome's scheme of this world, rather than of the next, forms her chief allurement."[59] Kingsley, of course, saw Newmanite conversion as a supremely personal act which was based on selfish asceticism.

The dispute with Newman's novel becomes clear when Luke enumerates in a letter to Lancelot all the churches and parties he had examined before he decided on the Roman Catholic Church. The chapter seems to react against the comical procession of representatives of different religious denominations who come to visit Charles Reding in *Loss and Gain* in order to convert him, although Luke's account is without the humour that characterizes Newman's passage. Kingsley had no time for joking and hurries on to show that the "Romish idea of man is a mistake—utterly wrong and absurd."[60] Luke's conversion is based on his rejection of "our animal nature."

[58] *Y* 33.
[59] *Y* 79.
[60] *Y* 79.

"I have not forgotten how that very animal nature, on the possession
of which you seem to pride yourself, was in me only the parent of
remorse," he writes to Lancelot, "I know it too well not to hate and
fear it. Why do you reproach me, if I try to abjure it, and cast away
the burden which I am too weak to bear?"[61]

Kingsley's condemnation increasingly concentrates on Luke's
effeminate rejection of his manhood. If Luke's ideal is "a soft cradle lying open for . . . with a Virgin Mother's face smiling down all
woman's love about it,"[62] Lancelot's response to this is Carlyle's
"Everlasting No", for he has seen

> in your fancy, at least, an ideal of man, for which you have spurned
> [. . .] the merely negative angelic—the merely receptive and indulgent
> feminine-ideals of humanity, and longed to be a man, like that ideal
> and perfect man.[63]

Lancelot's conversion is found in the wish to do social good, "to
regenerate one little parish in the whole world,"[64] a conversion which
springs from an inner urge towards an ideal active manhood. "Give
me the political economist, the sanitary reformer, the engineer,"
Kingsley concludes, "and take [you] your saints and virgins, relics
and miracles."[65]

The destinies of the two cousins needed to be separated. If in
Fraser's Magazine both cousins decide in the end to become artists,
we now read that Luke "had done with this world, and the painters
of this world,"[66] and he disappears from the novel. Kingsley voices
his final criticism of Roman Catholicism through Lancelot:

> here is the end of your anthropology! At first, your ideal man is an
> angel. But your angel is merely an unsexed woman; and so you are
> forced to go back to the humanity after all—but to a woman, not a
> man? And this, in the nineteenth century, when men are telling us
> that the poetic and enthusiastic have become impossible, and that the
> only possible state of the world henceforward will be a universal good-
> humoured hive, of the Franklin-Benthamite religion . . . . a vast prosaic
> Cockaigne of steam mills for grinding sausages—for those who can get

---

[61] *Y* 73–4.
[62] *Y* 74.
[63] *Y* 302.
[64] *Y* 309.
[65] *Y* 82.
[66] *Y* 261.

at them. And all the while, in spite of all Manchester schools, and high and dry orthodox schools, here are the strangest phantasms, new and old, sane and insane, starting up suddenly into live practical power, to give their prosaic theories the lie-Popish conversions, Mormonisms, Mesmerisms, Californias, Continental revolutions, Paris days of June. . . . . . Ye hypocrites! ye can discern the face of the sky, and yet ye cannot discern the signs of this time![67]

If Luke in the original had enjoyed a fair amount of sympathy from his creator, in the book version he mainly met with condemnation and is placed in the same class as his father-confessor Padre Bugiardo. This is underscored when Lancelot has to warn Luke that "there is a prejudice against the truthfulness of Romish priests and Romish converts."[68] When it turns out that Luke is unwilling to inform his father of his conversion, Kingsley proves the reality of what he had taken care to define as prejudice. Although such notions were clear from *The Saint's Tragedy*, these additions to *Yeast* in 1851 suggest that it was increasingly Kingsley's wish to establish the truth of the early-Victorian commonplace that saw Roman Catholics as essentially effeminate and hypocritical, and Anglican Protestants as 'manly' and true. Here we have all the ingredients for the confrontation with Newman that exploded publicly thirteen years later.

The denouement of the 1851 version of the novel was reworked along similar terms. Kingsley defends himself by asserting that he "can foresee many criticisms, and those not unreasonable ones, on this little book—let it be some excuse at least for me, that I have foreseen them. Readers will complain, I doubt not, of the very mythical and mysterious dénouement of a story which began by things so gross and palpable as field-sports and pauperism. But is it not true that, sooner or later, 'omnia exeunt in mysterium?'."[69] Notwithstanding this apologia, Kingsley introduced substantial changes to make the ending of his novel more credible. The prophet no longer remains anonymous but is now called Barnakill, a name of Gaelic origin, *Barr na cille*, and which stands for 'summit of the church.' Kingsley might also have played on the resemblance in the word to 'bairn ne kill' (children not killed), as he specifies that the prophet

---

[67] *Y* 261–2.
[68] *Y* 130.
[69] *Y* 311.

"save[s] the children alive whom European society leaves carelessly and ignorantly to die."[70] Having taken some of Ludlow's criticism to heart, the novel no longer ends with the mere announcement of the mystic departure for Prester John's country either. Twelve pages were added to explain why Lancelot will undertake such a "fearful journey." He is first urged to reason logically from experience to believe that he, like Tregarva, has a Father who loves him "in spite of his sin."[71] But although Lancelot remains sceptical about whether that knowledge is what he inwardly thirsted for—"Who is He to whom you ask me to turn? [. . .] I do not want cold abstract necessities of logic: I want living practical facts"[72]—Barnakill finally succeeds in "appeal[ing] to common sense and logic," and asks him to apply Baconian induction to his inquiry by gauging his ideals against the practical evidence of Prester John's country, from which he will bring home a message for England "which might help to unravel the tangled web of this strange time"[73] and the proof that a nation might be "all that England might be and is not."[74] To minimize the gap between the practical reality of England in 1851 and the vaguely utopian vision of Prester John's country, Kingsley adds that

> you will hear nothing new; you shall only see what you, and all around you, have known and not done, known and done. We have no peculiar doctrines or systems; the old creeds are enough for us. But we have obeyed the teaching which we received in each and every age, and allowed ourselves to be built up, generation by generation—as the rest of Christendom might have done—into a living temple, on the foundation which is laid already, and other than which no man can lay.[75]

When a bewildered Lancelot asks about this foundation, he gets the emphatic answer that it is "Jesus Christ—THE MAN." And as if this is still not satisfactory, Kingsley adds in the epilogue that he cannot say whether Lancelot and his spiritual guide

> have yet reached the country of Prester John; whether, indeed, that Caucasian Utopia has a local and bodily existence, or was only used by Barnakill to shadow out that Ideal which is, as he said of the

---

[70] *Y* 297.
[71] *Y* 300.
[72] *Y* 301.
[73] *Y* 297.
[74] *Y* 308.
[75] *Y* 309.

Garden of Eden, always near us, underlying the Actual, as the spirit does the body, exhibiting itself step by step through all the falsehoods and confusions of history and society.[76]

The religious ideal embodied in Christ-the-Man implied that man and the godhead had fundamental essences in common, which Kingsley had sensed in his spiritual and physical cravings. As we have seen, the organic and human which descend to the cradle of mankind in Alton Locke's dream were symbolically represented against a background of volcanic processes and eruptions of dark and unknown forces from the depths of the earth. That Kingsley saw the volcano as a symbol of creative (primordial) energy and instinct, with all its sexual connotations, is confirmed by his use of it in *Yeast*. The return to a primordial creative force was hinted at in the 1848 description of Prester John's country as "volcanic mountain ranges," where the earth's "bosom still heaves with the creative energy of youth, around the primeval cradle of the most ancient race of men." In 1851, how-ever, Kingsley wanted to give more prominence to this idea, as he suggests that, in the nineteenth century, they might all the time have been "over a volcano's mouth." There is a dubious attempt to link this to the title of his novel. Initially only two direct explanations were given for the title, namely that the novel was about questions that "are fermenting in the minds of the young of this day" and that "a wise man he will be able to bake for himself with" this yeast. These lines were kept in the book edition, but Kingsley added in the 1851 epilogue, directly addressing the reader:

> Do not young men think, speak, act, just now, in this very incoher-ent, fragmentary way; without methodic education or habits of thought; with the various stereotyped systems which they have received by tra-dition, breaking up under them like ice in a thaw; with a thousand facts and notions, which they know not how to classify, pouring in on them like a flood?—a very Yeasty state of mind altogether.[77]

The fermentation of yeast bears similarities to lava streams erupting from a volcanic crater, and just as the "the roaring of the fires within, the rattling of the cinders down the heaving slope" in *Alton Locke*[78] were a prelude to creation sequences of life, so the yeasty thawing

---

[76] *Y* 321.
[77] *Y* 312.
[78] *AL* 335.

ice-water invokes a picture of a primordial life-breeding miasma at
the bottom of creation:

> like a mountain burn in a spring rain, carrying with it stones, sticks,
> peat-water, addle grouse-eggs and drowned kingfishers, fertilising salts
> and vegetable poisons—not, alas! without a large crust, here and there,
> of sheer froth. Yet no heterogeneous confused flood-deposit, no fertile
> meadow below. And no high water, no fishing. It is in the long black
> droughts, when the water is foul from lowness, and not from height,
> that Hydras and Desmidae, and Rotifers, and all uncouth pseudor-
> ganisms, bred of putridity, begin to multiply, and the fish are sick for
> want of a fresh, and the cunningest artificial fly is of no avail, and
> the shrewdest angler will do nothing—except with a gross fleshly gilt-
> tailed worm, or the cannibal bait of roe, whereby parent fishes, like
> competitive barbarisms, devour each other's flesh and blood—perhaps
> their own. It is when the stream is clearing after a flood, that the fish
> will rise . . .[79]

A return to a dark primordial state is presented in *Yeast* as much as
a prerogative to regeneration as it was in *Alton Locke*.

VIII

When we bear in mind that Kingsley worked simultaneously on the
early instalments of "Bible Politics" for *The Christian Socialist* and on
his revision of *Yeast*, it is not surprising that affinities should emerge
between these writings. The addition of some of the material in the
last chapter invites comparison with the answers to Holyoake about
the existence of God in the early instalments of "Bible Politics" and
it is plausible that Kingsley's insistence here owes much to Holyoake's
perplexities regarding the existence of God. After all, the purpose of
the novel and the articles was just that.

Another parallel is also worth singling out. The tendency to describe
and interpret the development of society against the background of
the principles of natural history emerges powerfully. In the epilogue
of *Yeast*, Kingsley unequivocally offers the possibility of a universal
catastrophic system:

---

[79] *Y* 312–3.

What if the method whereon things have proceeded since the creation were, as geology as well as history proclaims, a cataclysmic method? What then? Why should not this age, as all others like it have done, end in a cataclysm, and a prodigy, and a mystery? And why should not my little book do likewise?[80]

This passage singles Kingsley out as a catastrophist, believing the earth to have come into existence through a series of sudden and violent changes, rather than a uniformitarianist, but he makes equally clear that in his view of (deep) time, catastrophes are part of the economy of a cyclical system.

Kingsley then moves to the micro-mechanisms working within such a system. The description of the village revel is of particular significance for the work as a Condition-of-England-novel. Kingsley had already remarked in *Fraser's* on the speech of the rural labourers as "half articulate, nasal, guttural, like the speech of savages." In the novel Lancelot is equally struck by their physiognomy, "by the lofty and ample development of brain in at least one half. There were intellects there—or rather capacities of intellect, capable, surely, of anything, had not the promise of the brow been almost always belied by the loose and sensual lower features." This argued that "they were evidently rather a degraded than an undeveloped race."[81] That Kingsley felt the need to insert this in his description shows that by 1851 he had firmly come to believe in the theory of degradation as a devolution of the species as outlined more in detail in his pieces for *The Christian Socialist*. That the labourers' speech was to Lancelot a "half-formed growl, as of a company of seals" is of course not just descriptive. Animal imagery to describe the social condition is indeed prevalent in the novel. The relics of promising features in a degraded race "testify against that society which carelessly wastes her most precious wealth, the manhood of her masses."[82] The Malthusian question, as we have seen in his articles for *The Christian Socialist*, was closely connected to such thinking. This was already apparent in 1848 when, after the experience of the fair, Kingsley attributed to Lancelot these thoughts:

---

[80] *Y* 312.
[81] *Y* 205.
[82] *Y* 206.

> A long silence followed, as they paced on past lonely farm-yards, from
> which the rich manure-water was draining across the road in foul black
> streams, festering and steaming in the chill night air. Lancelot sighed
> as he saw the fruitful materials of food running to waste, and thought
> of the "over-population" cry; and then he looked across to the miles
> of brown moorland on the opposite side of the valley, that lay idle
> and dreary under the autumn moon, except where here and there a
> squatter's cottage and rood of fruitful garden gave the lie to the lazi-
> ness and ignorance of man, who pretends that it is not worth his while
> to cultivate the soil which God has given him.

This passage was introduced in *Fraser's* to press the importance of
sanitary reform. As Lancelot is approaching a typhus-stricken cottage, and notices the "filthy open drain running right before the
door," the story of the Nun's Pool is revealed to Lancelot (and to
the reader). The moment is of pivotal importance for the plot. A
"presentiment of evil hung over him" as Lancelot witnessed the desolation. Of course, Argemone's doom is sealed in this instant, and
as at the end of the passage Lancelot finds out he has lost all his
fortune, he is firmly set on his path of conversion. Although the passage works well enough as it stood in the original version, Kingsley
seems in 1851 to want to highlight the Malthusian implication of it
by adding:

> Everywhere waste? Waste of manure, waste of land, waste of muscle,
> waste of brain, waste of population—and we call ourselves the work-
> shop of the world![83]

The parallels between the additions that Kingsley wrote for the novel
version of *Yeast* in 1851 and the various themes he touched on in
"Thoughts on the Frimley Murder," "Bible Politics," and "The
Church *versus* Malthus" confirm the fact that notions of (d)evolution
(and its related analysis of over-population and the survival of the
fittest) increasingly impinged on Kingsley's social thought in this
period. It is also clear that Kingsley's idea of progress was grounded
in the realization of manhood and work.

---

[83] *Y* 220.

IX

With the publication in book-form, Kingsley's first novel reached a much greater reading public than it did in *Fraser's Magazine*. It also meant greater public visibility for its author.

Yeast got a fair share of reviews in the national papers, the first of which came out on 22 March in *The Spectator*. The novel still appeared a "series of sketches, loosely strung together," a comment that most reviewers would make, but the purpose of the novel was much appreciated "as a life-like picture of the heavings of the mass, and the mental fermentation going on among individuals—of the yeast of society—the book displays great ability, and challenges careful attention."[84] *The Athenæum* followed a month later, and while it regretted the author's vehement expression, which is a "moral and logical weakness," it conceded that he had "a clear idea of what he wants to say." *The Athenæum* was ultimately positive: "truth must be uttered in every variety of speech and language, to convey its meaning to all. Honour to every man who does his part in the work of social reform in a true and fearless spirit."[85] This was an encouraging reception which seemed to prove to Kingsley that he had been right from the outset to insist on the republication of *Yeast* in novel form. After the success of *Alton Locke*, *Yeast* too fared well. A continental copyright edition was brought out by Bernard Tauchnitz, who announced it as "by the author of Alton Locke." Although *Yeast* was published anonymously, by this time is was public knowledge that it was by the same hand as that of the anonymous author of *Alton Locke*, and that this hand was the Rev. Charles Kingsley's.

As the author of two Condition-of-England novels, Kingsley increasingly started to attract attention in America. *Yeast* was published there by Harper and Brothers in April and was enthusiastically received by *The International Magazine* and *The American Whig Review*. Charles Dana, editor of the American newspaper *The Tribune*, had come in March with a "most liberal offer as to remuneration" and asked Kingsley to contribute with a new work on the social conditions of the nineteenth century, to be published in instalments. But, having

---

[84] *The Spectator*, 22/3/51, pp. 281–2.
[85] [Jewsbury] 428.

solved his financial problems with the Crowdy loan, Kingsley found himself in a position to decline the offer, as he deemed the novel which he had started writing (*Hypatia*) "hardly fit for your columns." Moreover, he no longer wanted to write "to order," being "a peculiarly slow workman in the process of elucubration," requiring a new subject to "welter & toss about in my head for months before I dare to put pen to paper." Instead, he recommended Froude to Dana as "one of the most perfect masters of English prose whom we possess."[86]

During the spring of 1851 Kingsley, Lees, and Hughes had been talking about plans to go trout-fishing for two days around Newbury, near where Hughes's father had bought a priory in 1833. Now, with Crowdy's money coming and the recent success of *Yeast*, Kingsley felt elated and exclaimed to Hughes that he was "thirst[ing] for the Newbury trout." An invitation for the Kingsleys to the Hughes family house at Donnington followed promptly. Thanking Hughes and his mother for the kind invitation, Mrs Kingsley, however, preferred to stay at Eversley. "[She] very seldom stirs from the house, & can hardly do it right now," her husband explained. Hughes was given elaborate instructions as to which flies (emphasizing that a brass minnow "is *the* gun trick here") to bring down from London for him and Lees, who, no doubt like he himself, was "with-of-trout-destroying-impossible-&-premature-dreams besmit." There was plenty of work to be done, such as preparing a lecture to be delivered to working men on 28 May, but first of all "I will fish."[87] That Kingsley felt comparatively buoyant by this time is also brought out by a small boisterous sketch that was added at the bottom of his letter to Hughes, showing a man with a scoop-net who runs to assist Kingsley, who has at least a four pounder on the hook.

But the popularity acquired by writing on "socialism" was inevitably going to cause adverse reactions from other parties. During the second week of May the bubble of triumph had started to burst. A devastating review of *Yeast* in the influential *Guardian* called for a letter to the editor, which was duly inserted on 21 May. In it Kingsley accused the reviewer of selective quoting to distort the moral of his novel, although he found that the specific allegations brought against him in the review were too outrageous to be worthy of detailed

---

[86] CK to Charles Dana, 24/3/1851, Martin (1950) 237–8.
[87] CK to TH, May 1851, Martin (1950) 244.

reply. Rather, with Father Valerian's answer to the Jesuits in Blaise
Pascal's *Lettres provinciales* (n. 15), he repeated three times "mentiris
impudentissimé," showing the extent of his exasperation.[88]

Hiding behind an anonymous "we", the reviewer of this high-
church paper, John Duke Coleridge, had vented sharp condemnation of both the novel and of Kingsley's morals. The book was to
him "a trashy and mischievous production." Of course, he knew that
it was written by the author of *Alton Locke*. But he posed as if he
were the first to find this out and to discover, moreover, that *Yeast*
had been written before *Alton Locke* (information which could easily
be gleaned from the preface): "otherwise," he wrote, "it would argue
not only a great declension of power and taste; but what is worse,
a declension in moral tone, and in definiteness and reality of religious faith and religious feeling."[89] Insult was added to this: there is
a tendency in the book, he maintained, to imply that "a certain
amount of youthful profligacy does no real and permanent harm to
the character: perhaps strengthens it for a useful and even religious
life; and that the existence of the passions is a proof that they are
to be gratified." And he concludes with a last shot that the author
of *Yeast* "has so skilfully and elaborately disguised his religion that
those who are best acquainted with the old one could discern no
traces of it in his."[90] Coleridge confessed in 1880 to Mrs Kingsley
that he was the author of this vicious review.

Relationships with *The Guardian* had suddenly and unexpectedly
deteriorated. In February it started a series of articles on the work
of the Christian Socialists in which it expressed itself essentially sympathetic to the movement—"we are with them in their labours"—
but it regretted that they sought to define their ideal of brotherhood
in terms of "socialism" and "cooperative principles." Notwithstanding
The Guardian's criticism of this approach, Kingsley, in a letter to its
editor, expressed his desire to cooperate with members of the so-
called high-church school, and Maurice, in two articles in *The Christian
Socialist*, reacted warmly to such "interest expressed in our operations"
by the religious press.[91] Maurice explained why "we have connected

[88] *LML* i.283–4.
[89] [Coleridge] 331.
[90] [Coleridge] 332.
[91] "The *Guardian* and Christian Socialism" 22/3/1851 *ChSoc* i.161.

the word Christian with Socialism."[92] The appreciation of an influential
church organ was encouraging. But the review of *Yeast* changed all
that. Kingsley's protest of "mentiris impudentissimé" in his letter to
the editor was answered in the same issue of *The Guardian* by the
blunt declaration that the Christian Socialists were henceforth to be
seen as "our opponents." Although they "had hoped at one time,
that this writer and others of his school, were, in a sense, fellow
labourers with us in the same great cause," they concluded that "that
delusion is now no longer possible." This aroused Maurice's ire.
Kingsley was right in wishing cooperation with High Churchmen,
he writes on the front-page of *The Christian Socialist* of 14 June.
Although they "are fullest of what seems to me crotchets, pettiness,
narrowness," they still are "a most precious and indispensable element in the English Church."[93] But Kingsley was wrong to court
The Guardian in this, because its party spirit "bring[s] out that which
is most disputatious, most evil, most untrue, in those who patronize
it, to weaken and undermine all those elements in it which might
make them fellow-workers with men of other schools for the good
of the whole nation." A newspaper like *The Guardian*, he continued,
"lives, therefore, for the promotion of self-deception and flattery."[94]
And in defence of Kingsley's novel, he added that its author had
nobly undertaken to show that the revelation of God contained in
the scriptures is "more capable of being presented as a Gospel to
the heart and conscience of suffering and sinful men of all classes,
than the different explanations of that revelation which are contained
in the theories and systems of our different parties."[95] Kingsley had
done so without "suppressing or altering facts which he knows to
exist, not hiding the weakness and sins of those who deal with them"
with the hope "that what he has said will reach the hearts of those
for whose sake it is spoken."[96] Maurice was rarely as eloquent as in
this article. However, notwithstanding the fact that he signed the
article with his own name, and notwithstanding the expression of
solidarity with which he concluded it (to him *The Guardian*'s "declaration of war against our friend" included all of "us, the Christian

---

[92] "The *Guardian* and Christian Socialism II" 5/4/1851 *ChSoc* i.178.
[93] "The Author of 'Yeast' and the *Guardian*" 14/6/1851 *ChSoc* i.257.
[94] "The Author of 'Yeast' and the *Guardian*" 14/6/1851 *ChSoc* i.257.
[95] "The Author of 'Yeast' and the *Guardian*" 14/6/1851 *ChSoc* i.257.
[96] "The Author of 'Yeast' and the *Guardian*" 14/6/1851 *ChSoc* i.258.

Socialists"), the affair was a heavy blow for Kingsley's reputation in the Church of England, and one from which it took him years to recover.

X

Although Kingsley felt keenly hurt by the attack in *The Guardian*, this public incident was followed up by another that was humiliating rather than infuriating. The Rev. G.S. Drew of St John's in Charlotte Street had decided on a series of discourses on the "Church and its Message to Different Orders of Society." Generally he had a congregation of young professional men, but as at the time many working men came to London for the Great Exhibition, he thought it opportune to address these workers specifically. He had followed with interest the movement around Maurice and asked him in late Spring to preach on one of these Sunday evenings. As he had also felt impressed by Kingsley's works, he asked Maurice if he could help to secure Kingsley for a sermon as well. Maurice proposed a sermon on the message of the church to labouring men and Kingsley agreed to another. Drew "intimated the most cordial approval of it" and had an advertisement placed on the front page of *The Times* announcing the sermon for 22 June.

Kingsley did not come up from Eversley in vain. A large congregation of mainly working men turned up to listen to the author of *Yeast*. Kingsley preached on Luke 4.18–19 and started by asserting that "the business for which God sends a Christian priest in a Christian nation, is to preach and practise liberty, equality, and brotherhood." The revolutionary stand imminent in these words was maintained throughout his subsequent explanation of the "acceptable year" as "one of the wisest of Moses' institutions, by which, at the expiration of a certain period, all debtors and bond-servants were released." Kingsley stressed that this was an "unparalleled contrivance for preventing the accumulation of large estates, and the reduction of the people into the state of serfs and day-labourers." When Kingsley halted a moment before moving on to give the blessing, Drew rose and addressed his congregation: "I have a duty to perform," he is reported to have said, "I must and do protest against much that he has said as extremely impudent and untrue. I may say, also, it is altogether different to what I had been led to expect." The excitement of the congregation was intense, and an eye-witness who wrote the next day to Mrs Kingsley attested that it was difficult to contain "knots of working men, who were beginning to hiss, or otherwise testify their disapproval."[97] Kingsley, however, managed to control himself and did not reply to the accusation the incumbent had thrown at him in front of the congregation, but bowed his head and left the pulpit, "passed straight through the crowd that thronged him with out-stretched hands," and never said a single word. "If he had," the eye-witness avowed, "I do not know what might have happened [. . .] a word from Charles, or, indeed, from any one on his behalf, might have raised such a storm as God only could have quelled."[98]

Biographers have explained Drew's crude intervention as a protest against the socialism in Kingsley's message. This is difficult to sustain. Drew knew from Kingsley's writing what to expect and was perfectly aware of the slant of the men who called themselves Christian Socialists. It is unlikely that it was this part that Drew objected to and which was so different from what he had been led to expect. It was more probably the following passage in Kingsley's sermon that made Drew's hair stand on end: "if you wish to know what the message of the Church really is, you must put out of your heads what the clergy of this particular time or of any other particular time may happen to say it is."

John Martineau recorded years later how Kingsley returned to Eversley the day after the sermon, "wearied and worn out, obliged to stop and rest and refresh himself at a house in his parish during his afternoon's walk" and that "that same evening he brought in a song that he had written, the 'Three Fishers,' as though it were the outcome of it all; and then he seemed able to put the matter aside."[99]

But the decision on Monday night to put the matter aside was premature. *The Daily News* on the following Tuesday used the episode to show that this was the result of the leniency Bishop Blomfield of London practised towards the clergy in his diocese and that he had better intervene if he did not want to deprive "himself of all moral respect and influence." The affair dragged on in the press. Again two days later, *The English Churchman*, while admitting not having

---

[97] *LML* i.290.
[98] *LML* i.290.
[99] John Martineau to FK, 24/12/1875, *LML* i.304.

read *Alton Locke*, concluded that its author was a rather "conceited, literary, intellectual young man" of "dubious principles." Friends had taken the sermon from Kingsley's hands as he left the church after Drew's declaration of disapproval, and they made sure it was printed to counter the many rumours that were growing daily. Not surprisingly, Blomfield was worried, and requested Kingsley to suspend any preaching in his diocese. Unfortunately Blomfield's letter does not survive, but from Kingsley's answer we can gather that the Bishop was distressed and perplexed rather than outraged. Kingsley thanked him "for the considerate & kind tone of [his letter]," and expressed "his sorrow for having, however innocently or unconsciously, added a moment's trouble to your Lordship's numerous anxieties." But not being aware of having said anything contrary to the doctrine or discipline of the Church of England, he made bold to send the bishop a copy of the sermon, as he felt "most deeply pained at finding that any hearsay report shd. have given you an impression of my sermon, quite contrary to that wh. the perusal of it will, I trust, & hope, produce in your Lordship's mind." And concluding his polite and balanced appeal, he asked Blomfield to "reconsider his request, & thus relieve me from my present delicate & humiliating position." Although the word "humiliating" was crossed out before the letter was sealed, its original presence shows its author's true feelings on the matter.

Blomfield read the sermon, and Kingsley was asked to see him at London House, where he met with a kind reception. The bishop was satisfied on all points, and the ban on preaching in his diocese was immediately lifted. Still, the experience was not easily forgotten by Kingsley or his friends. Amazingly, five months later the affair was still discussed. A reader of the *The Spectator* defended Kingsley's sermon in a letter to the editor and emphasized that after all the bishop had not objected to it.[100] Drew felt called upon to reply in turn that he had not remonstrated with Kingsley to the bishop, and that the bishop had never publicly prohibited Kingsley to preach in the diocese.[101] These two late reactions show how many rumours were still circulating.

---

[100] T.C.D., "The Christian Socialists," *The Spectator*, 15/11/1851, p. 1093.
[101] G.S. Drew, "Mr. Kingsley's Case," *The Spectator*, 29/11/1851, p. 1141.

But if the whole affair did much damage to Kingsley's reputation among his brethren of the cloth, and especially amongst its more conservative components, it made him highly popular with working men. Mrs Kingsley recorded in her biography how "letters of sympathy poured in from all quarters, from a few of the clergy, from many of the laity, and from numbers of working men."[102] Before Blomfield could lift the ban on Kingsley's preaching many of the latter met on Kennington Common and came with the proposal to start a "free church independent of episcopal rule, with a promise of a huge following," while the secretary of the John Street Lecture Hall, where Chartists and freethinkers met regularly, offered their premises. But acceptance, Kingsley and his friends realized, would link the Christian Socialists to freethinkers and make them suspect in the public eye. "As a churchman, such a suspicion would be intolerable to me," he wrote courteously but decisively, and he declined the "kind" offer.[103]

Exasperation with the controversies began to show through. When his parents asked him to join them on their holidays for a couple of weeks in Germany, Kingsley was glad to find a respite from the troublesome English scene. In 1848 he had buoyantly proclaimed that it was necessary for the people's cause to provoke and offend. By July 1851 he had fully experienced what that meant.

---

[102] CK to the Secretary of the John Street Lecture Hall, 26/6/1851, *LML* i.291.
[103] CK to the Secretary of the John Street Lecture Hall, 26/6/1851, *LML* i.291.

CHAPTER TEN

HE BADE HER CHANGE HER NUN'S DRESS
(JULY–DECEMBER 1851)

William Makepeace Thackeray, setting out with his family for their holiday to Weimar, crossed a stormy Channel to Antwerp on 10 July 1851. Anne Thackeray, the novelist's daughter, recorded in her memoirs, that it was a "sleety summer morning" and that, when they boarded a wet and slippery packet-boat at London Bridge, they were "kindly greeted by a family group already established there, an elderly gentleman in clerical dress and a lady sitting with an umbrella in the drizzle of rain and falling smuts from the funnel." The thirteen-year-old girl soon discovered that this was the Rector of Chelsea going abroad for health reasons and that he was accompanied by his wife and two sons Charles and Henry, both wearing "brown felt hats with very high and pointed crowns, and with very broad rims." But as the sea got rougher every minute, and most passengers started to feel sea-sick, conversation became impossible. Anne sat by Mrs Kingsley, feeling miserable and uncomfortable in the rough sea and anxious about her luggage. Still, she could not but watch "in a dazed and hypnotised sort of way the rim of Charles Kingsley's wide-awake as it rose and fell against the horrible horizon" as he "stood before us holding on to some ropes, and the steamer pitched and tossed." "I remember," she wrote in 1894, "that proud and eager head, and that bearing so full of character and energy."[1]

The trip to Germany was Charles Kingsley's first crossing to the continent. His parents had planned a two-month trip going down the Rhine from Cologne to Ems, and up the Moselle to Trier, visiting the celebrated sites and famed Kurhäuser on the route. Henry came down from Oxford for the summer holidays to join them, and as Fanny preferred to stay with relatives in England, the two brothers spent a great deal of time together. Although there was a difference

---

[1] Anne Thackeray Ritchie, *Chapters from Some Memoirs* (London: Macmillan, 1894) 101–8.

of eleven years, Henry had reached an age that made true companionship possible between the two, especially as both thoroughly
enjoyed physical exercise. Henry had enrolled at Worcester College
the previous year and turned into a young man who "gave himself
up to athletics and social pleasures."[2] His physical prowess was
described in his seeing a victorious boating race as the finality of
life itself: "He would fain fall back in his outrigger and expire suddenly at the close of a triumphant match with a champion sculler
of the whole universe. To perish of violent delight as his boat shot
past the goal, three clear lengths ahead of the universal champion's
outrigger, as the acclamations for the conqueror rent the air and
rose to the blue sky, would be a blissful exit."[3] Although much of
this must have been to the elder brother's liking (compare, for example, the description of the oarsmen in the boating episode in *Alton
Locke*), there was a darker aspect to Henry's life-style. As the boating sentiment shows, athletics was everything to him. Unlike Charles's
ideal masculinity, in his there was no space for Christianity. Moreover,
he utterly wasted his time at university and was eventually to leave
without a degree. He was also an excessive smoker (which would
later cause the throat cancer that killed him in 1876 at the premature age of 46), ran into debt, and showed some latent homosexuality in declaring himself, as a member of the Fez Club, to be a
hater of woman-kind. His elder brother could not but disapprove of
such behaviour and sentiments, and one can easily imagine the horror he must have felt when the rumour went round in Oxford that
the Fez Club was an society for the abolition of marriage which
advocated free love. However, Henry seemed a hearty enough fellow
and contemporaries who knew him at Oxford described him as
"always generous, manly, and of an inner temper nobler than his
external manners."[4]

The Kingsley family moved from Antwerp to Cologne and then
spent two weeks visiting the famous places along the Rhine from
Bonn up to Bad Ems. There was much that Charles wanted to see.
In Cologne, Wilhelm von Kaulbach's new stained-glass windows
impressed him, and the head of the Virgin in Koloffs' triptych made
him cry "like a child." And then there were the numerous castles

---

[2] Ellis 32.
[3] John Cordy Jeaffreson, in Ellis 33.
[4] Sir Edwin Arnold, in Ellis 32.

along the Rhine. The ruin Drachenfels just south of Bonn did not "overpower" him the way the Rolandseck Tower, right opposite, and the isle of Nonnenwerth did. Kingsley responded to the legend attached to the scene, which tells that when Roland was falsely reported fallen in battle, his betrothed retired to the convent Nonnenwerth on an island in the Rhine, and that, when he returned, Roland built the castle which now bears his name on the hills over the river so as to be able to watch constantly the place which harboured his inaccessible love. "*And that story*:—it seemed quite awful to find oneself in presence of it," Kingsley admitted to Fanny.[5] The powerful impression it made on Kingsley did not, of course, stem from his sentimental nature alone, but the tragically romantic story of Roland and his bride stirred intense memories of his own courtship of Fanny and her plans to enter a sisterhood. Roland's bride's untimely and hasty retirement to a nunnery was therefore more than just a tragic story to Kingsley.

For other reasons, the many ruins, symbols of former despotic times, contrasted with the fine sloping vineyards produced by diligent work—"every rock-ledge and narrow path of soil tossing its golden tendrils to the sun, gray with ripening clusters"[6]—that Kingsley saw a perfect symbol of the Chartist cause in them, which inspired him to write the following poem, "A Thought from the Rhine":

> I heard an Eagle crying all alone
> Above the vineyards through the summer night,
> Among the skeletons of robber towers:
> Because the ancient eyrie of his race
> Was trenched and walled by busy-handed men;
> And all his forest-chace and woodland wild,
> Wherefrom he fed his young with hare and roe,
> Were trim with grapes which swelled from hour to hour,
> And tossed their golden tendrils to the sun
> For joy at their own riches:—So, I thought,
> The great devourers of the earth shall sit,
> Idle and impotent, they know not why,
> Down-staring from their barren height of state
> On nations grown too wise to slay and slave,
> The puppets of the few; while peaceful lore
> And fellow-help make glad the heart of earth,

---

[5] CK to FK, 1/8/1851, *LML* i.292.
[6] *TYA* 397.

With wonders which they fear and hate, as he,
The Eagle, hates the vineyard slopes below.

Keeping the Kurort Ems in the dukedom of Nassau as their base, the two brothers went on excursions in the area. They went down "through cultivated lands, corn and clover, flax and beet, and all the various crops with which the industrious German yeoman ekes out his little patch of soil. Past the thrifty husbandman himself, as he guides the two milch-kine in his tiny plough, and stops at the furrow's end, to greet you with the hearty German smile and bow; while the little fair-haired maiden, walking beneath the shade of standard cherries, walnuts, and pears, all gay with fruit, fills the cows' mouths with chicory, and wild carnations, and pink saintfoin."[7] This idealistic perception of the German field labourer inspired Kingsley to express his socialist ideas in the poem above, and explains why Ehrenbreitstein, possibly then Europe's strongest fortress, "utterly disappointed" him. "The lying painters paint it just three times as high as it is, and I was quite shocked to find it so small," he complained to Fanny. On the other hand, it was Sonneck Castle, more to the south at Trechtingshausen, that fully caught his imagination, and which he thought "worth [. . .] all the other castles put together."[8] In after years, Kingsley responded more fully to the imposing military excellence of Ehrenbreitstein. In 1857 the description in *Two Years Ago* of one of its characters' wanderings from Ems to Koblenz was based on his own wanderings in the area with Henry. Coming down into a glen, the visitor pauses in awe, when he sees on his right "slope up the bare slate downs, up to the foot of cliffs" above which "gray slate ledges rise cliffs of man's handwork, pierced with a hundred square black embrasures; and above them the long barrack-ranges of a soldiers' town; which a foeman stormed once, when it was young: but what foeman will ever storm it again? What conqueror's foot will ever tread again upon the 'broad stone of honour,' and call Ehrenbreitstein his?"[9]

The two brothers went up the Rhine to Bingen by steamer, slept at Assmannshausen, and walked to St Goar on the right bank of the river, crossed and walked back on the other bank. Charles "scrambled up the face of the Lurlei to the nymph's own seat, and picked"

[7] *TYA* 396–7.
[8] CK to FK, 1/8/1851, i.292–3.
[9] *TYA* 397.

Fanny a little bouquet. They went fishing at Dausenau, caught "unspeakable butterflies" between Braubach and Marksburg, found numerous species of plants that were new to Charles, but "keeping them was no good, so I just picked specimens, and looked at them till I knew them thoroughly, and went on regretful."[10] The natural scenery and richness dazzled Kingsley while around him "the bright-eyed lizards hunt flies along the roasting walls, and the great locusts buzz and pitch and leap; green locusts with red wings, and gray locusts with blue wings [..] and the great 'purple emperors' come down to drink in the road puddles, and sit fearlessly, flashing off their velvet wing a blue as that empyrean which is 'dark by excess of light'."[11]

II

The Rhine Province had lived up to his highest expectations: "As for what I have seen and felt, I cannot tell you," he reported to Fanny, "it is all beautiful—beautiful. That vast rushing, silent river, those yellow vine slopes, and azure hills behind, with the thunder clouds lowering over their heads—beautiful; and the air! I have felt new nerves, as well as new eyes, ever since Cologne, the wonderful freshness and transparency of the colouring, and the bracing balminess of the atmosphere, make e understand now at once why people prefer this to England; there is no denying it." However, the separation from Fanny sorely pressed him. It was of some consolation that he could visit, and write about, the places she had visited in 1841 when they had been separated for the first time. It helped to appease the guilt he felt in enjoying such a beautiful country. "My comfort is that you have seen it already,"[12] he wrote in one letter, and in another: "it is delightful to think that you know it all! That thought recurs to me continually."[13] But the separation from Fanny, brought with it his intense physical longings for her body, and daily messages of passionate love were dispatched. In a letter from Ems his sexual frustration is manifest:

---

[10] CK to FK, 1/8/1851, i.293.
[11] *TYA* 397–8, 396.
[12] CK to FK, 1/8/1851, i.292.
[13] CK to FK, 1/8/1851, i.293.

> You do not seem to recollect how dreadfully I long for you in *body*—
> as well as mind. I kiss those two locks of hair till I am ready to cry,
> & think of you *all day long*—I don't believe you are out of my head
> for half an hour together by day—& I am always talking about you,
> & at night, unless I have walked myself tired, I cannot sleep for think-
> ing of you, & if I wake I begin longing & thinking & picturing you
> to myself.[14]

The language and import of this passage are not only reminiscent
of the letters they wrote in the early days of their courtship, but
even their mutual device of being imaginatively present in one
another's absence is evoked by the phrase "picturing you to myself."
A more ritualistic enactment of their sexual intimacy existed in kissing the two locks of hair: "I kiss *both* locks of hair every time I open
my desk—but the little curly one seems to bring me nearest to you."[15]
Now that he was away from her, visiting the very places she had
visited without him during their desperate days of passionate courtship
often brought the early days of the consummation of their marriage
to his mind:

> Oh that I were with you, or rather you with me here, & the beds are
> so small that we should be forced to lie inside each other, & the
> weather is so hot that you might run about naked all day, as well *as
> all night*—cela va sans dire! Oh those naked nights at Chelsea! How
> the memory of them haunts me yet! When will they come again?[16]

Although the associations with their days of courtship might have
come naturally, the insistence on repeating their early sexual bliss
might also indicate a latent fear of losing such perfect fulfilment with
age. Maybe Fanny, who was increasingly absorbed by a growing a
family, did not always respond to her husband's passion with the
same intensity.[17] To one of her letters from England he hastens to
specify that

> I fear you may think mine too exclusively physical—that I love your
> body—rather than your mind. But it is not so—only I cannot & will
> not analyze. I love *thee*—& I cannot divide thy body from mind or
> thy mind from thy spirit [...] your body is the sacrament of *you*, and
> thou art one![18]

---

[14] CK to FK, undated, MP-C0171–36914.
[15] CK to FK, 24–5/7/1851, BL-62553 f.210r.
[16] CK to FK, 24–5/7/1851, BL-62553 f.210r.
[17] Cf. Maynard 97.
[18] CK to FK, [23/8/1851], MP-C0171–36914.

It would be too much to say that there was a cooling of love on her part. When Charles came with the idea of a "second honeymoon," she readily joined her husband in planning to share a room in Chelsea upon his return, to which he enthusiastically responded: "I think your Chelsea plan is most excellent [. . .] but we must sleep without a dressing room, wh. of course will make you blush very much, & as my mother expresses it, 'wallow in each other's arms all night in a very narrow bed' but I do not think we shall be inclined to sleep very far apart, do you? And then *no nightdress* will take up less room, & there will be so much of us inside each other, that perhaps we shall be able to manage."[19] That Kingsley perceived his ecstatic sexual love for his wife as a sacramental reality made such frankness in his letters possible, and he willingly showed his epistles to his mother, who read them and added the occasional postscript. It was his love and respect for Fanny that made him at times rather impatient with the way his father treated his mother during the trip down the Rhine: "I confess it is hard to keep one's temper, when one sees her so bullied—& yet slaving on."[20]

There were letters to Rose and Maurice, in which Kingsley indulged in his by now idealistic infatuation with Germany. From Ems he wrote to them how opposite his window there was a "school where 300 little German children come every day, with knap-sacks on their backs to carry their books & slates" and how "the other day we had such fun here; it was the birthday of the Duke of Nassau, who is king over all this country, & he is a very good man, & the people are fond of him. So in the morning, all the children came to school, & the boys had flags, some blue & yellow, for Nassau, & some black & white & yellow, for Germany, & the little girls had garlands of flowers & oak-leaves round their heads."[21] In reality, Adolf of Nassau was far from popular in his dukedom, and the German flags waved in a dukedom that was nominally still allied to the Austrian empire belie Kingsley's representation.

[19] CK to FK, undated, BL-62553 f.211r.
[20] CK to FK, undated, MP-C0171–36914.
[21] CK to Rose and Maurice, 27/7/1851, Martin (1950) 250–1.

III

After the first three weeks of the trip, Kingsley's mother reported that her son was "in very rude health, & enjoying everything to the full extent of his powers, moral & physical." But a letter from Fanny saying that she had not yet heard from him, cast him down. Fanny had prepared for him letterheads with the places from which she expected to be written, and through July he had duly sent these letters home. The news, however, that they had been delayed destroyed Charles's happiness: "I have half a mind to come home, for I am so tormented by longing for you, & this has quite upset me," he wrote by return of mail, "[o]f course I wrote to you—There, I have no more to say, except that I wish I was safe at home." In the exasperation and despair of the moment he was unable to say more, and throwing down his pen he concluded the letter with: "I shall get my mother to fill up this sheet, & have a good cry."

This moment of severe disappointment, however, was overcome, partly because Charles and Henry had great plans of going on a week's walking trip in the Eifel. Mr and Mrs Kingsley chose to stay on at Bad Ems before moving to Trier, and Charles and Henry decided to wait no longer and go ahead on foot. As the plan was talked over the week turned into ten days and then into a fortnight. The prospect of "manly" exercise roused Charles from his despondency and three days later he wrote to Fanny: "so we start, and in a fortnight appear at Bonn, with beards, I suppose, as shaving is out of the question."[22] And, of course, that 'sleeping' landscape seen on the horizon from the Taunus mountains as "high in the air [. . .] with its hundred crater peaks"[23] had been beckoning Charles for weeks now.

After a whole day onboard a steamer sailing down the Moselle the brothers disembarked at Alf, and Kingsley felt glad "to find myself on my legs" and rather relieved of escaping from the steamer's "heat and confinement,"[24] and, if we may judge from the fictitious account Kingsley gives in *Two Years Ago*, eager "to jump into a carriage, and trundle up the gorge of the Issbach some six lonely weary miles" till they would at last turn "into the wooded caldron of the

[22] CK to FK, 4/8/1851, *LML* i.294.
[23] *TYA* 398.
[24] CK to FK, 7/8/1851, *LML* i.295.

Romer-kessel, and saw the little chapel crowning the central knoll, with the white high-roofed houses of Bertrich nestling at its foot."[25] From Bad Bertrich they went west toward Manderscheid. Charles walked with a rather heavy two-stone knapsack which contained, he detailed to Fanny, "a knapsack with a plaid, 2 clean shirts, clean trousers, clean brown holland coat, 2 prs of worsted socks, a little paper to write to you *twice* a week, my pipe, fishing tackle, a pair of slippers for the evening [. . .] a little german testament, word-book[,] map of Eifel, & note book [. . .] & *your locks of hair*, in a bag round my neck."[26] The excursion was a big adventure. The volcanic landscape was so dazzling that "craters filled with ghastly blue lakes, with shores of volcanic dust" made them forget time, so that almost right from the beginning of their walking-trip they found themselves somewhere above Manderscheid in complete darkness "at the top of a cliff 500 feet high, with a roaring river at the bottom, and *no* path. So down the cliff-face we had to come in the dark, or sleep in the forest to be eaten by wild-boars and wolves," an experience which "must not be repeated often if we intend to revisit our native shores."[27] But Charles loved it, and the physical exercise was of course to his taste: "I am exceedingly well and strong, though we did dine yesterday off *raw ham, and hock at 9d. a bottle.*—Oh! And had no katzenjammer after it."[28]

They turned toward Gerolstein and Hillesheim, and Kingsley thought it the most wonderful place he had ever been to in his life: "I have been stunned with wonders," he wrote to Fanny, "Mountains fallen in and making great lakes in the midst of corn-land; hills blown up with the wildest perpendicular crags, and roasted into dust; craters with the lips so perfect, that the fire might have been blazing in them twelve months ago; heaps of slag and cinder 2,500 feet above the sea, on which nothing will grow, so burnt are they; lava streams pouring down into the valley, meeting with brooks drying them up, and in the fight foaming up into cliffs, and hurling huge masses of trachyte far into the dells."

Kingsley's dynamic imagination of past volcanic activity in such descriptions is remarkable, and it shows how much the phenomenon

[25] *TYA* 469.
[26] CK to FK, 4/8/1851, MP-C0171–36914.
[27] CK to FK, 7/8/1851, *LML* i.294.
[28] CK to FK, 7/8/1851, *LML* i.295.

captivated him. The emotional quality which it held for him had
been formulated in Alton Locke's dream, where it was not only associated with the earth's generative power, but also with man's own
reproductive energy. As the volcano was to him a powerful representation of his own sexual instincts, which were again to him firmly
embedded in his Christianity, it is not surprising that he felt very
close to the ultimate mystery of life in the Eifel. He did not exag-
gerate when he quoted Dante's "wonderful, wonderful, and yet again
wonderful" in one of his letters, while in another it was "past all
words beautiful and wonderful and awful."[29] Unfortunately not many
of the volcanic specimens he collected could be carried in the knapsack, and "one could have filled a cart—as it was I could only fill
a pair of socks," but it all made a lasting impression. One of Kingsley's
most impressive pieces of description in *Glaucus*, written fully four
years later, makes his charged response to the scene tangible, linking it at the same time to the immeasurable and hidden aspects of
man's deepest emotions:

> the broad Rhine beneath flashed blood-red in the blaze of the light-
> ning and the fires of the Mausenthurm—a lurid Acheron above which
> seemed to hover ten thousand unburied ghosts; and last, but not least,
> on the lip of the vast Mosel-kopf crater—just above the point where
> the weight of the fiery lake has burst the side of the great slag-cup,
> and rushed forth between two cliffs of clink-stone across the downs,
> in a clanging stream of fire, damming up rivulets, and blasting its path
> through forests, far away toward the valley of the Moselle.[30]

Much of the attraction of the Eifel was the resemblance Kingsley
thought it bore to the landscape of Devon and Cornwall, "the whole
country the strangest jumble, alternations of Cambridgeshire ugliness
[. . .] with all the beauties of Devonshire."[31] In a sense it made him
feel at home, a notion he used in *Two Years Ago* when Tom Turnall,
visiting Bad Bertrich is suddenly reminded of his native shores: "The
likeness certainly exists; for the rock, being the same in both places,
has taken the same general form; and the wanderer in Rhine-Prussia
and Nassau might often fancy himself in Devon or Cornwall."[32]

---

[29] CK to FK, 13/8/1851, *LML* i.296.
[30] *G* 29–30.
[31] CK to FK, 7/8/1851, *LML* i.295.
[32] *TYA* 475.

Another week of criss-crossing from Daun to Birresborn, and then finally south through the Kyllwald towards Trier brought the walking trip to end, but only after a night in the town's prison "among fleas and felons, on the bare floor." The two brothers, with their stubble beards of just over ten days, had been arrested by a gendarme near Bitburg who had taken their "fishing-rods for 'todt-instrumenten'—deadly weapons—and our wide-awakes for Italian hats, and got into their addled pates that we were emissaries of Mazzini and Co. distributing political tracts." Anne Thackeray, who had heard from her father of the incident soon after it had happened, added in her Memoir a defence of the addle-pated gendarmes, apparently seeing (after half a century) more similarity between Mazzini and Kingsley than he ever did himself: "One can imagine the author of *Alton Locke* not finding very great favour with foreign mouchards and gendarmes, and suggesting indefinite terrors and suspicions to their minds."[33] However, the following morning it became clear that a mistake had been made, and the police-inspector, who was "a gentleman," sent the gendarme back to Bitsburg with a reprimand and the two brothers were "with many apologies" released. So there was time to visit the ancient town. Trier was 'wonderful' to Charles as everything else had been on his German trip, "but at first the feeling that one is standing over the skeleton of the giant iniquity—Old Rome—is overpowering."

Although Mrs Kingsley had originally planned to stay on at Ems while her sons went for a walking tour in the Eifel, she had suddenly changed her mind and had travelled as far east as Dresden, where she met with an adventure which was recorded fifty years later by Kingsley's niece Mary: "In after years his mother used to be fond of telling her grandchildren how another lady and herself had been extremely terrified, when they were once walking together in the vicinity of Dresden, by the sudden appearance, round a bend in the road, of a ragged, resolute, ruffian-looking young vagabond, who, fixing his wild gray eyes on them, and uttering an exclamation which they interpreted as a menace, had approached them with, as they had thought, the intention of peremptorily demanding alms; and how a close inspection had revealed that he was none other than her own son George, returning literally from Bohemia, with

[33] Ritchie, *Op. cit.*, 108.

his clothes in tatters, the remnants of his boots tied together with pieces of string, and his face burnt as brown as a gipsy's, radiant with his freedom and his joy at seeing her again."[34]

Coming back from Dresden, Mr and Mrs Kingsley discovered that their sons had just been released from prison and that as a consequence their imprisonment had become the talk all over Trier. The reunited family stayed long enough at Trier for the main attractions and then moved to Bad Bertrich for a couple of days. Although at the beginning of the walking trip Charles expressed his adulation for the "Kurhaus of all Kurhauses"at Bertrich, writing to Fanny that it was "so lovely, one longs to kiss it,"[35] it was presented in far less positive terms when the place was evoked in later years. It is likely that after the freedom and the emotions of the walking trip, and the novelty of these bathing places had worn off, Kingsley started to feel impatient with staying yet once more at the popular spa with its "black-petticoated worthies, each with that sham of a sham, the modern tonsure, pared down to a poor florin's breadth among their bushy, well-oiled curls, who sit at tables, passing the lazy day '*à muguetter les bourgeoises*'."[36]

IV

Kingsley continued to write poetry about the subject which had obsessed him during most of his stay abroad: his separation from Fanny and its related theme of the nun and the convent. A late nightingale, and a device borrowed from *Romeo and Juliet*, inspired him to voice his ill-borne separation from Fanny in the octave of a thirteen-line "sonnet"

> The baby sings not on its mother's breast
> Nor nightingales who nestle side by side:
> Nor I by thine: but let us only part,
> Then lips which should but kiss, and so be still,
> As having uttered all, must speak again—
> O stunted thoughts! O chill and fettered rhyme!
> Yet my great bliss, though entirely blest,
> Losing its proper home, can find no rest

[34] George Henry Kingsley, *Notes on Sport and Travel; With a Memoir by His Daughter Mary H. Kingsley* (London: Macmillan, 1900) 15–6.
[35] CK to FK, 7/8/1851, *LML* i.295.
[36] *TYA* 470.

while in "The Ugly Princess" the following lines are given to a deformed princess who is forced to retire to a convent and to deny her human desires. Kingsley plays here with elements of sexual longing and the fulfilment of motherhood in marriage, which are closely interwoven, and, it would seem, much on the same level:

> They little know how I could love—
> [. . .]
> They little know what dreams have been
> My playmates, night and day;
> Of equal kindness, helpful care,
> A mother's perfect sway.

Kingsley's point comes home in the irony of the last stanza but one, in which such earthly longings are only fit for secular life and are separated from religion:

> Now earth to earth in convent walls,
> To earth in churchyard sod:
> I was not good enough for man,
> And so am given to God.

These poems were enclosed in his letters to Fanny with the instruction to send them on to Ludlow for *The Christian Socialist*, where they were published over the following months.

The stay was now drawing to an end and the family started to move north, first to Andernach and then to Bonn before they slowly travelled back to England via Belgium. At Bonn they visited the museum and, although Kingsley felt frustrated that his German was not good enough to converse with the curator, he "was in ecstacies" at its well-arranged collection of minerals and fossils.[37] At the town of Andernach Kingsley composed his two Dolcino-poems, based on the dramatic tale of Fra Dolcino and Margaret, early fourteenth-century lovers condemned by the (Roman Catholic) church to the stake for their militant and heretical vow of poverty. Ideally, they represented an evangelical movement originating in the Franciscan order and known as the Apostolic Brethren, which tried to limit the church's temporal power and bring it back to the principles of apostolic times. By some the couple were simply seen as sensuous heterodox heretics. Probably sympathetic to their "protestant" cause, the moment of their inseparable love, even in the face of death, attracted Kingsley. As Margaret dramatically proclaims at the stake:

---

[37] CK to FK, undated, BL-62553 f.212.

> Ask if I love thee? Oh, smiles cannot tell
> Plainer what tears are now showing too well.
> Had I now loved thee, my sky had been clear:
> Had I not loved thee, I had not been here,
> Weeping by thee.
> ("Margaret to Dolcino")

Fra Dolcino firmly and unrepentantly replies,

> And the night will hallow the day;
> Till the heart which at even was weary and old
> Can rise in the morning gay,
>   Sweet wife;
> To its work in the morning gay.
> ("Dolcino to Margaret")

It is not clear what inspired Kingsley to write about these Italian lovers while he was visiting the Rhine. He might at one stage of his early life have read the story himself in *Historia fratris Dulcini heresiarche*, or a popular rendering of it, and heard it told or referred to in Andernach as the story had become a celebrated legend in Germany over the centuries. What is of interest, however, is that these poems once more stress the inseparable link between passionate love and religion, especially as the execution of Dolcino by order of the Pope on political grounds was staged as gruesome punishment for his (sexual) passion for a woman. To Kingsley the story represented all that he saw as sexually oppressive in Roman Catholicism.

From Bonn to Ostend there was time for briefly visiting sights in Brussels, Waterloo, Ghent and Bruges. Finally, Charles was reunited with Fanny, whom he had asked upon his arrival not to wear her glasses: "I *do* hate them so! I sat next the *first* woman today I have seen in them, & behold she was an Englishwoman! & I *shuddered*."[38]

The first trip abroad had been an enormous success. Kingsley now felt in great physical health—"I am very well indeed, and very strong, and my limbs are all knots, as hard as iron"[39]—and it had also bolstered his morale in general: "I cannot tell you what moral good this whole journey has done to me." The Rhine-Prussia and Nassau and its people were adorable: "Really this Germany is a wonderful country [. . .] and as noble, simple, shrewd, kindly hearts in it, as

---

[38] CK to FK, undated, MP-C0171–36914.
[39] CK to FK, undated, BL-62553 f.212.

man would wish to see." The statement was only slightly modified with the following qualification in the omission above: "—though its population are not members of the Church of England."[40]

V

Although the theme of nuns and convents, priests and monasteries, was often present at the outset of Kingsley's literary career, his interest in Roland's misfortune and Dolcino's tragedy during the German trip was stimulated by having re-read, just before leaving, his first prose fiction "The Nun's Pool." Although rejected once for *Politics For the People* in 1848, it was now going to be published in *The Christian Socialist*. It appeared in seven instalments in Kingsley's absence from 5 July to 30 August. The story is an insignificant one, running to approximately 10,000 words, and it was never reprinted or included in the *Complete Works*. It would hardly deserve discussion here, were it not for Kingsley's apparent fascination with it. And, although he repeatedly refers to it in *Yeast*, the story itself is left untold in that work.

"The Nun's Pool" tells of the passionate love of a yeoman and a nun in the "profligate" times of Henry VIII. When the lovers secretly meet one night in the fields around the convent, Kingsley has the nun say to the yeoman (but, of course, principally to the reader): "Why should I be ashamed of love? Did the evil one make me love you? Did *he* raise in me these longings which give me something to live for—which make me struggle to be wise, to be brave, to be useful—to be a woman? And yet my vows—my vows! Have I not promised myself to God? Why am I a nun—and yet here?" We then learn that the nun's earthly passions were awakened when she fell off her mule into a weir-pool and was saved by the yeoman, the scene being a thinly veiled form of baptism, "that first dawn of a new life."[41] At that moment the King's Commissioners arrive to seize the convent, and the nun hastens back to her cell, while the yeoman desperately tries to follow her. As he next finds a means to enter the convent himself with the help of a corrupt Franciscan friar, whom

[40] CK to FK, 13/8/1851, *LML* i.296.
[41] *ChSoc* ii.14.

"a good stick" would have taught "for once to work instead of beg-
ging,"[42] he finds many a noblemen spoiling the convent of it riches
in the king's name. This offers the occasion for the narrator to proclaim Kingsley's socialist message:

> No! The aristocracy have not yet atoned for the sins of their forefa-
> thers [. . .] Your fathers, by their robbery of the poor, first made a
> poor-law necessary. You, by your neglect and jobbing, converted that
> poor-law into a premium for profligacy, idleness, and beggary. And
> now you have improved upon that, by substituting in its place, a law
> which punishes, as a crime, the poverty which your own neglect, your
> own exactions, have produced. A law, which instead of work, offers a
> prison to English free-men [. . .] and if they point to the 10th of April,
> and cry 'Peace, peace' where there is no peace, tell them that the
> wind always falls dead before the thunderstorm; that the stream is
> always smoothest before it leaps into the abyss.[43]

The third instalment, from which this passage is taken, assumes with
such expressions the shape of a tract on vested rights in society, and
it clumsily interrupts what has so far been swift narrative. It is of
the same provenance as Kingsley's provoking "Letters to Landlords"
in *Politics for the People*. The artless intrusive voice of this instalment,
however, is soon forgotten when in the next similar sentiments are
proclaimed by the prioress of Whitford in her announcement of the
curse: "Woe to you and to your children! Woe! The curse of the
nuns of Whitford shall cleave to you night and day, till you have
learnt to do the works of the nuns of Whitford [. . .] you [shall] rue
the day when you drove us out, who stood in the gap between rich
and poor."[44]

The attention next shifts to an Earl who enters the scene with
"frightful reports of irregularities" against the convent. He summons
our yeoman, who the moment before had been seen discoursing intimately with a nun under the priory walls, and who is now recognized by another as a "pestilent and confessed heretic" who "kept
company with the Lutheran preacher who was burnt here." In a
scene of low comedy, the sheriff readily condemns him to be "racked,
till you confess your enormities, and then burned alive."[45] Kingsley

---

[42] *ChSoc* ii.30.
[43] *ChSoc* ii.47.
[44] *ChSoc* ii.79.
[45] *ChSoc* ii.95.

seems to be writing his own Dolcino but not without a touch of Roland's story. The suspicion of the yeoman being the prioress's lover is now uttered, and the earl addresses her with a sneer: "you who, among your celestial dreams, disdained ten years to be a count-ess petty, you have been content to be a petty Prioress and [whore]."[46] The last unpronounced word signals the climax. The nun steps for-ward to clear the prioress's name, but is caught by the yeoman, who disappears with her through the doorway into the darkness. The earl turns to rush after them, but is hit on the head by the monk and falls lifeless to the floor. As all the noblemen run after the murderer, the prioress stumbles out, murmuring the insulting word, and then throws herself into the whirling weir pool. The two lovers leave the country and the yeoman "bade her change her nun's dress."[47] Coming back to the scene from Germany after twenty years—"in the reign of good Queen Bess"—they contemplate the eddy in the pool where the prioress disappeared. "Do not the villagers say well, when they talk of the curse which lies upon Whitford, till the waters of the Nun's Pool shall flow up to Ash Down?" she asked, to which he replied, unwilling to exclude the impossible: "They may flow thither yet [. . .] We, His children, have a higher lot; we praise Him by progressing forward—forward, ever!"[48]

The short-story "The Nun's Pool" is a strange blend of questions of love and celibacy as well as of purely social ones. But the con-clusion makes clear that all is seen as part of darker ages from which man has since emerged. As Protestantism liberated man from a mis-guided ideal of celibacy, the yeoman and the nun's union signals the start of a religion which no longer contends the sanctity of mat-rimonial love. Similarly, the origin of the social evil of poverty is ascribed to the same dark period in English history. The advance-ment of English civilization is seen as the result of Protestantism, and nineteenth-century social evils would surely be eliminated if only man were willing to break with the pre-Elizabethan concept of prop-erty. This is at the core of the 'tract' instalment: as "England is still paying for this wholesale robbery of the poor," let the aristocracy "with the old monastic lands [. . .] obtain the old monastic spirit

---

[46] *ChSoc* ii.126.
[47] *ChSoc* ii.143.
[48] *ChSoc* ii.143.

[. . .] Let them be to England now, what the old monks were to England in the middle age—the pioneers of civilization and agriculture, the captains of industry, the discoverers of knowledge, the refiners of taste and art, the judges of the fatherless and the widow, the champions of the poor."[49]

VI

In Eversley there was plenty of work to do in the parish after Kingsley's return, especially as there was no curate, which, of course saved expense. On the other hand, there were no pupils either. William Lees had left at the beginning of the year, and John Martineau had parted with the family after eighteen influential months just before Kingsley went on his German tour. Almost all of the "The Nun's Pool" was published in Kingsley's absence. But immediately after his return from Germany he was driven back into the activities of the Christian Socialists. The September issue of *The Quarterly Review* carried a vitriolic attack on the movement, and Kingsley came in for his full share of offensive remarks. In a long article on "Revolutionary Literature," the anonymous writer, who was later identified as John Wilson Croker, heaped Kingsley's and Maurice's writings together, starting:

> Incredible as it may appear, there is, it seems, a clique of educated and clever but wayward-minded men—the most prominent of them two *clergymen of the Church of England*—who, from, as it seems, a morbid craving for notoriety or a crazy straining after paradox—have taken up the unnatural and unhallowed task of preaching, in the press and from the pulpit [. . .] under the name of '*Christian Socialism*'.[50]

Alton Locke came in for a good deal of abuse, and with its "ravings of rapine, blasphemy, and nonsense" was seen as the "manifesto of Kingsley-Mauricean Socialism."[51] Also using passages from *Politics for the People*, *Yeast*, and the Drew affair, Croker concluded that in the "detestable doctrinations [. . .] of Mr. Maurice's penny paper, and Mr. Kingsley's no-worth-a-penny novels [. . .] their greatest anxiety seems to insult and degrade the Church to which they belong."[52]

---

[49] *ChSoc* ii.47.
[50] [Croker] 524.
[51] [Croker] 530.
[52] [Croker] 531, 532, 533.

This time Kingsley refrained from answering the charges and, far from feeling dejected by a fresh assault on his reputation, he felt sanguine about the future of *The Christian Socialist*. In August the printing and publishing business of the movement had been given to John James Bezer, and Kingsley expressed his desire to meet Monops, as the one-eyed Chartist bookseller was known by his friends, wishing "that the periodical will prosper in your hands far better than it has yet done."[53] But serious discordance among the leaders of the Christian Socialist movement was emerging in the autumn of 1851.

In February 1850 Edward Vansittart Neale, a barrister of ample means at Lincoln's Inn, had become part of the band of Christian Socialists. He had originally been attracted to them when he heard of the Working Tailors' Association in Castle Street. Although he had known Maurice during his student days in Oxford, they had lost contact. But when their acquaintance was resumed, and Maurice found that he was sincerely interested in co-operation, the master, much to Ludlow's perplexity, proposed him as one of the members of their Society for Promoting Working Men's Associations. Neale immediately became an active and ambitious member, and within a few months advanced money to open a co-operative store which was to buy goods wholesale for its consumers. Kingsley saw this move as 'enormous,'[54] but Ludlow remained aloof and objected that although "production is essentially an unselfish act, consumption [is] a selfish one."[55] Nonetheless, a store was opened in October in Charlotte Street, and in the spring Neale founded a Central Co-operative Agency as a major wholesale centre for the whole nation. Ludlow painfully noted that the constitution of the Agency made no reference to Christian principles. Neale's projects did not end here. He started travelling all over England to promote the Agency, and found influential supporters in the north, and in such radical papers as *The Northern Star* and *The Leader*. A next step was to involve the trade unions, which could boost the popularity of the co-operative consumer project, and with the help of Lechevalier a circular was drawn up. Ludlow saw this as a further breach with the Society, which was barely mentioned. The Society and the Agency had started

---

[53] CK to John James Bezer, 15/9/1851, Martin (1950) 260.
[54] CK to TH, 31/5/1850, Martin (1950) 202.
[55] "Working Associations and Co-operative Stores" 31/5/1851 *ChSoc* i.241.

to become "two separate currents," he thought, as the Agency encouraged consumers to lose sight of the ideal of the Christian Socialists in cultivating a tendency to get goods at the lowest possible prices, which could not but lead to exploitation of the workers so that "the opposition of interests between producer and consumer would be exhibited in its nakedest from."[56] On 30 October 1851 he felt it was high time to speak out and he demanded that the Council of the Society expel the officers of the Agency as they perverted the ideal of the Society: "Live as brothers together, and you will free yourselves from the miseries of the competitive world."[57] His appeal, however, fell through, and Ludlow resigned from the Council.

Although Kingsley did not support Ludlow in his motion against the Agency, he too felt uneasy about Neale's new alliances amongst the journalists. Especially *The Leader* had dubious contributors, he warned Neale. He profoundly distrusted the paper's joint-editors George Henry Lewes and Thornton Hunt. For him, Lewes was an infidel and a bigamist, Hunt a narrow and ignorant "twaddler." Neither did he have any good words for its manager George Jacob Holyoake, who had become in his eyes a mere blackguard who gloried in calling himself an atheist. The attention the Christian Socialists were getting from *The Leader* was therefore embarrassing, but when Hunt started to praise Kingsley, quoted from his writings, and inserted him in the paper's list of contributors, he felt it was time to make it clear that he did not appreciate such publicity. He felt forced to impugn Hunt with "insolent and ungentlemanlike behaviour" in a letter to the editor which was inserted in the paper on 16 November. "Respectable people were naturally beginning to ask how far I favoured bigamy and atheism," he explained to Neale.[58] Kingsley's liberal sexual attitudes which had transpired from *The Saint's Tragedy*, *Yeast* and "The Nun's Pool" seem to have triggered positive responses in the more radical part of his reading public,[59] so much so that he now felt constrained to guard himself against too licentious interpretations and uses of his views. Thus, in a furious letter to the

---

[56] "Working Associations and Co-operative Stores" 31/5/1851 *ChSoc* i.242.
[57] "Working Associations and Co-operative Stores" 31/5/1851 *ChSoc* i.241.
[58] CK to Edward Vansittart Neale, 15/11/51, in Philip N. Backstrom, *Christian Socialism and Cooperation in Victorian England; Edward Vansittart Neale and the Co-operative Movement* (London: Croom Helm, 1974) 37.
[59] Cf. Maynard 101–2.

editor of *The Leader* he made clear that there are "things which are past argument," that a line had to be drawn somewhere:

> I happen to draw it at bigamy and atheism; & I am horribly afraid, as a married man who holds marriage to be sacred (while I feel just as strongly as you can do Woman's equal rights, & the injustices w. society & law often do to her) . . . that the public should think that I hold such matters as Mr. Holyoake's orations [. . .] For that w. I do believe, I will die please God. For that w. I do not believe but on the contrary abhor, I will not suffer a finger-ache.[60]

Although Kingsley did not react to the provocations from the *Quarterly*, silence became unbearable when, after the *Quarterly*, *The Guardian* too renewed its attacks. On 5 November it published an article in which it argued that Kingsley wrote for such dubious newspapers as *The Leader*. Kingsley once more wrote a letter to the editor, inserted in the paper on 12 November, in which he denied any such connection. It was exasperating that the press, and especially *The Guardian*, continued to harass him. But the German trip had invigorated Kingsley so much that, even with this, and "with parish, tithe dinner, Mrs. Kingsley's illness, & seven & forty other things," he felt that what the Christian Socialist cause needed was notoriety, "In plain English, we haven't had row enough yet."[61] In a long letter to Ludlow he outlined his idea of future tactics. As he thought that the devil was mainly hiding behind the anonymity of the press, "our plan will be, to take a periodical, & thrash it—thrash it like a sack, up & down, rough & tumble, & see if we can't kill it, & when we have killed it go on & try another." *The Economist* came in first as being "purely of the Devil," and he adds "I think we could do something towards making the editor's life a burden to him for the next few months [. . .] by [using] all the powers of sarcasm of w. I am master." Concluding, he instructs Ludlow "just [to] put down my name as a subscriber to the Economist, & order it to be sent to me weekly.' As Kingsley's eloquent offer was made late at night over a "brandy & water", having "put the wife to bed" and feeling "lonely as a gib cat,"[62] Ludlow would most likely have declined the offer anyway. But as it was, Ludlow was in no position even to consider

---

[60] Letter offered for sale in 2000 by Maggs Bros. Ltd, London.
[61] CK to JL, undated, Martin (1950) 262.
[62] CK to JL, undated, Martin (1950) 262–70.

the new tactics. The struggle between Ludlow and Neale for the leadership of the cooperative movement sharpened considerably at the beginning of November. After Ludlow's defeat on 30 October, Neale expressed his concern that Ludlow would use *The Christian Socialist* to oppose his Agency. Although, Ludlow immediately resigned his editorship, Maurice seized the occasion to express his disapproval of what, in his eyes, *The Christian Socialist* had become. He had read Ludlow's political pieces over the past year with growing distrust, and now became convinced that the editor was trying to raise what he feared most: a party spirit. Croker's scathing article in the *Quarterly* had had some effect on Maurice. He decreed, therefore, that their paper had henceforth to concentrate on technical matters only and therefore had to drop the first part of its title to become merely the *Journal of Association*. Ludlow obeyed, and the editorship passed into the hands of Thomas Hughes. The new editorial direction also meant the end of Kingsley's involvement with the movement. November saw his last contribution to *The Christian Socialist* in "The Long Game," a prophetic article in three instalments, on the sure advent of socialism. On 1 January 1852 Ludlow and Kingsley's "child of stormy dawn" ceased publication. Half a year later, the *Journal of Association* also came to an end. Kingsley, by then in the midst of getting out instalments of *Hypatia* in *Fraser's*, looked back in his poem "On the Death of a Certain Journal" on a period which had ended, realizing that he was putting part of his own life behind him. Yet he retained a muted optimism, borrowed from Tennyson's "crowning race":

> So die, thou. child of stormy dawn,
> Thou winter flower, forlorn of nurse;
> Chilled early by the bigot's curse,
> The pedant's frown, the worldling's yawn.
>
> [. . .]
>
> To grace, perchance, a fairer morn
> In mightier lands beyond the sea,
> While honour falls to such as we
> From hearts of heroes yet unborn,
>
> Who in the light of fuller day,
> Of purer science, holier laws,
> Bless us, faint heralds of their cause,
> Dim beacons of their glorious way.

VII

By the end of 1851, Kingsley had established a national reputation for himself as a writer, albeit a controversial one. He had drawn the attention of the influential Whig journals in Scotland and England, brought upon himself the ire of a leading High-Church organ, and found response to his writings in the radical press. He had fully emerged from the Christian Socialist movement, and his anonymity under the pseudonym Parson Lot had been broken. Countless letters from readers reached him, testifying to the influence his writings had upon the young. Henry James would later speak of it as a special disease, 'Kingsley fever.'[63] A young and still unknown George Meredith wrote: "I am driven with a spur to tell you the delight and admiration with which I read "Yeast", and the positive "Education" I have derived from it. It was the very book I was in want of and likely to do more good than any that I know."[64] It is in such a sense that 1851 was one of Kingsley's most successful years.

---

[63] Henry James, "Charles Kingsley's Life and Letters," *The Nation* 24 (1877), 60–1.
[64] Auctioned letter quoted in Martin (1959) 149.

MUSCULAR CHRISTIANITY

CHAPTER ELEVEN

THE ENERGETIC HEALTHY ANIMAL MAN (1852)

All through 1851 Kingsley had been reading up on fifth-century Alexandria, and had started to put his pen to paper on a new work during the autumn. In December he was "going on hard at it," planning to have six chapters ready by the beginning of the new year, and a first instalment was sent to Parker, urging him to return the proofs as soon as possible "for I cannot tell what the *style* looks like, unless I see it in print." Although Kingsley was obliged to Parker for advancing money for *Hypatia* and therefore felt bound to follow up his publisher's wishes, he, "& what is *a great deal more, Mrs. Kingsly*," thought a preface, which Parker desired, a bad idea: it would "only set peoples' ears & tails up, & make Mrs. Grundy suspicious."[1] Parker acquiesced in Kingsley's judgement, and the first instalment appeared in the January 1852 issue of *Fraser's Magazine* without a preface.

Relationships with his publisher were still fine when Kingsley started submitting the first chapters of *Hypatia* for publication, and Kingsley wrote that John Parker jr. was welcome to come over and stay at Eversley. But the friendship cooled considerably during the following two months. Ever in need of money to pay his debts, Kingsley was trying to get a second volume of sermons published. Parker objected that he did not like bringing out simultaneously two works by the same author, but offering to help Kingsley out financially, and unwilling to lose the sermons, he proposed forwarding £50 immediately for publication the following year. Kingsley did not like this: "I should only be spending next year's money this year," and publishing sermons had nothing to do with publishing "work[s] of pure art" as a "man is supposed to be always writing them." Moreover, just because *Hypatia* was "without any direct tendency or moral," he felt anxious to bring out his religious views in a set of sermons. Therefore, he informed Parker that "this set of sermons will go tomorrow to the Scotsman [John Joseph Griffin]."[2] Appearances

---

[1] CK to John Parker, December 1851, Martin (1950) 284.
[2] CK to John Parker, January 1852, Martin (1950) 293.

were kept up by Kingsley, but, notwithstanding his thanking Parker
for his "prompt friendly offer," it was clear that something had started
to go sour between writer and publisher. To Ludlow he wrote that
Griffin got the sermons which "that miserable boiled stockfish John
Parker would neither publish himself, nor let any one else publish."[3]

Kingsley also clashed with the anonymous editor of *Fraser's Magazine*
for having inserted in the first February issue alongside the instalment of *Hypatia* an article that accused the Christian Socialists of
"indirectly promoting a crusade against order and property." Kingsley
wrote to Parker and asked him to inform his editor that to allow
this "would be to fail as a gentleman & a man of honour, & to lose
the whole of that influence with the working men for w. I have ventured reputation, caste, even my position as a clergyman." A letter
to the editor was drafted and given to read to Hughes, Ludlow and
Maurice. However, there was no need for the letter as the contributor retracted his words in the next issue, probably following the
advice of the anonymous editor. Kingsley did not know that the
anonymous editor of *Fraser's* was no other than John Parker himself.

II

The *Sermons on National Subjects* were, apart from the 1849 sermons
on the cholera, mainly written (and preached) during 1850–51. They
are markedly different from the ones in Kingsley's first volume of
published sermons. The overall tone is less "muscular" and the subjects more conventional and references to personal sentiments are
rare. Most of the sermons, as the title of the volume indicates, deal
with notions of England and English civilization. The recurrent theme
is the sinfulness of England that lies in ignoring that English civilisation owed its greatness principally to the special covenant which
God had made with the English people ever since He blessed it with
a Protestant Anglican Church. But the superiority which was often
placed on English values over those of other nationalities had to
Kingsley a nasty ring of self-complacency if this was seen as an
achievement distinct from Christianity. "If we fancy that God's great
favours to us," he warned, "are a reason for our priding ourselves
on them, and despising papists and foreigners instead of remembering

---

[3] CK to JL, undated, Martin (1950) 298.

that just because God has given us so much, He will require more of us."[4] Thus, in an eloquent sermon preached at St Margaret's Church in Westminster in 1851 on behalf of its hospital, Kingsley gives the reader a concrete application of this. Running a hospital is a fine and noble enterprise, but it is high time to "begin to look on hospitals [. . .] in a sadder though in a no less important light:"

> When we remember that the majority of cases which fill their wards are cases of more or less directly preventible diseases, the fruits of our social neglect, too often of our neglect of the sufferers themselves, too often also our neglect of their parents and forefathers; when we think how many a bitter pang is engendered and propagated from generation to generation in the noisome alleys and courts of this metropolis, by foul food, foul bedrooms, foul air, foul water, by intemperance, the natural and almost pardonable consequence of want of water, depressing and degrading employments, and lives spent in such an atmosphere of filth as our daintier nostrils could not endure a day: then we should learn to look upon these hospitals not as acts of charity, supererogatory benevolences of ours towards those to whom we owe nothing, but as confessions of sin, and worthy fruits of penitence; as poor and late and partial compensation for misery which we might have prevented. And when again, taking up scientific works, we find how vast a proportion of the remaining cases of disease are produced directly or indirectly by the unhealthiness of certain occupations, so certainly that the scientific man can almost prophesy the average shortening of life, and the peculiar form of disease, incident to any given form of city labour—when we find, to quote a single instance, that a large proportion—one half, as I am informed—of the female cases in certain hospitals, are those of women-servants suffering from diseases produced by overwork in household labour, especially by carrying heavy weights up the steep stairs of our London houses—when we consider the large proportion of accident cases which are the result, if not always of neglect in our social arrangements [. . .] For whom have they been labouring, but for us?[5]

If England will not look after its poor, it will be severely punished for this, Kingsley warns. This "punishment will be seven times as severe as that of either France, Germany, and Austria, because we had seven times their privileges and blessings, seven times their Gospel light and Christian knowledge, seven times their freedom and justice in laws and constitution; seven times their wealth, and prosperity, and means of employing our population."[6] It echoes the apocalyptic

[4] "The Covenant" *NS* 182.
[5] "The Fount of Science" *NS* 127–9.
[6] "The King of the Earth" *NS* 5.

vein of his social thinking. Revolutions are a way God has to "execute justice and judgment for the meek of the earth."[7] But although he might envisage a Doomsday scenario in depicting his fear of terror, he stresses that he does not think that "what people commonly call the end of the world, that is, the end of the earth and of mankind on it, is not at hand at all."[8] What is at hand is the end of *this* "system of society, of these present ways in religion, and money-making."[9]

III

The weather was cold and wet in February 1852, and there was a lot of work to do in the parish that winter. Sir John Cope had died on 18 November the previous year, having left much property on his estate in bad repair. Kingsley helped to oversee the necessary work before his heir, William Cope, came down from London to take possession of Bramshill. But riding up and down the parish was made difficult by high water, and Kingsley often had to go round by the bridges, "the fords being up to your horses what do you call it & as cold as ever was ice."[10] Mrs Kingsley had gone with the children to stay with an elder sister of hers, and Kingsley had all the time to go surveying the parish for possible improvement on an old horse that Hughes had given him. The boggy places in the area were most treacherous, and he experienced himself what he had described with so much realism in Lancelot's fall at the beginning of *Yeast*. To his son Maurice he mentioned a fall from his horse that might well have ended worse:

> Black Prince fell upon daddy & bruised him very much in his leg & shoulder, for Black Prince is very heavy, & I had much sooner it had been Dandy [the dog]. When Daddy got up he thought his collarbone was broke, but he picked up the pieces & put them together, & rode on just the same.[11]

But Kingsley enjoyed such a hardy outdoor-life. The easterly winds were particularly attractive to him that year. Sir William Cope's

---

[7] "The King of the Earth" *NS* 2.
[8] "The King of the Earth" *NS* 3.
[9] "The King of the Earth" *NS* 4.
[10] CK to TH, undated, Martin (1950) 296.
[11] CK to Maurice Kingsley, February 1852, BL-41298 f.208v–209r.

Thames-boat (which had been temporarily stored in Chelsea on the premises of Mr Kingsley's rectory until it could be transported to the lake at Bramshill) had reached Eversley by mid-March, and Kingsley was "enjoying vigorous sculls" with it on the lake.

The 1851 publication of *Yeast* in book form induced a number of readers to discuss religious questions with its author. Kingsley went willingly into theological details with his correspondents, also because sophisticated discussion was impossible with the slow "Hampshire clods" that made up his congregation. To him these letters were "a recreation after book-writing and parish-visiting,"[12] although at times it was hard writing long theological letters "after two services and sermons, one *extempore*, and a class of confirmation candidates (all of which 'take it out of one,' when one is in earnest). Still, he would not complain of his parochial duty, as ultimately "it is wholesome, cheerful work [. . .] My people are silent and impassive, but sure— often surprising me by unexpected right-doing where I had suspected nothing but stupidity."[13] Much of this correspondence went into a discussion of philosophical notions of time ("I do not think time an instinctive idea, but altogether a conception from our own experience of the succession of natural phenomena'), and of evil ("merely a state of disharmony with and disobedience to a law"), but occasionally a more intimate exchange took place. In a letter to a nobleman who was instructing a carpenter to build a boat, Kingsley confessed that he himself had no "constructive genius," but saw himself merely as a destructive

> slayer of animals, which of course, as a clergyman, public opinion requires me to indulge in very little; and perhaps rightly. But luckily, shooting I hate; fishing is *par excellence* the parson's sport, and hunting I am preserved from, by double demurrers of an execrable hunting country, and pride, which forbids me to ride, unless I am as well mounted as the rest. So I am not a 'sporting parson' after all.[14]

This passage occurred in a letter written in early summer, when Kingsley felt particularly stressed. Fanny was confined to her rooms, as she had just given birth to their daughter Mary on 4 June. The "suffering of childbirth" was to Kingsley the "one thing which I hate

[12] CK to unidentified correspondent, 15/6/1852, *LML* i.325.
[13] CK to unidentified correspondent, 20/2/1852, *LML* i.319.
[14] CK to unidentified correspondent, 15/6/1852, *LML* i.325.

and curse, as the deepest paradox and puzzle upon earth."[15] Moreover, as the dangers of Victorian parturition to both mother and child were not to be underrated, the anxiety about Fanny had seriously worried him. Everything went well, however, as he wrote to Ludlow: "I have gotten a daughter. Fanny is safe through all her troubles, wonderfully well, & the baby too." But the silence of the rectory weighed on him all the same, and apart from letter writing there was not much to divert his nervousness. The "mere inability to sit quiet without a wife down stairs" sent him out on an "afternoon's pike-fishing."[16]

The confession of his destructive energies to his correspondent in June indicates some more or less unconscious and nervous feeling of guilt. If any thing, all through the spring of 1852 Kingsley had been a "sporting parson," enjoying boating on the lake and roaming the country on horseback in "a state of utter animalism."[17] Hughes's old horse proved a true delight to him and although "he is *not* fast, [. . .] in the enclosed woodlands he can live up to anyone." With it he felt "as well mounted as the rest" even for fox-hunting. He describes in a letter to Hughes how on 18 March, after a day's work he was sitting down at dinner at 4 o'clock,

> when the bow-wows appeared on the top of my mount, trying my patch of gorse: so I jumped up, left the cook shrieking & off. He was-n't there, but I knew where he was, for I keep a pretty good register of foxes (aint they my parishioners, & parts of my flock?) And as the poor fellows had had a blank day, they were very thankful to find themselves in five minutes going like mad. We had an hour & a half of it, scent breast high, as the dew began to rise.

As it was, they lost the fox, but Kingsley went back to his dinner feeling "three years younger today."[18]

IV

After Easter Kingsley went for three weeks to Plas Gwynant, the picturesque house in north Wales where the Froudes had taken up residence since the summer of 1850. The house stood on rising

---

[15] CK to unidentified correspondent, 15/6/1852, *LML* i.326.
[16] CK to unidentified correspondent, 15/6/1852, *LML* i.325.
[17] CK to JL, undated, Martin (1950) 329.
[18] CK to TH, undated, Martin (1950) 323.

woodland with the peak of Mount Snowdon scarcely two miles away. Across a lawn and meadow, the front window looked out upon Dinas Lake, while all round, through the gaps in the pines, blue and violet mountain ridges showed. At the bottom of the orchard a torrent poured with a waterfall in a deep pool at the foot of a rock ravine. Froude's years at Plas Gwynant were the happiest of his life. He loved the physically energizing mountain landscape and the place offered all the rest he needed for mental growth. Friends like Max Müller, Matthew Arnold, Arthur Clough, and Richard Powles came over to stay with the Froudes, sometimes for long periods, especially in spring and summer. Kingsley too had been invited, but although he could not come in the spring of 1851, this year he took time off from his parish duties, and from writing *Hypatia*, to join Froude in fishing, walking and boating in Wales. The "state of utter animalism" persisted: "I am in a perfect paradise here," he reported to Ludlow, "the trickling crystal at the bottom of the garden will probably be a roaring yellow torrent, & then tomorrow up to the vast mountain-wall above, & the crags of Llyn Llaggi, & 'kill! kill! kill!'."[19] Froude recalled Kingsley's visit that spring to Plas Gwynant as the "event of the season." Every morning, following Froude's habit, Kingsley would dive into the "liquid ice" of the pool at the bottom of the garden, and "come out like giants refreshed with wine."[20]

V

The political developments of 1852 roused in Kingsley an awareness of possible social reform. When, as Foreign Secretary, Lord Palmerston expressed his approbation of Louis Napoleon Bonaparte's *coup d'état* of 2 December 1851 without informing the Queen and cabinet, Lord John Russell was forced to dismiss him from his post. The Queen and Prince Consort had long been angered by the independent way in which Lord Palmerston conducted foreign policy, and Kingsley shared such views. He had a great personal dislike of the minister: "What can you expect of a man with that face," he wrote to Hughes. "If a nation knows no more of physiognomy than to make such men as him [. . .] its rulers—why it must take the

---

[19] CK to JL, undated, Martin (1950) 329.
[20] CK to JL, undated, Martin (1950) 329.

consequences of ignorance."[21] Russell's ministry was weakened by the loss of Palmerston, and soon after it fell in disagreement over a Militia Bill, Russell, who had governed England since 1846, resigned, and a conservative government was formed by Lord Derby on 26 February.

Derby's ministry offered the Christian Socialists a possibility of getting cooperative association the legal recognition that they had sought during the last two years. By law, in an association of up to twenty-five members, any of its members could pledge the credit of the association. This involved a certain risk, but, through a suit in Chancery, the society had the possibility of finding redress for loss caused by dishonest members. An association of over twenty-five members was, however, not protected at all against any member that absconded with its funds unless it registered under the Joint Stock Companies' Act, for which capital needed to be deposited. As such capital was not available to associations of workmen, Ludlow, Neale, John Stuart Mill and others had testified in 1850 to the necessity to change this situation, but Russell's commitment to total free trade had obstructed the introduction of a new bill. Derby's conservative administration offered hope.

Kingsley and Hughes agreed that the way to get at the new government lay through Cuthbert Edward Ellison, the "swell" (as Ludlow called him) amongst the Christian Socialists, who had been Lord John Manners's friend at university. Manners, conservative MP and follower of Disraeli's Young England, was, Kingsley maintained, a gentleman, Christian and friend of the poor. He therefore advised Hughes, in war-like imagery, to "pump him, sponge him, load him, fire him off," especially as there was no risk in doing so, because "if he bursts, or explodes at the wrong end . . . why—we are out of the way . . . & he can but 'shell' his own government with the bite."[22]

Whether Ellison was effective is not recorded, but the rumour that the new ministry was after all "going to bring a bill for legalizing us," set Kingsley on fire. By such a move, he wrote to Hughes, the ministry would "do more to carry out true Conservatism, and to reconcile the workmen with the real aristocracy, than any politician for the last twenty years has done."[23] In it he saw a possibility of

---

[21] CK to TH, undated, Martin (1950) 320.
[22] CK to TH, undated, Martin (1950) 319.
[23] CK to TH, undated, *LML* i.313.

fighting the true enemy of England and establish democracy against the "narrow, conceited, hypocritical, and anarchic and atheistic schemes" of the Manchester school of political economy:

> I have never swerved from my one idea of the last seven years, that the real battle of the time is—if England is to be saved from anarchy and unbelief, and utter exhaustion caused by the competitive enslavement of the masses—not Radical or Whig against Peelite or Tory [. . .] but the Church, the gentleman, and the workman, against the shopkeepers and the Manchester School.[24]

Such sentiments were publicly vented in an anonymous article Kingsley wrote for *The Morning Herald* of 15 March. "Don't say *I* wrote it," he asked Ludlow, "for there are many good radical friends of ours who might suspect one in consequence as a Tory in disguise."[25] Although the new administration could not rely on a solid majority in the Lower House, Kingsley advised Hughes to act "quickly, for the Derby ministry hangs on days, not on months,[26] Hughes and Neale (through Robert Slaney, MP for Shrewsbury) managed to get a new bill passed in June 1852, securing an important success for the Christian Socialist movement.

For a moment the new ministry also raised great expectations of parliamentary reform. Early in the spring of 1852, the Radical politician Lord Goderich, while campaigning to be elected MP for Hull, wrote a pamphlet in which he rejected any form of aristocracy, hereditary or intellectual, and saw universal suffrage as a basically Christian idea. As he had joined the Christian Socialists in 1850, he showed it to the publishing committee of *Tracts by Christian Socialists*, which consisted of Ludlow, Hughes, Kingsley and Maurice. All except Maurice liked it. Kingsley thought it "the best speech w. I have heard from a nobleman yet."[27] Maurice, however disapproved of it and maintained that monarchy reflected the divine kingship of God and that self-government would open the door to self-will. Maurice pointed out the specific passages that he thought were erroneous in Goderich's pamphlet. Much surprised by Maurice's reaction, and disagreeing with most of it, Goderich introduced a series of minor

---

[24] CK to TH, undated, *LML* i.314–5.
[25] CK to JL, undated, Martin (1950) 325.
[26] CK to TH, 25/3/1852, Martin (1950) 327.
[27] CK to TH, 29/5/1852, Martin (1950) 342.

changes. As Maurice's objections made it unfit for the *Tracts*, Hughes decided to have it printed independently. Ludlow and Kingsley apparently agreed; Maurice was away on holiday. Upon the latter's return, however, finding the pamphlet printed, Hughes got a "precious wigging" and was forced to suppress the pamphlet. All acquiesced to Maurice's decision, but the incident signalled that Maurice, Kingsley, Ludlow and Hughes were fast growing apart in politics. Weary with the question, and torn between his loyalty to Maurice and his socialist ideals, Kingsley wrote to Ludlow that he had "no heart to answer your letter [. . .] about Maurice. I don't care whether he is a socialist or not."[28]

Kingsley's socialist ideas were also different from Hughes's. When A.G. Stapleton saw the Derby government as an opportune moment to reprint his 1850 pamphlet *Suggestions for a Conservative and Popular Reform in the Commons House of Parliament*, in which he argued for direct representation in parliament of the professional classes and of the arts and sciences, Hughes called Kingsley a "muff" for liking it. To Hughes it tended to create a new intellectual class that seemed in direct contrast with Goderich's proposals. But Kingsley rebutted:

> I am not a muff: you are [. . .] I do hold Stapleton's notion not to be class legislation, but a great step toward deliverance from it, & that from that very worst form of it under w. England is now paralyzed, viz. Legislation by & for the SMALL SHOPKEEPERS [. . .] With out some device like S.'s to return a few of a higher & purer style of member [. . .] the extension of the suffrage will only open the door to more ignorant spouters.[29]

But soon it became clear that the new ministry was utterly disappointing in terms of parliamentary reform. "Did you ever see such a set as this Derby lot?" Kingsley wrote to Ludlow the same month the Association Bill was passed. "What confidence can I have," he asked Stapleton, "in a ministry who having come in on the simple ground of Protectionism, are now abandoning the only positive dogma w. gave them power or vitality?"[30]

But notwithstanding the spell of agitation during the Derby ministry, with the end of *The Christian Socialist* Kingsley's political enthusiasm

---

[28] CK to JL, 31/5/1852, Martin (1950) 345.
[29] CK to TH, 29/5/1852, Martin (1950) 342.
[30] CK to AS, 16/7/1852, MP-C0171–36919.

was waning too. Froude, always wary of Kingsley's "habit of thought and tone of feeling," reported to Arthur Clough that Kingsley had stayed with him after Easter and that he was finally "dropping out of the political into the poetic."[31] Froude's observation was not without foundation, and it seems that Kingsley indeed wanted to put his militant political persona behind him. He had concluded his role of Parson Lot in the last number of *The Christian Socialist* with the words: "And the spectacle of silent working faith is one at once so rare and so noble, that it tells more, even on opponents, than ten thousand platform pyrotechnics."[32] Even the correspondence with Ludlow that summer was predominantly about his proceeding work on *Hypatia* and about the suitability of hexameters in English poetry.

VI

After a physically energetic spring, Kingsley complained to Ludlow in June that he was lacking inspiration: "I cant settle again for a few days, & I cant work hard, because I cant play hard, on account of this mighty rain; & unless I get frantic exercises of body, my mind wont work."[33] This frustration lasted very briefly. June 1852, like most months of that year, was an exceptionally productive month. Apart from the fortnightly instalments of *Hypatia*, he was also working hard at a poem. If Kingsley's poetry after *The Saint's Tragedy* was mainly lyrical, he felt a strong urge to write on a bigger scale now. "When I have done "Hypatia" I will write no more novels," he announced to Ludlow, "I will write poetry [. . .] poetry is the true sphere, combining painting and music and history all in one."[34] One of the first results of this resolution was a poem written earlier that year: "Saint Maura, A.D. 304."

Although not their first child, Mrs Kingsley's giving birth to Mary in June greatly disturbed Kingsley. It confronted him once more with the great themes of his life. The fruit of their passionate love was to him the highest expression of divine creativity in man, but one which was reached through intense physical suffering. Kingsley

---

[31] JAF to Arthur Clough, 16/5/1852, Dunn i.185–6.
[32] *LML* i.330.
[33] CK to JL, undated, Martin (1950) 362.
[34] CK to JL, June 1852, *LML* i.338.

conceived of it in terms of sacrifice. It led him to translate in blank verse the celebrated scene from the sixth book of the *Iliad* where Andromache begs her husband to avoid impending death in battle and not to abandon her and her "playful-hearted babe." Ludlow thought the passage "flat" but to Mrs Kingsley it "was the first thing w. had ever made her feel what the real beauty & nobleness of Homer was."[35] Clearly to Charles and Fanny it possessed religious dimensions that it did not have to Ludlow. The passage was used for his novel as part of Hypatia's lecture which awakens in the monk Philammon sensations of the sublime "conquest of the spirit over the flesh."[36] Of course, to Kingsley, the notion of Hypatia's Neo-Platonism was as much a mistake as Philammon's celibacy. It is the physical reality of the matrimonial bond which is seen as the basic stimulant for spiritual courage. This had been explored earlier that year in the wider context of the meaning of suffering, martyrdom and saint-hood in Christianity. In the martyrdom of the early Christian saints Timothy and Maura he found an emblematic story to show that true sainthood is independent of celibate asceticism, and that true sanctity can be found in earthly love.

Kingsley must have known the story from the second chapter of Foxe's *Book of Martyrs*, where we read how after three weeks of mat-rimony, Timothy, a deacon of Mauritania, fell victim to the persecution of the Christians during the empery of Diocletian. He was apprehended and asked to deliver up the Holy Scriptures that were in his care so that they could be burned, something he sternly refused to do. The Governor Arrianus was much incensed and ordered him to have his eyes put out and to be hanged by the feet with a weight around his neck. When his newly-wed wife Maura implored him to give up the books for her sake, he reproved her mistaken love and declared he was willing to die for his faith. When Maura decided to follow her husband to glory, she was tortured too. "After this," Foxe con-cludes, "Timothy and Maura were crucified near each other."

In Kingsley's hands the final part of Foxe's story becomes a dra-matic monologue in blank verse in the tradition of Tennyson and Browning. The poem has a compelling immediacy in Maura's telling a silent and fainting Timothy how she had been tortured. When the two lovers are finally reunited and are left alone on their crosses

---

[35] CK to JL, undated, Martin (1950) 361.
[36] *H* 94.

("those gazers' eyes are gone at last!"), the reader is disturbed by being witness to Maura's deepest feelings and thus being very much like one of those deprecated gazers. This feeling is enforced by the way Maura's body is represented in the poem. As so often with Kingsley, the physical detail is startling:

> and I did not shriek—
> Once only—once, when first I felt the whip—
> It coiled so keen around my side, and sent
> A fire-flash through my heart which choked me—then
> I shrieked
> These little wrists, now—
> You said, one blessed night, they were too slender,
> [. . .] The cord has cut them through.

And to make the scene even more poignant, Kingsley makes Maura into a wife of three months (rather than three weeks) and hints that she might have been with child. "I can hardly bear to read it myself," he wrote to Ludlow, "but it is the deepest & clearest thing I have yet done."[37]

Not surprisingly, the physical tangibility of Saint Maura's fate appealed to Kingsley. It duplicates in poetry the drawing he made in 1842–3 of himself and Fanny going to Heaven, making love on a cross. "Saint Maura A.D. 304" is once more an expression of Kingsley's affirmation of the sanctity of the sexual act—"Come to thy bride-bed, martyr, wife once more"—which turns into a fore-taste of the eternal sexual bliss of "another body":

> —Oh, new limbs are ready,
> Free, pure, instinct with soul through every nerve,
> Kept for us in the treasuries of God.
> They will not mar the love they try to speak.

When he described to Ludlow his intention to turn to poetry as his artistic vocation, he added: "I feel my strong faculty is that sense of *form*, which, till I took to poetry, always came out in drawing."[38] Kingsley's "sense of form" is indeed a powerful feature of "Saint Maura A.D. 304."

---

[37] CK to JL, 2/5/1852, *LML* i.339.
[38] CK to JL, June 1852, *LML* i.338.

VII

But while "Saint Maura" was sent out to his father and to Hughes, Kingsley had started to give "colour and chiaroscuro" to a yet more ambitious work. He had first tried to draw its scenes, but "if I have made one drawing of Perseus & Andromeda, I have made 50, & burnt them all in disgust [. . .] the incompleteness of the pencil (for paint I cant) drives me to words."[39] But the composition in verse also caused him serious problems. "Oh!—Ah!—Eeeh!," he writes to Ludlow, "the children have come to the birth & there is not strength to bring forth. . . . I have laid a poem, & it won't hatch [. . .] I am with child of Perseus & Andromeda—and have got 'a wrong presentation!'."[40] What Kingsley was struggling with was the metre of the poem. He had tried unrhymed blank verse, as he had done in his translation from the *Iliad* and in "Saint Maura," as well as rhymed iambic pentameter, but neither could please him. He explained to Ludlow why:

> Rhymed metres run away with you, & you can't get the severe, curt, simple objectivity you want, in them—& unrhymed blank verse is very bald in my hands, because I wont write 'poetic diction', but only plain English—& so I can't get mythic grandeur enough. Oh for the spirit of Tennyson's Oenone![41]

The Poet Laureate clearly stood as a model for Kingsley in this artistic phase of his life and it did not escape the reviewers who sensed Tennyson's influence both in "Saint Maura" and in "Andromeda."

Ludlow suggested hexameters for the poem, but warned him that they were "foreign to our language." Kingsley picked up the idea, and although he "never had dreamed of daring to write hexameters," he sent Ludlow by return of post eighteen lines that he had "rattled off in the last 2 hours, in the act of dressing & breakfasting."[42] The first lines of the passage, which remained unaltered in the final version of "Andromeda," described in sensuous and erotic language Andromeda's ecstatic vision of the arrival of the Nereids, the young and beautiful daughters of the sea-god Nereus, mentor of Aphrodite.

---

[39] CK to JL, undated, Martin (1950) 368.
[40] CK to JL, undated, Martin (1950) 364–5.
[41] CK to JL, undated, Martin (1950) 365.
[42] CK to JL, undated, Martin (1950) 368.

Kingsley theorized at length on metre in his letters to Ludlow. He wrote to Parker to get copies of the articles on hexameters by William Whewell and W.S. Landor that had appeared in *Fraser's Magazine*. In the English language he found very few true diphthongs and consequently found it "a highly dactylic language" (i.e. a stress pattern of a stressed syllable followed by two unstressed ones) which made spondees (two stressed syllables) rather rare. But when scanning fifty lines of Homer, Lucretius, Virgil, Ovid and Goethe, he found respectively 48, 87, 116, 116, 66 spondees, while in his own "Andromeda" he came to only 32. As "Ovid always makes me inclined to vomit" the rule seems to be: "*in proportion to the badness of the poet, is the quantity of his spondees.*" Homer showed that his metre in "Andromeda" was fine. Moreover, his choice of sonorous words with "big vowels & lots of *liquids*" was a definite improvement on Whewell's "base noises" and their "verses [beginning] with 'and'!!!!!!"[43] All through June and July, Ludlow, who was experimenting with hexameters himself, joined in the discussion. Bits and pieces of "Andromeda" were forwarded to him, and sent back with comments and suggestions. Ludlow praised many passages, but on metre they could not agree. In one of his answers Kingsley included some boisterous doggerel (complete with stress-marks) at which Ludlow felt rather piqued. Kingsley hastened to apologize for these lines which he did "only in fun & fulness of heart" and he thanked Ludlow for all his precious criticisms of his poem. In the long run Ludlow did not resent this, since he recognized in Kingsley a great poet. In 1893, when decades of distance assured objectivity, he writes in an otherwise critical portrait of Kingsley that "in some of his poetry he rises higher than in all his prose, ay, to the level of his greatest contemporaries,"[44] and critics as different as Matthew Arnold and John Ruskin appreciated his poetry. Kingsley himself thought the art of poetry inferior to that of prose, and wrote in 1856: "Santa Maura is the poem, and Andromeda only the stalking horse. If my poetry lives, it will be by that and a song or two."[45] As it is, "Andromeda" must be reckoned amongst Kingsley's best poems and has earned a secure place in the canon of Victorian poetry for its fine use of hexameters. Unfortunately, Kingsley's decision in 1852 to become a poet

---

[43] CK to JL, undated, Martin (1950) 376.
[44] Ludlow (1893) 498.
[45] CK to Alexander Macmillan, undated, Kendall 98.

was short-lived, and after "Andromeda" he abandoned poetry for prose again.

The attraction of the Andromeda myth as Kingsley found it in Ovid was its matrimonial theme. When Perseus saw Andromeda bound on the rock, he exclaimed: "You should not be wearing such chains as these—the proper bonds for you are those which bind the hearts of fond lovers" and then turns to her parents, who had chained her to the rock, sacrificing a virgin, to ask whether he could have her hand if he saved her from the sea monster.[46] Kingsley responded to the story because he found in it an archetype of his own suit for Fanny, to whom the poem is dedicated: the eye-wedlock of Perseus resembled his own immediate attraction when he met Fanny for the first time, but, like Andromeda, Fanny's sexuality was bound by her parents' disapproval, and Kingsley-Perseus liberated her not only from her parents, but also from the "bulky and black" monster, viz. misguided religious celibacy. It is significant that, while in Ovid the parents are present throughout and immediately give their consent to marriage, in Kingsley's poem they disappear from the scene once they have chained and left their daughter to her fate. This gives Kingsley the possibility of exploring the growing intimacy between the two lovers. Similarly, whereas Ovid has a long dramatic passage describing Perseus' fight with the monster, Kingsley only borrows his eagle/osprey simile and states in a mere two lines that "thus fell the boy on the beast" in order to give ample space to the fulfilment of love through physical contact. This is so pervasive in "Andromeda," that it seems to constitute the real battle with the beast:

> [. . .] he kissed her, and clasped her yet closer and closer,
> [. . .] till her arms fell soft on his shoulder.
> [. . .] Then lifting her neck, like a sea-bird
> Peering up over the wave, from the foam-white swells of her bosom,
> Blushing she kissed him [. . .]
> Loosing his arms from her waist he flew upward, awaiting the sea-beast.
> [. . .]
> Leapt back again, full blest, towards arms spread wide to receive him.
> Brimful of honour he clasped her, and brimful of love she caressed him,
> Answering lip with lip; while above them the queen Aphrodité
> Poured on their foreheads and limbs, unseen, ambrosial odours,
> Givers of longing, and rapture, and chaste content in espousals.

---

[46] *Metamorphoses*, bk IV, transl. Innes 112.

The sensuous moves quickly to the erotic in the last passage, and though sexual passion seems safely sanctioned under the aegis of marriage, Aphrodite's claim to the lovers does not suffice as justification in itself. The theme of the Andromeda-myth worked on yet another level to Kingsley. When the goddess of love turns triumphantly to her sister Athene and says:

> 'Seest thou yonder thy pupil, thou maid of the Ægis-wielder?
> How he has turned himself wholly to love, and caresses a damsel,
> Dreaming no longer of honour, or danger, or Pallas Athene?
> Sweeter, it seems, to the young my gifts are; so yield me the stripling;
> Yield him me now, lest he die in his prime, like hapless Adonis'

Athene, goddess of practical reason, smilingly points out the social importance of marriage for civilization:

> 'Dear unto me, no less than to thee, is the wedlock of heroes;
> Dear, who can worthily win him a wife not unworthy; and noble,
> Pure with the pure to beget brave children, the like of their father.
> Happy, who thus stands linked to the heroes who were, and who shall be;
> Girdled with holiest awe, not sparing of self; for his mother
> Watches his steps with the eyes of the gods; and his wife and his children
> Move him to plan and to do in the farm and the camp and the council.
> Thence comes weal to a nation: but woe upon woe, when the people
> Mingle in love at their will, like the brutes, not heeding the future.'

This was an interpretation with which Kingsley was much taken. It made its beauty "unfathomable." As the myth represents these things at Joppa, Kingsley wrote to Ludlow, Andromeda "must have been a Canaanite" and this made it possible to see her plight as a "remnant of old human sacrifice to the dark powers of nature" and Perseus as a representative of "a higher race, with his golden hair & blue eyes" that saves her. When he discerns Andromeda he exclaims: "Tell me what barbarous horde, without law, unrighteous and heartless,/Hateful to gods and to men, thus have bound thee, a shame to the sunlight." Thus Kingsley's master-themes of sexual fulfilment and abhorrence of promiscuity are cast in a myth that reads the history of Christian civilization in terms of a "chaste content in espousals."

If both the translated *Iliad* passage and "Saint Maura" emphasized a submission of woman to man in a personal relationship which was both physical and spiritual, "Andromeda" seems to offer such submission as an explanation of Christian (protestant) progress. This has called forth the ire of modern feminist criticism. There is indeed a Victorian paternalistic attitude to society in much of Kingsley's writing

which often manifests itself in the female being liberated from bondage
when she submits to the male. This is also one of Kingsley's readings of the Andromeda-myth where woman cancels her self through
union with man. Still, this was not seen by Kingsley in terms of
sacrifice, but as realization of full womanhood. Similar rules applied
for man reaching his true manhood, and the poem is as much about
that as it is about Andromeda's submission. To maintain that "the
vision of Andromeda's torment, stripped naked, appealed to him as
a sign [. . .] of sexual servitude"[47] is to misunderstand Kingsley's
obsession with bondage. The sexual attraction Perseus feels for
Andromeda is manifest from the beginning, and he starts wooing
her before he thinks of liberating her. But rather than interpreting
this as evidence of Kingsley's attraction to woman's sexual servitude,
the emphasis is on Perseus who has to liberate her and slay the
black monster of his lust (sent by an incestuous goddess of the sea)
before his love will be sanctified by Athene. Kingsley would have
been sensitive to his use of "galley" (a Roman ship rowed by slaves
and convicts) to render Ovid's 'navis' to describe the approaching
monster when Perseus momentarily risks being *enslaved* by his sexual
passion for the beautiful Andromeda. As so often in Kingsley, being
bound represents the restraints upon sexual lust, to man as well as
to woman. Although Andromeda is chained naked to a rock, in
"Saint Maura" both lovers are chained, while in *Alton Locke* the male
is represented by Reni's bound St Sebastian. The restraint is, of
course, based on the sanction religion can give sexual love. Thus it
is not surprising that Perseus initially takes the chained Andromeda
for a "snow-white cross."

Adrienne Munich overshoots the mark when, in her otherwise
attentive reading of the poem, she jeers at Kingsley's galley as a
"great ocean liner,"[48] just as she misses the point when she affirms
that in the last line Kingsley's attitude to sex is ambivalent and that
it "contradicts the meaning of marriage as purification." Since he
represents Athene as "unsullied", she argues that Kingsley both
"sanctifies carnality" and "associates carnality with being sullied."[49]
However, the adjective does not reflect Andromeda's state. The goddess
is described as unsullied because she sanctions married love in contrast

---

[47] Munich 58.
[48] Munich 63.
[49] Munich 74.

with that of the incestuous queen of the deep to whom Andromeda is sacrificed by her backward (and incestuous) people. The poem thus makes an interesting case for Kingsley's own definition of love and lust and provides interesting psychological insight into the fragility of civilisation and the danger of a relapse into barbarism which ran parallel to his attempt to come to terms with his instinctive primordial sexuality. At the same time the black enslaving galley in "Andromeda" represents respectability's obstructive and hypocritical repression of sexuality, which makes Victorian men, as William Rathbone Greg put it in his assessment of Kingsley's erotic frankness, "slaves to what others think, and wish, to do, slaves to past creeds in which we have no longer pleasure."[50] And, to express his agreement with Kingsley on the question of the sexual hypocrisy of the age, Greg added that "in treating of the various questions arising out of the relations between the sexes, we lose much and risk much by a mischievous reticence and a false and excessive delicacy."[51] If there is ambivalence in "Andromeda," it is here, in the galley. The exploration of this theme in encounters with a primeval culture for a renewal of English culture was to be revisited three years later in *Westward Ho!*.

"Saint Maura A.D. 304" and "Andromeda" were not published in 1852. Although Kingsley was a hasty prose writer—an "improvisatore" as W.R. Greg put it[52]—he was strikingly reluctant to let poetry stand in its first version. When Ludlow argued for keeping original spontaneity and not to polish overmuch, Kingsley could not agree. "If you are a *verse-maker*, you will of course rub off the edges & the silvering, he argued, "but if you are a poet, & have an idea a one keynote running through the whole, w. you can't for the life define to yourself, but wh. is there out of the abysses defining you; then polishing is a bringing the thing nearer to that idea."[53] "Saint Maura" and "Andromeda" were such self-defining poems that needed polishing. "Saint Maura" was started at the beginning of the year and took some six months of polishing, and after a month of discussing hexameters with Ludlow, he wrote that he would "keep & work over this Andromeda till I have made it something that will live."[54]

---

[50] Greg (1860) 24.
[51] Greg (1860) 22.
[52] Greg (1860) 18.
[53] CK to JL, undated, Martin (1950) 382–3.
[54] CK to JL, undated, Martin (1950) 390.

Although during the following years Kingsley tried to get a volume of poetry out which included these cardinal pieces, it was not until 1858 that Parker finally decided to publish *Andromeda and Other Poems*, Kingsley's first volume of collected poetry after *The Saint's Tragedy*. By then, of course, Kingsley was at the height of his fame, having published a series of successful novels, and the contemporary judgement of his poetry in 1858 was necessarily coloured by the fame of *Hypatia* and *Westward Ho!* and does not reflect the fact that much of it was written back in 1852. Hexameters, for example, had come to be generally disliked in 1858. W.C. Roscoe in *The National Review* maintained that "perhaps there is no human being who reads it with pleasure,"[55] to John Skelton in *Fraser's* they were "these obnoxious English hexameters,"[56] and *Blackwood's* critic E.B. Hamley admitted "an ancient prejudice against hexameters."[57] Still, all agreed that "Kingsley handles it well,"[58] that "we forget, in the flow and music of many of Mr Kingsley's lines, our rooted objection,"[59] that after all "Andromeda" is "very exquisite," and "dewy, fragrant, and rosy."[60]

The reviewers were not indifferent to, but more reticent about, the intense and passionate love that emanates from the poems. *Fraser's* rather prudishly remarked on the "refined sensuousness" of "Andromeda" and its "warm and voluptuously idealized enjoyment of the powers of life,"[61] while Hamley wrote "No tame lovers these— no humdrum pair."[62] *The National Review* and *The Saturday Review* were more explicit on Kingsley's allusions to sex in "Andromeda." The reviewer of the *Saturday* called it "a glowing Etty-picture of the best kind," referring to the numerous small sensuous paintings of nudes that William Etty (1787–1849) turned out during the 1840s, while Roscoe took Kingsley seriously on this issue. He admitted that he felt mainly sympathetic to this "emphatic denouncer of prudery" and had "no quarrel with Mr. Kingsley for boldly handling subjects that seem to him to require it," but he questions Kingsley's delicacy in doing so: "As modesty veils the person, so it veils a thousand other

---

[55] [Roscoe] 131.
[56] [Skelton] 745.
[57] "Kingsley's Andromeda" *Blackwood's Magazine* 84 (1858) 222.
[58] "Mr. Kingsley's Poems" *National Review* 7 (1858) 132.
[59] "Kingsley's Andromeda" *Blackwood's Magazine* 84 (1858) 222.
[60] [Skelton] 747.
[61] [Skelton] 745.
[62] [Hamley] 225.

things; and it is no defence of an allusion to these in print to say that in themselves they are infinitely sound, pure, and healthy."[63] The danger of Kingsley's writing is that

> He has taken the energetic healthy animal man under his protection; but the healthy animal man is generally pretty well able to defend himself, and needs but gentle stimulants to his appetites, his anger, or even his love of physical excitement.[64]

The sentiment here coincides with that of the *Saturday Review*, which, in its review of "Andromeda," conferred upon Kingsley the title "the great Apostle of the Flesh."[65]

VIII

Mrs Kingsley did not feel well during the early summer of 1852. Although giving birth to Mary had proved without complications, towards the end of June she felt weak, suffered obscure pains, and fainted repeatedly. The previous summer, when she was unwell, the famed obstetrician Edward Rigby had been consulted, but this time Kingsley wanted none of the "London prigs," and a local physician was consulted. He prescribed "quinine & less baby."[66] This made her feel much better. She, however, still had to keep to her room, which was an ordeal in the excessive summer heat that year. It was also trying to Kingsley. "If you knew the miserable anxiety in w. I have been working the last week," he wrote to Ludlow.[67] And there was plenty of work to do beside the regular parish duties. New instalments of *Hypatia* had to be written. Parts were sent out to Froude, Ludlow, Maurice, Müller, Bunsen and others. Although suggestions were made by his friends, and although Kingsley promised he would rewrite pieces, in the end he very rarely found the time to do so. His relationship with Parker had improved momentarily and he agreed to do reviews for *Fraser's*, which implied a further demand on his time. Besides, his correspondence with friends as well as with complete strangers remained intense.

---

[63] [Roscoe] 136.
[64] [Roscoe] 137.
[65] [-], "Kingsley's Andromeda and Other Poems" *Saturday Review* 5 (1858), 594.
[66] CK to JL, undated, Martin (1950) 386.
[67] CK to JL, undated, Martin (1950) 382.

On one occasion the correspondence with one of those readers who, after the publication of *Yeast*, had turned to Kingsley for advice, inspired new literary work. Just before Easter 1852, a letter was received from "a young man who had been much perplexed by the Chapman doctrines about truth being merely subjective." Kingsley promptly answered this letter, but thought something more needed to be said on *religious truth*. In Kingsleyan fashion, if the story's account about its composition is to be taken seriously, he wrote a Socratic dialogue during the night, breaking it off occasionally to smoke a cigar on the terrace.[68] In late spring he read it out to Maurice who was "exceedingly delighted with it."[69] He suggested that Kingsley publish it. It was offered to Parker, but they declined it. At the beginning of August, therefore, Kingsley mailed the dialogue to Maurice, who had not yet seen it in written form, for advice as to another publisher. Maurice thought the Macmillan brothers, who had set up a publishing house at Cambridge, the right people, and promised Kingsley to forward it "with all high words from Hare and me."[70] Maurice kept his word, and three days later he wrote to Daniel Macmillan about Kingsley's manuscript, and explained the way it had come about. He added that Hare too thought greatly of it "as an imitation of Plato and for its direct purpose," and that Hare "is the best judge on such a subject."[71] Alexander Macmillan liked the dialogue, but thought that its shortness would make it difficult to market, and he suggested making it part of a story set in modern times to "explain the transition from Athens to Cambridge."[72] Kingsley conceded to Macmillan's wants, and the original 35 pages of dialogue were amplified to a story of a publishable 70 pages.

While the dialogue merely says that logic cannot but equate truth with the Godhead, the main interest of *Phaeton* lies in the "modern envelopment," which is a lively conversation between a country squire called Templeton and the first person narrator-clergyman, who is also the writer of the embedded Socratic dialogue. The occasion for the exchange of opinions is a dinner party the previous night at which the American Professor Windrush, the thinly veiled portrait of Ralph

---

[68] "Phaeton" *LGE* 363.
[69] FDM to Daniel Macmillan, 9/8/1852, Maurice 1.123.
[70] FDM to CK, 6/8/1852, Maurice i.123.
[71] FDM to Daniel Macmillan, 9/8/1852, Maurice i.124.
[72] FDM to CK, 13/8/1852, Maurice i.124.

Waldo Emerson that had already appeared in *Alton Locke*, was entertained. But whereas in his novel Kingsley was essentially concerned with Emerson's influence on working men, in *Phaeton* he explores the effect of American transcendentalism on the landed gentry. "How, in the name of English exclusiveness, did such a rampantly heterodox spiritual guerilla invade the respectabilities and conservatisms of Herefordshire?" the narrator incredulously exclaims. Templeton explains that the austere evangelicalism that his mother, "a great Low-Church saint," tried to instill in him was greatly responsible for "ripening" him for Professor Windrush's teaching. Evangelicalism was stifling to the "shrewd dashing boy, enjoying life to the finger-tips":

> she brought me up to pray and hope that I might some day be converted, and become a child of God—And one could not help wishing to enjoy oneself as much as possible before that event happened [. . .] I had no reason put before me for regarding such a change as anything but an unpleasant doom, which would cut me off, or ought to do so, from field sports, from poetry, from art, from science, from politics [. . .] from man and all man's civilization, in short.[73]

Such an exclusive notion of religion demanded certain fears, hopes and experiences that Templeton could not feel or experience. This estranged him from Christianity itself, and he had begun to

> suspect that religion and effeminacy had a good deal to do with each other. For the women, whatsoever their temperaments, or even their tastes might be, took to this to me incomprehensible religion naturally and instinctively; while the very few men who were in their clique were—I don't deny some of them were good men enough—if they had been men at all: if they had been well-read, or well-bred, or gallant, or clear-headed, or liberal-minded, or, in short, anything but the silky, smooth-tongued hunt-the-slippers nine out of ten of them were.[74]

The course of Templeton's notion of religion is similar to Alton Locke's, who was driven from his mother's suffocating puritanical views to be "entirely carried away" by Mr Windrush, as he records in his autobiography: "There was so much which was true, so much which it would have been convenient to believe true, and all put so eloquently and originally."[75] In both instances evangelical low-church

---

[73] *LGE* 403–4.
[74] *LGE* 403.
[75] *AL'* 211.

morale is blamed for driving people into the arms of a philosophy
that maintained that man contained everything that was essential in
himself and had his origins within himself, that sincere personal belief
had more authority for the revelation of the deepest truths than logic
and (scientific) experience.

Phaeton is a neglected work. Admittedly, the Socratic dialogue is
mainly a religious tract written without any real artistic inspiration,
but the story of Templeton and his pious wife Jane, who are growing ever more apart in their exclusive creeds, provides an interesting insight into the estrangement and the pain religious doubt caused
in the husband-wife relationship. As such, it merits inclusion in the
discussion of Victorian literature of unbelief.

What Templeton shares with Lancelot, Alton, and probably the
young Kingsley himself when he was at university, is the attraction
of a religious system that sees physical existence as "part and par-
ticiple of God."[76] Templeton's memories of boyhood remind us of
Kingsley's years first at Chelsea, and then at Cambridge, a part of
his life that later had to be repudiated. The reaction in *Phaeton* is
thus directed both at the Emersonians who are characterized as holding that "you may believe nothing if you like, and welcome; but if
you do take to that unnecessary act, you are a fool if you believe
anything but what I believe—though I do not choose to state what
that is,"[77] and at the narrowly evangelical background Kingsley knew
at Chelsea. That autobiographical significance can be read into this
is shown in the reluctance, soon after the publication of *Phaeton*, to
support a cause near his heart. When in November George Grove
appealed to Kingsley for the use of his pen and name in the campaign for keeping the Crystal Palace open on Sundays as a coun-
termeasure against drunkenness on the Sabbath, he declined. The
evangelical party in the Church objected to what they saw as dis-
couraging Sunday-observance, and although Kingsley agreed with
Grove, he had to apologize: "My great hitch is that my family are
strongly the other way, and that although my father himself is very
liberal on the matter, it would pain him dreadfully to see me in the
wars with the Evangelical party on that point. His health is bad,
and he is very nervous."[78] It is likely that the anti-Low Church tone

---

[76] Ralph Waldo Emerson, *Nature*, ch. 1.
[77] *LGE* 356.
[78] CK to George Grove, 28/10/1852, *LML* i.351–2.

of *Phaeton* had helped upset his father. Maurice too sensed that Kingsley had tended to make the Evangelical claim to truth too light, "at least so it will appear to many over whom you might have a healthful influence."[79] Kingsley tried to amend this before sending it to the printers, but the impression remains.

Although *Phaeton* was to Maurice's liking, reviewers and readers were less convinced of its qualities. A reviewer writing in *The Athenaeum* saw *Phaeton* merely as a quarrel between "two schools of thinking in our time" and on Kingsley's part, after having been accused of advocating Carlylism and Emersionianism in his writings, as "a formal announcement of his own orthodoxies," with which "we, as critics, have no concern."[80] Those whom Kingsley attacked—'Chapman and Co.' and the unitarians—were outraged by *Phaeton* A collaborator at Chapman's *Westminster Review*, George Eliot, Kingsley's exact contemporary, read the book in the first week of November and longed "to cut it up." "Kingsley provokes me more and more," she wrote to Charles and Caroline Bray.[81] A few months later she admitted to Mrs Peter Alfred Taylor that because Kingsley had great qualities as a writer, his faults truly vexed her: "But perhaps you may not be as much in love with Kingsley's genius, and as "riled" by his faults, as I am."[82] There is no doubt that she followed Kingsley's literary career with interest, and that, notwithstanding Kingsley's preaching, she did esteem his qualities as a novelist was confirmed when she directed one of the seven presentation copies of her first novel *Adam Bede* in 1858 to the Rectory at Eversley. Eliot's first novel may have owed more to Kingsley than is generally acknowledged. The *Saturday Review* seemed to have sensed as much in its review of *Adam Bede* when it asserted of its author that "evidently he has sat at the feet of Mr. Kingsley, and Mr. Kingsley may in many points be proud of his follower."[83]

All in all, *Phaeton* was not a success. It was not reprinted until its inclusion in the *Collected Works* in 1880, and the series of dialogues that Maurice had proposed came to nothing.

---

[79] FDM to CK, 11/9/1852, Maurice i.132.
[80] [-], *Athenaeum* 30/10/1852, 1168.
[81] George Eliot to Charles and Caroline Bray, 6/11/1852, Haight ii.66.
[82] George Eliot to Mrs Peter Alfred Taylor, 1/2/1853, Haight ii.86.
[83] [-], *The Saturday Review*, 26/2/1859, 250–1.

IX

The last two months of 1852 passed quietly. *Hypatia* was to continue
in instalments until April 1853, but most of the novel had been written by mid-October. "I do not know whether I have worked out
the £100 w. you advanced me," Kingsley wrote to Parker, "but if
I have, I should be very glad indeed (if it were convenient to your
house,) if you could advance me the rest as talked of doing when
we knew how long the book wd. be."[84] Relations with Parker had
decidedly improved, even though they had failed to accept the proposed volume of poetry, and Kingsley was asked to come over and
stay with him for the monumental funeral of the Duke of Wellington
in November. The publishing house also had plans of bringing out
a series of "standard authors" and asked Kingsley to do an introduction to Sidney's *Defense of Poesy*, to which he 'gladly' assented,
adding "I had better read the book, wh. I never did." Whether this
admission made Parker think the better of it or not is difficult to
say, but the book was never published.

---

[84] CK to John Parker, undated, Martin (1950) 403.

CHAPTER TWELVE

WHICH THE YOUNG AND INNOCENT WILL DO WELL TO LEAVE ALTOGETHER UNREAD (1853)

The winter of 1852–3 was again a period of bad health for Mrs Kingsley. Although the quinine-and-less-Baby cure helped her through her post-natal ailments, December brought her down with a form of influenza, and a persistent cough developed which necessitated a change of air. With Mrs Kingsley and the children at Ramsgate, Kingsley found himself alone at Eversley with "my pipe & my brandy & water being a widdered orphan." The weather was wet and the flooded country made fox-hunting and fishing impossible, so it was time to pour out his bile to Thomas Hughes in a remarkable passage of hunter's slang:

> I had a grind today: but I couldnt do anything: It was all neck & money, & a cheap screw like mine had no chance. I did some grew-some things in the first two miles, but the ground beat me, blew the old man before he could get his second wind, & trod his fore shoes almost off, & I had to go to the nearest forge & was beaten off beastly— horrid done & sold, & passed by base road riders who hadn't crossed a fence all day.

One should not infer from this that Kingsley did not perform his parochial duties, but the description of how an ordinary week-day (a Friday) was spent is suggestive of Kingsley's life-style. The picture of the evening alone at home is equally revealing. After the hunt described above, the lone rector went on foot ("my backside [. . .] sore" after the day's grind) to Bramshill to enquire after the Copes, and returned "sulky as a bear, having been thrown out, & as stupid as a pot, having just dined."[1]

In February Kingsley started negotiating the publication of *Hypatia* in book form, and asked Parker for payment upon publication. Notwithstanding the fact that they had obvious rights to the novel, Parker was quick to react. *Hypatia* was the Kingsley-novel they wanted

---

[1] CK to TH, 14/1/1853, Martin (1950) 427.

to publish that year, but, having refused *Alton Locke* in 1850 and having turned down a volume of sermons as well as *Phaeton* the previous year, they feared Kingsley might want to look elsewhere for publication. So they forwarded a check straightaway, adding that they would be loath to loose him as a writer. Even Kingsley was surprised: "I really did not want the cheque w. you sent so instantly," he apologized, "all I wanted was, a price for the book *when it came out*, in the regular trade way, instead of half profits at the years end." But, notwithstanding Parker's generosity, their publishing relationship needed some clarification:

> I don't think that you can say, my dear fellow that I left you. You yourself declined Alton Locke, when I offered it to you, & sent me kindly enough to Chapman, but you can't call that leaving you. And you declined also the sermons when I offered them you. And you declined Phaeton when I offered it to Frazer's. I would much sooner publish with you than with most other publishers: but I don't think that in a single case, *I* have left *you*.[2]

A fair warning that they would have done well to heed. They lost Kingsley's next novel in 1855, the best-selling *Westward Ho!*, to the Macmillan brothers and it would make that firm into a major fiction publisher that would long outlive Parker's.

The conduct of Kingsley's hero Rajah Brooke as Her Majesty's Commissioner in Sarawak again came under parliamentary investigation in 1853. Joseph Hume renewed his campaign against the use of the British flag in the suppression of the Dyaks, while a group of supporters of Brooke, amongst them Hughes and Kingsley, tried to lobby support for the white rajah. Kingsley went in "heart & soul," plotted with Thomas Hughes, and sent circulars to "many Belgravians," but his imagination at the time was chiefly captivated by a report in the newspapers of a spectacular fox-hunt of over fifty miles in the Lake District. "Oh that I cd. write a ballad thereanent," he concluded his letter to Hughes, "The thing has taken possession of me, but I cant find words. There was never such a run since *we* were born,—& think of hounds doing the last 30 miles *alone*."[3]

It is striking that Kingsley, who had corresponded so frequently with Ludlow about metre the preceding summer, had so little to say

---

[2] CK to John Parker, 20/2/1853, Martin (1950) 429.
[3] CK to TH, undated, Martin (1950) 436.

to him now—"I have nothing to tell you," he wrote on 14 July, after a long silence—while his epistles to Hughes remained eloquent and lively. What he shared with Hughes was the thorough physical enjoyment of the sportsman, which was the very bone and marrow of Kingsley's life. Hughes remembers how one evening, walking together in the London streets through a dense fog, philosophizing about the meaning of life, Kingsley abruptly asked him: "Tom, do you want to live to be old? [. . .] I dread it more than I can say. To feel one's powers going, and to end in snuff and stink." When Hughes tried to point out that some reached a great age with dignity and clarity of mind, Kingsley responded that that was no good "for an eager, fiery nature like mine, with fierce passions eating one's life out."[4]

The occasion of the foggy walk with Hughes through London was a meeting with Francis Thomas McDougall, whom Kingsley had invited to his father's rectory in Chelsea for dinner. McDougall, an "old college chum" of Hughes, had gone to Sarawak in June 1848 as a missionary and had briefly returned to England in 1853 to settle business with his London-based missionary society. He returned to Borneo soon after and in 1855 was appointed Bishop of Labuan and Sarawak. McDougall knew James Brooke well, and his first-hand experience of tropical exotic scenery made him a fascinating dinner guest. Kingsley's parents being away, the three had a quick dinner before they adjourned to the study. Seeing that Hughes wrote his Memoir twenty-seven years after the event, we cannot trust him too much as to the accuracy of the reported dialogues. Still, the general impression he gives of Kingsley that evening is probably near the truth. He describes how he and McDougall took the two fireside armchairs while Kingsley stood in his favourite attitude before the fire talking, now and then "taking a tramp up and down the room, a long clay pipe in his right hand (at which he gave an occasional suck; it was generally out, but he scarcely noticed it), and his left hand passed behind his back, clasping the right elbow." Hughes reports that they talked much of fishing, working-men's associations and Borneo. McDougall told wonderful stories of "apes, converts, and honey bears" and it struck Hughes that Kingsley seemed "as familiar with the Bornean plants and birds, as though he had lived there."

---

[4] Hughes (1876) xxxvii.

Kingsley that evening was very much "Parson Lot the Socialist Chief" to McDougall and Hughes. They took a lively interest in Kingsley's literary works and tried to draw him out as to his restless method of composition. He explained that he could not think "except in the dramatic form" and that he never put pen to paper unless he saw two or three pages as already printed in his mind while taking a "turn in the garden." Only then would he go in, write it down, and return to the garden, and so on.[5] But the religious establishment was not so sure about Kingsley's literary accomplishments as Hughes and McDougall were. Kingsley's reputation as an unconventional religious writer started to affect those who associated with him.

II

When in 1849 Kingsley was refused a chair at King's College, Maurice saw this decision as an "admonition to me to set my house in order."[6] He was not far wrong there. Maurice's connection with Kingsley was seen with suspicious eyes by the council of the College. The doubt the council felt about the suitability of Maurice for its Chair of Divinity had sharpened considerably since Croker brought against Maurice and Kingsley the public accusation that they acted out of "a morbid craving for notoriety" in the *Quarterly Review* in 1851. Principal Jelf wrote in no uncertain terms about the undesirability of his friendship with Kingsley, especially after the publication of *Alton Locke* and the Drew affair. Although Jelf had to admit that he could find nothing inconsistent in Maurice's socialist writings with his holding the Chair of Divinity, he could not "speak in similar terms of Mr. Kingsley's writings." He deemed his use of the Scriptures "irreverent," and his language generally "inflammatory" and "insurrectionary." When in November 1851 *The Guardian* hinted at Kingsley's connection with *The Leader*, it was time for Jelf to demand from Maurice that he would either resign or "openly disavow Mr. Kingsley." Otherwise people would be justified in drawing the conclusion that "Mr. Maurice is identified with Mr. Kingsley, and Mr. Kingsley is

---

[5] Hughes (1876) xxxviii–xxxix.
[6] FDM to Julius Hare, 28/5/1848, Maurice i.478.

identified with Mr. Holyoake, and Mr. Holyoake is identified with Tom Paine. . . . There are only three links between King's College and the author of the 'Rights of Man'."[7]

Maurice rose to the occasion when, in his answer to Jelf, he affirmed that he "knew that Mr. Kingsley *lived* for no other purpose than to assert the truths which Mr. Holyoake and the writers of the *Leader* deny," and that therefore admitting any of the charges made against Kingsley would be a "dastardly falsehood." Moreover, he concluded, while such suspicions circulated he would certainly not resign his office.[8] Jelf acquiesced for the time being. When, however, Maurice wrote in his *Theological Essays* in 1853 that he did not believe in eternal punishment, Jelf found sufficient reason to dismiss the Professor of Divinity without even giving him time to finish his series of lectures. Although his belief was supported by the fact that the notion of everlasting punishment had been discredited by the Anglican Church when it was removed from its articles in 1571, many Evangelicals tenaciously held to it. Maurice argued in his last essay that popular theology put too much emphasis on punishment rather than on evil itself, so that people were terrified more by the former than by the latter. Man needed to be delivered from sin not from punishment, he needed to believe in God, not in the Devil. Maurice's *Theological Essays* constituted an epoch for Kingsley: "If the Church of England rejects them, her doom is fixed," he wrote to an unnamed friend, "She will rot and die, as the Alexandrian did before her."[9]

One wonders whether without Kingsley as publicist of the Christian Socialist movement Maurice's Chair would have met the same fate. Maurice's dismissal also closely touched Kingsley's reputation. "Your cause is mine," he wrote Maurice when the crisis at King's was about to break, "we swim in the same boat, & stand or fall henceforth together." Needless to say Kingsley was on his master's side and ready for combat: "if you are condemned for these 'opinions' I shall & must therefore avow them, & they will have to squelch me as well as you. And I will not, please God, die unavenged in the true sense [. . .] As long as I have teeth & claws, I will die

---

[7] R.W. Jelf to FDM, 7/11/1851, Maurice ii.80.
[8] FDM to R.W. Jelf, 8/11/1851, Maurice ii.81–2.
[9] CK to unidentified correspondent, undated, *LML* i.371.

fighting like a good fox—". As to the reality of the threat which the outcry presented to Maurice, Kingsley joked:

> When old Cuvier died & went on his way, he came to the place where the upward & downward roads meet—& there behold the Devil. "Come along with me you old sinner!" says the Devil. "Hein? Hein? What's that you say?" quoth Cuvier, being somewhat deaf. "Come along with me, or I'll eat you, body & bones!" says the Devil. Cuvier took a large pinch of snuff; looked at him from head to foot; & then— "Hein? Hein? Hoofs & horns—Hoofs & horns—Ruminant—Can't do it!"—& he walked leisurely off up the upper road—[10]

Kingsley's own spiritual body and bones were equally difficult to ingest, although his ecclesiastical reputation had been compromised by his writings so far. And the reception of *Hypatia* did not improve the situation either.

Notwithstanding Kingsley's buoyant tone in his letters to Maurice, the public proceedings against the master were a true source of distress for him. Work in his own parish in 1853 was both successful and frustrating too. Incessant parochial work over the years in Eversley had started to bear fruit, but it had not been obtained without sacrifice. No pupils could be found to pay a curate, so all the parish-work fell on Kingsley himself. Although relationships between rector and Bramshill House seemed promising when the new Cope, also a clergyman, took possession of the estate the previous year, Kingsley soon discovered that he was "a mere bookworm" who knew "nothing how to manage an estate."[11] Personal friction seemed to have emerged soon after Sir William took residence. Cope was excessively irritable at times, and in September Kingsley was forced to speak hard words after the occurrence of an "unfortunate interview with Mrs. Kingsley." Information of what had happened between Cope and Mrs Kingsley is no longer extant, but Kingsley informed Stapleton almost a year later that he had "every reason to believe that he [Cope] was insane a few months ago."[12]

After the initial impression Sir William Cope had given of his willingness to invest in his property, not much was done once the preparations to make Bramshill comfortable in 1852 had been completed.

---

[10] CK to FDM, 21/7/1853, BL-41297 f.42.
[11] CK to AS, 6/9/1854, MP-C0171–36919.
[12] CK to AS, 6/9/1854; see also CK to FK, undated, BL-62554 f.65.

In November 1853 "a great piece of the wall of the long gallery, fell down on the terrace, with such a dreadful crash" that it was necessary to prop up that side of the house with beams "for fear more should fall."[13] Cope's property in Eversley hardly fared any better under the new owner. In October 1853, the local Sanitary Committee reported "nuisances" that had to be removed from some of these cottages. In November Kingsley had to remind Cope of his duty in these "small sanitary repairs" and it seems from a letter of February 1854, when cholera was raging in England again, that nothing sanitary had yet been done to the "dear old treacherous" Eversley.[14] Sir William Cope seems to have been more interested in receiving the Bishop of Oxford for the inauguration of the new national school at Eversley with a full choral service cathedral style. Of course, the opening of the first real school in the parish was the result of Kingsley's exertions, but he graciously waived any claims to conducting the service and put it entirely in Cope's hands.

III

Hypatia; or, New Foes with an Old Face came out in book form in May 1853. George Henry Lewes in *The Leader* had been attacking the serialized version as it was appearing in its monthly instalments in *Fraser's*. In January 1852 he wrote that he entirely disapproved of its "*wilful* mingling of the quite modern with the ancient colouring," which he could not but see as a mistake. In March he thought that Kingsley's ambitious novel was becoming somewhat wearisome, while in April, not yet a third through the novel, he pronounced the whole project to be the "failure of a remarkable writer."[15] On the other hand, Kingsley's other enemy, the high-church *Guardian*, expressed doubts about the novel's respectability. Parker felt uneasy with such criticism, and informed Kingsley that they feared it would injure the sales of their magazine. Kingsley replied that the next instalment (chapters 9 and 10 in May) would even have "satisfied the Guardian & respectability." About Lewes he was more outspoken. He was "an ignorant charlatan, who dislikes me, because I have boldly shaken

---

[13] CK to Maurice Kingsley, 10/11/53, BL-41298 f.210v.
[14] CK to FK, February 1854, *LML* i.420.
[15] Martin (1959) 146.

off the Leader, & therefore snarls & snaps."[16] Still, Kingsley was touchy about Lewes's criticism, and he constantly updated Parker on all the positive reactions he got to the historical veracity of *Hypatia* from people like Maurice, Hare, Froude, Bunsen and Müller. Artistically, the novel was of great importance to Kingsley. In an early letter of January 1852 he pointed out that *Hypatia* was "a work of pure art" and in the spring he felt he had to set Hughes right, because the latter thought *Hypatia* an allegory of the present time: "It is strictly a historic tale, & I have, in the character of Hypatia & every incident, worked out all the historic facts I found."[17] Charles Kegan Paul remembered in later life how he stayed with the Kingsleys through the summer of 1852 and how he was struck by the "extraordinary pains" Kingsley took to be accurate in detail: "We spent one whole day in searching the four folio volumes of Synesius for a fact he thought was there, and which was found there at last." He added: "The hard reading he had undergone for that book alone would furnish an answer to some who thought him superficial."[18]

The subtitle of the novel and its conclusion that the reader had been shown his "own likenesses in toga and tunic, instead of coat and bonnet"[19] has tended to obscure the artistic and aesthetic qualities of the work. Kingsley's third novel posed enormous challenges. Whereas for *Yeast* and *Alton Locke*, he could draw on his own direct knowledge and experience of the social and sanitary condition of England, for *Hypatia* he had to set his imagination to work with the historical facts of a country he had never visited. The result has called forth very different comments, from accusations in *Blackwood's Magazine* in 1855 that Kingsley "systematically overworks his materials" and thus produced "about the wildest book that ever was written"[20] to Joseph Ellis Baker's view seventy-five years later that "the historical imagination has seldom achieved anything so magnificent."[21] Indeed, although it is not difficult to pinpoint its numerous defects, *Hypatia* is a most remarkable novel.

For his setting Kingsley chose the events of the Christian Church in early fifth-century Alexandria, using as a pivotal character the

[16] CK to John Parker, undated, Martin (1950) 334.
[17] CK to Th, undated, BL-41298 f.62.
[18] C. Kegan Paul to FK, undated, *LML* i.229.
[19] *H* 345.
[20] [Aytoun] (1855) 631–2.
[21] Joseph Ellis Baker 95.

Greek Neo-Platonic philosopher Hypatia, whose fate was well-known to the nineteenth-century reader through the graphic description of it in *The Decline and Fall of the Roman Empire*.[22] "Hypatia was torn from her chariot," Gibbon wrote, "stripped naked, dragged to the church, and inhumanly butchered by the hands of Peter the reader, and a troop of savage and merciless fanatics."[23] This was enough to engage Kingsley's imagination. He filled in his historical details with what he found in the seventh book of Socrates Scolasticus' *Ecclesiastical History*[24] and introduced a series of historical characters, such as Hypatia's father Theon, the Roman prefect Orestes, the Patriarch Cyril, bishop Synesius of Cyrene (Ptolemais), and Augustine of Hippo. To these he added the fictional characters Philammon (a Christian monk brought up in the desert), his sister Pelagia (a high-class dancer and courtesan), Raphael Aben-Ezra (a rich Jewish libertine), Miriam (an old Jewish sorceress), Victoria (the daughter of a Roman officer) and a group of ill-mannered, but courageous, Goths. The plot of the novel follows the mounting tensions in Alexandria between the Neo-Platonist Greeks, the Christians, and the Jews of the city, which result in Hypatia's death at the hands of the monks. The Goths are outsiders in the city. While they have a significant role in the lives of the novel's main characters, historically they are of little importance. Their physical prowess is provided as a foil to the effeminate and over-civilized peoples of Kingsley's Alexandria.

When Kingsley started to toy with the idea of his third novel in January 1851, he wrote to Maurice that he wanted "to set forth Christianity as the only really Democratic creed, & Philosophy, above all Spiritualism, as the most exclusively aristocratic creed."[25] With spiritualism he was thinking of the "Emersonian Anythingarianism" that MacKaye in *Alton Locke* had so sharply and eloquently condemned: "That every puir fellow as has no gret brains in his head will be left to his superstition, an' his ignorance, to fulfil the lusts o' his flesh; while the few that are geniuses, or fancy themselves sae,

---

[22] Cf. Frank M. Turner, "Christians and Pagans in Victorian Novels", in Catharine Edwards ed., *Roman Presences: Receptions of Rome in European Culture, 1789–1945* (Cambridge: Cambridge University Press, 1999), 173–87.

[23] Edward Gibbon, *The Decline and Fall of the Roman Empire*, ed. David Womersley, 3 vols. (London: Allen Lane,1994), ii.946.

[24] Kingsley further refers his readers "for further information about the private life of the fifth century" to Synesius' and Isidore's letters (*H* xvi).

[25] CK to FDM, 19/1/1851, BL-41297 f.16r.

are to ha' the monopoly o' this private still o' philosophy—these
carbonari, illuminati, vehmgericht, samothracian mysteries o' bottled
moonshine."[26] What is at the bottom of this condemnation of transcendentalism is Kingsley's understanding of the reality of the
Incarnation which determined his entire theological outlook. What
had been the emphatic element of conversion in *Yeast*, viz. "Christ—
THE MAN," is also the perspective from which all the characters
in *Hypatia* are seen. Closely related to this is Kingsley's belief that
the family and the nation are the "two divine roots of the Church,"[27]
something that he saw threatened by the Tractarian ideals of the
monastic system of the early Church. Cyril and his Alexandrian
monks, "like all weak ones, found total abstinence easier than temperance, religious thought more pleasant than godly action; and a
monastic world grew up all over the East, of such vastness that in
Egypt it was said to rival in numbers the lay population"[28]—a veritable spectre to Kingsley. Thus, in Emersonianism and Tractarianism
Kingsley found his "New Foes with an Old Face."

IV

Early on in the novel, Hypatia lectures to her elect public that the
"soul is all with which our souls must deal" and she contends that in
Homer each detail has "spiritual meaning." It is therefore absurd to
suppose that "the divine soul of Homer could degrade itself to write
of actual and physical feastings," and she concludes: "As soon believe
the Christian scriptures, when they tell us of a deity who has hands
and feet, eyes and ears, who condescends to command the patterns
of furniture and culinary utensils, and is made perfect by being born—
disgusting thought!—as the son of a village maiden, and defiling himself with the wants and sorrows of the lowest slaves!"[29] The passage
she reads to her audience is the above-mentioned fragment Kingsley
had translated from *The Iliad*. The discrepancy between its contents,
celebrating matrimonial bonds, and the vestal philosopher Hypatia,
who reads the passage, is crucial to the central theme of the novel.

---

[26] *AL¹* 213.
[27] *H* xiv.
[28] *H* xiv.
[29] *H* 99.

The reader is introduced to the monk Philammon who wants to go out into the world and yet promises "to hide my face in the dust whenever I approach a woman,"[30] and it is he who is amongst Hypatia's audience the day she lectures on Homer. In their spiritual aspirations both deny the body, albeit on different metaphysical principles. But, the health of a Church depends, Kingsley reminds us in his Preface, on the conviction that "the *mens sana* must have a *corpus sanum* to inhabit [. . .]; bodies untainted by hereditary effeminacy."[31] The emphasis on '*corpus*' derives from a conviction that the divine is incarnated in each human *body*. Kingsley works this out in the Jew Raphael Aben-Ezra, Hypatia's most promising disciple, whom her philosophy had plunged into scepticism.

Raphael is probably the novel's finest creation. Being a wealthy and cunning merchant living in deliberate and consistent luxury, he stoically loses all his possessions when Cyril and his parabolani (lay helpers) oust the Jews from their prominent public position in Alexandria and sack their property. He decides to leave Egypt a beggar, to find a passage on board a ship to Cyrene (Libya), and to go thence to study life in Italy. Crossing the Mediterranean with Heraclian's military expedition against the Emperor Honorius for the "empire of the world," he is landed in a scene of desolation and destruction in the "Campagna of Rome." Heraclian's army is routed and Raphael finds himself "at the very bottom of the bottomless" and disports himself "on the firm floor of the primeval nothing"[32] amidst the corpses littering the burn-scarred battlefield south of Rome, "covered with broken trees, trampled crops, smoking villas, and all the ugly scars of recent war."[33] He is gradually brought back to humanity, not by any philosophic system, but first by his dog's uncon-ditional and instinctive care for her litter of puppies, and then by the practical Christianity of Victoria, the self-sacrificing daughter of one of the officers of Heraclian's defeated legions. Raphael falls in love with her, and returns to Alexandria a wiser man and a Christian. It is he who returns to Hypatia with true wisdom and "solemn thoughts about Victoria, and about ancient signs of Isaiah's, which were to him none the less prophesies concerning The Man whom

---

[30] *H* 6–7.
[31] *H* xi–xii.
[32] *H* 145.
[33] *H* 148.

he had found, because he prayed and trusted that the same signs might be repeated to himself, and a child given to him also, as a token that, in spite of all his baseness, 'God was with him'."[34]

Kingsley was very much taken with the character he was creating. The inspiration for Raphael was Alfred Hyman Louis, the young and able Jewish barrister at Lincoln's Inn whom Kingsley had brought to the band of Christian Socialists, where he became very close to Ludlow. In November 1851 he was converted to Christianity and on that occasion was baptized in Eversley Church by Kingsley. "Raphael was suggested to me by Louis," Kingsley admitted to Hughes whilst he was in the midst of writing his novel, "& am so fond of him that he who touches him, touches me."[35]

William Edmondstoune Aytoun in *Blackwood's Magazine* in 1855, however, did not think Raphael worthy of analysis and dismissed him as a character who "is intended to be a mystery, affects nonchalance, walks about Alexandria with a British mastiff-bitch at his heels, declares himself to be utterly used up, and is rather richer than Rothschild. We have met this personage before in *Coningsby* and *Tancred*. He is therein denominated Sidonia."[36] The influence of Disraeli's enigmatic character has been noted before in *Yeast*. But while Kingsley seems to have been inspired by Disraeli's Jewish mentor for Barnakill, Raphael is of another stamp. Far from a 'prophet,' he is a picture of Kingsley's own self. On his return to Alexandria towards the end of the novel, Raphael tells Hypatia that "through every form of human thought, of human action, of human sin and folly, have I been wandering for years, and found no rest—as little in wisdom as in folly, in spiritual dreams as in sensual brutality. I could not rest in your Platonism [. . .]. I went on to Stoicism, Epicurism, Cynicism, Scepticism, and in that lowest deep I found a lower depth, when I became sceptical of Scepticism itself."[37] This emblematic description of the Victorian doubter (another "new foe"), is, as we have seen, also an accurate portrayal of Kingsley's own student days at Cambridge. Perhaps unaware of the similarity to the author's own university experience, one attentive reader, the reviewer

---

[34] *H* 346.
[35] CK to TH, undated, BL-41298 f.62r.
[36] [Aytoun] (1855) 634.
[37] *H* 338.

for the *Westminster Review*, picked up something of the nineteenth-century Oxbridge student in Raphael's language: "such phrases as a 'four in hand', and 'horses are a bore', are especially out of place in the mouth of an Alexandrian Jew, and bring us down unpleasantly to the 'fast' undergraduate."[38]

Raphael's conversion also has much in common with Lancelot in *Yeast* and thus with Kingsley himself. Lancelot, Kingsley and Raphael are converted to Christianity by Argemone, Frances Eliza Grenfell and Victoria respectively, all young women destined for a spiritual celibate life in a beguinage or convent. When about to be converted, Raphael discovers that Victoria's father intends to "place my dear child in the safe shelter of a nunnery."[39] "What benefit or pleasure your Deity will derive from the celibacy of your daughter," he asks bewildered and then concludes with a truly Kingsleyan stand on Christianity:

> half an hour ago [I] was fearfully near becoming neither more than less than a Christian. I had actually deluded myself into the fancy that the Deity of the Galileans might be, after all, the God of our old Hebrew forefathers—of Adam and Eve, of Abraham and David, and of the rest who believed that children and the fruit of the womb were an heritage and gift which cometh of the Lord—and that Paul was right—actually right—in his theory that the church was the development and fulfilment of our old national polity. . . . I must thank you for opening my eyes to a mistake which, had I not been besotted for the moment, every monk and nun would have contradicted by the mere fact of their existence, and *reserve my nascent faith for some Deity who takes no delight in seeing his creatures stultify the primary laws of their being.* Farewell![40]

Notwithstanding this extreme abandonment of Christianity, Raphael travelled to Cyrene to seek out its bishop and to unburden his soul to one who had refused to give up his lawfully wedded wife when he was made a bishop. On a hunting expedition with Synesius, he happened to meet Augustine of Hippo, escorted by Victoria's father's legion. Augustine captivated Raphael by the evangelizing power of his sermons. One evening a heated discussion on celibacy and matrimony took place in which Victoria's father set Raphael and Synesius up against Augustine, while in an adjacent room "lay Victoria, wrestling all night long for him in prayer and bitter tears, as the

---

[38] [-], "The Progress of Fiction as an Art" *Westminster Review* 4 (1853) 367.
[39] *H* 202.
[40] *H* 203; my italics.

murmur of busy voices reached her eager ears, longing to catch the sense of words, on which hung now her hopes and bliss."[41]

The discussion with Raphael and Synesius on one side, and Victoria's father and Augustine on the other, ends when "Augustine had to save himself from his friends by tripping the good Prefect['s dogmatic faith] gently up."[42] On a second occasion, Augustine delivered "an encomium on virginity" to Raphael, but, as neither Raphael nor Victoria seemed to him to have any call for celibacy, he followed it up with a "eulogium on wedlock as I never heard from Jew or heathen,"[43] and Raphael found himself "to my astonishment, seized by two bishops, and betrothed, whether I chose or not, to a young lady who but a few days before had been destined for a nunnery."[44] This seals his final conversion to Christianity. In Victoria's love Raphael now "found at last the hated and dreaded name of God: and found that it was Love! . . . To possess Victoria, a living, human likeness, however imperfect, of that God; and to possess in her a home, a duty, a purpose, a fresh clear life of righteous labour, perhaps of final victory."[45]

Introducing into the novel Saint Augustine, who thought celibacy "the higher life," might seem contradictory to Kingsley's plea for marriage. Augustine's opinion of celibacy would carry decisive authority. However, it soon becomes clear that he is no match for Raphael's and Synesius' argument about marriage. Kingsley does not explain this to the reader straightaway. It is only at the end of the novel that this wooden didactician comes to life in retrospect, when Raphael recounts to Hypatia what had happened to him in Cyrene. After the "eulogium on wedlock" Raphael had remarked innocently enough to Augustine that it was a pity he had not married and made some woman happy. "I saw an expression on his face which made me wish for the moment that I had bitten out this impudent tongue of mine, before I so rashly touched some deep old wound . . . That man has wept bitter tears ere now, be sure of it."[46] Kingsley here made use of the passage in *Confessions* where Augustine admitted his bitter regret

---

[41] *H* 274.
[42] *H* 274.
[43] *H* 340.
[44] *H* 339.
[45] *H* 372.
[46] *H* 340.

for having left for reasons of secular ambition the concubine with whom he had lived for fifteen years and who had borne him a son:

> my concubine being torn from my side as a hindrance to my marriage, my heart which clave unto her was torn and wounded and bleeding. [. . .] Nor was that my wound cured, which had been made by the cutting away of the former, but after inflammation and most acute pain, it mortified, and my pains became less acute, but more desperate.[47]

This puts Augustine's views of love for a woman in a different light. Kingsley fully responded to this passage, and by using it manages to provide some depth for this character who appears only very briefly in the novel but has a key-role in the process of Raphael's conversion.

The fact that Kingsley chose to make his ideal character in the novel a Jew is striking. Although there was direct and real-life inspiration for Raphael in Alfred Louis, this would not necessarily have meant that he was to represent Kingsley's Christian ideals. In theory, Kingsley could have shown the religious transformation in a character belonging to any other race. One of the pagan Goths Kingsley admired would have been a plausible alternative. His choice of a Jew, however, was deliberate, and there is some justification that Aytoun should have seen a Sidonia in Raphael Aben-Ezra. Disraeli in his Young England Trilogy celebrates in Sidonia the Hebrew foundation of Christianity, and he does so with pride. Kingsley does something very similar with Raphael, as the outburst against religious celibacy quoted above illustrates. For Kingsley, Raphael embodies the prototype of the Jewish Nation that has a "culminating [. . .] part to play in the history of the race" and in "teach[ing] us the real meaning of the Old Testament and its absolute unity with the New [. . .] For if we once lose our faith in the Old Testament, our faith in the New will soon dwindle to the impersonal 'spiritualism' of Frank Newman, and the German philosophasters." Kingsley wrote this to Adolph Saphir, a Jew who had enthusiastically written to him about his books, when he had finished the instalment for *Fraser's* where Raphael discusses celibacy with Synesius and Augustine.[48] It is Kingsley's belief that a Christian Jew alone can provide the key to both testaments because "he alone can place himself in the position

---

[47] *The Confessions of S. Augustine*, transl. E.B. Pusey (J.H. Parker: Oxford, 1838) VI.25.
[48] CK to Adolph Saphir, 1/11/1852, *LML* i.353–4.

of the men who wrote them, as far as national sympathies, sorrows, and hopes, are concerned."[49] In his inaugural lecture as Professor of Modern History at Cambridge in 1860, Kingsley told his students that history was made up of "the history of men and women,"[50] and that it therefore needed an imaginative understanding of men and women acting out their lives according to certain laws, which "are to be discovered, not in things, but in persons; in the actions of human beings."[51] Such was his reading of the Hebrew Bible, while German Higher Criticism and Neo- Platonism reduced the real men and women of the Bible to lifeless myth or mere spiritual qualities, which was unacceptable for Kingsley's view of Christianity. In the same letter to Saphir, Kingsley added: "I owe all I have ever said or thought about Christianity as the idea which is to redeem and leaven all human life, 'secular' as well as 'religious,' to the study of the Old Testament, without which the New is to me unintelligible."[52]

Although Kingsley was particularly fond of Raphael, he also felt enchanted by what he discovered about Synesius. The private letters were "charming"and he concluded from them that the Bishop

> was one of those many-sided, volatile, restless men, who taste joy and sorrow, if not deeply and permanently, yet abundantly and passionately. He lived [. . .] in a whirlwind of good deeds, meddling and toiling for the mere pleasure of action; and as soon as there was nothing to be done, which, till lately, had happened seldom enough with him, paid the penalty for past excitement in fits of melancholy. A man of magniloquent and flowery style, not without a vein of self-conceit; yet withal of over-flowing kindliness, racy humour, and unflinching courage, both physical and moral; with a very clear practical faculty, and a very muddy speculative one—though, of course, like the rest of the world, he was especially proud of his weakest side, and professed the most passionate affection for philosophic meditation; while his detractors hinted, not without show of reason, that he was far more of an adept in soldiering and dog-breaking than in the mysteries of the unseen world.[53]

The description also fitted Kingsley himself, and as if to acknowledge the affinity, he is turned into a sporting squire-bishop. Synesius comes to life in the memorable hunting scene, in which Kingsley

---

[49] CK to Adolph Saphir, 1/11/1852, *LML* i.354.
[50] "The Limits of Exact Science as Applied to History" *RT* 308.
[51] "The Limits of Exact Science as Applied to History" *RT* 310.
[52] CK to Adolph Saphir, 1/11/1852, *LML* i.353.
[53] *H* 251.

found an outlet for his passion for hunting during the early part of 1852. "Here," Synesius announced, "are our hunting-grounds. And now for one hour's forgetfulness." When two Ostriches are spotted, Synesius' "face and limbs [are] quivering with delight [...], tears of excitement glittering in his eyes."[54] The killing instinct of the passage, however, becomes disturbing when Synesius spots a group of Ausurians attacking a train of Christians, and "rushed into the thickest of the fight" and came out victorious "wiping a bloody sword."[55] The dividing line between sport and war disappears, as when the Crimean War broke out in 1854 and Kingsley wrote to Hughes that he was going rabbit shooting, adding: "Would that the Rabbits were Russians, tin pot on head & musquet in hand!"[56]

V

Although Raphael and Synesius are Kingsley's favourites, the story of *Hypatia* develops mainly around the groups of characters that interact with each other in Alexandria. The number of those who embrace celibacy is dazzling. The reader approaches Alexandria through the impressions of Philammon, a monk who wants to leave his monastery in the desert to be "in the forefront of the battle of the Lord."[57] He is received by Cyril, the Patriarch, and his monks, and then falls under the influence of Hypatia, a vowed Neo-Platonist virgin philosopher. But there is no mistake about the tension around the celibacy of these characters. Philammon is introduced as "full of life and youth and beauty" who in an early man-fight felt how "a new sensation rushed through every nerve, as he grappled with the warrior [...] which, strange to say, as it went on, grew absolutely pleasant."[58] The sensation becomes recurrent in the various scuffles in which Philammon becomes involved throughout the novel. Hypatia herself, when she meets Philammon, finds in him what she had lost with Raphael's departure from Alexandria: "to find one such man, among the effeminate selfish triflers who pretend to listen to me." His beauty

---

[54] *H* 263.
[55] *H* 265
[56] CK to TH, 18/12/1854, Martin (1950) 567.
[57] *H* 10.
[58] *H* 35.

is to her that of "the young Phoebus himself, fresh glowing from the slaughter of the Python."[59] The physical and sexual attraction is barely covered by the scanty clothing of both.

The repression of the sexual urges takes on frightening dimensions in Cyril's monks. They vent their frustration on the naked body of Hypatia in a (rape-) scene of chilling ferocity:

> [she] rose for one moment to her full height naked, snow-white against the dusky mass around-shame and indignation in those wide clear eyes, but not a stain of fear. With one hand she clasped her golden locks around her; the other long white arm was stretched upward toward the great still Christ appealing—and who dare say, in vain?—from man to God. Her lips were opened to speak: but the words that should have come from them reached God's ear alone; for in an instant Peter struck her down, the dark mass closed over her again . . . and then wail on wail, long, wild, ear-piercing, rang along the vaulted roofs, and thrilled like the trumpet of avenging angels.[60]

Contemporaries were shocked by such pictures and language. Alfred Tennyson, for one, could not bear the depiction of Hypatia's death. He "was really hurt at having Hypatia stript at her death," he admitted. Lewis Carroll also thought her death "outrageous" and condemned Kingsley's faulty taste in parts of the novel, "especially the sneers at Christianity" that he put in the mouths of his characters.[61] But such passages are Kingsley's verdict on the Christians of the early Church in Alexandria, those that the Tractarians tended to idealize. In a hardly less dramatic passage the Jewish sorcerer Miriam reveals to Raphael that to avoid being "a slave, a plaything, a soulless doll, such as Jewish women are condemned to be by their tyrants, the men," she had taken the vow and became a Christian nun, because the Christian priests were willing to give her what she wanted: "They pampered my woman's vanity, my pride, my self-will, my scorn of wedded bondage, and bade me be a saint, the judge of angels and archangels, the bride of God":

> But they lied, lied, lied! I found them out that day. . . . Do not look up at me, and I will tell you all. There was a riot—a fight between the Christian devils and the Heathen devils—and the convent was sacked, Raphael, my son!—Sacked! . . . Then I found out their blasphemy. . . .

---

[59] *H* 125.
[60] *H* 362.
[61] Martin (1959) 144.

Oh, God! I shrieked to Him, Raphael! I called on Him to rend His heavens and come down—to pour out His thunderbolts upon them—to cleave the earth and devour them—to save the wretched helpless girl who adored Him, who had given up father, mother, kinsfolk, wealth, the light of heaven, womanhood itself for Him—who worshipped, meditated over Him, dreamed of Him night and day. . . . And, Raphael, He did not hear me . . . He did not hear me . . . did not hear me! . . . And then I knew it all for a lie! a lie! [. . .] There was no mistaking that test, was there? . . . For nine months I was mad. And then your voice, my baby, my joy, my pride—that brought me to myself once more![62]

As a character who has for most of the novel been depicted in negative terms, she suddenly obtains the reader's sympathy at the further cost of the early Christians. When, moreover, in a final interview between Cyril and Raphael it becomes clear that Hypatia's murderers will go unpunished, the latter's prophetic words ring with extraordinary power at its close: "I advise you honestly to take care lest while you are busy trying to establish God's kingdom, you forget what it is like, by shutting your eyes to those of its laws which are established already [. . .] My only dread is, that when it is established, you should discover to your horror that it is the devil's kingdom and not God's."[63] Kingsley's narrating voice emphasizes that, even though Hypatia's death showed that man "had done with" Neo-Platonism,

in the hour of that unrighteous victory, the Church of Alexandria received a deadly wound. It had admitted and sanctioned those habits of doing evil that good may come, of pious intrigue, and at last of open persecution, which are certain to creep in wheresoever men attempt to set up a merely religious empire, independent of human relationships and civil laws;—to 'establish,' in short, a 'theocracy' and by that very act confess their secret disbelief that God is ruling already.[64]

VI

The weakness of Alexandrian Christianity was for Kingsley determined by an excessive and fanatical emphasis on monastic abstinence, which had to give way in western civilization to the Christian Gothic type

---

[62] *H* 374–5.
[63] *H* 380.
[64] *H* 381.

with its "sacred respect for woman, for family life [. . .] bodies untainted by hereditary effeminacy."[65] Kingsley points this reading of history out in his preface and makes it the pivotal force of the novel. Still, the ultimate promise the Goths presented to Christianity is much obscured by their "boyish rollicking strength and animalism," and Froude in a letter of 14 July 1852 urged Kingsley to pay more attention to this for the book edition. In the nature of the Goths, he wrote, "lay all the germs of character which, when impregnated with Christianity, were to grow out and exhibit Christianity in its real depth and power as it was for eight centuries in Western Europe."[66] Kingsley failed to do so and stuck to a mainly 'muscular' image of those who would propagate true Christianity during the following centuries. Effeminacy similar to that of fifth-century Alexandria was the danger of the present state of Christianity: "I have shown you New Foes under an old face," he, therefore, concludes his novel, "your own likenesses in toga and tunic, instead of coat and bonnet."[67]

The nineteenth-century "cloak and bonnet" of Kingsley's characters is most tangible when Philammon is introduced to the "city fashions" of Alexandria by a poor old priest, who points out that most influential priests are always at the beck and call of a rich lady "for the sake of her disinterested help toward a fashionable pulpit, or perhaps a bishopric. The ladies settle that for us here." The description that follows is that of a Victorian cathedral service:

> Do you suppose that a preacher gets into the pulpit of that church there, without looking anxiously, at the end of each peculiarly flowery sentence, to see whether her saintship there is clapping or not? She, who has such a delicate sense for orthodoxy, that she can scent out Novatianism or Origenism where no other mortal nose would suspect it. She who meets at her own house weekly all the richest and most pious women of the city, to settle our discipline for us, as the court cooks do our doctrine.[68]

Notwithstanding such examples, R.A. Vaughan in the *British Quarterly Review* deplored the fact that parallels with his own time were not more explicit in Kingsley's novel.[69] He saw the High Church Bishop

---

[65] *H* xiv.
[66] CK to JAF, 14/7/1852, Dunn i.188.
[67] *H* 389.
[68] *H* 88.
[69] [Vaughan] 126.

of Exeter, Henry Phillpotts, as the unquestionable reincarnation of
Cyril, while he also recognized in John Henry Newman's ambitious
religious sentiments an aspiration to be, like Cyril, a "religious man
without being a Christian." Only deference to "the dictate of taste"
could have withheld such a fearless writer as Kingsley from drawing the parallels clearer, Vaughan maintained. Such a response shows
the interest of the novel for the early Victorian reader.

Vaughan also took up Kingsley's historical debate with Neo-
Platonism, and praised the author, above all, for having artfully contrived "to render the incidents of the story themselves indicative of
the character and fortunes of the philosophy he has to depict." In
this respect, the reviewer adds, "the tale may be read as history"
and no one will be able to accuse his "portraiture of untruthfulness."[70] The *New Quarterly Review and Digest of Current Literature* held a
similar view. *The Westminster*, however, was hostile. True, the author
displayed great knowledge of the time, but it still remained a finely
executed novel with a purpose merely expressing the author's own
special theory, allowing no space for true observation of human
nature. Especially Hypatia is a character whom "if we did not pity,
we should almost despise":

> According to Mr. Kingsley's system, no woman, however wise and
> pure, can withstand the will of any man, however base and vile. If
> she loves,—as in the case of Argemone,—her subjugation is total—
> reason, conscience, choice, are mute and powerless; and if she hates,
> like Hypatia, she is equally at the mercy of the man who thinks it
> worth to subdue her.[71]

This puts the finger on the weakness of Kingsley's female protago-
nists in both *Yeast* and *Hypatia*. Their reactions and behaviour are
produced to bring out the author's own conviction of the unnatu-
ralness of celibacy. As such, both remain characters in a novel of
purpose, although Hypatia is undoubtedly an improvement on
Argemone.

Mr Kingsley "has almost an eleventh commandment against the
sin of celibacy," *The Westminster* remarked perceptively. But although
it sympathized with Kingsley's "righteous onslaught" upon the presumably holy notion that sees "animal nature as utterly unclean," it

---

[70] [Vaughan] 154.
[71] [-], "The Progress of Fiction as an Art" *Westminster Review* 4 (1853) 364.

still feared that teaching that the appetites and passions may be indulged in without checks because they are natural incurs the risk that "everything good, and fair, and lovely in the world, sinks and perishes under the blight of sensuality."[72] *The Westminster* had thus strong moral objections to the surrender of women to men in Kingsleyan terms. It failed to appreciate Kingsley's emphasis on marriage, and it failed to pinpoint the emphasis on conjugal love represented by Synesius and Raphael.

Although one late-Victorian would maintain that "probably *Hypatia* is the one book which is now considered indispensable in the education of a complete gentleman,"[73] the three reviews mentioned above were all that appeared when the novel came out in 1853. No reviews appeared in *The Times, The Athenaeum, The Spectator, The Guardian* or *The Quarterly Review.* Nobody in *Fraser's Magazine*, Parker's own journal, discussed their author's work. As a major novel, and as a serious work of art, it is strange that it should have received far fewer reviews than, for example, *Yeast.* Still, the novel begged for a reaction from the Anglo- and Roman Catholics. It could not be passed over in silence by those who had in the first place inspired Kingsley's treatment of early Christianity. To correct what he saw as a biassed and selective picture of the early Christian Church, Cardinal Wiseman published in 1854 the novel *Fabiola; or, The Church of the Catacombs.* It was the first volume of the *Popular Catholic Library*, a series of tales illustrating the condition of the Church in different periods. With a plot that unrolls in Rome during the reign of Diocletian—the glory of the Christian martyrs well in the foreground—Wiseman hoped to restore some "admiration and love" of those primitive times of the Christian Church.[74] Moreover, he emphatically assures his readers that in *his* novel the "worst aspect [of the pagan world] has been carefully suppressed, as nothing could be admitted here which the most sensitive Catholic eye would shrink from contemplating."[75] *Fabiola* was by no means as good a novel as *Hypatia*, and, although historically as impressive as Kingsley's, Wiseman's novel failed to rouse contemporary interest in the scenes it described.

---

[72] *Ibid.* 365.
[73] Joseph Ellis Baker 88.
[74] *Fabiola; or, The Church of the Catacombs* (London: Burns, Oates & Washbourne, 1922) viii.
[75] *Fabiola; or, The Church of the Catacombs* (London: Burns, Oates & Washbourne, 1922) viii.

John Henry Newman's novel *Callista; A Tale of the Third Century* was more of a match for *Hypatia*. Back in 1848, after the success of *Loss and Gain*, Newman had started on a novel to "express, from a Catholic point of view, the feelings and mutual relations of Christians and heathens,"[76] but could not manage to get beyond the first two chapters. The manuscript was put away till, in 1854, Wiseman asked him to write a sequel to *Fabiola*. Newman complied, and now resumed his story about third-century Roman Africa. He finished it the following year and it came out in 1856. What Wiseman did not do, Newman does superbly. The unobtrusive analogy in *Callista* between his third-century Christian and nineteenth-century Roman Catholics in England represents, like *Hypatia*, a "new foe with an old face." As *Yeast* was Kingsley's answer to the religious questions addressed in Newman's *Loss and Gain*, *Callista* was Newman's rejoinder to Kingsley's representation of Christianity in *Hypatia*. It constitutes another phase in the profound controversy Kingsley felt there existed between Newman and him.

VII

With *Hypatia* Kingsley gained a reputation as a historian. On the strength of it he was invited to deliver a series of four lectures on Alexandrian Neo-Platonism at the Philosophical Institution of Edinburgh in February 1854. Before the first lecture Kingsley was "dreadfully nervous" and "actually cried with fear," but he thought that he "got through it very well, being very cheered & clapped."[77] His second lecture went off even better than the first, and the third "better than ever." He was complimented on his "power of condensing,"[78] he wrote to Fanny, and added, when it was all over, that "altogether it has been [...] one of the most pleasant and successful episodes in my life."[79]

The lectures were published "at the special request of my audience"[80] as *Alexandria and Her Schools*. It is in the preface of this work that

---

[76] *Callista: A Tale of the Third Century* (London: Longmans, Green, 1889) Advertisement.
[77] CK to FK, undated, BL-62554 f.16r.
[78] CK to FK, 22/2/1854, BL-62554 f.23v.
[79] CK to FK, undated, BL-62554 f.25r.
[80] "Alexandria and Her School" *HLE* 3.

Kingsley once more expressed that he felt modern civilization was at a crossroads:

> Europe, and England as an integral part thereof, is on the eve of a revolution, spiritual and political, as vast and awful as that which took place at the Reformation; and that, beneficial as that revolution will doubtless be to the destinies of mankind in general, it depends upon the wisdom and courage of each nation individually, whether that great deluge shall issue, as the Reformation did, in a fresh outgrowth of European nobleness and strength, or usher in, after pitiable confusions and sorrows, a second Byzantine age of stereotyped effeminacy and imbecility. For I have little sympathy with those who prate so loudly of the progress of the species, and the advent of I know-not-what Cockaigne of universal peace and plenty, as I have with those who believe on the strength of "unfulfilled prophecy," the downfall of Christianity, and the end of the human race to be at hand.[81]

It is a passage which explains why Kingsley wanted to write a novel about fourth-century Alexandria, and next with *Westward Ho!* a novel about the immediate aftermath of the Reformation. "Only by understanding what has happened, can we understand what will happen; only by understanding history, can we understand prophecy," he reiterates. This meant "trying to discover its organic laws, and the causes which produce in nations, creeds and systems, health and disease, growth, change, decay and death."[82] Thus the decay of the Roman Empire, the defeat of the Spanish Armada, and the revolutions of mid-nineteenth-century Europe were seen by Kingsley as crucial moments in the history of mankind, moments of "universal fermentation of human thought and faith,"[83] "bubbles, as they formed and burst on every wave of human life."[84] As in *Yeast*, Kingsley describes in *Hypatia* a time when "the minds of men, cut adrift from their ancient moorings, wandered wildly over pathless seas of speculative doubt."[85]

In his preface, Kingsley had warned that "a picture of life in the fifth century must needs contain much which will be painful to any reader, and which the young and innocent will do well to leave altogether unread." This great but hideous age is a time of virtues and

---

[81] "Alexandria and Her School" *HLE* 5–6.
[82] "Alexandria and Her School" *HLE* 6–7.
[83] *H* x.
[84] *H* x.
[85] *H* x.

vices manifest "side by side—even, at times, in the same person" whether Christian or pagan.[86] The picture of the Christians, in fact, is far from complimentary. *The Princeton Review* was outspoken in this respect and in a short notice expressed the wish that the young and innocent should indeed leave the book unread.[87] Individual readers trembled. Elizabeth Sewell, who thought the novel "a marvel," admitted that it made her feel unhappy, and Miss Mitford thought *Hypatia* "a work of great power" but dreaded "what the Bishops may say."[88] In an address to the Society of Authors in 1909, Sir Oliver Lodge cautioned against contemporary criticism and hasty censorship that proposals of Library censorship entailed, and he reminded his audience that, "amazing as the fact sounds now," *Hypatia* created a religious outcry when it appeared.[89] Kingsley himself admitted in 1873, that it was met "with curses from many of the very Churchmen whom I was trying to warn and save" and that it seriously compromised his ecclesiastical career.[90] Moreover, the novel cost him an honorary degree of D.C.L. at Oxford in 1863. Pusey at Oxford opposed it because he thought *Hypatia* unfit to be read by "our wives and sisters," with which verdict he much offended Dean Stanley, as he had read the book upon Mrs Augustus Hare's recommendations and then urged his own mother to read it.[91]

It would seem that contemporaries were less disturbed by Kingsley's representation of the latent inhumanity of the pagan populace of Alexandria. Although Tennyson and Carroll, for example, felt squeamish at Hypatia being murdered naked, they did not seem to mind this passage:

> The boy had just arrived at the altar in the centre of the orchestra, when he saw a gladiator close upon him. The ruffian's arm was raised to strike, when, to the astonishment of the whole theatre, boy and dog turned valiantly to bay, and leaping on the gladiator, dragged him between them to the ground. The triumph was momentary. The uplifted hands, the shout of 'Spare him!' came too late. The man, as he lay, buried his sword in the slender body of the child, and then rising, walked coolly back to the side passages, while the poor cur stood over

---

[86] *H* vii.
[87] [-], "Short Notices" *The Princeton Review* 27 (1855) 367.
[88] Pope-Hennessy 121–2.
[89] Oliver Lodge, *Modern Problems* (London: Methuen, 1912) 83–4.
[90] Lodge, *Op. cit.*, 84.
[91] Rowland E. Prothero, *Life and Letters of Dean Stanley* (London: Thomas Nelson & Sons, n.d.) 351.

the little corpse, licking its hands and face, and making the whole building ring with his doleful cries. The attendants entered, and striking their hooks into corpse after corpse, dragged them out of sight, marking their path by long red furrows in the sand; while the dog followed, until his inauspicious howlings died away down distant passages. [. . .] The people were coolly sipping wine and eating cakes . . .[92]

The social situation of Alexandria is seen as symptomatic of all that brought about the decay of the Roman Empire: "a great tyranny, enslaving the masses, crushing national life, fattening itself and its officials on a system of world-wide robbery" that barred the human race from future hope. Similarly, Spain's world power in the sixteenth century was crushed because it based itself on slavery. The "accursed and destroying sin [. . .] of treating their brother-men like beasts that perish"[93] had been Kingsley's key in justifying the destruction of the Canaanites in his articles for *The Christian Socialist.* Canaan, Alexandria and Spain were a writing on the wall. He warned that "the Southern United States will surely fall" because of it,[94] and in *Alton Locke* he felt alarmed at England's "ever widening pit of pauperism and slavery"[95] amongst its working classes. Thus, although at first sight very different, because historical, *Hypatia* is thematically closely bound up with *Yeast* and *Alton Locke*, and it forms a prelude to Kingsley's next novel, *Westward Ho!*.

Hypatia is hailed by most modern critics as Kingsley's best novel. It certainly presents the reader with a rich canvass of characters who all contribute to the furtherance of the plot. The graphic descriptions of Egypt are as intense as the hunting-scene in *Yeast* or the creation of Jacob's Island in *Alton Locke*. No critic can deny Kingsley's remarkable evocative power as a novelist. Time passes swiftly in *Hypatia* and in un-narrated time between chapters enormous geographical shifts take place. This made the novel suitable for adaptation for the stage, which was done at least twice in the two decades following Kingsley's death. Ex-cathedra preaching in *Hypatia* is almost absent, and as such the novel seems less of a novel with a purpose than his earlier ones. The characterization in the novel, however,

---

[92] *H* 279.
[93] "Bible Politics: or God Justified to the People No. VIII" 19/4/1851 *ChSoc* i.193.
[94] "Bible Politics: or God Justified to the People No. VIII" 19/4/1851 *ChSoc* i.193.
[95] *AL¹* 195.

has often been criticized. Admittedly, Hypatia remains lifeless, and Philammon, with whom the novel begins and ends, remains uninterestingly flat, even though the novel's final scene inspired the Royal Academician Arthur Hacker for his oil painting *Pelagia and Philammon* (1887). Froude found in Philammon the same fault as in Alton Locke and advised Kingsley to take him out of the novel altogether: "He is merely passive to influences. Everything and everybody work on him. He works on nothing and on nobody."[96] With his emphasis on 'body', Froude might well have made a point which justified the creation of these two bodiless characters to Kingsley.

---

[96] JAF to CK, 14/7/1852, Dunn i.188.

CHAPTER THIRTEEN

A LITTLE OF THE WOLF-VEIN (1854)

The year 1853 had been an especially difficult one. Church work, schools and lectures pressed heavily on Kingsley's time. The last instalments of *Hypatia* were published in April in *Fraser's Magazine* and the book version was seen through the press later that year. Illness among his parishioners required constant visiting. Then there were private worries. Fanny was laid up with a cold after a bad miscarriage in September. She needed a change from the damp Eversley setting again, and the doctor advised her to spend the winter in the mild south-Devon climate. As the Froudes were living at Babbacombe at Torbay, they were asked to find lodgings. Fanny moved with the children to Torquay while Charles remained alone in Eversley to settle his affairs. Debts were growing daily and he bore the separation from his family badly. His letters betray impatience with Fanny's constant demands for money. He finally managed to follow them at the end of December, having obtained leave from the bishop to absent himself from his parish for six months, although it remained difficult and costly to find curates. Moreover, Fanny's cures were expensive and often Kingsley had to travel back to Eversley during the weekends to attend to the Sunday services. Although the idea of settling in Devon was cheering, he left Eversley with a heavy heart. Prospects of advancement in his clerical career looked bleak, debts were pressing on him, and his idealistic plans for his parish would come to nothing now that he was leaving it for who knew how long. Eversley "is like a grave [. . .] & the grave, too, of so many hopes of what the parish might have been," he wrote to Fanny.[1] The good thing of leaving Eversley, though, was that it also offered much wanted rest to Charles. He now had spare time on his hands, and used it well.

Torquay, originally a Channel Fleet port, had rapidly grown into a fashionable sea-side resort for the rich. At the beginning of the

---

[1] CK to FK, undated, BL-62554 f.36r.

century the Napoleonic wars and the blockade of the French ports had made it difficult for the rich to go abroad and the south Devon coast with its mild climate and invigorating sea air was discovered to be a suitable alternative for the wealthy invalid in which to spend the winter months. The 1848 railway to Torquay had opened the West and in 1850 it boasted about 2,000 lodgings for visitors while the number of inhabitants had grown over the years to more than 11,000.

The Kingsleys lodged at Livermead, a fashionable house near the sea front, originally built in 1820 by the Reverend Roger Mallock for his guests, but considerably enlarged by the mid-fifties. Mrs Kingsley hoped that her husband's presence in Torquay would lead to invitations to preach in its churches, so that he could impress some of the wealthy and influential church-going families staying there for the winter and find the favour which was necessary for preferment to a more lucrative parish than Eversley. But "all parties in the Church stood aloof from him as a suspected person; and the attacks of the religious press [. . .] had so alarmed the clergy of Torquay, High Church and Evangelical, that all pulpit doors were closed against the author of 'Alton Locke', 'Yeast', and 'Hypatia'."[2] In a private letter to her sister, Fanny exclaimed that the situation was the doing of the old-fashioned High Churchman Bishop of Exeter, Henry Phillpotts, who disapproved of Kingsley's religious views and objected to his preaching in his diocese—"hanging is too good for him," she concluded.[3] In defence of her husband's religious opinions she added in her biography:

> Once only he was asked to preach in the parish church for a charity, and once at St. John's, in a Lenten week-day service, when he surprised the congregation, a High Church one, by his reverent and orthodox views on the Holy Eucharist.[4]

Thus Kingsley was left with plenty of time on his hands in Torquay. While Mrs Kingsley stayed indoors to convalesce of the sofa, he and the children went combing the coast for natural treasures. Torbay offered good possibilities for a naturalist. Philip Henry Gosse, an amateur zoologist and populariser of science who was much respected

---

[2] *LML* i.404.
[3] FK to unidentified sister, undated, Chitty (1974) 166.
[4] *LML* i.404.

in scientific circles, had made the Devon shore popular in a series
of books on natural history, and his *Naturalist's Rambles on the Devonshire
Coast* had just come out. Kingsley had read it with enthusiasm and
felt stimulated to go to Devon to investigate for himself. Fanny's
forced permanence at Torquay gave him the opportunity to pick up
marine zoology.

In July Kingsley had written to Gosse with his usual enthusiasm
for natural history, highly praising his *Naturalist's Rambles*. Unfortunately
the letter is lost, but from Gosse's reply we can reconstruct Kingsley's
letter of introduction, which seems to have conveyed his enthusiasm
for natural history as well as some reference to the profitable study
of God's works. Gosse, who belonged to the Plymouth Brethren, a
stern and unimaginative sect, generally kept aloof from all society,
but on this occasion was roused and wrote back that "independently,
however, of the gratification of my *amour propre*, there is that in your
letter which could not fail to elicit my warm sympathies [. . .] I shall
esteem it a favour & a privilege to continue the correspondence you
have commenced."[5]

It was his curiosity in natural history that drove Kingsley to explore
the sea-shore in the first place, but the constant need for money
might have stimulated his studies in marine zoology as well. Gosse
had found a gap in the book market with his sea-side studies. The
studies he conducted of marine life at St Mary Church, a small village of wooden houses half a mile inland parallel to the cliff-line just
north of Torquay led, in 1852, to successful experiments with the
"aquarium," a word he introduced into the English language. The
idea became popular, and his descriptions, pictures, and instructions
of the sea-aquarium created quite a rage for the rich. The aquarium
at Regent's Park, the first institutional aquarium to be opened to the
public, was set up according to Gosse's guidelines a year later in 1853.

Thus Kingsley found himself exploring the rock pools around
Corbyn Head, just below Livermead. Finally free from the strain of
sermon writing and parish work, the Kingsleys spent the first real
holiday they had had for years: "the quiet peaceful Sundays with his
wife and children were most welcome," Mrs Kingsley writes, no doubt
revealing her own sentiments as much as her husband's.[6] But the

---

[5] PHG to CK, 28/7/1853, L-BC Gosse Correspondence.
[6] *LML* i.404.

days were not spent in idleness. Every low-tide Kingsley sallied out with his children to explore rock-pools and collected all the curiosities that had been washed ashore. Some of the happiness of these expeditions is caught in the father's words:

> Wanderings among rock and pool, mixed up with [. . .] the laugh of children drinking in health from every breeze and instruction in every step, running ever and anon with proud delight to add their little treasure to their father's stock.[7]

Jars were filled with sea-creatures and carried to Livermead to be dissected in the evening and studied under the microscope. The material was systematically arranged, drawings made, and all discoveries duly entered in a daily journal. The verandah of Livermead House was littered with jars and a vivarium was set up in the drawing room to study the habits of many of the rarest species of molluscs, annelids, crustacea and polyps they found. Kingsley searched out Dr Robert Battersby, a physician in Torquay who was interested in marine life. He pointed out for him the best locations for "sea-beasts" and lent him dredging equipment. Gosse was not forgotten. The correspondence was renewed, and Kingsley asked him to forward hampers with glass jars to Livermead to transport some of the more interesting specimens back to London for Gosse's inspection. The hampers arrived, and the Kingsleys filled them. Towards the end of January he wrote in a letter accompanying a hamper of jars: "I must add my thanks to you for giving not *me* only, but Mrs. Kingsley & my children, this occupation—We are as busy as bees about the animals all day, & the little ones full of desire to find something worth sending you."[8] On the other side of the line, in Gosse's dreary house in Islington, the hampers were eagerly anticipated and opened by the whole family, and Gosse warmly thanked the sender for a few cheerful moments in an otherwise rather stern and gloomy religious household.[9]

Kingsley's letters to Gosse remained impersonal, scribbled in haste and written without imagination. Sometimes they were just lists of contents accompanying the hampers; often they contained mere scientific queries or observations illustrated by minute sketches. Only one letter, recently come to light, shows Kingsley's more poetic capacities

[7] CK to PHG, undated, *LML* i.405.
[8] CK to PHG, [28/1/1854], L-BC Gosse Correspondence.
[9] PHG to CK, L-BC Gosse Correspondence.

in observing nature. The following description of an ascarid found its way into the book Kingsley was to write about the sea and is typical of its lively tone:

> I don't know whether you know, or *want*, any of those strange long ascarids, black & brown, w. lie knotted up under stones. I have got them 1/4 in diam, and more than 2ft. long. Today one astonished me. Poking about the bottom of the vase, he nosed out a Sabella-animal writhing about out of his tube, seized him instantly in spite of his furious struggles, & commenced bolting him whole. He got him at first by a knot, but at last shifted to his head, drawing him home by retracting himself, all across the glass; & then began. [...] He was near ten minutes getting him down, packing him into the funnel shaped mouth [...]. He is now reposing, like a Boa or a Czar gorged with slaughter.[10]

Kingsley and Gosse were very different men, and although Gosse only found this out years later, Kingsley had little sympathy for his narrowly Christian beliefs, and what the Plymouth Brother saw as friendship, which really amounted to little more than a common interest in marine zoology, eventually foundered when Kingsley fully embraced the outcome of the discovery of geological time on the eve of the publication of *The Origin of Species* a few years later.

II

Although Kingsley was not asked to the pulpits of the area and was not invited by fashionable Torbay society, the Kingsleys were not debarred from social life. The Froudes were regular guests, but some of the other visitors who came over to stay at Livermead include Charles Mansfield, Max Müller, his schoolfriend Richard Powles, his brother George, and all were initiated in the wonders of the shore. The Foxes of Falmouth were also staying at Torquay at the time, and Kingsley decided to pay them a visit. Unfortunately the Foxes were out, but a few days later the visit was returned. Robert Were Fox (1789–1877), head of a prosperous Quaker family running a ship agency business in Falmouth, was also a man of science. In 1848 he was made FRS and often attended meetings of both the Royal Society and the British Association, accompanied by his daughter Caroline.

---

[10] CK to PHG, 11/4/1854, private collection.

No doubt the Foxes had heard much of the author of *Alton Locke* through F.D. Maurice, whom the family got to know in the early 1840s through John Sterling. The daughter, Caroline (1819–1871), is known for her journals in which she described her meetings with many of the foremost figures of the day in literature and science. Of Kingsley she wrote in her journal: "A very happy call, he fraternising at once, and stuttering pleasant and discriminating things concerning F.D. Maurice, Coleridge and others. He looks sunburnt with dredging all the morning, has a piercing eye under an overhanging brow, and his voice is most melodious and his pronunciation exquisite. He is strangely attractive."[11] In a letter to Elizabeth Carne, who had asked for her impressions of the novelist, she admits that she saw very little of him herself but had had the possibility of discussing his novels with Mrs Kingsley, who talked about *Yeast*, how it was written with "his heart's blood," how it "cost him an illness," and about how the letters from whom his books had rescued from infidelity "console[d] him greatly for being ranked among his country's plagues."[12]

Although the shore offered as much as could be desired, Kingsley began nevertheless to be tired of the foppery of fashionable society in Torquay, of "the ignoble army of idlers, who saunter the cliffs, and sands, and quays; to whom every wharf is but a 'wharf of Lethe,' by which they rot 'dull as the oozy weed',"[13] and consequently in May the family moved to Babbacombe where they were nearer the Froudes. Here the study of marine zoology was continued.

III

In July Fanny needed a change of air and the Kingsleys left the south coast for Bideford on the Torridge in the north of Devon, a location which offered further occasions to amass material for his sea-side studies. By this time Kingsley must have been considering the idea of publication, and in November he published an article in *The North British Review*, which was at the same time a review of Gosse's popular *Rambles* and an account of Kingsley's own research. The review lent itself well for separate publication, and Macmillan

---

[11] Wilson Harris, *Caroline Fox* (London: Constable, 1944) 241.
[12] *Ibid.* 242.
[13] *G* 1.

became interested in bringing it out as an enlarged book edition, which was completed a year later at Bideford during the first months of 1855.

The book, *Glaucus; or, Wonder of the Shore*, remained popular until the end of the nineteenth century, and was illustrated by one of that family of great illustrators of nature, the Sowerbys. It earned Kingsley the attention of the Prince Consort, was vilified by George Henry Lewes to his publisher Blackwood, and was praised more than a century later by critics as one of Kingsley's finest books for children.[14] For Kingsley it was a book which records some of his happiest periods, written with passion, a financial success which went through five revised, and beautifully illustrated, editions during his lifetime. Still, the importance of *Glaucus* has been underrated. Although often mistaken for a mere book of popularizing natural history and noted only cursorily for preceding some of the elements of *The Water-Babies*—Chitty writes, for example, that it is "chiefly of interest today as a less fanciful forerunner of *The Water-Babies*"[15]—it is in reality a book which introduces, analyses, and links many themes of Kingsley's thought. It propagates his views of cleanliness, his concepts of education, his moral stand, his patriotic pride. On a more philosophical plain, it discusses the relationship between the Creator, creation and man. Above all, with it Kingsley participated in the most lively debate about design in nature which preceded the publication of *The Origin of Species*.

In his novels *Yeast* and *Alton Locke* Kingsley had repeatedly dwelled on the importance of a grounding in natural history, but nowhere had he tried to work out any of the religious premises that underlay such a stance. Although the fact that Lancelot Smith is presented as a geologist was of obvious significance to a contemporary reader, Kingsley had not yet found an occasion to be as outspoken as he wished to be about the role of science in religion. *Glaucus* now offered such an occasion.

As in his student days Kingsley had been an ardent follower of Adam Sedgwick's courses, much of his early geological knowledge can safely be ascribed to the "field-lectures which, in pleasant bygone Cambridge days, Professor Sedgwick used to give to young geologists."[16]

---

[14] Edna Johnson, Evelyn R. Sickels, and Frances Clarke Sayers, *Children's Literature* (Boston: Houghton Mifflin, 1959) 1099.
[15] Chitty (1974) 167; but see also Uffelman (1979) 70.
[16] *G* 57.

Of course, he also followed with interest William Buckland and Charles Lyell's contrary systems of explaining geological phenomena. The progress made in the 1830s in the science of geology convinced Kingsley that the Biblical account of Creation in seven days could not hold, let alone its initial creation by a single act of God. "Let us speak freely a few words on this important matter," he writes, "Geology has disproved the old popular belief that the universe was brought into being as it now exists, by a single fiat."[17] Lyell's uniformitarian interpretations were controversial when he published them in the early 1830s, but by the mid 1850s much of his system had been accepted by other geologists—although the exact meaning and application of his principles remained under discussion—and Kingsley's geological ideas tended towards the direction of Lyell's system, according to which all the former change of the earth had been "gradual". The importance of Lyell's work also lay in his application of his principles to the organic creation. Although most scientists held that God's separate creations had proceeded progressively in time till, as Tennyson put it, "at last, arose the man," Lyell maintained that such reasoning implied direction and was therefore very little removed from Lamarck's self-contained system of transmutation which endangered the concept that species were fixed entities. Denying the fixity of species might lead to denying divine intervention altogether. Creations of species should therefore, Lyell argued, still take place, albeit invisibly. Lyell rehearsed most of his argument in 1851 in his Anniversary Address as President of the Geological Society of London, of which Kingsley must have heard. Although Lyell belittled the occasion that caused him to repeat things he had been urging for twenty years, the address was part of the general outcry against principles of transmutation and "the favour which they have acquired of late, with the general public, in consequence of the eloquent pleading of the anonymous author of the 'Vestiges of Creation'."[18]

Mid-nineteenth-century reasoning in science was still subject to a view of nature based on Natural Theology which argued that—on the principle that design implies the existence of a designer—because creation is a coherently and efficiently working system, it follows that there is a creative intelligence behind it. This approach to the divinity

---

[17] G^3 66.
[18] Charles Lyell, "Anniversary Address of the President," *The Quarterly Journal of the Geological Society of London*, 7 (1851), xxxiii.

greatly influenced English divines, and William Paley's *Natural Theology* (1802) had become a set text at the universities. Kingsley, who had studied *Evidences of Christianity* as an adolescent, found Paley's philosophy convincing. Actually, few naturalists in the first half of the nineteenth century were willing to abandon the concept of order implicit in the basic idea of perfection of the divine organisation underlying all existence. But carried to the extreme, such reasoning on the perfection of a system runs the risk of describing the system as self-sufficient, thus removing the importance of a First Cause. And in introducing a rudimentary principle of evolution, this is basically what *Vestiges of Creation* did in 1844. A storm of protest broke out in which most clergymen and scientists took part. Kingsley's geology professor thundered from Cambridge that the "foul book" could not be read without "feelings of loathing and deep aversion" and prepared a reply to the anonymous author in his fifth edition of his *Discourse on the Studies of the University of Cambridge* (1850), which was originally the text of a 94-page sermon held before the university in 1833, but which now "swelled out of all common measure"[19] into a treatise of over 800 pages written over a period of four years. Charles Darwin, who was hatching his own ideas about development in nature, admitted that he read Sedgwick's attacks with "fear and trembling."[20]

Kingsley's growth as a naturalist coincided with the tumultuous years following the publication of *The Vestiges of Creation*, during which a flood of narrow-minded apologetic religious literature was unleashed, and in *Glaucus* he did not want there to be any doubt about his own scientific position as a clergyman. He had no patience with those "cowardly" and "fanatic" brethren of the cloth, he wrote, who saw in science the enemy of revelation, "sure that God could take better care than they of His own everlasting truth,"[21] and praised the steadfast work of inductive science:

> Heavy and uphill was the work [. . .] of those who steadfastly set themselves to the task of proving and of asserting at all risks, that the Maker of the coal seam and the diluvial cave could not be a "Deus quidam deceptor," and that the facts which the rock and the silt revealed were

[19] Adam Sedgwick, *A Discourse on the Studies of the University of Cambridge*, 5th edn. (London: John W. Parker; Cambridge: Deightons, and Stevenson, 1850) ccxli, 314.
[20] *The Life and Letters of Charles Darwin*, (London: John Murray, 1888) i.334.
[21] *G³* 12.

sacred, not to be warped or trifled with for the sake of any cowardly and hasty notion that they contradicted His other messages.[22]

But Kingsley's implicit faith in truth was not the only reason for his defence. He clearly saw that if the speculations of "well-meaning" pseudo-scientists were accepted, no grounds remained to refute the reasoning of *The Vestiges of Creation*. Inductive science was needed in the defence of religion itself. Kingsley, therefore, regularly mentioned his admiration for "brave" men like Sedgwick, Lyell and Hugh Miller and emphasized that they had "wielded in defence of Christianity the very science which was faithlessly and cowardly expected to subvert it," that they "will be looked back to as moral benefactors of their race."[23]

These premises need further analysis. As Sedgwick showed in his 1850 *Discourse*, and Lyell in his 1851 address to the Geological Society, scientific views on development and progression in the organic world were not easily proved in the early 1850s. Kingsley's own, essentially Paleyan, struggle with the question was based on the concept of design in creation. He argued in *Glaucus* that "there has been, in the Creative Mind, as it gave life to new species, a development of the idea on which older species were created, in order that every mesh of the great net might gradually be supplied, and there should be no gaps in the perfect variety of Nature's forms." And "this development is the only one of which we can conceive, if we allow that a Mind presides over the universe, and not a mere brute necessity," he added.[24] The *Quarterly Review* rejoiced that Kingsley's "references to the great First Cause of all these marvels are in the true spirit of a Christian philosophy."[25]

Kingsley's objections to *Vestiges* hinge on the following two points: first, he accuses the advocates of the book of falsely maintaining that all criticism against them is *odium theologicum*, as if churchmen were in no intellectual position to reason inductively in science; and second, that the "Transmutation theory is not one of a progress of *species* at all." The first point was very dear to Kingsley, and made it possible for him to accept evolution ten years later. The verdict

---

[22] *G³* 11.
[23] *G³* 11–12.
[24] *G³* 65–6.
[25] [-], "Brief Literary Notices" *London Quarterly Review* 4 (1855) 556.

on the theory itself is an example of Kingsley's distinguishing between species and individuals of the species. When Chambers wrote that

> The idea, then, which I form of the progress of organic life upon the globe—and the hypothesis is applicable to all similar theatres of vital being—is, *that the simplest and most primitive type under a law to which that of like-production is subordinate, gave birth to the type next above it, that this again produced the next higher, and so on to the very highest,* the stages of advance being in all cases very small—namely, from one species only to another.[26]

Kingsley maintained that "what the Transmutationists really, if they would express themselves clearly, or carefully analyse their own notions, is a physical and actual change, not of species, but of *individuals,* of already existing living beings created according to one idea, into other living beings created according to another idea." And of such change, he retorted, "nature has as yet given us no instance."[27] What is of interest in his analysis, however, is that it left open the possibility of the continued creation of species. He admitted that, in studying nature, order is observed and progress in time seems implied (lower animals appearing first, and man one of the latest in the series), but, he cautioned, such progress is not proved: "as we know that species of animals lower than those which already existed appeared again and again during the various eras, so it is quite possible that they may be appearing now, and may appear hereafter." This is in line with Lyell's "steady-state" system, and the continuation of creation of species in time necessary to sustain such a system. Thus the expectation "that for every extinct Dodo or Moa, a new species may be created, to keep up the equilibrium of the whole"[28] appealed to Kingsley because it posited a perfect idea of creation and sets before us a God who is a *living* God.[29] Remarkably little needed to be changed in the ground plan of this argument when, in 1873, Kingsley prepared for the fifth edition of *Glaucus,* which was the first edition of the book to include the implications of Darwin's *Origin of Species.*

---

[26] [Robert Chambers], *Vestiges of the natural History of Creation* (New York: Harper, 1875) 115.
[27] G^3 68.
[28] G^3 67.
[29] G^3 70.

IV

Although Kingsley views nature as the expression of an active divine mind, his attitude, unlike Buckland's, is not anthropocentric. The concept that man is not the measure of all things surfaces repeatedly in *Glaucus*: "This planet was not made for man alone," he writes at one point, explaining that the ocean teemed with beautiful and perfect life-forms countless ages before the appearance of man.[30] It is a "conceited notion" which makes "man forsooth the centre of the universe."[31] It is tempting to read an early form of ecological awareness into such words, which is perhaps not entirely misplaced in Kingsley's case. The German naturalist Ernst Haeckel and the American chemist Ellen Swallow Richards are often seen as the founders of modern ecology. Haeckel was to coin the word *Oekologie* in 1866 to describe the intricate interrelationships of organic and inorganic elements, while Richards was to apply her chemical training to sanitary engineering. "One of the most serious problems of civilization is clean water and clean air," she wrote shortly after the turn of the century. Her early studies were on sewage water and water supplies for the Massachusetts Board of Health in 1872, and when she later turned to the subject of healthier buildings, she emphasized the importance of proper ventilation systems.[32] Both Haeckel's biological sense of the term and Richard's environmental attitude are central to the Kingsleyan view of nature. Jonathan Bate has argued that "scientists made it their business to describe the intricate economy of nature; Romantics made it theirs to teach human beings how to live as part of it,"[33] and Kingsley was in fact both a scientist and a (post)romantic.

Such an ecological stance is closely linked to Kingsley's sanitary work. When at the end of February 1854 he was forced to return to Eversley and wait for a new curate, he put all his energy into collecting sanitary statistics for a deputation to the House of Commons.

---

[30] *G* 88.

[31] *G* 133.

[32] See Martha Moore Trescott, "Women in the Intellectual Development of Engineering: A Study in Persistence and Systems Thought," in *Women of Science: Righting the Record*, ed. by G. Kass-Simon and Patricia Farnes (Bloomington & Indianapolis: Indiana University Press, 1990) 150–57.

[33] Jonathan Bate, *Romantic Ecology: Wordsworth and the Environmental Tradition* (London: Routledge, 1991) 40.

Later in the spring he went up to London to pass his information on to Lord Palmerston "which I trust may save many lives." He also used his time setting up an Anti-Cholera Fund and wrote a pamphlet on sanitary reform, but Eversley was dreary in spite of the bright sun and the crocuses in full bloom.

Alone in Eversley on his thirty-fifth birthday Kingsley was in a pensive state: "It is a very solemn thought that *half* one's earthly career is over—perhaps more. God grant that the next 35 years may see more work & less folly come out of me than the last 35. I *hate* the remembrance of all of it, except what has been spent in your beloved arms."[34] In Eversley he felt "dreadfully lonely & unhappy,"[35] and therefore he often stayed in London and travelled to do duty in Eversley. He spent the evenings with Maurice and Ludlow, and paid Bunsen and Carlyle visits. One day he went to see Gosse's aquarium and recognized many of the sea animals he had collected with Rose and Maurice on the Devonshire coast. He was invited to Monckton Milnes's parties where he met many literary celebrities of the time. He talked to Mrs Gaskell, was introduced to Edward George Bulwer-Lytton, and met Charles Dickens. Bulwer-Lytton he thought had "a devilish face," but he liked Dickens: "He is a really genial loveable man with an eye like a hawk, not high bred, but excellent company, & very sensible." "But Mrs Dickens!" he wrote to Fanny, "Oh the [. . .] vulgar vacancy."[36]

Back on the Devon shore happiness returned, but it was not easy to forget "the festering alleys of Bermondsey and Bethnal Green," and the question of sanitary reform eventually found its way into his work for *Glaucus* too. Notwithstanding his jubilant letter to Fanny, delusion and frustration could not be hidden for long as he thought over the "whole hapless question of sanatory [*sic.*] reform," how "the very cholera they had been striving for years to ward off" had re-appeared.[37] If before going to London Kingsley was hopeful that with Palmerston's help in the Commons "we may by one great and wise effort save from ten to twenty thousand *lives* in London alone!",[38] he realized that bureaucracy was still one of the main obstacles in

[34] CK to FK, undated, BL-62554 f.30.
[35] CK to FK, undated, BL-62554 f.60v.
[36] CK to FK, undated, BL-62554 f.52v.
[37] *G³* 128.
[38] CK to FK, undated, *LMLM* 157.

advancing their objects of sanitary reform. He could not help not-
ing the "sublime irony" in nature's processes, which he presents in
his wonderful illustration of the spider crab *Maia squinado*, a slow-
moving scavenger with long legs, which had been taken out of a
lobster pot by fishermen and left in Kingsley's boat to die. Kingsley
turned it into a masterpiece of satire on the human efforts at sanitary reform, revealing at the same time his utter frustration with
English legislation:

> in the boat at the minute of which I have been speaking, silent and
> neglected, sat a fellow-passenger, who was a greater adept at removing
> nuisances than the whole Board of Health put together [. . .] he was
> at that moment a true sanitary martyr, having, like many of his human
> fellow-workers, got into a fearful scrape by meddling with those exist-
> ing interests, and "vested rights which are but vested wrongs," which
> have proved fatal already to more than one Board of Health. [. . .]
> For last night, as he was sitting quietly under a stone in four fathoms
> water, he became aware [. . .] of a palpable nuisance somewhere in
> the neighbourhood; [. . .] He needed not to discover the limits of his
> authority, to consult any lengthy Nuisances' Removal Act, with its
> clauses, and counter-clauses, and explanations of interpretations, and
> interpretations of explanations. [. . .] so finding a hole, in he went, and
> began to remove the nuisance, without "waiting twenty-four hours,"
> "laying an information," "serving a notice," or any other vain delay.
> The evil was there,—and there it should not stay.[39]

Kingsley believed as firmly as Ellen Swallow Richards that "fresh
air and pure water" did much towards removing the ills of society.
This idea is based on a kind of environmental awareness which stems
from an adequate knowledge of the workings of natural processes.

Such a quest for knowledge is maybe not without its own ethical
difficulties. Chitty comments that the seashore fashion of the 1850s
led to "permanent denuding of the rockpools."[40] This may be so,
and the reckless chiselling away at rocks to extract sea-anemones
would horrify a modern environmentalist. But we should not interpret nineteenth-century collecting with twentieth-century sensibility
and experience. When the contemporary reviewer of *Glaucus* for
Blackwood's Magazine, Margaret Oliphant, writes: "We came away,
alas! pricked in our conscience, because of a hapless living thing

---

[39] *G³* 130–2.
[40] Chitty (1974) 166.

which we had unwittingly detached from its rock,"[41] this expresses regret for a single living being and does not reflect an ecological position. It would also be wrong to classify Kingsley as a reckless collector. After all, he warned his parishioners at Eversley not to kill the slow-worm that lived in the churchyard, and even in *Glaucus* itself there is an unmistakable undercurrent that nature is the property of "generations yet unborn."[42] First and foremost his attitude to nature was reverence coupled with an unwavering trust in its "awful permanence."[43] Moreover, that the "perfection of the natural world" could ever be threatened by man seemed beyond the comprehension of the mid-Victorian mind.

V

When Kingsley with a heavy heart sold the cow and left the rectory in Eversley in December 1853, he probably thought they would return to the parish once the winter was over. In March 1854 he wrote that Fanny was getting stronger slowly but steadily. But in May plans had to be changed. Trouble and anxiety returned; the children were ill and Fanny was so poorly that the doctors still thought her much too weak to travel and they disapproved of any plan to return to the damp rectory in Eversley.[44] A new curate was found for the parish, when, in July, they moved to the North Devon coast where they rented Northdown House in Bideford. In September Kingsley wrote to Stapleton that the children were fine but "as for Mrs. Kingsley's health, I wish I could say more than that she is safe at present, as long as she takes great care: but she cannot walk a quarter of a mile, & even in this summer heat, we have to watch every blast."[45] An eventual return to the rectory in Eversley was unattractive if not scaring, and in October ideas were hatched of rebuilding the rectory on different and higher ground. In a dramatic letter to his patron, Sir William Cope, Kingsley finally broached the subject and pointed out that one of the main faults of the present

---

[41] [Oliphant] (1855) 218.
[42] *G* 159.
[43] *G* 124.
[44] CK to AS, 8/3/1854; CK to AS, 19/5/1854, MP-C0171–36919.
[45] CK to AS, 6/9/1854, MP-C0171–36919.

site was that it lay on a level with the water course that drained the nearby Coombes' bogs. From time to time the house was visited by "those heavy floods, of w. we have had three in the last five years, in one case breaking down the yard wall, & standing a foot deep in the kitchen, & in every case coming into the back part of the house, & laying the whole premises & garden under water, thus saturating the foundation of the house."[46] Dampness invaded the rectory and, notwithstanding constant burning of stoves for the greater part of the year, books and clothes were ruined by mildew, and prints on the walls were spoilt.

As the living was in Sir William's hands, Kingsley needed his, as well as the bishop's, consent to rebuild the rectory. Although Sir William firmly declined contributing to the building costs, he did not seem opposed to Kingsley's plans at first, no doubt because, as Kingsley himself well realized, some day one of Cope's own sons might succeed him as Rector of Eversley.

Kingsley proposed rebuilding the rectory basically on the same plan on the glebe in front of the present site, using the materials and fittings of the old house. Approximately £1,000 was to come from Queen Anne's Bounty (a fund for the building and repair of parsonage houses), to be repaid by the living in instalments of £35 per year plus 4 per cent interest, while Kingsley himself offered to contribute £200 out of his own pocket, which was all he could manage "under present circumstances" (he had already spent over £1,000 on fruitless repairs to the old house). When an architect was consulted, however, it became clear that only a much smaller rectory could be built for the money available, and Sir William started to demur when in April 1855 Kingsley sent him the plans of the new house in which the front entrance was eliminated. "It is really a question of money. I have not money to make an entrance in the front elevation," Kingsley lamented. Details of building material and the size of various rooms were discussed between rector and patron by mail, but when Sir William remained firm and refused a smaller rectory than the present one, concluding that "the house is a good house as it stands and has been sufficient for many many Rectors, and indeed for yourself for many years,"[47] Kingsley's tone too sharpens:

[46] CK to WC, 16/10/1854, MP-C0171–36908.
[47] WC to CK, 16/4/1855, MP-C0171–36908.

"The arguments on my side for [a] license to build a smaller house w^d. be, the very large sums £1000 first & last, w. I have vainly spent in trying to patch the old house, dilapidate by the neglect of my predecessors, & wanting, when I entered it, the commonest decencies of civilization."[48] Although a few more letters on the subject followed, Kingsley realized that Cope's conclusion was final: "You of course have a perfect right to decide whether these pleas are sufficient; & you have decided that they are not [. . .] So the matter must rest." The new rectory was never built.

VI

The Turkish fleet in the Black Sea had been destroyed by Russia barely a month before Kingsley arrived in Torquay to join his family at Livermead in December 1853. The conflict had started when the Ottoman Empire declared war after Russia had occupied the Danubian principalities of Moldavia and Walachia. In England, the Russian aggression caused general consternation and fear of an extension of Russian power in the Balkans and Palestine, and, together with France, it demanded immediate evacuation of the principalities. Russia refused and the allied forces declared war on 28 March 1854. Kingsley's soldierly and fighting spirit was immediately kindled and on reaching the south of Devon he mused on England's glorious naval history: "We cannot gaze on its blue ring of water [. . .] without a glow passing through our hearts," he writes in *Glaucus*.[49] As much of the Crimean war was a conflict over the rights of the Russian Orthodox Church and the Roman Catholic Church in the holy places in the Middle East, Kingsley's heart warmed when he saw England intervening in the name of Western Christianity, but when towards the end of February he read in *The Times* that the government had only decided to sent 10,000 Guards, while the French sent 60,000 men, it made his "blood boil."[50]

The early stages of the war were marked by indecision and bad organization. When forces reached Gallipoli and were about to liberate

---

[48] CK to WC, 18/4/1855, MP-C0171–36908.
[49] *G³* 49.
[50] CK to FK, undated, BL-62554 f.27v.

the Principalities by attacking Varna, the action was held up by officials who doubted whether troops could be supplied with food there. When Varna was reached, the Russians had already retreated after having received threats from Austria. Moreover, the allies were badly affected by malaria and cholera. The English Government considered an attack on Sebastopol, but military advisors objected. A wavering cabinet finally decided to go ahead all the same, and towards the end of August 1854 the campaign was resumed. There was not much left of the heroic in the enterprise at this point. "What a muffy war!" Kingsley exclaimed in a letter to Thomas Hughes, "God grant we may not fail at Sebastopol, or the ministry will go out; & muffs as they are, whom can we put in their place?"[51] But this changed when troops finally landed on the Crimea in September, and the allies won an early victory on the heights south of the Alma River. Public opinion cheered, and Kingsley wrote in a letter to Maurice:

> I am afraid I have a little of the wolf-vein in me, in spite of fifteen centuries of civilization; [. . .] This war would have made me mad, if I had let it. It seems so dreadful to hear of those Alma heights being taken and not be there; but God knows best, and I suppose I am not fit for such brave work.[52]

At times Kingsley felt ashamed of himself, quietly naturalising on the Devon shores while England's honour was at stake in the Crimea, and, as if to justify his employments, in writing *Glaucus* he feels it necessary to stress repeatedly the courage and hardiness of the naturalist. In 1847 Thackeray had pictured the figure of the naturalist with his usual humour in *Vanity Fair*—

> "If you were a man of any spirit, Mr. Eagles, you would box the wretch's ears the next time you see him at the Club," she said to her husband. But Eagles was only a quiet old gentleman, husband to Mrs Eagles, with a taste for geology, and not tall enough to reach anybody's ears.[53]

—and such an image of the naturalist must have stung Kingsley. One of the first things he clarifies in *Glaucus* is that the pursuit of natural history is a truly honourable one, that it is no longer looked upon as fit for him "who went 'bug-hunting' simply because he had

---

[51] CK to TH, 11/9/1854, Martin (1950) 542.
[52] CK to FDM, 19/10/1854, *LML* i.162.
[53] William Thackeray, *Vanity Fair*, (Harmondsworth: Penguin, 1968) 745.

not spirit to follow a fox."[54] "The coarse, fierce, hard-handed training of our grand-fathers" was suited to different times, he explains, but "let us be thankful that we have had leisure for science; and show now in war that our science has not unmanned us."[55]

This was not just empty rhetoric. The times were indeed changing. In the middle of the century, the individual life had become more important in a society which was beset by religious doubt, and more and more educated people saw fighting as essentially barbaric. No doubt the all-pervading idea of progress in Victorian society squared badly with a war, which many saw as a step backwards in civilisation. Kingsley's own comment in his letter to Maurice indicates that he shared the basic belief in the progress "of fifteen centuries of civilization," but at the same time found much to lament in the spirit of the age. In Torquay he witnessed the frivolity of the fashionable classes, and even "a frightful majority of our middle-class young men are growing up effeminate, empty of all knowledge but what tends directly to the making of fortune."[56] It is in the pursuit of science that both body and mind are properly trained; that a man learns to be brave and enterprising, patient and undaunted; that the mind learns to observe free from "haste and laziness, from melancholy, testiness, pride, and all the passions which make men see only what they wish to see;" that he will never rashly discredit reports.[57]

Parallels between soldiers and naturalists are constantly drawn in *Glaucus* and sustained by many examples of famous officers who turned to science. Moreover, Kingsley stresses that the kingdom of nature "must be taken by violence,"[58] that it is "an epos of the destruction and re-creation"[59] that some botanists bemoan "themselves, like Alexander, that there are no more worlds left to conquer."[60] Nature itself is one big battle and the language used in *Glaucus*, maybe unconsciously, creates the idea of continuous struggle in the mind of the reader: saxifrages 'retreat', rocks are furrowed as if scratched by 'iron talons'. Sometimes this leads to some of the most evocative passages of the book. In the following example of volcanic

---

[54] G^3 6.
[55] G^3 8.
[56] G^3 43.
[57] G^3 37–9.
[58] G^3 38.
[59] G^3 22.
[60] G^3 23.

fury, the smoke and blasts of cannon are expressed in a dazzling sequence of sibilants, fricatives and plosives:

> the broad Rhine beneath fashed blood-red in the blaze of the lighting and the fires of the Mausenthurm—a lurid Acheron above which seemed to hover ten thousand unburied ghosts; and last, but not least, on the lip of the vast Mosel-kopf crater—just above the point where the weight of the fiery lake has burst the side of the great slag-cup, and rushed forth between two cliffs of clink-stone across the downs, in a clanging stream of fire, damming up rivulets, and blasting its path through forests.[61]

And this was just to describe Kingsley's elated emotion of finding for the first time in his life a yellow fox-glove.

George Henry Lewes, who was often maddened by Kingsley's "would-be manliness," noticed the muscularity of such passages, and reacted to such an ideal of English male prowess in his own book on marine zoology, *Sea-side Studies*. The following can be seen as a response to Kingsley's book:

> Nay, even when he is sea-sick—as unhappily even the Briton will some-times be—he goes through it with a certain careless grace, a manly haughtiness, or at the lowest a certain "official reserve," not observ-able in the foreigner. What can be a more abject picture than a Frenchman suffering from sea-sickness—unless it be a German under the same hideous circumstances? Before getting out of harbour he was radiant, arrogant, self-centred; only half an hour has passed, and he is green, cadaverous, dank, prostrate, the manhood seemingly spunged out of him. N.B.—In this respect I am a Frenchman.[62]

No doubt part of Lewes's attitude to Kingsley was influenced by the success of *Glaucus*, and his envy is ill-concealed in a letter to his publisher: "If Kingsley could sell 3 editions of Glaucus which had nothing whatever new in it, nothing of his own except the preaching, we ought to be able to get off 1250, but it's a horrid bore having a weight of unsold copies on one's shelf."

VII

The letter to Maurice in which Kingsley regrets not having been in the Crimea when the Alma Heights were taken was written about

---

[61] *G³* 25–6.
[62] George Lewes, *Sea-side Studies* (Edinburgh: William Blackwood, 1858) 199.

a week before the battle of Balaclava, when the Crimean War itself
turned into a "dreadful nightmare, which haunted him day and
night."[63] The war had begun to take its toll on the British army: after
the early victory on the Alma Heights it did not proceed well and
dragged on without success, while the number of casualties grew.
While the new intellectual and, to Kingsley, effeminate attitude to
war was still that of a minority in Victorian society, the suffering of
the British troops had more impact. For the first time in British history public opinion about war was moved. In a sense the Crimean
war changed the idea of war for those who remained at home.
People were better informed about the horrors while it was going
on, as newspaper correspondents followed the campaign in the field
and sent back home reports which the postal system allowed to reach
them in only a couple of days. Especially *The Times*, expressing the
ideas of the middle classes, thundered in its columns against the
shortcomings of the officials and the mismanagement of the administration at home. Moreover the decline of religious belief which
made death look horrible in the eyes of the doubtful helped to undermine the idea of gallantry and heroism which had still underlain the
Napoleonic wars. Add to this the obvious blundering in organization,
and it is not difficult to sense the contradictions in the hearts of
many of the people at home.

When in "The Charge of the Light Brigade" Tennyson transformed
both the gallantry and the blundering into poetry and wrote about
the six hundred English cavalrymen who were slaughtered by Russian
artillery because of confusing orders, Tom Hughes urged Kingsley
to employ his poetic genius in a similar way. Kingsley impatiently
dismissed the idea; much as he admired Tennyson, he retorted: "oh!
my dear lad, there is no use fiddling while Rome is burning."[64] No
fiddling, but vigorous prose, as he had already made clear to Maurice:
"But I can fight with my pen still [. . .] in writing books which will
make others fight."[65] Early in 1853, Kingsley had in fact started
planning a novel to rouse national feeling against French naval expan-
sion, a "most ruthless bloodthirsty book," "just what the times want,"[66]

---

[63] *LML* i.439.
[64] CK to TH, 18/12/1854, *LML* i434.
[65] CK to FDM, 19/19/1854, *LML* i.433.
[66] CK to FDM, 19/19/1854, *LML* i.433.

and he was well underway with what was to become *Westward Ho!*
when England blundered into war with Russia.

But while reports of the disgraceful conditions of the sick and
wounded reached the English through the papers, and the controversy about the war started, the soldiers were still out there, suffering
and dying for the honour of their country. This discussion would
do them no good, Kingsley decided. They, and the people at home,
needed rallying. *Westward Ho!* might do the trick, but the book was
only half written. When, however, he heard that most of the pamphlets which were sent out to the troops were left unread, he sat
down and wrote a 1400-word tract himself and gave it the title *Brave
Words to Brave Soldiers and Sailors*. The anonymous tract—a perfect
specimen of Muscular Christianity—was sent out to the Crimea in
December 1854. In it Kingsley does not play on the patriotic element, but gives the fighting a firm religious direction. He admits
that, although the people at home felt for the soldiers who had to
"face delay, and disappointment, and fatigue, and sickness, and
hunger, and cold, and nakedness,"[67] it is only natural for the soldier
out there to think: "My people at home feel for me, but they cannot know, they never will know, the half of what I have gone through
[. . .] Who can make up to me for my life?"[68] It is important, therefore, he urges, to be aware that "if the nation cannot reward you
for sacrificing your life in a just war, there is One above who can,
and who will, too,"[69] and that He who is the Prince of Peace is also
the Prince of War, that "whosoever fights in a just war, against
tyrants and oppressors, [. . .] is fighting on Christ's side, and Christ
is fighting on his side."[70] Then, to stimulate courage, he quotes St
John's vision of Christ clothed in a garment dipped in blood riding
a white horse, whose name is the Word of God with which he will
smite nations (Revelation 19.11), and asks "Is not this a general
worth following?"[71]

Such words might smack of shallowness in a debate that touched
the profound issues of a changing attitude to war. But a letter to
Ludlow and Hughes written in February 1855 shows that Kingsley's

---

[67] *TW* 200.
[68] *TW* 201.
[69] *TW* 203.
[70] *TW* 204.
[71] *TW* 206.

ideas on the issue were far from unimaginative. He explained to
Ludlow and Hughes, who had somehow found out that Kingsley
was the author of *Brave Words*, why he had written the pamphlet.
The Church, he explained, will pray only for "the sick, wounded,
nurses, every one but the fighting men as fighting men, every thing
but the War itself," while they are careful not to pronounce any
opinions on the justice of the war. This is not to be marvelled at,
Kingsley admits, as this is "*not* a just war. It began in a lie & and
a cant. We pretended to go to war for liberty [. . .] We went to war
because the ministry wanted to keep in, & thought that by yielding
to the popular cry they wd have administration, & all wd be over
in 6 months."[72]

What Kingsley proclaimed in his pamphlet to the soldiers as a
"just war" was not an unconditionally "just war." One might sense
a misleading contradiction in Kingsley's words: when he used "just"
to the soldiers he meant "honest and manly in a just cause." But it
was the way the war was managed, all the political wrangling around
it, and the effeminate comments on the war back home in England
that disgusted him, that made it "not a just war." The fighting had
turned out "grim earnest"; so "we are in it and shall have to carry
on the war honestly."

The letter to Ludlow and Hughes contained some more pungent
views of the war which Kingsley proposed to use for a second pamphlet and which show that he had a much better grasp of its political
background than *Brave Words* revealed. The second tract was never
finished, and, therefore, never published. "Let us bide our time," he
noted, and even Mrs Kingsley, when she prepared her husband's
biography in 1875, wrote on the draft: "Pray do not publish this—
it wd be misunderstood." When *Brave Words* came out the political
situation had not yet come to a head. But in December the outcry
against the mismanagement of the war grew, and when John Arthur
Roebuck, Radical MP for Sheffield, presented a motion to enquire
into the conditions of the army, the government fell. The fall was
the result of the resignation of Lord John Russell, officially over the
rejection of a reform bill he had brought in, but it was seen by
many middle class voters as a result of the bad management of the

---

[72] CK to TH and JL, 25/2/1855, BL-62557 f.18v–19r. The transcription of this
letter in Appendix 1 of Chitty's biography (298–301) is particularly corrupt.

war. A strong man was wanted to save England's image abroad, and, in the eyes of the people, Lord Palmerston seemed the right person to become Prime Minister. But many able politicians discredited Palmerston's new government, "a Cabinet of All the Mediocrities," Disraeli grumbled. Roebuck complained that no complete change of ministers was effected and the army and administration still needed investigation.

Kingsley echoed these sentiments and was disappointed that Lord John Russell's reform had been shelved. "My children," he writes in a letter to Ludlow and Hughes, "the English nation is simply insulted and humbugged. Insulted, by the putting in again of the men it turned out."[73] What had happened was that Palmerston had formed a cabinet with exactly the same ministers except for Lord Aberdeen and the Duke of Newcastle, Prime Minister and Secretary at War respectively. But when Palmerston decided that Roebuck would have his committee of enquiry, three ministers, amongst whom the former Chancellor of the Exchequer Gladstone and the War Secretary Sidney Herbert, would not accept the idea and resigned. Kingsley saw all this as suspicious, and grimly commented on the responsibilities for the mismanagement of the war that, notwithstanding the humbug change of Parliament, in the end truth would out, and the time was now for "an eye for an eye":

> We have thrown away the Gospel, & put ourselves formally under The Law. And what says the Law? Without shedding of blood there is no remission of sin. And who so sheddeth man's blood by him shall man's blood be shed. And the blood of that Crimean Army cries from the ground against—I don't know whom: but God knows; & God will demand that blood; & with such a sin committed in the face of our Light & knowledge & by men who are full of religiosities & virtuosities [. . .] Don't ask me to prophesy on it: because there is no use recommending the gallows, till one has settled a little who should be hanged on it. Sidney Herbert & Gladstone I do see my way toward hanging (but no further).[74]

The interest of this letter to Ludlow and Hughes lies in the fact that it shows us Kingsley's twofold attitude to the war. If on the one hand he had little patience with the popular interest in Florence Nightingale, whose exploits at the throughly inadequate and overcrowded hospitals

---

[73] CK to TH and JL, 25/2/1855, BL-62557 f.11v–12r.
[74] CK to TH and JL, 25/2/1855, BL-62557 f.13v–14r.

at Scutari had made her a heroine at home, and whose success Kingsley saw as overshadowing the more important issues of the war, on the other he was actually willing to go a long way with Roebuck's motion and the general tone of protest in the harshly condemnatory articles on the government that appeared in the war-columns of *The Times*.

CHAPTER FOURTEEN

A MOST RUTHLESS BLOODTHIRSTY BOOK
(JANUARY–JUNE 1855)

The patriot in Kingsley warmed towards England's glorious history in *Glaucus* with

> a glow passing through our hearts, as we remember the terrible and glorious pageant which passed by in the glorious July days of 1588, when the Spanish Armada ventured slowly past Berry Head, with Elizabeth's gallant pack of Devon captains [. . .] following fast in its wake, and dashing into the midst of the vast line, undismayed by size and numbers, while their kin and friends stood watching and praying on the cliffs, spectators of Britain's Salamis.[1]

He did so not only to criticize the effeminacy of the youth of his day, but also to give us a glimpse of what had been passing in his mind since his arrival in Torbay, if not during most of the previous year. Since he finished *Hypatia*, his interests had focussed on the heroes of the Elizabethan period. In July 1852 Froude had written an article on "England's Forgotten Worthies" for the *The Westminster Review* which was based on a new edition of Richard Hakluyt's *Divers voyages touching the discouerie of America*, and, impressed with both his brother-in-law's essay and Hakluyt's narrative, Kingsley recommended a selection of the voyages, with a preface by Froude, to his publisher. It is possible that Kingsley started having some vague ideas about a novel on the period himself, and his anti-Catholic sentiments, which the weak foreign policy of Lord Derby's ministry nurtured through the following year, invited constant comparisons with the time of "Good Queen Bess" when men were of "another stamp."[2]

Political developments in France from 1848 onwards had kindled English patriotism, and when Louis Napoleon, President of the Second Republic, started meddling with affairs in Italy, took power to change the French constitution with a coup d'état in 1851, and managed

---

[1] *G³* 49.
[2] CK to AS, December 1852, MP-C0171.

to get himself proclaimed emperor Napoleon III at the end of 1852, many Englishmen felt alarmed about a possible invasion. Added to this, his decisive help in restoring the papacy by suppressing Mazzini's and Garibaldi's short-lived Roman Republic made him suspicious in Protestant eyes. The press voiced its fears in numerous alarming and nationalistic writings, and Alfred Tennyson contributed as poet laureate in various 'newspaper pieces,' of which the following is a good example:

> Shall we fear *him*? Our own we never fear'd.
> From our first Charles by force we wrung our claims.
> Prick'd by the Papal spur, we rear'd,
> We flung the burthen of the second James.
> I say, we *never* feared! And as for these,
> We broke them on the land, we drove them on the seas.
>   ("The Third of February 1852")

Tennyson's lines show how much Napoleon's military threat was linked to religious sentiments about the threat of continental Roman Catholicism. This had been growing steadily in England since the re-introduction of the Roman Catholic hierarchy and the elevation, at the end of 1850, of Dr Wiseman to the Roman Catholic See of Westminster, an event which many in the Anglican Church saw as an act of papal aggression.

To Kingsley too the threat of war with France loomed large on the horizon, and when the Foreign Secretary Lord Malmesbury announced in the Lords that England recognized Napoleon III as Emperor of France, Kingsley cried out against a government which, "from some suicidal blindness, did more to back Popery than any government I have ever seen, by petting & tampering with Louis Napoleon, the utter, willing, notorious tool of the Jesuits, the most frightful incarnation of Antichrists triple power—money, sword, & priestcraft, wh. our age has seen." England's weak international politics forced Kingsley, Tennyson and others to look back to the glorious courage of the past. Thus, when the ministry fell over Disraeli's budget barely a month later and was substituted by a coalition of Whigs and Peelites, Kingsley expressed his absolute trust in Gladstone, who had taken Disraeli's place in the new ministry, as he "& his fellows are not in the hands of the Jesuits." This was reassuring for Kingsley because he was convinced that "the whole continent *is* so." The comparison with England in the late sixteenth century came naturally: Derby's ministry had been deservedly turned out of power

as it fawned on "a villain who has vowed to invade England & re-
establish the Romish faith in it," a ministry which would "as soon
have fawned on Philip of Spain while he was fitting out his Armada."
There was more likelihood in the new coalition, Kingsley thought,
of finding a "ministry who will face the new Armada."[3]

These internal and foreign political matters, and not the Crimean
War in the following year, gave birth to *Westward Ho!*, a novel which
has gone down to history as Kingsley's Crimean novel. Critics and
biographers have, in fact, confused the influence of the events in
France and Russia on the shaping of the novel, and sometimes
ignored the importance of the former altogether. Such an approach
to the novel undoubtedly owes much to Mrs Kingsley's biography
in which she says that Torbay inspired her husband to write the
novel[4] and that the writing itself commenced when the family moved
to Bideford in July 1854.[5] This would indeed imply that the novel
came into being as the main events of the Crimean war occurred,
and would be in line with two much-quoted comments by the author
himself, one in a letter to Macmillan in which he announces the
novel as "a book which people will read in these war-times,"[6] another
in a letter to Hughes that the novel he was writing was "a sanguinary
book: but perhaps containing doctrine profitable for these times."[7]
But these comments are misleading. They are late expressions when
Kingsley's blood was up about the miserable performances of the
English on the Crimean peninsula and when the book was well
underway. What many critics have overlooked when calling *Westward
Ho!* a war novel is Kingsley's contempt for the Jesuits and his outrage at the Spanish Inquisition, themes which feature centrally in
the novel, but which have little to do with the Russian aggression
in the Crimea and there is no doubt about it that the underlying
sentiments which initially spurred him on to write it had been fermenting in his mind ever since Louis Napoleon's interventions in
Italy. They had contributed to an ever more solid aversion to Rome:
"I am becoming more & more Protestant the longer I live," he wrote
to Stapleton in September 1853, "& if I have little sympathy with

---

[3] CK to AS, 5/1/1853, MP-C0171–36919.
[4] *LMLM* 155.
[5] *LML* i.428.
[6] CK to Macmillan, 1/6/1854, BL-54911 f.31.
[7] CK to TH, 18/12/1854, Martin (1950) 567.

Dr. Cumming & the Exeter Hall school, I am nevertheless persuaded that Rome is utterly of the Devil, & that not only she, but all w. approaches to her, is to be held anathema by every one who does not intend to give up merely his status, but his very feeling, as an Englishman."[8]

Moreover, although it is easy to find echoes of, and even direct comments on, the Crimean War in the narrator's voice, and although his writing in North Devon during the war months was prompted by contemporary events, so that it was easy for a contemporary reader, such as Caroline Fox, to see the novel as being against Russia, Kingsley never transferred his hostile feelings for France, now ironically an ally, to Russia. Thus, at the beginning of the novel Kingsley contemplates in his authoritative narrator's voice, that, had it not been for Devon's "forgotten worthies," England would be a "Popish appanage of a world-tyranny."[9] Similarly, one of the first pieces of English savage bravery we are told of in the novel is how its hero, Amyas Leigh, insulted by a Frenchman who spoke slightingly of Queen Elizabeth, "got mad, and leapt upon him, and caught him by the wrist, and then had a fair side-blow; and, as fortune would have it, off tumbled his head on to the table, and there was an end of his slanders."[10] The parallel between the early 1850s and the late sixteenth century is that the Jesuits "had as stoutly persuaded themselves in those days, as they have in these [. . .] that the heart of England was really with them, and that the British nation was on the point of returning to the bosom of the Catholic Church."[11] Rather than to his worries about Russia's 'godless' aggression on the Crimea, it is to these early lines of the novel that the original intention of the book can be traced. They unequivocally reflect Kingsley's reaction to both the efforts to restore the Roman Catholic hierarchy in England, and Louis Napoleon's reinstating the Pope to his seat in Rome. "What is one to do, if the whole country is full of [Papist spies]?" Amyas is made to exclaim.[12]

---

[8] CK to AS, 13/9/1853, MP-C0171–36919.
[9] *WH* 2.
[10] *WH* 56.
[11] *WH* 66.
[12] *WH* 59.

II

Only a few months after recommending the selection from Hakluyt's voyages to Parker, Kingsley was seriously planning a novel which was going to be "the autobiography of a knight of Queen Elizabeth's time" and he specified to Macmillan, who, after the success of *Phaeton*, had apparently asked for a novel, that "considering these times of *The Pope & the French Invasion*, it may make a hit, & do good." The seafaring Elizabethan heroes had always captivated Kingsley's imagination—he had known the "the West Indian part of it [. . .] from a child" through the stories his maternal grandfather had told him—and Froude "who knows that period better than any man" supplied him with a wealth of material on the English part.[13]

Westward Ho! was offered to Macmillan at an early stage. Kingsley's relation with Parker had cooled considerably after the review on *Phaeton* in *Fraser's Magazine* (which was owned by Parker), and when they failed to pick up his schemes on Hakluyt, Kingsley felt free to publish with the Scottish Macmillan brothers. But Chapman still had an option on a second novel, and Kingsley warned the Macmillans that they "shall have it [only] if I can fairly get off Chapman without damage to my pocket."[14] As it was, Chapman released Kingsley, and the Macmillans brought out the book which was to establish them as a major novel publisher.

The move to Devon for Mrs Kingsley's health had come at an ideal moment for further inspiration and to be staying near the Froudes was a great attraction. Kingsley went for long walks on the beaches and cliffs around Babbacombe with his brother-in-law to discuss the Elizabethan "forgotten worthies." In June 1854, Macmillan was informed that the book "thrives apace" and that he had written "up & down, several chapters, whereof Froude approves much."[15] Kingsley wanted the novel to take an autobiographical form and he intended "to call it *The Tracey Papers* or some such name, and cooly and impudently to assume the reality of the whole story." Macmillan, who had no tradition of publishing novels as yet, were "greatly taken" with all Kingsley told them about his project, but urged him not to try to invent a "pseudo-antique manner" as Thackeray had done in *Esmond*.

13 CK to Macmillan, 17/2/53, BL-54911 f.18v–19r, italics mine.
14 CK to Macmillan, 17/2/53, BL-54911 f.18r.
15 CK to Macmillan, 1/6/1854, BL-54911 f.31r.

The "free march" of Kingsley's own style would be more Elizabethan in tone, they thought.[16] Kingsley talked it over with Thackeray himself, who admitted that the archaic form of *Esmond* had probably injured the sales of his novel. It is likely that this made Kingsley abandon his initial first person narrative and use omniscient narration instead. He now sat down in Northdown House in Bideford to get it out by January the following year.

But if Macmillan was "sure it will be a right brave and noble book, and do good to England,"[17] they feared Kingsley's belief in the didactic calling of his writings and asked him not to hold forth in his own person and preach, as he had done in his previous novels. Kingsley acknowledged the advice offered and reassured them that he would "expunge all preachments,"[18] which was only partially effected.

Although Kingsley's blind and overtly muscular enthusiasm for the war is often discussed and criticised, much of Kingsley's views on England's military prowess and his own role in sustaining such courage suffered severely as the fighting stalled during that horrible winter in the Crimea, and he was at times full of misgivings and doubt about his own stand. At the beginning of the year, when England declared war on Russia, his Elizabethan narrative seemed just the thing his country needed. When in September the war had become "muffy," Mrs Kingsley writes that it all "weighed heavily" on him, a "dreadful nightmare" which "haunted him by day as well as night."[19] In October he admitted he felt more than guilty for not being there— "sometimes very sad; always very puzzled"—and realizing that he was "not fit for such brave work" he learned about himself what he suspected all along, namely, that he was "a poor queasy, hysterical half-baked sort of fellow." As a result, he added, the book is "only half as good as I could have written."[20] In such moments he seemed to resign himself to the fact that all his courage amounted to was writing a blood-thirsty book and rabbit shooting, pretending "that the Rabbits were Russians, tin pot on head & musquet in hand!"[21]

---

[16] Macmillan to CK, June 1854, Nowell-Smith 37.
[17] Macmillan to CK, 18/6/54, Nowell-Smith 37.
[18] CK to Macmillan, 29/9/54, BL-54911 f.37.
[19] *LML* i.439.
[20] CK to FDM, 19/10/1854, *LML* i.433.
[21] CK to TH, 18/12/1854, Martin (1950) 567.

Writing *Westward Ho!*, moreover, had become more than a mere interest in the "men of good Queen Bess's time": it had become a financial necessity. Fanny was not strong enough to return to Eversley and needed a much longer sojourn in Devon. Kingsley needed a new book out soon and to sell well—which explains why, never much perturbed by publishers' wants, he was so willing to listen to Macmillan's advice on style and preaching—but the pressure was beginning to tell. "We never have really wanted yet," he pleads with Fanny when looking for accommodation in north Devon, "Oh! let us be content."[22]

Although Kingsley worked hard on the manuscript and despatched it in bits and pieces to Macmillan, Clay, the printer had problems keeping up with such a rhythm, and both author and publisher had to "kick up" the "snail."[23] But when the novel came out at the end of March 1855, it was an immediate success. The historian of the House of Macmillan records how, in 1855, 2,000 copies were printed of two expensive three-volume editions at a guinea and a half, and in 1857 a further 6,000 of a one-volume edition, for which Kingsley received a total of £850.[24] This was a considerable amount of money, and in the long run, long after Kingsley's death, the family continued to profit from its sales which were stimulated by the cheap six-penny editions from 1889 onwards.

The success of *Westward Ho!* gave the Macmillans the name of a major publisher of fiction and this would bring the firm such novelists as Thomas Hughes, Henry James, and Thomas Hardy, the famous and influential essayists Thomas Henry Huxley and Matthew Arnold, and poets such as Alfred Tennyson and Arthur Hugh Clough.

III

Of all Kingsley's novels, the epithet 'Muscular Christianity' fits most closely in *Westward Ho!*. Because the novel was sent out to the front in the Crimea, its nationalistic spirit and glorified scenes of battle were often remembered as representing its true spirit, a quality that soon relegated it to the domain of boys' literature. This approach has tended,

---

[22] CK to FK, undated, 62554 f.38v.
[23] CK to Macmillan, 19/4/1855, BL-54911 f.54v; 1/2/1855, BL-54911 f.48v.
[24] Morgan 42–3.

during much of the century following publication, to obscure the fact that it is also an ambitious and sophisticated work of art. In it Kingsley dealt with themes that were of central interest to himself and to his time, raising questions of origins, race, history, slavery, empire and nationality. Neither is the novel devoid of Kingsley's more personal concerns with religion and matrimonial love.

To Kingsley *Westward Ho!* was a natural sequel to *Hypatia*. It epitomized the second historical phase in a progressive pattern towards freedom and emancipation, the final phase of which Kingsley saw as imminent in nineteenth-century socialism in the form of a Christian brotherhood. This last stage was hinted at in the narrator's last words in *Yeast*: "my heroes go on as they have set forth, looking with single mind for some one ground of human right and love."[25] If his novel about fourth-century Alexandria represented to him a turning point in the history of the Christian Church, an "infusion of new and healthier blood into the veins of a world drained and tainted by the influence of Rome," the Elizabethan Era, with its victory over the Spanish Armada, represented more than any other period a pivotal moment where the health of the Church depended "not merely on the creed which it professes, not even on the wisdom and holiness of a few ecclesiastics; but on the faith and virtue of its individual members."[26] But for "the glorious fight of 1588, what had we been by now, but a Popish appanage of a world-tyranny," Kingsley writes. To him it was an epic national subject, "fit rather to have been sung than said, and to have proclaimed to all true English hearts."[27]

The momentous events of the 1580s are shown in *Westward Ho!* on two separate, but intertwining, levels: the national and the individual. And it is through the tension between these levels that Kingsley explores his main themes.

The story starts in the year 1575 as Amyas Leigh, a tall and fair Bideford schoolboy, listens to the wild tales told by sailors about fighting the Spaniards and the marvellous riches which could be captured. The sentiment is crude enough at the outset. "I tell you," the captain says, "those Spaniards are rank cowards, as all bullies are. They pray to a woman, the idolatrous rascals! and no wonder they

---

[25] *Y* 378.
[26] *H* xi.
[27] *WH* 2.

fight like women."[28] But it is the right stuff to make a lasting impression on the boy, who from that day starts dreaming of the days he himself will serve his country at sea, and see brave sights and do brave deeds. Although he is still too young to enroll, Amyas, Kingsley anticipates, "is a symbol, though he knows it not, of brave *young England* longing to wing its way out of its island prison, to discover and to traffic, to colonise and to civilise, until no wind can sweep the earth which does not bear the echoes of an English voice."[29] This seems boisterous rhetoric in all respects, but Kingsley does not want there to be any doubt about the moral centre of the novel, and vents an early warning that will ring throughout as the plot unfolds. When Amyas tells of his fancies to become an adventurer, his godfather, Sir Richard Grenville, admonishes him: "to be bold against the enemy is common to the brutes; but the prerogative of a man is to be bold against himself [. . .] To conquer our fancies, Amyas, and our lusts, and our ambition, in the sacred name of duty; this it is to be truly brave, and truly strong; for he who cannot rule himself, how can he rule his crew or his fortunes?"[30] And for the time being Amyas has to be content to finish his education, until at seventeen he will be allowed to sail for three years with Sir Francis Drake.

The narrative power of *Westward Ho!* is created, as in *Hypatia*, by Kingsley's clever interweaving of fictional characters with historical ones. Historical persons like the adventurers Grenville, Hawkins, Oxenham, Raleigh and Drake, or the poet-courtiers Sidney and Spenser form an effective backdrop of veracity that is convincing, while much of the direct liveliness of the narrative is sustained in the reader's interest in Amyas's personal adventures.

Although the events in South America form the core of the novel, it takes Kingsley almost half the book to get his characters there. This delay is part of a deliberate strategy to explore the *otherness* that South America represents. The adventures that the novel recounts are also a careful investigation of primitive cultures, in terms both of origins and of reinvigorating energy.

Before Amyas sails to the West Indies, he has to do duty in Ireland under Sir Walter Raleigh. The confrontation with Ireland is ambiguous,

---

[28] *WH* 4.
[29] *WH* 10; my italics.
[30] *WH* 16.

as it represents a primitive country that is not England yet is part of the British Isles. The description of Amyas's journey to "the land of Ire" (and its "children of wrath") is described in terms of a descent into a savage world of mud and bog, inhuman and brutish:

> The grey March skies are curdling hard and high above black mountain peaks. The keen March wind is sweeping harsh and dry across a dreary sheet of bog, still red and yellow with the stains of winter frost. One brown knoll alone breaks the waste, and on it a few leafless windclipt oaks stretch their moss-grown arms, like giant hairy spiders, above a desolate pool which crisps ans shivers in the biting breeze, while from beside its brink rises a mournful cry, and sweeps down, faint and fitful, amid the howling wind.[31]

This is not a volcanic primeval world from which Ireland is being born, but one that has been visited by the sins of man. Its degradation, which hangs in the air as venom, is feared and condemned by Amyas. Raleigh, however, points out that the "venom" is as much caused by past conduct of the English, as it is a danger to their future. Kingsley probes into the meaning of race and civilisation when Amyas maintains that what is needed there is "sword and bullet [. . .] Until a few more of these Irish lords are gone," and Raleigh rejoins:

> Humph! not so far wrong, I fear. And yet—Irish lords? These very traitors are better English blood than we who hunt them down [. . .] Strange, Amyas, is it not? Noble Normans sunk into savages—Hibernis ipsis hiberniores! Is there some uncivilising venom in the air?

Kingsley had political insight enough not to offend his Irish readers, and Raleigh asserts that it is without doubt that "the Irish themselves are well enough." This distinction was important, and Kingsley did not want to let it go by unnoticed. Therefore, an intrusive footnote was added at the end of the chapter, explaining that:

> It has been reserved for this age, and for the liberal policy of this age, to see the last ebullitions of Celtic excitability die out harmless and ashamed of itself, and to find that the Irishman, when he is brought as a soldier under the regenerative influence of law, discipline, selfrespect, and loyalty, can prove himself a worthy rival of the more stern Norse-Saxon warrior. God grant that the military brotherhood between Irish and English, which is the special glory of the present war, may be the germ of a brotherhood industrial, political, and hereafter, perhaps,

---

[31] *WH* 217.

religious also; and that not merely the corpses of heroes, but the feuds and wrongs which have parted them for centuries, may lie buried, once and forever, in the noble graves of Alma and Inkerman.[32]

This affirmation of Englishness was, of course, dictated by the fact that many Irishmen were right then dying in the Crimea for Britain. Kingsley's apology should not, however, obscure the fact that Raleigh's words also reveal that this confidence and national pride is little more than a brittle layer of civilisation. With Conradian clarity Kingsley fears the danger that colonisation might bring to the coloniser: "Are even these men worse than we might be, if we had been bred up masters over bodies and souls of men, in some remote land where law and order had never come?"[33] Such considerations show that Kingsley had conflicting thoughts about English colonisation. English imperialism had two fearful predecessors in that of Rome and that of Spain. But while these empires were built on slavery, England's was to be based on freedom. This difference is constantly alluded to by Kingsley in the novel and is used to justify England's battle against the "West-Indian devilries of the Spaniards."[34] But with this Kingsley was writing against history, and he knew it. He was well-read enough in Elizabethan history to know of John Hawkins's slave-trading voyage to the West Indies in 1562–3, which was supported and financed by prominent London merchants, and that the expedition turned out to be so successful that many noblemen, as well as Queen Elizabeth herself, subscribed to back a second enterprise in 1564–5. The enterprise is glossed over in a farcical passage in an early chapter. Yeo, the memorable Anabaptist gunner, admits having been with Hawkins on his expeditions "to Guinea for negro slaves, and thence to the West Indies," and Sir Richard Grenville reminds him that Captain Hawkins came to a bad end. Yeo voices his racist opinion of black man:

> I doubt—about the unlawfulness, I mean; being the negroes are of the children of Ham, who are cursed and reprobate, as Scripture declares, and their blackness testifies, being Satan's own livery; among whom therefore there can be none of the elect, wherefore the elect are not required to treat them as brethren.

---

[32] *WH* 111.
[33] *WH* 218–9.
[34] *WH* 12.

Grenville, who, as Fanny's illustrious forebear, is an authoritative voice in the novel, exclaims:

> What a plague of a pragmatical sea-lawyer have we here? And I doubt not, thou hypocrite, that though thou wilt call the negroes' black skin Satan's livery, when it serves thy turn to steal them, thou wilt find out sables to be Heaven's livery every Sunday, and up with a godly howl unless a parson shall preach in a black gown, Geneva fashion. Out upon thee![35]

Kingsley playfully deplores Hawkins's involvement in the slave-trade (without reference to Queen Elizabeth, of course), and then cursorily dismisses it from his mind. But the historic dilemma of England and slavery was not limited to Hawkins alone. When Amyas and his crew witness a train of slaves being maltreated by their Spanish tyrants, Kingsley brings out the difference between the Spanish and the English:

> a low murmur of indignation rose from the ambushed Englishmen, worthy of the free and righteous hearts of those days, when Raleigh could appeal to man and God, on the ground of a common humanity, in behalf of the outraged heathens of the New World.

The English heroes slay the Spanish and set the slaves free, but Kingsley, this time in more serious vein, feels bound to add that these were times

> when Englishmen still knew that man was man, and that the instinct of freedom was the righteous voice of God; ere the hapless seventeenth century had brutalized them also, by bestowing on them, amid a hundred other bad legacies, the fatal gift of negro-slaves.[36]

Slavery was an important colonial question for Kingsley, who also condemned, as he made clear in *Alton Locke*, the "condition of England" very much in terms of masters and slaves. So, Kingsley at times had reservations about the capacity of the English to civilise the world. And this emerges in the Irish part of *Westward Ho!*. If, on the one hand, he sees for Britain a God-given mission to build up "the weal of the Reformed Churches throughout the world, and the liberties of all nations, against an enemy more foul and rapacious than that of Nero or Caligula,"[37] on the other hand, the dark part in man is

---

[35] *WH* 129.
[36] *WH* 435.
[37] *WH* 13.

feared, whose "genius of tyranny and falsehood [will] find soil within thy heart to grow and ripen fruit" and will cause its "children [to] sink downwards"[38] once it comes in contact with a culture in which instinctive impulses are not gilded over by civilisation but still lie at the surface. It is the example that Ireland supplied as internal proof that savagery could easily surface in British civilisation itself that underscores the necessity of consolidating the notion of Britain's own civilization before it was morally entitled to venture to colonize overseas. One thing the condition of the poor in England had taught Kingsley was that British civilization was still more an ideal than a reality.

The part in Ireland provides the necessary preparation for the adventures in the second half of the novel, which are set in a New World often represented in scenes of paradisiacal beauty. There is a pristine quality to this world that contrasts sharply with the barrenness of Ireland. But there is always an element of danger and death lurking below its enticing surface. The scene where two of Amyas's crew desert to live with their Indian women a life of drugged felicity makes Amyas pause: "Such, he thought, was Paradise of old; such our parents' bridal bower! Ah! If man had not fallen, he too might have dwelt for ever in such a home."[39] For a moment he envies the blissful unmarried savagery, until his thoughts are suddenly interrupted by a black jaguar killing one of the men: "O Lord Jesus [. . .] And this is the selfish rest for which I would have bartered the rest which comes by working where Thou has put me!"[40] Similarly, Amyas meets his Eve (Ayacanora) on a paradisiacal river island, ten yards from where "the cataract fell sheer in thunder."[41] The quest for primordial inspiration to renew English civilization that emerged in Lancelot's desire to follow the prophet to Prester John's country, in Alton Locke's dream-return to the cradle of mankind, and in *Hypatia*'s infusion of new Gothic blood, can be read in *Westward Ho!* in the confrontation with Ayacanora's primitive culture. The Indian girl represents the fresh blood that will invigorate British civilisation, but she will have to be transferred to England to be able to exercise her inner wealth. Submitting to it in its original primitive culture,

---

[38] *WH* 219.
[39] *WH* 425.
[40] *WH* 425.
[41] *WH* 407.

however tempting, will only lead to degradation and extinction for the English.

Still, much of this view is undone when Kingsley's finally abandons this ideal union and makes Ayacanora of English-Spanish descent. This might indicate the author's doubt about the real possibility of such a renewal through primitive cultures, or that he is ultimately unable to make up his mind about whether the primitive otherness represents degradation or unspoilt innocence. His indecision as to Indian nature might have dictated Kingsley's subsequent use of Ayacanora in the novel. But her newly discovered identity is not less problematic—it is her Spanishness that now forms an insurmountable moral barrier to Amyas. Ayacanora now becomes linked to the part of the plot in which Amyas's hatred for Don Guzman stands central. But before exploring this new development, we must first have a look at how Kingsley represents his Spanish nobleman and how he emerges from his encounters with Amyas, Frank, and Eustace Leigh.

In the serial *Yeast*, Kingsley gives his main character Lancelot an alter ego in his Tractarian cousin Luke, who represents Lancelot's, and Kingsley's own, early fascination with Roman Catholicism. Although at one point the two cousins seem to share similar destinies, Luke has to leave the novel when Lancelot is about to discuss with the prophet "the true idea of Protestantism."[42] Luke is the part of Lancelot's personality which has to be shed, as the former's ideals "will repeat themselves and caricature themselves more weakly and more narrowly every succeeding exhibition, and dwindle down into hopeless mannerism, admired not for what they are, but what they were, like the rest; till one day both tapers will lie snuffed out, and the world will never guess what a brace of undeveloped possibilities it has lost."[43] This device of representing different parts of the main character's psyche by creating contrasting characters who are cousins appealed to Kingsley. In *Alton Locke* we are thus confronted with a much more complex relationship between Alton and his cousin George, who represents the more opportunistic and lascivious element that is absent in Alton. Their antagonistic roles are built up with painful insight, and if Alton might at times appear

---

[42] *Y*^{F} 699.
[43] *Y*^{F} 711.

sterile to the reader, George fully makes up for that part of his personality. It is interesting that in the end neither Alton nor George will be allowed by Kingsley to survive. In rewriting *Yeast* for book publication, Kingsley mainly returned to the relationship between Lancelot and Luke, which is given more religious depth and results in a more aggressive condemnation of Luke's position. But as this remains essentially an addition to an already written novel, the contrast is contrived and has merely pamphlet quality. In *Westward Ho!*, however, the device is again carefully set up, and Amyas is given not only a cousin Eustace, but also a brother Frank, who is again a cousin of Eustace. And the unravelling of the novel's plot hinges upon the tensions between the three.

Frank is a fashionable scholar, poet and well-travelled humanist at the court of Queen Elizabeth, "of so rare and delicate a beauty, that it seemed that some Greek statue, or rather one of those pensive and pious knights whom the German artists too delight to paint, had condescended to tread awhile this work-day earth in living flesh and blood." Frank has everything in terms of intellect, culture and spirituality, but the red spots on his cheeks are early indications of "sad possibilities, perhaps not far off."[44] Eustace, on the other hand, is educated by the Jesuits, a "hapless scapegoat [. . .] made a liar of at Rheims," a man "trying to be good with all his might and main, according to certain approved methods and rules, which he has got by heart; and like a weak oarsman, feeling and fingering his spiritual muscles over all day, to see if they are growing."[45] Amyas is contrasted with these two as a man "not even knowing whether he is good or not, but just doing the right thing without thinking about it, as simply as a little child, because the spirit of God is with him."[46] What brings them together in the novel is that they all fall in love with Rose Salterne, the beautiful daughter of a Bideford trader. However, the Rose of Torridge, as she is known to the Devon worthies, elopes with the Spanish nobleman Don Guzman de Soto. When Amyas and Frank, sworn in a brotherhood with others, follow the two lovers to La Guayra to avenge the deed, and are betrayed by Eustace, their intertwining destinies become the prime cause of final calamity. Frank and Rose end up martyred by the Spanish Inquisition. Guzman

[44] *WH* 38.
[45] *WH* 51, 53.
[46] *WH* 53.

and his ship founders on Lundy island after the defeat of the Armada. And Amyas, who had long since lost his humanity and righteousness in his all-consuming desire for revenge, provokes divine punishment and is struck blind by lightning.

In the three Leighs different approaches to love are explored, forming the backdrop of Kingsley's master-theme: the sanctity of matrimonial love. Although Eustace "wasted miserable hours in maddening thoughts, and tost all night upon his sleepless bed, and rose next morning fierce and pale,"[47] his passion is no more than perversion that stems from the teachings of the Roman Catholic Church, which Kingsley accuses of sanctioning lust in the name of love. Eustace serves to bring out all that Kingsley saw with disgust in a church which taught that celibacy was its highest religious ideal:

> [Eustace] looked on her as a lamb fallen unawares into the jaws of the greedy wolf, which he felt himself to be. For Eustace's love had little or nothing of chivalry, self-sacrifice, or purity in it; those were virtues which were not taught at Rheims. Careful as the Jesuits were over the practical morality of their pupils, this severe restraint had little effect in producing real habits of self-control. What little Eustace had learnt of women from them, was as base and vulgar as the rest of their teaching. What could it be else, if instilled by men educated in [. . .] the age in which the Romish Church had made marriage a legalized tyranny, and the laity, by a natural and pardonable revulsion, had exalted adultery into a virtue and a science? That all love was lust; that all women had their price; that profligacy, though an ecclesiastical sin, was so pardonable, if not necessary, as to be hardly a moral sin, were notions which Eustace must needs have gathered from the hints of his preceptors; for their written works bear to this day fullest and foulest testimony that such was their opinion; and that their conception of the relation of the sexes was really not a whit higher than that of the profligate laity who confessed to them. He longed to marry Rose Salterne, with a wild selfish fury; but only that he might be able to claim her as his own property, and keep all others from her. Of her as a co-equal and ennobling helpmate; as one in whose honour, glory, growth of heart and soul, his own were inextricably wrapt up, he had never dreamed.[48]

When Eustace realizes that Rose will never be his, the suppression of his sexual energy ensues in an unmanning deceit. His distorted

---

[47] *WH* 63.
[48] *WH* 63–4.

love drives Rose into the arms of the Inquisition, where she is accused of having used witchcraft to ensnare Don Guzman. Under torture she defends herself: "Witchcraft against Don Guzman? What need of that, oh, God! what need."[49] These are significant words, after which Eustace can only sneak away ashamed and hide himself in a Jesuit order. The final dismissing of Eustace stresses a significant point in Kingsley's views of love and religion, notwithstanding the fact that it is rather inelegantly done. "Eustace Leigh vanishes hence-forth from these pages," he suddenly writes, justifying this (in)artis-tic choice with: "This book is a history of men,—of men's virtues and sins, victories and defeats; and Eustace is a man no longer."[50]

But if Eustace's love is condemned on moral grounds, Frank's sophisticated notions of spiritual love do not fare much better. Frank's love for Rose is lofty enough and is not condemned as Eustace's is, but it still has no chance of surviving without the more physical counterpart natural to Amyas's constitution. Rose, for example, laments that Frank "had never given her a sign of real love, nothing but sonnets and compliments."[51] Being in love, more than anything, perhaps, with love itself, Frank's understanding of love is far too idealistic and will never lead to the creation of the true English home that Kingsley sees as the cornerstone of a free society.

As Amyas seems to possess instinctively all the right qualities of the true Englishman, we might expect him to be the suitable hus-band for Rose. But Kingsley makes it clear that Rose never had any real interest in Amyas apart from sentiments which were no more than "girl's fancies."[52] Amyas's infatuation with her, notwithstanding his honourable intentions, has a slight resemblance to Eustace's "selfish fury." He never seems to realize that Don Guzman and Rose might actually have chosen each other as co-equal lovers. It is this cardi-nal mistake that makes Amyas desert the Queen's cause and which, after his brother's death, increasingly blinds him with private justifications, risking more than once crew and ship for his willful desire for revenge. This misguided behaviour also allows Ayacanora's Spanish blood to stand in the way of his feelings for her. But, as suggested above, the relationship with Ayacanora is troubled from

---

[49] *WH* 394.
[50] *WH* 395–6.
[51] *WH* 76.
[52] *WH* 77.

the very beginning, and this might be seen as responsible for the shape and tone the telling of Kingsley's story ultimately takes.

IV

The graphic descriptions of physical violence in *Westward Ho!* have troubled many readers, past and present. A critic in *Blackwood's* objected to the novel that "deep, abiding, and inveterate hatred of the Spaniards and the Pope, and lust for blood and plunder, are expressed in almost every page."[53] Kingsley's attitude to violence in the novel is ambivalent. At times it is described in high-spirited language that seems to indicate approval, while at other times the gruesome action is intended to shock the reader into condemnation. Alexander Macmillan feared that some of the scenes of violence would damage sales of the book, and when preparing for the second imprint in May, sounded Kingsley out as to whether two questionable passages could be omitted. He thought Amyas's boisterous knocking his teacher unconscious distasteful, especially as Kingsley expressed his own approval by making Richard Grenville laugh heartily at this. "Excuse me," Macmillan objected, "but it does not look like the act of a brave boy to hurt a poor old man even though he was a dominie." He also disapproved of the passage in which Salterne beat his daughter. "They are the fly in the ointment to me. I daresay I am squeamish," he apologized to Kingsley.[54]

It is odd that Macmillan should have felt squeamish about these passages, and apparently thought the later scenes of torture part of the ointment. The scene of an old Indian falling down with exhaustion in a Spanish slave-train becomes to Kingsley an emblem of Spanish inhumanity—"The blade gleamed in the air, once, twice, and fell: not on the chain, but on the wrist which it fettered. There was a shriek—a crimson flash—and the chain and its prisoner were parted indeed." Of course, such violence is not laughed at as Amyas's boyish feats with his teacher were, and "one moment more, and Amyas's arrow would have been through the throat of the murderer." There is no question about Kingsley's moral stand. But what has disturbed readers here is that in the description of the atrocity there is an

---

[53] [Aytoun] (1855) 639.
[54] Macmillan to CK, 21/4/1855, Sutherland 127.

uncanny combination of masculinity and violence. The moment immediately before the repellant event, Kingsley writes of the Spanish officer:

> The man was a tall, handsome, broad-shouldered, high-bred man; and Amyas thought that he was going to display the strength of his arm, and the temper of his blade, in severing the chain at one stroke.[55]

The whole passage is not gratuitous violence and it is meant to mirror an earlier scene in the novel when Amyas goes to Ireland with Raleigh "in brilliant inlaid cuirass and helmet, gaudy sash and plume, and sword hilt glittering with gold" while beside him, "secured by a cord which a pikeman has fastened to his own wrist, trots a bare-legged Irish kerne, whose only clothing is his ragged yellow mantle."[56] Both Raleigh and the Spanish officer represent European civilization, and Raleigh's fear of what lust of power might do to it is unfolded in the Spanish officer's cruelty later in the novel.

Notwithstanding the thematic relevance of his representation of violence in this and other scenes, there is no denying that there is a physical quality in Kingsley's writing that is startling to the reader. This is, as we have seen, by no means a unique quality of *Westward Ho!*. Kingsley had displayed in his prose and poetry a constant pre-occupation with the (naked) body, but it began to assume an unsettling association with physical violence in both *Hypatia* and in *Westward Ho!*. It is as if Kingsley, unconsciously, finds in it an outlet for repressed sexual energy in the novel's main characters. Although, the relationship Amyas-Ayacanora in *Westward Ho!* is meant by Kingsley to prefigure the ideal union between man and woman, it remains strikingly sterile in its physical reality. A repression of sexual attraction becomes tangible from the very first in the static icons of femininity and masculinity that represent Ayacanora and Amyas upon their first meeting:

> And full of simple wonder, he gazed upon that fairy vision, while she, unabashed in her free innocence, gazed fearlessly in return, as Eve might have done in Paradise, upon the mighty stature, and the strange garments, and above all, on the bushy beard and flowing yellow locks of the Englishman.[57]

---

[55] *WH* 437.
[56] *WH* 217.
[57] *WH* 408.

Ayacanora and her paradisiacal world offer unlimited sexual gratification which Amyas, and Kingsley, feel constrained to suppress, as it is not sanctioned by Christianity. Consummation of their love has to wait for England. John Maynard has suggested that the alternative of violence in the novel might actually be motivated by an unconscious sense of punishment for such repression.[58]

The self-destructive attitude in Amyas's relations to Guzman and Ayacanora makes the final crisis become tangible long before it happens. Kingsley is here at his best, moving to a climax with such artistry as Coleridge used in "The Rhyme of the Ancient Mariner": "Amyas had got the hone out of his pocket, and was whetting away again at his sword-edge, as if there was some dreadful doom on him, to whet, and whet forever."[59] And as the mist rises, clouds gather, and a thunderstorm approaches, the object of revenge, Don Guzman's galleon, which they had desperately chased for weeks, is seen just before it is smashed to pieces on the shallows at the south end of Lundy.

> "Shame!" cried Amyas, hurling his sword far into the sea, "to lose my right, my right! when it was in my very grasp! Unmerciful!"
> A crack which rent the sky, and made the granite ring and quiver; a bright world of flame, and then a blank of utter darkness, against which stood out, glowing red-hot every mast, and sail, and rock, and Salvation Yeo as he stood just in front of Amyas, the tiller in his hand. All red-hot, transfigured into fire; and behind, the black, black night.[60]

And, on an epic scale, this moment of hubris is completed when a stone-blind Amyas comes to himself the following days. The dramatic climax of the book overwhelmed an otherwise unimpressed Edward Fitzgerald, who confessed that, although he could never read *Westward Ho!* all through, he thought the end of it "a really *sublime* thing. "Kingsley is a distressing writer to me," he adds, "but I must think this (the inspiration of it) of a piece with Homer and the Gods."[61]

The moment of Amyas's repentance removes all obstacles with regard to Ayacanora, who, as his wife, will now fulfil the initial promise of cultural rebirth for English civilization, which Kingsley, as in *Alton Locke*, once more saw embodied, not in England itself,

---

[58] Maynard 132.
[59] *WH* 575.
[60] *WH* 578–9.
[61] Cruse, *The Victorians and Their Books*, 275; quoted in Sutherland 132.

but in a *new* England, or, literally, New England. The final words of the novel are:

> From that hour Ayacanora's power of song returned to her; and day by day, year after year, her voice rose up within that happy home, and soared, as on a skylark's wings, into the highest heaven, bearing with it the peaceful thoughts of the blind giant back to the Paradises of the West, in the wake of the heroes who from that time forth sailed out to colonize another and a vaster England, to the heaven-prospered cry of Westward-Ho![62]

V

In a letter to Ludlow Kingsley revealed that the hero of *Westward Ho!*, Amyas, was modelled on his college friend Frank Penrose. "He is cold & unimaginative: but his eye is single, & his heart is mighty in warmth," he explained, and added: "I believe him incapable of meanness or vanity."[63] This admission was prompted by an accident that befell Kingsley's other Cambridge friend, Mansfield, on 16 February 1855, and which cost him his life. Experimenting in his laboratory with the boiling of coal tar, Mansfield had discovered how to distill benzene (C_6H_8) from naphtha below the temperature of 100°C. Although benzene had been discovered in 1825 by Faraday, production of it remained difficult. Mansfield's suggestion of how to extract it from coal tar was a breakthrough in the field and his boiling process is still generally followed in the production of aniline. Originally it was used in combustive oil lamps, for dissolving rubber, and in the dye industry. Nowadays it is also used to make drugs, explosives, plastics, and photographic chemicals.

Mansfield had patented his discovery, but while refining the distilling process, a still boiled over and caught fire. He acted immediately, but with disastrous results. Carrying the vessel out to save the premises, he caught fire himself. Fearfully burnt, he was taken to the Middlesex Hospital where he struggled for his life. When Kingsley heard what had happened he wanted to rush to London to help nurse Mansfield, but Ludlow and Penrose assured him that

---

[62] *WH* 591.
[63] CK to JL, 27/2/1855, Martin (1950) 577.

there was nothing he could do and had better stay in Devon. The
news of Mansfield's death nine days later was a tremendous blow
to Kingsley. To Ludlow he wrote:

> oh John Ludlow, if he was so much to you, what was he to me? He
> was my first love. The first human being, save my mother, I ever met
> who knew what I meant. To him & to Frank Penrose what do I not
> owe. They two were the only heroic souls I met during those dark
> Cambridge years. They two alone kept me from sinking in the mire,
> & drowning like a dog. And now one is gone.[64]

Mansfield was buried in Weybridge cemetery, Maurice read the service. Kingsley wanted to come down for the funeral, but then decided
not to: "I am better where I am, for many reasons," he explained,
"Mrs. Kingsley has felt it much, too much. She loved him as well
as any of us, perhaps better."[65] But with the death of Mansfield,
Kingsley became a much lonelier man. He lost the only friend with
whom he had been truly intimate. Kingsley implored Ludlow to tell
Penrose "that now Mansfield is gone, he must be my friend, & I
his, in a way that we never yet have been." Perhaps it is the sense-
lessness of this proposal which sums up the despair Kingsley felt at
losing Mansfield.

VI

Westward Ho! was published in the last week of March 1855. Perhaps
because of the stalling of the war in the Crimea, the Macmillans
were cautious about venturing into novel-publishing, and while they
asked the printer a series of estimates for print-runs ranging from
1,000 to 2,000 copies, they settled on 1,250 only, a comparatively
small number for a new novel in the 1850s. The Macmillans, however
did not risk anything with *Westward Ho!*. The book proved popular
from the very outset. Three hundred-and-fifty copies went in one
go to Mudie's circulating library, who got a ten per cent discount
on the batch, and Alexander Macmillan offered discounts to book-
sellers who were willing to buy numbers of advance copies.

---

[64] CK to JL, 27/2/1855, Martin (1950) 577.
[65] CK to JL, 27/2/1855, Martin (1950) 578.

Notwithstanding its apparent popularity, reviewers did not like the book as much as its ordinary readers. The first review that came out was in *The Athenaeum* of 31 March. It admitted that the book had been set up with care, and that it contained many fine things, "scenes which will make the pulse beat, and passages that will make the reader feel choked and miserable, and force tears from him in spite of himself," but that on the whole "the spirit in which the book is written is neither good nor pleasant." The reviewer thought "the story straggling, tumultuous and incoherent" and the book's capital error is that "Mr. Kingsley never, for a single page, forgets himself, nor keeps himself out of sight: he is all along in a pulpit preaching at his readers." But this being Kingsley's intention, he admits, "must as such be accepted." On the other hand, what the reviewer can- not excuse is "that the whole spirit and tendency of this book is, to excite that bitter and most relentless of hatreds,—theological sensi- bility, which, when once wounded, can never heal—once offended, can never forget."[66] This largely negative review, however, did not damage the book's sales. Within two weeks a jubilant Alexander Macmillan wrote to Mrs Kingsley that they had already sold over nine hundred copies, and that they were thinking of a reprint for the next month. The temporary unavailability of the book caused silence on the review-front, and it was not until the novel's second impression in May that other magazines and newspapers followed *The Athenaeum*.

The reviewer in *Fraser's Magazine* thought *Westward Ho!* "almost the best historical novel [. . .] of the day." Comparisons with Sir Walter Scott came naturally. The accuracy of "costume" in *Westward Ho!* reminded *Fraser's* reviewer of *Kenilworth*,[67] *The Times* referred to Scott but mentioned shortcomings, and the critic writing for *The British Quarterly Review* not only asserted that "*Westward Ho!* is a learned book, a trustful book, a book which only a man of real genius could have written"[68] but that its didactic element made him far superior to Scott: "It is the grand defect of Sir Walter that he did everything simply as an artist."[69] Few critics were prepared to go along with the *British Quarterly* in the comparison with Scott. William Edmondstoune

---

[66] [-], "New Novels" *Athenaeum* 31/3/1855, 376.
[67] [Whyte-Melville] 517.
[68] [-], "Our Epiligue on Books," *British Quarterly Review* 22 (1855) 260.
[69] *Ibid.*

Aytoun in a long article in *Blackwood's Edinburgh Magazine* in which he
assessed Kingsley's literary career to date, also described Kingsley as
a "fascinating writer" and "a most beautiful depicter of scenery,"
but compares him unfavourably to Scott: "In the hands of Scott,
the preparation for receiving the Armada would have resolved itself
into a most noble and animated picture; in the hands of Mr Kingsley,
it is a stupid Dutch daubing, suggestive of sack, tobacco, and bowls."[70]
Arguably, however, it is in scenes like this that Kingsley was a fair
match for Scott.

Kingsley's descriptive powers received praise from most of the
reviewers. *The Times* asserted that Mr Kingsley was "no mean artist"
in "scenes which Humboldt has hardly described with more of local
atmosphere." In his twelve-page article, *Fraser's* reviewer deliriously
praised the novel's romantic beauty, which was to him the work of
a painter, "a pen-and-ink picture flooded with golden light, soft and
sunny as a Claude or a Gainsborough."[71] The depiction of Salvation
Yeo "affords much such a study of character as does some fine old
Rembrandt."[72] He did not like Kingsley's representation of the Jesuits,
but concedes that Kingsley is a "good hater."[73] But *Fraser's* reviewer
does not shine in his critical ability. He lauds in Rose Salterne
Kingsley's "deep insight into the recesses of the female heart," while
he admits that "Ayacanora we do not so entirely like." For this he
expresses the following piece of Victorian priggishness: "there is
difficulty in reconciling the character of a half-reclaimed savage with
that softness of disposition and refinement of feeling which are indispensable to constitute a *loveable* woman; and if a woman is not loveable, we will have none of her."[74]

In *The Westminster Review*, however, Kingsley got a reviewer of great
critical ability and insight, and a woman at that. Kingsley's "scene-
painting" was noted by her too: "One sees that he knows and loves
his Devonshire at first hand," she writes, "and he has evidently lingered over the description of the forests and savannahs and rivers
of the New World, until they have become as vividly present to him
as if they were part of his own experience."[75] In this he clearly is a

---

[70] [Aytoun] (1855) 642.
[71] [Whyte-Melville] 508.
[72] [Whyte-Melville] 515.
[73] [Whyte-Melville] 515.
[74] [Whyte-Melville] 515.
[75] [Eliot] 290.

"poet and artist in a rare degree."[76] Comparing it to recent novels
in general, the reviewer, who was no other than George Eliot, maintains that "It seemed too long since we had any of that genuine
description of external nature, not done after the poet's or novelist's
recipe, but flowing from spontaneous observation and enjoyment."[77]
This is generally a point where the reviewers' praise of Kingsley's
novel stops. He "sees, feels, and paints vividly," George Eliot continues, "but he theorizes illogically and moralizes absurdly." She
would rather have lingered over Kingsley's beauties than point out
his faults, "but unhappily, Mr. Kingsley's faults are likely to do harm
in other ways than in subtracting from the lustre of his fame."[78] His
moralizing view of history seems essentially that of our childish days,
Eliot explains, where the champions of the Reformation are heroes
and the adherents of popery viciously base. "Mr. Kingsley would
have carried with him all minds in which there is a spark of nobleness, if he could have freed himself from the spirit of the partisan,
and been content to admit that in the Elizabethan age, as in every
other, human beings, human parties, and human deeds are made
up of the most subtly intermixed good and evil."[79] Eliot is equally
severe on his logic, pointing to the passage where Kingsley accuses
Alexander von Humboldt of overrating scientific knowledge, and
supressing his instinctive feelings, when judging the barbarous state
of savages. It is "cool arrogance" in Kingsley to assert that "the
patriarch of scientific investigators, is 'misled by the dogmas of a so-
called science."[80]

George Eliot's perplexity about Kingsley was shared by all the
reviewers, except the one writing for *The Times* who rather admired
Eustace and Kingsley's "talent and truth of the analysis out of which
it has grown," and concluded that "Mr. Kingsley has this time
selected a good subject, and has written a good novel to an excellent purpose." But in this he stood virtually alone. To all Kingsley
was a man of genius but with ideas that were disagreeable. The
reviewers were unanimously impressed by Kingsley's extraordinary
descriptive talent, but his 'muscularity' baffled and irritated them.

---

[76] [Eliot] 289.
[77] [Eliot] 288.
[78] [Eliot] 291.
[79] [Eliot] 292.
[80] [Eliot] 294.

The Guardian, openly hostile to Kingsley's moral views ever since it
reviewed *Yeast* in 1851, perceived also in *Westward Ho!* the writer's
"dangerous tendency" to "recommend a hearty, fearless following of
generous impulses, with a dash of buoyant recklessness which dis-
dains Christian watchfulness as a restraint on its liberty and a hin-
drance to its vigour."[81] Aytoun in *Blackwood's* was more outspoken
still. With Kingsley, he warns, we are not only "in the company of
an accomplished master"[82] but also in that of "a man of extreme
and unsafe opinion."[83] He accuses Kingsley of falsifying the history
of the Elizabethan heroes, as "no considerations of Protestantism or
humanity dictated those marauding expeditions [. . .] booty was the
main object."[84] Aytoun does indeed put his finger on one of the
weak spots of *Westward Ho!* as a historical novel, as we have already
seen concerning the problem of Hawkins's involvement in the slave
trade. However, Aytoun weakens his point of criticism considerably
when he ultimately reads history himself in terms of Scott's noble
and animated pictures. George Eliot shared this impression: "the last
word we have to say of 'Westward Ho!' is to thank Mr. Kingsley
for the great and beautiful things we have found in it, as our dominant feeling towards his works in general is that of high admiration."[85]

But literary praise was one thing. Quite another was the indelible and dubious distinction Kingsley had earned as Apostle of the
Flesh. His aggressive views of religion, which were to become known
as "Muscular Christianity," had made Kingsley notorious rather than
celebrated. One critic wrote in 1855, after the publication of *Westward
Ho!*, that "Mr Kingsley, with all his liberality, has a strong propensity to persecution. We would rather keep out of his reach were he
armed with ecclesiastical powers."[86]

---

[81] *Guardian*, 23/5/1855, 404.
[82] [Aytoun] (1855) 626.
[83] [Aytoun] (1855) 627.
[84] [Aytoun] (1855) 639.
[85] [Eliot] 294.
[86] [Aytoun] (1855) 643.

SANITARY REFORM

ALONE AMONG MANKIND, ON A CLIFF WHICH IS CRUSHING BENEATH ONE (JULY 1855–DECEMBER 1856)

At the age of thirty-six, notwithstanding the fame his novels had earned him, Kingsley was far from the man whom the critics had branded the champion of confident Protestant manliness. He felt insecure and depressed. Although he had celebrated the excellence of the righteous English character in *Westward Ho!*, his nationalistic pride was hurt by the way the events of the Crimean war unfolded. The future of England looked unpromising to him. "Master, terrible & sad thoughts haunt me," he wrote to Maurice, and added, "I cannot escape that wretched fear of a national catastrophe, w. haunts me night & day. I live in dark nameless dissatisfaction & dread, w. has certainly not diminished during the last few months."[1] Fanny's weak constitution added to his unease of mind. The Kingsleys had returned to Eversley for the summer, but it was clear that the rectory was unfit for her during the damp winter months. Although Kingsley wrote in April that Fanny's indisposition was "nothing alarming,"[2] in August she was still reported ailing[3] and in autumn he wrote that "Mrs. Kingsley has been very ill indeed."[4] It was necessary to look for alternative accommodation for the winter months. Something was needed which would both allow Kingsley to do his parish work in Eversley and at the same time would not be too great a drain on his insufficient income. He consulted Stapleton about Farley Court, which was reported vacant for the winter. As it was a spacious house in a high and dry spot in the nearby village of Farley Hill, it was ideal for Kingsley's needs. But when Kingsley inquired about the rent he discovered that they asked the absurdly high sum of eight guineas a week. After negotiations, however, he managed to get it for less, and although it is no longer possible to discover on how

---

[1] CK to FDM, 6/8/1855, BL-41297 f.80v, 79r.
[2] CK to FDM, undated, BL-41297 f.72v.
[3] CK to AS, [16/8/1855], MP-C0171–36919.
[4] CK to Macmillan, undated, 54911 f.76r.

much they settled, he reported to Stapleton on 19 October that they had "taken Farley Hill for the winter—cheap, I think—& are moving up thither piecemeal."[5] The prospect cheered Fanny, so much that Kingsley shortly afterwards wrote that "it is quite surprising how quickly she has rallied."[6]

The parish in August 1855 was very quiet, and although Cope's sulky behaviour to Mrs Kingsley had somehow led to the circulation of a false rumour that he had struck her in public, Kingsley found him "quite rational & civil, & all goes merrily enough."[7] Cope's mental coherence, however, soon deteriorated again. In September his condition was "frightful" and in October he went "off on a 'tour'." Exasperated with his patron, Kingsley wished "his eccentricities wd. either cease, or take a more decided form."[8]

Added to these national and family worries were profound doubts about his role as a writer and a minister of the church. With the completion of *Westward Ho!* he felt he had come to a turning point in his life, a moment of crisis. "The period of collapse has come to me," he wrote to Maurice at the beginning of August, "I look back upon earlier years with longing, as a sort of Eden—I mean the years from 1844–1848 & sigh." He realized that through aging he had outlived his immature ideals and rash reactions of those years, but he still saw this essentially as a loss:

> I suppose if I lived them over again with my present experience I should be ashamed of them: of my vanity & haste, my reckless laying down the law & fault finding, my conceited dream that I knew everybody's business better than they themselves did—And yet—I have not lost that vanity, often it seems ready to take baser & more childish forms than ever—of w. I am ashamed to speak even to you, & meanwhile I have lost the good side of my other faults, my hatred of evil, my longing to make everything I came to fulfil itself in its vocation.[9]

This confession shows mature humility, as well as a profound sense of uncertainty about his future public role:

> And then I cry—It is the devils voice slandering my countrymen to me, slandering priests, statesmen, rich & poor, & I am a devil myself,

---

[5] CK to AS, 19/10/1855, MP-C0171–36919.
[6] CK to AS, undated, MP-C0171–36919.
[7] CK to AS, [16/8/1853], MP-C0171–36919.
[8] CK to AS, 19/10/1855, MP-C0171–36919.
[9] CK to FDM, 6/8/1855, BL-41297 f.73v–74r.

who am sinning against the Holy Ghost, & calling good mens' works evil. And yet the [. . .] nation is going right, the Bishops are right in not denouncing the governors who allowed Crimean tragedies; evey one is right in leaving well alone—even in leaving ill alone, where it is so inextricably mixed up with good that you cannot root up the tares without rooting up the wheat also.[10]

But he felt utterly unable to decide whether the voice that prompted such reflections was "God's voice, or the devil's."

Kingsley told Maurice not to fear that "ultimately I shall be content with being 'an artist.' I despise & loathe the notion from the bottom of my heart," and he promised to "leave fame to take care of itself." Still, he did not see his way clearly: "I am losing a zest for work—Everything seems to me not worth working at—except the simple business of telling poor people [about God's love]." But even in his ministerial office he felt insecure at times: "I darent say what I think—I darent preach my own creed, w. seems to me as different from what I hear preached & find believed, everywhere, [. . .] as St Paul—horrible thought!—seems to me at moments from the plain simple words of our Lord." The denial of Christ as the "ideal & perfect man" made him tremble and he dreaded without that to "lose all." The thought tormented him and he felt that "when my trust in the Bible as a whole seems falling to pieces it is [. . .] terrible work for a poor soul to know where the destructive process must stop: & one feels alone in the universe, at least alone among mankind, on a cliff w. is crumbling beneath one, & falling piecemeal into the dark sea."[11] Such religious doubt Kingsley had not felt for years.

Kingsley had started to review his role in social reform as well and retreated from active prominence in the cause. As a result Maurice thought it necessary to exhort Kingsley to use his imaginative powers to God's "higher trust of being manly and of caring for your fellow-men and their miseries and sins,"[12] and Ludlow reproached him for deserting the people's cause in his courting of public esteem. Kingsley replied by urging his own mistaken arrogant and self-conceited past behaviour with which he had offended people, not caring what they might say, simply because he felt convinced that "the word of God had only come to me."[13] Especially as a father, he continued, he would

---

[10] CK to FDM, 6/8/1855, BL-41297 f.79.
[11] CK to FDM, 6/8/1855, BL-41297 f.74r–77r.
[12] FDM to CK, 4/8/1855, Maurice ii.261.
[13] CK to JL, 30/12/1855, *LML* i.459.

not set an example to his children that would turn them in "insolent and scoffing radicals, believing in nobody and nothing but themselves" by making the watchword of his house "Never mind what
people say."[14]

But Ludlow was right in more than one way in his surmise that
Kingsley was no longer willing to stake his reputation in a revolutionary cause. Kingsley could no longer afford to scorn the support
of those who had influence in public life. The problem that kept
irking Kingsley during the first half of 1856 was the unhealthy site
of his Rectory. With Fanny's delicate health, the prospect of having
to return with his family to Eversley after a comfortable and dry
winter at Farley Court was a gloomy one. Notwithstanding numerous costly repairs, the damp of the place remained, and as Sir William
Cope had made it quite clear that rebuilding the rectory on Kingsley's
terms was out of the question, he realized that preferment elsewhere
was the only solution left. But he was reluctant to leave Eversley,
and would rather look for an additional appointment to an ecclesiastical post, such as a canonry at a cathedral, for the winter months.
Hughes, who had friends in the right places, was repeatedly pressed
by Kingsley to use his influence. After failing to secure one of the
vacant canonries at Hereford and at St Paul's, Kingsley set his mind
on Westminster Abbey, which he thought "the sort of place for a
literary man especially one who is interested in social & sanitary
questions." He had singled out Westminster where "2 canonries may
be or must be vacant any day," as Canon Monk's fragile health at
the age of 72 indicated imminent death, while another canon was
likely to succeed the Oxford Professor of Geology William Buckland
as dean. Buckland, after years of insanity, was now about to die.

Kingsley thought he had some influence with Lord Palmerston
through his wife's family—with which relations had improved over
the years—and through his support of the Crimean War by writing
Westward Ho!. He had Riversdale Grenfell write to Palmerston. But
"what is wanted," he wrote to Hughes, "is someone beside Ld.
Palmerston aware of what few claims I may have personally, & what
effect on the working men's mind, & their feeling toward the Church
& the status in quo, the government's patronizing me would have."
Kingsley marked this letter "Private even from *Ludlow*."[15] Hughes

---

[14] CK to JL, 30/12/1855, *LML* i.460.
[15] CK to TH, 28/2/1856, Martin (1950) 645.

was asked to exert his influence on William Cowper, MP for Hertford, heir to Palmerston, and future Baron Mount-Temple. Hughes, who was obliging, suggested asking Lord Goderich (who had joined the Christian Socialists at an early stage and had become an active component in 1852) to use his influence. He also approached Cowper. Kingsley himself decided to approach Monckton-Milnes on the subject. He hoped he was not impertinent to think that, as "the Government are under obligations to you," he could help him to get the canonry. To justify his candidacy, he added, "I do not think it so very pre-posterous a hope on my part, that I may get one of those places which were originally meant for literary parsons."[16] Monckton-Milnes was not provoked and would gladly have helped Kingsley, had he not already been pressing Palmerston for a bishopric for Richard Trench. He could hardly "ask for 2 things," he said.[17]

Cowper, who was willing to support Kingsley for the canonry, told him that he expected a canon to be actively present in the run-ning of a cathedral. Hughes, or Cowper through Hughes, also advanced the possibility of taking a London living and giving up damp Eversley. Kingsley hastened to specify that although he shared Cowper's idea of a canon's duty—"to be a popular preacher [. . .] & talk to the working men & cockneys in plain English, & to try gradually, & *cautiously* [. . .] to make a cathedral a centre of civi-lization, *physical* as well as moral"—but that "as for being a London Rector, I should be in my grave, or in a madhouse, in 12 months."[18] Kingsley's idea was to keep his living, to reside the necessary term of three months in winter in London, and then return for the rest of the year to Eversley. The prospect of being a London rector like his father was stifling, and the three months in a cathedral had no attractions to him either. Cathedrals had always oppressed Kingsley. "I have often fancied," he wrote to Maurice later that year, "I should like to see the great useless naves & aisles of our cathedrals turned into museums & winter gardens, where people might take their Sunday walks, & yet attend service."[19] A canonry was a necessity for Fanny's health rather than a sincere wish for preferment. But Kingsley need not have worried about a future in London. When James Henry

---

16 CK to R. Monckton Milnes, 11/6/1856, Pope-Hennessy 147.
17 CK to FK, 12/6/1856, BL-62554 f.90v.
18 CK to TH, March 1856, Martin (1950) 650.
19 CK to FDM, July 1856, BL-41297 f.88v.

Monk died on 6 June, it was decided not to fill the vacancy, while Buckland, who died two months later on 14 August, was not succeeded by a Westminster canon, but, ironically, by Richard Trench.

Although much of Kingsley's aspirations and lobbying were held secret from Maurice and, especially, from Ludlow, both had noticed a change in attitude and told him so. Kingsley answered both Maurice's and Ludlow's reservations in long and detailed letters. But while he gracefully took Maurice's "lecture" to heart, he felt annoyed by the tone of Ludlow's letter. To Hughes he wrote:

> You may, meanwhile, tell Ludlow to mind his own business. If you or I don't do it gently, some one will some day *un* gently. But I have had a correspondence with him lately, w. will be the last *earnest* one between us for some time, so censorious, & so infallible in his own eyes does he seem to have become. I do not like pistol shots & Bowie thrusts on Sunday mornings as I am going to church, to make me miserable all Christmas day, under the plea that they are "works of piety, charity, & necessity."[20]

This shows the growing rift between two men who had become such close friends in the socialist cause following the chartist Petition in April 1848.

What both Maurice and Ludlow realized was that the end of Christian Socialism as a movement coincided with the peak of Kingsley's literary fame. It is interesting that both recognized the turning point in Kingsley's social activities the very moment it happened. Hughes, looking back at this moment after twenty years, could not but confirm that this was indeed the moment when "he laid aside his fighting name and his fighting pen, and had leisure to look calmly on the great struggle more as a spectator than an actor."[21]

When, in the spring of 1856, Hughes lamented the failure of the Christian Socialist movement in which they had all lost much money, energy and public esteem, he was more generous than either Maurice or Ludlow when he wrote that Kingsley too had dutifully done his part and borne the brunt of the critics during its active years—as, of course, he had. He had often damaged his reputation in the movement's cause, Hughes maintained. However, half ashamed of his

---

[20] CK to TH, undated, BL-41298 f.82.
[21] Hughes (1876) lviii.

literary success and of his change as a public figure, Kingsley answered Hughes:

> you are green in cottoning to me about the '48 mess'. Because why? I wasn't hit, who ever was. I lost nothing—I risked nothing. You fellows worked like bricks, spent money, did the dirty work, & got midshipman's half pay (nothing a day & find yourself & monkey's allowance (more kicks than halfpence). I risked no money—cause why I had none: but *made* money out of the movement, & fame too. I've often thought what a dirty beast I was. I made £150 by Alton Locke, & never lost a farthing by anything—& I got, not in spite of, but by, the rows, a name & standing with many.[22]

When he wrote this magnanimous acknowledgment of what the movement had done for him, Kingsley seemed to want to forget for a moment the stress of overwork, Jelf's veto of his nomination at King's College, the Drew affair, the condemnatory tone of many articles in the *Guardian*, or the humiliating atmosphere of ecclesiastical distrust of his person when he was resident in Torquay.

Hughes ultimately saw Kingsley's assessment of 1848 as one of the last letters of the Parson Lot period. It showed, he argued, not that Kingsley had "deserted his flag," but rather that his "battle rolled away to another part of the field."[23]

The letter to Maurice in which Kingsley had opened his heart, concluded with expressing a profound longing to put away his "disjointed unmanly wailings." Kingsley made up his mind to "put [them] away in simple silent homework," which consisted in "settling quietly here again, & write my sermons, & books for my children."[24] The book for his children he had started writing was a series of stories about ancient Greek heroes.

II

It is difficult to believe that the man who wrote *Hypatia* in 1852–3, and *Westward Ho!* in 1853–4, next wrote such a book as *The Heroes; or, Greek Fairy Tales for My Children*. Not that *The Heroes* was not a successful book—it has long been, with *The Water-Babies*, Kingsley's

---

[22] CK to TH, undated, Martin (1950) 678.
[23] Hughes (1876) lviii.
[24] Hughes (1876) lviii.

only book never to go out of print—but for the first time all Kingsley's social and religious purposes were set aside for a straightforward story without the Kingsleyan energy and preaching that made his earlier works so lively and controversial. The flatness of *The Heroes* reflects a moment of creative stasis and his increasing doubts about his calling as a writer, a moment of retreat from the controversial public reputation he had earned since 1848. Even the fact that he started writing for children seems to signal a certain fatigue with the professional world of letters and an intention, as Maurice's and Ludlow's fears indicated, to rest upon his laurels.

The Heroes was ostentatiously written for Rose, Maurice and Mary, to whom it is dedicated. Fanny, in her biography, reinforced this impression by writing that her husband "in the intervals of parochial work and lectures at the various diocesan institutes [. . .] wrote a book of Greek fairy tales for his children."[25] and Kingsley himself repeatedly referred to it in his letters as a series of "Greek Stories for my Children."[26] However, the book had above all financial attractions. At an early stage he had promised the book to the Macmillan brothers, who were keen to bring it out as a Christmas book. In September, with the first of the three parts written, he asked them: "How big will you have the book? & how much will Perseus make? & how many illustrations wd. you have?"[27] And when the Boston publishers Ticknor and Fields sent him a copy of their edition of *Wesward Ho!*, he was quick to offer them *The Heroes* as well. Although he admitted he was rewriting "the same myths w. Hawthorne took [. . .] in his 'wonder-book' [*Tanglewood Tales*]," he stressed that he was "treating them in a somewhat more classical fashion," a fashion which he expected to boost a "large sale" in America as well as in England.[28]

The story of Perseus gave Kingsley ample scope to explore the ideal of masculinity that critics were to define as "muscular Christianity." At the beginning, Perseus, at the age of fifteen, is presented to the reader as "the most skilful of all in running and wrestling and boxing, and in throwing the quoit and the javelin, and in rowing with the oar, and in playing the harp, and in all which befits a man."[29]

---

[25] *LML* i 455–6.
[26] CK to Ticknor and Fields, 15/10/1855, Martin (1950) 622.
[27] CK to Macmillan, 3/9/1855, BL 54911 f.73v–74r.
[28] CK to Ticknor and Fields, 15/10/1855, Martin (1950) 622.
[29] *Heroes* 9.

Pallas Athene promises him that "to those who are manful I give a might more than man's." Such manfulness is given to heroes who fight "the enemies of God and men,"[30] and Perseus is destined to become one of these. His main task lies in slaying the Medusa and carrying off her head in a goat-skin. Although this near impossible act is anticipated with skill, creating the central piece of suspense in the story, the crucial moment is described with a few unimaginative strokes:

> Then he came down and stepped to her boldly, and looked steadfastly on his mirror, and struck with Herpé stoutly once; and he did not need to strike again.
> Then he wrapped the head in the goat-skin, turning away his eyes, and sprang into the air aloft, faster than he ever sprang before.[31]

At this point the reader is only half-way through the story. Kingsley's ideal of masculinity, of course, embraced more than mere physical prowess and athletic skill. With the myth of Perseus Kingsley also revisited his much cherished Andromeda. To this he dedicated most of the second half of his story, which, as in his poem of 1852, celebrated Kingsley's idea of marital love. In fact, although hardly noticeable to the reader who comes with *The Heroes* to Kingsley for the first time, the story, under its surface, makes it possible to trace its author's master-themes. Before asking Andromeda's hand, Perseus has to break the chains with which she is tied to the rocks by her people and turn the sea monster into stone. The monster in his earlier version could be seen as an image of man's instinctive sexual lust that needed to be conquered before pure love could be celebrated. Such a reading can be applied here as well. Kingsley describes how the monster, before coming to devour (deflower) the chained Andromeda, stopped "at times by creek or headland, to watch for the laughter of girls at their bleaching, [. . .] or boys bathing on the beach."[32] He is, moreover, explicit that only after turning the monster into stone, i.e. by petrifying his lust, will he be awarded by having Andromeda as his wife. As Pallas Athene remarks: "Perseus, you have played the man, and see, you have your reward."[33] And as it

---

[30] *Heroes* 12.
[31] *Heroes* 37.
[32] *Heroes* 53.
[33] *Heroes* 58.

was a barbarous and superstitious people that wanted to sacrifice Andromeda's virginity to an old deity, Perseus, sustained by the powers of the new gods, saves her in marriage. In *The Heroes* Kingsley did not argue his views on love and marriage consciously, and, of course, they would have been inappropriate in a book for children, but the physical fitness needed for the make-up of a man is put in deliberately so as to feature prominently. Thus, the story of Perseus concludes as it started, and describes the hero at the games where he "was the best man of all, at running, and leaping, and wrestling, and throwing the javelin."[34]

The second story of *The Heroes*, telling of the adventures of the Argonauts, is more linear than the first and swift action characterizes the telling of Jason's quest for the Golden Fleece and how, after many hardships and losses, the Argonauts returned home to Iolcos. Kingsley here chose a more epic style for his story and left no occasion unused to mention and explain ancient names, geography, or genealogy. There is much less emphasis on "manliness," and Kingsley's master-themes are absent. The deeds of the Argonauts are presented as generally noble, as were those of "the ladies, who went out last year, to drudge in the hospitals of the East, making themselves poor, that they might be rich in noble works. And young men too, whom you know, children, [. . .] went out to the war, leaving wealth, and comfort, and a pleasant home, and all that money can give, to face hunger and thirst, and wounds and death, that they might fight for their country and their Queen."[35] There is a temptation to read Kingsley's account of the Argonauts as a parable of the Crimean War, in which the Golden Fleece stands for Christianity, which England was going to defend there. The fact that much of the story takes place in the Black Sea encourages such an interpretation. Though successful in their quest for the Fleece, the heroes that sail with Jason have to pay a heavy price for it in terms of victims and the survivors have to go through severe agony and suffering. Although Kingsley might have played with the pertinence of this story in the year 1855, he never takes up such a comparison with consistence and, apart from the early reference to the nurses and soldiers "who went out last year," further parallels remain vague.

---

[34] *Heroes* 65.
[35] *Heroes* 72.

The book concludes with the adventures of Theseus, which provide the characteristic zest for fighting that is lacking in Kingsley's first two stories. Slayings of monsters and of sinful men come in thick succession, and they are described with far more gusto than Perseus' severing the Gorgon's head in the first story of the book. As the three stories of *The Heroes* were written in the sequence in which they appear in print, this seems to indicate that Kingsley's fighting mettle was rekindling towards the end of the autumn. And, if in the first two stories Kingsley seemed to feel almost reluctant to point the moral, indicative of the misgivings he felt about moralising during the late summer of 1855, at the end of *The Heroes* Kingsley had regained some confidence in his public role. He concludes his book with the following paragraph of warning:

> So it is still, my children, and so it will be to the end. In those old Greeks, and in us also, all strength and virtue come from God. But if men grow proud and self-willed, and misuse God's fair gifts, He lets them go their own ways, and pitifully, that the glory may be his alone. God help us all, and give us wisdom, and courage to do noble deeds! but God keep pride from us when we have done them, lest we fall, and come to shame![36]

What is remarkable is that such Kingsleyan preaching is otherwise absent in *The Heroes*. It can also be read as a reflection on the author's feelings about fame earned in the cause of Christianity.

Although *The Heroes* was dated 1856 on its title-page, the book was written at Farley Court during the autumn of 1855, and it was marketed just in time for the Christmas of that year. The book was advertised when it came out as "with eight illustrations by the author." Macmillan had agreed to publish it with Kingsley's own illustrations. The illustrations are not without merit. Although there is a lot of heroic action narrated in the three stories, they rarely depict any of this. There is only one picture with Greek heroes in action, but it is hardly clear what that action refers to. The other drawings are for the most part static sketches of the characters. Half of them present the reader with images that picture the hero in the company of a womanly figure of beauty, such as Perseus with his mother at sea, Perseus approaching Andromeda in shackles, Jason awed by Hera's appearance, and Theseus with his mother when he finds

---

[36] *Heroes* 254–5.

Illustration 3. Kingsley's drawing of Perseus
and Andromeda (from: *The Heroes*)

Hermes' and Athene's sandals and sword. The drawing of Perseus
and Andromeda shows remarkable resemblance to a young Kingsley
in a wide-awake approaching a Fanny-like woman chained to rock.
That this was the most important part of the Perseus story is borne
out by the fact that Kingsley made no drawing of Perseus with the
Medusa head, whereas for the second story he did make an illustration of Jason reaching over the enchanted serpent for the Golden
Fleece, and for the third story a drawing of Theseus with his foot
an the slain Minotaur. That Kingsley moreover took great pains with
his pen-and-ink drawing of Perseus and Andromeda becomes clear
from his instructions to the engraver in a letter to Alexander Macmillan:
"here is a patchy bad shadow behind the woman's wrist, & the man's
left thigh seems to me a little too short for the leg. if he ever chooses
to give *less* shading he may: & the man's right hand is quite loveable." He also asked Macmillan to "see a specimen of his powers
before going ahead,"[37] but the skills of Macmillan's craftsman did
not live up to his standards. "What a brutal mess the engravers have

[37] CK to Macmillan, 3/9/1855, BL 54911 f.73v.

made of my drawings," he lamented to Hughes when the book had come out.[38]

With *The Heroes* Kingsley consolidated his role as a Macmillan author, and although it was not such an instant hit as *Westward Ho!* had been, numerous editions and reprints followed. The book opened for Macmillan possibilities as a publisher of children's books with a repertoire which was to include in coming years not only *The Water-Babies*, but also that other Victorian classic, *Alice's Adventures in Wonderland*. *The Heroes* became a classic gift-book for children, and in 1868 the publishing house even marketed an expensive edition with coloured illustrations. In America, where a publisher had to reckon with Hawthorne's successful version of the same Greek myths, Kingsley's book did reasonably well, and Ticknor and Fields did not regret investing in it. The book was issued in the firm's juvenile binding style, and they commissioned a craftsman of their own for three illustrations· They sold more than three thousand copies in three editions over eight years.[39]

Notwithstanding its lasting popularity with readers, *The Heroes* received very little contemporary critical acclaim. Apart from a handful of literary notices and advertisements, the book got no proper reviews. Twentieth-century critics have preferred it to Hawthorne's *Tanglewood Tales*, as they think Kingsley's language more true to the classical spirit of Greek mythology. Critics and historians of children's literature have indicated the high standing it has long had in England and some have hailed it as Kingsley's finest book for children.

III

Kingsley had admitted in his "unmanly wailings" to Maurice in August that, in this period of self-doubt, he could not study at all but only try to forget his misgivings about his own public role in moments of amusement. Such amusement consisted in fishing. As so often before, fishing was to Kingsley an outlet of repressed agitation and distress, an unconscious attempt to channel his frustrations in socially accepted diversion. At the end of the year he started planning

---

[38] CK to TH, 26/12/1855, Martin (1950) 636.
[39] Winship 219.

a fishing holiday with Hughes and Froude in Wales for the following summer. A long series of epistles followed all through the winter, spring and early summer of 1856 in which his thirst "to kill" occurs with a startling frequency. For example, on Boxing-Day 1855 he wrote to Hughes: "I conceive that *humanly* speaking, if we went to work judgmatically, we could live for 15s. a day each at the outside [. . .] And kill an amount of fish perfectly frightful;"[40] or again in a letter written in early summer, "*I* only think of the trouts—which the last I saw killed in Llyn Melch was 3 1/2 pounds, & will kill his wife & family."[41] Towards the end of winter he was "organizing a series of 'leaves' from every body round," and he managed to get "8 or 9 leaves for [a] d[a]y's fishing."[42] All his piscatorial exploits were detailed in his letters to Hughes, as for example:

> It is raining 'sicut inferna et Thomam' from dead south, & will blow a sou-wester tomorrow, so I'm off again to my happy fishing ground, & if the water is a *leetle* coloured, expect a stone of fish [. . .] I killed a beast there 3 years ago.[43]

But it was not just the thrill he got out of fishing that was important to him. It was what kept him sane when his ministerial office confronted him with the incomprehensibility of human suffering, as the following extract from an account in another letter to Hughes reveals:

> I have had a sorter kinder sample day. Up at 5, to see a dying man [. . .] Was from 5.30 to 6.30 with the most dreadful case of agony— (insensible to me: but not to his pain). Came home, got a bath & a pipe, & away again to him at 8, found him insensible to his own pain with dilated pupils, dying of pressure on the brain—going any moment, prayed the commendatory prayers over him. & started for the river with West, fished all morning in a roaring N.E. gale, with that dreadful agonized face between me & the river, pondering on *the* mystery. Killed 8 on March brown & governor, by drowning the flies, & *taking 'em out gently, to see if aught was there*—w. is the only dodge in a N. Easter [. . .] Clouds burn up at 1. P.M. I put on a brass minnow & kill 3 more [. . .] Came off the water at 3.30. Found my man alive: & thank God, quiet. Sat with him & thought him going once or twice. [. . .] Got back at 10.30 & sit writing to you. So goes one's day. All manner of incongruous things to do—& the very incongruity keeps one beany & jolly.[44]

[40] CK to TH, 26/12/1855, Martin (1950) 635; my italics.
[41] CK to TH, undated, Martin (1950) 715.
[42] CK to TH, undated, Martin (1950) 656.
[43] CK to TH, undated, Martin (1950) 670.
[44] CK to TH, undated, Martin (1950) 678-9.

Through killing fish Kingsley was momentarily in control of the powers of life and death, with this modest practical activity restoring the calm that his professional difficulties were threatening to undermine. Such moments usually came when Kingsley was on the brink of a depression, and 1856 was no exception to that. Overwork was causing a strain on his mind once more. After two productive years of writing for his new publisher, plans for a new novel stalled, even though Macmillan pressed him for something more substantial than *Glaucus* and *The Heroes* to follow up the success of *Westward Ho!*.

Moments of gloom alternated with outbursts of intense elation. The latter were found in rapturous fishing sprees. But, as the passage above shows, such excitement was often a mere escape from everything that frustrated and oppressed Kingsley in 1856. It is significant that he wrote to Hughes in spring that he was "almost the only cove I care to hear from, because you don't *write* wisdom, but write nonsense, & does wisdom [. . .] Blow genius & give me a brick."[45] And what they wrote about was the weather, flies, tackle, and the gains of a fishing day. Week by week they "dreamed" about their August fishing holiday with Froude in Wales. It was envisaged as a vigorous expedition far from the civilized world, a holiday during which all they would want were "an ordnance map, a compass, fishing tackle, socks & slippers." And there was going to be no need for shirts, for "who would wear them?" Bodily comfort was not to be counted on. Kingsley warned Hughes at an early stage of their planning that "we must depend on our own legs, & on stomachs w. can face braxy mutton young taters, Welsh porter—wh. is the identical drainings of Noah's flood turned sour, & brandy of more strength than legality. Bread horrid. Fleas MCCCC ad infinitum." They would bathe in "ye mountain brook" and have for a towel "a wisp of any endogen save Scirpus triquetor, or Juncus squarrosus." Fanny disapproved of the holiday—she disliked North Wales ever since her sister Charlotte's experiences there as a newly wedded wife—but if Hughes could make "a vow & keep it strong" to go to Snowdon, she would allow her husband to go with him.[46]

The enthusiasm for the Snowdon holiday was fuelled by fishing experiences all through the spring in "ye happy fishing grounds," as he called his favourite fishing water near home at Eversley. If he could not fish with West, or with the guest who came over to stay

[45] CK to TH, undated, Martin (1950) 672.
[46] CK to TH, 26/12/1855, Martin (1950) 636.

at Eversley, Kingsley went on his own as soon as the Southwester started blowing. On 15 May he managed to have some fine fishing with Hughes at Wotton. At Wotton House, the birthplace of John Evelyn, Kingsley and Hughes were joined by the poet Martin Tupper, friend of the inhabitant of Wotton House, W.J. Evelyn. Kingsley had formed a negative image of Tupper, presumably for his reputation of philosophizing in ridiculous verse, but his prejudices vanished as soon as the two men met, and Kingsley admitted to Hughes afterwards that he had been "unjust to the man: & we have made great friends."[47] Tupper reveals in his autobiography that there was a "strong sympathy" between him and Kingsley when they discovered that they both suffered from stammering. He added that, although Kingsley had, like himself, conquered his infirmity when he had to speak in public, "privately his speech would often fail him."[48]

The plans for the fishing holiday in Wales changed towards the end of April when Froude proposed salmon fishing in Ireland instead. Killarney, Froude maintained, would "cost no more money, if as much, & be much more glorious" than Snowdon.[49] As Froude had stayed there in his dark days of 1848 for a period of ten weeks, he boasted he knew "every inch of it." Kingsley enthusiastically responded to Froude's plan. However, when in July it became clear that Froude was too busy on his *History of England* and could not join them on their vacation, Kingsley's enthusiasm for Killarney waned quickly, and he wrote to Hughes: "as I get old, somehow, I don't like *new* places; I like to thump over the same book, & trot over the same bog, & feel *"homey"* wherever I be."[50]

Now that Froude was not going to join them, and the "auspicious time" drawing near, Kingsley and Hughes were on the look-out for a third companion. Kingsley much desired to have the playwright Tom Taylor as "salvidge man", and communicated, through Hughes, that he could show him views of the Welsh mountains that no "mortal cockney knows, because though the whole earth is given to the children of men, none but we jolly fishers get the plums & raisins of it."[51] Taylor accepted, and it was agreed he would join them

---

[47] CK to TH, undated, Martin (1950) 690.
[48] Martin Farquhar Tupper, *My Life as an Author* (London: Sampson Low, 1886) 347.
[49] CK to TH, [25/4/1856], Martin (1950) 667.
[50] CK to TH, 10/7/1856, Martin (1950) 700.
[51] CK to TH, undated, Martin (1950) 715.

during the second week on 18 August. Fanny and the children would go to stay with her brother Riversdale at Ray Lodge. Now that everything had been decided on, Kingsley wrote his famous "Invitation" to Hughes which later found its way into all editions of Kingsley's collected poems. With its contemporary allusions, its references to Kingsley's hobby-horses and idiosyncrasies, and as an example of his humour, it is worth quoting at length:

Come away with me, Tom,
Term and talk are done;
My poor lads are reaping,
Busy every one.
Curates mind the parish,
Sleepers mind the court;
We'll away to Snowdon
For our ten days' sport:
Fish the August evening
Till the eve is past,
Whoop like boys, at pounders
[. . .]
Homer's heroes did so,
Why not such as we?
What are sheets and servants?
Superfluity!
Pray for wives and children
Safe in slumber curled,
Then to chat till midnight
O'er this babbling world—
Of the workmen's college,
Of the price of grain,
Of the tree of knowledge,
Of the chance of rain;
If Sir A. goes Romeward,
If Miss B. sings true,
If the fleet comes homeward,
If the mare will do,—
[. . .]
Down, and bathe at day-dawn,
Tramp from lake to lake,
Washing brain and heart clean
Every step we take.
Leave to Robert Browning
Beggars, fleas, and vines
Leave to mournful Ruskin

Popish Apennines,
Dirty Stones of Venice
And his Gas-lamps Seven—
We've the stones of Snowdon
And the lamps of heaven.
Where's the mighty credit
In admiring Alps?
Any goose sees 'glory'
In their 'snowy scalps.'
Leave such signs and wonders
For the dullard brain,
As aesthetic brandy,
Opium and cayenne.
[. . .]
Though we try no ventures
Desperate or strange;
Feed on commonplaces
In a narrow range;
[. . .]
Tho' we earn our bread, Tom,
By the dirty pen,
What we can we will be,
Honest Englishmen.
Do the work that's nearest,
Though it's dull at whiles,
Helping, when we meet them,
Lame dogs over stiles;
See in every hedgerow
Marks of angels' feet,
Epics in each pebble
Underneath, our feet;
Once a year, like schoolboys,
Robin-Hooding go,
Leaving fops and fogies
A thousand feet below.

On 11 August Kingsley and Hughes set out from Eversley early in the morning to catch at Reading the 5.30 train to Wolverhampton. Here they had to wait for more than four hours before getting on the train to Bangor, which they reached at five the following morning. Kingsley wrote to Fanny upon their arrival at Pen-y-gwyrd that the train journey had been tiring, and that they "never slept 40 winks last night." They had set out on foot from Bangor at five, fishing on the way. However, the "fish would not rise (though *you* don't care for that)," but there was good hope for the following days as all "the rivers are flooded, & therefore we *shall* have noble sport." And he added off-hand that that first day they merely "had 20 showers."[52]

Kingsley and Hughes found lodgings at the little inn of Pen-y-gwyrd "which standeth in the meeting of noble valleys three" ("Pen-y-gwryd") with Snowdon towering overhead. The inn's kitchen—"a low room, ceiled with dark beams, from which hung bacon and fishing-rods, harness and drying stockings, and all the miscellanea of a fishing inn"—and its landlord, Henry Owen, and wife were to feature in *Two Years Ago*, where Kingsley remembered the place and its owners with fondness as "the central heart of the mountains." "And a genial, jovial little heart it is, and an honest, kindly little heart too, with warm life-blood within. [. . .] There was Harry Owen, bland and stalwart, his baby in his arms, smiling upon the world in general."[53]

Kingsley had been to Wales before, but the grandeur of the mountains did not fail to impress him once more. To Fanny he wrote that "the glory was what I never saw before, all those grand mountains 'silver-veined with rills.' Cataracts of snow—*white cotton threads*, if you will, zigzagging down every rock-face—sometimes 1000 feet & the whole air alive with the roar of waters,"[54] and to his children he wrote of "great walls & crags of lava, & ashes wh. have come out of volcanoes at the bottom of the ancient sea,"[55] and of going up the 3300 feet of the Glydyr Vawr past a formation of volcanic rock which "was just like one of the antediluvian seamonsters at the Crystal palace" until he reached "the great jagged giants standing

---

[52] CK to FK, [12/8/1856], BL-62554 f.96.
[53] *TYA* 372.
[54] CK to FK, [12/8/1856], BL-62554 f.96r.
[55] CK to Rose Kingsley, [17/8/1856], Martin (1950) 718.

up in the clouds."[56] The Welsh mountains stimulated a sensation of perfect harmony between the primordial physical (and spiritual) urge to conquer them (i.e. climbing them) and the symbol of the volcanic "creative energy of youth."[57]

Notwithstanding their undiminished high hopes after the first day of rain, fishing the following days did not prove very successful. "We are on our legs 10 hours a day, the weather was far too stormy for sport," and "the cold & wet are extreme," Kingsley complained when the holidays were half-way through, "& we catch ve[r]y few fish."[58] This, after six long months of great expectation, was disheartening. Something else contributed to dampen Kingsley's high spirits. As had happened often before while alone on holiday, the separation from Fanny killed Kingsley's enthusiasm for the place he was visiting, especially when on 18 August he had received no letters from Fanny for five days. He had "wretched dreams" about her and fancied she must be ill. "If I do not hear tomorrow," he threatened, "I shall come right home."[59] Fanny had written, but the letters had been held up at Beddgelert. In her husband's absence she felt wretched too. She regretted she had not been able to share her husband's enthusiasm for Wales and even reproached herself for appearing unfeeling to him. She wrote about her doubts to him, to which he in turn humbly replied: "I am a foolish careless man, who will never grow old, & who vexed you (treasonably) by foolishly boyish crowing over going to Snowdon, & I am wrong & you are right—& for goodness sake say no more, only love me, love me, love me."[60] Still, hearing from Fanny was enough to make him "quite happy again."

Tom Taylor had arrived in the meantime, and he found himself "abandoned to two wild men—mountain-climbers, salmon-seekers, plant-pickers, rock-renders." "If I come back with whole bones," he wrote to Lord Goderich, "it will be a crowning mercy. I write cheerful letters home, not to alarm my wife, but, in truth, I go in fear of my life between this Socialist lawyer and this Socialist parson."[61]

---

[56] CK to Maurice Kingsley, [20/8/1856], BL-41298 f.216v.
[57] *Y* 296.
[58] CK to FK, [19/8/1856], BL-62554 f.100v.
[59] CK to FK, 18/8/1856, BL-62554 f.99r.
[60] CK to FK, [20/8/1856], BL-62554 f.101.
[61] Tom Taylor to Lord Goderich, 20/8/1856, Mack and Armytage 83.

With improved weather Hughes reported that now "we certainly enjoyed ourselves famously."[62] Kingsley scribbled in the guest-book:

> I came to Pen-y-gwryd in frantic hopes of slaying
> Grilse, Salomon, 3 lb. red-fleshed trout, and what else there's no saying:
> But bitter cold and lashing rain, and black nor'eastern skies, sir,
> Drove me from fish to botany, a sadder man and wiser.[63]

IV

In her chapter "The Years of Drought, 1856–58," arguing from evidence from a period which stretched from the summer of 1855 to August 1856, Susan Chitty described 1856 as the year during which Kingsley's "creativity dried up."[64] Although Kingsley felt increasingly perplexed about his role as a writer, Chitty's thesis is difficult to sustain. As a matter of fact, after finishing *The Heroes* for Christmas 1855, Kingsley returned with relish to writing poetry and then, during the second half of 1856 matured the idea for, and set to work on, his next novel. Moreover, during that year he contributed lengthy reviews to *The North British Review* and *Fraser's Magazine*.

The poems of 1856, as always with Kingsley's poetry, reflect their author's moods and emotions. If his earlier poems featured heroic knights, misguided nuns, women in distress, or victims of social injustice, the subject and ambition of these new poems is more homely. In February, for example, when Riversdale Grenfell came with his family to stay at Farley Court, Kingsley wrote "Farewell." This poem, dedicated to Grenfell's daughter Charlotte Elliot, has a subdued opening that reflects Kingsley's disillusionment with the times and his uneasiness about his artistic calling:

> My fairest child, I have no song to give you;
> No lark could pipe in skies so dull and gray.

And the muted message of the final stanza, which contains the famous line "Be good, sweet maid, and let who can be clever," indicates perplexities about the moral righteousness and usefulness of speaking out in the world similar to those that Kingsley had communicated

---

[62] TH to Lord Goderich, 20/8/1856, Mack and Armytage 82.
[63] *LML* i.495.
[64] Chitty (1974) 187.

to Ludlow in the long letter written during the last days of the previous year.

During his brother-in-law's visit Kingsley also realized that Grenfell's other daughter, Georgina Adelaide, who just turned 21, was no longer the young child he had known twelve years before when he courted Fanny, but that she had grown into a woman. This led to a short lyric. The occasion was a playful jest about the importance of high-society life to her. Kingsley's treating her as a mere girl with childish fancies triggered "a silent tear" of reproach and shame in her. She "In that one look to woman grew/ While with child, I thought, I played" ("to G.A.G."). It emphasized the passing of time and that he himself too was growing old. If the year before he had remarked that his life was half over, he now wrote to Fanny, on his thirty-seventh birthday, that "God grant I may spend the *lesser* half of my life w. remains better than I have the former."[65] The very same day he bought Fanny "a bottle of *hair-wash* to keep your dear head nice, & to keep off grey hairs!!!"[66]

The other poems Kingsley wrote in 1856 reflect the delight he took in fishing that year. At the beginning of April he celebrated the South Wind:

> O bless'd South wind that toots his horn
>   Through every hole and crack!
> I'm off at eight to-morrow morn,
>   To bring *such* fishes back!

Such occasional pieces, like the ones about fishing in Wales or Ireland quoted above, were written to be included in his letters to Thomas Hughes and do not share the muted sentiment of the poems written for his nieces. Still, notwithstanding the exulting tone of joy, they are no less homely than these. "The Find," a poem celebrating a neck-breaking fox-hunt, develops in its rhythmical pattern the frenzied chase—

> Yon sound's neither sheep-bell nor bark,
> They're running—they're running, Go hark!
> The sport may be lost by a moment's delay,
> So whip up the puppies and scurry away.
> Dash down through the cover by dingle and dell,

---

[65] CK to FK, 12/6/1856, BL-62554 f.90r; my italics.
[66] CK to FK, 12/6/1856, BL-62554 f.90v; my italics.

> There's a gate at the bottom—I know it full well;
> And they're running—they're running,
>   Go hark!

—but finishes on this homely note:

> Then shog along homeward, chat over the fight,
> And hear in our dreams the sweet music all night
> Of—They're running—they're running,
>   Go hark!

The reviews Kingsley wrote in 1856 are remarkable for the enormous amount of reading that went into them. In "Plays and Puritans," written for the *North British Review*, Kingsley reviewed no fewer than fifteen books. In this review Kingsley regretted a tendency in literary criticism to acquit the seventeenth-century playwrights of the accusation that they delighted in their coarse language and immoral plots. Critics argued that the immorality should be seen as the natural outcome of a free-spoken and fearless age which at bottom was based on an energetic principle of virtue, that the stage merely presented vices which men did not practise in reality, that "the language of the stage is purified in proportion as our moral deteriorated."[67] As a result of such reasoning, the Puritans with their condemnation of the stage could only be seen as barbarians of art. Kingsley retorted that "there is a mass of unanimous evidence which cannot be controverted, to prove that England, in the first half of the seventeenth century, was far more immoral than in the nineteenth" and that the reaction to the stage was "a natural and necessary revolt against [. . .] luxury and immorality [. . .] a protest for man's God-given superiority over nature, against that Naturalism which threatened to end in sheer animalism."[68] But it was virtually useless to urge this on his readers, Kingsley lamented, as the "easy-going and respectable multitude, in easy-going and respectable days like these" were not willing to listen to historic truth and preferred to "shut their ears prudishly to his [the historian's] painful facts." And, with at the back of his mind the criticism he himself had received upon the publication of *Westward Ho!*, Kingsley added:

> Thus if any one, in the justification of the Reformation, and the British hatred of Popery during the sixteenth century, should dare to detail the undoubted facts of the Inquisition, and to comment on them

---

[67] *PP* 44.
[68] *PP* 72.

dramatically enough to make his readers feel about them what men who witnessed them felt, he would be accused of a "morbid love of horrors."[69]

It was such criticism that had contributed to Kingsley's doubts about his public role as a historian and had led to a retreat to the sphere of the home and the family. Moreover, he asked himself elsewhere: "is [a man] the wiser and stronger for being told by a reviewer that he has written fine words, or has failed in writing them; or to have silly women writing to ask for his autograph, or for leave to set his songs to music?" And he answered his own question in the negative.[70] Kingsley's private withdrawal from the heroic and the national is betrayed by his arguing later in "Plays and Puritans" that the Puritans were by no means the sour, narrow, inhuman persons that they were often made out to be, but that they indubitably possessed a taste, sense of poetry and feeling of their own; he explained: "We do not mean now the unwritten tragedy of the battle-psalm and the charge; but simple idyllic poetry and quiet home-drama, love-poetry of the heart and the hearth, and the beauties of every-day human life."[71]

A passage in another review Kingsley wrote in 1856 is equally revealing of his state of mind. In a highly acclaiming piece on Froude's *History of England*, after having traced the book's representation of the English character in Tudor England as reflecting a strong national sense of military-like discipline, he turned to the nineteenth century and concluded that the forty years of peace following the Battle of Waterloo had induced the English to think that peace is a natural state of modern life. But the "fearful fact" was that "war, in some shape or other, is the normal condition of the world."[72] And on this pessimistic note he warned his readers that it would be unwise and dangerous not to recognize that a "rottenness" on the continent was rapidly becoming intolerable to God, and that the Crimean War was "but the prologue to a fearful drama."[73] The English may only pray, therefore, that "in that day we have chosen for our leaders, as our forefathers of the sixteenth century did."[74] Such reasoning was in tune with the patriotic and nationalistic gist of *Westward Ho!*,

---

[69] *PP* 7.
[70] *TYA* 57.
[71] "Froude's History of England" *PP* 74.
[72] "Froude's History of England" *PP* 267.
[73] "Froude's History of England" *PP* 269.
[74] "Froude's History of England" *PP* 270.

but it lacked in enthusiasm. What was different in 1856 is that Kingsley had abandoned most of his hope for England as a civilizing world-power. He now limited himself to asserting that England's "true military greatness lies in the power of defence" only.[75]

V

Although the Christian Socialist movement could be said to have ceased to exist in 1854, the energy of many of its promoters was not wasted. It was channelled into a new project, the Working Men's College. Although the ideal of providing education for working men had been part of the Christian Socialists' plans since at least 1852, and although popular lectures and weekly classes for working men had been given regularly by its members, it was not until the expulsion of Maurice from King's College as a result of his *Theological Essays* that the moment seemed ripe for the foundation of a college. Premises were available in Red Lion Square due to the closing of the Needlewomen's Association, and Maurice, who was asked to become the college's principal, accepted the proposal as "divine direction."[76] A Council of Teachers was created including many of the most ardent old Christian Socialists who offered their services for teaching the evening classes. Thus, Maurice lectured three days a week on theology and English Literature, Ludlow taught on "the Law of Partnership", Frederick Furnivall held English grammar classes, and Charles Walsh discussed questions of public health and hygiene. One of the new recruits, attracted by a circular Furnivall had written to promote their new enterprise, was John Ruskin, who offered himself for drawing classes. His presence did much for the College's popularity and success.

It is striking that Kingsley's name is missing in both the Council of Teachers and the list of lecturers. Although Kingsley had complained at times that Ludlow would not give him an adequate share in their doings,[77] his prolonged residence in Devon had made it impossible to participate in the setting up of the Working Men's

---

[75] "Froude's History of England" *PP* 266.
[76] Raven 350.
[77] Raven 346.

College. He had approved of the College project as a "noble plan" when Maurice had written to him at Bideford, where he was still "shut up like any Jeremiah,"[78] and he did give a lecture at the "Needlewoman's Institution" in 1855 on "Woman's Work in a Country Parish," but after his return to Eversley he offered his friends no permanent help at the college. In the Christian Socialists' last project Kingsley wanted to be, in Hughes's words, more of a spectator than an actor. His enthusiasm for the brotherhood and its cause had unmistakably faded. His social interest had shifted to questions of sanitary reform and to problems in his own parish.

When in Wales Kingsley joined Hughes and Taylor in writing a letter to Lord Goderich, he was unable to be as informal and jocular as his friends were. With Buckland's canonry still pending, and needing the nobleman's support for preferment, he addressed Goderich with his title. Hughes playfully suggested that Kingsley only applied the principle of brotherhood to those below him but kept a respectful reverence for those above him. "The Parson has all the prophesy knocked out of him," he added.[79] Although Hughes's comments were uttered in jest, there was more truth in them than he probably suspected at the time. In 1856 Kingsley no longer wanted to be considered a mocking Lot in the English Cities of the Plain.

---

[78] CK to FDM, 19/10/1854, *LML* i.433.
[79] TH to Lord Goderich, 20/8/1856, Mack and Armytage 83.

CHAPTER SIXTEEN

A LITERARY MAN, A MODERN HERCULES, AND A COUNTRY CLERGYMAN (1857)

Before continuing in her biography with the events of 1857, Mrs Kingsley interrupts her narrative with a brief sketch of her husband's domestic life, "in his home, where his children had the best of everything."[1] This was, in a sense, a felicitous choice. Whether she did so deliberately, marking the shift in Kingsley's interest from the public to the home, or whether her chapter simply came conveniently as an introduction at the beginning of her second volume, is impossible to say. However, seeing the growing emphasis on his family, and on his parish work, from 1856 onwards, and his own confessions that he no longer wanted to spend his life attacking and condemning others, there is no reason not to adopt Mrs Kingsley's approach and have a closer look at how Kingsley's family life unrolled at Eversley.

Rose, Maurice and Mary were now thirteen, ten, and four years old. From the evidence that remains there seems to be little doubt that the children had a perfectly happy childhood. They had large and sunny rooms in the Rectory, and Rose remembered in 1907 that her father had built them a play place at the end of the straight walk that crossed the back garden, and which was bordered on both sides with flowerbeds in which old damask roses "simply ran riot" with paeonies and pinks.[2] Later, in the sixties, Kingsley built a new hut on the "Mount", the highest point of the sloping woodland on one side of the house, where the younger children kept books, toys and "tea-things" and where they would play in the warmer seasons. For Rose, then in her late teens, he had part of the Mount cleared and levelled for "a charming croquet-ground."[3]

After work Kingsley would often join his children at the play house, and bring in all kinds of natural curiosities which he had

---

[1] *LML* ii.3.
[2] Rose Kingsley, *Eversley Gardens and Others* (London: George Allen, 1907) 264.
[3] *Ibid.* 267.

picked up during his weekday walks through the parish. Sundays were never associated with gloom or restrictions. These always ended with an evening or afternoon stroll on the moor which Maurice remembered vividly in 1877: "I can *feel* him striding by me in the narrow path, while from the bright sky and the look of the country he drank in nature, till his eye lit up, his chest expanded, his step grew elastic, and he was a boy again with me."[4] But what Maurice remembered as "perhaps the brightest picture of the past" were the moments when after morning service on Sundays, or in the evenings on weekdays, Kingsley gathered with his children and their picture books and made drawings of whatever they asked him: "There he sat, with one hand in mother's, forgetting his own hard work and worry in leading our fun and frolic, with a kindly smile on his lips, and a loving light in that bright grey eye that made us feel that, in the broadest sense of the word, he was our father."[5] Although John Martineau, when he came to board with the Kingsleys in 1850, remarked that Mr Kingsley was a rather grave man who never laughed, Fanny described the family gatherings as the brightest hours of the day and quotes her late husband saying "I wonder [. . .] if there is so much laughing in any other home in England as in ours."[6] Maurice, too, remembered these days as a period of "perpetual laughter."[7] What pained Kingsley deeply was to see his children in grief. "A child over a broken toy is a sight I cannot bear," he admitted,[8] while his own moments of depression and doubt were concealed from them. Corporal punishment was not allowed in his household, Mrs Kingsley writes. He had a true horror of flogging ever since "his own childish experience of the sense of degradation and unhealthy fear it produced."[9] Instead, he tried to instill a profound sense of justice, mercy and self-control in his children, by gaining their confidence, giving them much freedom and laying out only a few "broad, distinct laws of conduct."[10]

If his attitude to his children made him a lovable parent, it made him less suitable as their tutor and taskmaster. Although Kingsley

---

[4] *LML* ii.8.
[5] *LML* ii.9.
[6] *LML* ii.5.
[7] Chitty (1974) 189.
[8] *LML* ii.6.
[9] *LML* ii.4.
[10] *LML* ii.5.

might have had good reasons not to send Maurice to a boarding school—"he *shall not* go to school to be made a beast of"—it was also the decision of a parent who looked with dismay and anxiety at the prospect of his child leaving the parental nest for the first time. "Nature must be right & if home education is not natural, what is?" he concluded. But his proposal to "work at him & for him" himself was a mistake. He distrusted his own character and temperament, and resolved to change: "I will restrain my temper, & speak & act deliberately, more & more—you will see a change in me, I trust, in many things."[11] As it was, Kingsley was unable to effect such a change in himself, and when the boy was sent to school after all, the teachers found him backward in knowledge.[12]

In her description of the family life at Eversley, Mrs Kingsley underscores her husband's profound love for animals. She mentions the Scotch terrier Dandy, who through the 1850s accompanied his master on all his parish walks and attended at the cottage lectures and school lessons. Kingsley's love for animals extended to wild animals as well. He was intensely interested in a family of natter jacks that lived in a spot of the rectory lawn which "the scythe was never allowed to approach,"[13] and he would tempt them out from their hole and admire "the colours on their backs, while the little creatures sat contentedly in his hand."[14] He felt affection for a pair of sand wasps that he had saved from drowning and whose descendants lived for years in a crack of the window of his dressing room, and he warned his parishioners not to kill the slow-worm that could occasionally be seen in the churchyard. This profound love for nature Kingsley imparted to his children. "I am bringing up my children as naturalists," he wrote in 1857 to his old friend Peter Wood. And especially Maurice was to be brought up as both naturalist and sportsman to give him a pursuit for the future and "to keep him from cards and brandy-pawnee, horse-racing, and the pool of hell."[15] Thus Kingsley invited his children to share his observation of the wild animals and plants, and often his letters to them when he was away from home abounded with details of natural history. There is a passage in his *Life* which recounts how his daughter (presumably Rose)

[11] CK to FK, 15/6/1856, BL-62554 f.91r, 92r.
[12] Chitty (1974) 191.
[13] *LML* ii.10.
[14] Rose Kingsley, *Op. cit.*, 275.
[15] CK to Peter L.H. Wood, 5/4/1857, *LML* ii.21.

ran up to the window of the breakfast room with a long worm in her hands when guests where staying at the rectory, saying: "Oh! daddy, look at this *delightful* worm."[16] An American visitor upon his return home still saw in his mind's eye how "Maurice comes by with an insect or a flower, or just a general wonder and life in his eyes."[17] Neither did Kingsley fail to communicate his passion for field sports, especially to Maurice, and many letters to the boy included reference to feats of hunting or hard cross-country riding, often illustrated with small but brilliant pen-and-ink sketches in the style of Bewick. Harriet Beecher Stowe, who came to stay for three days in the autumn of 1856, unaware of her host's sporting tastes, unwittingly spoke out against foxhunting during a meal and maintained that hunting the 'poor' animals was a very unmanly business, a remark which tempted Maurice to throw the water bottle at her head.

II

The months after Kingsley's return from Snowdon passed uneventfully, and the routine of parish work and writing was only broken by a series of American visitors who came to stay at Eversley for a few days at a time. "My life runs on here," he had written in July to F.D. Maurice, "in a very simple easy way, what with the parish & the children, & Mrs Kingsley, & a little literary work."[18] This "little literary work," however, was to become quite voluminous during the last four months of 1856. Having failed to obtain one of the Westminster canonries, he needed extra income. He worked on reviews of Froude's *History* and on Mansfield's posthumous book on South America, and wrote, upon invitation, a preface to Susanna Winkworth's *History and Life of the Reverend Doctor John Tauler of Strasbourg*, a task about which he felt rather diffident. But most of his time went into a new novel. Although Kingsley had long wanted to write a book called *Letters from Snowdon* for his children, the experiences of his fishing trip with Thomas Hughes and Tom Taylor went into his fifth novel, *Two Years Ago*. He started writing soon after his return to Eversley and wanted to get the novel out early in January 1857.

---

[16] *LML* ii.10.
[17] Unidentified correspondent to CK, undated, *LML* i.497.
[18] CK to FDM, 30/7/1856, BL-41297 f.95v–96r.

Such haste was, on the one hand, dictated by his publisher's demand for a new novel, on the other by his financial straits. When the novel was well under way Macmillan promised "to print 3000, & make it a 7/6 book, & to give us for the edn. Will you believe it? between £100 & £150—he thinks nearer the latter sum. So we shall get on well this winter thank God. It seems that Westward Ho & Glaucus have put my name up so that anything I write will sell. So if God gives me health I can soon clear off all debts."[19] To finish the book as soon as possible Kingsley now moved to London, where he could work undisturbed by parish and family on his manuscript, while he could at the same time oversee Clay (Macmillan's printer) who had started setting those chapters that had already been written. Thus, while *Two Years Ago* was not written for serialization in a magazine, the procedure of composition was very similar: at no time did Kingsley see the manuscript complete for corrections. The book was written in bits and pieces at a neck-break speed and sent straight off to the printer, for Kingsley "never indulged in 'rough copy'."[20] While Clay had "100 pages & more set up & I gave him about 30 more today, & shall do as much, I hope, tomorrow," Kingsley was still trying to get the facts "abt. ye cholera" which he needed for the second half of his novel.[21]

The last proofs were going through the press in January, and Kingsley felt "better off now than I have been for years!"[22] He had good reason to feel satisfied. His new novel received ample and instant attention from the reviewers. Even if there was plenty of praise of his descriptive powers, most reviewers found fault with the structure of *Two Years Ago*. The *Athenaeum*, quick as always in getting out reviews of new novels, remarked in its issue of 14 February that "Mr Kingsley writes with an impatient pen." The reviewer regarded the narrative "disconnected, irregular, confused; the characters frequently pass, repass, and hold long colloquies, without any evident object; the plot is dim." As a result the book was "dull and disappointing," and he concluded that "We cannot help thinking that Mr. Kingsley might advantageously allow his imagination some rest."[23]

[19] CK to FK, undated, BL-62554 f.106v–107r.
[20] Rose Kingsley *Op. cit.* 257.
[21] CK to FK, undated, BL-62554 f.108v.
[22] CK to TH, January 1857, *LML* ii.16.
[23] [St. John] 212.

But not all reviews were as devastating as this. The *Athenaeum* was just a bad start. It was followed a week later by Thomas Collett Sandars in the *Saturday Review* who asserted that "this appears to us much the best work that Mr. Kingsley has written."[24]

Many reviewers were willing to overlook the weakness of structure and concentrate on Kingsley's stronger qualities. "Homeward Ho!" wrote an anonymous reviewer in the *British Quarterly Review*, "We welcome Mr. Kingsley as an old friend, on his return to England and the nineteenth century."[25] He admitted that Kingsley was not generally successful in the development of plot, but that there were many points of excellence in the book. He concentrated especially on Kingsley's views of marriage and on his "righteous contempt" of "male hysterics" and that he was absolutely right to "demand the healthful discipline of the body by manly exercise."[26] George Meredith too, writing for the *Westminster Review*, detected "a sense of hurry in the book" and was unable to dispel the idea that it was "hastily thrown off." Still, he could not but express admiration for those parts of the novel where Kingsley spoke in person, and he concluded that "the bold and beautiful manliness of his remarks on marriage, and love in marriage, will be appreciated."[27] It is such keynotes in *Two Years Ago* that led Sandars in his piece for the *Saturday Review* to formulate his famous description of "muscular Christianity" as that of "a man who fears God and can walk a thousand miles in a thousand hours—who [. . .] breathes God's free air on God's rich earth, and at the same time can hit a woodcock, doctor a horse, and twist a poker round his finger." This characterization not being meant as condemnation, he adds that he "should be sorry to say that this ideal is not a very good ideal [. . .] let Mr. Kingsley encourage us all to pursue the path that leads to so blessed a possibility."[28]

The main plot of *Two Years Ago* follows the vicissitudes of Tom Thurnall, a young doctor who, during a shipwreck on the coast of the West Country, loses the money he had scraped together as a gold digger in Australia. The prime suspect of having taken Tom's belt with £1,500 when he was washed ashore is Grace Harvey, a

---

[24] [Sandars] 176.
[25] [-], "Kingsley's *Two Years Ago*" *British Quarterly Review* 25 (1857) 399.
[26] *Ibid.* 414.
[27] [Meredith] 611.
[28] [Sandars] 176.

pious Methodist schoolmistress of beauty. When Tom decides to remain in the small fishing village of Aberalva, the two meet and fall in love with each other. The belt with money, however, stands between them. When in the end truth comes out, and Grace is proved innocent, they marry. Neither the cliché romantic plot, nor the unravelling of the events in the relationship between Tom and Grace, make *Two Years Ago* an engaging novel. It is a series of themes and realistic backgrounds that lend interest to the book. Amongst these there are questions of sanitary reform, slavery in America, the Crimean War, the figure of the artist, and faith and church. All are considered from the point of view of Kingsley's muscular Christianity.

Two Years Ago is Kingsley's most homely novel, and, like *Yeast*, it contains references to many of his personal hobbyhorses and private opinions. From the beginning there is mention of Thurnall being not "a Christian"[29] and that Grace, whose saintliness had "made her free of that 'communion with the saints'," "could do nothing for him but pray for his conversion."[30] The parallel with Lancelot and Argemone, and with Kingsley's early life, is evident. Kingsley also introduced the Whitbury of *Yeast*, mentioned the fate of the Lavingtons, referred to Minchampstead, and re-featured Claude Mellot. Moreover, there are numerous other, less obtrusive, biographical references that can be lifted from Kingsley's text, For example, the volume of poetry which is not published because "it is not as long as the publisher thinks fit"[31]—a terse comment on Parker's unwillingness to bring out a new volume of Kingsley's poetry—and the description of "a true American review, utterly extravagant in its laudations, whether from over-kindness, or from a certain love of exaggeration and magniloquence" which might owe something to the reviews Kingsley received on his American volume of poetry in the *New York Daily Times* and in *Putnam's Monthly Magazine* during the spring of 1856. The point that such reviews were thought of as very flattering but that it would be better still "if they would send one a little money, instead of making endless dollars by printing one's books, and then a few more by praising one at a penny a line"[32] also has an authentic ring. Then there is the allusion to the evenings that Kingsley was invited at Richard Monckton Milnes's dinner parties, "where you may meet,

[29] *TYA* 93.
[30] *TYA* 93.
[31] *TYA* 147.
[32] *TYA* 148.

on certain evenings, everybody; where duchesses and unfledged poets, bishops and red republican refugees, fox-hunting noblemen and briefless barristers who have taken to politics, are jumbled together for a couple of hours."[33] While many of these autobiographical fragments are good-natured observations and are presented with a gentle touch of humour, others reach deeper feelings. The parenthetic assertion in the description of the poet Vavasour as "tired, too—as who would not be?—of the drudgery of writing for his daily bread" brings the narrative exceptionally close to Kingsley's own predicament.

Those who knew Kingsley must have recognized the originals of many of the events and characters in the novel. Although *Two Years Ago* is not autobiographical in the sense that *Yeast* was, the use of such personal experiences and the ample material that he drew from the memories of his 1851 trip to Germany and his more recent Welsh holiday invited readers to see it as a *roman à clef*. The surmise that Tom Thurnall was inspired by Kingsley's brother George, the banker Armsworth by George Carr Glyn, husband of Fanny's sister Marianne, and that Valentia was based on his niece Georgina Adelaide, contributed further to this sensation. The impression was so strong that it led Tennyson to believe that he himself stood model for the poet Elsley Vavasour, especially as Kingsley had written in his recent review of Tennyson's *Maud* that he was disappointed with the laureate's new volume, that in its "gloom-pampered" hero—"discontented with his fate, his poverty"—he found a "tone of effeminacy."[34] Although Kingsley aimed at Shelley and those of his followers that had been dubbed the Spasmodic school of poetry, Tennyson had reasons to be suspicious. It is indeed possible to argue that Vavasour was inspired by Tennyson's 'mad' hero, who, in turn, owes much to the Spasmodics.[35] Vavasour is introduced by Kingsley as being "not man enough," his "ribs growing over his backbone," and suffering from "dyspepsia, brought on by his own effeminacy."[36] Moreover, the terms in which Kingsley analyses the male character of *Maud* in his review fit Vavasour in *Two Years Ago* strikingly well: of Tennyson's character, for example, Kingsley wrote that he "only

---

[33] *TYA* 179–80.
[34] "Tennyson's Maud" *Fraser's Magazine* (Sept 1855) 266.
[35] An alternative candidate for the character would be Richard Monckton Milnes, who featured as Vavasour in Disraeli's *Tancred* (1849).
[36] *TYA* 128.

feed[s] his wrath inwardly" until his "dark undercurrent of suspicion, pride, contempt" of the people around him become "a fixed idea" and results in "the entire withdrawing of a man into self," and moreover that he "has neither outward nor inward strength to fight his calamity" and that his madness becomes "the absolute triumph of self-will and selfishness."[37] On the whole Kingsley made clear that he disliked the "unrest, and unhealth, inability to find a purpose and a work" in Tennyson's poem.[38] Arguably, it was this notion of work and purpose which he found lacking in *Maud* (and perhaps in Tennyson) that stimulated Kingsley to write *Two Years Ago* in the first place. For Kingsley, only active, individual work of a practical and social kind to help one's fellow human beings defined a man. It was the purpose of this novel to show that this must done in a Christian spirit. To demonstrate this he created Tom Thurnall.

Although the model of the muscular Christian in *Two Years Ago*, as Sandars maintained in his review, is represented by the interaction of "a literary man, a modern Hercules, and a country clergyman," the novel's main character Tom Thurnall has come to be seen as the fictional prototype of Muscular Christianity, and critics have tended to fasten on his physical vigour and prowess. This is hardly surprising considering the overstated description Tom Thurnall gives of himself:

> I have some practical reason for wearing as my motto "never say die." I have had the cholera twice, and yellow-jack beside; five several times I have had bullets through me; I have been bayoneted and left for dead; I have been shipwrecked three times—and once, as now, I was the only man who escaped; I have been fatted by savages for baking and eating, and got away.[39]

This portrait informs his character for the rest of the novel and leads to a tendency to rate his muscular aspects over his Christian ones. Admittedly, like Amyas Leigh, Thurnall does the right thing without thinking about it, but is entirely wanting in Christian faith. When the curate Headley is puzzled why Thurnall cares for the lot of the villagers of Aberalva, he receives as an answer that

> I hate to see a woman's gown torn; I hate to see her stockings down at heel; I hate to see anything wasted, something awry, anything going

---

[37] "Tennyson's Maud" *Fraser's Magazine* (Sept 1855) 268–70.
[38] "Tennyson's Maud" *Fraser's Magazine* (Sept 1855) 271.
[39] *TYA* 77.

wrong; I hate to see water-power wasted, manure wasted, land wasted, muscle wasted, pluck wasted, brains wasted; I hate neglect, incapacity, idleness, ignorance, and all the disease and misery which spring out of that.[40]

Although Kingsley liked Thurnall's moral courage, he is, and increasing becomes, a sceptical stoic. As such he is not a complete man. As in *Yeast*, this is supposed to be the main theme in the novel. The gist of the purpose in creating Thurnall is clear. Still, Kingsley only rarely manages to convey his disapproval of Thurnall's one-sided actions and opinions. Only when condemnation is absolutely necessary, Kingsley interrupts the narrative with preachy and inartistic premonitions like: "Take care, Tom Thurnall. After pride comes a fall."[41] When in the end he runs out of luck and ends up in a Russian prison—events which are only vaguely referred to—he is converted to Christianity. Subdued, he returns to England and marries Grace. This conclusion is one of the worst parts of the novel. Although Thurnall comes to appreciate Headley's humane Christian ethos when they fight the cholera together, his conversion is all too sudden and carries little conviction with the reader. In the end, the spiritual is barely visible in the solid physicality of Thurnall's heroic feats, and it is not surprising that, in the public opinion, muscular Christianity received through him a more muscular than Christian imprint.

That Kingsley had difficulty in creating a more profound personality in Thurnall is also brought out by an obscure comment in a letter dated 19 March 1857. Kingsley explained that

I fear you take Tom Thurnall for a better man than he was, and must beg you not to pare my man to suit your own favourable conception; but consider that *that* is the sort of man I want to draw, and you must take him as you find him. My experience is, that men of his character (like all strong men till God's grace takes full possession of them) are weak upon one point—every thing can they stand but that; and the more sudden and violent is the temptation when it comes. I have indicated as delicately as I could the world-wide fact, which all know and all ignore; had I not done so, Thurnall would have been a mere chimera fit only for a young lady's novel.[42]

---

[40] *TYA* 223.
[41] *TYA* 445.
[42] CK to JB, 19/3/1857, *LML* ii.19.

Whatever it was that Kingsley exactly had in mind here, it is hardly brought out by the novel. But the failure to delineate Thurnall's conversion in a more convincing way is easily forgotten in the interest for another theme for which Kingsley needed Thurnall: sanitary reform.

When Tom Thurnall settles in Aberalva to find out who had taken his belt, he becomes an instrument in Kingsley's propaganda for sanitary reform. During the summer Thurnall averts that cholera cannot be far off. He warns the villagers of the impending danger, but is met by "that terrible front of stupidity."[43] He prevails over the curate, who, though he foresees resistance to talking about secular subjects from the pulpit, preaches "a noble sermon." But he is set upon by the Brianite Methodist preacher of the place, "a fanatic whose game it was—as it is that of too many—to snub sanitary reform, and hinder the spread of plain scientific truth, for the sake of pushing their own nostrum for all human ills."[44] As slowly but inevitably the disease advances—the Nuisances Removal Act is shown to be inadequate because there are no measures to implement it— Kingsley turns his novel into an urgent pamphlet for sanitary reform and shows in a chapter entitled "Baalzebub's Banquet" the terrible results of withstanding preventive action. With a small group of friends Thurnall works without rest, and without fear for his own life, until the epidemic passes, but a great number of men, women and children die all the same. What Kingsley wants to show is that such deaths are caused by the religious blindness which passively accepts epidemics as God's visitation for sin. He underscores this through a piece of poetic justice in which the Methodist preacher is taken ill with cholera and dies soon after having imbued his congregation with notions of sin, while Thurnall and his friends all survive the epidemic. Notwithstanding the overtly didactic purpose, the urgency with which Kingsley writes is convincing and this part of the novel makes good reading.

For a further theme that Kingsley wanted to discuss he needed to introduce a subplot. *Uncle Tom's Cabin* (1852) was enjoying tremendous success when its author Harriet Beecher Stowe came on her second visit to England in 1856. She stayed at the Eversley Rectory for three days, and Kingsley, who had admitted once to Elizabeth

---

[43] *TYA* 213.
[44] *TYA* 218.

Gaskell that *Uncle Tom's Cabin* was "too painfully good,"[45] discussed slavery with her until she felt quite tired. Kingsley also met the American journalist W.H. Hurlbert the same autumn, and got much political information about the abolitionist case. Impressed with what Beecher Stowe and Hurlbert had told him, Kingsley decided to make place in *Two Years Ago* for the anti-slavery movement and, as he had by now a wide American readership, he hoped that his novel would be influential in solving the problem. Thus, the novel starts with Claude Mellot and the American Stangrave, a rich sleeping partner in a New York firm and Frémonter loosely modelled on Hurlbert, who holds that, to avoid disruption of the Union, moderation in anti-slavery measures is needed. When Claude urges that it is a Christian's duty to "free those slaves at once and utterly,"[46] Stangrave replies that the cruelty of slaveholders fills his "heart with fire" but that conscience has also taught him "to feel for the Southerner as a brother."[47] To strengthen the anti-slavery debate in his novel Kingsley introduces Marie Cordifiamma, a beautiful American actress who stays with the Mellots. When Stangrave meets her they fall in love, but Marie resists him. She has a secret: "in her veins were some drops, at least, of the blood of slaves. When one moment "her eyelid slope[d] more and more, her nostril shorten[ed] and curl[ed], her lips enlarge[d], her mouth itself protrude[d],"[48] Stangrave divines the truth and "shuddered as saw [it],"[49] and suddenly has important business to do on the continent. With Marie's following confession the slavery theme becomes more pungent in Kingsley's novel: "I was born a slave. My father was a white gentleman of good family: my mother was a quadroon; and therefore I am a slave; a negress, a runaway slave, [. . .] who if I returned to America, should be seized, and chained, and scourged, and sold."[50] But it is ultimately Stangrave's love for Marie that sets him working in the anti-slavery cause. After much solitary contemplation in Germany, and a violent quarrel with Thurnall, he comes to the conclusion that "Life is meant for work, and not for ease; to labour in danger and in dread, to do a little good ere the night comes, when no man can work."[51] He realizes

---

[45] CK to Elizabeth Gaskell, 25/7/1853, *LML* i.370.
[46] *TYA* ii.
[47] *TYA* iii.
[48] *TYA* 138.
[49] *TYA* 138.
[50] *TYA* 196.
[51] *TYA* 402.

Marie "had awakened in him [. . .] noble desires to be useful," "that abolition was the Sangreal in the quest of which he was to go forth."[52] Kingsley's ethics of work, duty and love seem to point to an easy solution. His position, however, on racial otherness, as it was in *Westward Ho!*, remains ambiguous when he makes Marie so light-skinned that she passed easily for a south European. Kingsley unconsciously recoiled from stronger Negro features, as he reveals for a moment in the description of the face of Marie's grandmother which was "withered as the wrinkled ape."[53]

In *Yeast* Kingsley had described a tableau called "The Triumph of Woman." It stood as an emblem for the saving power that Kingsley felt women have over men. Without female guidance man is lost in purpose. This is the master theme of *Two Years Ago*. Thurnall's conversion through Grace's unwavering example, is duplicated in Headley's love for Valentia, which makes him realize that his passive Puseyite notions were based on mere selfishness. "I tried to be good, not knowing what good meant," he explains to her, "I tried to be good, because I thought it would pay me in the world to come."[54] On the other hand, Elsley's withering love for his wife and consequent growing self-centeredness lead to destruction, and Major Campbell, a good Christian, dies on the Crimea as his purpose in life remains sterile because of unfulfilled love. The archetype of this perception of love was, of course, Kingsley's own love for Fanny, which, he repeatedly pointed out, gave his life purpose and saved him from a life of errant atheism.

III

The winter of 1856–57 was the first in years the family spent at Eversley. Most of the time Kingsley worked quietly in his parish. His novels and sermons, however, had brought him so much fame that Eversley was hardly the secluded and unfrequented place it had long been. People started to seek Kingsley out either by letter or by coming in person to his Sunday services. Although he gladly received visitors at the rectory, he felt dismayed and annoyed by all the strangers flocking to his church, especially as many tried to have a

---

[52] *TYA* 139.
[53] *TYA* 138.
[54] *TYA* 347.

word with him after the service. He saw it as a breach of privacy. "I cannot bear having my place turned into a fair on Sundays, and all this talking after church," he commented. A little back gate leading into his garden was therefore made so that he could escape unobserved via the vestry door after service.

In January Kingsley went in therapy with Dr James Hunt for his stammering. Hunt's breathing techniques and emphasis on physical exercise seemed to have good results with his patient. Although Mrs Kingsley remained reticent in her biography about her husband's stammer, it was something which pained Kingsley all through his life. In a revealing article published in 1859, Kingsley admitted that "a stammerer's life is (unless he be a very clod) a life of misery."[55] As a boy he suffered "the mockery of his wanton schoolfellows,"[56] while as an adult he was at times still afraid of meeting new people. The last was the case with John Bullar, a London lawyer much interested in sanitary reform, and to whom he admitted "that the fearful curse of stammering, now, thank God, all but gone, which has been my misery from childhood, has always made me avoid an introduction to men, to whom [. . .] I should inevitably stammer."[57] Bullar, who fully sympathized with Kingsley's plight, tried to discuss it with him. Kingsley was won over and gave him the full story of his defect which

> came from an under jaw contracted by calomel, and nerves ruined by croup and brain fever in childhood. That prevented my opening my mouth, that gave me a wrong use of the diaphragm muscles, till I got to speak inspiring, and never to fully inflate my lungs; and that brought on the last and worst (yet most easily cured) spasm of the tongue. All the while, I could speak, not only plain but stentorially, while boxing, rowing, hunting, skating, and doing any-thing which compelled deep inspirations.[58]

Kingsley's confidence in Hunt's theory of breathing was such that in August he even decided to follow the doctor to Swanage. From "this delicious place, a ring ve[r]y like Babbacombe, with noble chalk cliffs," he wrote full of hope to Fanny: "if I cd. be with this man for 3 weeks right on end, I should never stammer again, over &

---

[55] "The Irrationale of Speech" *Fraser's Magazine* (July 1859) 6.
[56] "The Irrationale of Speech" *Fraser's Magazine* (July 1859) 6.
[57] CK to JB, 23/1/1857, *LML* ii.17.
[58] CK to JB, 27/1/1857, *LML* ii.18.

above the *elocution* w. I shd. learn [. . .] I cannot tell you how hopeful I am about myself & the stammering, & how desirous to perfect a cure once & for all."[59] Of course, Hunt's therapy was just to Kingsley's heart. He made this clear in his 1859 review of the doctor's *Manual of the Philosophy of Voice and Speech*:

> But, over and above what Mr. Hunt or any other man can teach: stammerers, and those who have been stammerers need above all men to keep up that *mentem sanam in corpore sano*, which is now-a-days called, somewhat offensively, muscular Christianity—a term worthy of a puling and enervated generation of thinkers, who prove their own unhealthiness by their contemptuous surprise at any praise of that health which ought to be the normal condition of the whole human race.

Of all men especially a stammerer "must make a man of himself," he reiterated. Such masculinity was defined as follows:

> Let him, if he can, ride, and ride hard [. . .] Let him play rackets, and fives, row, and box [. . .]; Above all, let him box; And let him, now in these very days, join a rifle-club, and learn in it to carry himself with the erect and noble port which is all but peculiar to the soldier, but ought to be the common habit of every man; let him learn to march; and more, to trot under arms without losing breath; and by such means make himself an active, healthy, and valiant man.[60]

Although Kingsley's stammer never fully disappeared, his consultations with Hunt seemed to have given him more control over his speech than before. As a result the energetic "raciness" that many had remarked upon as characteristic of, and charming in, his speech disappeared and was substituted by a rather monotonous and slow mode of recitation. As he himself admitted to a lady who consulted him upon stammering in 1858: "[I] went down & staid in his [Hunt's] house at Swanage for 12 dys—& came away cured. I don't say I have not hesitated since [. . .] But I can always & instantly stop it."[61]

While Kingsley was staying at Swanage, he was shown "some letters from an Indian Colonel" which disturbed him mightily. By the late 1850s British colonization was starting to have far-reaching consequences on the structure of Indian society and its traditions. Christian missionaries, the introduction of British systems of education, and the replacement of the old Indian aristocracy by British officials

---

[59] CK to FK, undated, BL-62554 f.116v–117r.
[60] "The Irrationale of Speech" *Fraser's Magazine* (July 1859) 11.
[61] CK to unidentified correspondent, 10/11/1858, BL-41298 f.94v–95r.

of the East India Company caused increasing friction between colonizers and colonized. When a new rifle was introduced in the Bengal army with cartridges that were greased with pig's and cow's lard of which the ends had to be bitten off before loading, both Hindu and Muslim Indian troopers saw this as an outrageous insult to their religion. It was in a sense the final straw, and when a group of sepoy soldiers at Meerut were punished and imprisoned for refusing to use the cartridges, their comrades revolted and shot many of their British officers. They marched on Delhi, which they captured without much resistance. The mutiny then spread to northern India, until peace was officially re-enforced in July 1858.

Although the sepoys rose against an arrogant and insensitive attitude to their traditions, the brutality with which they killed British officers and massacred their wives and children infuriated English public opinion at home, and many justified the scale of the British bloodshed of retributory killings. Kingsley reacted with the mainstream opinion. His wife starts her description of 1857 with the "terrible trouble" that came over him at the awful news of the Indian Mutiny, but, understandably, gives only the more human side of his reaction to it when she excerpts part of a letter to F.D. Maurice:

> I can think of nothing but these Indian massacres. The moral problems they involve make me half wild. Night and day the heaven seems black to me, though I never was so prosperous and blest in my life as I am now.
>
> I can hardly bear to look at a woman or child—even at my own beloved ones sometimes. It raises such horrible images, from which I can't escape. What does it all mean? Christ is King, nevertheless. I tell my people so. I should do—I dare not think what—if I did not believe so. But I want sorely some one to tell me that he believes it too. Do write to me and give me a clue out of this valley of the shadow of death.[62]

Another side of his reaction is revealed in his letter to Fanny from Swanage. The accounts he had heard of the mutiny were "too dreadful in their details," he wrote, and to make clear on whose side the atrocity lay, he added "I do trust that neither Brahmin or Mussulman Sepoy will be left alive in 3 months. Mercy is injustice, as well as folly."[63] Kingsley's reaction to the Sepoy Mutiny duplicated his attitude

---

[62] CK to FDM, 3/9/1857, *LML* ii.34.
[63] CK to FK, undated, BL-62554 f.120.

to the Canaanite question, his acceptance of Brooke's violence in Sarawak, and his representation of the 1579 wholesale extermination of the rebellious Irish army in *Westward Ho!*. He instinctively justified brutal suppression of insurgents where (English) civilization was threatened, and became blind to the horrors of retaliation. Even if some critics have identified such instinctive reactions with Kingsley's ideal of Christian manliness, they were caused in part by the fear that resulted from the imminent threat they posed to such ideals. This innate fear he articulated in a letter to Bullar, who could not share Kingsley's approval of bloody vengeance: "Show me what security I have that my wife, my children, should not suffer, from some unexpected outbreak of devils, what other wives and children have suffered, and then I shall sleep quiet, without longing that they were safe out of a world where such things are possible."[64] And in a sermon on the Creed which he preached to his parish, he further explained where his problems lay in the question: "For men, and men's sufferings, that is a slight matter comparatively [...] But the poor women and children!"[65] To attenuate her husband's extreme position on repressing "barbarous" peoples, Mrs Kingsley inserted this justification in a late 1901 edition of her biography.

But notwithstanding the "terrible trouble" and the sense of anxiety for the future that the Indian Mutiny caused in Kingsley's mind throughout the summer of 1857, on his birthday he wrote a buoyant letter to Hughes: "Eight & thirty years old am I this day [...] Well, Tommy, God has been ve[r]y very good to me: & I cant help feeling a hope that I may fight a good fight yet before I die, & get something done."[66] Although Kingsley does not specify it, it is likely that part of the fight included new literary work which was stimulated by Hughes's first novel. "Now isn't it a comfort to your old bones to have written such a book," he wrote to Hughes, "and a comfort to see that fellows are in a humour to take it in?"

Soon after the publication of *Two Years Ago* Hughes had put a manuscript novel in his friend's hand. Kingsley was impressed and recommended it warmly to Daniel Macmillan: "I have laughed and cried over the book to my heart's content [...] I should have been

[64] CK to JB, undated, *LML* ii.35.
[65] *LMLM*.ii.63.
[66] CK to TH, 12/6/1857, BL-41298 f.86r.

proud to have written that book, word for word as it stands."[67] But Macmillan did not need any convincing, and Hughes's novel *Tom Brown's Schooldays* became an instant success when it appeared in the last week of April. In a long letter to Hughes, Kingsley explained that *Tom Brown* and its positive reception had given him back some confidence in the English middle-class ethos. *Tom Brown's Schooldays*, a book which celebrates Thomas Arnold's Rugby as a miniature world preparing middle class boys (the "living embodiment of the nation") for the responsibility of ruling England by instilling a standard of manliness which is based on hard work and a team spirit, was to Kingsley the true expression of "Young England." "The day of 'Pietism' is gone, and 'Tom Brown' is a heavy stone in its grave," he explained, "I have good hopes, and better of our class, than of the class below. They are effeminate, and that makes them sensual. Pietists of all ages [. . .] never made a greater mistake (and they have made many), than in fancying that by keeping down manly θμυός, which Plato saith is the root of all virtue, they could keep down sensuality."

When Kingsley wrote about how much he appreciated the "manly thumos" in his friend's novel, he could not dream that his and Hughes's names would henceforth be associated with a rising cult of masculinity. In the history of literature *Tom Brown's Schooldays* is linked to *Two Years Ago* as the two most influential literary expressions of Muscular Christianity. Although the label had been but recently coined by Thomas Collett Sandars to describe the characters in *Two Years Ago*, the term could be, and soon was, applied to everything Kingsley had written since *The Saint's Tragedy*. The public and the critics found the term "Muscular Christianity" a very apt epithet and it quickly caught on. It came to embrace much more than Kingsley was, or would be, willing to accept as the precepts of a true Christian's life. In an assessment of Hughes's novel in the *Edinburgh Review*, Fitzjames Stephen saw *Tom Brown's Schooldays* as representative of "a school of feeling rather than thought" which he saw as becoming very influential in England. Stephen described it as upholding a "deep sense of the sacredness of all the ordinary relations and all the common duties of life" and as contending "the great importance and value of animal spirits, physical strength, and a hearty enjoyment of all the pursuits and accomplishments which are connected

---

[67] CK to Macmillan, February 1857, Mack and Armytage 89.

with them."[68] "It is a school," he writes, "of which Mr. Kingsley is the ablest doctor; and its doctrine has been described fairly and cleverly as 'muscular Christianity'."[69] And, concluding his review of *Tom Brown's Schooldays*, Stephen congratulated Kingsley "on a disciple who reproduces so vigorously many of his own great merits."[70]

Although Kingsley and Hughes had much in common in their Christian outlook, as Kingsley's comments on *Tom Brown's Schooldays* show, with the emphasis on team sports and "healthy" competition in Hughes's novel, their ideal of Christianity assumed a meaning that would slowly, but steadily, erode the ideal of its Christian basis and put an increasing emphasis on mere physical health, prowess and achievement. Evangelical boys' movements that have been associated with Muscular Christianity, such as the Boy's Brigades and the Young Men's Christian Associations, movements which wanted to show that Christianity was not an effeminate pietistic matter, played a major role in this process. For example, the YMCA, founded in London in 1844, was originally an evangelical movement to combat drunkenness and gambling amongst young workers newly arrived in the industrial cities from the country. It wanted to provide for their spiritual needs by organizing street Bible-readings and prayer-meetings, but during the second half of the nineteenth century it increasingly turned to mere physical exercise as the antidote to male idleness. Similarly, in their ideal of Christian manliness, the working-class members of the Boy's Brigades received drill and discipline modelled on the army, and were introduced to team sports such as league football. Although in their Christian outlook the youth movements reflected a view that religion can be a robust and manly business Kingsleyan style, it was sports that became the means par excellence for building (the British or the American) character. Of course, Kingsley and Hughes were not personally involved in the setting up of these influential youth-organisations. They shared the underlying ideal of making young men better citizens by giving them a practical religion, but they would never have conceded to the late nineteenth- and early twentieth-century cult of sport which arose from it.

As the term Muscular Christianity rapidly gained popularity and as the cult of the healthy body with which it became identified

---

[68] [Stephen] 190.
[69] [Stephen] 190.
[70] [Stephen] 193.

spread, Kingsley felt it was time to speak out on the subject, especially, since with the mention of Muscular Christianity, "either Tom Hughes or I rise to most folks minds." His refusal to endorse the term was categorical: "I consider the term as silly and offensive," he wrote in 1860 in a letter to the editor of *Fraser's Magazine* in which he denied that he had ever thought, or spread the belief, that the healthy and strong make the best Christians. If he could discover who propagated that he believed such a notion, he would "bestir" himself to give them "such a dressing in *Fraser* as would show them that my tongue was still sharp enough."[71] Kingsley had good reason to feel uncomfortable about being called the champion of Muscular Christianity.[72] By the time he spoke out, he had such a dubious disciple as George Alfred Lawrence. In 1858, Lawrence, who made no secret of his admiration of Kingsley's muscular tales of adventure, had published his ideal of masculinity in his novel *Guy Livingstone*. To Kingsley it must have seemed mere brutal self-indulgence. Lawrence's novel of action about the exploits of the so-called 'manliness' of a decadent duelling aristocrat in a masculine world, is a forerunner of the all-masculine worlds in the late-Victorian novels by George Alfred Henty and John Buchan, novels which came to be associated with Muscular Christianity but in which the spiritual constituent is minimized to make place for a practical patriotism. Kingsley objected to the absence of a Christian purpose, but, unconsciously, he might also have felt writers like Lawrence failed to appreciate that his ideal of manliness included traits of the feminine, the feeling of tenderness and the display of emotion not being the least of these. Seeing what Muscular Christianity had come to stand for in the hands of writers like Lawrence, it was not surprising he felt uneasy about it and rejected it so fiercely in his letter published in *Fraser's Magazine*. But, notwithstanding his criticism of Muscular Christianity, over the years the appellation was to cling to Kingsley and in 1865 he found it wiser to discuss the term publicly in front of the students of the University of Cambridge, and argued that its only meaning "may be simply a healthful and manly Christianity; one which does not exalt

---

[71] *New York Times*, 25/2/1877, 4d; reprinted from *Fraser's Magazine*.

[72] Hughes felt equally uncomfortable about Muscular Christianity, and published in 1879 *The Manliness of Christ* in which he emphasized the importance of thoughtfulness for others and that patience, rather than action, was the truly Christian virtue that leads to manliness.

the feminine virtues to the exclusion of the masculine." One wishes
for clarity's sake that Kingsley had added that the contrary also held
true for him.

If, on the one hand, Kingsley's "healthy animalism" led to popular
interpretations of his theology in the terms of a muscular Christianity
as outlined above, theologians construed it as proof of his unorthodox
views about the Holy Spirit. In April 1857 the *London Quarterly Review*
featured a long article on Kingsley's writings. This was the most
complete treatment of his work that had appeared so far, and the
only review that linked his fiction to his sermons and other works
of non-fiction. The unsigned article was written by James Harrison
Rigg, a Wesleyan minister and divine who had written ably in defence
of the polity of Methodism during the disruptive years 1849–1852
that led to the Wesleyan split. In his article Rigg righted the reputation
of the evangelicals whom Kingsley had accused of a theology of
selfishness, and concentrated on the implications of the "Mauricean
heresy" in Kingsley's writings which tended to "confound the human
and the Divine personality."[73] Rigg had already criticized the theology
of Coleridge, Jowett, Hare, and Maurice in 1856, but he now turned
with relief to one who "speaks out much more plainly and intelligibly
than his mysterious fellow-labourer [Maurice] has generally thought
proper to do"[74] and who lay bare the pantheistic implications and
contradictions in the theology of "his more cautious and cloudy
friend:"[75] "It is well to have a plain-speaking colleague like Mr.
Kingsley, to tell what a misty writer like Mr. Maurice does not choose
clearly to speak out.[76]"

Rigg maintained that Kingsley's theology secularized the kingdom
of Christ by according with the half-paganized Christian Neo-Platonist
philosophers who, in the words of Coleridge, "paganized Christianity
to christen paganism."[77] To him it seemed that Kingsley argued that

> the root from which Christianity is the legitimate and orderly devel-
> opment, 'the bright, consummate flower,' was planted before the Fall
> or the Creation, the apostasy of man being but a subordinate parenthesis
> in the history, progress, and destinies of the race. Thus Christianity is

---

[73] [Rigg] (1857) 33.
[74] Rigg (1856) 7.
[75] [Rigg] (1857) 21.
[76] [Rigg] (1857) 45.
[77] [Rigg] (1857) 25.

made to be, only in a subordinate and accommodated sense, a means and power of redemption. The reconciliation of *man* to God was never needed, seeing that the Eternal Word, ever and essentially one with the Father, has been from eternity and is essentially the Root and Archetype of humanity. As the Word or Son is by necessity of nature one with the Father, so, it is the doctrine of Mr. Kingsley, man is always one with the Son.[78]

Thus, although Kingsley professed to criticise material pantheism, Rigg concluded, "we fear that, logically, the distinction between Mr. Kingsley and a [spiritual] pantheist is not very great."[79] It is arguably Rigg's equation of Platonism with pantheism which is logically questionable, but his reaction to Kingsley's liberal theology indicates how easily it was misconstrued by more orthodox (evangelical) thinkers to whom his "animalism" seemed in contradiction with notions of spirituality.

Rigg's review is a strange mixture of a critique of Kingsley's theology and an unhidden admiration for the sincerity of his expression: "All his works, noble though they be," he concludes, "are poisoned; and this poison will, ere long, hasten their passage into oblivion."[80] As Kingsley had made it "a rule to answer no public attacks," he personally, and rather patronizingly, wrote to Rigg that "I cannot believe that you have studied the Neo-Platonists at first hand [. . .] I fear that you have got your notions on the point at second-hand [. . .] Be warned in time, and study these subjects, whatever be your conclusions, more rigidly and scientifically, that you may be no longer misled yourself or mislead others by catchwords and epithets." And when Rigg communicated to Kingsley that he intended to use his review for a book he was writing, the latter warned him "that if you publish anything which accuses Hare, Maurice, or me of rationalism, you will be venting a falsehood and a slander." At the same time Kingsley assured Rigg that he would remain silent on any charges he would make against his person. "My business is attack, and not defence," Kingsley concluded.[81] This exchange of letters, Mrs Kingsley remarks, led to a "personal acquaintance and warm friendship" and in later editions of her biography she thought it more befitting such a friendship to suppress the initial "angry correspondence" on her husband's part.

---

[78] [Rigg] (1857) 35.
[79] [Rigg] (1857) 33.
[80] [Rigg] (1857) 49.
[81] CK to James H. Rigg, 30/5/1857, *LML* ii.22–3.

CHAPTER SEVENTEEN

A MINUTE PHILOSOPHER (1858)

In 1858 Parker finally ventured to bring out the volume of poems that Kingsley had wanted to publish ever since 1852. One of Parker's objections six years before had been a lack of material to fill a volume. But, although some recent work was now added, the bulk of the poems still consisted of "Santa Maura", "Andromeda" and other poems written at least half a decade before. Parker's initial unwillingness was, of course, overcome now that Kingsley had become an established author. Moreover, the volume of poetry brought out by Ticknor and Fields in America in 1856 had proved a moderate success. Although the reviews that appeared were only partially positive, the publication of a volume of poetry by Parker proved important. Beside that of novelist, Kingsley henceforth also acquired a reputation as poet, and some of his poems would be anthologized for over a hundred years after his death.

But while Kingsley's fame as an author had been consolidated by 1858, his brother's was about to start. After the summer holiday in Germany in 1851, Henry Kingsley returned to Worcester College, Oxford, but he continued wasting his time with athletics, a bit of gambling, and with the Fez Club. In 1853 he suddenly left Oxford to seek his fortune as a gold-digger in Australia, a move which has been seen as testimony of his being sent down from university when his strain of homosexuality had become apparent to the authorities. There is, however, no further evidence of this, and, although his biographer S.M. Ellis does not deny Henry's latent homosexuality, he points out that Henry had come to the end of the usual three years of residence and that his father might well have refused to pay any longer for his idleness. Thus, in 1853 he said a difficult farewell to Chelsea Rectory. "One more look around the room. The last for ever," he wrote almost ten years later, "I looked once into a room which had been my home ever since I was six years old [. . .] knowing that I should never see it again."[1] In Australia, Henry was down on

---

[1] From *Ravenshoe*, quoted in Ellis, 39–40.

his luck and had a rough time. By 1858 he had been reduced to a "sun-downer," a vagabond riding the country who arrives at farms in the evening, offering a day of work in exchange for supper and a bed for the night. Before he decided he had better return to England, and while staying at sheep farms in the neighbourhood of Langa-willi and Ballarat, he started writing a novel of Australian life.

The story goes that he returned to London but had no courage to ring the bell at the Chelsea Rectory, fearing that during the years of absence his parents might have died. When he finally brought himself to ring, he was told that his father had left London due to ill health and had moved with his family to a cottage in Eversley. Henry immediately repaired to his brother's parish, where, according to his biographer, he was welcomed with great joy by his parents and brother. There was news to be exchanged, and Charles was very interested in the novel his brother had started. It was decided that Henry too would live in Eversley, and they found him a small cottage next to his parents', where he could work at ease on the manuscript he had brought back from Australia. With Charles's help Henry's first novel, *The Recollections of Geoffry Hamlyn*, was published by Macmillan in 1859 and it was the beginning of a successful literary career. The two brothers were close again in interests and brotherly affection. In his fiction Henry was influenced by the muscular Christianity of Charles's last two novels, and although his first novel was duly dedicated to his parents, his second, and most famous, *Ravenshoe*, which earned him unconditional critical acclaim, was dedicated to his brother, "in token of a love which only grows stronger as we both get older." Curiously, Mrs Kingsley remains silent about all this, and never mentions her brother-in-law's residence at Eversley or his literary success.

In spring Kingsley's fourth child was born. "It seems too good to be true," he had exclaimed the previous autumn when Fanny told him she was pregnant once more, "surely God is Love, & gives with one hand, if he chastises with the other!"[2] The child was called Grenville Arthur after his ancestor Richard Grenville and Arthur Penrhyn Stanley, Dean of Westminster. Fanny was now forty-four, and Grenville was to be their last child.

Kingsley spent the winter of 1858 at Eversley. In a letter to John Bullar he had spelled out what Ludlow had feared for some time,

---

[2] Martin (1959) 207.

namely that with the failure of Christian Socialism as a movement
he had no zest to be politically active anymore. "Politics and political economy may go their way from me," he explained, especially
as the latter with its *laissez-faire* seemed to establish selfishness and
chance, real as they might be, as the only existing laws. But to allow
them to become the "root laws" of human society, and the foundation
for empire—and, "tired of the helplessness of *laissez-faire*, educated
men are revolting fast to Imperialism"—means fostering "a state of
society more rotten, because more physically cunning and wealthy,
than that of old Rome." Such a state of England Kingsley never
hoped to witness, and never would, as "I shall be either at rest in
the churchyard, or founding for myself a family of free landowners
in the valley of Ottawa."[3] Thoughts of emigration occasionally crossed
Kingsley's mind during the 1860s and early 1870s, revealing his frustration with the prominence given to economics in English religious
and political thought, with what Steven Schroeder in his study of
F.D. Maurice has recognized as the sidetracking of an important
philosophical and theological discussion of *value* ever since the middle
of the nineteenth century when descriptive economics started to define
value as the "necessary outcome of natural processes."[4] "The being
who merely obeys the laws of nature," Kingsley argued, "is *ipso facto*
a brute beast. The privilege of a man is to counteract (not break)
one law of nature by another. In the exercise of that power stands
all art, invention, polity, progress."[5]

Counteracting nature, by studying it, was to be Kingsley's task
from now on, and in this alone lay his future social work. "I see
one work to be done ere I die, in which [. . .] nature must be coun-
teracted, lest she prove a curse and a destroyer, not a blessing and
a mother; and that is, Sanitary Reform."[6] Of course, ever since his
acquaintance with his brother-in-law Osborne, and through the
Christian Socialist years, Kingsley had been working on sanitary
questions. The change from politics to sanitary reform was, starting
with Hughes, seen as a falling off in Kingsley's involvement in the
condition-of-England question, but it is often forgotten, however, how
conscious this shift was on Kingsley's part. He had come to conclude
that the freedom God had given to man consisted mainly in man's

---

[3] CK to JB, 26/11/1857, *LML* ii.37.
[4] Steven Schroeder, *The Metaphysics of Cooperation* (Amsterdam: Rodopi, 1999) xiii.
[5] CK to JB, December 1857, *LML* ii.38.
[6] CK to JB, December 1857, *LML* ii.38.

power to counteract fixed laws by using other fixed laws, and because man had this power to counteract, the study of nature was of central importance. Such an approach to life and society was probably represented best, but not exclusively, in the field of medicine, where disease caused by the existence of one law is cured by the (counter-) application of another. Hence Kingsley's choice of making Tom Thurnall in *Two Years Ago* a doctor.

After the success of *Two Years Ago*, Parker asked Kingsley for an article for *Fraser's Magazine* on sanitary reform, which is some measure of how popular he had made it in his novel. Kingsley accepted, and in January "A Mad World, My Masters" appeared. It was signed: "by a Sanitary Reformer." The article has a startling opening, in which Kingsley lashes out at those who would readily condemn the blood-shed and loss of Indian life in the British suppression of the Sepoy Mutiny, but who keep silent when English lives at home are imperilled:

> Those who demand mercy for the Sepoy, and immunity for the Coolie women of Delhi, unsexed by their own brutal and shameless cruelty, would, one fancies, demand mercy also for the British workman, and immunity for his wife and family. One is therefore some-what startled at finding that the British nation reserves to itself, though it forbids to its armies, the right of putting to death unarmed and unoffending men, women, and children.[7]

However outrageous the comparison might be, it was effective in drawing the attention of British readers to the subject of cleanliness.

"A Mad World, My Masters" is a brilliant tirade, vented in ener-getic language, but completely free of religious cant. In it Kingsley enumerates all the obstacles to sanitary reform. First, he remarks with biting sarcasm on the trust that people had far too long placed in the clergy for sanitary reform, as if to "preachers the mortal lives of men would be inexpressibly precious; that any science which held out a prospect of retarding death in the case of 'lost millions' would be hailed as a heavenly boon, and would be carried out with the fervour of men who felt that for the soul's sake no exertion was too great in behalf of the body."[8] Not even the "religious public," with its principle of doing good works ("spiritual capital, to be paid with interest at the last day"),[9] would exert itself in this direction, as "sanitary

---

[7] "A Mad World, My Masters" *SSE* 271–2.
[8] "A Mad World, My Masters" *SSE* 274.
[9] "A Mad World, My Masters" *SSE* 286.

reform makes no proselytes. It cannot be used as a religious engine."[10] To "religionists" sanitary reform had, moreover, suffered a fate similar to that of the science of geology. "Like geology, it interferes with that Deus e machinâ theory of human affairs which has been in all ages the stronghold of priestcraft. That the Deity is normally absent, and not present; that He works on the world by interference, and not by continuous laws."[11] Kingsley stressed that seeing epidemics as visitations of the deity upon sinners was detrimental to the cause of sanitary reform. Political economists, on the other hand, with their "bugbear" theory of overpopulation, had added other insurmountable obstacles to the progress of sanitary reform. They "cannot be expected to lend their aid in increasing the population by saving the lives of two-thirds of the children who now die prematurely in our great cities; and so still further overcrowding this unhappy land with those helpless and expensive sources of national poverty."[12] Finally, and, ironically, not unlike Matthew Arnold's famous criticism of the philistines of English society in *Culture and Anarchy* (1869), Kingsley lamented the cultural and scientific ignorance of the electorate of the 1850s and the consequent "deterioration of our House of Commons towards such a level of mediocrity as shall satisfy the ignorance of the practically electing majority, namely, the tail of the middle class."[13]

It is interesting that Kingsley ostentatiously abandoned the cause of association because he thought it had failed, and that at the same time he decided to exert himself in the cause of sanitary reform while admitting that whereas that too had "been before the world for more than twenty years, nobody believes in it enough to act upon it."[14] What "A Mad World, My Masters" makes clear is that underlying the shift of attention in Kingsley's social thinking lay an increasing distrust of democracy. In discussing the failure of sanitary reform so far, he scornfully concluded that democracy was to blame for the dismal hygienic housing conditions of the poor: "The immense majority of the British nation will neither cleanse themselves nor let others cleanse them: and are we not governed by majorities? Are not majorities, confessedly, always in the right, even when smallest,

---

[10] "A Mad World, My Masters" *SSE* 288.
[11] "A Mad World, My Masters" *SSE* 276.
[12] "A Mad World, My Masters" *SSE* 277–8.
[13] "A Mad World, My Masters" *SSE* 296.
[14] "A Mad World, My Masters" *SSE* 272.

and a show of hands a surer test of truth than any amount of wisdom, learning, or virtue?"[15]

Kingsley's article is ultimately a powerful plea for man's right to enjoy clean "water, air, light,"[16] but his jingoistic notions about everything English that transpires from the opening of the article and his strong dislike of democracy contrast with the magnificently humane stamp of his attack on a society which remained idle in its moral duty to do something to alleviate the suffering of so many. Such contrasts help us to appreciate Ludlow's frustrated feelings about his friend's reasoning, feelings which increasingly veered from great admiration to utter bewilderment.

Kingsley's campaign for sanitary reform was not merely theoretical activity. When later in 1858 a new fatal disease, diphtheria, appeared in Eversley and made many victims amongst the children of his parish, he studied the disease and "took counsel with medical men" as to what preventive measures could be taken. "Some might have smiled," Mrs Kingsley writes, "at seeing him, going in and out of the cottages with great bottles of gargle under his arm, and teaching the people [. . .] to gargle their throats [. . .] but to him it was grim earnest."[17]

As there was no money for a curate, during the spring all the parochial and sanitary work fell to Kingsley's hands. With an enlarged family too, he had hardly any time to rove beyond the Eversley neighbourhood. But he seemed content with his homely existence. In his attitude to church matters, however, a certain amount of fatigue with controversy transpires. "You dislike the tone and officiality of the clergy now. When you have been eighteen years in orders you will detest it," he wrote to George Boyle, a fellow clergyman who came to consult him in 1858 about the perplexity he felt about the work of the ministry. And rather low-key, Kingsley added that "it is a comfort often to feel there is one little spot, the parish, to which thoughts and prayers are for ever turning."[18]

Other people beside Ludlow and Hughes must have remarked on their friend's retiring into the every-day routine of a country parish, and Kingsley, as if to justify his new choice of life, felt compelled

---

[15] "A Mad World, My Masters" *SSE* 273.
[16] "A Mad World, My Masters" *SSE* 299.
[17] *LML* ii.47.
[18] George Boyle to FK, 20/11/1875, *LML* ii.50.

to describe the richness of it in an article called "My Winter Garden." The secret lies, Kingsley writes, in the fact that he is "a minute philosopher [. . .] content with small pleasures,"[19] that he had discovered long ago that "my lot was to stay at home and earn my bread in a very quiet way."[20] It is true, he admits, that "this little patch of moor [. . .] looked at moments rather like a prison" and that he would often sigh that he could wing away to adventure as an eagle. But those urges had passed with time and "when one finds one's self on the wrong side of forty, and the first grey hairs begin to show on the temples, and one can no longer jump as high as one's third button—scarcely, alas! to any button at all; and what with innumerable sprains, bruises, soakings, and chillings, one's lower limbs feel in a cold thaw much like an old post-horse's, why, one makes a virtue of necessity."[21]

In "My Winter Garden", Kingsley tells of his riding in his parish and how the minutest details of natural history can claim his attention. The flora, fauna and geological formations around our homes are all infinite miracles of nature, "if we have only eyes to see it."[22] He gives the reader various examples of this, and describes a fox-hunt which happens to cross his path. However, by keeping the progress of the hunt in the background of the description of his lonely passage home through treacherous bog land, he effectually conveys that his own "hunting days are over."[23] Moreover, in a contribution on fishing published in *Fraser's Magazine* in September 1857, the Minute Philosopher even rejected energetic mountain fishing for the "more homely pleasures" of fishing in the low-lands.[24] These are revealing admissions. Although there is some exaggeration in the representation of his age—he was still only thirty-eight when he wrote this—it indicates an increasing awareness and preoccupation that he was growing too old for active battle or adventure. It contributed to the sense many had that he was consciously putting one part of his life behind him.

---

[19] "My Winter Garden" *PI* 135.
[20] "My Winter Garden" *PI* 138.
[21] "My Winter Garden" *PI* 139.
[22] "My Winter Garden" *PI* 140.
[23] "My Winter Garden" *PI* 161.
[24] "Chalk-Stream Studies" *PI* 32.

One reason why Kingsley relinquished most of his revolutionary activities for sanitary reform has been overlooked in the various accounts of his life. When in April 1848 Kingsley set out to talk to Ludlow about doing something for the working men, England was still reeling from the severe economic depression of the 1844–45. By the late 1850s, however, economic growth had made possible vast improvements in working-class housing, working conditions, and education, and social evils were less pressing than they had been a decade before. This was clearly the way Kingsley saw it. When in 1859 a fourth edition of *Yeast* was published, he pointed out in the preface that in the twelve years since the book was written most of the social, religious, and political questions had been mightily improved. But while Kingsley triumphed with the fact that the "liberal principles, for which the Whigs have fought for the last forty years"[25] had led to the "improved tone" of workers, landlords and clergy alike, he regretted that sanitary reform was still "going on at a fearfully slow rate." The apathy of the educated classes in this respect, he added, was "most disgraceful."[26] Thus, Kingsley's shift of attention from socialism to sanitary reform was not only a private decision but was also dictated by the larger effects of economic progress.

On the other hand, it is also true that Kingsley consciously wanted to shun political controversy. When Hughes briefed him about a new magazine in which each writer would sign with his own name and which in a sense would fill the void left by the *Christian Socialist*, Kingsley's reaction was only lukewarm. Early in 1858 Macmillan had decided to trade on the success of muscular Christianity with the reading public and start a new quarterly magazine, which was meant "to speak the truth to this wretched old dead state of things."[27] Maurice was approached for it, and in March Macmillan talked to Hughes about the editorship. Of course, Kingsley too was an essential ingredient of such a publication, but when, in May, he heard from Hughes that Austen Henry Layard, the famous excavator who had just lost his parliamentary seat for Aylesbury, was to contribute with an article on facts which sullied the role of the English in the Indian Mutiny, he retracted: "I have a ve[r]y grave objection to writing for

---

[25] *Y* viii.
[26] *Y* iv.
[27] TH to Fanny Hughes, 16/3/1858, Mack and Armytage 107.

a periodical in wh. Mr Layard is to give us his views of Indian matters." He explained:

> [I] was disgusted with what I heard. I don't believe his assertions in the first place, & in the next, if they are true, it is folly & wickedness to make statements about his mother country w. will be published with exaggeration & comments by all her foreign enemies. Such facts (if facts) shd. be kept private, & put into the hands of the government as secretly as possible. But patriotism & respect for one's native land are dead, & Layards, Brights & Derbys are alike careless of her honour, if they can make a noise, or wreak their spleen & envy. We shall have to hang some of these home-traitors yet, ere we get England governed.[28]

In 1858 the quarterly did not come into being as a result of Kingsley's unenthusiastic attitude and his final refusal to be involved in anti-England sentiments. Macmillan, however, was still eager to start a journal, and, in 1859, ultimately decided on a monthly. Layard never became a contributor to this journal.

II

In "My Winter Garden" Kingsley had overstated in his homely contentedness his "never requiring a six-weeks' holiday." As spring arrived, and Kingsley started playing with ideas for a novel, plans were made for a trip to the north of England. F.D. Maurice had suggested to him a novel about "The Pilgrimage of Grace"—the 1536 Yorkshire rising of 30,000 men, led by Robert Aske, against Henry VIII's Reformation policies—for which local colour and historical details would need to be collected.

In the summer Kingsley left for the north. He first stayed with William Edward Forster at Burley in Wharfedale. Bolton Abbey provided good material for his novel, and Forster, who had a taste for genealogy, helped him to find out as much as possible about the Askes and Cliffords. The people and the industry in the area impressed him. He felt "in a state of bewilderment" at the clothes manufacturing industries. The machinery he saw "no tongue can describe, about three acres of mills." His enthusiasm was such that everything looked marvellous and perfect to him, even the people all seemed

---

[28] CK to TH, 19/5/1858, BL-41298 f.92–93.

"healthy, rosy, and happy." "The country is glorious,"[29] he concluded, "the people are the finest I ever saw."[30]

After a few days in Burley, Kingsley was invited by Walter Morrison for three days to Malham House. Around Malham Tarn research for his novel was set aside. Time was spent there botanizing, and trout fishing turned out to be the "best in the whole earth." "Unfortunately it wants all my big lake flies, which I, never expecting such a treat, left at home."[31] Malham House, with its idiosyncratic architecture inspired him and was to appear in the book he was researching, but it ended up in both *The Water-Babies* and in *The Tutor's Story* as a "house [which] looked like a real live house, that had a history, and had grown and grown as the world grew,"[32] a house whose architectural incongruities had "an historic value of unity, of progressive development, and of life."[33] The surroundings of Malham Tarn did not fail to make an impression either. He had often heard people talk of Godale Scar and Malham Cove, and seeing with his own eyes that "awful cliff filling up the valley with a sheer cross wall of 280 feet, and from beneath a black lip at the foot, the whole river Air coming up, clear as crystal"[34] found that its famed grandeur was no exaggeration. Malham Cove is supposed to have provided Kingsley with the scenery for the turning point in Tom's life in *The Water-Babies*. He imagined the dark spots in the limestone acclivity to be the trace left by a sooty chimney sweeper stumbling down the cliff. A house with a sloping garden at Bridge End on the river Skirfare became the place where Tom changed from a land-baby into a water-baby.

Although Kingsley soon started to feel restless and longed to be back with Fanny, he stayed on: "It would be folly to go home without the materials for which I came."[35] From Malham Tarn he returned to Burley, and then continued east with his search for material in Ripon, Fountains Abbey, York, the East Riding, and Hull. In the end he felt satisfied: "I have done my work well. The book grows on me. I see my way now as clear as day. How I will write when

---

[29] CK to FK, July 1858, *LML* ii.57.
[30] CK to FK, 6/7/1858, *LML* ii.58.
[31] CK to FK, 5/7/1858, *LML* ii.58.
[32] *WB* 24.
[33] *TS* 53.
[34] CK to FK, 6/7/1858, *LML* ii.58.
[35] CK to FK, undated, *LML* ii.59.

I get home.”[36] But before returning to his “ve[r]y pretty woman with darke eyes & hair, & a skin like satin,” he decided that he “must be in London some hours Saturday morning to hunt the London Library.”[37]

After his return to Eversley, Kingsley set to work on his novel. Part of the work was written during the summer and autumn and was forwarded to Macmillan, who had offered him £2000 for a new novel. However, Kingsley felt unable to continue his story. It is possible that he felt dissatisfied with the Catholic-Protestant relations he was delineating in his book. To a Roman Catholic lady who had helped him with historical facts, but who feared that Kingsley's Protestantism would distort history, he wrote that he would try “in this book [to] do the northern Catholics ample justice,” but that he could not “withdraw what I said in ‘Westward Ho’.”[38] But, of course, his heroes Robert and Christopher Aske were still “Romanists.” The very lack of a true English Protestant hero might have caused his increasing difficulties with the story. When, soon after this letter, Kingsley decided to abandon the Pilgrimage of Grace, he proposed to Macmillan a Yorkshire novel set in modern times, and gave it the provisional title *Alcibiades*. In a modern variation of the Socrates-Alcibiades theme, Kingsley purposed to explore the moral influence of a clubfooted Cambridge scholar (Mr Brownlow) who had been charged with the education of a handsome, intelligent, but profligate young nobleman. The early parts of the novel contrast the good-natured Yorkshire people with the decadence and corrupt morals of an aristocratic household. The novel, written in the first person singular, is strikingly devoid of the implications of Kingsley's deeper social, religious, and political convictions. The story is carried along by flat dialogue, and the characters fail to interest the reader. The Yorkshire characters are not nearly as attractive as the Devonshire characters in his previous novels, and even that at which Kingsley is generally very good—local colour—is uninspired description. The impressions of Yorkshire, about which Kingsley wrote so enthusiastically in his letters home and which were effectually used in *The Water-Babies*, remained unused. Kingsley would not finish this Yorkshire novel either. He told Macmillan that he abandoned it because “I

---

[36] CK to FK, undated, *LML* ii.59.
[37] CK to FK, undated, BL-62554 f.124r.
[38] CK to C. Kegan Paul, October 1858, *LML* ii.59.

Illustration 4. Late nineteenth-century illustrated frontispiece of sheet music of "The Three Fishers," set to music by John Hullah

have been too much behind the scenes of court, fashionable, and intellectual circles [. . .] and would introduce personal portraits,[39] but to F.D. Maurice he complained of headaches and admitted that "I found that the novel wh I had been wearily trying to write was twaddle & a failure."[40] The unfinished manuscript was found half a century later by his daughter Mary who decided to complete the work. It was published as *The Tutor's Story* in 1916.

The failure to produce a new novel confirmed to Kingsley that he was much better at writing poetry. In 1857 John Hullah had asked for permission to set some of his poems to music, and, when a year later Kingsley heard "The Three Fishers" sung for the first time, he congratulated Hullah with the song, saying that it "rendered what I wanted to say, and entered into the real feeling of the words." He added: "I feel more and more inclined to suspect that they are what I can do best, and that I am [. . .] only likely to get myself into the wars by meddling with politics and lofty matters."[41] Such were his feelings when he tried to write his Yorkshire novel.

Notwithstanding this assessment of himself as a poet, there is no evidence that Kingsley tried hard to write new poetry, and the verse published over the next few years is scanty. It is clear that by 1858 the inspiration for literary work entirely failed him. But vision also lacked him in non-fiction. When, in October 1859, Kingsley explained to F.D. Maurice why he had stopped writing fiction, he promised that he "shall write nothing but sermons."[42] This promise followed the publication of a new volume of sermons earlier that year. On 30 December 1858 he had informed Maurice that he was in the middle of preparing the sermons for the press and that "I purpose to call them sermons on "The Good News of God"—a clumsy title, but the only one w. expresses what I mean."[43] The volume was an important one to Kingsley. The sermons were selected with care and he had taken "far more pains with them than with any former ones." He asked Maurice whether he would be willing to see them in proof as "I am much afraid of being doctrinally wrong here & there, & leaving a word on wh. a charge of heresy might be grounded, w. could do

[39] Chitty (1974) 187.
[40] CK to FDM, 25/10/1859, BL-41297 f.119v.
[41] CK to John Hullah, March 1858, *LML* ii.60–1.
[42] CK to FDM, 25/10/1859, BL-41297 f.119v.
[43] CK to FDM, 30/12/1859, BL-41297 f.113v.

no good, & might do harm. And as I speak far more boldly in them than I ever yet have done, I have to be all the more careful."[44] What is revealing about *Good News of God* is that the sermons do not have the bold quality Kingsley thought they had. They make flat reading. Kingsley's characteristically energetic language in preaching comes to the surface only very rarely, and the themes are uncontroversial explanations of such ecclesiastical concepts as eternity, love of one's neighbours, God's goodness, and repentance. To some Protestant readers the notion that he believed with Maurice in "the termination of future punishment" remained irksome, but otherwise, the *New Englander and Yale Review* remarked, "these thirty-nine sermons might be profitably studied by all ministers."[45] It is the uncontroversial all-purpose appeal of these sermons that diminish the historical and biographical importance of the volume. There are very few references to contemporary social or political issues, and allusions to private opinions or feelings are carefully avoided. There are no affirmations of masculinity, and even the comparison between the Biblical locust-swarms and the present plight of cholera, although mentioned, is not worked out. As it is, *Good News of God* is probably Kingsley's least interesting collection of sermons. Apart from the short notice in the *New Englander and Yale Review*, it was not reviewed in the periodical press and remained one of Kingsley's lesser-known volumes of sermons. The inability to write with inspiration seemed to extend to virtually all his writings.

III

When the summer came to an end, the happiness of the family was destroyed. It had become clear that the eleven-years-old Maurice needed to be sent to school after all. Ever since the publication of Hughes's book about public-school boys the age of his own son Kingsley must have contemplated Maurice's future schooling, especially as the plans of educating him at home had not borne much fruit. The spectre of a boarding school loomed large on the horizon, and

---

[44] CK to FDM, 30/12/1859, BL-41297 f.114r.
[45] [-], "The Rev. Charles Kingsley's Sermons. The Good News of God," *New Englander and Yale Review* 18 (February 1860) 222.

although, in a review for the *Saturday Review*, Kingsley praised Hughes's vision of "Young England," he remained strikingly reticent about public school life itself. The lack of enthusiasm in the review—perhaps the shortest and most lifeless Kingsley ever wrote—might well be an indication of Kingsley's unease about his own son's future. The value of a boarding school in preparing a boy for life had been redeemed for him by *Tom Brown's Schooldays*, but the prospect of Maurice being bullied made Kingsley squirm.

When in September 1858 it was decided that the boy had to go to school, the choice did not fall on Rugby, but on his old friend Cowley Powles's school at nearby Blackheath. Notwithstanding the reassuring fact that Maurice would be in kind hands with the Powleses, parting with him proved traumatic for both Charles and Fanny. Kingsley accompanied his son to Blackheath and stayed for almost a week, Maurice creeping into his father's bed at night. Fanny wrote heartbreaking letters from Eversley. "The house is sad & lonely without our darling boy," she wrote, "but the comfort of feeling *you are there* is so beyond all words that I am sure you will stay if only for *my* sake. Tell me every little particular, & whether he cries *at night*."[46] Maurice did cry at night, and when Charles told Fanny, she knew that this was her "first *real* grief & trial [. . .] The feeling he was unhappy perhaps crying in his little bed among strange boys seemed more than I could bear."[47] Kingsley too admitted that "I have felt intensely—more than I ever expected to feel, & was ready to cry again & again,"[48] and in his first letter to Maurice he confessed that "I was ready to cry when I left you there in the bedroom, though I know it is for your good."[49] There was in fact no doubt about it that the boy needed proper instruction. "His ignorance is pretty total, it seems," Kingsley had reported home[50] and Maurice was put in the lowest class.[51] Nevertheless he had many misgivings which were badly concealed in the reassuring advice to his boy in another letter: "Keep up your heart [. . .] never mind if

[46] CK to FK, undated, BL-62554 f.125r.
[47] CK to FK, undated, BL-62554 f.131v.
[48] CK to FK, undated, BL-62554 f.127r.
[49] CK to Maurice Kingsley, undated, BL-41298 f.236.
[50] CK to FK, undated, BL-62554 f.126v.
[51] CK to FK, undated, BL-62554 f.132.

boys bully a little; they mean no harm."[52] To keep up the boy's spirits Kingsley sent him frequent accounts of hunting in Eversley which he illustrated with humourous pen-and-ink drawings. Although Maurice came home in the holidays in good health and with good reports, the separation was felt by both parents as "a crisis—the beginning of a new life for us."[53]

[52] CK to Maurice Kingsley, undated, BL-41298 f.238.
[53] CK to FK, undated, BL-62554 f.135v.

CHAPTER EIGHTEEN

AN EXCELLENT DARWINIAN (1859–1860)

The new year promised well for Kingsley. Over Christmas Fanny had felt strong enough to "dance & dig in the garden" and Maurice had been more successful at school than had been anticipated. "Your Godson [has] come home with an admirable character & 2 prizes," Kingsley wrote to F.D. Maurice, and he concluded: "My cup runs over—God grant that I may *not throw it over* as I expect surely to do some day by my own laziness, thanklessness & self indulgence."[1] But he need not have worried as yet. Literary fame was about to give him recognition in high quarters. On 17 April 1859 he was asked to preach at Buckingham Palace on Palm Sunday. To Macmillan he wrote that this was because of *Two Years Ago*, which the Prince Consort had liked exceedingly. Royal interest in the Protestant mettle of Kingsley's writings, however, was of some years standing. The Prince had given *The Saint's Tragedy* to the Crown Princess of Prussia to read, and *Hypatia* was a great favourite of the Queen.

As befitting the occasion, Kingsley preached on the meaning of Passion Week. Its meaning, he argued in direct and conversational language, was not shutting oneself up in one's closet to meditate, as some people do. "Amid the roar of the busy world, which cannot stop (and which ought not to stop)," Christ's suffering should stir up feelings of "obedience, usefulness, generosity, that I may go back to my work cheerfully."[2] From Christ, he concluded, we get "all sense of duty, obedience, order, justice, law; [...] regardless of what it costs us in the station to which each of us has been called by his Father in heaven. Amen."[3] It was a proper sentiment to preach before Queen Victoria, who did not like difficult, long or controversial sermons, and royal appreciation came a few weeks in the appointment as one of the Queen's chaplains in ordinary. He wrote to Fanny that "I had a v[er]y cordial letter from Ld Sydney offering

---

[1] CK to FDM, 30/12/1858, BL-41297 f.115r.
[2] "How to Keep Passion Week" *VTCS* 198, 197.
[3] "How to Keep Passion Week" *VTCS* 200.

it to me from *Her*." It was the public recognition that Fanny had longed for: "From this time there was a marked difference in the tone of the public press, religious and otherwise, towards him," she comments.[4] Of course, he too felt much flattered and accepted the post immediately, but, unsure of how to style his answer, he first took it to Stapleton "to correct."[5]

The note of emphasis on duty and the common good that Kingsley had struck in his first sermon had been appreciated by the Queen. Thus in the sermons that followed, delivered as the Queen's Chaplain, he reiterated the idea. When he preached on "Divine Hunger and Thirst" he explained these as the satisfaction which comes from becoming better and more righteous men and women; "as the life of our bodies grows cold and feeble, the life of our souls may grow richer, warmer, stronger, more useful to all around us."[6] In yet another sermon he discussed true modesty as that of a man who does his business in public, "simply because the thing has to be done; and then quietly withdrawing himself when the thing is done."[7] The conversational tone with which he contemplated these subjects was just right, and on 13 November Kingsley was invited to preach to the court in the private chapel at Windsor Castle. It was on this occasion that he was finally presented to the Queen, the Prince Consort, and to the Crown Princess of Prussia. He detailed to Fanny that the experience was "ve[r]y like a dream when one awaketh, though a not unpleasant one."[8] When Kingsley was taken to the Queen he "had to kneel & kiss hands, & didn't dislike it."[9] In a slightly foreign accent she remarked they all "had great delight in my books" but that she liked *Hypatia* best of all. When Prince Albert asked whether he was working on anything new, Kingsley pleasantly answered "that I had spent all the wits I had in climbing up *hither*, & must lay on my oars & be content with my present honours."[10] The Prince Consort impressed him. He was to Kingsley "one more strong good man," one of those that he "like[d] to look in the faces"

---

[4] *LML* ii.72.
[5] CK to FK, undated, BL-62554 f.144.
[6] "The Divine Hunger and Thirst" *VTCS* 206.
[7] "The Transfiguration" *VTCS* 210.
[8] CK to FK, 14/11/1859, BL-62554 f.151r.
[9] CK to FK, 14/11/1859, BL-62554 f.151v.
[10] CK to FK, 14/11/1859, BL-62554 f.154r.

and "love[d] to contemplate." "I have fallen in love with that man," he confessed.[11]

But notwithstanding the royal honours he had received, which were gratifying, Kingsley's spirits were low in the autumn of 1859. His failure to write a new novel had started to fret him. He realized that it was over two years and a half since he had finished *Two Years*. If Mrs Kingsley's date is correct, only a week after meeting the Queen and Prince Albert, he wrote to John Bullar about his state of mind:

> I am a slack hand now. I can't think; I can't write, I can't run, I can't ride—I have neither wit, nerve, nor strength for anything; and if I try I get a hot head, and my arms and legs begin to ache. I was so ten years ago: worse than now. I have learnt by that last attack, and have, thank God, pulled up in time. Do not fancy that I am going to fret myself about anything. I have infinite power left of doing two things, which are generally necessary to earthly salvation, viz., eating and sleeping, and to them I am paying great attention. When I tried to work, and yet could not, I had over and above a nasty craving for alcohol—for more wine than I have usually found necessary to digest my food. Since I have left my brain alone, that craving is going off.

Not even physical activity offered relief any more, and he had even come to think it pure folly "trying to cure mental fatigue by bodily [exercise]":

> I tried that experiment a fortnight ago, and was miserably ill for three days. I had used up the grey matter of my brain by thought (my head feels at times like a pumpkin), and then had used up still more by violent volition, running to hounds on foot, and leaping hedges and ditches for five hours, calling the same fresh air and exercise! I was a great fool, and found it out. No, my dear Bullar, I will be a pig for twelve months. There is nothing in my parish to raise me out of the state of pigdom; save three services for Sunday, to help in which I shall get a curate, while as for writing, &c, the world got on tolerably without me for six thousand years (I hold for a great many more), and therefore there is a fair presumption that it will get on without me for one.[12]

Kingsley had been feeling very low for some time now. In January his father had fallen seriously ill. It was the beginning of a long and lingering process of suffering. "Miserable to see life prolonged when

---

[11] CK to JB, 16/11/1859, *LML* ii.94.
[12] CK to JB, 16/11/1859, *LML* ii.93–4.

all that makes it worth having (physically) is gone," he wrote to an old friend when the end was coming near.[13] It had a dampening effect on the success he had earned with the royal family. On his fortieth birthday in June he wrote to Hughes: "What a long life I have lived! and silly fellows that review me say that I can never have known ill-health or sorrow. I have enough to make me feel very old."[14] In August 1859 he had offered the parish part of the Rectory ground as an extension of the churchyard, and when preparatory work was begun six months later, he reserved in it a spot for his own grave.

The sentiment of growing old went hand in hand with a longing for death which to a modern reader at times might seem to border on morbid obsession. But a series of deaths in 1860 had a powerful claim on Kingsley's emotional resources. Kingsley's father died in March 1860, creating the awful feeling "of having the roots which connect one with the last generation seemingly torn up, and having to say, 'now *I* am the root, I stand self-supported'."[15] With the passing of the years the relation with his father had considerably changed. Especially during the last few years of his life much mutual understanding between father and son had been established, and notwithstanding a feeling that "every word & deed towards that good old man, & every sorrow I caused him—rise up in judgement against one," Kingsley could rest assured in the end that his father had "died loving me."[16]

Soon after his father's death the news of the decease of others who were very dear to Kingsley shocked him. First, in April, a desperate letter from Froude reached him that his wife Charlotte was alarmingly ill. By the time Kingsley read the letter, the end had come. She was one of the first to be buried in the new churchyard in the vacant space next to the spot Kingsley had chosen for himself. "Before our window lies the grave of [. . .] my wife's favourite sister," he wrote to John Skelton.[17] Amongst those who stood beside her grave during the burial service were John Ashley Warre, the husband of Fanny's sister Caroline; Charles Grenfell, son of Fanny's brother; and Froude's and Kingsley's friend John Parker jr. All three

---

[13] CK to James Montagu, February 1860, *LML* ii.102.

[14] CK to TH, 12/6/1859, *LML* ii.73.

[15] *LMLM* 234.

[16] CK to FDM, March 1860, BL-41297 f.125.

[17] CK to John Skelton, undated, *LML* ii.105.

died before the year was over. Parker's death greatly affected Kingsley: "His was a great soul in a pigmy body," he told Skelton, and, thinking of poor Parker's small stature he added rather archly and with unintended humour: "those who know I loved him, know what a calumny it is to say that I preach 'muscular Christianity'."[18]

As death took away many of Kingsley's dearest friends and relatives in 1860, it is hardly surprising that he was feeling that most of his own life was over. With it also came the sense that his literary career, which had lain stagnant for years now, belonged to the past. "All that book-writing and struggling is over, and a settled position and work is before me," he told Fanny in 1860, and added: "Would that it were done, the children settled in life, & kindly death near, to set one off again with a new start somewhere else."[19] "The 'far off look,' and longing for rest and reality, and for the unfolding of the mystery of life grew stronger upon him, and he said more frequently to his wife 'How blessed it will be when it is all over!' "[20]

To make sense of Kingsley's premature yearning for death it is also important to put it in the context of how he understood life and marriage after death. Ever since his love for Fanny had saved him in his student days from "sensuality and dissipation"[21] by sealing his sexual longings in a sacred union with her, he had nurtured a feeling of repugnance to re-marrying. When during the years of courtship Fanny expressed her doubt in her journal, which she gave to Charles to read, he chided her for supposing he could ever marry again if she died: "I would never never marry another [. . .], till I found my own own Blessed only wife in heaven," for the idea that

> communion with you is to be a mere temporary self-indulgence wh. may be replaced, if taken away, is so horrible to me, that if I thought you really believed so, I could never bring myself to touch your body! But your having given vent to the thought in absence & fear of death, only adds to my love for you, my knowledge of your Love for me! Bless you, my wife! My only Love! Mine to all eternity! My twin-sister![22]

In a theology which promises life after death, this naturally leads to the question of whether marriage exists in heaven. In November 1843

---

[18] CK to John Skelton, undated, *LML* ii.105.
[19] CK to FK, undated, MP-C0171.
[20] *LML* ii.73.
[21] CK to FK, undated, *LML* i.53.
[22] CK to FK, [30/10/1843], BL-62552 f.100.

Charles had discussed this with Fanny. "Is not marriage the mere approx*imation* to a unity, w. shall be *perfect* in heaven?" he argued in a long letter:[23] "Here the physical body can but strive to express its love[24]—its desire of union. Will not one of the properties of the *spiritual* body be that it will be able to express that w. the natural body only *tries* to do? Is this a sensual view of heaven?"[25]

Kingsley's reasoning and phraseology are reminiscent of the eighteenth-century mystic Swedenborg, who asserted that "a spiritual wedding means being linked with the Lord, something that happens on earth, and if it has taken place on earth, it has also taken place in heaven. The wedding therefore cannot be repeated in heaven, nor can they be given in marriage again."[26] However, when Kingsley wrote to Fanny about marriage in heaven, he was only a 24-year-old clergyman who was about to be married to the woman he was madly in love with, and, as he had not read Swedenborg yet, his contemplations then owed nothing to Swedenborg's theology. It was not until 1847, when he was feeling lonely at Chelsea trying to sell his Life of St Elizabeth, that Kingsley read *Delitiae Sapientiae de Amore Conjugiale.* "I have been reading a mad book of Swedenborg's on conjugal love, wh. has made me love you more & more, & taught me many deep things. I must introduce you to bits of it."[27] "The reason why a person's sexual love remains after death," he found in Swedenborg, "is that a male remains a male and a female a female, and the male's masculinity pervades the whole and every part of him, and likewise a female's femininity, and the impulse to be joined is present in every detail down to the smallest."[28] Although Kingsley realized that Swedenborg's theology was full of "peculiarities,"[29] he cherished his work on conjugal love. "There are many noble and beautiful things in that text-book of his," he admitted to an unidentified correspondent in 1859.

As at the end of the 1850s Kingsley increasing felt that the best part of his life was over and when he started to long for rest, he

[23] CK to FK, [26/10/1843], BL-62552 f.147r.
[24] CK to FK, [26/10/1843], BL-62552 f.148r.
[25] CK to FK, [26/10/1843], BL-62552 f.148v.
[26] Emanuel Swedenborg, *The Delights of Wisdom on the Subject of Conjugial Love*, transl. John Chadwick, (London: Swedenborg Society, 1996) 41.
[27] CK to FK, undated, BL-62553 f.98v–99r.
[28] *Conjugial Love* 37.
[29] CK to Horace Field, 3/11/1867, *LML* ii.259.

returned to the study of those verses where the Bible speaks of marriage in heaven. The passage in Matthew 22 where Jesus replies that "in the resurrection they neither marry, nor are given in marriage" had always inspired Kingsley and now he longed to know what Swedenborg made of it. As Swedenborg devotes a full paragraph in *Amore Conjugiale* to Matthew 22, it is obvious that Kingsley was not a habitual reader of this book. It would, therefore, be more appropriate to note Kingsley's appreciation of some of Swedenborg's ideas rather than affirm that he was influenced by them in his own theology.

II

A short holiday in the autumn of 1859 broke the parish drudgery for a few days. The family went to stay with the Tennysons, with whom all misunderstandings regarding the inspiration for Elsley Vavasour in *Two Years Ago* had been clarified. But the holiday was far too short to alleviate Kingsley's wearied mind. As there was no curate who could be employed, the strain of overwork made itself felt again as soon as they returned to Eversley. Mrs Kingsley writes in her biography that her husband "shrunk from the bustle of London, refused all sermons there, and withdrew from politics."[30] Public appearances were indeed kept to a minimum. If on the one hand, as Mrs Kingsley explains, Kingsley was coping badly with the strain of overwork, on the other hand he was not willing to compromise his newly acquired position in the royal household by revolutionary activities. *Vanity Fair* was to write in the text accompanying their cartoon of Kingsley in 1872: "Time and opinions move so fast that it is difficult to recall the period, though it is really so recent, when the Rev. Charles Kingsley, sometime author of "Alton Locke" and now Chaplain to the Queen [. . .] was one of the most daring and advanced revolutionists of his cloth."[31] This could have been said of Kingsley as early as 1859.

In 1859 Kingsley wrote even less than in the preceding years. It was the year of reprints. Parker brought out a fourth edition of *Yeast* with a new preface, as well as a volume that collected essays and reviews that Kingsley had contributed to *Fraser's Magazine* and to the

---

[30] *LML* ii.72.
[31] *Vanity Fair* 30 March 1872.

North British Review. Meanwhile, Kingsley corrected and enlarged *Glaucus*, which now came out with twelve splendid colour lithographs, but unfortunately it was too early to incorporate the implications of *The Origin of Species* (a book Kingsley immediately read and admired) and much in the new edition of *Glaucus* was dated even before it appeared in print. These revised texts, and the sermons in *The Good News of God*, were all he produced in 1859. "So much life had actually gone out of him," Mrs Kingsley commented.[32]

However, when necessary, Kingsley could still rise to the occasion. Although "I am tired of most things in the world," he wrote to Lady Harding, "Of sanitary reform I shall never grow tired."[33] At the first meeting of the Ladies' National Association for the Diffusion of Sanitary Knowledge, where he spoke together with Lord Shaftesbury, he employed his irony to attack once more the dubious culture of the lower middle classes and their deplorable influence on popular opinion which impedes a true understanding of nature, namely that "she kills, and kills, and kills, and is never tired of killing" until man has learnt how to obey her.[34] He felt grateful that the ladies who attended the meeting had "discovered that human beings have bodies as well as souls, and that the state of the soul too often depends on that of the body."[35]

Kingsley's campaign to bring sanitary reform to the public's attention brought him respect from a number of men of science. When during the summer of 1860 England had incessant rain for almost three months, and the crops were threatened, Kingsley felt irritated that all over the country prayers for fair weather were read in the churches. From his own pulpit he contended that praying for a change in the weather was preposterous. As the climate and the weather are the outcome of God-created, but fixed, natural laws, asking for a change in nature's ground plan would mean a lack of respect for the Creator. But what exasperated him above all was the short-sightedness and presumption in not recognizing the blessing of that year's rain. After years of drought and cholera, it was "washing away, day by day, the seeds of pestilence in man and beast, and vegetables, and sowing instead the seeds of health and fertility, for

---

[32] *LML* ii.87.
[33] CK to Lady Harding, 22/7/1859, *LML* ii.86.
[34] "The Massacre of the Innocents" *SSE* 266.
[35] CK to Lady Harding, 22/7/1859, *LML* ii.86.

us and for our children after us."[36] Praying for fair weather would be tantamount to asking God to send back the disease.

As the sermon provoked much discussion, Kingsley convinced Parker to publish it. Fellow men of the cloth did not take kindly to the sermon, and numberless angry letters were delivered to Eversley Rectory. To one correspondent Kingsley had to point out some of the facts about the incessant heavy rains. "Are you aware, dear sir," he wrote, "what they have done? Have you read the Registrar General's reports for the last quarter? [. . .] This the rains have done. They have saved (by the returns compared with those of the same quarter last year) in the three months ending October, 18,000 English lives, besides the seeds of future disease. The doctors and apothecaries have been saying they never had so little to do."[37]

Kingsley's sermon in defence of rain and bad weather was associated in the public mind with his "Ode to the North-East Wind" which included the following line: " 'Tis hard gray weather/Breeds hard English men." It was ridiculed as part of the muscular Christianity he preached. George Eliot playfully referred to it in a letter to Mrs William Cross: "Just now the chill east wind has brought a little check to our pleasure in our long afternoon drives, and I could wish that Canon Kingsley and his fellow-worshippers of that harsh divinity could have it reserved entirely for themselves as a tribal god."[38] This was written in 1874, but as early as 1861 Kingsley complained that he had been "called names, for a foolish 'Ode to the North-East Wind'," and added: "If my cockney critics had been country parsons, they would have been more merciful, when they saw me, as I have been more than once, utterly ill from attending increasing sick cases during a soft south-west November of rain and roses."[39]

On the other hand, Kingsley's views on the weather met with the immediate approval of some leading scientists. Richard Owen praised Kingsley as the only person who, as a priest, "had the honesty and courage to utter the truth in references to its subject,"[40] while Charles Lyell thanked him for an excellent sermon and he admitted ashamedly

---

[36] "Why Should We Pray for Fair Weather" *LML* ii.112.
[37] CK to unidentified correspondent, 12/11/1860, *LML* ii.116.
[38] George Eliot to Mrs William Cross, 14/6/1874, Haight, vi.55.
[39] CK to CB, undated, *LML* ii.117–8.
[40] Richard Owen to CK, undated, *LML* ii.110.

that he too, in a private conversation, had made "an idle and thought-less speech" apropos of the incessant rains.[41]

During the late 1850s Kingsley was moving increasingly in scientific circles and made friends of many of the leading scientists of the day. In 1857 he was elected a fellow of the Linnean Society, and the various editions of *Glaucus* had brought him many "pleasant letters, & self-introductions, from scientific men."[42] Moreover, his friendship with Charles Bunbury led to other introductions, amongst whom Lyell and Joseph Hooker. At the same time his friendship with Gosse stranded on evolutionary concepts.

In the winter of 1857–1858 Philip Henry Gosse compromised his scientific reputation. When, after the meeting of the Royal Society in the summer of 1857, he was acquainted by Hooker with the impending publication of Darwin's views of the evolution of species, he felt alarmed at what this meant for Christianity and he hastened to write a book on the fixity of species. In *Omphalos: An Attempt to Untie the Geological Knot* Gosse controverted the conclusions of the geologists who saw in the fossil sequences of creatures confirmation of constant change of species within the animal kingdom. Instead he argued that such evidence only indicated an *illusory* past. Just as Adam was born complete with a navel, yet was never born of woman, the Creation too was complete at once with fossils and strata. *Omphalos* was published at the end of the year, and during the winter of 1858 Gosse impatiently awaited the reactions of gratitude (which he thought would come from all quarters) for having saved religion in the face of modern science. But his jubilant mood turned to blackest despair when his book was rejected wholesale by the reading public, scien-tists and churchmen alike. The press ridiculed his theory as imply-ing "that God hid the fossils in the rocks in order to tempt geologists into infidelity," while "atheists and Christians alike looked at it, and laughed, and threw it away."[43]

In May 1856, upon the publication of Gosse's *Tenby*, Kingsley had expressed his admiration for Gosse's scientific rigour as well as for the religious lessons which could be learned from it. As Kingsley also appreciated Gosse's thorough Protestantism and had once told him that he fancied that "you & I should agree there as well as we

---

[41] Charles Lyell to CK, 23/9/1860, *LML* ii.114.
[42] CK to PHG, 13/5/1856, L-BC Gosse Correspondence.
[43] Edmund Gosse, *Father and Son*, (Harmondsworth: Penguin, 1970) 77.

do on sea-beasts,"[44] Gosse now wrote to Kingsley for approval. But
Kingsley felt no sympathy for Gosse's theory. He could not "give
up," he replied, "the painful and slow conclusion of five and twenty
years' study of geology, and believe that God has written on the
rocks one enormous and superfluous lie."[45] To make his dissociation
from Gosse's book as clear as possible, he wrote in the fourth edition of *Glaucus* that "it is with real pain that I have seen my friend
Mr. Gosse [. . .] make a step in the direction of obscurantism, which
I can only call desperate," and added: "If Scripture can only be vindicated by such an outrage to common sense and fact, then I will
give up Scripture, and stand by common sense [. . .] For my part,
I have seen no book for some years past, which I should more carefully keep out of the hands of the young."[46] This was another public blow to Gosse and might seem gratuitously unkind on the part
of Kingsley if we forget that *Glaucus* had grown directly out of Gosse's
books on marine zoology, and that Kingsley throughout refers to
Gosse's works. To safeguard his own scientific reputation he could
not but take his distance from Gosse. Stephen Jay Gould has argued
that the point of *Omphalos* is not whether its theory is right or wrong,
but that Gosse's fundamental error lay in his failure to understand
the essential character of science by sustaining an unprovable and
untestable, and therefore useless, hypothesis, thus placing "himself
outside the pale of science."[47] Kingsley perceived as much, and that
was why he said he was not willing to give up "five and twenty
years' study of geology."

On 22 November 1859 Charles Darwin's long-awaited book on
the origin of species came out. About ten days before it was launched,
Darwin had sent out complimentary copies to leading botanists and
geologists at Oxbridge and Harvard. With the indignant outcry that
followed *Vestiges of Creation* fresh in his mind, Darwin awaited the
reactions to his book in trepidation. Although he had been careful
not to mention man's origins in his text, he still feared the protests
that would no doubt come from religious quarters. In the letters that
accompanied the complimentary copies for those scientists he knew
to be stern believers, he even humbly apologized for views which

---

[44] CK to PHG, 13/5/1856, L-BC Gosse Correspondence.
[45] Edmund Gosse, *Father and Son*, (Harmondsworth: Penguin, 1970) 77.
[46] *G⁴* 15.
[47] Stephen Jay Gould, *The Flamingo's Smile* (Harmondsworth: Penguin 1985) 111.

they would very likely be unwilling to embrace. For unknown reasons, Kingsley was sent a complimentary copy too.

Kingsley, much honoured to have received a book from "the Naturalist whom, of all naturalists living, I most wish to know and to learn from," replied almost by return of post on 18 November after a quick look at the text. Although "I am so poorly (in brain), that I fear I cannot read your book just now as I ought," he felt both enthusiastic and impressed.

This was a nice surprise for Darwin, and from an unexpected quarter. As the 1250 copies of *The Origin of Species* were practically sold out on its very first day, Darwin had already started on a second corrected edition, and when he received Kingsley's letter he realized its value. He jubilantly told those scientists who were willing to defend his theory, Thomas Henry Huxley and Charles Lyell, that "Rev. C. Kingsley has a mind to come round"[48] and that he had written him "a capital paragraph on such notions as mine being NOT opposed to a high conception of the Deity."[49] He had not lost time and had written back to Kingsley to ask him whether he was allowed to quote his "admirable sentence" in the new edition of his book. Kingsley felt delighted and the following passage was inserted at the end of the second edition of *The Origin of Species*:

> A celebrated author and divine has written to me that "he has gradually learned to see that it is just as noble a conception of the Deity to believe that He created a few original forms capable of self-development into other and needful forms, as to believe that He required a fresh act of creation to supply the voids caused by the action of His laws."

Darwin kept the passage in all successive editions.

In 1855 Huxley had been put in touch with the Working Men's College through Frederick Daniel Dyster, a retired doctor in South Wales, who, in 1851, had contributed to *The Christian Socialist* with a number of short pieces on healthy living and on the principles of hygiene. The two men had met during Huxley's visit to the area and they searched the tidal rock pools together. They talked about marine zoology, religion, and socialism, and back in London Huxley

---

[48] Charles Darwin to THH, 27/11/1859, Francis Darwin, *The Life and Letters of Charles Darwin*, 3rd edn. (London: John Murray, 1887), vol. 2, ch. 1.

[49] Charles Darwin to Charles Lyell, 2/12/59, Francis Darwin, *The Life and Letters of Charles Darwin*, 3rd edn. (London: John Murray, 1887), vol. 2, ch. 1.

offered the Working Men's College free tickets to his lectures. Of course, word about Huxley reached Kingsley, who promptly decided to seek him out. Unfortunately there is no record of their meeting in 1855, but when four years later the implications of Darwin's book kept turning in Kingsley's mind, he felt free to discuss his doubts and perplexities to Huxley, although he had been "forbidden by my doctors to write a word." Huxley had just started his career as Darwin's bulldog with a powerful piece in defence of *The Origin of Species* in Macmillan's new monthly, and seemed an obvious person to turn to to discuss Darwin's book. "There is much in his book wh. impresst me deeply," he admitted, even if it "startled many pre-conceived judgements of mine." He fully approved of Huxley's arti-cle—it would "keep the curs from barking"—and he promised that "the day will come [. . .] when my brain will have sufficiently recovered to enable me to say my say."[50] Huxley appreciated Kingsley's open-mindedness and he wrote in a letter to Dyster that he thought him

> a very real, manly, right minded parson but I am inclined to think on the whole that it is more my intention to convert him than his to convert me. He is an excellent Darwinian to begin with, and told me a capital story of his reply to Lady Aylesbury who expressed her astonishment at his favouring such a heresy—"What can be more delightful to me Lady Aylesbury, than to know that your Ladyship & myself sprang from the same toad stool." Whereby the frivolous old woman shut up, in doubt whether she was being chaffed or adored for her remark.[51]

Huxley's intention to convert Kingsley to Darwinism was facilitated by Kingsley's belief in a progressive perfection in creation, while what Kingsley would insist on as he made evolution his own was "that the belief in a good and just God is the foundation, if not of a scientific habit of mind, still of a habit of mind into which science can fall, and seed."[52] Kingsley's ground plan remained theistic.

Huxley had long since abandoned his faith that a good and just God was the foundation of nature's plan and the teleological notion of a sublime Providence seemed to him completely out of tune with Darwin's "clumsy, wasteful, blundering low & horrible cruel works

---

[50] CK to THH, 7/12/1859, IC-19.160.
[51] THH to Frederick Daniel Dyster, 29/2/1860, IC-15.110.
[52] CK to CB, undated, *LML* ii.118.

of nature."[53] A personal tragedy that befell Huxley later that year led to an intense correspondence in which the two men confronted agnostic and theological world views. These unique letters have been completely overlooked by Kingsley's biographers, and have only been partially used by those on the Huxley side.

In September Huxley's three-year-old son Noel fell ill with scarlet fever and died within three days. It was a devastating blow, and Huxley found little or no relief in the sympathetic reactions that arrived. He had long been a religious doubter and his idea of providence now received its final blow. A long emotional letter from Kingsley, however, roused him to open his heart. In the address to the first meeting of the Ladies' National Association for the Diffusion of Sanitary Knowledge Kingsley had stressed that, notwithstanding his faith in heavenly recompense, "a dying child is to me one of the most dreadful sights in the world [. . .] it does make me feel that the world is indeed out of joint, to see a child die."[54] Thus, when Huxley wrote to him, detailing the news of the death of Noel, Kingsley felt "exceedingly" shocked: "I always have been unable to face the thought of what has happened you. It looks something horrible intolerable, like being burnt alive."[55]

Huxley's first letter to Kingsley is no longer extant, but from Kingsley's answer it is possible to gather what he had expressed there. When Huxley's mother suddenly died in April 1852, he had written to his sister "I offer you no consolation, my dearest sister, for I know of none;"[56] all one could count upon to bear tragedy was one's inherent strength and their mutual sympathy, he added. It is likely that Huxley had expressed similar sentiments in his letter to Kingsley. But, of course, to Kingsley there *was* consolation, and he felt obliged to tell his correspondent of it. This was a delicate business, but Kingsley wrote from the depth of his heart, and succeeded by not offering the "professional commonplaces" that he felt Huxley could not but despise. Still, his instinct made it impossible for him to doubt the existence of a higher future state of man which fell in with a spiritual idea of an evolutionistic progress of species, the very same scientific principles to which Huxley owed his

---

[53] Adrian Desmond, *The Devil's Disciple* (London: Michael Joseph, 1994) 228.
[54] *LML* ii.83–4.
[55] CK to THH, 21/9/1860, IC-19.162r.
[56] THH to his sister, 17/4/1852, Leonard Huxley I.99.

agnosticism. There might seem to be a contradiction in interpreting principles which tie man to the animal kingdom in terms of a metaphysical destiny, Kingsley admitted, but "I dare say that I am descended from some animal from whom also the chimpanzee has sprung—I accept the fact fully, & care nothing about it [. . .] but this I know: that I am what I am; & that I am nearer to a God than to a chimpanzee."[57] The very fact that man can think of his immortality, and that the majority of people in all ages have done so, makes a good case "for believing the sense of immortality to be an universal natural law of our species [. . .] & therefore surely a true thought, to be fulfilled hereafter, unless the fountain of the universe be a Deus quidam deceptor, whom I had best curse, & die."[58] Kingsley excused himself for pressing these thoughts on Huxley, but he felt that "you & I have a common standing ground [as men of science]" and that he himself had "had trial enough in the last year to make me think terribly hard about what I am, & what this strange universe means."[59]

Huxley, who was generally reticent about his deepest feelings, answered Kingsley's frank letter and spoke "more openly and distinctly to you than I ever have to any human being except my wife."[60] Years before, Dyster had recommended Kingsley as the person to speak to about his religious doubts "because, as he [Dyster] said, you [Kingsley] were the only man who would do me any good. Your letter leads me to think he was right, though not perhaps in the sense he attached to his own words." Discussing the meaning of life with Kingsley helped him to take some philosophical distance from the immense tragedy that had just befallen him. At the same time it was a close examination of his (un)belief. Although he admitted he could not disprove the immortality of man, he, unlike Kingsley, could find no scientific reason for believing in it either. To him affirmation of awareness of personality had nothing to do with immortality. Nor did the infinite dissimilarity between man and the animals make any difference in the argument: "I do not know whether the animals persist after they disappear or not," he contended, and slyly added, "I do not even know whether the infinite difference

---

[57] CK to THH, 21/9/1860, IC-19.165v–166r.
[58] CK to THH, 21/9/1860, IC-19.166v.
[59] CK to THH, 21/9/1860, IC-19.167v–168r.
[60] THH to CK, 23/9/1860, Leonard Huxley I.221.

between us and them may not be compensated by THEIR persistence and MY cessation after apparent death, just as the humble bulb of an annual lives, while the glorious flowers it has put forth die away." But, Huxley continued in a more serious vein, if many arguments for the immortality of man were to him simply delusive, others were downright harmful: "The one is the notion that the moral government of the world is imperfect without a system of future rewards and punishments. The other is: that such a system is indispensable to practical morality. I believe that both these dogmas are very mischievous lies." Morality was a thoroughly human quality and could stand well without religion. " 'Sartor Resartus' led me to know that a deep sense of religion was compatible with the entire absence of theology," he concluded. And this objection bore directly upon his latest contemplations of Christianity and its promise of after life:

> As I stood behind the coffin of my little son the other day, with my mind bent on anything but disputation, the officiating minister read, as a part of his duty, the words, "If the dead rise not again, let us eat and drink, for to-morrow we die." I cannot tell you how inexpressibly they shocked me. Paul had neither wife nor child, or he must have known that his alternative involved a blasphemy against all that was best and noblest in human nature. I could have laughed with scorn. What! because I am face to face with irreparable loss, because I have given back to the source from whence it came, the cause of a great happiness, still retaining through all my life the blessings which have sprung and will spring from that cause, I am to renounce my manhood, and, howling, grovel in bestiality? Why, the very apes know better, and if you shoot their young, the poor brutes grieve their grief out and do not immediately seek distraction in a gorge.

Kingsley amply repaid Huxley for his letter. The frankness touched him and he realized they had much in common in their social views. The importance Huxley gave to the nobility of life here on earth was shared by Kingsley. This explained why Huxley felt attracted by the Christian Socialists. Although he professed not to understand their theology, "I have always said I would swear by your truthfulness and sincerity, and that good must come of your efforts."[61]

Kingsley thought, however, that Huxley had misinterpreted St Paul's words. A further problem with Huxley's stand was that he

---

[61] THH to CK, 23/9/1860, Leonard Huxley I.221–2.

did not think it wise to throw away the old before the new had disproved it. Moreover, their common ground of humanity would make it wrong to mock the belief in a future state "because it wd make many poor people miserable, & take from them a source of innocent happiness, without giving them anything in return; & it is not right to make mankind the poorer."[62] But if Huxley's and Kingsley's arguments had thus reached a state of stalemate, Kingsley's answer to Huxley's warning about the future of the Anglican Church, and his appeal to Kingsley's role in it, adds interest to their correspondence. Huxley concluded that "it must be by the efforts of men who, like yourself, see your way to the combination of the practice of the Church with the spirit of science" that the Church of England was "to be saved from being shivered into fragments by the advancing tide of science."[63] Kingsley answered in a passage which is worth quoting in its entirety. It provides unequalled insight into the way Kingsley groped with the consequences of the new discoveries in science on his theology, and the war-metaphor he employed, and which became firmly embedded in the nineteenth-century discourse of science and religion, indicates that Kingsley's stand on truth was not less sincere than Huxley's.

> What you say about scientific men & the Church of England I am well aware of. All I can answer is, that standing, as I do (rightly or wrongly) on *both* grounds, I will do my little best to see fair play for the men of science. Them I love, them I trust, with them I should live, had I my wish, with them I should die: but I suppose that God has put me where I am, that I may keep hold, in these confused times, on something w. they are in danger of losing; & perhaps, by doing them & their science full justice, learn from it at last some fruits toward reconciling two forms of human thought w. are now at open war—and as openly at war within my poor distracted head, my dear Huxley— as they are in the world around. Do not think of me as a dogmatist. No man is less so at heart: I need more knowledge on every possible subject. I need discussion, advice, comfort, from every side—& get very little. Mr. Maurice's ignorance of physical sciences prevents his helping me on many of the points w. I have most at heart; & I cannot find a man in England who is fighting the same battle exactly as I am—the attempt to grasp the new without hastily throwing away the old. I am engaged in a very serious struggle of w. I never talk,

---

[62] CK to THH, 26/9/1860, IC-19.184v.
[63] THH to CK, 23/9/1860, Leonard Huxley I.221.

just because it is so serious; I never opened my mind to any one as I have now to you, & you must have patience with me, as I have with you, for as with poor St Paul (whom you calumniate) so with me 'without are fightings, & within are fears.'[64]

What both men agreed on in their correspondence in September 1860 was the importance of human sympathy in the face of suffering, and it was such sympathy which ultimately stood out in their feelings for each other.

III

Although Kingsley's literary production had come to a near stand-still, his name had become synonymous with successful sales in the publishing world. When the illustrator Charles Henry Bennett was trying in vain to find a publisher for an illustrated edition of *The Pilgrim's Progress*, he sought Kingsley's help, and the latter's promise to write a preface for it immediately secured Bennett the willingness of Longman to venture on such a publication.

The new connection with the royal family led to further public advancement. The Regius professorship of Modern History at the University of Cambridge was vacant and Kingsley had shown Prince Albert he was interested in it. Through his influence, Lord Palmerston was won over and in May 1860 he asked Kingsley to fill the chair. Although Kingsley felt immensely honoured, there was an underlying sense of contrition in his reaction. It was all "very awful and humbling" and he could not but think of his own "unworthiness." His mixed feelings were the result of his uncertainty whether he would do well to accept the professorship. His "diffidence" did not come, as Mrs Kingsley suggests,[65] from professional qualms. Fanny had expressed her complete disapproval of the appointment from the very beginning. Her husband was overworked and she doubted whether he could bear the extra work at the University. Moreover, she did not like the idea of residence in Cambridge during term, the place being too far from Maurice's school. Kingsley tried to get a more objective view from John Parker, but he too was against the professorship. He feared it would interfere with his career as a writer,

---

[64] CK to THH, 26/9/1860, IC-19.186.
[65] *LML* ii.101.

which would make him lose money. But Kingsley knew it was too late to renounce it now. "The thing is *done*, rashly or not," he wrote to Fanny, "To decline a thing after having asked for it would offend the Prince deeply."[66] Moreover, he argued, Cambridge offered so many opportunities that he could not refuse. Residence in the university town would enable him to get "first rate masters for the girls" while they could return for Maurice's holidays to Eversley. "Consider," he further urged, "the noble honour of the thing & the status w. it gives me & you & the children henceforth—besides relieving me from the need of writing."[67] As he warmed to the prospect of the addition of the £371 that the appointment would bring to his income, and the idea of spending much time with the young men of the university, he felt "that my work for the rest of my life is clear before me."[68] In the end he accepted the post, and, the day before going to Cambridge to settle it all by getting his MA degree, he had a fierce quarrel with Fanny. This dampened what would otherwise have remained in his mind as a dream-like experience. But the Cambridge environment soon convinced him that he had made the right decision. Upon taking his MA he wrote to Fanny: "I have been thinking and praying a good deal over my future life. A new era has opened for me: I feel much older, anxious, & full of responsibility; but more cheerful & settled than I have done for a long time."[69]

As his course of lectures would start in November, Kingsley thought it a good idea to muster some energy (and brush up some history) during a summer fishing holiday in western Ireland with a sorrow-stricken Froude. Although his brother-in-law was a cause for anxiety—"He has quite broken down, won't fish, is v[er]y miserable, & takes the darkest view of his future prospects[70]—Kingsley's spirits were roused when he caught the first salmon of his life. "I have done the deed at last," he wrote home, "Killed a real actual live salmon, over 5lbs weight."[71] The excitement did Kingsley good, and Froude rallied too. The scenery was stunning, the weather glorious and the people hospitable and kind. They had "plenty of sea-boating

[66] CK to FK, undated, BL-62554 f.184r.
[67] CK to FK, undated, BL-62554 f.185v.
[68] CK to FK, undated, BL-62554 f.186r.
[69] CK to FK, undated, MP-C0171.
[70] CK to FK, undated, BL-62554 f.189v–190r.
[71] CK to FK, undated, MP-C0171–36913.

& yachting," but Kingsley hardly cared for that: "Since I have caught salmon," he explained, "I can think of nothing else [. . .] There is nothing like it. The excitement is maddening."[72] The holiday was a success. "I never felt so well & strong in life," he wrote to Fanny, "Anthony is looking & feeling v[er]y well."[73]

To reach the west coast, they had crossed large parts of Ireland, and had seen the signs of past and present poverty. Especially the stretch from Markree Castle in Sligo to Westport distressed him. "You cannot conceive," he wrote to Fanny, "to my English eyes the first shock of ruined cottages [. . .] what an amount of human misery each of those unroofed hamlets stands for!"[74] "Ireland is a v[er]y depressing place," he concluded, "it is so dreary & neglected,"[75] "It is a land of ruins & of the dead."[76] Still, in the Irish countenance Kingsley discerned a "look of ruddy health & plenty," and, contrary to expectation, the people all had "plenty of good clothes on their backs," and he hardly saw "a ragged person."[77] Yet the Irish physiognomy upset him. It revealed, he thought, an "idiotic brutality"and he "never saw lower specimens of humanity than the average men."[78] As the Irish children looked beautiful enough to him, he decided that "degradation" accounted for what he saw in the people. The feeling grew on him, and from Markree Castle he wrote

> I am haunted by the human chimpanzees I saw along that 100 miles of horrible country. I don't believe they are *our* fault. I believe there are now only many more of them than of old, but that they are happier, better, more comfortably fed than they ever were—but to see *white* chimpanzees is dreadful. If they were black one wouldnt feel it so much: but their skins, except where tanned by exposure, are as white as ours.[79]

As the condition of the English peasantry had improved much over the last decade, Kingsley had been led to expect a more prosperous state of the Irish peasantry as well. But although the bitter years of starvation were past, the country was still far from prosperous,

---

[72] CK to FK, 15/7/1860, BL-62554 f.194r; undated, BL-62554 f.190v.
[73] CK to FK, undated, MP-C0171–36913.
[74] CK to FK, undated, BL-62554 f.191v.
[75] CK to FK, undated, BL-62554 f.188v.
[76] CK to FK, undated, BL-62554 f.191v.
[77] CK to FK, undated, BL-62554 f.187v; f.188r.
[78] CK to FK, undated, BL-62554 f.187v.
[79] CK to FK, undated, MP-C0171–36913.

and what Kingsley interpreted as a sign of degradation in the Irish people, was in effect the indications of a state of poverty which was only just above the famine threshold. Moreover, the ruined cottages Kingsley saw were the monuments that testified to the massive emigration by which the population of Ireland had decreased by about two million people during the previous decade, an exodus which had drained the country of many of its more able-bodied men and women.

The passage quoted above has become notorious for the racist implication that most twentieth-century critics have read in it. However, there is some historical distortion in singling out this instance to emphasize Kingsley's racial opinions. That Mrs Kingsley freely published the passage after her husband's death indicates that the notion was hardly considered controversial or shocking at the time. Seeing the depressing standard of life of the Irish peasantry, Kingsley succumbed to the popular Victorian notion that the Irish Celts were an inferior race that came close to filling the missing link between man and the animal kingdom in the great chain of being. As in the fictional encounters with non-Teutonic cultures in his novels, the otherness of the Irishman caused in him a fear of losing in the underdeveloped effeminate Roman Catholic Irishman everything that stood for Kingsley's view of a civilization based on a prosperous Protestant culture. As we have seen, such an attitude lays bare deeper psychological complexities in Kingsley. Just as he was consistently opposed to slavery and reached out in sympathy to suffering working classes, closeness or intimacy with them unconsciously opened up fears of primitive feelings that find expression in rejection or in such commonplace prejudices as in the passage above. Claiming kin with other peoples continued to threaten his own carefully constructed cultural, social and religious identity, which increasingly voiced itself in jingoism. It also pressed upon him the possibility that the principle of evolution, apart from a progressive and forward succession of forms, might also be considered in terms of degeneration and degradation. It was to become a major point on which his interpretation of Darwinism hinged.

IV

Kingsley's appointment as Regius Professor of Modern History had not been received very well at the University of Cambridge. Although William Whewell, then Master of Trinity, had given Kingsley a hearty welcome in May, his private reaction was considerably less generous. Rumour got about that, when the news of Kingsley's appointment reached him, he exclaimed that the man was "a howling idiot."[80] Many of the dons remembered with horror Kingsley's devastating denunciation of the immorality and hollowness of Cambridge University life in *Alton Locke*, a novel which had remained popular over the years. Such aggression was not easy to forgive. J.S. Howson, then Hulsean Lecturer at Cambridge, and Kingsley's future friend and colleague at Chester, reacted in a way that must have been representative of the feelings many Cambridge men had towards receiving Kingsley in their midst: "I must confess that at that time I had a strong prejudice against him. I had read 'Alton Locke,' on its first appearance, and had thought it very unjust to the University of which both he and I were members. It seemed to me quite out of harmony with my recollections of a place, from which I was conscious of having received the utmost benefit."[81]

Kingsley was well aware of such animosity among the members of the university, and it was with some trepidation that he embarked on his new duty. "I cannot but be aware (it is best to be honest)," he said in his inaugural lecture on 12 November, "that there exists a prejudice against me in the minds of better men than I am, on account of certain early writings of mine."[82] But if the dons had reservations about Kingsley, the appointment of the new professor stirred up great interest in the undergraduates. One of them remembered "the thrill one felt as one November evening a man announced 'in Hall'—'Kingsley is come; I saw him to-day in the streets; my father knows him, and I knew him in a moment'." And he added "the man whose father knew Kingsley was a man to be envied, and to be asked to one's rooms at once."[83]

Kingsley found the inaugural lecture in the Senate House quite an ordeal. His former pupil John Martineau, by now a Cambridge graduate himself, decided to come to Cambridge to hear the lecture and saw on Kingsley's face a "strange half-frightened look" that he had never seen on him before. The atmosphere in the overcrowded Senate House was unruly. F.D. Maurice had come up too and was

---

[80] Chadwick, "Charles Kingsley at Cambridge" 304.
[81] J.S. Howson to FK, undated, *LML* ii.409.
[82] *RT* 342–43.
[83] Unidentified correspondent to FK, undated, *LMLM* 240.

recognized by an undergraduate who promptly shouted "Three cheers for Mr. Maurice," which was received with approval. This was followed by "three groans for Mr. Bright" and "three cheers for Garibaldi," both of which were endorsed by the students.[84] Deafening cheers were heard when Kingsley was announced and when he entered. Cheering would become a feature that regularly attended his lectures, and which Kingsley himself found most painful. "He would beckon for quiet," an undergraduate recalled, "and then in a broken voice and with dreadful stammering say, 'Gentlemen, you must not do it. I cannot lecture you if you do'."[85] Although Kingsley's rasping voice was not audible in all the building, on the whole, the inaugural lecture of nearly two hours seemed to go well. After the lecture Kingsley retired to his rooms near the Fitzwilliam Museum where an ailing Fanny (she had broken her leg) was awaiting him. When Martineau went to see Kingsley in the evening after the lecture he found him "very tired and rather low in spirits."[86]

Kingsley's inaugural lecture, which was printed with the title "The Limits of Exact Science as Applied to History," was meant to "warn you off from the too common mistake of trying to explain the mysteries of the spiritual world by a few roughly defined physical laws."[87] He refused to accept that "man was the creature of circumstances; and denied [. . .] the possession of freewill, or at least the right to use freewill."[88] Human welfare was founded on morals—"the fruit of righteousness is wealth and peace, strength and honour; the fruit of unrighteousness is poverty and anarchy, weakness and shame"[89]— and morality was theologically subject to the exercise of freewill. Therefore, history to Kingsley was created by individuals exercising their freewill of employing laws to counter other laws, and as the outcomes of counteracting are so numerous, history is far from a predetermined sequence of events: "So far removed is the sequence of human history from any thing which we can call irresistible or inevitable. Did one dare to deal in epithets, crooked, wayward, mysterious, incalculable, would be those which would rather suggest themselves."[90]

---

[84] Martineau 68.
[85] Unidentified correspondent to FK, undated, *LMLM* 240.
[86] Martineau 68.
[87] *RT* 334.
[88] *RT* 326.
[89] *RT* 334.
[90] *RT* 333.

Instead, Kingsley advocated that history could only be understood through the study of the men and women who made history. Thus, biography was the proper approach to history, while it was useless to try to find fixed laws of society to understand the course of history, just as it was impossible to give an average definition of man, as sooner or later an individual would break such patterns. It was like Babbage's calculating machine: the results it turned out may be predictable for thousands of numbers, but sooner or later it would turn up an unexpected number. And this was important in Kingsley's approach to history, as history was made by great men, not by little men. Moreover,

> those who offer us a science of little men, and attempt to explain history and progress by laws drawn from the average of mankind, are utterly at sea the moment they come in contact with the very men whose actions make the history, to whose thought the progress is due. And why? Because (so at least I think) the new science of little men can be no science at all: because the average man is not the normal man, and never yet has been; because the great man is rather the normal man, as approaching more nearly than his fellows to the true 'norma' and standard of a complete human character.[91]

Kingsley's great example of his theory was Luther. To say that his age made him what he was meant overlooking the question why the average monk, exposed to the same circumstances as Luther was, did not become like Luther. Although he approached the "standard of a complete human character," Luther clearly was not average.

Kingsley's inaugural lecture is closely connected to, and partly the result of, the views of nature and of humanity he had been discussing with Huxley. It seems as if the following passage from the end of the lecture was directly addressed to Huxley and the question of freewill and (immortal) personality they had discussed:

> mankind seems, at moments, the mere puppet of those laws of natural selection, and competition of species, of which we have heard so much of late; and, to give a single instance, the seeming waste, of human thought, of human agony, of human power, seems but another instance of that inscrutable prodigality of nature, by which, of a thousand acorns dropping to the ground, but one shall become the thing it can become, and grow into a builder oak, the rest be craunched up by the nearest swine. Yet these dark passages of human life may

---

[91] *RT* 331.

be only necessary elements of the complex education of our race; and as much mercy under a fearful shape, as ours when we put the child we love under the surgeon's knife. At least we may believe so; believe that they have a moral end.[92]

At the end of October, when Kingsley was preparing his lecture, he had written to Huxley that "Spinozaism contains a great truth and is only false when [. . .] it ignores the opposite pole of human thought," but that "I think it wrong in hoping man to apply exact science to [. . .] the history of mankind."[93] "Science indeed is great: but she is not the greatest,"[94] he concluded his lecture.

A grumbling Registrar wrote in his diary that day that the lecture "excited no applause" and that Kingsley appeared merely "solemn" when he intended to be pious, but his remained one of the very few negative comments. Because of the lecture, he had got home late for dinner and he was, moreover, one of those who had disapproved of Kingsley's appointment from the very beginning. Otherwise, Kingsley's warm personality was reported to have won over many of those undergraduates who had remained sceptical,[95] and the press described Kingsley's lecture as a "triumph."[96] The Prince Consort too, when a printed version was read out to him, was full of praise, and expressed approval of his view of Luther. However, a review published the next year in the *Westminster and Foreign Quarterly Review* written by Edward Spencer Beesly, the positivist professor of history at University College, London, thundered against Kingsley's language, logic, terminology and ideas. Beesly, who had always admired *Alton Locke*, found Kingsley's lecture but a "feeble, confused, and pretentious performance"[97] and felt irritated by "the slipshod, ungrammatical sentences, the mannerisms and the egotism which peep out in every page."[98] Kingsley was a first-rate novelist, but a lamentable historian. The very title of his lecture was absurd: "If Mr. Kingsley means that history will never be raised into an exact science, we perfectly agree with him, and only wonder why he should think it necessary to disprove so elaborately what no one, either wise or foolish,

---

[92] *RT* 339–40.
[93] CK to THH, 31/10/1860, CL-19.195.
[94] *RT* 335.
[95] Unidentified correspondent to FK, undated, *LMLM* 240.
[96] Chadwick, "Charles Kingsley at Cambridge" 308.
[97] Beesly 306–7.
[98] Beesly 321.

has ever been known to assert."[99] History was not a string of biographies, because that would imply that there was no scientific method in history. In sociology, Beesly maintained, observation, experiment, and comparison were valuable means of investigation, the last method of which was firmly rooted in history. Cultivating history scientifically, therefore, helped to discover or verify sociological laws. While such premises had long since been recognized on the Continent, England remained deplorably behind in historiography: "Nowhere but in England—we might perhaps say but in an English University—would Mr. Kingsley find listeners when he asserted that Luther caused the Reformation."[100]

Beesly knew he had to reckon with Kingsley's success with the undergraduates, and he was honest enough to admit that, whatever Kingsley's shortcomings in theorizing, he had qualities as a professor: "When he has done philosophizing, and reverted to story-telling, they will probably listen to many a brilliant and interesting sketch of men, manners."[101] The main problem with Kingsley's lectures, however, Beesly added, did not lie in the general appreciation of Kingsley's ethics, but in seeing them as permanent contributions to the study of history: "however laudable they may think his spirit, however sound his principles, they will view with some apprehension his confirmed habit of publishing."[102]

Beesly's warnings were appropriate. Although Kingsley's romantic and spirited presentation of history was popular with the undergraduates, who "crowded him out of room after room, till he had to have the largest of all the schools, and [. . .] crowded that—crammed it,"[103] Beesly's review was the first of a long series of criticisms from the professional historians. Derogatory reviews would dog Kingsley as, during the nine years that he held his Cambridge professorship, he insisted on publishing his lectures. In the end they would force him to resign the post.

---

[99] Beesly 312.
[100] Beesly 324.
[101] Beesly 307.
[102] Beesly 336.
[103] Unidentified correspondent to FK, undated, *LMLM* 240.

ENEMIES

CHAPTER NINETEEN

CAMBRIDGE IN MAGNIFICENT REPOSE (1861–1862)

In 1860 six clergymen of the Church of England and a layman published a collection of articles with the meaningless title *Essays and
Reviews*. The book was meant to encourage a liberal and candid
exchange of ideas on Biblical questions, a frank discussion that would
try to "attempt to illustrate the advantage derivable to the cause of
religious and moral truth, from a handling, in a becoming spirit, of
subjects peculiarly liable to suffer by the repetition of conventional
language, and from traditional methods of treatment."[1] Instead, it
triggered a fierce public reaction which bordered on hysteria, and,
punning on Aeschylus' tragedy about the downfall of Thebes by its
own men, the book's seven authors were condemned as "septem
contra Christum."

The authors, all Broad Church liberals of the Coleridgean school,
included Frederick Temple (Headmaster of Rugby), Baden Powell
(Oxford Savilian Professor of Geometry), Benjamin Jowett (Oxford
Regius Professor of Greek), and Mark Pattison (Rector of Lincoln
College, Oxford). The Oxford philologist Max Müller, who had married Kingsley's niece Georgina Adelaide Grenfell in 1859, was to
contribute too, but never sent in his article. The general tenet of
most of the articles was that a "gap" had grown between what the
Church held as religious doctrine and what educated men at the
universities really believed. This regarded both what new scientific
discoveries and new historical method had discerned as truth. The
truth of Christianity did not depend on the historical truth of the
recorded word, and the truth of revelation was reflected in its moral
impact rather than proven by miracles or prophesy. The implication was that it was ultimately irrelevant for the truth of Christianity
whether the Bible as the word of God was genuine or not. If
The Origin of Species had started to create a sharp controversy in the

---

[1] *Essays and Reviews*, "To the Reader."

religious world in 1859, the publication of *Essays and Reviews* caused
a complete uproar.

One would expect Kingsley to have sided with the authors of
Essays and Reviews. He himself had long been a thorough Broad
Church liberal and accepted the implications of the new discoveries
in geology and biology. What he could not accept, however, was
their defence of the new critical methods in history. To Kingsley,
notwithstanding his openness to the progress of learning, the Old
Testament remained fundamentally true, and the Higher Critics and
Comtean positivists were rank atheists to him. Thus, when the bubble burst after a highly approving review of *Essays and Reviews* by
the positivist Frederick Harrison, Kingsley recoiled. However, when
he received a circular from the archdeacon of his diocese asking him
to sign a petition for synodical action against its writers, he refused to
join his brethren of the cloth, but he found it necessary to explain
to the bishop that his unwillingness to sign arose from doubts about
the legality of the archdeacon's initiative and not because he agreed
with the authors of *Essays and Reviews*. Its publication was "deplorable",
he wrote, as "all the essays deny but do not affirm." It raised afresh
"doubts and puzzles which [. . .] have passed through the mind of
every thinking man in the last twenty-five years [. . .] without any
help to a practical solution."[2] Thus, when his curate at Eversley,
Septimus Hansard, who had just been ordained, asked him whether
he should read the notorious volume, Kingsley's answer was a stern
"By no means."[3] He also feared a negative influence on the undergraduates at the university, because "young men are only too glad
to fly off on intellectual disquisitions, from the plain requirements of
Christian faith and duty."[4] It would disturb the "magnificent repose"
he discerned in religion at the University. Still, in a letter to his new
friend Arthur Stanley, author of Arnold's *Life*, Kingsley recognized
there was some affinity between the authors of *Essays and Reviews*
and himself and the liberal Cambridge environment. He felt he was
fighting on the same side of the authors of *Essays and Reviews*. But
although "we wish them all well," he thought their action irresponsible and imprudent: "What the plague had these men to do, starting

---

[2] CK to J.B. Sumner, undated, *LML* ii.130.
[3] CK to J.B. Sumner, undated, *LML* ii.131.
[4] CK to J.B. Sumner, undated, *LML* ii.131.

a guerilla raid into the enemy's country, on their own responsibility? We are no more answerable for them, than for Garibaldi. If they fail, they must pay the penalty. They did not ask us—they called no Synod of the Broad Church—consulted no mass of scholars, as to what could be done just now."[5] Focussing on the gaps in theology, Kingsley felt, would only bring religion down in the end. No doubt Kingsley's stand-offish reaction to *Essays and Reviews* also reflected his wish to stay out of religious controversy.

Maurice, Ludlow and Hughes all shared Kingsley's fears that *Essays and Reviews* would do the Broad Church movement no good. Especially Hughes deplored the book's destructive criticism of faith. But he likewise deplored the synodical prosecution of its authors. Free expression of ideas was threatened by such measures. With Ludlow he therefore decided on a course of action. Two weeks later he read out a draft version of a pamphlet that stated the importance of basic beliefs and which was called *Religio Laici*. Maurice approved and suggested it was published as the first of a series of tracts with the title *Tracts for Priests and People*. It was the last effort of the Christian Socialists to set up an organ to promulgate their beliefs, but, notwithstanding Hughes's literary fame and the pamphlet's direct and feeling expressions of faith, very few people read it. Kingsley liked it—"it is clear, hearty, and honest"—but when he was asked to contribute to the series, he declined: "For me, I bide my time. I have always asserted, rather than denied. I have nothing more to say now than what I have said in print a dozen times."[6] This is one more instance of the fact that Kingsley had tired of Christian Socialist activities. The lack of reactions to the *Tracts for Priests and People* also shows how much the movement had depended for publicity on Kingsley's controversial pieces. Hughes seemed to realize that if something of their ideals was to be reached, it was to be done through different channels. They could no longer count on Kingsley's public support. Towards the end of the year Hughes made up his mind to stand for Parliament. He became Liberal MP from 1865 to 1874.

---

[5] CK to A.P. Stanley, 19/2/1861, *LML* ii.129.
[6] CK to TH, 21/4/1861, *LML* ii.132.

II

Kingsley enjoyed the residence at Cambridge during his lecturing terms in 1861 and 1862. Owen Chadwick has written that the "first three years as a professor were the happiest of Kingsley's life."[7] Although the statement needs some qualification, the dark brooding of 1859–1860 had indeed disappeared, and Kingsley felt more secure. Everything and everybody was described as "jolly" in his letters. The university environment clearly stimulated him, and royal favour continued to fall on him. At the beginning of 1861 Kingsley received a message from the Prince Consort, asking him to form a class on the constitutional history of England from 1688 to 1832 for the Prince of Wales, who had showed a rather lackadaisical approach to academic studies the previous year at Oxford. Beside the classes with the small group of selected undergraduates twice a week, the Prince was also to receive private tuition from Kingsley at his Cambridge residence. This added to Kingsley's sense of responsibility, a sense which, rather than weighing on him, he seems to have cherished. It meant, however, that Kingsley had to stay in residence at Cambridge for all the terms and only returned to Eversley for the summer.

Notwithstanding the weight of the "confidence [that] has been reposed in me", Kingsley found the Prince of Wales an easy person to get on with. He was interesting to talk to about politics and the press, and he "made up my mind to speak plain truth as far as I know it."[8] There was soon a mutual sense of friendship between tutor and pupil, and the Prince even asked his tutor to go with him to the races, something Kingsley said he could not very well do. Although the young Prince had a reputation for wild escapades, Kingsley was not scandalized at his behaviour. On the contrary, the professor gloried in the Prince's company. In December, when England was shocked by the sudden death of Prince Albert, his son was taken away from Cambridge, and Kingsley's appointment as the Prince's tutor came to an end. However, Kingsley remained on close terms with the Royal family. When the Prince left Cambridge, as a token of friendship he made Kingsley his private chaplain. In 1863 he and

[7] Chadwick, "Charles Kingsley at Cambridge" 313.
[8] CK to AS, 9/2/1861, MP-C0171-36919.

Illustration 5. Regius Professor of Modern History (photography by John Watkins, London, 1860s)

Mrs Kingsley were invited to the Prince's wedding, and in after years
he was often invited to stay at the Royal couple's residence at
Sandringham.

Most of Kingsley's time went into preparing his lectures. The first
two years of his professorship he lectured on early medieval Europe,
while the outbreak of the American Civil War inspired him in 1862–3
to do a course on the history of the United States. None of these
lectures, however, was published. Kingsley's writing for the press had
come to a near standstill. Apart from his inaugural lecture and a
series of sermons, no other works were published in 1860 and 1861.
He wrote no fiction, and submitted no reviews to the magazines.
This had partly to do with the lack of inspiration from which he
had suffered ever since 1858, partly with the fact that lecture-writ-
ing left him no time for other projects. The double duties at Cambridge
and at Eversley were not always easy to combine. At the end of
1861, for example, upon returning to Eversley for the Christmas holidays, he wrote to Charles Bunbury that "the heavy work of last
term, and the frightful catastrophe [Prince Albert's death] with which
it ended, sent us all home to rest, if rest is possible, when, on coming home, one finds fresh arrears of work waiting for one, which
ought to have been finished off months since." And he added that
"the feeling of being always behind hand, do what one will, is second only in torment to that of debt."[9] So there was hardly any time
left for writing. Moreover, it would seem that with his Cambridge
chair Kingsley felt relieved from "the need of writing."

The only book Kingsley brought out in 1861 was a collection of
sermons called *Town and Country Sermons*. The early sermons in the
volume were written in 1859. It contained the first three sermons
preached before the queen, as well as a handful of sermons which,
judging from a similar emphasis in them on discipline, authority,
and hard work, in all probability belong to the same year. Most of
the remaining sermons can safely be attributed to 1860.

If *Good News of God* provided little insight into what was going on
in Kingsley's mind, the sermons of 1860 are of considerably greater
importance to the biographer. They seem to reflect Kingsley's fascination with the question of evolution. One sermon starts with the
notion that "chance and change—there seems to us, at times, to be

---

[9] CK to CB, 31/12/1861, *LML* ii.134.

little else than chance and change,"[10] while another asserts that science can tell what God does but not how He does it.[11] There is no systematic analysis or appraisal of evolution in these sermons, but there is a dark shadow hovering over many pieces of Biblical exegesis, and a recurrent fear of brutes and savages runs as a red line through the volume.

Kingsley often expresses his fear of coming into contact with primitive or savage man: "if he looks at base and low things, he becomes base and low himself."[12] The end would be utter dissolution of civilization: "the savages will (as all savages are apt to do) destroy each other off the face of the earth, by continual war and murder."[13] Although he praises the London Diocesan Board of Education for raising "rude settlers [overseas] and ruder savages [. . .] and [for] help[ing] to sow the seeds of civilization and Christianity, wherever the English flag commands Justice, and the English Church preaches Love,"[14] he also realizes that the superficial polish of civilization is easily removed by gratifying the appetites: "if you would see how low man can fall, you must go to the tropic jungle, where geniality of climate, plenty and variety of food, are in themselves a cause of degradation to the soul."[15] Like Marlow in *Heart of Darkness*, he finally urges work as a restraint from indulging in contemplating the darker animal instincts. English civilization was built on work, he insisted, "not like the brutes, who cannot work, and can therefore never improve themselves, or the earth around them."[16] The idea of degradation absorbed Kingsley's mind increasingly, and almost became an obsession.

Behind all this there is a palpable sense that man and ape could, after all, be more similar than his theology allowed for. At moments this fear expands into an awareness of man's closeness to the apes: "in the rich forest, wanders the true savage, eating and eating all day long, like the ape in the trees above his head; and (I had almost said), like the ape, too, with no thoughts save what his pampered

[10] "The Victory of Faith," *VSTCS* 231.
[11] "The Hearing Ear and the Seeing Eye," *VSTCS* 226.
[12] "The Loftiness of Humility," *VSTCS* 327.
[13] "Antipathies," *VSTCS* 292.
[14] "Religious Dangers," *VSTCS* 261.
[15] "Religious Dangers," *VSTCS* 252.
[16] "Work," *VSTCS* 274.

senses can suggest."[17] In at least two sermons Kingsley resorts in such contexts to "Let us eat and drink; for to-morrow we die" (1 Corinthians 15.32), the very phrase which had triggered the correspondence with Huxley in 1860. It indicates the affinity of these sermons with the questions he had been discussing with Huxley, and that he thought they merited further consideration.

III

The friction in American society caused by the very different economic conditions of the manufacturing northern states and the south with its system of plantations had grown over the decades. At the end of 1860 the confederate Southern States broke up the Union by seceding. The following spring civil war broke out. Although the economic discord between North and South concerned various rights of trade and tariffs, they were above all closely related to the question of free labour as opposed to slavery, and it is this latter point which, thanks to an influential Anti-Slavery Society, found most resonance in England. As Kingsley had made the detrimental effect of slavery on the progress of civilisation a major theme in several of his novels, as well as in many of his other writings, the event of the American Civil War engaged him. "As for the American question," he wrote in December 1861 to Bunbury, who had asked his opinion on the war, "I have thought of nothing else for some time." He felt that it concerned him directly as professor of modern history, "so strongly do I feel the importance of this crisis, that I mean to give as my public lectures, next October term, the History of the American States."[18]

Early on in his literary career, Kingsley had summed up the view of slavery that recurs in most of his fiction: "every nation in the world which lives by slave-labour" will gradually be "corrupted down to the moral and intellectual level of their own slaves," and fall "by them, as Athens fell, as Rome fell; as the Spaniards in America have fallen, as the Southern United States will surely fall, unless they cast away, as an accursed and destroying sin, their present madness of

---

[17] "Religious Dangers," *VSTCS* 252.
[18] CK to CB, 31/12/1861, *LML* ii.134.

treating their brother-men like beasts that perish."[19] Thus, to people who had followed his denunciation of the sweat system in *Alton Locke*, his sharp condemnation of the Spanish in *Westward Ho!*, and his recent anti-slavery sub-plot in *Two Years Ago*, Kingsley would seem to make for a natural ally of the Northern States. The champion of freedom and equality could hardly do otherwise, they thought. "Charles Kingsley was to most boys in Great Britain who read books," Justin McCarthy reminisced in 1872, "a sort of living embodiment of chivalry, liberty, and a revolt against the established order of baseness and class-oppression in so many spheres of our society."[20] It was with amazement, therefore, that readers saw Kingsley take sides with the Southern slave-holding states. It caused a lasting dent in Kingsley's reputation. "The apostle of liberty and equality, as he seemed to me in my early days, has of late only shown himself to my mind as the champion of slave-systems of oppression and the iron reign of mere force," McCarthy concluded.[21]

Much misunderstanding has persisted about Kingsley's attitude to the American Civil War. Margaret Thorp thought that Kingsley had "altered the violent abolitionist sentiments with which he wrote *Two Years Ago*,[22] while Robert Bernard Martin, Una Pope-Hennessy, Guy Kendall and Susan Chitty seem to have preferred to gloss over the apparent inconsistencies in Kingsley's attitudes and keep complete, or near, silence about the Civil War. Brenda Colloms's comments are decidedly more helpful. She does not sense a contradiction in the fact that Kingsley sided with the South against the Northern "money-grabbing 'arithmocracy'." She adds that Kingsley believed the outcome of the war would be the end of slavery,[23] but leaves the question how Kingsley envisaged such a result unexplored. Still, almost twenty years earlier John Waller had done some groundbreaking research on Kingsley's ideas about the American Civil War and unearthed a reliable eye-witness report of Kingsley's America lecture. A report by Samuel Robert Calthrop, a unitarian clergyman, in the *Christian Examiner* of November 1863 contributes to a better understanding of Kingsley's position.

---

[19] "Bible Politics: or God Justified to the People No. VIII" 19/4/1851, *ChSoc* i.193.
[20] McCarthy 181.
[21] McCarthy 182.
[22] Thorp 150.
[23] Colloms 253.

In his lecture Kingsley argued that the Southern states had a "moral" right to secede, from which statement Calthrop inferred that Kingsley thought that the North was morally wrong in opposing them.[24] As in the long battle of power between North and South, the Northern free states had conceded slavery to the Southern States in the Compromises of 1820 and 1850, the more recent Crittenden Compromise of 1860, which with similar measures tried to forestall the war, should have been accepted by the North as well. Since to enlarge the Union, the North had subscribed in the Omnibus Bill of 1850 to the provision that runaway slaves should be returned to their masters, they had now no right to oppose Southern secession. Otherwise, Kingsley argued, the North should have broken up the Union in that year.

So where does that put Kingsley with regard to the anti-slavery question? Does such an approach to the Civil War mean that, in McCarthy's words, Kingsley had indeed become "the champion of slave-systems of oppression and the iron reign of mere force"? What we have is Kingsley's life-long stand against slavery, while it is significant that, nowhere during the years of the Civil War, did he declare he was in favour of it. As Calthrop's outline of the lecture shows, Kingsley was above all concerned with the right of the North to interfere in the political and economic situation of the South. Although this concerned questions of slavery, there is no judgment of slavery itself in his argument. Rather, Kingsley, as has been seen, had a profound distrust of the Manchester school of political economy of Richard Cobden and John Bright. This seems to have influenced his support of the Southern states with its aristocratic economy, and his disdain for the free market economy of the Northern states, which, as he had showed in *Alton Locke*, led to a slavery of its own. Kingsley thought that the central question of the war was one of economic hegemony. Tom Thurnall, for example, professes that he sees "the whole of the northern states so utterly given up to the 'almighty dollar,' that they leave the honour of their country to be made ducks and drakes of by a few southern slave-holders. Moral superiority?"[25] That was Kingsley's opinion in 1857. But little had changed on the eve of the Civil War four years later. Abraham

---

[24] Waller 563.
[25] *TYA* 400.

Lincoln, when he promised in his inaugural address of March 1861 not to interfere with slavery in the South, proved to Kingsley that keeping the Union together was more important to the North than the question of slavery itself. That Kingsley was mainly thinking in terms of economy is also shown by his reaction when the Civil War broke out. Kingsley cynically thought that it could only lead to a breaking up of the Union, which "will be a gain to us."[26] Kingsley thus saw the American Civil War in a perspective in which the issue of slavery was only of secondary importance. As to the question of Negro-slavery, Kingsley believed that that was a problem they would solve themselves. In *Two Years Ago* one character proposes to isolate the "tainted" Southern states "and leave the system to die a natural death, as it rapidly will."[27]

It would be wrong to label Kingsley as the black sheep in the English reaction to the American Civil War. Voices discerning hypocrisy in the English pro-Northern anti-slavery lobby were not infrequent. Charles Greville, the political diarist, for example, had commented in January 1861 that "with all our virulent abuse of slavery and slave-owners, and our continual self-laudation on that subject, we are just as anxious for, and as much interested in, the prosperity of the slavery interest in the Southern States as the Carolinian and Georgian planters themselves, and all Lancashire would deplore a successful insurrection of the slaves, if such a thing were possible."[28] Kingsley echoed such views. When, in 1862, as a result of the American Civil War, the Lancashire cotton-industry crashed, and nation-wide financial help was mustered to help the starving cotton-spinners, he wrote a letter to the *Times* in which he wanted the readers to remember that, although he and all poor-rate payers in the south would contribute to the aid project, "these very Lancashire men have directly helped to cause the present distress and the present war, by their determination to use exclusively slave-grown cotton; developing thereby, alike slavery itself, and the political power of the slave owners."[29] Charles Dickens, too, while he had condemned slavery in his *American Notes* (1842), believed "the

---

[26] CK to CB, 31/12/1861, *LML* ii.134.

[27] *TYA* ii.

[28] Quoted in Llewellyn Woodward, *The Age of Reform 1815–1870* (Oxford: Oxford University Press, 1962) 312.

[29] CK to the editor of the *Times*, undated, *LML* ii.145–6.

Federal cause to be based on dollars and cents with the anti-slavery cry as no more than mere camouflage for the grosser economic motives."[30] Kingsley was thus far from alone in his support of the Confederate States. Similarly, the undergraduates at the University of Cambridge received his views in his last lecture on America with applause and "wild cheers," and while the professor "almost sobbed as he sat down amidst the storm," many students went away with the feeling that "something in our lives was over."[31] On the other hand, his position estranged him from some friends of long standing. Those who sustained the views of the North included Hughes and Ludlow.

Kingsley's letter to the *Times* about the Lancashire cotton famine triggered an intense correspondence on the question. J. Thompson, a Manchester mill owner, protested that Kingsley had grossly misrepresented the industrial North. Kingsley's letter to the *Times*, he thought, implied that ruthless selfishness was "the mark of a Manchester man"and that there were no high-minded manufacturers among them. To show him that this image was false, Thompson invited Kingsley to come and see the condition of the workers in his mills, many of whom had worked for his father and grandfather. Kingsley's answer to Thompson's letter reveals some interesting points of opinion. He denied that he believed that there were no "excellent men in Lancashire as elsewhere" who had created an atmosphere of "wholesome feudal feeling," but he pointed out that, on the other hand, "during the last few year, new men have sprung up in hundreds—investing their all in new mills, and their profits in new mills again, till the bubble burst and left them [the workers] paupers."[32] It would be meaningless, he wrote in another letter, to come and see that the workers in Thompson's factories were "a picture of industrial health." That would be like judging "American slavery from the men who would ask one" to see the situation at their plantations.[33]

Although Kingsley's disdain of the Manchester school of economics was based on his social objections to the system, it also had roots in strong personal feelings of repugnance to factory labour and his

---

[30] Peter Ackroyd, *Dickens* (London: QDP, 1990) 1010.
[31] *LMLM*.247.
[32] CK to J. Thompson, 8/4/1863, *LML* ii.146.
[33] CK to J. Thompson, 14/4/1863, *LML* ii.148.

conviction that it was effeminate work that risked unmanning the nation. "Another great evil [. . .] is that mill-labour effeminates the men," he told Tompson, and further explained that

> large bodies of men should be employed in exclusively performing day after day, the same minute mechanical operation, till their whole intellect is concentrated on it, and their fingers kept delicate for the purpose, is to me shocking. I would gladly see such men emigrate, even though they fared badly at first, because the life of a colonist would, by calling out the whole man, raise them in body and mind enormously.[34]

This is a key to explaining why Kingsley had created a mostly bodiless character in *Alton Locke* and why, at the end of the novel, he is made to emigrate, "leave [. . .] physically decrepit races"[35] and find "physical perfection."[36]

IV

In the summer of 1862 Kingsley took Fanny and Maurice for a month's holiday to Scotland, where they enjoyed both fashionable society and the scenery. In one breath he writes to his mother about fishing, of the grandeur of the Tay, and of the "reels [they] had last night, Lord J. Manners & Sir Hugh Cairns figuring aw[a]y."[37] He did a lot of fishing with Maurice, and was in ecstasy about Dhu Loch which contained, he said, "salmon, salmon trout, brown trout, salmo-ferox, sythe, lythe, herrings, sticklebacks, flounders, grayling [. . .] and all other known and unknown fresh and salt-water fish, humbled together in thousands. Such a piece of fishing I never saw in my life."[38] The few letters from Scotland that survive show that Kingsley was in great spirits and had left all sense of fatigue behind. Mrs Kingsley confirms that "the visit to Inveraray was one of the bright memories and green spots of his life."[39]

In October Kingsley attended the annual meeting of the British Association for the Advancement of Science, which was held that

---

[34] CK to J. Thompson, 14/4/1863, *LML* ii.148.
[35] *AL¹* 384.
[36] *AL¹* 385.
[37] CK to MK, August 1862, BL-41298 f.128v.
[38] CK to MK, undated, *LML* ii.139.
[39] *LML* ii.140.

year in Cambridge. Huxley, who was working on his provocative book that would carry the title *Evidences as to Man's Place in Nature*, had told Kingsley that man and the gorilla shared the same ancestors. Although such notions were bound to raise a storm of protest from religious quarters, they could safely be discussed with Kingsley. "If so," he placatingly told Huxley, "I compliment my ancestors on having had wits enough to produce *me*, while my cousins have gone & irremediably disgraced themselves, by growing *four* hands instead of 2; & not being able to do the 3 Royal R's to this day."[40]

The question of man's animal origin had become a public question which was followed with avid interest by the press. Ever since the publication of *The Origin of Species* Richard Owen had maintained that there were unique anatomical characteristics in the human brain, something Huxley publicly doubted. At the famous Oxford meeting of the British Association in 1860 such preconceptions about man's unique nature were behind Samuel Wilberforce's well-meant, but unfortunately flippant, question in support of Owen whether Huxley's apes were on his grandfather's or grandmother's side, which triggered Huxley's legendary and devastating answer: "If then, said I the question is put to me would I rather have a miserable ape for a grandfather or a man highly endowed by nature and possessed of great means of influence & yet who employs these faculties & that influence for the mere purpose of introducing ridicule into a grave scientific discussion, I unhesitatingly affirm my preference for the ape."[41]

The debate about the origin of man was resumed when, in 1862, the heads of decapitated gorillas were shown on tour through England by the gorilla hunter Paul de Chaillu. Owen, who bought the heads for the British Museum, concluded from them that men and apes were essentially different by virtue of the absence of the hippocampus, a small lobe at the back of man's brain. Although Huxley had already exposed Owen's conclusions in print as "mendacious humbug,"[42] he decided to have the last word at the Cambridge meeting of the British Association. During the Zoological Section (Section D), to which he stood as chairman, he had an ape's brain dissected and showed that, like man's, it did contain a hippocampus.

---

[40] CK to THH, 28/2/1862, IC 19.203.
[41] Adrian Desmond, *The Devil's Disciple* (London: Michael Joseph, 1994) 279.
[42] Adrian Desmond, *The Devil's Disciple* (London: Michael Joseph, 1994) 307.

Kingsley had been informed that Huxley was going to speak on the hippocampus question during the meeting of the British Association in Cambridge, and, thinking it likely that the Huxley-Wilberforce scenario would be reenacted, assured Huxley in August that "if any body tries to get up a "religious" controversy, (w. I think no Cambridge man will) then will I show you that I have teeth & claws, & especial pleasure in worrying a parson, just *because* I am a good churchman."[43] A few weeks later he wrote again to Huxley to let him know that Darwin's theory of evolution had completely conditioned his way of thinking about God and nature. He sent Huxley a self-invented anecdote of a Khan who asks two Moolahs to tell of their gods so that he will be able to choose the wisest. The first Moolah offers a god who has created all things, while the second offers a god who "makes all things make themselves." " 'Wah wah! Said the Khan. 'He is the Sultan of all sultans; he is the wisest of all master-builders. He is the God for me henceforth, if he be wise enough'."[44] Kingsley meant this anecdote "as a hint of the effect on my natural theology Darwin has had on me," and he added that, if Huxley found it worthwhile, he might "send it on to the good man, as it may please him."[45]

Of course, Kingsley kept thinking about a theistic explanation of evolution, and it is hardly surprising that he found much of the discussion about the hippocampus beside the point. Anatomical details were irrelevant in his conception of man, and the narrowing down of the ultimate difference between man and ape to the absence or presence of a small lobe of the brain was ludicrous to him. The absurdity of the discussion in Section D of the British Association led him to write an imaginary speech of a Lord Dundreary at the meeting and circulate it among his friends. Dundreary's slight wit first mistakes hippocampus for hippopotamus, and when he corrects himself wanders off like this:

> There's a mistake somewhere. What was I saying? Oh, hippopota-
> muses. Well, I say, perhaps mine's dead. They say hippopotamuses
> feed on water. No, I don't think that, because teetotallers feed on
> water, and they are always lean; and the hippo's fat, at least in the

---

[43] CK to THH, 4/8/1862, IC 19.207v.
[44] CK to THH, 20/12/1862, IC 19.211.
[45] CK to THH, 20/12/1862, IC 19.209r.

Zoo. Live in water, it must be; and there's none in my brain. There was when I was a baby, my aunt says; but they tapped me; so I suppose the hippopotamus died of drought. No—stop. It wasn't a hippopotamus after all, it was hip—hip—not hip, hip, hurrah, you know, that comes after dinner, and the section hasn't dined, at least since last night, and the Cambridge wine is very good. I will say that No. I recollect now. Hippocampus it was. Hippo-campus, a sea-horse; I learnt that at Eton; hippos, sea, and campus, a horse—no—campus a sea, and hippos, a horse, that's right. Only campus ain't a sea, it's a field, I know that; Campus Martius—I was swished for that at Eton.[46]

For those who had followed the debate—the "famous tournament," as Mrs Kingsley called it—it must have made hilarious reading. In *The Water-Babies* it was condensed in a more lasting, and completely rewritten, form to become one of Kingsley's best pieces of satire.

But apart from all the fun, the implications of evolution for man were of great concern to Kingsley. In a more serious mood, for example, he wrote to Professor George Rolleston, who had long sustained Huxley's thesis, about the possibility of a theory of degradation. The theory was attractive to him. Rather than seeing primitive races, brutes, and savages as evolutionary precursors of civilized man, it was more congenial to him to think in terms of degradation. It saved the idea of man created in God's image, and did not hint at the dark and primitive instincts of man as a reality merely gilded over by civilization, and allowed for the existence of the soul in a process which now seemed essentially soulless. Of course, the idea of degradation had occurred to many theologians over the centuries, but Kingsley tried to reconcile it to the scientific evidence for the evolution of organic forms. It led to a belief, "which I hardly dare state in these days," he wrote to Rolleston after the meeting of the British association, "that the soul of each living being down to the lowest, secretes the body thereof, as a snail secretes its shell, and that the body is nothing more than the expression in terms of matter, of the stage of development to which the being has arrived." He wished Huxley and Rolleston would try for a change to conceive of the brain of a gorilla or a baboon "under the fancy of their being *degraded* forms." In conclusion, he playfully threatened that "I shall torment you and your compeers with my degradation theory,

---

[46] *LML* ii.141.

till you give me a plain Yes or No from facts."[47] It was a promise he kept.

In his proposition of a degradation theory Kingsley committed the same scientific error for which he had dismissed Philip Henry Gosse's ill-fated refutation of organic development in *Omphalos*. The existence of the soul and its moral state is scientifically as undemonstratable as Gosse's prochronism. What saved Kingsley, however, from the scorn of the men of science was the fact that contemplating degradation in the plan of evolution was perfectly legitimate in terms of scientific hypothesis and testing, and that the existence, or non-existence, of the soul was irrelevant in such discourse.

V

The circumstance of the genesis of *The Water-Babies* has become almost as famous as the book itself. Mrs Kingsley tells that

> Sitting at breakfast at the rectory one spring morning this year, the father was reminded of an old promise, "Rose, Maurice, and Mary have got their book, and baby must have his." He made no answer, but got up at once and went into his study, locking the door. In half an hour he returned with the story of little Tom. This was the first chapter of "The Waterbabies," written off without a correction.[48]

In May Kingsley sent Macmillan some chapters of his work. The publisher, longing to bring out a new book by Kingsley, immediately seized upon the project. "I have read a great deal of it," Alexander Macmillan wrote when he visited Eversley a few weeks later, "it is the most charming piece of grotesquery, with flashes of tenderness and poetry playing over all, that I have ever seen."[49] He proposed to run it as a serial in *Macmillan's Magazine* as soon as Henry Kingsley's second novel *Ravenshoe* was concluded. It appeared in instalments from August 1862 to March 1863.

An early reviewer writing for *The Times* realized that Kingsley's new book was different from other books for children and predicted that it would soon become something of a classic: "That the *Water-Babies* will outlive many generations of ordinary gift-books would

[47] CK to G. Rolleston, 12/10/1862, *LML* ii.143–4.
[48] *LML* ii.137.
[49] Alexander Macmillan to James MacLehose, [June 1862], Morgan 65.

probably be no unsafe prophecy."[50] He was proved right. Hundreds of editions have since appeared, often lavishly illustrated,[51] and, more than a hundred-and-thirty years later, the Oxford World's Classic edition of 1995 advertised that Kingsley's book "has claim to being the most peculiar book ever to achieve the status of a children's classic."[52] *The Water-Babies* is Kingsley's most successful work and much of his fame today rests on this novel alone.

The Water-Babies was, and still is, a book that calls forth reactions that vary from unbounded enthusiasm to intense aversion. Edward Lear, for example, wrote in 1871 to thank Kingsley "for so much gratification given me by your many works—(Perhaps above all—'Water Babies'."[53] Alexander Macmillan read the book to his children as it came to him, piece by piece, and his daughter recalled those readings as "the greatest excitement in the nursery world that I remember."[54] However, another contemporary, Charles Eliot Norton, wrote in a private letter of 1875 that his children were "deep in 'Tales from Shakespeare,' and in 'Tom Brown'," and that he was "glad of it, for I do not like the style of most recent story books for children." Disparagingly he added "I don't want anything from the professional writers of stories, the John Halifax Mulock Craiks, or the Charles Water Kingsley Babies [. . .]. May they never be read!"[55]

Tom Brown's Schooldays, the novel Kingsley would have liked to have written, provides a helpful starting point for a discussion of Kingsley's children's classic. In their books, both Hughes and Kingsley wanted to argue the importance of moral fortitude. The influence of Hughes's book is palpable in a number of elements in the first pages of *The Water-Babies*. For example, the fact that the main characters in both novels are called Tom is an early indication of the link that Kingsley saw between *The Water-Babies* and *Tom Brown's Schooldays*. Kingsley's main character is introduced as follows: "Once upon a time there was a little chimney-sweep, and *his name was Tom*. That is a short name, and *you have heard it before*, so you will not

---

[50] *The Times*, 26/1/64, 6.
[51] Cf. Anna Maria Ricci, "The Water-Babies: una fiaba di successo e le sue variazioni testuali e paratestuali", http://www.scintille.it/, 2002.
[52] *WB¹* backcover.
[53] Alderson ix.
[54] Morgan 65.
[55] Charles Eliot Norton to Constance Hilliard, 5/4/1875, *The Letters of Charles Eliot Norton* (London: Constable, 1913) ii.50–1.

have much trouble in remembering it."[56] To make sure that his choice of the name Tom for his hero is no casual coincidence, Kingsley follows this up with a reference to the wearing of velveteen trousers. The use of the plural form "velveteens" is first recorded in the *OED* for Hughes's novel, and next for Kingsley's. Indeed, in *The Water-Babies* Tom is looking forward to the days he will be wearing velveteens and be a man: "And he would have apprentices, one, two three, if he could. How he would bully them, and knock them about."[57] The association of velveteens and bullying is striking. Tom Brown's encounter with an under-keeper called Velveteens is an instance of the growth of "gentlemanliness" in the boy. When he gets caught fishing on private grounds, Tom admits he is in the wrong and stoically accepts the consequences when he is brought before the headmaster. He bears Velveteens no ill-will when he gets flogged and afterwards "they became sworn friends."[58] Kingsley's Tom is equally stoic in enduring punishment. When he was beaten by his master he "stood manfully with his back to it till it was over."[59] However, Tom's notions of justice are still muddy. The code of honour and justice that Hughes wanted to make explicit in the Velveteens episode is meant to contrast with the pernicious practices of the fifth-form boys who bully the smaller boys at Rugby. The tyrannical liberty the older boys take with the smaller boys exceeds their "legally determined limits."[60] Thus, where Velveteens represents legal and righteous exercise of authority, the fagging of the small boys by the fifth form stands for abuse of power. As his purposed beating of his future apprentices indicates, in Kingsley's Tom there is much confusion about the real meaning of authority. Until that is learnt, Tom cannot be "like a man."[61] Of course, what also stands central in Hughes's novel is that the growth of a boy towards full manhood cannot take place without the recognition of the body of Christ. The physical and spiritual are closely intertwined in this perception and this vision is aptly representative of Hughes's and Kingsley's Christianity.

---

[56] *WB* 3; my italics.

[57] *WB* 5.

[58] Thomas Hughes, *Tom Brown's Schooldays* Prt 1, Ch ix.

[59] *WB* 4–5.

[60] Cf. David Elliston Allen, *The Naturalist in Britain: A Social History* (London: Allen Lane, 1976) 125.

[61] *WB* 5.

Indeed, it also stands at the heart of Kingsley's novel. The reader is told at the beginning of *The Water-Babies* that his Tom "never had heard of God, or Christ."[62] His idea of manhood needs to be completely overhauled, just as much as Tom Brown's, and this is what Kingsley hints at in the opening paragraph of *The Water-Babies*.

Kingsley prefaces his novel with two stanzas from Wordsworth's "Lines Written in Early Spring." The passage emphasizes the "fair works of Nature" that Kingsley wanted to explore in his novel, but the line "what man has made of man" also strikes another key-note in *The Water-Babies*. Throughout his narrative Kingsley makes abundant use of the words *boy* and *man*, both in addressing his reader and in setting an example. At the beginning Tom is described as a boy who aspires to be a *man* and *manfully* stood his punishment, but who at the end of the first paragraph is still no more than the "jolliest *boy* in the whole time". The reader too is addressed from the very beginning as "my dear little boy." Only at the end of the first chapter, after having emphasized at least twice that Tom was a "brave boy", does Kingsley describe his action as that of "a brave little *man*."[63] The moment is important. It comes when Tom, church bells pealing in his head, goes down the rocky slope of the mountain to reach the "clear stream" he had seen in the valley down below. It anticipates his moment of baptism and regeneration (i.e. becoming a water-baby), the first stage of a process of growth towards the ideal of man, Christ. The reader, following Tom's process of regeneration, at this moment becomes a "little man" too.[64]

In the early stages of Tom's conversion Kingsley's use of the words *boy* and *man* oscillates considerably, but, although Kingsley is at times careless in his use of the two terms, on the whole there is a growing emphasis on *man*. This reflects Tom's moral progress. Half-way through the novel the attention even shifts at one point from *little* man to *big* man. In chapter six it is made clear that Tom's physical and spiritual journey is a testing ground of his manliness, of those qualities which were deemed necessary "if he intended ever to be a man."[65] The notion is defined within the parameters of the plucky, dutiful, hardworking, clean, and God-loving English*man* and gentle*man*.

---

[62] *WB* 4.
[63] *WB* 47.
[64] *WB* 56.
[65] *WB* 264.

In *The Water-Babies* Kingsley was as much concerned with the constitution of a "Young England" as Hughes was.

The stern and improving purpose underlying *The Water-Babies* might seem to make the novel an unattractive book for children. It is not. One quality of the novel that makes it attractive for children is the way adults are throughout presented as foolish individuals who are ridiculed for their unimaginative attitude to life. Moreover, there is so much fun on the surface-level of the novel that the didactic purpose is easily forgotten. Kingsley's dazzling array of verbal frolicking makes *The Water-Babies* unparalleled in its kind. His flow of words is marked by carefree spontaneity, and the scenes evoked are based on intense and vivid sense experiences. The course of the narrative is constantly interrupted by digressions into all kinds of Victorian questions. These again would seem over-serious if they were not balanced by a Rabelaisian exuberance of language. A mere description of Kingsley's style can hardly do justice to its effervescent spirit, and although examples cry out to be quoted, the following passages must suffice to illustrate Kingsley's method in *The Water-Babies*.

After sneering at the current debate about the importance of the hippocampus during the meeting of the British Association for the Advancement of Science, Kingsley confronts the professor whom Lord Dundreary had failed to understand with a water-baby. Professor Ptthmllnsprts (Put-them-all-in-spirits), "a very great naturalist, and chief professor of Necrobioneopalaeonthydrochthonanthropopithekology," refuses to accept the existence of a water-baby. This leads Kingsley to comment on bigoted and unimaginative scientists (drawn by Linley Sambourne in the likenesses of Thomas Henry Huxley and Richard Owen for the illustrated Macmillan edition of 1886). His satire starts as follows:

> And this is why they say that no one has ever yet seen a water-baby. For my part, I believe that the naturalists get dozens of them when they are out dredging; but they say nothing about them, and throw them overboard again, for fear of spoiling their theories. But, you see the professor was found out, as every one is in due time. A very terrible old fairy found the professor out; she felt his bumps, and cast his nativity, and took the lunars of him carefully inside and out; and so she knew what he would do as well as if she had seen it in a print book, as they say in the dear old west country; and he did it; and so he was found out beforehand, as everybody always is; and the old fairy will find out the naturalists some day, and put them in the Times, and then on whose side will the laugh be. [. . .] So she [the fairy] took

the poor professor in hand: and because he was not content with things as they are, she filled his head with things as they are not, to try if he would like them better; and because he did not choose to believe in a water-baby when he saw it, she made him believe in worse things than water-babies—in *unicorns, fire-drakes, manticoras, basilisks, amphisbae-nas, griffins, phoenixes, rocs, orcs, dog-headed men, three-headed dogs, three-bodied geryons*, and other pleasant creatures, which folks think never existed yet, and which folks hope never will exist, though they know nothing about the matter, and never will; and these creatures so upset, terrified, flustered, aggravated, confused, astounded, horrified, and totally flabbergasted the poor professor that the doctors said that he was out of his wits for three months; and perhaps they were right, as they are now and then.[66]

Although Kingsley has amply underscored his point here about dog-matism in science and the unimaginative public reception of new discoveries in science, he is not content to leave it at this. At such moments the more playful aspect of *The Water-Babies* takes over and the serious and factual adult world is mocked in and out, creating a sense of solidarity with the child-reader:

So all the doctors in the county were called in to make a report on his case; and of course every one of them flatly contradicted the other: else what use is there in being men of science? But at last the major-ity agreed on a report in the true medical language, one half bad Latin, the other half worse Greek, and the rest what might have been English, if they had only learnt to write it. And this is the beginning thereof—
   The subanhypapaposupernal anastomoses of peritomic diacellurite in the encephalo digital region [. . .] But what they proceeded to do My Lady never knew; for she was so frightened at the long words that she ran for her life, and locked herself into her bedroom, for fear of being squashed by the words and strangled by the sentence. A boa constrictor, she said, was bad company enough: but what was a boa constrictor made of paving stones? [. . .] So she made Sir John write to the Times to com-mand the Chancellor of the Exchequer for the time being to put a tax on long words.[67]

But moments like these are given a further Rabelaisian brilliance in page-long rhythmic catalogues of words and concepts that turn "the commonsense notion that all experience is true and reliable into ridicule."[68] Moreover, by drawing on erudite knowledge, it is with

---

[66] *WB* 183–4.
[67] *WB* 184–6.
[68] Coleman 514.

these pieces of learned humour that Kingsley manages to draw in
the adult reader again. The digression on Professor Ptthmllnsprts's
realization that water-babies did exist after all continues with the
doctors' opinions as how to cure the professor, prescribing medicines
based on hellebores ("to wit—Hellebore of Aeta. Hellebore of Galatia.
Hellebore of Sicily"), trying on him the methods of "Hippocrates,
Aretaeus, Celsus, Coelius Aurelianus, And Galen." But finding this
too much trouble they had recourse to

> Borage. Cauteries. Boring a hole in his head to let out fumes, which
> (says Gordonius) "will, without doubt, do much good." But it didn't.
> Bezoar stone. Diamargaritum. A ram's brain boiled in spice. Oil of
> wormwood. Water of Nile. Capers. Good wine (but there was none
> to be got). The water of a smith's forge. Ambergris. Mandrake pil-
> lows. Dormouse fat. Hares' ears. Starvation. Camphor. Salts and senna.
> Musk. Opium. Strait-waistcoats. Bullyings. Bumpings. Bleedings.
> Bucketings with cold water. Knockings down. Kneeling on his chest
> till they broke it in, etc. etc.[69]

Such playing with words explains why the Menippean satire of *The
Water-Babies*, as Northrop Frye has called it, is often coupled with
that in *Alice in Wonderland*.[70]

The Water-Babies has been described as a Victorian fantasy crowded
with Kingsley's hobby-horses. The fantasy genre seemingly allowed
him to pour out whatever he had on his mind—"he is prattling out
of a full heart," *The Times* commented.[71] The book indeed abounds
with references to fishing grounds, the importance of hygiene, the
fascination with the natural world, the mistakes of Victorian education, abhorrence of eternal punishment, acceptance of evolution, condemnation of the American Civil War, and the necessity of social
reform. Because Kingsley interrupts his story with endless digressions
on these subjects and further irrelevant material, the unfolding of
Tom's story is never straightforward. C.N. Manlove has estimated
that as much of three-quarters of the book has no relation to Tom
and his history at all.[72] Many early critics, in fact, blamed Kingsley
for the undisciplined way the story is told and concluded that *The
Water-Babies* failed in structural unity. The reviewer in *The Times*

---

[69] *WB* 188–190.
[70] Northrop Frye, *Anatomy of Criticism* (Princeton University Press, 1957) 310.
[71] [-], "Mr. Kingsley's *Water-Babies*", *The Times* 26 January 1864, p. 6b.
[72] Manlove, p. 20.

summed up the early reaction to the book as follows: "The whole story was absurd, without rhyme or reason, beginning or end, and a sort of thing that no man could understand."[73] Although *The Times* was willing to brush such objections aside, and appreciate the humour of the book, *The Spectator* was not. Its reviewer explicitly points out that the structural deficiencies of Kingsley's story-telling mar the quality of the final product:

> we arraign Mr. Kingsley of that half-animal impatience which cannot be satisfied with working out patiently a single distinct idea,—but must interpolate arrogant inarticulate barks at a hundred things which have no business at all in his tale [. . .] Mr. Kingsley has, as he too often does, spoiled a good story by his undisciplined and ill-concentrated imagination, which induces him to interrupt one train of thought just to vent his disgust at a dozen follies or crimes which occur to him while he is at work.[74]

But such comments missed the very essence and attraction of *The Water-Babies*. It is the vigorous presence of Kingsley's authorial voice that makes it special as children's literature. It is the personality of the author that stands out as a main quality of the book.

The central theme of *The Water-Babies* is cleanliness. It increases in importance as the story unfolds and firmly stands out at the end of the book in lines such as "thank God that you have plenty of cold water to wash in" and "stick to hard work and cold water."[75] On the surface level it represents Kingsley's crusade against the unhealthy sanitary situation of the time. Kingsley, for example, explains that water-babies are "all the little children in alleys and courts, and tumble-down cottages, who die by fever, and cholera, and measles, and scarlatina, and nasty complaints which no one has any business to have."[76] Similarly, when Ellie is taken to the seaside to improve her health, Kingsley's gloss on this is that her mother might have saved her money by keeping her children at home rather then taking them "to some nasty smelling undrained lodging, and then wondering how they caught scarlatina and diphtheria." This is closely followed by a comment on the craze for the sea-aquarium

---

[73] [-], "Mr. Kingsley's *Water-Babies*", *The Times* 26 January 1864, p. 6a.
[74] [-], "Mr. Kingsley's Water-Babies", *The Spectator* 23 May 1863, pp. 2037, 2038.
[75] *WB* 388.
[76] *WB* 221.

in which young ladies let sea-beasts "die of dirt and neglect."[77] In *Glaucus* Kingsley had already dwelt on the power of nature to clean up its dirt, and it is not surprising that he returned to it here in *The Water-Babies*:

> Only where men are wasteful and dirty, and sewers run into the sea [. . .] or in any way make a mess upon the clean shore [. . .] the sea-anemones and the crabs [. . .] clear away everything, till the good tidy sea has covered up all the dirt in soft mud and clean sand, where the water-babies can plant live cockles and whelks and razor shells and sea-cucumbers and golden-combs, and make a pretty live garden again, after man's dirt is cleared away.[78]

Sequences like this take the theme of cleanliness to deeper levels. They show the course of nature to be in a state of equilibrium, and the actions of man as a disrupting force. The anticipation of the aquarium in which sea-beasts are allowed to "die of dirt" prepares for the aquarium the water-babies build where the water is truly clean. Thus the reader is confronted with the opposing worlds of man's "wasteful and dirty" earthly condition and the water-babies' ideal paradisiacal state, the worlds of adulthood and of childhood, and, as an extension, the worlds of sin and of innocence. Placing such dichotomies against the background of Kingsley's life one can read into *The Water-Babies* deeper personal issues of the author, especially where the relationship between Tom and Ellie reflects that of Charles and Fanny.

The first meeting between Tom and Ellie is dramatic in the symbolism which surrounds its description. Coming down one of the flues of the chimneys he was cleaning Tom finds himself in Ellie's bedroom. His sooty intrusion in the girl's white bedroom is described in startling terms: "[He] stood staring at her, as if she had been an angel out of heaven [. . .] She cannot be dirty. She could never have been dirty, thought Tom to himself. [. . .] And looking round, he suddenly saw, standing close to him, a little ugly, black, ragged figure, with bleared eyes and grinning white teeth. He turned on it angrily. What did such a little black ape want in that sweet young lady's room? And behold, it was himself, reflected in a great mirror."[79] In

---

[77] *WB* 167–8.
[78] *WB* 213.
[79] *WB* 30.

this passage there are various tensions at work. Ellie's angelic appearance is enhanced by a picture on the wall "of a man nailed to a cross," at which Tom feels "sad, and awed," even if he does not know who the figure represents. It is easy to find parallels in Tom's heathen and 'dirty' state with Kingsley's when he met Fanny. The guilt and unworthiness Tom feels upon intrusion, which Maureen Duffy has reconstructed as a scene of "attempted rape,"[80] resembles Kingsley's early reactions as a dissolute university student to his love and sexual passion for Fanny. It is because of Ellie that Tom wishes to be clean again and starts on his pilgrimage to true holiness. However, notwithstanding the remarkable progress Tom makes on the road to regeneration, this is something he fails to reach. Only when Tom unites his quest for doing good with his love for Ellie can a state of holiness (after a period of separation) be reached and is he truly worthy of Ellie. The parallelism to Kingsley's own courtship of Fanny is palpable. It reflects Kingsley's belief that he owed his return to Christianity principally to his love for her. Sexuality, which in the prudery of the Victorian Age was considered as the manifestation of the animal in man, is relocated by Kingsley within Christianity in such a way as to become an expression of it.

With all its references to sticks, snakes, truncheons, pipes, flues, crevices and anemones, the book lends itself well to a Freudian interpretation, such as the one in Duffy's *Erotic World of Faerie*, where Tom is seen as a symbol of "the questing penis and the unborn foetus in its in its amniotic fluid."[81] But it would be wrong to read *The Water-Babies* exclusively in such a way, and to over-emphasize this element is to distort Kingsley's main purpose in writing the book, which is mainly a work about childhood and nature in a rapidly changing industrial society. Kingsley does not hide that his theme owes much to Wordsworth, and half of the chapters in the book are prefaced by lines from the late Poet Laureate. Like Wordsworth Kingsley felt in nature "a presence that disturbs me with the joy/Of elevated thoughts; a sense sublime/Of something far more deeply interfused."[82] In *The Water-Babies* this presence is both an

---

[80] Maureen Duffy, *The Erotic World of Faery* (London: Hodder and Stoughton, 1972), 284.

[81] Maureen Duffy, *The Erotic World of Faery* (London: Hodder and Stoughton, 1972), 283.

[82] "Lines Composed a Few Miles Above Tintern Abbey" lines 94–6.

awe-inspiring—"Nature can do, and has done, beyond all that man's poor fancy can imagine"[83]—and moral presence. Like Wordsworth too, Kingsley turns to childhood to explore the moral presence, and meditates on the inevitable loss of direct contact with nature and its related loss of vision as one grows into an adult. In this Kingsley closely follows Wordsworth's *Intimations of Immortality from Recollections of Early Childhood*, a few lines of which are quoted at the beginning of chapter six. But Kingsley is not so much interested in the Platonic process of alienation from the preexistent soul, as with a modern Victorian society which denies children their childhood and thus takes away their moments of divine vision which are so necessary in order to see nature as "The anchor of my purest thoughts, the nurse,/The guide, the guardian of my heart, and soul/Of all my moral being."[84] It is in this sense that Kingsley in *The Water-Babies* grieves with Wordsworth to think "What man has made of man." This is obvious in the overlying plot-element of the book, namely that of returning to Tom as a water-baby the childhood which had been taken away when society had turned him into a chimney sweeper. The book abounds with condemnations of the ill-treatment of children, which Kingsley generally depicts as deforming constraints on the spontaneity of childhood. The following is a playful example of this, but much harsher comments can be found:

> And then [Mrs Bedonebyasyoudid] called up a whole troop of foolish ladies, who pinch up their children's waists and toes; and she laced them all up in tight stays, so that they were choked and sick, and their noses grew red, and their hands and feet swelled; and then she crammed their poor feet into the most dreadfully tight boots.[85]

There is a good deal of punishment in Kingsley's fable, and the birch rod is never far off. It is, however, represented as the perverse symbol of the corrective power of Victorian society. Kingsley abhorred corporal punishment, and those who used it are given in the book "a taste of their own rods"—"She birched them all round soundly with her great birch rod."[86] But there is no satisfaction in the act of whipping, just as there is none in any kind of punishment; Mrs

---

[83] *WB* 180.
[84] "Lines Composed a Few Miles Above Tintern Abbey" lines 109–11.
[85] *WB* 229–30.
[86] *WB* 232.

Bedonebyasyoudid's retribution is a fixed law of nature, as she explains to Tom: "I cannot help punishing people when they do wrong. I like it no more than they do [. . .] I work by machinery."[87] And, of course, from *The Water-Babies* it is clear that Kingsley denies the possibility of eternal punishment in Hell.

Kingsley's text is also imbued with a latent fear for the frailty of Christian civilisation, which is encoded in Kingsley's interpretation of evolution. This is behind the uneasy tension of the intrusion in Ellie's room between the angelic white Ellie and the black dirty Tom, who is negatively compared to a Negro with a "little ugly, black, ragged figure, with bleared eyes and grinning white teeth" and next to a "little black ape." The people who disrupted the equilibrium of nature in the example above, and who will not listen to St Brandan to become "peaceable Christians," "were changed into gorillas, and gorillas they are until this day,"[88] and, later in the book, when Tom grows prickles all over his body, like a hog, we are reminded of Kingsley's repeated mention of hogs in his descriptions of the lower classes in *Yeast*. One can go even further down the evolutionary scale to the eft: "You were very near being turned into a beast once or twice Tom. Indeed, if you had not made up your mind to go on this journey, and see the world, like an Englishman, I am sure but that you would have ended as an eft in a pond."[89] It serves as an illustration for a central idea in Kingsley's interpretation of evolution: "people's soul's make their bodies, just as a snail makes its shell."[90] Nothing in the story is stable, and nature is in a constant flux: "There are two sides to every question, and a downhill as well as an uphill road."[91] The presence of this creative urge in all things is one of the leitmotifs of the story. It is personified in Mrs Carey, who makes new beasts out of old, and who tells Tom that "I am never more busy than I am now," but never stirred a finger. "I sit here and make them make themselves," she explains.[92] It is a playful expression of Kingsley's construction of evolution.

Much has been written on Kingsley's imaginative representation of evolution, his poetic appropriation of Darwinism. His explanation

---

[87] *WB* 226.
[88] *WB* 215.
[89] *WB* 277.
[90] *WB* 251.
[91] *WB* 277.
[92] *WB* 314–5.

of his purpose in writing *The Water-Babies* in a 1862 letter to F.D. Maurice has been quoted over and over again (albeit never from the original):

> When you read it, I hope you will see that I have not been idling my time away. I have tried, in all sorts of queer ways, to make children & grown folks understand that there is a quite miraculous & divine element underlying all physical nature; & that nobody knows any thing about any thing, in the sense in w[h]. th[e]y may *know* God in Christ, & right & wrong. And if I have wrapped up my parable in seeming Tom-fooleries, it is because so only could I get the pill swallowed by a generation who are not believing with anything like their whole heart, in the Living God [. . .] Meanwhile remember that the Physical science in the book is *not* nonsense, but accurate earnest, as far as I dare speak yet.[93]

Gillian Beer has remarked that "Kingsley, in his images of extinction, of degeneration, and of recapitulation and development, mythologises Darwinian theory with remarkable insight."[94] Although Kingsley never abandoned his creationist view of life, he ably assimilated the newness of Darwin's discoveries. Darwin's emphasis on random change in the animal and vegetable kingdoms was introduced in Kingsley's fable as proof of the infinitely *wonderful* quality of creation. Darwinism contained for Kingsley a valid mythology of existence. In its appropriation of evolution, and speculation on devolution, it embraces his insistence on the link between the moral and the physical in nature. Witness, for example, the conclusion of *The Water-Babies*:

> these efts are nothing else but the water-babies who are stupid and dirty, and will not learn their lessons and keep themselves clean; and, therefore (as comparative anatomists will tell you fifty years hence, though they are not learned enough to tell you now), their skulls grow flat, their jaws grow out, and their brains grow small, and their tails grow long, and they lose all their ribs (which I am sure you would not like to do), and their skins grow dirty and spotted, and they never get into the clear rivers, much less into the great wide sea, but hang about in dirty ponds, and live in the mud, and eat worms, as they deserve to do.
>
> But that is no reason why you should ill-use them: but only why you should pity them, and be kind to them, and hope that some day

---

[93] CK to FDM, 17/5/1863, BL-41297 f.147–8r.
[94] Gillian Beer, *Darwin's Plots; Evolutionary Narrative in Darwin, George Eliot and Nineteenth Century Fiction* (London, Boston, Melbourne, Henley: Routledge & Kegan Paul, 1983) 138.

they will wake up, and be ashamed of their nasty, dirty, lazy, stupid life, and try to amend, and become something better once more. For, perhaps, if they do so, then after 379,423 years, nine months, thirteen days, two hours, and twenty-one minutes (for aught that appears to the contrary), if they work very hard and wash very hard all that time, their brains may grow bigger, and their jaws grow smaller, and their ribs come back, and their tails wither off, and they will turn into water-babies again, and perhaps after that into land-babies; and after that perhaps into grown men.[95]

If Thomas Hughes envisioned a Christianity which seamlessly joined the moral and physical qualities that make up "a true Englishman,"[96] Kingsley casts it in the spiritual ground plan of an evolutionary creation myth. In so doing, he darwinized his muscular Christianity.

VI

The exuberant style of *The Water-Babies* reflects Kingsley's happiness during 1862. The book's pace, originality and constant humour, in which the author is always present, convey that he enjoyed writing it. Although Mrs Kingsley enhanced her story by saying that the first chapter was written in only thirty minutes (which would be physically impossible even for the fastest of writers), her remark that "the whole thing seemed to flow naturally out of his brain and heart, lightening both of a burden without exhausting either,"[97] is no exaggeration.

Kingsley's position at Cambridge was also gratifying. He liked teaching the undergraduates, and his popularity did not diminish. The recollections of one undergraduate who attended his lectures in 1862–63 reveal that Kingsley was in his element at Cambridge. One February afternoon a group of undergraduates was waiting along the river for the return of one of the rowing boats when

> through the deepening twilight come two figures more; one tall, felt-hatted, great-coatless, with a white comforter, slinging along at a great pace. He is among us before we are well aware of it. In the pipes go into the pockets, and the caps are lifted. He passes down a little below

---

[95] *WB* 386–7.
[96] *WB* 388.
[97] *LML* ii.137.

us, and returns smoking a cigar, and goes a little above us and waits. Then the sound of the thrashing oars—up comes the boat—[. . .] As she passes him he throws his cigar into the river, and begins to run too. I shall never forget it. The crew are tired and row badly, as they did at Putney afterwards. He ran with us to Grassy Corner. I remember the boat stopped there for an 'Easy all,' and his short comment, 'I'm afraid that won't do, gentlemen.'

"We all loved him," the account concluded, "we would have carried him back to Cambridge with delight. The boat went on again, and away we ran and left him to his walk. But in many a hall that evening the story was told how he had been running with the boat."[98]

Kingsley felt full of gratitude to Cambridge, and he expressed this by writing an installation ode for the Duke of Devonshire, the new Chancellor of the University, in which he lamented the death of Prince Albert, but also celebrated his Alma Mater as the place where

> Gliding wherries come and go;
> Stalwart footsteps shake the shores;
> Rolls the pulse of stalwart oars;
> Rings aloft the exultant cry
> For bloodless victory.
> There she greets the sports, which breed
> Valiant lads for England's need
> [. . .]
> Spreading round the teeming earth
> English science, manhood, worth.

For the occasion, the Ode was set to music by William Sterndale Bennett and performed in the Senate House. For unknown reasons Kingsley was not present during the ceremony itself, but was briefed of its success with the undergraduates by a satisfied Bennett, who recorded that "the last thing I heard was the ringing cheer for Professor Kingsley."[99]

The lines from the Ode quoted above reminded many persons present of the notorious Cambridge boating scene in *Alton Locke*. But there could be no greater contrast between the celebration of the true English manhood here and the decadent representation of it twelve years before. To Kingsley the contrast was a painful one, and when Macmillan proposed to print a new edition of his first published novel he profited from the occasion to rewrite the scenes which

---

[98] *LMLM* 247–8.
[99] William Sterndale Bennett to CK, [June 1862] *LML* ii.138.

had given offence, and add an apologetic preface. The change was effected in no uncertain terms. In the "Preface to the Undergraduates of Cambridge" Kingsley announced that, because many "of our own fellow-countrymen [. . .] have taken umbrage at certain scenes of Cambridge life drawn in this book", "I have re-written all that relates to Cambridge life."[100] The reason he did so was dictated by his conviction that much had changed since 1838–42 when he himself was an undergraduate there, but above all because "I have received at Cambridge a courtesy and kindness from my elders, a cordial welcome from my co-equals, and an earnest attention from the undergraduates with whom I have come in contact." What has made historians cry out at this recantation is the sense that Kingsley emasculated his first published work of prose just as Alton emasculated his first volume of poetry. The following statement in the Preface is indeed as ugly as it is uncritical: "[my reception] would bind me in honour to say nothing publicly against my University, *even if I had aught to say*."[101] Understandable as his expressions of gratitude may be, one wishes Kingsley had left this out.

Although the affirmation that all the Cambridge scenes were rewritten is not true, the changes that were effected were startling. At times the mere omission of a short phrase sufficed to change the general atmosphere. Thus, the "bold, bedizened women"[102] along the river and "the yelling of the most sacred names, intermingled too often with oaths"[103] disappeared from the text. In other parts Kingsley added considerably to his text to change its tone. When, for example, Alton is pushed into the river and curses himself for "getting among you cursed aristocrats," Kingsley adds in the new edition that "the reader may say that I was in a very unwholesome and unreasonable frame of mind. So I was."[104] The description of the supper party, that "invention of bacchanalian luxury" where they sang "of the most brutal indecency"[105] had to go too, but rather than re-writing the offending "scene of frivolity and sin,"[106]

---

[100] *AL* xxvii.
[101] *AL* xxviii; my italics.
[102] *AL¹* 130.
[103] *AL¹* 131.
[104] *AL* 103.
[105] *AL¹* 136.
[106] *AL¹* 137.

Kingsley makes Alton absent himself to wander untainted among the "noble buildings."[107] The text was also purged of the numerous negative references to the university dons. Cambridge had become a place of "earnestness and high-mindedness, increased sobriety and temperance."[108]

The rewriting and the preface did not convince his enemies nor did it please his admirers. Even such a moderate friend as Howson, who, as a Cambridge man, initially had felt hostile to the author of *Alton Locke*, questioned whether the "pendulum of his strong feeling did not, on this last occasion, swing too far in its new direction."[109] Even today critics still question the moral implications of Kingsley's changes. But in their haste to condemn two things are often lost sight of. First, although Kingsley's revisions change the picture of Cambridge substantially, the impact on the novel as a whole is minimal. Second, there are no grounds to suspect Kingsley of hypocrisy. He felt sincere gratitude to the university and was convinced he had overdone his criticisms of Cambridge life. It was a place which had given him recognition, friendships and happiness. That we regret such changes in one of the most outspoken condition-of-England novels is quite another matter.

---

[107] *AL* 107.
[108] *AL* xxxviii.
[109] J.S. Howson to FK, undated, *LML* ii.409.

CHAPTER TWENTY

TRUTH, FOR ITS OWN SAKE (1863–1864)

Notwithstanding the congenial Cambridge atmosphere during the early years of his professorship, in 1863 Kingsley decided to give up his house in St Peter's Terrace and come up to Cambridge from Eversley for lectures and exams only. The reason Mrs Kingsley gives for this unexpected decision is that keeping a second house in Cambridge had become far too expensive for "the salary of his Professorship."[1] Her explanation, however, hardly reflects the complete truth. There is no evidence for this in the correspondence. Moreover, Owen Chadwick points out that Macmillan, who in 1863 bought up the works Kingsley had published with Parker (who went out of business that year), had started to pay Kingsley a respectable amount of money over the years. Moreover, a lack of money would have prompted Kingsley to publish more than he did during the early years of his professorship. Although residence in Cambridge during term entailed extra expense, it was above all the professorial salary of £371, an amount which almost equalled that of his living, as Kingsley repeatedly pointed out, which made it possible to escape from the drudgery of writing for money. There were more pressing reasons, therefore, which made a return to Eversley necessary. One of them was that the climate of the Fen Country did not agree with the Kingsleys. Mrs Kingsley reports that by the beginning of 1864 "for more than a year past Mr. Kingsley had been suffering from chronic illness increased by overwork of brain."[2] She herself felt ill most of the time in Cambridge too. Although it is difficult to assess what exactly it was that ailed Kingsley—Mrs Kingsley's description "overwork of brain" is too generic for that—in later letters there is repeated reference to malarial infection. Chadwick also suggests that gout had started to trouble Kingsley.[3]

Maurice's stay at Cowley Powles's school St Neot's had been short.

---

[1] *LML* ii.154.
[2] *LML* ii.192.
[3] Chadwick, "Charles Kingsley at Cambridge" 316.

In 1859 he had been transferred to the newly founded Wellington College, a national boarding school in Crowthorne, Berkshire, only 7 miles from Eversley. The Prince Consort had done much to promote the new school, and although Wellington College was, in the first place, "more consonant to his views for his son,"[4] Kingsley's decision to send him there also grew out of his respect for the Royal family. After Prince Albert's death he felt bound to do all he could for the college "because he looked upon the place as a memorial of the great Prince."[5] His friendship with the headmaster, Edward White Benson, moreover, made close involvement with the school possible. And when Kingsley gave up his Cambridge house and returned to Eversley, the school's proximity to his parish allowed him to lecture to the boys during school term. He was keen on helping to set up a museum of natural history and instill in the boys a habit of observation that would enable them to become men of science, because the interest he had at heart in his connection with Wellington College, he said, was "the interest of Science itself":

> Ah, that I could make you understand what an interest that is. The interest of the health, the wealth, the wisdom of generations yet unborn. Ah, that I could make you understand what a noble thing it is to be men of science; rich with a sound learning which man can neither give nor take away; useful to thousands whom you have never seen, but who may be blessing your name hundreds of years after you are mouldering in the grave, the equals and the companions of the noblest and the most powerful. Taking a rank higher than even Queen Victoria herself can give, by right of that knowledge which is power.[6]

That Kingsley had clear visions about promoting science in boys is borne out in a letter to the influential geologist Charles Lyell, whom Kingsley had met through Charles Bunbury, Lyell's brother-in-law. As Lyell wanted to see a greater role for science in school curricula, Kingsley did not hesitate to write to him about his plans for a museum at Wellington College. "As most of the boys," he explained, "go abroad in after life, it seems to open a great door for your scheme, of having educated gentlemen-naturalists spread abroad, and in communication with each other and with the societies at home."[7]

---

[4] *LML* ii.72.
[5] *LML* ii.156.
[6] Lecture at Wellington College, 25/6/1863, *LML* ii.166.
[7] CK to Charles Lyell, 28/4/1863, *LML* ii.168.

Mrs Kingsley allots much space in her biography to Benson's reminiscences of this time ("those evenings at Eversley—certain lyings on the grass")[8] and to her husband's natural history lecture to the boys which overflowed with glowing enthusiasm and bliss in its descriptions of the pursuits of the naturalist. Well might she give such a full account of this, because one of the last happy periods of Kingsley's life was fast drawing to an end. Public disappointment and humiliation were soon added to his growing ill-health. Conservatives still eyed the author of *Alton Locke* with suspicion while many radicals and socialists had not sympathized with the changes in the new edition. His connections with the royal family also made many of those anti-establishment men, who had once admired the stammering "Chartist" parson, doubt his sincerity. By 1863 Kingsley had made critics and enemies on the left and on the right. Many churchmen abhorred his religious views and deprecated *Hypatia*. His history lectures, when published in 1864, were ridiculed. Only with scientists did Kingsley seem at ease, and he corresponded intensely with men such as Lyell, Bunbury, Darwin, Huxley, William Pengelly, and Henry Walter Bates. Topics included such unlikely ones as the erosion of geological strata, traces of volcanic activity, mocking butterflies, the filament at the petiole-end of *Lathyrus nissolia*, the analogy of language and natural history, and the relationship between humans and apes. The men of science appreciated Kingsley's intelligent participation in the scientific debate, and, as a sign of recognition, he was made a Fellow of the Geological Society in 1863 upon a proposal advanced by Bunbury, who was seconded by Lyell.

In a famous passage in a letter to F.D. Maurice, himself a hopeless scientist, Kingsley explained his trust in the present generation of scientists, a trust which hinged on an honest perception of truth:

> I am v[e]ry busy working out points of Natural Theology, by the strange light of Huxley, Darwin, & Lyell. I think I shall come to something worth having, before I have done. But I am not going to reach into fruit this 7 years. & for this reason. The state of the Scientific mind is most curious: Darwin is conquering everywhere, & rushing in like a flood, *by the mere force of truth & fact*. The one or two, who like Owen hold out [. . .] are forced to do so by all sorts of subterfuges as to fact, or else by evoking the *odium theologicum*.—as Owen himself is said to have done in a Review [. . .]

---

[8] E.W. Benson to FK, 11/7/1875, *LML* ii.157.

> But—they find that now th[e]y have got rid of an interfering God—a master-magician, as I call him—th[e]y have to choose between the absolute empire of accident, & a living, immanent, ever-working God.[9]

Kingsley's study of science subserved his religious convictions, and, in conclusion, he reassured Maurice that his interest in scientific debate had not lead him "astray into materialism as yet."

Kingsley's open views in science contrast oddly with his rigid resistance to the study of the historical truth of the Bible. Much of his resistance, of course, stemmed from the fact that many of the historians who questioned the truth of the Bible to him were uncongenial materialists. His loathing of everything connected to Straussism has been amply noted. The Higher Critics that the *Westminster Review* school of "materialists" such as George Eliot championed could easily be brushed aside as immoral individuals. But when John Colenso, a follower of Maurice and a bishop in the Church of England, argued in 1862 that the Pentateuch was post-exilic forgery, things stood differently.

Colenso, a liberal Norfolk rector, had in 1853 been appointed Bishop of Natal in South Africa. Struck by many questions his Zulu converts asked him about the Old Testament, he logically examined the evidence of truth the Bible presented him with and concluded that the many numerical discrepancies in the text warranted doubts about its historicity. As he had long regarded Maurice as his theological mentor, and had even dedicated a volume of sermons to him, he felt surprised to find, when he detailed his opinions in correspondence, that Maurice disapproved of his conclusions. Still, Colenso decided to publish them in a volume entitled *The Pentateuch and Book of Joshua Critically Examined*. The result of this was a row between the two men of the cloth. Maurice urged that Colenso should give up his bishopric if he held such views. To this Colenso retorted that "if it comes to that, there are plenty of people who say that you have no business to hold your living."[10] This launched Maurice in a crisis of tormented self-investigation in which, to clear his lofty purposes, he considered giving up his living. But although Maurice felt muddled about his own conscience, he saw clearly in his theology that science offered no confirmations for revelation, that numerical

---

[9] CK to FDM, 17/5/1863, BL-41297 f.148; italics mine.
[10] John Colenso to FDM, undated, Brose 270.

evidence did not affect the historical evidence of the Bible. "You cannot shake faith or understanding by criticism," he wrote in a rejoinder to Colenso's book, "But you by criticism or without it, make men doubt and reject that which they have ceased to understand as connected with themselves."[11]

Kingsley was against Maurice's giving up his Vere Street living and felt anger at Colenso for having harassed the Master with undue scruples. From such premises Colenso could not be expected to get a fair hearing from Kingsley. Although he was not willing to speak out in the periodical press on the Colenso question, as he would have done ten years before, he did "burn to say something worth hearing" about the Pentateuch in a series of sermons to be preached at Eversley. "I cannot help hoping that what I say may be listened to by some of those who know that I shrink from no lengths in physical science," he wrote to Maurice, concluding that "I am sure that science and the creeds will shake hands at last."[12]

For these sermons, which were published "by request" in 1863 as *Sermons on the Pentateuch*, Kingsley wrote a preface in which he made clear that he thought that Colenso's book "was altogether negative; was possessed too often by that fanaticism of disbelief which is just as dangerous as the fanaticism of belief; was picking the body of the Scripture to pieces so earnestly, that it seemed to forget that Scripture had a spirit as well as a body."[13] The Bible has a unique effect upon the "human heart, life and civilization," he argued, which cannot be altered or cancelled by "all possible deductions for 'ignorance of physical science,' 'errors in numbers and chronology,' 'interpolations,' 'mistakes of transcribers'."[14] And such effects originate in the "noble acts" of God, not in man's noble thoughts, and therefore "the value of the Bible teaching depends on the truth of the Bible story."[15] In a letter of acknowledgement to Llewellyn Davies, who reviewed Kingsley's new volume of sermons for *The Reader*, he asserted: "You will understand that I have read much and hard on these critical questions about Scripture, and that I am sick of them, because they do not touch vital religion, which is all in all to me."[16] This might

[11] FDM to John Colenso, undated, Brose 271.
[12] CK to FDM, undated, *LML* ii.181.
[13] "Preface" *GPD* xii–xiii.
[14] "Preface" *GPD* xiv.
[15] "Preface" *GPD* xv.
[16] CK to J. Llewellyn Davies, 3/8/1863, *LML* ii.187.

seem to express Kingsley's wish not to enter further religious controversy. He was in no state for battle. "I have to preach the divine-
ness of the whole manhood," he wrote to Maurice, "and am content
to be called a Muscular Christian, or any other impertinent name,
by men who little dream of the weakness of character, sickness of
body, and misery of mind, by which I have bought what little I
know of the human heart."[17] But there was going to be no respite
from religious battle. His reputation for muscular controversy had
been formed and his name was inseparably linked to Maurice's.

Shortly after the Colenso affair, Maurice was once more attacked
on his disbelief of eternal damnation, this time by Oxford professor
Edward Bouverie Pusey. An exchange of letters in *The Times* followed between the two divines in which Maurice had the better of
it. After an especially acute letter in which Maurice protested against
Pusey's treatment of Benjamin Jowett, one of the authors of *Essays
and Reviews*, Kingsley congratulated him on defeating Puseyism once
and for all:

> You have burst out of the thicket upon poor old Pusey like a 'Reem'
> of Bashan, horning him hip & thigh, tossing him over your back like
> any buffalo or borellé, & rushing on triumphant through the scrub,
> not caring to look back for your victim. He will answer, "exili voce",
> like the witch's ghost out of the earth, or Homer's suitors with a "bat-
> like squeak": but I do not think you need mind a voice from the world
> below. That letter is quite enough for English commonsense. I hope
> you will back it up by silent disdain, if he rejoins.
>
> Puseyism is dead, & knows it: & is therefore, like an evil sprite, ven-
> omous & querulous. But remind it that it is a sprite, as you have done,
> & dead & d-.
>
> [. . .] I have seen enough of the poor ghost for the last 10 years,
> to know its w[a]ys intimately. Ahimé![18]

Pusey could still bite though. An opportunity offered itself when the
Prince of Wales showed his gratitude to his former tutor and private chaplain by proposing his name for an honorary D.C.L. at the
University of Oxford. Pusey threatened a "non placet," explaining
he could not allow the conveyance of such an honour to an author
who, with *Hypatia*, had written an immoral book unfit to be read
by "our wives and daughters." The situation was embarrassing for

---

[17] CK to FDM, 18/9/1863; *LML* ii.186.
[18] CK to FDM, 23/2/1863, BL-41297 f.139–40.

Kingsley and for those who supported his nomination. Arthur Stanley especially had cause to remember the controversy. He had liked the book and had given it to his mother to read.[19] For once Kingsley had the press on his side. The *Spectator* deplored Pusey's behaviour and saw his action against Kingsley as "another opportunity for gratifying his rabid theological tastes."[20] Although Kingsley appreciated the stand of the University Council on the matter, he wanted to avoid the "fracas before the Prince's face" and decided to withdraw his name. He decided that "it was an honour that must be given, not fought for." But, notwithstanding Mrs Kingsley's words that he soon rooted out the unpleasant memory, the public offence rankled in his mind long after.[21] When Bishop Wilberforce of Oxford invited Kingsley in 1866 to preach a course of sermons in the University of Oxford, he declined.

The humiliation at Oxford aggravated Kingsley's depression. But more humiliation was in store for him when, at the end of 1863, he unwittingly blundered into offending an old enemy: John Henry Newman.

II

In a review of the seventh and eighth volume of Froude's *History of England* in *Macmillan's Magazine*, Kingsley discussed the immorality caused by the Pope's arbitrary dispensing of power in Tudor England, and mentioned in passing that

> Truth, for its own sake, had never been a virtue with the Roman clergy. Father Newman informs us that it need not, and on the whole ought not to be; that cunning is the weapon which Heaven has given to the saints wherewith to withstand the brute male force of the wicked world which marries and is given in marriage.[22]

This was a blunt and gratuitous accusation. But because it was so, it reveals much of what Kingsley had come to feel about Newman

---

[19] Prothero, Rowland E., *Life and Letters of Dean Stanley* (London: Thomas Nelson & Sons, n.d.) 351.

[20] In Martin (1959) 232.

[21] *LML* ii.180.

[22] "Froude's History of England Vols. VII and VIII" *Macmillan's Magazine* (January 1864) 217.

and of what he took for granted about the Roman Catholic Church. It was not meant as a public and malicious attack on Newman— Kingsley was in no mood to enter public controversy—and the allegation therefore expresses a genuine conviction (and prejudice) in him which had been formed so long ago as to have become habitual in his consideration of the Roman Catholic question.

Newman, who confessed he was not a reader of *Macmillan's Magazine*, was sent the January issue of the magazine by a friend, the slanderous passage underlined in pencil. He wasted no time in addressing the publisher and in a letter dated 30 December 1863 drew attention to the passage in question, specifying that

> I should not dream of expostulating with the writer of such a passage, nor with the editor who could insert it without appending evidence in proof of its allegations. Nor do I want any reparation from either of them. I neither complain of them for their act, nor should I thank them if they reversed it. Nor do I even write to you with any desire of troubling you to send me an answer. I do but wish to draw the attention of yourselves, as gentlemen, to a grave and gratuitous slander, with which I feel confident you will be sorry to find associated a name so eminent as yours.

Although Newman was amply justified in reacting against Kingsley's remarks concerning him, there is a quality of uncanny evasion in Newman's protest that characterizes the confusion Kingsley felt as the correspondence, and the controversy, between the two men thickened. To borrow from his later pamphlet, Kingsley might well have asked himself at this early stage "What, then, does Dr. Newman *want?*".

The story of what followed has been told many times, almost invariably at Kingsley's expense. As Kingsley's accusation was the direct cause of Newman's celebrated spiritual autobiography *Apologia pro vita sua*, Kingsley, as the *Quarterly Review* put it, was to go down in history as "the embedded fly in the clear amber of his antagonist's apology."[23] Susan Chitty has helped to conserve this picture of Kingsley when she affirms that in responding to Newman Kingsley could "only appeal to the lowest prejudices of his readers."[24] This is ungenerous. It perpetuates a verdict which has long obscured much

---

[23] [Wilberforce] 529.
[24] Chitty (1974) 231.

of what Kingsley really accused Newman of: not recognizing the value of truth *for its own sake*. G. Egner, a pseudonym for the Roman Catholic philosopher Fr Patrick James FitzPatrick, tried to set the record right in 1969 by examining to what extent Kingsley was more consistent than Newman in his argument, and he concluded that Kingsley "raised genuine objections which Newman did not and could not answer."[25] However, Egner's work was ignored in Chitty's 1974 biography, and Colloms makes but scanty use of it in her biography of 1975 and comes to the equally fruitless conclusion that Kingsley "flung in a careless and ill-researched jeer at Dr. Newman."[26] Although there is little doubt that Kingsley blundered his way through the exchange of letters and pamphlets that followed Newman's protest, some sympathy for Kingsley's case may surely be found.

When Macmillan forwarded Newman's reaction to Kingsley, the latter did not hesitate to write to Newman that the alleged accusations were made in good faith, and that no slander was intended, that some passages of Newman's writings had led him to believe so, but that

> I am most happy to hear from you that I mistook (as I understand from your letter) your meaning; and I shall be most happy, on your showing me that I have wronged you, to retract my accusation as publicly as I have made it.

For the passages in Newman's writings that had led Kingsley to his accusation he made reference to Newman's sermon "Wisdom and Influence" of 1844. Kingsley, thus, thought there were grounds for what he had affirmed about Newman's attitude to truth, and this makes the accusation less gratuitous than it is often supposed to be.

Newman, by return of post, acknowledged Kingsley's letter, and wrote that he had nothing to add to what he had already communicated to Macmillan, except that "no person whatever, whom I had ever seen or heard of, had occurred to me as the author of the statement in question. When I received your letter, taking upon yourself the authorship, I was amazed." This is an astonishing affirmation. The review of Froude's book was signed C.K., while the cover of the magazine cited in the list of contributors Kingsley's full name

---

[25] Egner xiii.
[26] Colloms 268.

and professorial title. It is hard to believe that Newman, after what he considered a "grave and gratuitous slander" against his person, made no attempt to check who the slanderer might be. Although we might give Newman the benefit of the doubt and accept at face value his remark that he "lived out of the world," that the initials had meant nothing to him and that he had not seen the table of contents, it is also understandable that the unlikeliness of such ignorance made Kingsley, if only unconsciously, conceive of it as yet another example of Newman's disregard for truth. This misconception grew as the correspondence continued and Kingsley increasingly felt Newman was trifling with his words. In a letter to an intermediary, who was none other than Alexander Macmillan, Newman expressed his hope the accusation would be withdrawn in total and without reserve. But in case of admission of error "if I will convince them, [. . .] they had better let it alone, as far as I am concerned, for a half-measure settles nothing." He also warned that "any letter addressed to me by Mr Kingsley, I account public property." Newman thus rejected Kingsley's apology and intention to retract his accusation if Newman showed him he had wronged him. In that case he preferred to "let it alone." The warning that further correspondence with Kingsley would be considered public property, however, seemed to indicate future intentions on Newman's part and that, contrary to what he asserted in the same letter, he might not remain as one who "look[s] on mainly as a spectator" at how Macmillan would solve "so grave an inadvertence." This conditioned the tone of Kingsley's next letter, the one which precipitated the controversy into a public disaster for Kingsley. He expressed his pleasure that his "opinion of the meaning of your words was a mistaken one" and proposed to publish the following retraction in the next issue of *Macmillan's Magazine*:

> Dr Newman has, by letter, expressed in the strongest terms, his denial of the meaning which I have put upon his words.
>
> No man knows the use of words better than Dr Newman; no man, therefore, has a better right to define what he does, or does not, mean by them.
>
> It only remains, therefore, for me to express my hearty regret at having so seriously mistaken him; and my hearty pleasure at finding him on the side of Truth, in this, or any other, matter.

Some exasperation with Newman's playing with words was beginning to show through, and Newman's criticism of his proposed retraction did not increase his sympathy for Newman's case. Newman objected that the common reader would interpret Kingsley's words as meaning:

> I have set before Dr Newman, as he challenged me to do, extracts from his writings, and he has affixed to them what he conceives to be their legitimate sense, to the denial of that in which I understood them.
>
> He has done this with the skill of a great master of verbal fence, who knows, as well as any man living, how to insinuate a doctrine without committing himself to it.
>
> However, while I heartily regret that I have so seriously mistaken the sense which he assures me his words were meant to bear, I cannot but feel a hearty pleasure also, at having brought him, for once in a way, to confess that after all truth is a Christian virtue.

Although Newman presents this as an "unjust, but too probable, popular rendering of it," Kingsley felt Newman's paraphrase more likely reflected what he thought to be Kingsley's real meaning behind the retraction.

Kingsley, again, was willing to omit the beginning of the second paragraph and the last half of the third, but maintained that

> by referring publicly to the Sermon on which my allegations are founded, I have given not only you, but every one an opportunity of judging of their injustice. Having done this, and having frankly accepted your assertion that I was mistaken, I have done as much as one English gentleman can expect from another.

What is clear from this exchange of letters is the continual and mutual distrust of the honesty of each other's intentions. Newman evidently believed that Kingsley really thought he had mistaken his assertions in his sermon, while Kingsley remained with the impression that his opponent was indeed "a great master of verbal fence, who knows, as well as any man living, how to insinuate a doctrine without committing himself to it." This is where the correspondence between Kingsley and Newman finished. Kingsley duly published his retraction (with the modifications as detailed in his last letter) in the February issue of *Macmillan's Magazine*.

Kingsley might well have wished this to be the end of the controversy. It was not. Macmillan, as intermediary, had not improved matters when he confessed to Newman that he himself "had read the passage, and did not even think that I or any of my communion would think it unjust." "Most wonderful phenomenon!" Newman exclaimed, "An educated man, breathing English air, and walking in the light of the nineteenth century, thinks that neither I nor any members of my communion feel any difficulty in allowing [Kingsley's charge]." What Macmillan's self-defence did was to bring to the fore the general Anglican prejudice about Roman Catholic morality. This goes some way to explaining why Newman felt it necessary to go to the very bottom of the affair. The chronology of events is that Newman now consulted Edward Badely, a Roman Catholic lawyer who had assisted Newman in the past, on whether Kingsley's public retraction was sufficient or not, and when Badely's answer was a resolute negative, he proceeded by publishing the whole correspondence, adding an analysis of the exchange of letters in a piece of superb sarcasm cast in the form of an imaginary dialogue in which he turned the tables on Kingsley. It was for the sake of this "Reflection" alone that Newman seemed to have published the whole correspondence. Kingsley felt now forced to explain why he had accused Newman of dishonesty. He did so in his notorious *What, Then, Does Dr Newman Mean?*

Kingsley's pamphlet appeared on 20 March. Froude, to whom Kingsley had shown it, had approved of it and thought that Newman would not answer it. Kingsley himself was far less sanguine. "It has made me quite ill with anxiety & I must run off to Scotland to recruit," he admitted to Macmillan.[27] Froude was to be proved wrong, and Kingsley's anxiety proved justified. Newman struck back with all his power.

Kingsley's pamphlet was far too hot-headed to bear out the logic on which his accusations were based. Moreover, his haste to expose Newman to the reading public as the worst example of a hypocritical liar resulted in language which damaged the explanation of why he had come to his initial charge. The pamphlet is interspersed with affirmations that "the atmosphere of the Romish priesthood has degraded his notions,"[28] that Newman talks "stuff and nonsense, more materialist than the dreams of any bone-worshipping Buddhist,"[29] that Newman had worked himself into a "pitch of confusion,"[30] that Newman's mind was in "that morbid state, in which nonsense is the

---

[27] CK to Macmillan, 17/3/1864, BL-54911 f.158v.
[28] *WTDNM?* 23.
[29] *WTDNM?* 36.
[30] *WTDNM?* 37.

only food for which it hungers,"[31] that it is impossible to find motives "for Dr Newman's eccentricities,"[32] that Newman's statements strike "at the root of all morality,"[33] that Newman had "gambled away" his human reason,[34] that Newman was no more than a "subtle dialectician" practising "cunning sleight-of-hand logic."[35] Kingsley's urge to make Newman out as the archenemy—"How art thou fallen from heaven, O Lucifer"—overrides all attempts at a logical and well-organized defence of his accusations. The uncharitable and patronising denigration of his adversary was an unprofitable way to tackle such a quick and able writer as Newman. It is true that Newman might not have been universally admired in England after his defection from the Anglican Church, but to make him out as essentially evil and dishonest was not going to work.

The controversy between the two divines was unduly blown up and became a nationwide drawing-room topic. Kingsley, "like the burglar, who touches unaware the alarum-spring, has awoke around himself a crashing peal which it is quite clear he heartily wishes he had left to slumber in its former repose," the *Quarterly Review* commented.[36] When subsequently Newman started systematically to refute the allegation of the "furious foolish fellow"[37] against him in the first instalments of *Apologia pro vita sua*, there was no way to stem the flow of articles in the periodical press. The *Apologia* steadily grew into a masterpiece of spiritual autobiography, for whose undeniable quality it is deservedly still read today. In it the author vindicated his own personal honesty, and it has been generally accepted that "Kingsley is held to have been resoundingly defeated by Newman."[38] The success of the *Apologia* has weighed heavily in Newman's favour. Compared to Kingsley's poorly argued pamphlet there is indeed no doubt as to which of the two is more convincing. Add to this the fact that Newman as a theologian is still of supreme interest for Roman Catholics today—while Kingsley's role as a divine in the

---

[31] *WTDNM?* 38.
[32] *WTDNM?* 39.
[33] *WTDNM?* 42.
[34] *WTDNM?* 43.
[35] *WTDNM?* 51.
[36] [Wilberforce] 529.
[37] *The Letters and Diaries of John Henry Newman*, ed. C.S. Dessain *et al.* (London/Oxford: 1961–) xxi.100.
[38] Egner 3.

Church of England dwindled at the beginning of the twentieth century and all but disappeared after the Great War—and it is not difficult to see how such an appraisal of the controversy (and of Kingsley's defeat), persists.

III

Although we are not concerned here with the success of Newman's method of vindicating himself, it is of interest in a Life of Kingsley to investigate what exactly led Kingsley to express such ill-reasoned and vehement accusations, why confronting Newman was so important to him personally, and how his contemporaries reacted to the controversy. Some of the ridicule which is bestowed on Kingsley's part in the controversy might thus be profitably turned into an understanding of Kingsley's own consistent intellectual (and religious) honesty. It is sometimes ingenuous, but never despicable.

To many contemporaries Kingsley's name was not just "the embedded *fly* in the clear amber of his antagonist's apology."[39] "A theological controversy between Professor Kingsley and Dr. Newman cannot but have a special interest," *The London Quarterly Review* wrote, "they are two of the greatest living masters of English."[40] Even *The Westminster Review*, which did not want to dwell on the controversy but only on the issue at stake, admitted that interest was roused in the first place because it was connected with "two eminent divines."[41] In the eyes of his contemporaries, Kingsley's theological standing in England warranted his crossing swords with Newman. Moreover, to many his objections to Newman's conceptions of truth did not seem as preposterous as they seem today, and the controversy was followed with great seriousness for the arguments on either side. Before discussing these reactions it is necessary to explain on what Kingsley's accusations in *What, Then, Does Dr Newman Mean?* really hinged, especially since they confirm that, as he himself pointed out, his "opinion of him [Newman] was not an 'impulsive' or 'hastily-formed' one."[42]

[39] [Wilberforce] 529; italics mine.
[40] [Rigg] (1864) 115.
[41] [Cox] 137.
[42] *WTDNM?* 33.

In his first letter to Newman, Kingsley had referred to Newman's
Sermons on Subjects of the Day. Newman retorted that the sermon
Kingsley objected to was "a Protestant sermon of mine" published
when he was still a clergyman of the Church of England. In his
pamphlet Kingsley defies the exoneration implied by Newman's
answer. "It is not a Protestant, but a Romish sermon," he retorted.
Kingsley made a pertinent point here. Newman's equation of Protestant
with Anglican was not justified, especially as the Oxford Movement,
with its search for a "catholic" tradition, reacted overtly against an
ultra-Protestant conception of the Church of England. Next, Kingsley
berated Newman for maintaining in another sermon in the same
volume that a real Christian should be a "humble monk" or a "holy
nun."[43] This accusation, as it stands, ("What Dr Newman means by
Christians"), was not warranted by Newman's sermon, and Kingsley
was wrong to generalize from a passage in which Newman discussed
monks and nuns, who he thought were "Christians after the very
pattern given us in Scripture."[44] Of course, such an affirmation did
not exclude other people from being Christians. Still, it is easy to
see how Kingsley reached his conclusion. Newman continues with
the following lines. As they explain much of Kingsley's disgust for
Newman, they deserve to be quoted in full.

> But, if the truth must be spoken, what are the humble monk, and the
> holy nun, and other regulars, as they are called, but Christians after
> the very pattern given us in Scripture? What have they done but this—
> continue in the world the Christianity of the Bible? Did our Saviour
> come on earth suddenly, as He will one day visit, in whom would He
> see the features of the Christians He and His apostles left behind them,
> but in them? Who but these give up home and friends, wealth and
> ease, good name and liberty of will, for the kingdom of heaven? Where
> shall we find the image of St Paul, or St Peter, or St John, or of Mary
> the mother of Mark, or of Philip's daughters, but in those who, whether
> they remain in seclusion, or are sent over the earth, have calm faces,
> and sweet plaintive voices, and spare frames, and gentle manners, and
> hearts weaned from the world, and wills subdued; and for their meek-
> ness meet with insult, and for their purity with slander, and for their
> gravity with suspicion, and for their courage with cruelty . . .[45]

---

[43] *WTDNM?* 24.
[44] *WTDNM?* 24.
[45] *WTDNM?* 24.

In this passage Newman gives a special place to nuns and monks as Christians and then singles them out as the only Bible Christians in an apostolic sense. Although Newman in his rejoinder in *Apologia* denied that his text bore such an interpretation and called it a blot of logic in Kingsley, the repetition of 'but' surely enforces such a meaning.

The partiality to celibacy in the passage above lay for Kingsley at the heart of the flaw in Newman's theology: the separation of world and church. Kingsley pointed out that Newman in his sermon "Wisdom and Innocence" argued that, because "the servants of Christ are forbidden to defend themselves by violence,"[46] they had to employ other means to defend themselves. Moreover, Kingsley noted that Newman continued that

> those who would be holy and blameless, the sons of God, find so much in the world to unsettle and defile them, that they are necessarily forced upon a strict self-restraint, lest they should receive injury from such intercourse with it as is unavoidable; and this self-restraint is the first thing which makes holy persons seem wanting in openness and manliness[47]

—and concluded that "religious men are a mystery to the world; and being a mystery, they will in mere self-defence be called by the world mysterious, dark, subtle, designing."[48] Thus, Newman said, on the one hand, that Christians must resort to means of defence different from those of the world—which he terms "restraint"—and, on the other, he maintained that the world interpreted such behaviour as "dark, subtle, designing." Again, in such a train of argument, Kingsley was not justified in accusing Newman of teaching his congregation deceit and double-dealing as morally acceptable means of defence. Still, the ambiguity in which Newman defined, explained and justified that which the world called "dark, subtle, designing" seems to admit Kingsley's doubts. Kingsley warned of the danger of delivering such words "before fanatic and hot-headed young men, who hung over his every word."[49] Although Newman denied the initial charge of untruth, Kingsley added that his impression of Newman's sermon was reasonable: "All England stood round in those days, and saw

---

[46] *WTDNM?* 25.
[47] *WTDNM?* 26.
[48] *WTDNM?* 26.
[49] *WTDNM?* 29.

that this would be the outcome of Dr Newman's teaching. How was I to know that he did not see it?"[50] That Newman did not realize what position he held in the eyes of the young clergy is indeed hard to believe.

These examples are symptomatic of the controversy between Kingsley and Newman. Although Kingsley was constantly wrong in his accusations, his underlying reasons were not ungrounded and display genuine objections to Newman's religious views.

After having stated his objections to *Sermons on Subjects of the Day*, Kingsley moved to Newman's idea of historical truth. Here Kingsley seems to be on firmer ground. He questioned Newman's role as editor of the series *Lives of the English Saints*. The defect of the series is that some volumes treated legend or myth as fact, and the editor fully endorsed such a representation. One example is the *Life of St Walburga*. Kingsley exposed the credulity of many of the miracles around the saint and then mentioned that Newman in his preface to the work affirmed that these miracles "are to be received as matter of fact [. . .] there is no reason why they should not be. They are the kind of facts proper to ecclesiastical history. There is nothing, then, *prima facie*, in the miraculous accounts in question to repel a properly-taught or religiously-disposed mind."[51] In another sermon, Kingsley quoted Newman as writing about miracles that, "If the alleged facts did not occur, they ought to have occurred, if I may so speak."[52] The implication seemed again that truth for the Christian is different from that of the world. It is not unreasonable, therefore, that Kingsley should have objected that "to talk nonsense of this kind [. . .] saps the very foundation of historic truth."[53]

Another work by Newman to which Kingsley gave much prominence in adducing evidence for his adversary's dishonesty is *Lectures on Anglican Difficulties*, published as a Roman Catholic in 1850. Two passages in particular irritated him. As, again, these are important for a proper understanding of Kingsley's reaction, they will be quoted in full:

> [the Catholic Church] holds it better for sun and moon to drop from heaven, for the earth to fail, and for all the many millions on it to

---

[50] *WTDNM?* 30.
[51] *WTDNM?* 36.
[52] *WTDNM?* 47.
[53] *WTDNM?* 34.

die of starvation in extremest agony, as far as temporal affliction goes, than that one soul, I will not say should be lost, but should commit one single venial sin, should tell one wilful untruth, or should steal one poor farthing without excuse.

Take a mere beggar woman, lazy, ragged, and filthy, and not over-scrupulous of truth—(I do not say she has arrived at perfection)—but if she is chaste, sober, and cheerful, and goes to her religious duties (and I am not supposing at all an impossible case), she will, in the eyes of the Church, have a prospect of heaven, quite closed and refused to the State's pattern-man, the just, the upright, the generous, the hon-ourable, the conscientious, if he be all this, not from a supernatural power (I do not determine whether this is likely to be the fact, but I am contrasting views and principles)—not from a supernatural power, but from mere natural virtue.[54]

To Kingsley the teaching of these lectures was "utterly beyond my comprehension." He could not but see that such statements strike "at the root of all morality."[55] Apart from finding them anti-scrip-tural, he felt obliged to add:

If he answer, that such is the doctrine of his Church concerning 'nat-ural virtues', as distinguished from 'good works performed by God's grace', I can only answer, So much the worse for his Church. The sooner it is civilized off the face of the earth, if this be its teaching, the better for mankind.[56]

A final point to be mentioned here is Kingsley's perplexity about Newman's justification of telling half-truths, or, as Newman calls it, 'economy'. This point concerns the difficulty of conveying to the uninitiated the complexity of religious truth. Newman was probably right when he maintained that in most complex religions selective simplification ('economy') is unavoidable "if we are to gain admis-sion into their minds at all."[57] Although Kingsley, unreasonably, might not have accepted the basic need for it at all, it is important to note that the point he made is not against economy itself, but to the extent in which Newman allowed it in his teaching. In being deemed not to be able to comprehend the whole truth, "we are to be treated like children," Kingsley complained. To him it came down

---

[54] *WTDNM?* 40–41.
[55] *WTDNM?* 42.
[56] *WTDNM?* 42.
[57] *WTDNM?* 48.

to justifying the "equivocation and dishonest reticence"[58] with which
the priest is endowed through his holy office. This kind of dialec-
tics was what Kingsley had condemned for over a decade as "priestcraft" and it explains why he had come to the conclusion that
Newman was not interested in "truth, for its own sake."

Kingsley thought he had good reasons for challenging Newman,
but his feeling of (subconscious) repugnance to him was just as much
conditioned by Newman's conception of the world and the church,
which struck at the root of basically everything that Kingsley himself had come to see as essential in Christian life. Kingsley's careful
selection of passages from Newman's works brings this out. First, to
a student of Kingsley it can come as no surprise that he could and
would not accept Newman's views of celibacy. For Kingsley marriage, in its sanctification of the sexual alongside the spiritual, embodied the essence of religion. Newman's hint at the apostolic purity of
celibacy undermined his acceptance of man's animal nature, a question which had occupied Kingsley emotionally for years, and to which
he believed he owed his salvation. The use of the word "purity" in
the passage about nuns and monks as true Bible Christians, and the
implication that Newman held that purity can be found only in
celibacy, roused his sensibility to a view which saw sex as merely
sinful. That Newman viewed sex as contamination—"those who
would be holy and blameless, the sons of God, find so much in the
world to unsettle and *defile* them"[59]—was beyond doubt to Kingsley.
Added to this there was, of course, Fanny's pre-nuptial wish to enter
a kind of religious sisterhood, the realisation of which, Kingsley always
thought, would have destroyed his happiness (as well as his mental
sanity and morality) forever. It caused his lasting distrust of "father
confessors" and the power they could exercise over their flock. A
celibate priesthood thus continued to constitute one of Kingsley's
main objections to Roman Catholicism. Hence his initial charge that
Newman maintained that saints have to "withstand the brute male
force of the wicked world which marries and is given in marriage."
This charge would hardly have surprised the readers of *Macmillan's
Magazine*. Of course, it was a master-theme which was present in all
Kingsley's works of fiction.

---

[58] *WTDNM?* 48.
[59] *WTDNM?* 26; my italics.

Closely linked to this is the way Kingsley projected his idea of manhood. Newman's ideal of "calm faces, and sweet plaintive voices, [. . .] and hearts weaned from the world" was so contrary to Kingsley's energetic and restless nature that it undercut the very meaning of life itself. This perhaps brings out the greatest difference between the two men. Whereas Newman was essentially searching for inward spiritual truths, Kingsley exteriorized most of his religion. Newman's affirmation, therefore, that it is better millions on earth starve "in extremest agony" than that one soul "should commit one single venial sin" was received by Kingsley, first with amazement, and finally with scorn. This is not surprising in one who had worked throughout his clerical career to improve the social and sanitary conditions of people. The contrast between Kingsley and Newman is here so sharp that even Egner seems to be thrown off-balance when he interrupts his analysis of their controversy to "record my admiration for the compassion and understanding he [Kingsley] showed towards specific social problems" and to "record my embarrassment at political and social opinions [. . .] expressed by Newman."[60] The statement is partly unfair to Newman, but it is useful to highlight Kingsley's, rather than Egner's, estimation of Newman's non-existent social commitments. Better no church at all than a church which shuns its social (and political) duties.

From here it is only a small step for Kingsley to the charge of dishonesty. Newman's distinction between the world and the church and the affirmation this distinction warrants, namely the exercising of that "self-restraint" which "makes holy persons seem wanting in openness and manliness," led Kingsley to conclude that "Father Newman informs us that it [truth, for its own sake] need not [be a virtue with the Roman clergy], and on the whole ought not to be." Newman's texts, moreover, implied to Kingsley that religious justifications of dishonesty exist. Newman condemned telling an untruth "without excuse," thus giving space for speculation about when he might have justified untruths which, in his view, had some excuse. Kingsley also picked on Newman's example of the chaste beggar woman who is "not over-scrupulous of truth." Newman's point that she had a better prospect of heaven than "the State's pattern-man, the just, the upright, the generous, the honourable, the conscientious,

---

[60] Egner 79–80.

if he be all this, not from a supernatural power" was abominable theology to Kingsley. All this was absorbed by Kingsley in his critique of Newman's "economizing," which made him conclude that Newman finally maintained "that cunning is the weapon which Heaven has given to the saints."[61]

From such premises Kingsley could not but distrust Newman's intentions when he wrote to Macmillan a letter of protest which featured *denials* of his reasons for writing rather than *affirmations*. When Newman finally published the correspondence with his reflections, to Kingsley the point had been proved. In a controversy where truth was discussed Kingsley could only see Newman as playing with fine and subtle rhetoric against his blunt and forward statements. Newman's unjust (but witty) jeer that after all it was Kingsley "who did not mean what he said" left the latter with no doubts about his life-long suspicions of Newman's double-dealing.

Although Newman was not a popular figure with the English reading public, at the outset the public verdict of the dispute was that Kingsley had grossly insulted Newman with gratuitous slander and that his apology to Newman a month later was inadequate. But when Kingsley published his pamphlet in which he substantiated his charges, the opinion of some journals started to sway, if not slightly in Kingsley's favour, at least decidedly in Newman's disfavour. This attitude is brought out by the early reactions after the publication of *What, Then, Does Dr. Newman Mean?* On 26 March the *Athenaeum* belittled the affair as "yet another controversy of the season, a subject for club-gossip, and a dinner-table tattle."[62] The reviewer castigated both Kingsley and Newman in an analysis of the controversy. It is true that he blamed Kingsley for an unreasonable charge of dishonesty, but he also questioned why Newman took "the trouble to remonstrate" if he did not require any reparation from either author or publisher. He agreed that many of the passages from Newman's works that Kingsley quoted were impressive, but that "to be foolish is not necessarily to be false" or that because "Dr. Newman is credulous, [it follows that] he is also dishonest."[63] Thus, although the *Athenaeum* did think Newman foolish and credulous, it deplored the "light rattling style" of Kingsley's exposition. It concluded that

---

[61] *WTDNM?* 30.
[62] [-], *Athenaeum* (26/3/1864) 432.
[63] [-], *Athenaeum* (26/3/1864) 432.

accusations against Roman Catholics were generally so common that they were best passed over in silence, only this time they were uttered by "the Oxford Professor of History." For dinner-table tattle, it would seem, whether Kingsley was professor of history at Oxford or at Cambridge was altogether irrelevant.

Although the *Athenaeum* was dismissive of the theological importance of the controversy, W. Cox in the *Westminster Review* discerned issues that went well beyond the merely trivial. The literary duel "which has lately been amusing the world, has a serious and permanent as well as an ephemeral and entertaining side," he stated at the outset: "any exhibition of the irascible passions is welcomed in this decorous age, [. . .] at an early stage in this debate it was evident that it had deeper and worthier sources of interest."[64] The modes of thought which had "come in collision" in the dispute were worthy of serious attention. There was no doubt that Kingsley's charge was "sweeping" and "too absurd to make it worth refuting,"[65] but the reviewer recognized the virtue of Kingsley's "exceptional and irrepressible admiration of and passionate devotion" to truth.[66] Still, Kingsley himself had repressed this zest for truth in his condemnation of Colenso's critique of the historicity of the Pentateuch. Kingsley's apology, Cox argued, amounted to his admitting that he had made a mistake in accounting Newman "a knave when he was only a fool." But Kingsley himself was "foolish" enough to believe in the miracles of the Old Testament. The *Westminster Review* was hostile to Kingsley's part in the controversy, but the point to be noted here is that, although Cox meant to deny Kingsley his right to castigate Newman on the question of miracles, the implication of his critique on miracles was as devastating for Newman as it was for Kingsley. In March the *Spectator* too published an article in which it exposed both Kingsley's prejudices and Newman's casuistry.

Kingsley was no match for his adversary's rhetorical abilities. Newman had no difficulty in exposing in *Apologia pro vita sua* most of Kingsley's weaknesses in logic and in making his pamphlet seem feeble and absurd. But another factor was to damage Kingsley's reputation in the long run. A comparison of Kingsley's pamphlet with Newman's masterly spiritual autobiography is necessarily unequal.

---

[64] [Cox] 137.
[65] [Cox] 139.
[66] [Cox] 140.

The very depth with which Newman describes the developments of his inner life cannot but be at Kingsley's expense. Such an attitude is brought out by, for example, George Eliot's reaction to Newman's book:

> I have been reading Newman's Apologia pro Vita Suâ, with such absorbing interest that I found it impossible to forsake the book until I had finished it. I don't know whether the affair between him and Kingsley has interested you, or whether you have shared at all my view of it. I have been made so indignant by Kingsley's mixture of arrogance, coarse impertinence and unscrupulousness with real intellectual *in*competence, that my first interest in Newman's answer arose from a wish to see what I consider thoroughly vicious writing thoroughly castigated. But the Apology now mainly affects me as the revelation of a life—how different in form from one's own, yet with how close a fellowship in its needs and burthens—I mean spiritual needs and burthens.[67]

The *Apologia* was, and indeed still is, much admired for the "absolute revealing of the hidden life in its acting,"[68] but Newman's unequalled powers of language did not convince everybody. Especially the part which carried an "Answer in Detail to Mr Kingsley's Accusations", and which equalled his "Reflections" in sarcasm, hardly promoted the idea of sincerity that the autobiographical account of his spiritual life was meant to prove. Newman realized this and dropped this part in future editions of *Apologia* from 1865 onwards.

Moreover, the "Answer in detail" did not convince the critics. Some acknowledged that there was surely some foundation for Kingsley's accusations. Even before the publication of the *Apologia*, such convictions had been voiced by the Rev. Frederick Meyrick with a pamphlet entitled *But Isn't Kingsley Right After All?* Meyrick, who had published an article on "St Alfonso De Liguori's Theory of Truthfulness" in 1854, had no doubt that Kingsley's personal accusations were unjust and that Newman's "reflections" had defeated his opponent, but that Kingsley's complaints of Newman's lack of truthfulness pointed to the fact that the Roman Catholic Church, and Newman its representative, is "unable to declare what we in England mean by untruthfulness to be immoral."[69] Samuel Wilberforce

---

[67] George Eliot to Sara Sophia Hennell, 13/7/1864, Haight iv.158.
[68] [Wilberforce] 529.
[69] Egner 226.

in the *Quarterly Review* was influenced by Meyrick's pamphlet. He recognized the *Apologia* as a "gift of undoubted genius"[70] but found that in the early parts "the calm dignity of Dr. Newman is painfully ruffled by the angry gusts of personal invective and defence."[71] On the whole he thought Newman's argument "laboured" and maintained that "the Jesuits especially, and Roman Catholic divines generally, have taught their disciples to act rather on the principles of casuistry than on the dictates of conscience."[72] When, in defence of the "lazy beggar" passage, Newman cited from his own work that "the publicans and harlots go into the kingdom of God before you," Wilberforce could not but conclude that "surely such statements as these tend to subvert all the principles of morality."[73]

More outspoken still was a long article by J.H. Rigg in the *London Quarterly Review* of October 1864. Rigg held in the main that Kingsley had not been wrong in his accusations and could "not sympathize in Dr. Newman's indignation against Professor Kingsley *because of his imputations*."[74] Moreover, he felt particularly annoyed by Newman's analysis in the *Apologia* of Kingsley's logical blots: "We know of nothing in the way of quibbling more abjectly poor, more puerile and sophistical,"[75] he wrote. The difference between the two opponents was that "Mr. Kingsley excels in insight—insight into the hearts of men, into the power of principles" while "Dr. Newman excels in detailed exposition and analysis, in subtlety of hypothesis, in logical fence, in intellectual persuasion."[76] And weighing such qualities the *London Quarterly* came to the conclusion that "Dr. Newman's intellectual perversity is much more to be blamed than Mr. Kingsley's uncharitableness."[77] The *London Quarterly* expressed feelings about Newman that were shared by many prominent Victorians. An Anglican, Benjamin Jowett, said about Newman that "in speculation he was habitually untruthful, and not much better in practice," while a Roman Catholic archbishop, Henry Manning, held that Newman "simply twists you round his little finger. He bamboozles you with

---

[70] [Wilberforce] 529.
[71] [Wilberforce] 530.
[72] [Wilberforce] 530.
[73] [Wilberforce] 531.
[74] [Rigg] (1864) 116; my italics.
[75] [Rigg] (1864) 119.
[76] [Rigg] (1864) 115.
[77] [Rigg] (1864) 117.

his carefully selected words, and plays so subtly with his logic that your simplicity is taken in."[78] In 1889, only a year before Newman's death (and fifteen after Kingsley's), an ageing Thomas Henry Huxley returned once more to the question of Newman and (scientific) truth. While reading up for an article on Christianity and agnosticism that he was writing for the *Nineteenth Century*, he wrote to J. Knowles that his "satisfaction in making Newman my accomplice has been unutterable. That man is the slipperiest sophist I have ever met with. Kingsley was entirely right about him."[79] In a further letter Huxley specified: "That a man of his intellect should be brought down to the utterance of such drivel—by Papistry, is one of the strongest of arguments against that damnable perverter of mankind, I know of."[80]

IV

There was little consolation for Kingsley in the solidarity of such remarks. Under the stress of the controversy, his health broke down. Alexander Macmillan took pity on him and wished he "had a yacht and I would go and get Mr. Kingsley and take him to see Garibaldi— that would do him good."[81] Other friends too urged Kingsley to leave the country. Although he himself had thought of Scotland as a place of refuge, Froude happened to be going to Spain for research, and Kingsley decided to go with him. Without awaiting the reaction to *What then Does Dr. Newman Mean?*, and before March was over, Kingsley was in Paris. The French capital surprised Kingsley. His jingoistic notions of unique British progress were belied by everything he saw: "The splendour of this city is beyond all I could have conceived, and the beautiful neatness and completeness of everything delight my eyes. Verily these French are a civilised people."[82] This impression of the French lasted. From Bordeaux he wrote of the "thrivingness and improvement everywhere" and exclaimed "What a go-a-head place France is!";[83] and from Biarritz: "I am quite in

---

[78] Egner 4.
[79] THH to CK, 23/9/1860, Leonard Huxley II.226.
[80] THH to CK, 23/9/1860, Leonard Huxley II.227.
[81] Morgan 72.
[82] CK to FK, 25/3/1864, *LML* ii.193.
[83] CK to FK, 26/3/1864, *LML* ii.194.

love with these Frenchmen. They are so charmingly civil and agreeable."[84] Everything he saw did away with many of his old prejudices, as he himself recognized towards the end of the holiday: "I
have learnt, I hope, more tolerance, and wider views of man and
God's purpose in putting him here. I cannot say that I have become
more tolerant of the *cafards*, who set up on every high place their
goddess-virgin. But I have learnt to love these French people, and
to feel that we have much to learn from them."[85] Kingsley's appreciation of the French at times ill-concealed the frustration he felt
with his own countrymen. He found the French such pleasant people to talk to, and at Biarritz he complained "alas! I have fallen
among English at the *table d'hôte*."[86]

Kingsley did not follow Froude into Spain, but stayed at Biarritz—
then a newly developed seaside resort on the Bay of Biscay in southern France, "a cross between Bude and Scarborough"—to "botanize
and breathe sea-champagne."[87] The drinking water had made Kingsley
ill, and he decided to stay in France as Froude continued alone to
Madrid for his research. Kingsley could well do with a bit of relaxation and there was plenty to enjoy between Biarritz and the Pyrenees.
After breakfast he generally "lounge[d] the rocks till one," smoking
cheap cigars and watching lizards, to the extent that "I start sometimes and turn round guiltily, with the thought, 'Surely I ought to
be doing something'."[88] The flowers he found bewildered him, and
the natural scenery of the Pyrenees was breath-taking: "What I have
seen I cannot tell you. Things unspeakable and full of glory." Going
up the Pic du Midi to "the eternal snow holding on by claws and
teeth where it could above" was a new sensation. The peaks stunned
Kingsley—"I could have looked for hours. I could not speak. I cannot understand it yet." It was the first time he was in eternal snow,
and the view did not reassure him. It was "very horrible. Great
white sheets with black points mingling with the clouds, of a drea-
riness to haunt one's dreams. I don't like snow mountains."[89] One
night at Pau "a dear little sucking earthquake, went off crash—bang,

[84] CK to FK, [April 1864], *LML* ii.196.
[85] CK to FK, [April 1864], *LML* ii.205.
[86] CK to FK, [April 1864], *LML* ii.196.
[87] CK to FK, [April 1864], *LML* ii.195.
[88] CK to FK, [April 1864], *LML* ii.196–7.
[89] CK to FK, [April 1864], *LML* ii.199.

just under my bed." This real-life experience of an earthquake did not stimulate his imagination and made less impression than the snow-capped mountains. Unlike the volcanoes in the Eiffel, the event led to no further contemplation of the interior energy of the earth. "Hearing no more, [he] guessed it, and went to bed."[90]

The holiday did his health good. From Pau, during the second week, he reported that "my nerve and strength have come back,"[91] from Nîmes that "my brain is getting quite clear and well,"[92] and on the way back to England he wrote from Lyon: "I believe, shall bring home a stock of health with me. My brain never excites itself or tries to work."[93] But these expressions were calculated to reassure Fanny at home. Shortly after his return he wrote to F.D. Maurice that "I am come back (from France) better, but not well, and unable to take any mental exertion."[94]

Kingsley was now confronted with Newman's *Apologia*. Although the subject of Newman had been carefully avoided in his letters to Fanny, the controversy had lingered at the back of Kingsley's mind. When Macmillan told him of his opponent's final move, he answered that he was not ready to answer Newman yet: "I shall not read him yet till I have recovered my temper about Priests—w. is not improved by the abominable idolatry wh. I have seen in France."[95] That he originally meant to strike back is borne out by a letter to Stapleton's son, in which he wrote that in France he had "seen enough to enable me to give Newman such a *revanche* as will make him wince."[96] Maybe Froude convinced him not to answer Newman. When Froude read *Apologia pro vita sua* in June, he told Kingsley that

> there is nothing in it which requires from you a word of reply [. . .] No sane person could ever have divined the workings of his mind, or could have interpreted them otherwise than you, in common with so many others, did. [. . .]
>
> Still, if you wish to set yourself perfectly right with the world, I would write a very few words to Macmillan, that the original expression which gave offence, was not such as in cool blood you would

[90] CK to FK, [April 1864], *LML* ii.200.
[91] CK to FK, [April 1864], *LML* ii.199.
[92] CK to FK, [April 1864], *LML* ii.203.
[93] CK to FK, [April 1864], *LML* ii.205.
[94] CK to FDM, undated, *LML* ii.207.
[95] CK to Macmillan, undated, BL-54911 f.110.
[96] Martin (1959) 251.

have used, or would attempt to defend. That being hit hard and called on to explain yourself, you had given as it seemed to you sufficient reasons for your bad opinion of him. That you retain your opinion, so far as it concerns the nature of the absurdities which Catholicism requires men to believe, but that as regards Newman personally you see you were mistaken, concluding with a sentence of frank and unreserved apology for the pain which you have given him.

This (judging from the tone of conversation) is what those who agree with you heartily in the main question would wish you to say, and if you only say it without qualification, I think you will have every one on your side. Your answer—as an answer—remains unshaken.[97]

Kingsley' reputation would probably have gained much had he followed Froude's advice. As it was, in the end he merely succumbed to a feeling of impotence in countering such a "treacherous ape" as Newman, who, when he "lifts to you meek & suppliant eyes [. . .] springs, gibbering & biting, at your face."[98] He therefore wrote to Macmillan on 8 June that "I have determined to take no notice whatever of Dr. Newman's apology," because "I have nothing to retract, apologize for, explain. Deliberately after 20 years of thought I struck as hard as I could. Deliberately I shall strike again, if it so pleases me, though not one literary man in England approved." But, Kingsley added, "If I am to bandy words, it must be with sane persons."[99] The bitterness of the defeat Kingsley felt was not only caused by his own frustration at being unable to answer Newman adequately. He feared further public condemnation. "The world seems inclined to patronize Dr. Newman & the Cafards just now, because having no faith of its own, it is awed by the seeming strength of fanaticism. I know them too well either to patronize or to fear them." He lamented the death of Thackeray, as he thought this "genial satirist" only would have been able to "take a tone about this matter, w. would have astonished too many literary men."[100]

Kingsley's reactions show that he was aware that his reputation as a man of letters had been damaged by the controversy with Newman, and when, in the autumn, he was asked to be one of the preachers at the University of Cambridge for 1865, he accepted with trepidation. "Wish me well through these sermons," he wrote to F.D.

---

[97] JAF to CK, 3/6/1864, Dunn ii.306–7.
[98] CK to Macmillan, 8/6/1864, BL-41298 f.145.
[99] CK to Macmillan, 8/6/1864, BL-41298 f.144.
[100] CK to Macmillan, 8/6/1864, BL-41298 f.145.

Maurice as he was preparing the sermons. He need not have worried about the undergraduates. Students crowded round the church-door before it was opened, and listened to Kingsley with "rapt attention." One of them, Evelyn Shuckburgh remembered "the thrill of half-expectation, half-amusement, which seemed to go round the church" as he opened his first sermon with a discussion of the meaning of Muscular Christianity. He also noted Kingsley's "keen, fiery, worn face."[101]

The first of the four sermons on David is of interest as a meek, and belated, answer to Newman. Kingsley did not have the courage to attack Newman openly, but the decision to accept the term Muscular Christianity as what distinguished him from his antagonist is significant. He strongly repudiated Muscular Christianity as it was presented by novelists like George Alfred Lawrence:

> There are those who have written books to shew, that provided a young man is sufficiently brave, frank, and gallant, he is more or less absolved from the common duties of morality and self-restraint.[102]

But if Muscular Christianity "may be simply a healthy and manful Christianity, one which does not exalt the feminine virtues to the exclusion of the masculine," the term, although presenting nothing new, might be accepted. He further justified this in a passage in which the references to Newman could not have gone unnoticed:

> That certain forms of Christianity have committed this last fault cannot be doubted. The tendency of Christianity, during the patristic and Middle Ages, was certainly in that direction [. . .] As time went on, and the monastic life, which, whether practised by man or by woman, is essentially a feminine life, became more and more *exclusively the religious ideal*, grave defects began to appear in what was really too narrow a conception of the human character. [. . .] Their unnatural attempt to be wiser than God, and to unsex themselves, had done little but disease their mind and heart. They resorted more and more to those arts which are the weapons of crafty, ambitious, and unprincipled women. They were too apt to be *cunning, false*, intriguing.[103]

---

[101] *LMLM* 267.
[102] "David" *GDP* 261.
[103] "David" *GDP* 257–8; my italics.

CHAPTER TWENTY-ONE

IN MUCH MIRE (1865–1866)

One of the oddest omissions in Mrs Kingsley's biography is the complete silence on her husband's sixth and last novel, *Hereward the Wake*. There were obvious reasons to forget the unhappy aftermath of the Newman controversy, and she evaded her duty as biographer by simply saying that "the letters of 1865 that have been recovered are few." This is true, but she, of all people, would have known how to fill in the events of that year. Instead, she merely hinted at this painful year by saying that her husband "was so broken in strength, that to get through his professorial and parish work was as much, nay, more than he could manage, and in the summer he was forced to leave home with his family for three months' rest, and settle quietly on the coast of Norfolk."[1] The holiday is not recorded, and probably was not a happy one. A disconsolate passage in a letter to Thomas Hughes dated 21 May reveals what Kingsley had been going through for over a year:

> I am getting better after fifteen months of illness, and I hope to be of some use again some day; a sadder and a wiser man, the former, at least, I grow every year. I catch a trout now and then out of my ponds (I am too weak for a day's fishing and the doctors have absolutely forbidden me my salmon). I have had one or two this year, of three and two pounds, and a brace to-day, near one pound each, so I am not left troutless . . .[2]

Kingsley's depression had not been caused by his defeat by Newman alone. A series of history lectures he had published the previous year as *The Teuton and the Roman* had got short but vicious reviews in the *Times* and in the *Saturday Review*. Kingsley's history writing was no more than "a sort of spasmodic groping," the latter wrote, "rant and nonsense—history, in short, brought down to the lowest level of the sensation novelist."[3] This cruel attack was made by E.A. Freeman,

---

[1] *LML* ii.214.
[2] CK to TH, 11/5/1865, *LML* ii.215.
[3] [-], "Mr Kingsley's Roman and the Teuton" *Saturday Review* (9/4/1864) 446–8.

a young historian who would come to be called a "liberal racist" for his ethnocentric emphasis on the Teutonic component of English civilization. Although Kingsley probably realized that Freeman's invective owed to personal envy, his public attack cast a shadow over his Cambridge professorship. He wanted to resign, but as he intended his son Maurice to enroll at the University the following year, he decided not to.

When in the late 1850s and early 1860s Kingsley decided to abandon his antagonistic public role for a quieter and more homely life, this change seemed justified to him because of the literary fame he had gained over the years, which was confirmed by Royal preferment in 1859 and his appointment at Cambridge the following year. All this was now put into question. After the Newman affair, Kingsley felt he had the whole literary world against him, while the negative reviews of his history lectures filled him with self-doubt about his role at the university. The happiness of the days as the tutor of Prince of Wales had come to an abrupt end with the death of the Prince Consort, and although he still enjoyed royal favour, it was not as intense and gratifying as it had been five years before. Add to this physical illness, and it is hardly surprising that Kingsley felt his world was once more falling apart in 1864–1865. The concluding lines of a poem he wrote in 1864, "The Knight's Leap", seem to reflect the author's mood after boldly riding against Newman:

> He spurred the old horse, and he held him tight,
> And he leapt him over the wall;
> Out over the cliff, out into the night,
> Three hundred feet of fall.
> They found him next morning below in the glen,
> With never a bone in him whole—
> A mass or a prayer, now, good gentlemen,
> For such a bold rider's soul.

The same year he also composed "The Song of the Little Baltung," a poem about a courageous young Balt whose destiny it was to help bring down the Roman empire. The final lines again may be read in reference to Kingsley's Protestant battle against Newman's Roman Catholicism:

> And when he is parting the plunder of Rome,
> He shall pay for this song of mine.

Read together, these poems create both a sense of defeat and an unmistakable vein of heroic, but (as yet) unrecognized, sacrifice.

At about the same time Kingsley wrote these verses, he had also started reading for a new novel. Kingsley reacted to his literary misfortunes in 1864 by returning to poetry and fiction. It indicates that he thought he had been very much wronged by the critics. The new novel he was projecting (eight years after his previous one) also indicates that he meant to vindicate himself.

Kingsley had been inspired by the reading he had done on Teutonic peoples for his university lectures, and had decided on a novel set in the low Fen country in Anglo-Saxon times. The heroic deeds of Highlanders "have been told in verse and prose [. . .] but we must remember, now and then, that there have been heroes likewise in the lowlands and in the fen," Kingsley affirmed in the "prelude" to his new novel. Although Walter Scott is not mentioned, his name comes to mind when reference is made to the heroes of the Highlands. If reviewers had equated *Westward Ho!* to Scott's works, Kingsley now seemed consciously to exploit this comparison. He had requested Macmillan to send him the essential books and all the necessary ordinance maps of Cambridgeshire. The best part of 1864 after his return from France, Kingsley spent studying the *Anglo-Saxon Chronicle*, Geoffrey Gaimar's *Metrical Chronicle*, the prose *Life of Hereward* based on Leofric's account, and other material he could lay his hands on, such as the "valuable" fragment *The Family of Hereward*, edited by Thomas Wright (to whom the novel was to be dedicated). For the historical context Kingsley consulted Francis Palgrave's *History of the Anglo-Saxons* and E.A. Freeman's *History of the Norman Conquest*. The novel was meant to be published in instalments starting from January 1865 in *Macmillan's Magazine*. However, just as the story started to materialize in his mind, he received an offer of £1500 from Norman McLeod for the mere rights of serializing "a story by me" in *Good Words*.[4] This was a tempting sum, but Kingsley decided he could not refuse the publisher who "got" him and who had treated him so well lately in terms of money. Moreover, Alexander Macmillan was a personal friend of long standing. To McLeod, Kingsley, therefore, "replied v[y] kindly that I have no intention of writing one, & if I had, am bound to offer it first to Macmillan."[5] However, it is clear from Kingsley's letters that his wife thought otherwise, and he was forced to justify his refusal to her: "I do not see," he wrote,

---

[4] CK to FK, undated, BL-62555 f.31.
[5] CK to FK, undated, BL-62555 f.33r.

"how I can refuse Mac. Hereward for the Magazine, if he pays me as much as the Scotchman. Moreover, I shall not get the money from Good Words till it is all finished, whereas I can draw on Macmillan when I like."[6] He told Macmillan too of having refused the £1500 that *Good Words* had offered him "& he opened his eyes, & said he was exceedingly obliged, & I should never have to repent it."[7]

Good Words was a magazine with a distinctively Christian spirit which printed edifying articles (and also fiction) which were suitable not only for family reading in general but also made acceptable Sunday reading. Kingsley was not averse to publishing in a magazine that shared his Christian ideals. In fact, in January 1863 he had published "The Monks and the Heathen" in *Good Words*, an article based on his university lectures. Its circulation was much wider than *Macmillan's Magazine*, and Macmillan could not offer anything like the sum McLeod offered. In the end Fanny prevailed and Kingsley had to set old friendship aside. In January *Hereward, the Last of the English* started to appear in *Good Words*. The novel in volume form, however, was promised to Macmillan, to be published as soon as McLeod's magazine finished serialization in December 1865.

By the end of December 1864, Kingsley seemed to have had much of the idea of his novel ready, as he wrote to Macmillan: "I have nearly done now. How I wish the book was all received, & safe in your hands. Th[e]y s[a]y it is quiet & likely to do well. I don't know, & hardly care,"[8] and mid April the following year, when Macmillan came to stay at Eversley while Fanny was away, author and publisher discussed the rest of the plot. Macmillan was "v[er]y hopeful about the new novel," Kingsley wrote to Fanny.[9]

Hereward the Wake is the least Kingsleyan of Kingsley's novels. It is a straightforward and painstakingly researched story with very few interpolations of the author's own opinions and hobbyhorses. This makes it Kingsley's best-structured novel as well as his least interesting one. As Stanley Baldwin remarked in 1934, it is not a book one would care to read twice.[10]

---

[6] CK to FK, undated, BL-62555 f.33.
[7] CK to FK, undated, BL-62555 f.33v.
[8] CK to Macmillan, 12/12/1864, BL-54911 f.127r.
[9] CK to FK, undated, BL-62555 f.43.
[10] Baldwin 173.

Kingsley tells the story of how an eighteen-year-old unruly Hereward is outlawed by the king and how after numerous adventures in Cornwall, Ireland and Flanders, where he proves his unparalleled courage and physical strength, returns to England to fight the Norman invader William the Conqueror. Most of the first half of the novel is a mere episodic succession of Hereward's 'heroic', but above all bloodthirsty, exploits, which make unpleasant reading. As modern critics have found, in closely following the material he got from the chroniclers, Kingsley created more a prose saga than a novel. It is only with Hereward's return to England, accompanied by his wife Torfrida, that the author manages to invest his main characters with some depth. This has to do with the passion Kingsley felt towards the theme he introduced with Torfrida. As Hereward's wife she is the civilizing complement of the rugged and pagan hero, and, as Hereward often points out, she will pray while he must fight. It is Torfrida who admonishes Hereward: "Boast not, but fear God,"[11] a warning which assumes growing importance in the second half of the novel. With this Kingsley revisits the theme of the limitations of merely physical prowess that he had already explored with Amyas in *Westward Ho!* and with Tom Thurnall in *Two Years Ago*. As in all his earlier novels, it is woman who must lead and inspire the truly chivalric in man. But, unlike the earlier novels, it is not the budding love for a young woman that stands central in *Hereward the Wake*. This novel, written at the age of 46 shows a maturer view. Hereward's fortunes start to turn when a middle-aged Torfrida looks at the reflection of her own "wan coarse face"[12] and knows that "her beauty was gone, and that he saw it."[13] When Hereward abandons her for the younger and beautiful Alftruda, being "utterly besotted on her,"[14] his, and old England's, lot is sealed: from that moment he is "not the same man" anymore,[15] "his nerve was gone, as well as his conscience."[16] At this point Kingsley comments that

> The truth was, that Hereward's heart was gnawed with shame and remorse [. . .] He had done a bad, base, accursed deed [. . .] No man

---

[11] *HW* 158.
[12] *HW* 365.
[13] *HW* 360.
[14] *HW* 383.
[15] *HW* 388.
[16] *HW* 396.

could commit such a sin without shaking his whole character to the root [. . .] All his higher instincts fell from him one by one.[17]

Soon after this Hereward is defeated and his head put on the gable of Bourne manor. Kingsley's depicts Hereward's destruction with urgent passion, and to make his point on matrimonial fidelity, he has the novel end with Hereward's and Torfrida's granddaughter and husband in old age sitting "side by side, and hand in hand, upon a sunny bench" contemplating their work of drainage of the Bourne fens, whose "lonely meres, foul watercourses, stagnant slime" were now rich corn and grass lands. They represent the beginning of a new creative (not destructive) England that in time would lead to the magnificence of the nineteenth century: "So there the good man, the beginner of the good work of centuries, sat looking out over the fen."[18] With this Kingsley defined on what terms he was willing to accept "muscular Christianity," an label which by now firmly clung to all his writings. Physical prowess unsustained by monogamous Christianity leads to destruction only: the need to define this once and for all seems to be behind Kingsley's urge to write *Hereward the Wake*. It was the last novel he ever wrote. Whether Kingsley's last novel managed to convince his readers of his restrained views of muscular Christianity is doubtful. Although a young Henry James, as well as an anonymous reviewer for the *Athenæum*, thought *Hereward the Wake* Kingsley's best book,[19] J.R. Wise in the *Westminster Review* exclaimed against Kingsley's "blood-and-thunder mood": "instead of being gladdened with a tale of honour and high bearing, we are drenched with blood and sickened with villainy [. . .] To our thinking there is nothing worse than this mere love and strength and lust of ferocity such as are depicted in 'Hereward'."[20]

II

Kingsley's health remained weak during 1865. "I am on the whole better [. . .] but [still] weak & in bad health," he wrote to Macmillan

---

[17] *HW* 407.
[18] *HW* 421–22.
[19] James 115; [-] *"Hereward the Wake," Athenæum* 2007 (14/4/1866), 493.
[20] Wise 268.

in September.[21] The year passed uneventfully, except for a royal visit to the Kingsley house. In the autumn of 1865, the widowed Queen Emma of the Sandwich Islands was a guest at Eversley Rectory for two days. Emma's late husband, the Hawaiian sovereign Kamehameha IV, has gone down in history as a benevolent monarch who was much interested in social, sanitary and economic reform. He distrusted American capitalism and exerted himself to keep the islands independent. He also invited the Church of England to establish itself on his territories to limit the power of American puritan missionaries. After the death of his four-year-old son in 1862 he withdrew from public life and died the following year. Kingsley, no doubt, admired the social and religious outlook of the late king, who had read *The Water-Babies* to his son shortly before the child's premature death.

Although Mrs Kingsley presents the visit as stemming only from the queen's wishes to meet the author of *The Water-Babies*, Robert Bernard Martin[22] has shown that the initiative of the invitation was entirely on the Kingsleys' side. Fanny went out of her way to ask the widowed Queen over to her house, making sure they had her completely to themselves for two days. Fanny had been unduly modest in promising in her invitation only "plain hospitality" in the "ménage of a plain country clergyman."[23] Instead, she organized a more than royal reception with flowers and elaborate meals during which pineapples were served. Although it was hard work for Fanny and the servants, it all turned out to be a gratifying visit. She scribbled on the back of a letter of her husband's to Macmillan that the queen was "one of the most charming women I ever met" and that all in all it had been "one of the most interesting visits of our life." The queen had flattered Mrs Kingsley so much by repeatedly expressing the late king's delight in her husband's work that she had promised the queen "a copy of each of *novels & poems*" and asked Macmillan to order a set "*plainly*—not expensively bound in calf."[24] The royal visit helped to lift Kingsley's sombre mood, as did a short stay at Windsor Castle the second week of November, during which he preached to the court.

---

[21] CK to Macmillan, 5/9/1864, BL-54911 f.135r.
[22] Martin (1959) 254–6.
[23] Martin (1959) 255.
[24] CK to Macmillan, 11/10/1865, BL-54911 f.137v.

Illustration 6. The Rectory in 1865 (photograph published in Rose Kingsley's *Eversley Gardens* (1907))

III

In October 1865 an insurrection broke out in Morant Bay, Jamaica. After a quarrel about paying rent, Paul Bogle, a black preacher, received a warrant for having participated in the riot, during which a policeman had been beaten. About 400 black men armed with cutlasses came to Bogle's rescue, while a crowd burnt the court house, broke open the jail, and sacked a number of stores. A general rising of the black population seemed imminent, especially as armed groups of insurgents had started to move inland to attack the plantations, driving the white inhabitants out and killing some of them. The Governor of the island, Edward John Eyre, declared martial law over the district, and, in the military action that followed, suppressed the revolt with force. As a measure to avoid future unrest, he had 439 of the insurgent blacks executed and more than 600 men and women flogged.

The Jamaica riots and the ensuing reprisals brought the controversy about colonial rule once more to the attention of the English public. Although slavery had been abolished in 1838, Jamaica, with its population of approximately 13,000 whites, who were mainly planters, and 350,000 black labourers, had become a testing ground for mid-Victorian abolitionists who wanted to establish in the British colonies a free-labour economy in which blacks could freely participate. Not surprisingly, as with James Brooke in the early 1850s, Eyre's extreme action was condemned by English philanthropists who protested against the Governor's dubious use of English military power. Objections and concerns were voiced in Parliament, and the Government was forced to nominate a Royal Commission to inquire into Eyre's behaviour. However, when the official report of the commission cautiously expressed approval of Eyre's military promptitude in re-establishing order, but condemned his use of martial law and the excessive punishments he inflicted on the black population, a group of British intellectuals, who had been shocked by Eyre's use of force, set up a Jamaica Committee with the purpose of prosecuting the Governor for murder. This took place in July 1866. Amongst those who were ardent promoters of a trial against Eyre were John Stuart Mill, Thomas Henry Huxley, and Thomas Hughes. Others who sympathized with their cause, and subscribed to the Committee, included John Ludlow, Charles Darwin, and Charles Lyell.

But there were others who maintained that Eyre had acted hero-
ically and justly. With the Indian Mutiny fresh in their minds, they
claimed that Eyre had saved thousands of whites from massacre. In
September this led to the setting up of an Eyre Defence Committee
which undertook to raise money for the Governor's legal defence in
court. The counter-committee was led by Thomas Carlyle, who criticized those on the Jamaica Committee as "a knot of nigger philanthropists" who were unwilling to recognize that the riots proved
that blacks were born to be mastered. Carlyle gathered around him
a group of prominent men as formidable as those he opposed. Among
those who subscribed were Charles Dickens, who condemned with
Carlyle "that platform-sympathy with the black—or the Native, or
the Devil,"[25] and Alfred Tennyson, who thought that "We are too
tender to savages, we are more tender to a black than ourselves."[26]
John Ruskin and John Tyndall also took Carlyle's view. Seeing
Kingsley's reaction to Brooke and the Sepoy Mutiny, it is not surprising that he too sympathized with their cause, but he was "still
laying back afraid" of joining their ranks. Henry Kingsley, still unaware
of the Jamaica violence, had published in October 1865 a rhapsodic
article in *Macmillan's Magazine* in which he exalted Eyre's heroic
exploration of Australia during the years 1833–1845. Coinciding with
the reports of the Jamaica insurrection, Henry's assessment of Eyre's
humanity—"eminently kind, generous, and just"; a man who "pleaded
for the black, and tried to stop the war of extermination which was
[. . .] carried on by the colonists against the natives"[27]—could not
fail to trigger reaction, and an exchange of letters in *The Times* signalled the beginning of a controversy that would divide the Victorian
intellectual world the following year and during which many friendships would be severely tried by the asperity of tone on both sides
of the debate. Huxley, for example, regretted that he and Tyndall
"should be ranged in opposite camps in this or any other cause,"
but exerted himself to save old friendships. He ended a letter to
Tyndall:

> Thus there is nothing for it but for us to agree to differ, each sup-
> porting his own side to the best of his ability, and respecting his friend's

---

[25] Peter Ackroyd, *Dickens* (London: QDP, 1990) 971.
[26] R.B. Martin, *Tennyson: The Unquiet Heart* (Oxford: Clarendon Press, 1980) 459.
[27] Henry Kingsley, "Eyre, the South-Australian Explorer," *Littell's Living Age* XXXI
(1865) 482.

freedom as he would his own, and doing his best to remove all petty bitterness from that which is at bottom one of the most important constitutional battles in which Englishmen have for many years been engaged.

If you and I are strong enough and wise enough, we shall be able to do this, and yet preserve that love for one another which I value as one of the good things of my life.[28]

Kingsley, who had finally been won over by his brother Henry and Carlyle, heard of a letter Huxley had published in the *Pall Mall Gazette* of 31 October in which he had explained his reasons for being a member of the Jamaica Committee. He took up his pen and wrote to Huxley that Eyre was essentially a humane and coura-geous person, something Carlyle's personal acquaintance with Eyre had confirmed for him, and that his prosecution by the Committee savoured to him of a vindictive party spirit. "Mr. Eyre's personality in this matter," Huxley retorted, "is nothing to me; I know nothing about him, and, if he is a friend of yours, I am very sorry to be obliged to join in a movement which must be excessively unpleas-ant to him." It was also going to be unpleasant to Kingsley. One wonders what Kingsley felt when in a powerful passage of the same letter Huxley castigated his uncritical enthusiasm for the heroic:

> I daresay he [Eyre] did all this with the best of motives, and in a heroic vein. But if English law will not declare that heroes have no more right to kill people in this fashion than other folk, I shall take an early opportunity of migrating to Texas or some other quiet place where there is less hero-worship and more respect for justice, which is to my mind of much more importance than hero-worship [. . .] The hero-worshippers who believe that the world is to be governed by its great men, who are to lead the little ones, justly if they can; but if not, unjustly drive or kick them the right way, will sympathise with Mr. Eyre.
>
> The other sect (to which I belong) who look upon hero-worship as no better than any other idolatry, and upon the attitude of mind of the hero-worshipper as essentially immoral; who think it is better for a man to go wrong in freedom than to go right in chains; who look upon the observance of inflexible justice as between man and man as of far greater importance than even the preservation of social order, will believe that Mr. Eyre has committed one of the greatest crimes of which a person in authority can be guilty, and will strain every

---

[28] THH to John Tyndall, 9/11/1866, Leonard Huxley I.283.

nerve to obtain a declaration that their belief is in accordance with the law of England.[29]

Huxley was not going to change his opinion because friends thought otherwise and he acquiesced in differing therefore with many people who were dear to him. "People who differ on fundamentals," he reminded Kingsley, "are not likely to convert one another. To you, as to my dear friend Tyndall, with whom I almost always act, but who in this matter is as much opposed to me as you are, I can only say, let us be strong enough and wise enough to fight the question out as a matter of principle and without bitterness." But not all friends managed to put personal resentment aside. Ludlow was adamant when he heard of Kingsley's subscription to the Defence Fund, and he overreacted by writing to him "to say that our paths now ran so divergent that it was useless to correspond any longer."[30] Of course, the two men had steadily grown apart over the years, and Ludlow's final breaking off of all contact between them was more painful as a gesture than as a real loss of friendship. But with Hughes this lay rather differently. In the controversy over Eyre, Kingsley lost a friend and fishing companion who had been close to him during many moments of depression. From 1866 onwards the men would only seldom exchange letters or go fishing together.

The public condemnation of Kingsley's stand in the controversy was as disturbing as the loss of old friends. The press seized upon Kingsley's presence at a banquet given to Eyre in Southampton, and denigrated the social reform for which he had worked for over twenty years. Although Eyre was eventually acquitted of the charges brought against him, Kingsley's alliance with the Eyre Defence Committee probably damaged his public reputation more than it ever damaged Dickens's or Ruskin's. This is partly because Kingsley was identified with a Muscular Christianity that was increasingly criticized as immoral, while the others were not. "Muscular Christianity looked less amiable when it applauded the proceedings of Governor Eyre in Jamaica," *Vanity Fair* commented in a summary of Kingsley career in 1872, "Carlyle, with his worship of strength, and Society, with seductions of which this quondam Radical has undergone all the spell, seem to have given him other thoughts and other sympathies

---

[29] THH to CK, 8/11/1866, Leonard Huxley I.282.
[30] JL to CK, undated, Martin (1959) 261.

than of old." Kingsley keenly felt the injustice of such criticism. The public treatment of his support for Eyre made him write full of bitterness that

> I have been cursed for it, as if I had been a dog, who had never stood up for the working man when all the world was hounding him (the working man) down in 1848–9, and imperilled my own prospects in life in behalf of freedom and justice. Now, men insult me because I stand up for a man whom I believe ill-used, calumniated, and hunted to death by fanatics.[31]

Kingsley's distress at being misunderstood in 1866 would have been increased still further had he known that in an appropriately entitled section "Nebulae" in *The Galaxy*, an American family magazine, the authorship of *Ecce Homo* had been attributed to him. *Ecce Homo*, an anonymous book by J.R. Seeley, professor of Latin at University College, London, was a life of Christ written in startlingly fresh language, which seemed to make Christ merely human and was therefore condemned by many for evading both criticism of the Biblical texts and theological implications. Lord Shaftesbury called it the "most pestilential book ever vomited [. . .] from the jaws of hell."[32] It is easy to see why the writer for *The Galaxy* indicated Kingsley as a possible candidate for the authorship of *Ecce Homo*—after all, *Yeast* emphatically concluded with the affirmation that the foundation of Christianity was "Jesus Christ—THE MAN"[33]—but the attribution was put in far from flattering terms, charging Kingsley for that "loose thinking" which he had attacked with all his might a decade before:

> The book [. . .] is filled with loose thinking and a looser use of language. It is in particular not new to us; but it has startled our more closely retrained British cousins, and no little of our interest in it is a reflex of theirs. Judging entirely from internal evidence, we should not be surprised at learning that "Ecce Homo" was written by Charles Kingsley.[34]

The public press willfully misrepresented Kingsley's views of religion, defamed his principles in the controversy with Newman, denigrated his historical methods as professor of history, and openly suspected

---

[31] CK to T. Dixon, 27/10/1866, *LML* ii.235.
[32] Chadwick (1987) ii.65.
[33] *Y* 309.
[34] [-], "Nebulæ," *The Galaxy* 1 (August 1866) 745.

him of inhumanity in his support for Eyre. Moreover, by 1867 it seemed to have become common practice in the press to ridicule Kingsley. Martin mentions how in a review of Gregory Smith's *Faith and Philosophy* the reviewer expresses his feeling of amusement at Smith's tone towards Kingsley. "He evidently looks upon him quite seriously," the reviewer added.[35] Similarly representative are William Stubbs's 1871 lines on Kingsley and Froude, who had been appointed Rector of St Andrews University. Stubbs sent John Richard Green "a hymn on Froude and Kingsley" which proved so popular that it was published with slight variations the following year in *Vanity Fair*. As the original version has at various times been reproduced in histories and biographies, the *Vanity Fair* variant will be given here:

BROTHERS-IN-LAW
Froude informs the Scottish youth
That no divine can care for truth;
The Reverend Canon Kingsley cries,
That history is a parcel of lies.
What cause their judgment to malign?
    A brief reflection solves the mystery:
Froude believes Kingsley a divine,
    Kingsley believes that Froude is History.[36]

Although these lines were written towards the end of 1871, they describe what many Victorians felt about Kingsley's role as divine and historian during the mid and late 1860s. No wonder public opinion sickened Kingsley and that he longed to retire quietly to Eversley. Cambridge was no longer a place that rendered him happy. He shunned London society too: "I am seldom or never in London, & have called on no one for twelve months past, in that Babylon which I fear & hate," he wrote to Miss Ingelow in June 1867.[37]

---

[35] Martin (1959) 265.
[36] *Vanity Fair*, 3/2/1872, 40.
[37] CK to Miss Ingelow, 11/6/1867, BL-41298 f.162.

CHAPTER TWENTY-TWO

GOD'S FACTS, INSTEAD OF MEN'S LIES (1866–1867)

The meteor shower which was visible during the night of 13–14 November 1866 made a profound impression on Kingsley. In "trembling excitement he paced up and down the churchyard"[1] and called Fanny and the children out when it began to be visible. Although he wrote to professor Adams about how fortunate nineteenth-century man was in being able to look on the spectacle rationally and with a cool head, he was conscious of the mid-Victorian malady of living in a pitiless universe. The meteor shower led to profound contemplations on the course of nature: "We were swept helpless, astronomers tell us, through a cloud of fiery stones, to which all the cunning bolts which man invents to slay his fellow-man, are but slow and weak engines of destruction."[2] Such events forced upon Kingsley the fact that nature had sides which are dark and ugly, that it was "most playful, and yet most treacherous; most beautiful, and yet most cruel."[3] Although science had taught that nature did not crush by caprice or ill-will, the natural laws it had discovered only substituted quirky behaviour with a "brute necessity." Just as Hardy had stated in his early poem "Hap", to Kingsley the "purblind doomsters" created merely a "moral terror which is far more overwhelming."[4] The scientific aspect of nature was horrible if it caused one to ask: "Are we only helpless particles, at best separate parts of the wheels of a vast machine, which will use us till it has worn us away, and ground us to powder?"[5] Such questions were morally so ghastly to Kingsley that he concluded that he could not but believe in a living God superintending his creation still, that those meteor bolts "did not fall to the ground without our Father."[6] Kingsley distinguished between

---

[1] *LML* ii.239.
[2] "The Meteor Shower" *WoL* 181.
[3] "The Meteor Shower" *WoL* 179.
[4] "The Meteor Shower" *WoL* 180.
[5] "The Meteor Shower" *WoL* 180.
[6] "The Meteor Shower" *WoL* 181.

science and natural theology, a distinction which allowed him to be
a good scientist and a good churchman at the same time. Although
science should be free of theological speculation, a true natural theology, he emphasized, should begin with the attributes of the Creator,
and not with the laws of nature, if it was not to drift into pantheism.[7]

The second half of the 1860s signalled a renewed interest in science and nature in Kingsley's writings. Although Kingsley had never
lost interest in natural theology since the publication of *The Water-
Babies*, the preparation for his history lectures left him little time for
the pursuit of this intellectual passion. In the spring of 1866, however, Kingsley was invited to hold two lectures for the Royal Institution.
As his subject he chose "Superstition and Science," and he boldly
set out that the subject seemed to him especially fit for a clergyman:
for a man of the cloth, of all men, should be able, by knowing what
was theology and religion, to state what was *not* theology or religion.
Superstition and science did not belong to either. Superstition was
not a corruption of religion but an irrational fear of the unknown
which can only be dispelled by the rationality of science. The first
lecture abounded with examples of "barbarous man" and fetishism
that expressed Kingsley's fears about man's deepest and darkest inner
instincts. In moments of intoxication, he pointed out, superstitious
men "had seen something they should not have seen; done something they would not have done" and for which they would be punished.[8] This resulted in such an irrational dread of woman, of "her
who brings him into the world," that brute force in the form of
"terror, torture, murder" was the only kind of deliverance from her.
Where superstition ruled, "woman must be crushed, at all price, by
the blind fear of the man."[9] Kingsley's reading of women's inequal-
ity in society as originally caused by superstition is as curious as it
is revealing. It uncovered both Kingsley's latent and subconscious
fears of primitive instincts, which at the same time defined and
destroyed virility, and his celebration of an ordered and progressive
civilization based on the democratic powers of science.

But if superstition unmanned, science enhanced masculinity. The
starting point here was that "courage is the child of knowledge."

---

[7] "The Meteor Shower" *WoL* 186.
[8] "Superstition" *SLE* 223.
[9] "Superstition" *SLE* 225.

Kingsley's lecture on science was, in fact, throughout drafted in terms of masculine strength. Prying into nature's secrets was dangerous, and to reach knowledge one had to look nature in the face with "an unquailing glance." For the early Greek and Roman pioneers of physical science "the mud-ocean of ignorance and fear in which they *struggled so manfully* was too strong;"[10] the "practical, hard-headed" Teutons had "a *sore battle*: a battle against their own fear of the unseen,"[11] modern scientists "have discovered that they are *engaged in a war—a veritable war*—against the rulers of darkness" and they "get their shilling a-day of *fighting-pay*."[12] Historians of science nowadays agree that the early twentieth-century conflict thesis between science and religion, which emphasized a triumphant view of the former and a dismissive view of the latter, is a crude misrepresentation of facts and that there has never been any real and consistent war between the two fields that could justify such views. Kingsley's stand is relevant in the new conception of this relationship. While he never maintained there existed a war between religion and science, he still evokes the image of war to describe the relationship of science with what he saw as *imperfect* or *deviant* forms of religion. To Kingsley that war was real enough and had retarded the progress of science. A few years later, in 1871, he returned to this point and blamed the impulse Wesleyanism had given to the earnest mind to concentrate mainly on questions of personal religion. This was responsible for the "popular war [that] arises between the reason of a generation and its theology."[13] Of late, it had impeded this reciprocal enterprise of science and religion: "that the religious temper of England for the last two or three generations has been unfavourable to a sound and scientific development of natural theology, there can be no doubt."[14] Still, "the *clergy of the Church of England*, since the foundation of the Royal Society in the seventeenth century, have done more for sound physical science than the clergy of any other denomination."[15]

Thus, at the beginning of his first lecture for the Royal Institution, Kingsley maintained that, although theology and religion are subjects

---

[10] "Science" *SLE* 235.
[11] "Science" *SLE* 236.
[12] "Science" *SLE* 253; all italics mine.
[13] "The Natural Theology of the Future" *SLE* 315.
[14] "The Natural Theology of the Future" *SLE* 316.
[15] "The Natural Theology of the Future" *SLE* 315; italics mine.

which were rightly excluded from that scientific organization, a relationship between science and theology needed to be urged:

> There is a scientific reverence, a reverence of courage, which is surely one of the highest forms of reverence. That, namely, which so reveres every fact, that it dare not overlook or falsify it, seem it never so minute; which feels that because it is a fact it cannot be minute, cannot be unimportant, that it must be a fact of God; a message from God; a voice of God, as Bacon has it, revealed in things; and which therefore, just because it stands in solemn awe of such paltry facts as the Scolopax feather in a snipe's pinion, or the jagged leaves which appear capriciously in certain honeysuckles, believes that there is likely to be some deep and wide secret underlying them, which is worth years of thought to solve. That is reverence, a reverence which is growing, thank God, more and more common; which will produce, as it grows more common still, fruit which generations yet unborn shall bless [. . .] after all, as with animals, so with nature; cowardice is dangerous. The surest method of getting bitten by an animal is to be afraid of it; and the surest method of being injured by Nature is to be afraid of it.[16]

This view was closely bound up with the view that scientific training needed to be provided to the people. This ideal had found an application in Kingsley's attempt to involve great scientists in setting up a natural history museum at Wellington College. When, in 1867, he took over the editorship of *Fraser's Magazine* for the few months that Froude was abroad for research, he tried to make the journal "a vehicle for advanced natural science" and to "get a little real natural science into folks' heads."[17] He therefore invited his scientist-friends to collaborate, but received few acceptances. He even asked Darwin for an article, but the naturalist declined because he was too busy getting *Variations of Animals and Plants Under Domestication* ready for the press. In the end, only Charles Bunbury and Alfred Newton, the ornithologist, obliged. Kingsley himself contributed with the article "A Charm of Birds." "Some day," he wrote to Newton, "ere I grow too old to think, I trust to be able to throw away all pursuits save natural history, and die with my mind full of God's facts, instead of men's lies."[18]

---

[16] "Science" *SLE* 230–31.
[17] CK to Alfred Newton, April 1867, *LML* ii.246.
[18] CK to Alfred Newton, May 1867, *LML* ii.246.

Although Kingsley's science was grounded on premises of an ultimate metaphysical aim in nature, he tried to be perfectly Darwinian in his natural theology. While he was the editor of *Fraser's* and preparing his bird article, he wrote to Darwin to ask for his help in locating a pamphlet which had appeared shortly after *The Origin of Species* and which enumerated some forty "phenomenal puzzles" which could only be explained by evolution. "I may specially want it in your defence," he added. He also asked Darwin to have a look at his lectures given at the Royal Institution, so that could he rest assured that "I am not unmindful of your teaching."[19]

Kingsley had often remarked on the humour in God's creation. Similarly he had stressed the value of beauty for its own sake and a creator who rejoiced in creating. Such beliefs were easily adopted within the Darwinian framework of evolution, and he even scolded Darwin for underrating the application of it. In discussing the Duke of Argyll's anti-sexual-selection book *Reign of Law*, Kingsley added this piece of reasoning:

> Why on earth are the males only (to use his teleological view) ornamented, save for the amusement of the females first? In his earnestness to press the point (which I think you have really overlooked too much), that beauty in animals and plants is intended for the aesthetic education and pleasure of man, and (as I believe in my old-fashioned way), for the pleasure of a God who rejoices in His works as a painter in his picture—in his hurry, I say, to urge this truth, he has overlooked that beauty in any animal must surely first please the animals of that species, and that beauty in males alone is a broad hint that the females are meant to be charmed thereby—and once allow that any striking new colour would attract any single female, you have an opening for endless variation.[20]

But apart from personal feelings on the question of the beauty of God's creation, evolution also kept attracting Kingsley from a theological point of view. On the Paleyan premises of a designer—"if there be evolution, there must be an evolver"[21]—it proved in its continuing forms of creation that God was a present and living reality. To the published version of his lecture "The Natural Theology of the Future," Kingsley therefore added a footnote in which he expressed his admiration for Saint George Mivart's book *The Genesis of Species*

---

[19] CK to Charles Darwin, 12/7/67, *LML* ii.249.
[20] CK to Charles Darwin, 6/6/1867, *LML* ii.248.
[21] "The Natural Theology of the Future" *SLE* 330.

(1870). Mivart, a Roman Catholic anatomist, argued that evolution
was directly controlled by God. "I found him, to my exceeding pleasure, advocating views which I had long held," Kingsley wrote of
him.[22] When Darwin in his *Descent of Man* (1871) explained human
behaviour as subject to the evolution of animal instinct, Kingsley
was less sanguine about Darwin's interpretation of evolution. The
main purpose of Mivart's book had been to show that there existed
a crucial distinction between the human body and the human soul.
Although the body might be subject to natural processes, the soul
was something divinely created. Kingsley subscribed to that too.
Kingsley's eccentric fancy for the body-secreting soul had apparently
passed and was substituted by a theologically more satisfactory interpretation of evolution. Ironically, Mivart's view was to become almost
a century later the official stand of the Roman Catholic Church on
evolution and creation.

II

By the beginning of 1866 Kingsley had come to dread the time necessary to deliver his series of lectures at Cambridge. The prospect
of the Lent term of 1866 was gloomy. Fanny had complained for
some time about pains in the head, which she attributed to a bad
tooth. Her physician, however, thought otherwise and advised her
to leave Eversley for a rest on the coast. She left with Mary and
Grenville for Bournemouth. Although the February weather was cold
and breezy, she soon felt better, and a somewhat reassured Kingsley
concluded that her infirmity was caused by "the damp & general
malaria, & of that you can have none at Bournemouth."[23] However,
he bore the separation from Fanny badly and in her absence remained
over-anxious about her health. Above all, he made himself miserable with reproaches that he had "left you ill & in such pain."[24]
Although he had numerous invitations for dinner, he felt lonely at
Cambridge and was looking forward to joining Fanny and his youngest
children in Bournemouth. "I am v[er]y near the end of my widow-
hood now," he wrote when the term was nearing its close.[25]

---

[22] "The Natural Theology of the Future" *SLE* 313.
[23] CK to FK, undated, BL-62555 f.85v.
[24] CK to FK, undated, BL-62555 f.94r.
[25] CK to FK, undated, BL-62555 f.109r.

The end of term was marked by William Whewell's death. A fall from his horse had left him half paralysed for days before he died. As Vice-Chancellor of the university, Whewell had done much for progress and reform at Cambridge, and Kingsley keenly felt the "awful suddenness" of his death[26] and "spoke a few words to the lads before lecture" about Whewell's scientific standing.[27] He also felt personally touched by the event: "He was v[er]y kind to me, & I am fond of him."[28] It would seem that any misunderstanding that had existed between the two men upon Kingsley's appointment as professor of modern history in 1860 had disappeared and that in time they had learned to appreciate and respect each other.

The presence at the University of Cambridge of his son Maurice (who had gone up in the autumn of 1865 to Trinity as a rather unwilling student), made Kingsley's 1866 residence more bearable than he had expected. Kingsley spent much time with his son, who joined him on his walks "of his own accord."[29] Still, a year later, when the Lent term of 1867 neared, Kingsley again dreaded the separation from Fanny, and the work the university lectures brought with them weighed on him. However, the Lent term of 1867 proved in the end as successful as the previous year. His son's presence at Cambridge remained a delight to him. "I am so happy with my boy," he wrote on 15 February to Fanny, "he comes unto me continually as a matter of course, & walks with me ev[er]y afternoon."[30] In the autumn of 1866 Kingsley had managed to get F.D. Maurice appointed Knightsbridge Professor of Casuistry, Moral Theology, and Moral Philosophy, and Cambridge even turned into something of a pleasure again for Kingsley. Both Maurices made it worth while for Kingsley to reconsider his "purpose of residing more in Cambridge."[31] Kingsley enjoyed Maurice's lectures, and in the evening resorted to the Master's rooms. Sometimes he brought promising undergraduates with him, doing his utmost to make them feel at ease with the shy theologian.

---

[26] CK to FK, undated, BL-62555 f.106r.
[27] CK to FK, undated, BL-62555 f.107v.
[28] CK to FK, undated, BL-62555 f.96v.
[29] CK to FK, undated, BL-62555 f.19r.
[30] CK to FK, 15/2/1867, BL-62555 f.150v.
[31] FDM to CK, 17/12/1866, Maurice ii.552.

Illustration 7. Charles Kingsley (photography by Eliott & Frye, London, c. 1866)

But notwithstanding the pleasant company of friends and son at the university during the 1866 and 1867 terms, there were factors that increased Kingsley's diffidence at his public role. In the autumn of 1867, he wrote to F.D. Maurice about his intentions of giving up the professorship. This was caused by a negative review of his history lectures on "The Ancien Régime" in *The Times*. The reviewer— Mrs Kingsley suspected Woodham, who had coveted Kingsley's professorship for himself[32]—admitted that "this little book contains some ingenious reflections, acute remarks, and original views," but that on the whole Kingsley did not, and never could, grasp the whole of a subject. Kingsley's lectures "bear marks of hurried and shallow thought; they betray knowledge crammed for the occasion; they are full of incoherence and irrelevance [. . . which] will not add to his reputation as a commentator on history." This was bad, but what really stung was the allegation that the *Saturday Review* had been right about Kingsley all along: "We cannot say that it [Kingsley's book] will silence the calumnies of the uncharitable persons who have insinuated that the appointment of Mr. Kingsley to the Chair of Modern History at Cambridge was a sign that the University despised the subject."[33]

F.D. Maurice told Kingsley not to succumb to the tyranny of the press. The new Vice-Chancellor, W.H. Thompson, when informed of Kingsley's intention to resign, answered Kingsley "to the same effect as [Maurice]" about the press.[34] But their reassuring advice was to no avail. Kingsley's next letter to Maurice revealed the amount of self-doubt the reviews had wrought in him. He admitted that "I feel more & more my own unfitness for the post," and complained that his "memory grows worse & worse, & I am only fit for a preacher or poetaster: not for a student of facts (moral & historical at least). I feel so strongly that what the press urges against me is, on the whole, true." He, therefore, felt inclined to accept the verdict of the press and wanted to resign his professorship, but he promised Maurice not to do anything rashly,[35] and first to "talk it out with" him and Thompson before coming to any final decision.[36] Since he no longer had a fixed residence at Cambridge it was hardly

---

[32] Martin (1959) 267.
[33] *The Times*, 7/11/67, 6c–d.
[34] CK to FDM, 12/11/1867, BL-41297 f.221r.
[35] CK to FDM, 12/11/1867, BL-41297 f.220.
[36] CK to FDM, 12/11/1867, BL-41297 f.221r.

worth his while to keep the professorship, and residence at Cambridge was by now out of the question because of both Kingsley's and Fanny's weak health. He added in his letter to Maurice:

> Would that I could reside more. But Mrs. Kingsley has been always ill at Cambridge & I caught my illness there, & alw[a]ys returns when I go there. I cannot live in that relaxing air, & the malaria of the river acts as poison on my insides.[37]

Although Chitty maintains that Kingsley was getting over the last profound depression of his life by the spring of 1865,[38] complaints of a weak and overworked brain continued till far into 1868. Mrs Kingsley, in a long letter about her husband's intention to resign his professorship, explained to F.D. Maurice that she had "*long* wished him to give up the Professorship, simply because it is too much for his brain." Still, that she pressed him to stay on a bit longer is clear from the following passage: "if I had not felt he wd. so like to be at Cambridge while our dear boy Maurice was there, I shd. have persuaded him to give it up."[39] More likely than not, this reflected Mrs Kingsley's own reasons for convincing her husband not to resign.

The mental stress caused by overwork was also the result of Kingsley's renewed literary activities. If the Cambridge professorship had once liberated him from the obligation of writing for money, by 1867 the family required more money than his fixed income could cover. He had to pay for the education of three children—although Rose had ended her education, Maurice needed money at university, Grenville was sent to a public school and Mary received an expensive education at home—and a rebuilding of the rectory to put in central heating meant that Kingsley had had to take up his pen again and write for deadlines to supplement his income. The Cambridge lectures interfered with his parish work, and the parish with the lectures, and both with the "wretched necessity of writing for the *Children's* sake," Mrs Kingsley complained. She prophesied that "combined together [they] are too much for him—& will kill him." But the professorial stipend could not be dispensed with, she realized, "unless he is relieved from a great deal for it by the Queen's giving him a Canonry."[40]

---

[37] CK to FDM, 12/11/1867, BL-41297 f.221.
[38] Chitty (1974) 239.
[39] Martin (1959) 267.
[40] Martin (1959) 267.

Some relief for the mental stress of 1867 was found in a September holiday in Scotland. Notwithstanding Kingsley's jingoism, he often hankered to get away from England and the English. To Professor Skelton, for example, he announced his plans to be present at the British Association at Dundee "to see all you good Scotch *savans*." "I am afraid," he added, "I am a bad Englishman, for I like you Scots far better than my own countrymen."[41] It was a feeling that recurred with increasing frequency during the last years of Kingsley's life.

From St Andrew's Kingsley wrote how his presence was celebrated during the meeting of the British Association and how he was asked, "against my express entreaty," for a speech during a dinner offered by the University and the City to the attendants of the Association. Professor Campbell proposed a toast to the "literature of science" and coupled it with Kingsley's name. A contemporary account reported that Kingsley felt honoured but that he could not "speak for those honoured names which Professor Campbell had mentioned, but only for what he would call the camp-followers of science, hanging on to the outskirts, perhaps taking care of the sick and wounded, perhaps foraging and plundering a little."[42] Although he generally tried to keep a low profile—"I hate being made a lion of"—he could not avoid receiving numerous invitations, amongst others from Blackwood ("of the magazine"), and Grant-Duff. He was also asked to preach in Boyd's church, but even if he realized that it was "quite legal," he wished to avoid "a sudden and uncalled for row with the Puseyites."[43] The public picture of Kingsley that emerges during his visit to Dundee in 1867 is that of a humbled, but celebrated, man of letters.

September 1867 was not a very opportune time for Kingsley to leave his family behind at Eversley. Maurice's future weighed on his and Fanny's minds. At the end of 1864, Maurice, then almost eighteen, had contemplated what he would do when he finished school the following year. Fearing his father's reaction, he wrote a letter to his mother to express his wish to become an explorer in India or Australia. As Fanny was away from home at the time, Kingsley happened to open the letter, and, rather piqued at not being taken into

---

[41] CK to John Skelton, undated, *LML* ii.230.
[42] CK to FK, 19/9/1867, *LML* ii.252.
[43] CK to FK, 7/9/1867, *LML* ii.251.

his confidence, replied: "Don't try to hide anything from me. You will find me—not as reasonable as she is—no one can be that—but quite reasonable enough a fellow who has a skin, & can stand a prick" and he stipulated that, although India or Queensland might offer a fine opening in life, "Before you go [...] any where else, you will go to Cambridge. There you will stay till you take your degree."[44] Kingsley hoped that Cambridge would change his son's mind, at least "3 or 4 times," but during his third year at university, it became clear that Maurice was not interested in taking a degree and still felt inclined to explore new continents. Maurice had decided to try to make his fortune in South America. Realizing he could not keep his son in England, Kingsley acquiesced and tried to make the best of it, and, while at Dundee, he talked to Bates of the Geographical Society who "s[a]ys that if Maurice will call on him a[n]y d[a]y at the Geographical Society, / Whitehall, he will give him all information ab[ou]t S. America—will show him v[er]y [...] maps of the Southern States of the Panama, Monte Video & will take him to his own house & show him his collections.[45]

To Fanny, who bore separation from her children badly, all this was distressing. Added to this, Grenville had reached school-going age, and the prospect of her youngest son leaving the family nest plunged Fanny into great anxiety. She worried about their son's fragile health (he had a weak liver) and about the melancholy stare in his eyes. While her husband was in Scotland, Grenville left Eversley for his first term at Winton House, a private school for boys in Winchester. The school was run by Kingsley's one-time master and friend C.A. Johns, and the delicate boy was entrusted to the care of Mrs Johns who "is like a mother to them all."[46] However, parting with Grenville made Fanny quite ill, and she wrote a disconsolate letter to her husband, which, in turn, made him feel wretched. He tried to reassure her: "Pr[a]y do not fret about the boys sad look. I have observed it for years, & have made up my mind that it came from just those unsatisfied energies & that longing for companionship, w. school will satisfy. It was to me."[47]

[44] CK to Maurice Kingsley, 12/12/1864, BL-62557 f.36.
[45] CK to FK, undated, BL-62555 f.166.
[46] Chitty (1974) 251.
[47] CK to FK, undated, BL-62555 f.176r.

Notwithstanding the anxiety at home, Scotland was a success. At Dundee Kingsley had made friends with the emerging geologists Archibald Geikie and John Lubbock. After the meeting of the British Association he was invited to many of the noble estates of the area. He also did some invigorating salmon fishing while he was the guest of the Prince of Wales at Abergeldie, and he reported to Fanny that "I am quite well, better than I have been for 4 years"[48] and that "I am picking up more health & strength than I have done for years past."[49] Much of his happiness, however, was destroyed when he received from Fanny the news that Grenville had run away from school within a week and had returned to Eversley.

III

After the financial success of *Hereward the Wake*, and the relative ease with which it was written, Kingsley seemed to have got over his writer's block which had followed the publication of *Two Years Ago*. He was full of plans for a new novel, which had again become necessary to complement his inadequate income. Early in 1866 he wrote to Fanny from Cambridge: "Pr[a]y don't fret yourself for a moment about money matters. I see my way to earning a deal of money this year, with real pleasure to myself. All it will require is a little wandering ab[ou]t the New Forest."[50] Alexander Macmillan was briefed by Kingsley that the "New Forest novel is hatching slowly but well."[51] A year later, however, progress on the novel had stalled and Macmillan had to press him "to try again at the New Forest novel." He also tried to enlist Fanny's help to convince Kingsley to persevere with writing new fiction.[52] Nothing ever came of the New Forest novel.

At the beginning of 1868, however, Kingsley came with another idea of a novel, which he outlined to Macmillan as "the autobiography of a poor English Scholar from abt 1490"[53] He started research, and Mrs Kingsley shortly afterwards wrote to Macmillan that her

---

[48] CK to FK, undated, BL-62555 f.172v.
[49] CK to FK, undated, BL-62555 f.173v.
[50] CK to FK, undated, BL-62555 f.101v.
[51] Martin (1959) 263.
[52] CK to FK, undated, BL-62555 f.154v.
[53] CK to Macmillan, undated, BL-54911 f.177.

husband had gone to Norfolk for a week. She hoped "his week in Norfolk will do him good," and she added, "*he is so overdone* that I quite shrink from the novel. I believe it will just finish him! & I am *very* uneasy."[54] Although money matters pressed him, by the beginning of 1868 Kingsley knew he would never write fiction anymore, and, therefore, in April he tried to sell the copyright of some of his most successful works to Macmillan:

> When the illustrated Edition of the Heroes comes out, I shd. like to sell the book to you out & out as I must part with any copyrights I can this year, owing to the necessity of finding money for my boy's Emigration Capital. Think over this please. I am willing—or rather unwillingly forced—to offer you the Waterbabies out & out likewise. But necessity is ruthless.[55]

It was painful to part with the rights of these works, but there was no energy left in Kingsley for new novels. Towards the end of the year, he had no curate so that all the parish work fell to himself, and next year's lectures still had to be written. He gave Macmillan a dramatic account of his mental state: "I have been so overworked & am about to sick & dying."[56]

In October 1866, Kingsley had set about negotiating a new volume of sermons with Macmillan. The publisher showed immediate interest (anything Kingsley wrote was selling well by now) and Kingsley forwarded some sermons "verbatim, from memory" for Alexander Macmillan to read, asking him to send them next to F.D. Maurice for an opinion on them.[57] To prepare a volume of sermons required less energy from Kingsley, and the following year a collection of twenty sermons called *The Water of Life* appeared. It included a number of longish sermons preached on special occasions at Westminster Abbey, Whitehall, and the Chapel Royal, as well as a series of shorter ones delivered at Windsor before the Queen. Very few of the sermons were delivered before his own Eversley congregation.

The interest of the volume lies in the sermons dealing with natural phenomena and the progress of science. Kingsley, for example, discussed the following subjects: "The Physician's Calling", "The Earthquake", "The Meteor Shower", and the "Cholera, 1866." These

[54] FK to Macmillan, undated, BL-54911 f.180.
[55] CK to Macmillan, 30/4/1868, BL-54911 ff.181–2.
[56] CK to Macmillan, 6/12/1868, BL-54911 f.183.
[57] CK to Macmillan, undated, BL-54911 f.153.

sermons concentrate on the feelings of nineteenth-century man about the modern notion of such concepts and events, and Kingsley compares it to the "ignorant" reaction of previous ages. In other, more theoretical, sermons Kingsley developed the implications of these comparisons. The nineteenth century was not yet the glorious century some liked to call it, although man's gain in true qualities of civilization had been invaluable. In a sermon called "Progress," which was preached before the Queen on 3 June 1866, Kingsley affirmed that "it is not true of Christian nations that the thing which has been is that which shall be; and that there is no new thing under the sun."[58] The true spirit of God was that of "improvement, discovery, progress from darkness to light,"[59] and therefore one should not regret past times, Kingsley warned: "if we long to be back in those so-called devout ages of faith, we long for an age in which witches and heretics were burned alive."[60] He admitted in another sermon that it is natural for nineteenth-century man to feel "How simple, and easy, and certain, it all looked to our forefathers! How complex, how uncertain, it looks to us!"[61] and he recognized that it was true that faith in progress had brought with it hopes that were never realized, but "if we are better men than we were in former times, then is the present better than the past, even though it be less happy."[62]

Kingsley's contemplations on progress constitute a fine piece of Victorian perplexity about change, which at the same time is balanced by an optimistic awareness of living in an age of momentous transition. Anticipating Freud's famous description of the three crises with which modern man has had to come to terms, Kingsley writes:

> Our conceptions of them [the heavens and the earth] have shaken. The Copernican system shook them, when it told men that the earth was but a tiny globular planet revolving round the sun. Geology shook them, when it told men that the earth has endured for countless ages, during which whole continents have been submerged, whole seas become dry land, again and again. Even now the heavens and the earth are being shaken by researches into the antiquity of the human race, and into the origin and the mutability of species, which, issue in what

[58] "Progress" *WoL* 137-8.
[59] "Progress" *WoL* 138.
[60] "Progress" *WoL* 139.
[61] "The Shaking of the Heavens and the Earth" *WoL* 70.
[62] "Progress" *WoL* 141.

results they may, will shake for us, meanwhile, theories which are venerable with the authority of nearly eighteen hundred years, and of almost every great Doctor since St. Augustine.[63]

Instead of geology, Freud added his own achievements in psychology as the third crisis.

The Water of Life also reveals the extent of Kingsley's clerical, but extra-parochial, engagements during the period from June 1864 to the end of 1866, and it helps us to understand why Kingsley suffered periodically from the strain of overwork. Of the twenty sermons included in the volume, only eight can be considered parish sermons, while four were preached before the Queen, five at the Chapel Royal before the court. Three sermons were written and preached for special occasions at Westminster Abbey, at Whitehall for St George's Hospital, and in St John's Church, Nottinghill, for the Bishop of London's Fund. Further extra-parochial sermons of 1866 that are not published in this volume include one preached at Wellington College, one at St Olave's Church, Hart Street, and a sermon delivered before the Prince of Wales at Sandringham. The pattern of 1867 was much the same. With his parish duties, the work for his Cambridge chair, and his literary activities, it is not surprising that Kingsley was severely tried by this load of work. At the end of 1867, at the age of only forty-eight, Kingsley felt old and outlived. He was in a dark mood when, in November, he wrote these lines:

> I watch them drift—the old familiar faces,
> Who fished and rode with me, by stream and wold,
> Till ghosts, not men, fill old beloved places,
> And, ah! the land is rank with churchyard mold.
> ("Drifting Away; A Fragment")

---

[63] "The Shaking of the Heavens and the Earth" *WoL* 72–3.

CHAPTER TWENTY-THREE

THE UGLY AFTER-CROP OF SUPERSTITION
(1868–1869)

Although Kingsley was unable to write a new novel after the publication of *Hereward the Wake*, he devoted himself to plenty of other literary work. During his 1868 term at Cambridge he wrote a life of St Anthony which appeared as the first part of *The Hermits* in Macmillan's *Sunday Library for Household Reading* in April 1868. According to Una Pope-Hennessy, Kingsley had got the idea for a book on the lives of the hermit-saints during his summer holiday in Scotland the previous year. The weather being too dry for salmon fishing, he listened to his gillie's stories about the Celtic hermits of Scotland.

The Hermits is one of Kingsley's most forgotten books. Mrs Kingsley refers to it in her biography merely as her husband's "little history of the Hermits for the 'Sunday Library',"[1] and of all later biographers only Una Pope-Hennessy seems to have thought it worth-while to discuss the book, even if she does so in one paragraph only. Chitty uncritically copied the outline from Pope-Hennessy, while Thorp, Martin, and Colloms remained silent about it. The book fares even worse in the works of the literary critics. After Kingsley's enemy *The Saturday Review* declared it dull, it is not mentioned again in the vast literature on Kingsley. This silence is strange, as *The Hermits* is Kingsley's answer to Newman's *Apologia*. As such, even Egner missed it in his *Apologia Pro Charles Kingsley*. Admittedly, *The Hermits* in itself does not make exciting reading, and is dull by the standards of *Hereward the Wake*. *The Saturday Review*, in its meagre review of a mere two pages, criticized Kingsley for omitting from his accounts of the hermits' lives the rude and savage details of the original stories! These, of course, would hardly have been appropriate for Sunday family reading. Still, for the student of Kingsley, *The Hermits* is far from uninteresting, even though the first hundred pages tend to put the reader off.

---

[1] *LML* ii.267.

Since Newman's *Apologia* proved a lasting success and went through one revised edition after another, Kingsley might well have felt the need to speak out on one of his central accusations, especially as his name in the popular memory remained inseparably linked to the *Apologia*, notwithstanding the fact that Newman eliminated many of the original points of the controversy in his 1865 edition. Kingsley felt that the press had not seriously considered his points, while Newman's answers to his charges were inadequate for him. Although he did not want to open the controversy again, he still felt the need to vindicate his own position. Since much of Kingsley's accusation rested upon Newman's use of hagiography, this field was chosen to put the record straight.

In *What, Then, Does Dr. Newman Mean?* Kingsley had drawn attention to the *Lives of the English Saints*, in which Newman, as its editor, seemed to sanction some of the puerile miracles recounted in them. In particular, in the preface to the Life of St Walburga, on the question whether the miracles in the narrative should be recorded as a matter of fact, Newman wrote: "there is no reason why they should not be. They are the kind of facts proper to ecclesiastical history [. . .] there is nothing, then, *prima facie*, in the miraculous accounts in question to repel a properly-taught or religiously-disposed mind."[2] In the fourth and fifth parts of Newman's "Answer in detail to Mr Kingsley's Accusations" and appended to the first book edition of the *Apology*, these charges were only weakly refuted. Newman declined editorial responsibility for any of the lives published after the second number, ignoring that the life Kingsley so much objected to *was* in the second number. Moreover Newman quoted at length from a lecture of his in which he affirmed that "miracles to the Catholic are historical fact, and nothing short of this; and they are to be regarded and dealt with as other facts [. . .] They may or may not have taken place in particular cases; he may be unable to determine which; he may have no distinct evidence; he may suspend his judgment."[3] To Kingsley this was dallying with the meaning of the word "fact", while "judgment" was out of place in assessments of truth. Newman also asserted that "the Incarnation is the most stupendous event which ever can take place on earth; and after it and henceforth, I do not see how we can scruple at any miracle on the mere

---

[2] *WTDNM?* 36.
[3] Newman 344.

ground of its being unlikely to happen."[4] The two are not comparable events, and Kingsley could not accept Newman's argument.

It is not to be supposed that in *The Hermits* Kingsley consciously set out to answer Newman (there is no evidence for this in the correspondence with Macmillan or with others), but rather that while working on *The Hermits* he suddenly saw an innocuous way to do so. Of course, Kingsley was aware that with the subject of his book he was going over ground which Newman had gone over before him. Writing a "Lives of the Hermit Saints," could not but invite comparison with Newman's *Lives of the Saints*, especially as the fourth volume in Newman's series was called the "Hermit Saints." Kingsley, therefore, proceeded very cautiously in *The Hermits*, and made sure that neither Newman nor the controversy were mentioned in it. He stated that the original biographies he translated were not written as "religious romances," that

> there is not the slightest evidence that such was the case. The lives of these, and most other saints [...] were written by men who believed the stories themselves, after such inquiry into the facts as they deemed necessary; who knew others would believe them; and who intended that they should do so; and the stories were believed accordingly, and taken as matter of fact for the most practical purposes by the whole of Christendom. The forging of miracles [...] belongs to a much later and much worse age.[5]

But, in his introduction, he emphasized above all that, in this volume, he wanted to give the lives "translated as literally as possible." *The Hermits* was thus presented as a work of translation only. Kingsley was prudent and wanted to avoid another public chastisement in a crossing of swords with Newman. For those readers who perceived the affinity to Newman's *Lives of the Saints* (and some must have perceived them), such premises were disappointing. The first Life, that of St Anthony of Egypt, which runs to almost a third of the book, does not touch upon any of his disagreements with Newman. Trier, for example, where the original manuscript of Anthony's life was discovered, is vividly described in the early pages of the volume, but the relic of the holy coat, which had featured in Kingsley's accusations of Newman's credulity in *What, Then, Does Dr. Newman Mean?*

---

[4] Newman 343.
[5] *Herm* 20.

as well as in Newman's *Apologia*, is not mentioned. With hardly any editorial comment Kingsley next gives his translation of St Athanasius' account of St Anthony.

At the conclusion of the Life of St Anthony, however, something got the better of Kingsley, and the purpose of *The Hermits* seemed to have changed. Kingsley suddenly anticipated "What we are to think of the miracles and wonders contained in it, will be discussed at a later point in this book."[6] He then gave St Jerome's representation of St Anthony in his Life of St Paul, as well as the anecdotes collected about him by the Desert Fathers. Kingsley refrained from comment here.

The next life in *The Hermits* is that of Anthony's pupil St Hilarion, the founder of anchoritic life in Palestine. Kingsley's text is again St Jerome's, but after only five pages of translation there is a significant editorial interpolation. "It is unnecessary," Kingsley writes, "to relate more wonders which the reader cannot be expected to believe."[7] In a long and rambling meditation on the monks in the East Kingsley, on the one hand, envied their escape into solitude—

> It is the bustle and hurry of our modern life which causes shallow thought, unstable purpose, and wasted energy, in too many who would be better, and wiser, stronger and happier, if they would devote more time and silence and meditation.[8]

while, on the other, he admitted that

> the average monk, even when well-conducted himself and in a well-conducted monastery, was, like average men of every creed, rank, or occupation, a very common-place person, acting from very mixed and often very questionable motives.[9]

Although Kingsley admired some of the aspects of monastic life, in the end he did not like monks. The conviction was as strong as it had been twenty-five years before. Worthy of consideration is also the fact that Kingsley had attacked Newman on singling out monks and nuns as the only apostolic Bible Christians.[10]

After these affirmations a decided change of tone sets in. In the following passages Kingsley abandoned his method of translation and

---

[6] *Herm* 81.
[7] *Herm* 110.
[8] *Herm* 127.
[9] *Herm* 137.
[10] *WTDNM?* 24.

briefly narrated in his own words the lives of the hermits of Asia. After only a few pages, speaking of John Chrysostomus, he remarked: "A story like this may raise a smile in some of my readers, in others something like indignation or contempt." But, Kingsley pointed out, as long as such legends are told with gravity as proof of the holiness and humanity of the saint, "an honest author is bound to notice some of them at least, and not to give an alluring and really dishonest account of these men and their times, by detailing every anecdote which can elevate them in the mind of the reader, while he carefully omits all that may justly disgust him." With this Kingsley justified his own approach to the lives of the saints. "Yet," he added, "after all, we are not bound to believe this legend."[11] Thus, while Kingsley rightly recognized the symbolical value of legend and myth, he made clear that such stories have nothing to do with historical reality. The dialogue with Newman is becoming palpable at this stage.

Half-way through *The Hermits*, in his account of the life of Basil, Kingsley remarked that "as the years went on, the hermit life took a form less and less practical, and more and more repulsive also,"[12] and in the next life, that of St Simeon Stylites, Kingsley's comments build up a tension between the narrated material and the opinion of the author that indicates that a climax cannot be far off. The hermits have become "mere self-torturing fakeers" and the reported miracles and penances "can only excite horror and disgust."[13] Unsure of how to proceed, Kingsley resorted to the safe emotional distance of the translator, and alternatively gives the texts of St Simeon's disciple Anthony and of Theodoret, both of which he found in Rosweyde's *Vitæ patrum* (1628), omitting "some painful details unnecessary to be translated,"[14] and "more painful stories, which had best be omitted."[15] Kingsley's patience with the saints was running out, and at the end of St Simeon's life he added a twenty-page tirade against the puerility of preposterous miracles and against the people who believe in them. This is how it starts:

> After such a fantastic story as this of Simeon, it is full time (some readers may have thought that it was full time long since) to give my

[11] *Herm* 157.
[12] *Herm* 163.
[13] *Herm* 169, 170.
[14] *Herm* 178.
[15] *Herm* 189.

own opinion of the miracles, visions, daemons, and other portents
which occur in the lives of these saints. [. . .] In this age, as in every
other age of materialism and practical atheism, a revulsion in favour
of superstition is at hand; I may say is taking place round us now.
Doctrines are tolerated as possibly true,—persons are regarded with
respect and admiration, who would have been looked on, even fifty
years ago, if not with horror, yet with contempt, as beneath the serious notice of educated English people. But it is this very contempt
which has brought about the change of opinion concerning them. It
has been discovered that they were not altogether so absurd as they
seemed; that the public mind, in its ignorance, has been unjust to
them; and, in hasty repentance for that injustice, too many are ready
to listen to those who will tell them that these things are not absurd
at all—that there is no absurdity in believing that the leg-bone of St.
Simon Stock may possess miraculous powers, or that the spirits of the
departed communicate with their friends by rapping on the table. The
ugly after-crop of superstition which is growing up among us now is
the just and natural punishment of our materialism—I may say, of
our practical atheism.[16]

Although this was not specifically aimed at Newman, it is a significant
passage about Newman's and Kingsley's contention about truth in
1864. A direct snipe at Newman, therefore, does seem implicit in
the following remark: "Very few people decide a question on its
facts, but on their prejudices as to what they would like to have
happened [. . .] They tell you quite honestly, not what they saw, but
what they think they ought to have seen."[17] This echoes one of those
statements concerning miracles by Newman that Kingsley found
highly objectionable, viz. that "if the alleged facts did not occur,
they ought to have occurred, if I may so speak." If by 1868 public
opinion had long since forgotten the details of the Newman-Kingsley
controversy, Kingsley had not. He wanted to vindicate his conviction that "these good hermits worked no real miracles and saw no
real visions whatsoever,"[18] that their visions were no more than the
products of "a more or less unhealthy nervous system,"[19] that

> these good hermits, by continual fasts and vigils, must have put them-
> selves (and their histories prove that they did put themselves) into a
> state of mental disease, in which their evidence was worth nothing; a

---

[16] *Herm* 196–8.
[17] *Herm* 202–3.
[18] *Herm* 202.
[19] *Herm* 206.

state in which the mind cannot distinguish between facts and dreams; in which life itself is one dream; in which (as in the case of madness, or of a feverish child) the brain cannot distinguish between the objects which are outside it and the imaginations which are inside it.[20]

That people in the past accepted the miracles in the stories of the hermit saints was because previous ages had not yet acquired "the habit of looking cooly, boldly, carefully, at facts."[21] Kingsley specified that he did not think miracles *per se* impossible, but that his refusal of post Biblical miracles rested on the test that none had happened recently. "When we are told," as Newman seemed to imply in ushering in the comparison with belief in the Incarnation, "that the reason why we see no prodigies is because we have no faith, we answer (if we be sensible), Just so."[22] To Kingsley such faith amounted to beliefs that people could be magically cured of a disease, that ghosts existed, that daemons transformed themselves into the shape of animals, that witches had the power to curse, and so forth. To Kingsley, such beliefs had nothing whatsoever to do with the real spiritual world of Christianity.

Newman's biographers have pointed out that, in the end, Newman bore Kingsley no ill-will, that Kingsley's accusation in *Macmillan's Magazine* merely gave Newman the opportunity to do what he had long wished to do. Similarly, Kingsley reacted in a magnanimous way to Newman's *Dream of Gerontius*. Although there was much in the book which shocked and pained him, he read it with "awe and admiration." "However utterly I may differ from the *entourage* in which Dr. Newman's present creed surrounds the central idea," he wrote in May 1868 to William Cope, "I must feel that that central idea is as true as it is noble."[23] Thus, in *The Hermits* Kingsley did not want so much to attack once more Newman's puerile attitude to miracles as to make clear to the reading public what he himself thought about such attitudes in general. Since Newman had omitted any mention of Kingsley in his autobiographical account in the second edition of the *Apologia*, Kingsley avoided mentioning Newman in *The Hermits*. Still, albeit two widely different texts, they are both closely linked in being the authors' vindications of their religious

---

[20] *Herm* 205.
[21] *Herm* 200.
[22] *Herm* 200.
[23] CK to WC, 2/5/1868, *LML* ii.270.

positions (and opinions) in the aftermath of their original controversy
over truth.

Kingsley felt there were also other records to set right. Early in
1868 Kingsley asked Alexander Macmillan to send him Auguste
Comte's works. "I must know something of Comte, if I am to be
of any further use in the world, to your friend John Morley, or any
body else who thinks," he explained.[24] Mrs Kingsley writes that her
husband "got through nearly sixteen volumes of Comte's works, in
preparation for his next year's lectures at Cambridge."[25] Studying
Comte in detail, however, did not change Kingsley's opinion of him.
He did not like Comte's style and rhetoric—"it is difficult not to be
cowed by his self-sufficient glibness and cheerfully naïve sophistry"—
and his theory of the development of religion did not convince him
at all. "My notion is," he wrote to F.D. Maurice in September "to
take your 'Kingdom of Christ,' Carlyle's 'French Revolution,' and
Bunsen's 'God in History,' and show the men how you all three
hold one view (under differences), and Comte and all who are on
his side an absolutely different one."[26] A month and a half later, he
was more than convinced that he had chosen the right subject for
his lectures: "in Cambridge [. . .] the very air seems full of Comtism.
Certainly the press is; and how to make head against the growing
unbelief in any God worth calling a God is more than I can see."[27]
His last course in 1869 was thus on the philosophies of history as
held by Comte, Bunsen, Carlyle and Maurice. The subject confirmed
Kingsley's heroic view of history, and, in reflecting the premises for
the study of history which he had outlined in his inaugural lecture,
it brought his university career to a coherent end. Unfortunately
there are no detailed records of how the lectures were received, nor
were any of these final lectures ever published.

II

In September 1868 Kingsley's son Maurice sailed for South America.
In the end he had left Cambridge without taking a degree, and,

---

[24] CK to Alexander Macmillan, undated, BL-54911 f.185v–186r.
[25] *LML* ii.268.
[26] CK to FDM, 10/9/1868, *LML* ii.274.
[27] CK to FDM, 23/10/1868, *LML* ii.274.

after having acquired some basic agricultural knowledge at the Royal Agricultural College in Cirencester, he decided to try his luck as a breeder of cattle. Although Kingsley was hopeful that Maurice would make his fortune abroad, parting with his first-born child was difficult. When the first Christmas without the complete family neared, he expressed his thought and feelings in poetry: "How will it dawn, the coming Christmas Day?" he asked himself. The poem compares the traditional Christmas in the northern hemisphere with a Christmas in the middle of summer south of the equator. But wherever on earth, even in a South American wilderness, at Christmas God

> reminds us, year by year
> What 'tis to a man: to curb and spurn
> The tyrant in us; that ignoble self
> Which boasts, not loathes, its likeness to the brute.

The fictional encounters with bare nature and the primitive animal instinct which had fascinated and worried Kingsley in *Westward Ho!* were now a real-life experience for his son. It brought once more to his mind the flimsy polish of civilization and the danger to give in to mere animal nature. In lines which are highly reminiscent of Tennyson's *In Memoriam* he reflected on evolution and the place of man in creation:

> Are we as creeping things, which have no Lord?
> That we are brutes, great God, we know too well:
> Apes daintier-featured; silly birds who flaunt.
> Their plumes unheeding of the fowler's step;
> Spiders, who catch with paper, not with webs;
> Tigers, who slay with canon and harp steel,
> Instead of teeth and claws;—all these we are.
> Are we no more than these, save in degree?
> No more than these; and born but to compete—
> To envy and devour, like beast or herb;
> Mere fools of nature; puppets of strong lusts,
> Taking the sword, to perish with the sword
> Upon the universal battlefield
> Even as the things upon the moor outside?

Tennyson's reply to such dark views was that he "was born to higher things" and this line comes to mind when reading Kingsley's "Christmas Day." After all, Tennyson's coming to terms with Hallam's death (and the consequent meditations on the man's forlorn and futile life in an indifferent plan of nature) also works through a series of

Christmas celebrations, which stand for the symbol of "what 'twas to be a man."

If Kingsley lost a son in 1868, he unwittingly gained a future son-in-law. With all the work he had on his hands during his lent term at Cambridge, a curate at Eversley was indispensable. In October he asked Alexander Macmillan for information about a certain William Harrison, with whom Kingsley was in negotiation for the following term. He wanted to know whether Mr Harrison was: "1. good tempered 2. Honest 3. Reasonable."[28] Harrison met Kingsley's standards, and in 1868 he remained at Eversley to help out with the parish work. He was to marry Kingsley's youngest daughter Mary in 1876, a year after Kingsley's death. There is no evidence that Mary Kingsley and William Harrison expressed their feelings for each other during the last years of Kingsley's life.

Kingsley's youngest son continued to cause anxiety. Grenville needed constant attention and guidance. He suffered from a weak liver and was spoilt at home by both parents. After a letter of apology in which Kingsley explained his son's running away from C.A. John's school as that of "a child who has never met his equals and had been much petted and spoilt," Grenville returned to Winton School.[29] As he had done years before when Maurice went to school, Kingsley made it a habit to visit his son at Winchester regularly and lecture to the boys. Many of the lectures given at Winston School were published in *Good Words* from November 1868 to October 1869 as *Madam How and Lady Why*. After *Hereward the Wake* relations with McLeod and Strahan of *Good Words* had remained excellent. Although Macmillan ultimately kept the right to publish Kingsley's works in volume, most of what he wrote during the last years of his life first appeared in the Scotsman's magazine. There were, for example, the sketches of nature "From the Ocean to the Sea" and "The Fens" that were to be collected by Macmillan with earlier pieces as *Prose Idylls* in 1873 and a series of lectures and sermons on educational matters written between 1866 and 1874 were finally published as *Health and Education*. Thus, *Madam How and Lady Why* too went for serialization to *Good Words*. And no wonder. In the summer of 1868 Kingsley was able to inform Fanny that "Strahan offers me £1000

---

[28] CK to Alexander Macmillan, 7/10/66, BL-540911 f.148.
[29] Chitty (1974) 252.

for twelve papers of How & Why."[30] Macmillan could not advance such sums for magazine serialization.

Although dedicated to "my son Grenville Arthur and to his school-fellows at Winston House," *Madam How and Lady Why* was part of Kingsley's wider agenda of scientific education. The subtitle—*First Lessons in Earth Lore for Children*—gives some indication of the work's generical contents, but does not do full justice to what Kingsley wanted to teach. Like most of his later publications, it is only cur-sorily mentioned in Kingsley studies and is not given proper weight in Kingsley's appropriation of evolution. Admittedly, the book has no attraction for children today, but as a mid-Victorian attempt to teach boys in their early teens to think about nature along the prin-ciples of Lyell's uniformitarianism and Darwin's natural selection, *Madam How and Lady Why* is of historical interest. Although the book abounds with the typical phraseology of natural theology—such as "reading the book of nature" or "nature's footprints"—and tells chil-dren that to observe nature is the devout duty of a Christian, Kingsley's 'fairy tale' goes far beyond the traditional natural theology for chil-dren in such popular books as Mrs Gatty's *Parables from Nature*. Kingsley's approach is descriptive of the processes of nature (Madam How) while, without denying the possibility, he avoids framing such knowledge in a teleological design (Lady Why). As Kingsley would have put it himself, his was an aspiration to teach how to think in a scientific (inductive) way.

The first part of *Madam How and Lady Why* seems faithful to the original text of the lectures—many interpolations where Kingsley addresses his schoolboy audience enforce this impression—while the later chapters are cast in the form of an imaginary dialogue between father and son who are travelling together. The invention of the characters Madam How and Lady Why and the natural wonders they work, convey the sensation of a fairy-tale world. Indeed, Kingsley encourages a view of the marvellous in nature by repeatedly using the word fairy tale in his text. Fearing, however, that he was over-emphasizing the element, he pointed out that his story of nature is "the true fairy tale."[31]

Kingsley's object in writing these lessons in earth lore seems to have been to offer in a playful way the principles of modern

---

[30] CK to FK, 7/10/1866, BL-62555 f.217.
[31] *MHLW* 145.

natural science in an inconspicuous and traditional form, thus hiding the controversial elements and the far-reaching implications of the new discoveries in the earth sciences. The descriptions of a geological uniformitarian system and the workings of natural selection in passages like

> Every thing round you is changing in shape daily and hourly, as you will find out the longer you live [. . .] Madam How is making and unmaking the surface of the earth now, by exactly the same means as she was making and unmaking ages and ages since[32]

and

> But among these trees in a sheltered valley the larger and stronger would kill the weaker and smaller [. . .] So they would fight, killing each other's children, till the war ended. [. . .] And the competition of species means, that each thing, and kind of things, has to compete against the things round it; and to see which is the stronger; and the stronger live, and breed, and spread, and the weaker die out[33]

are carefully embedded in a context which forces upon the reader the presence of a higher purpose in studying nature. The following excerpt is a good example of this:

> It is your duty to learn His lessons: and it is your interest. God's Book, which is the Universe, and the reading of God's Book, which is Science, can do you nothing but good, and teach you, nothing but truth and wisdom. God did not put this wondrous world about your young souls to tempt or to mislead them.[34]

This remained Kingsley's last word on the study of nature. In a letter to F.D. Maurice, who had read *Madam How and Lady Why*, he explained why he had written the book: "I wished to teach children—my own especially—that the knowledge of nature ought to make them reverence and trust God more, and not less [. . .] they are meant more as prolegomena to natural theology, than as really scientific papers."[35]

---

[32] *MHLW* 13,108.
[33] *MHLW* 253–4.
[34] *MHLW* xii.
[35] CK to FDM, 16/1/1869, *LML* ii.292.

III

Although Kingsley differed with Hughes, Huxley, and Mill over the Eyre controversy, this did not mean that he ceased to count them among his friends. Kingsley was not the kind of person to bear lasting ill-will. Even towards Newman surprisingly little personal resentment was felt during the years that followed the blows he had received from him. The estrangement from Ludlow was a process which had been going on since the mid-fifties and became complete when Kingsley sided with the Southern States in the Civil War in America and had proclaimed himself pro-Eyre. But otherwise, as Huxley had hoped, friendships persisted. Kingsley continued to correspond with Huxley about science and education, and in 1869 John Stuart Mill thought Kingsley a suitable person for a complimentary copy of his just published *The Subjection of Women*.

It is likely that Mill remembered Kingsley's endeavours for equality in the Chartist cause. Although Kingsley in his lecture on "Thrift" earlier that year had written that he had no wish for any "social revolution in the position of women," he still urged the importance of their education.[36] This emphasis on a solid education for both sexes must have drawn Mill's attention and convinced him that he was the right person to engage in the battle of women's rights. This means that notwithstanding their contrasting opinions over Eyre, the humiliation Kingsley had received at the hands of Newman, and the denigration of his qualities in the field of history, a man like John Stuart Mill still thought Kingsley worth having on his side in a public cause.

Kingsley thanked Mill for the "honour" and wrote that "it seems to me unanswerable and exhaustive, and certain, from its moderation as well as from its boldness, to do good service in this good cause." And he added that "I shall continue to labour, according to my small ability, in the direction which you point out."[37] Mill took Kingsley up on his promise. He asked him to speak at the first meeting of the Women's Suffrage Society in London and invited him to stay at his house for the occasion. Kingsley accepted the invitation, and although he was not keen on speaking at the meeting, he assured

---

[36] "Thrift" *SSE* 77.
[37] CK to J.S. Mill, 3/6/1869, *LML* ii.294.

Mill that he was "completely emancipated from those prejudices which have been engrained into the public mind by the traditions of the monastic or canon law about women, and open to any teaching which has for its purpose the doing woman justice in every respect." There was much he longed to discuss with Mill, as "I have arrived at certain conclusions thereon, which (in the face of British narrowness) I have found it wisest to keep to myself."[38] The two men were dissimilar in temperament and differed on points of religion, but Kingsley was impressed by Mill and remarked afterwards: "When I look at his cold, clear-cut face [. . .] I think there is a whole hell beneath him, of which he knows nothing, and so there may be a whole heaven above him."[39]

In October, at the Social Science Congress in Bristol, Kingsley acted as President of the Educational Section. Kingsley himself spoke vehemently against the denominational school system, and pleaded instead for national compulsory male and female education for all social classes. One hundred thousand copies of the address were subsequently printed and distributed by the National Education League. At the congress, Kingsley met Elizabeth Blackwell, the first woman to receive an M.D. degree from a medical school in America. From a family of English immigrants, Blackwell had studied and practised in America, but had returned to England in 1869 to found the London School of Medicine for Women. When Kingsley was introduced to Blackwell during the Bristol congress, he won her over with his first words "You are one of my heroes." They became instant friends and Blackwell became a regular guest at Kingsley's house where they ardently discussed the emancipation of women in the field of medicine. In 1874, shortly before his death, Kingsley was asked to become the chairman of a committee for securing medical degrees for women, and he enthusiastically accepted. After his death Blackwell wrote that, although the movement did not depend on the accomplishments of a single individual worker, "our cause has suffered a heavy loss."[40]

Still, as Kingsley was drawn into the movement for women suffrage there was much that he could not, and would not, uphold. In 1870 he discerned a militant line in the suffragist societies that, as in the

---

[38] CK to J.S. Mill, 17/6/1869, *LML* ii.295.
[39] *LML* ii.295.
[40] Elizabeth Blackwell to FK, undated, *LML* ii.305.

Chartist Movement of 1848, he thought would be self-defeating. He objected to the "hysteric element," by which he meant, as he explained to Mill, "the fancy and emotions unduly excited by suppressed sexual excitement."[41] What irked Kingsley was that the movement for suffrage was not led by married women, but by "foolish women, of no sound or coherent opinions, and of often questionable morals."[42] "Our strength," he told Mill, "lies not in the abnormal, but in the normal type of womanhood."[43] To Kingsley true womanhood, like true manhood, could only be realized in marriage, and comparisons of "emancipated" free women with the monastic life which he had made it his life's mission to deprecate, came naturally:

> Prurience, sir, by which I mean lust, which, unable to satisfy itself in act, satisfies itself by contemplation, usually of a negative and seemingly virtuous and Pharisaic character, vilifying, like St. Jerome in his cell at Bethlehem, that which he dare not do, and which is, after all, only another form of hysteria.[44]

John Stuart Mill also discovered that Kingsley was not unconditionally in favour of women's rights. As he had objected twenty years before to indiscriminate political rights for the Chartists, he now opposed the right of women to vote or to work before they could enjoy the same practical and scientific education as men. Just as Kingsley had posited Christian premises to freedom for Chartist emancipation, he now posited scientific requisites for female emancipation.

Moreover, for women to be successful in their cause the *public* should first become accustomed to their ministrations, "as to show them that they are the equals of men in scientific knowledge and practical ability (as they are)."[45] Thus he urged Mrs P.A. Taylor, a co-founder of the first women's suffrage society, "that unless this movement is kept down to that tone of grace, and modesty, and dignity, [. . .] and which would make it acceptable to the mass of cultivated and experienced, and therefore justly powerful, Englishmen and Englishwomen, it will fail only by the faults of its supporters."[46]

---

[41] CK to J.S. Mill, undated, *LML* ii.328.
[42] CK to J.S. Mill, undated, *LML* ii.328.
[43] CK to J.S. Mill, undated, *LML* ii.330.
[44] CK to J.S. Mill, undated, *LML* ii.330.
[45] CK to J.S. Mill, undated, *LML* ii.329.
[46] CK to Mrs Peter Taylor, 27/5/1870, *LML* ii.327.

IV

After the lent term of 1869 Kingsley resigned his professorship. The preparatory work for his last course of lectures had taken up so much of his time and energy—"I worked eight or nine months hard for the course of twelve lectures"—that it had left him "half-witted." In April, therefore, he wrote to the Master of Trinity College that he had "obtained leave from the Queen to resign at the end of the academic year" and that he had "told Mr. Gladstone as much."[47] Although Kingsley regretted leaving Cambridge because of the many friendships he had made there, he was relieved to withdraw from "doing what others can do better." Notwithstanding the success his lectures on Comte had with the students, Kingsley never managed to overcome the feeling that he was ultimately unfit for the post. The public denigration he had suffered in the press by a handful of critics had a lasting effect on him.

Kingsley undoubtedly had qualities as a professor of modern history. Max Müller, in his preface to the *Roman and the Teuton*, reminds the reader that Kingsley's lectures "were more largely attended than almost any other lectures at Cambridge." The novelty of Kingsley's lectures had not worn off after nine years, and his last lectures on Comte attracted almost as many students as his early ones. One undergraduate who attended in 1869 wrote to Kingsley to tell him of the "good you have done me, and I have no doubt many others, by your English lectures. Your whole series last term, and especially the grand concluding one on Comte, have made an expression just at the moment when it was needed [. . . and] put into the minds of many young men the same living belief in a living God."[48] Such a contemporary response justifies Müller's view that "History was but his text, his chief aim was that of the teacher and preacher."[49] Kingsley's lectures were not what academic lectures ought to be, they were not a critical appreciation of consulted authorities, they were not even always impartial, Müller continued, but they managed to stir up "the interest of young men, and made them ask for books which Undergraduates had never asked for before at the

---

[47] CK to William Hepworth Thompson, 1/4/1869, *LML* ii.293.
[48] Unidentified correspondent to CK, undated, *LML* ii.293.
[49] *RT* xii.

University libraries."[50] This was in itself no mean achievement. And, after all, Kingsley had announced in his inaugural lecture that "I am not here to teach you history. No man can do that. I am here to teach you how to teach yourselves history."[51] Kingsley's qualities as a lecturer were such that Thompson is alleged to have stood up after the inaugural lecture of Kingsley's successor J.R. Seeley and to have said: "Dear, dear, who would have thought that we should so soon have been regretting poor Kingsley!"[52] Moreover, in retrospect, Kingsley's academic standing might need some further qualification. His theories of an English nationalism based on a spiritual coherence of its history and an instinctive acceptance of hierarchy in its people probably deserve more attention in English historiography than they have received so far.

Giving up the Cambridge professorship was a severe cut in Kingsley's income that could only with difficulty be compensated for by writing. Kingsley hoped that the Royal family would help him to obtain ecclesiastical preferment. In 1868 the queen had suggested a vacant canonry at Worcester, but the interim prime minister Disraeli objected. With a new government under Gladstone there seemed the possibility of obtaining a deanery at Durham, which fell vacant in the summer of 1869. While on holiday with Rose in Ireland, during a visit to Froude, Kingsley wrote home to Fanny that he had written to the Prince about Durham. Of course it would "be a great shock to leave Eversley: but there is hardly a spot in England that I would sooner be in than Durham," he added. The appointment was rumoured to be worth £3000 a year, and although Kingsley believed this would be cut down under the new law to £2000, even such a sum would amply solve all their financial problems: "Quite enough that, though, with a house in that high healthy situation."[53] The deanery, however, went to W.C. Lake, who, Kingsley thought, deserved it. He felt almost relieved when he found out that the appointment meant "v[er]y hard work in the management of the University of Durham," which was not attractive, especially as he had learnt from Trench, the son of the Archbishop of Dublin, that

---

[50] *RT* x–xii.
[51] "The Forest Children" *RT* 1.
[52] Martin (1959) 268.
[53] CK to FK, undated, BL-62556 f.1–2.

the university was "a failure."[54] Kingsley remained full of hope that preferment was near: "The Bp. of Salisbury's death, & the Bhs' retirement bill," he reassured Fanny, "will make plenty of vacancies, and then our time will come."[55] He was right. While sailing back in a yacht from Ireland to Penzance, a letter from Gladstone was delivered at Eversley. A canonry at Chester, which was vacated when George Moberly was appointed to the See of Salisbury, was now offered to Kingsley. "If you agree," Gladstone added, "I need not impose on you any obligation of even temporary secrecy, as I know that the act will be very agreeable to her Majesty."[56] The canonry, which was worth only £500, was gratefully accepted. As there were four canons at Chester, the Kingsleys could remain at Eversley, and move for only three months a year to the cathedral town where a well-furnished house was provided. "We are well-satisfied & very thankful," Mrs Kingsley wrote to a friend, "it will indeed be a blessed rest, after the heavy work & responsibility of the Professorship."[57] In November Kingsley was officially installed as Canon of Chester, and would take residence in May the next year.

---

[54] CK to FK, undated, BL-62556 f.3.
[55] CK to FK, undated, BL-62556 f.3v.
[56] William Ewart Gladstone to CK, 13/8/1869, *LML* ii.296.
[57] FK to unidentified correspondent, undated, Martin (1959) 268.

OLD AND NEW WORLDS

CHAPTER TWENTY-FOUR

THE DREAM OF FORTY YEARS (1870–1872)

Kingsley had always felt a desire to visit the Spanish Main and the Caribbean islands, where his maternal ancestors had lived. When, at a party at the Shaw-Lefevres, Kingsley met Sir Arthur Gordon, the governor of Trinidad, he showed him such a lively interest in the West Indies, that he received an invitation to come and stay with him in Trinidad. The offer was accepted. Early in 1869 plans matured to visit South America as soon as Kingsley had resigned from his Cambridge professorship, but it was not until 2 December 1869 that Kingsley, accompanied by his daughter Rose, set out on board the steamer *Shannon* for a trip of three months. The impressions and sensations of visiting the tropics for the first time were meticulously recorded in the letters that Kingsley sent home to Fanny. Kingsley had secured a contract with *Good Words* for a travelogue. As the first instalment was forwarded to Strahan direct from the West Indies for inclusion in the March issue, the task of correcting the proofs fell to Fanny. Later instalments, which ran all through the year until December, were prepared for the press by Kingsley himself, and the text was revised completely for publication as a volume the following year by Macmillan as *At Last; A Christmas in the West Indies*. Although Kingsley had feared he "should never again write a saleable book," it sold well and the reviews were positive. "A better tourist could not possibly have gone on a better tour," *The Times* commented. "Our only regret [. . .] has been that a great novelist should have gone so far, should have seen so much, should have described all he saw so admirably, and yet should have been content to leave his descriptions bare [. . .] instead of using them as the accessories and ornament of another noble fiction—perhaps a modern Westward Ho!"[1]

"At last the dream of forty years, please God, would be fulfilled," Kingsley wrote in the opening paragraph of his travel account: "From

---

[1] *The Times*, 18/1/75, 9c.

childhood I had studied their Natural History, their charts, their Romances, and alas! their Tragedies."[2] The stories he had been told when still a boy by his grandfather, and the information he had gathered later from books, had found their way into his fiction in the dreamland chapter of *Alton Locke* and, more fully, in the West Indian part of *Westward Ho!*. "Now, at last, I was about to compare books with facts, and judge for myself of the reported wonders of the Earthly Paradise."[3] The prospect of visiting the West Indies was a stimulating one, and during the tedious voyage Kingsley impatiently pictured the new world in his imagination. Talking to other passengers helped to pass the time, but "the very names of their different destinations, and the imagination of the wonders they would see" only raised further expectations.[4] He liked to think that he was in the track "of the old sea-heroes; of Drake and Hawkins, Carlisle and Cavendish, Cumberland and Raleigh, Preston and Sommers, Keymis and Whiddon," to which formidable list he added the following meditation: "Yes. There were heroes in England in those days. Are we, their descendants, degenerate from them? I, for one, believe not."[5] The visit to the West Indies was above all confronted in a spirit of heroic Englishness and in a desire to retrace the steps of his own forebears. The line that divides the two becomes at times so subtle as to ignore all distinction. His own ancestors become part of England's heroic past in whose continuity Kingsley pictured himself as the explorer of natural history, or rather, in the person of a voyaging scientist like Darwin or Huxley, who, as he had repeatedly pointed out in his writings, were the modern equivalents of the English hero. Out of such feelings grow the numerous complacent, but often disturbingly ambiguous, reflections on Englishness and Negroes with which the text of *At Last* is interspersed. This, rather than the "picturesque adventures" that Chitty discerns as the only interest of his travel account, is the relevance of Kingsley's book.

On 17 December *The Shannon* reached the first island of the Lesser Antilles, St Thomas, "all pink and purple in the sun,"[6] and then, after a few hours' stop, continued due south towards Trinidad.

---

[2] *AtL* 1.
[3] *AtL* 1.
[4] *AtL* 4.
[5] *AtL* 6.
[6] *AtL* 14.

Kingsley admitted that he was "altogether unprepared for their beauty and grandeur,"[7] and explored small stretches of the land whenever he could leave *The Shannon* during the brief visits to the islands. Running into the harbour of Antigua Kingsley speculated on the formations of the craters and volcanic cliffs of the island that "nature, for the time being at least, has handed over from the dominion of fire to that of water."[8] On St Lucia he tried to capture for the London Zoological Gardens a live specimen of the Fer-de-lance, a rat-tailed venomous snake that was reported to be a pest on the island, but he had no luck. Passing St Vincent he had tantalizing views of the volcano Souffrière, half hidden in the clouds, and having had its "facts on my memory since my childhood," Kingsley regretted that he could not visit it.[9] The next stop was at Grenada, and there was the possibility of a short visit to George Town before the steamer set off for its ultimate destination, Port of Spain, which they reached on the shortest day of the year. "Amid Negroes, Coolies, Chinese, French, Spaniards, short-legged Guaraon dogs, and black vultures"[10]—a list from which the English are conspicuously missing—he and Rose made their way to Governor Gordon's country house, which served as a base for the numerous expeditions with his host that were made during the rest of their stay. As part of the Governor's suite it was possible for them to explore spots that would remain hidden to the normal visitor, and during the trips through jungle, mud plains and mangrove swamps, Kingsley could indeed demonstrate that, in courage, he did not belong to 'degenerate' modern man.

Apart from the simple surface emotions caused by the thrill of adventure or the delight in the beauty of tropical life, the West Indies also provoked feelings in Kingsley that went much deeper. These reflections are present from the very beginning of *At Last*. As the steamer sailed into St Thomas Kingsley had his first real-life impressions of the West Indies. While the ship was loading coal before continuing its journey to Trinidad, he asked to be rowed to a little cove a quarter of a mile away, a white line of sand with behind it hills of impenetrable jungle. The impact of its vegetative richness

[7] *AtL* 26.
[8] *AtL* 36.
[9] *AtL* 55.
[10] *AtL* 66.

swallowed up all other emotions: "the massiveness, the strangeness, the variety [. . .] was a wonder."[11] But while absorbed in the bliss of his botanizing in this "paradise", he experienced the first of a series of psychological backlashes: "Then we shrank back from our first glimpse of a little swamp of brown foul water, backed up by the sand-bush, with trees in every stage of decay [. . .] We turned, in wholesome dread, to the white beach outside."[12] This passage is followed immediately by Kingsley's observations on a group of singing blacks who were reloading *The Shannon* with coal, "a scene which we would fain forget":

> These were all the scraps of negro poetry which we could overhear; while on deck the band was playing quadrilles and waltzes, setting the negro shoveller dancing in the black water at the barge-bottom, shovel in hand; and pleasant white folks danced under the awning, till the contrast between the refinement within and the brutality without became very painful. For brutality it was, not merely in the eyes of the sentimentalist, but in those of the moralist; still more in the eyes of those who try to believe that all God's human children may be somewhen, somewhere, somehow, reformed into His likeness.[13]

Notwithstanding his enthusiasm in encountering the primeval setting, Kingsley only barely disguised his unconscious fear of the instinctive and the primitive. This piece of racial prejudice reveals Kingsley's unease at otherness, and made him for a moment cling desperately to his own English and Christian background. The sensation of latent danger in the encounter with the New World is repeated in the display of a brilliant nosegay of flowers that Rose had collected. One of the flowers, however, turned out to be "a very deadly poison."[14] The descriptions of both the blacks and the nosegay are anticipated by the unconscious indications of repulsion in his first encounter with the West Indian natural scene. Kingsley narrates his reaction as an escape from the jungle with its "*brown foul* water" to the "*white* beach outside".

Latent feelings of the evil of hidden blackness (darkness) are frequently expressed in Kingsley's text. An emblematic example is a visit to a pitch lake, which is described as a sudden coming to "the

---

[11] *AtL* 18.
[12] *AtL* 19.
[13] *AtL* 21.
[14] *AtL* 24.

very fountains of Styx," and the return journey as "a single step out of an Inferno into a Paradiso."[15] Such examples enforce a general sensation of the menace posed by the otherness of the New World in which it is the white man's pride and contentment to bring order and security. In this respect, it becomes clear that many of Kingsley's observations are based on an underlying belief in the importance of the English Protestant imperial mission. Kingsley deliberately underscores this at different stages of his narrative. He writes, for example, that British rule had been "a solid blessing to Trinidad" and that its present prosperity spoke well for "the mildness and justice of British rule."[16] Although Kingsley reminds the readers continually that the tropical setting is like paradise, it was agreeable to find during one of their adventures in the "remotest" wilderness a planter's house which was tastefully furnished with "pretty things, a piano, and good books, especially Longfellow and Tennyson."[17] At times such attitudes become almost preposterous, as when, in visiting the woods of Port of Spain, a Scottish guide is picked up, "fresh from his bath," to row them over "the muddy mirror" and under the blazing sun "we were glad to cool ourselves in fancy, by talking over salmon-fishing in Scotland and New Brunswick."[18] These might be frivolous examples, but Kingsley's delight in the white plantations are a paradigm of complacent colonialism. He fervently approves of the "activity and high cultivation" which is reached "under the superintendence of gentlemen who are prospering, because they deserve to prosper."[19]

However, Kingsley's is not the typical colonial perspective of the liberal Christian humanitarian who recoils from primitive culture once he gets into direct real-life contact with it.[20] There is a latent ambiguity in Kingsley's feelings in his encounter with the New World, in which, as in *Westward Ho!*, the tropics represent a primeval paradisiacal world dominated by a pristine energetic vitality which English civilisation has long since lost. There are frequent comparisons between Negro "health, strength, and goodly stature"[21] and the "small,

---

[15] *AtL* 185–6.
[16] *AtL* 84.
[17] *AtL* 331.
[18] *AtL* 148.
[19] *AtL* 221.
[20] Cf. Gikandi.
[21] *AtL* 33.

scrofulous, squinny, and haggy" appearance of the English.[22] Although
in a second meeting with the blacks, Kingsley again drew attention
to their barbarous "screaming and jabbering,"[23] this negative depiction is balanced by the awareness that "we have at home here tens
of thousands of paupers, rogues, whatnot, who are not a whit more
civilised, intellectual, virtuous, or spiritual than the Negro."[24] "The
Negro may have the *corpus sanum* without the *mens sana*," he added
drily, "but what of those whose souls and bodies are alike unsound?"[25]
Such comparisons echo convictions that Kingsley had held since the
beginning of his literary career about the effeteness of modern English
civilisation. In his first published novel he had idealized Alton's final
journey as that of "one who should leave the routine imagery of
European civilisation, its meagre scenery, and physically decrepit
races, for the grandeur, the luxuriance, the infinite and strongly-
marked variety of Tropic humanity,"[26] and he concluded *Alton Locke*
with the despondent question-exclamation: "Oh, England! stern
mother-land, when wilt thou renew thy youth?"[27] The text of *At Last*
reproduces such sentiments and repeatedly condemns "our hasty,
irreverent, wasteful, semi-barbarous mercantile system, which we call
[. . .] civilisation."[28] Kingsley "looked at the natural beauty and repose;
at the human vigour and happiness [. . .] leaving behind [. . .] false
civilisation and vain desires, and useless show."[29] The tropics literally offered Kingsley "safety and returning health,"[30] "as the noble
heat permeated every nerve, and made us feel young, and strong,
and blithe once more."[31] And he sighed: "One would have liked to
build, and live and die [there]."[32] Moreover, as Kingsley travelled
from Antigua, Guadeloupe, St Lucia, and finally to Trinidad, he witnessed the direct results of earthquakes and volcanic activity, tangible signs of a continent "where her [nature's] bosom still heaves with
the creative energy of youth, around the primeval cradle of the most

[22] *AtL* 87.
[23] *AtL* 32.
[24] *AtL* 33.
[25] *AtL* 33.
[26] *AL¹* 384.
[27] *AL¹* 388.
[28] *AtL* 16.
[29] *AtL* 130.
[30] *AtL* 14.
[31] *AtL* 201.
[32] *AtL* 142.

ancient race of men."[33] The simile of energetic youth and decrepit old age is consciously developed in *At Last*. After the initial confrontations, Kingsley poses the difference in explicit terms: "in the Tropics [. . .] the so-called 'powers of nature' are in perpetual health and strength, and as much stronger and swifter, for good and evil, than in our chilly clime, as is the young man in the heat of youth compared with the old man shivering to his grave."[34] Comparing such passages from *Yeast*, *Alton Locke*, and *At Last* it becomes clear that not much had changed in Kingsley's attitude to the attraction of the New World since the beginning of his literary career.

As in *Westward Ho!*, there are also Kingsley's unmistakable misgivings as to whether the "civilized" Englishman could cope with the overpowering energy of primeval life. Early on in *At Last* Kingsley reminds his reader of the excitement which had overpowered the European "reason and conscience" upon discovering the New World, and that "frenzied with superstition and greed, with contempt and hatred of the heathen Indians [. . .] they did deeds which, like all wicked deeds, avenge themselves, and are avenging themselves, from Mexico to Chili, unto this very day."[35] At a later stage of his account Kingsley wistfully asks himself what the West Indies might have been "had men—calling themselves Christian, calling themselves civilised— possessed any tincture of real Christianity, of real civilisation."[36] Such contemplations define the dominating tone of the book. Towards the end of his narrative Kingsley pressed this view once more. Speaking of the Trinidad Negroes, he remarked: "We white people bullied these black people quite enough [. . .] If, like Frankenstein, we have tried to make a man, and made him badly; we must, like Frankenstein, pay the penalty."[37] The stark horror of this vision stands out amongst all the other reflections about the West Indies in the book, and it is in passages like this that Kingsley revealed his trepidations about the possibility and auspiciousness of the English imperial mission.

Although Kingsley knew his letters home constituted important documents to complete his West India book once he came back, much of the underlying ambiguity is not yet present in the original

---

[33] *Y* 296.
[34] *AtL* 100.
[35] *AtL* 27.
[36] *AtL* 187.
[37] *AtL* 298.

letters. Towards the end of the trip, for example, he bluntly asserted
in a letter to his mother "I am afraid I don't like the negroes, specially the women."[38] The final tone of his travel experiences was
brought out after Kingsley had turned back to England "after getting so far along the great path of the human race"[39] and expanded
his material into a two-volume travel book for Macmillan.

Kingsley also came home with lots of curiosities, including a live
kinkajou and a parrot, "and lots of snakes" in spirits.[40] The change
of climate was felt most "cruelly", but there was ample material to
keep his memories of the tropics alive. For the rest of the winter he
prepared new instalments for *Good Words* and transmitted his experiences in his penny readings in his parish. To Charles Bunbury,
however, he had to write that he had not brought home the wealth
of material he had promised. "I found collecting plants, riding through
the forest, to be almost impossible," he apologized.[41] Those specimens of plants that he did manage to bring back were duly sent to
Bunbury, but they proved virtually useless as they had been dried
"in an atmosphere charged with water," and "carried either at my
back, or jammed among clothes."[42] But notwithstanding this loss, the
trip had been very successful. At the age of fifty Kingsley felt "wonderful improvement in my health" and remarked on the "renewed
youth of my mind."[43]

II

There was little time to regret the West Indies for long. Maurice
came home from South America, and there was much to talk about
before he left again to "try his own manhood" in the Rocky
Mountains.[44] Public commitments also required Kingsley's attention.
In April he was asked to become the President of the Devonshire
Scientific Association, an honour which he gratefully and enthusiastically accepted. But above all, he was to go into residence in Chester

---

[38] CK to MK, 25/1/1870, *LML* ii.312.
[39] *AtL* 388.
[40] CK to FK, 23/1/1870, *LML* ii.310.
[41] CK to CB, 15/3/1870, *LML* ii.316.
[42] CK to CB, 28/5/1870, *LML* ii.331.
[43] CK to CB, 15/3/1870, *LML* ii.317.
[44] CK to W. Pengelly, 15/4/1870, *LML* ii.318.

for his new canonical duties on 1 May. Kingsley had never liked cathedrals much, and he must have looked forward with some trepidation to his new ecclesiastical appointment. Although Mrs Kingsley reports that "the Sunday services, including the vast nave congregation in the evening were exciting and exhausting; but through all, he experienced an abiding satisfaction of soul, a sense of the fitness of things, which was quite unexpected to himself and to those who had known his previous habit of life and feeling,"[45] his feelings went out to quite other activities. In a small room of the city library he started evening lectures for "middle-class young men" on physical science, "the only thing I care for much now—for it is the way of God who made all."[46] "I believe not only in 'special providences',," he wrote to Alfred Wallace in reaction to his newly published *Contributions to the Theory of Natural Selection*, "but in the whole universe as one infinite complexity of providences."[47] The classes on botany and geology, which included excursions, became the basis for the Chester Natural History Society, founded in 1871, and which at the time of Kingsley's death boasted between five and six hundred members. Natural science had now taken such a hold of Kingsley that even during the rest of 1870, after his return to Eversley, he mainly worked on natural history. In a letter written on 1 November he thanked Matthew Arnold for the "moral tonic" and "intellectual purge" of "Culture and Anarchy," and added: "Ah, that I could see you, and talk with you. But here I am, trying to my quiet work; and given up, now, utterly, to physical science—which is my business in the Hellenic direction."[48]

There were numerous domestic, national and international events that happened in 1870. When a heath fire broke out on the Eversley Flats, a messenger entered the church, interrupting the service, to call out the men because the Bramshill firs were threatened. Kingsley left the rest of the service to Harrison and was seen "taking a flying leap, in surplice, hood, and stole, over the churchyard palings"[49] to help put out the fire with the help of a billhook. On a larger scale, the Franco-Prussian War occupied his mind completely at times. He

[45] *LML* ii.319–20.
[46] CK to JAF, undated, *LML* ii.321.
[47] CK to Alfred Wallace, 22/10/1870, *LML* ii.338.
[48] CK to Matthew Arnold, 1/11/1870, *LML* ii.338–9.
[49] Unidentified correspondent to FK, undated, *LML* ii.316.

thought it was the most important event since the French Revolution: "it will work good for generations to come. But at what an awful price."[50] Kingsley justified the provocation of war for "all that Germany has suffered for two hundred years past, from that vain, greedy, restless nation."[51] To professor Max Müller, who had married his niece, he sent his "loving congratulations to you and your people" and added he was "full of delight and hope for Germany." He only feared the Germans would march on Paris, "which cannot concern them."[52] Part of Kingsley's interest in the war was his friendship with the Prussian embassador Bunsen, who had died in 1860. He used to say to Kingsley with tears in his eyes that "the war must come" and that he only prayed "it might not come till Germany was prepared."[53] In 1870, Germany *was* prepared, and Kingsley foresaw that the outcome of the war would mark the end of the supremacy of France on the continent and the realization of a unified Germany.

All these opinions were duly reproduced by Mrs Kingsley in her biography. What she did not say was that Henry Kingsley, who was married by now, was desperately trying to scrape an income together for himself and his wife. He had lost favour with the reading public, and had gone to the Franco-Prussian war as a reporter for the *Edinburgh Daily Review*. When he returned to England, he was dismissed by the paper, and tried to raise money wherever he could until he had a new book ready for publication. At one stage he had even written to Lord Houghton for a modest sum of money: "If you could help to keep me alive and slightly free from worry [. . .] I honestly venture to think that you would have served literature by £40." He insisted on complete secrecy from his brother and "never [to] hint to him about this letter."[54] Charles and Fanny felt ashamed when the secret leaked out, and they hastened to write to Houghton and offered to pay the money back. Two years later poverty was still dogging Henry. He had been forced to move to London where he found shabby lodgings in Kentish Town. Henry was not able to write another successful novel, and supplications for money started to arrive at the Eversley Rectory. Although Kingsley was willing to

---

[50] CK to unidentified correspondent, undated, *LML* ii.337.
[51] CK to CB, 31/8/1870, *LML* ii.335.
[52] CK to Max Müller, 8/8/1870, *LML* ii.332–3.
[53] CK to CB, 31/8/1870, *LML* ii.335.
[54] Pope-Hennessy 266.

help his brother at first, the requests for money became so frequent that Charles started to feel annoyed. When rumours of scandals in which Henry got involved reached Eversley, Kingsley's patience ran out. Mary Kingsley told Henry's biographer, S.M. Ellis,[55] that the conclusion of her father's poem which celebrated the serenity of his own homely life in 1872 was a reference to Henry:

> Ah, God! a poor soul can but thank Thee
> For such a delectable day:
> Though the fury, the fool, and the swindler,
> To-morrow again have their way.
> ("The Delectable Day")

Henry's behaviour during these years might well have made Mrs Kingsley decide to drop any mention of her late husband's brother in her biography. She had never liked Henry, and probably never forgave him for harassing her husband for money or for trading on the Kingsley name.

Mrs Kingsley writes that the years 1870–73 were among the happiest of her husband's life. Although the beginning of a professorial career at Cambridge was probably an even happier period, it is true that Kingsley enjoyed being at Chester at first. He was more than willing to devote his time to Chester and bordering south Lancashire. He agreed to preach in Liverpool for the Kirkdale Ragged School. He continued his lifelong battle against the modern system of political economy which allowed that "a certain amount of waste is profitable." He applied this principle to the nineteenth-century social system by maintaining that "capital is accumulated more rapidly by wasting a certain amount of human life, human health, human intellect, human morals, by producing and throwing away a regular percentage of human soot." Kingsley's indignation and warnings in "Human Soot," as the sermon was entitled, attracted a great deal of attention in the Liverpool papers. He could only hope that a higher civilization, because more truly scientific, would yet address such wrongs and that the river would "once more run crystal clear."[56]

Kingsley sustained a lively interest in the Natural History Society. Even when his three-monthly residence was over, he returned during the second half of the year to his natural history class there to

---

[55] Ellis 100.
[56] "Human Soot" *LML* ii.323.

give lectures. These lectures grew in popularity the second year, especially as he allowed each man to bring a lady-companion. The subject in 1871 was geology, and the field trips were a huge success. Geological hammer in hand and botany box slung over his shoulder, Kingsley would sometimes guide as many as a hundred men and women, first by train, and then on foot, to interesting and instructive sites. Moreover he lectured eloquently on the geological history of such everyday realities as the soil in the field, the pebbles in the street, the slates on the roof, or the coal in the fire. These lectures were published in 1872 as *Town Geology*. In its long preface Kingsley summarized the aim of these lectures and he hoped to see the day "when ignorance of the primary laws and facts of science will be looked on as a defect, only second to ignorance of the primary laws of religion and morality."[57] There are three key notions underlying these lectures: first, science, by studying the great book of God, can never be antagonistic to religion;[58] second, knowledge of geology is important as people's comfort, wealth and health depend so much on the constitution of the planet they live on; third, science is essentially democratic. The last point is worked out in some detail: "And I tell you—that in becoming scientific men, in studying science and acquiring the scientific habit of mind, you will find yourselves enjoying a freedom, an equality, a brotherhood, such as you will not find elsewhere just now." Real freedom, to Kingsley, is "that we may be each and all able to think what we choose," and not merely pick up opinions at second hand. It is science alone that can teach man such freedom of mind, "the art of connecting facts together in your own mind in chains of cause and effect, and that accurately, patiently, calmly, without prejudice, vanity, or temper." Natural science is the poor man's science by excellence, as the rich have "neglected it hitherto [. . .] so that they have not the start of the poor man." Moreover, it is a science that does not need teachers: the student must teach himself by patient observation and a few books. More expensive books or equipment could be bought in co-operative natural science clubs, thus generating a wholesome ground of brotherhood as well as the possibility of mixing "with men, and men, too, eminently worth mixing with."[59] The deliberate

---

[57] "Town Geology" *SLE* 7.
[58] "Town Geology" *SLE* 22.
[59] "Town Geology" *SLE* 13–7.

phrasing of this final assertion shows that, by the early 1870s, Kingsley's idea of democracy and emancipation had entirely come to be based on education and knowledge. On the importance of education he completely agreed with John Stuart Mill. On other questions, however, he differed with England's foremost thinker on Ireland.

In 1868 John Stuart Mill published his *England and Ireland*, in which he pressed what he had advocated since the 1840s, namely that peasant proprietorship of land was the most efficient path to bring justice to Ireland. When, during the late 1860s, with the rise of Fenianism (the secret revolutionary movement assisting the overthrow of the English in Ireland) Mill feared disruption of the United Kingdom, he questioned the moral standing of England in its relationship to Ireland, its partner in the Union, and re-proposed the solution of land-proprietorship. The urgency and belligerent tone of Mill's pamphlet caused an upheaval in political circles, and Mill, who was liberal MP for Westminster, was forced to respond in Parliament. The debate did not escape Kingsley, who was interested in both Mill and Ireland. His acquaintance with Mill had led to scrutiny of Mill's writings and Kingsley found he fully agreed with Mill's idea of personal liberty,[60] but he did not subscribe to land-proprietorship as a solution to the problems of Ireland. It went counter to his Carlylean faith in a feudal society. In a reaction to Mill's *Chapters and Speeches on the Irish Land Question* (1870), Kingsley wrote to Charles Bunbury that "the landlord is a necessary element, first in civilization, because he ensures the presence and influence of an educated man [. . .] and next, in agriculture, because by him alone can large and central works be carried out."[61] Of course, Kingsley knew that this was more idealistic than realistic: "I have no words for the conduct of our universities, in passing through their course yearly the *élite* of the English land-owners without teaching them a single fact—or warning them of a single duty—which belongs to their station."[62] Although he had clear notions about Ireland, by the early 1870s Kingsley had grown wary of speaking out in public on any aspect of this subject. "I, as I too often do, hold views which will please no one [. . .] and which, therefore, I keep as much as possible out of sight."[63] Betting and

---

[60] "Town Geology" *SLE* 14.
[61] CK to CB, 27/7/1871, *LML* ii.356.
[62] CK to CB, 27/7/1871, *LML* ii.357.
[63] CK to CB, 27/7/1871, *LML* ii.356.

gambling were more innocuous subjects than Ireland to expound on in public. As the beginning of the residence at Chester coincided with the races, Kingsley had witnessed the immoral pandemonium that attended the festivities. With the approval of the Dean, he decided to write a series of short papers for the SPCK on the social and private evils attending betting on horses. These writings attracted much interest, but they were not controversial. Only on matters concerning sanitary reform did Kingsley dare to speak of shame and disgrace to the nation. In a sermon delivered at the Chapel Royal he stressed once more "the scandalous neglect of the well-known laws of health and cleanliness" and that England left its poorest men and women "to sicken and die in dens unfit for men—unfit for dogs."[64]

The routine of Kingsley's activities in 1872 was much the same as that of the previous year. Few events broke this routine. In ecclesiastical matters he discussed hymnology with Dr J. S. B. Monsell, and joined the Committee for the Defence of the Athanasian Creed. In the main, Kingsley objected to the adoption of many hymns, especially those that combined "the faults of Puritanism, Mysticism, and Romanism." Especially those that put individual confessions into the mouths of a general congregation were distasteful to him.[65] Many popular hymns were proofs of "an unhealthy view of the natural world, with a savour hanging about them of the old monastic theory of the earth being the devil's planet instead of God's."[66] Moreover, that many of those hymnals were compiled by components of the Oxford Movement contributed to Kingsley's disdain. On the question of whether the Church should reject the Athanasian Creed Kingsley was equally outspoken. Although he had never liked its damnatory clauses, he thought it infinitely more harmful to the tradition of the Anglican Church to take the Creed out of its Articles and the Prayer Book. Rejecting the Creed because of its damnatory clauses would mean throwing away "all the practical purposes" of the Creed itself. He wrote a letter to the Committee in which he explained this. He also urged the necessity of "a somewhat neglected Catholic doctrine—that of the intermediate state, or states"[67] and he

---

[64] *LML* ii.369.
[65] *LML* ii.386.
[66] *LML* ii.346.
[67] CK to the Committee for the Defence of the Athanasian Creed, November 1872, *LML* ii.395.

added that he thought the English mind "specially ripe just now for receiving once more this great Catholic doctrine [of Purgatory]."[68] Una Pope-Hennessy remarked that no one present at the meeting where this letter was read out knew how to take it or how to reply.[69] Of course, Kingsley's view stemmed from his unwillingness to conceive of a God who inflicted eternal punishment, a controversial notion he had inherited from F.D. Maurice.

Mrs Kingsley writes that when her husband was commenting on hymnology he was again "over-worked." He lectured very little for the Natural Science Society, because, she explains, it was by now well established on a basis of its own. But this is not like Kingsley. In fact, more serious reasons can be found for his retiring from lecturing and leading field expeditions. What had happened was that "over-work of brain had brought on a constant lassitude and numbness of the left side, which led him to apprehend coming paralysis."[70] When Norman McLeod died in March that year, he took it as an omen of his own impending end: "He is an instance of a man who has worn his brain away, and he is gone as I am surely going."[71] It was at this stage of his life that a cartoon of Kingsley appeared in *Vanity Fair*. It almost reads as an obituary.

III

In 1869 *Vanity Fair* started inserting their now famous coloured lithographs of caricatures of the famous people of the day. Politicians, statesmen, professors, novelists, scientists, and churchmen were drawn by such able caricaturists as Leslie Ward, Max Beerbohm, Adriano Cecioni, and Carlo Pellegrini. Series after series followed until 1914. The full-length portraits were captioned and accompanied by short descriptions of the persons in question in the main text. The prints were originally issued on separate sheets and folded into the periodical. At the end of the year they were collected and published in book form with separate sheets giving information on the life and career of its subjects.

---

[68] CK to the Committee for the Defence of the Athanasian Creed, November 1872, *LML* ii.397.
[69] Pope-Hennessy 256.
[70] *LML* ii.353.
[71] *LML* ii.379.

Illustration 8. "Men of the Day No. 42: Apostle of the Flesh" (*Vanity Fair* lithograph, 30 March 1872)

Kingsley's portrait was inserted as one of the 'Men of the Day' on 30 March 1872 with the caption "The Apostle of the Flesh." Although the portrait itself is far from flattering, Kingsley seems to have accepted to have his caricature taken. Vincent Brooks, the lithographer and printer of *Vanity Fair*, relates how he was walking down Endell Street with Carlo Pellegrini ('Ape') one day when they spotted Kingsley coming towards them. Pellegrini took out his sketch book while Brooks stepped up to Kingsley and asked his permission to have his portrait sketched. Kingsley assented and, being a good draughtsman himself, looked at the sketching with interest. He thought the caricature was not bad, but objected to the hat, which was easily removed.[72] Although the subjects of Ape's clerical portraits often wear hats, Kingsley appeared hatless in *Vanity Fair*.

The unsigned print shows a gaunt figure in black looking fiercely over his right shoulder. Although the face displays a certain intensity, maybe irritability, it gives at the same time an impression of haggardness. The lean old figure contrasts sharply (and ironically) with the caption. The accompanying text comments on the beginnings of Kingsley's public career when he "wrote and preached with ardent sympathy for the cause of the labouring and oppressed," which was followed by a humbler phase of practical social improvement in sanitary reform which finally diminished with the growth of his worldly success. Although Kingsley's merit in reform was not doubted, the main point of the comment comes with the following assertion: "That somewhat grotesque intimacy with the counsels of Heaven, which his religious language always implied, seems to have grown closer and closer with his worldly success, till the attitude of the Canon towards Providence and the aristocracy are almost equally puzzling to the ordinary mind." Devastating as this comment might seem, the text concludes that "if all this were so and worse, there remains [. . .] respect due to a chivalrous, manly, and genial character." As a contemporary comment on Kingsley towards the end of his life this is interesting, as most people who knew him were trying to play down his inconsistencies and emphasize his genial and energetic character.

But not all critics were as generous as to overlook Kingsley's faults with the same kind of goodwill. In August of the same year the

---

[72] Row 226.

Vanity Fair cartoon appeared, a devastating analysis of Kingsley's career came out in the New York based *Galaxy*, a "magazine of entertaining reading." The article was written by the politician-journalist Justin McCarthy, a Roman Catholic Irishman.

McCarthy vividly remembered the influence Kingsley had on young men in 1850—he was at the time a man of twenty—with a "youthful spirit of revolt" in them, dreaming of republics and the equality of man: "Charles Kingsley was to most boys in Great Britain who read books at all a sort of living embodiment of chivalry, liberty, and a revolt against the established order of baseness and class-oppression in so many spheres of our society." He added that, when it was reported that the author of *Alton Locke* had delivered a sermon in which he protested against the wrongs done to the poor in the presence of his "spiritual chief," who arose and denounced the preacher, "this excited our youthful enthusiasm into a perfect flame for the minister of the State Church who had braved the public censure of his superior in the cause of human right. For a long time Charles Kingsley was our chosen hero."

McCarthy's sense of disillusion with Kingsley makes place for scorn for his intellectual qualities. He senses a discrepancy between Kingsley's achievements and his "feminine" character, and writes, after emphasizing that "I never heard any one question his sincerity and his honest purpose to do good," that

> he is often terribly provoking. His feminine and almost hysterical impulsiveness, and his antiquated, feudal devotion to rank, are difficult to bear always without strong language. His utter absence of sympathy with political emancipation is a lamentable weakness. His self-conceit and egotism often make him a ludicrous object. Still, he has an honest heart, and he tries to do the work of a man.[73]

This assessment is remarkably similar to that reached in *Vanity Fair*. In his conclusion, however, McCarthy, diverges significantly from such sympathizing attitudes. After thirty years, he had come to feel that the hero of his youth was merely

> the most perverse and wrong-headed supporter of every political abuse, the most dogmatic champion of every wrong cause in domestic and foreign policies [. . .] I hardly remember, in my practical observance of politics, a great public question but Charles Kingsley was at the

---

[73] McCarthy 190.

wrong side of it. The vulgar glorification of mere strength and power, such a disgraceful characteristic of modern public opinion, never had a louder-tongued votary than he.[74]

Undoubtedly this voiced the opinion of many Victorians and McCarthy stuck to this judgement when, in 1899, and long after Kingsley's death, he included the article in his *Reminiscences of an Irishman*.

---

[74] McCarthy 181–2.

CHAPTER TWENTY-FIVE

THE GREAT YOUNG FREE NEW WORLD (1873–1874)

"I have to propose to you, with the sanction of her Majesty, that in lieu of your canonry at Chester, you should accept the vacant stall in Westminster Abbey," Gladstone announced at the end of the winter of 1873. The Prime Minister added that he "was sorry to injure the people of Chester; but I must sincerely hope your voice will be heard within the Abbey, and in your own right." Mrs Kingsley comments that her husband received this news with "mingled feelings" and that "there was a strong battle in his heart between the grief of giving up Chester and the joy of belonging to the great Abbey."[1] By inserting a letter written 24 March, in which Kingsley refers to his preparation for his to return to Chester, she creates the impression that the offer of the Westminster stall came unexpectedly. That impression is not correct.

Kingsley's son Grenville had left Winton school and, after a brief preparation for public school, decided that, instead of Winchester, he wanted to go to Harrow. Fanny's reaction to this decision was almost hysterical, and she insisted that the family took a house at Harrow, so that she need not leave her son to "that sea of vice."[2] Kingsley found a house in Harrow-on-the-Hill and got permission from the bishop to be absent from his parish for reasons of health. To make up for the extra expenses Kingsley once more tried to obtain a more remunerative post in the Church. He expressed his wishes to the Prince of Wales, and set Osborne and his patron, Lord Portman, to work on Gladstone when a deanery became vacant at Winchester and a canonry at Windsor, neither of which he managed to obtain. Thus, Kingsley had been actively trying to change Chester for something more rewarding, and although he might have resigned his first canonry with a rueful feeling, there was never any question of choosing between Chester and Westminster. The Abbey, with its £1000 income, was just what he desired.

---

[1] *LML* ii.405–6.
[2] Chitty (1974) 280.

Kingsley went in residence at Westminster in September and October 1873. He felt taken aback by the large congregations in the City and admitted that "the responsibility is too great for me, and I am glad I have only two months' residence."[3] His duty at the Abbey weighed on him. Although he appreciated the beauty of the place and the comfort of the house in the cloisters, towards the end of his term he wrote to Fanny, who was ill at Eversley, that "I do not think I could have stood the intense excitement of the Sundays much longer."[4] These admissions sound ominous, as they are reminiscent of the words he had written in 1856, namely that a ministerial office in London would kill him in twelve months.[5] Although the stall at Westminster was the recognition he had longed for all his life, it came too late. "The candle had already burnt down," Mrs Kingsley commented, "and though light and flame still flared up, it flared as from the socket."[6] Kingsley himself saw the preferment to the canonry of Westminster Abbey as quiet retirement: "What better fate than to spend one's old age under the shadow of that Abbey [. . .] with leisure to cultivate myself, and write, if I will, deliberately, but not for daily bread?"[7] This expression lacks Kingsley's characteristic fire and energy, and confirms that, although only 54, Kingsley felt his hyper-active life beginning to take its toll on his health. When his son Maurice, who had been railway-surveying in Mexico, returned home, he was shocked by his father's haggard appearance, and the doctors, too, strongly advised a long sea voyage before he entered upon his new responsibilities in London. But Kingsley declined to leave the country because his 86-year-old mother was ailing. Also his brother Henry noticed Charles's state of exhaustion when they met soon after at their mother's funeral. Kingsley knew that he was overworked and in need of a change and he finally decided on a trip to America with his daughter Rose, who had been to America in 1871 with John Saul Howson, Dean of Chester. They embarked on 29 January in Liverpool, called on Queenstown and reached New York on 11 February.

---

[3] *LML* ii.417.
[4] CK to FK, November 1873, *LML* ii.418.
[5] CK to TH, March 1856, Martin (1950) 650.
[6] *LML* ii.416.
[7] CK to CB, undated, *LML* ii.415.

II

To many successful English writers, an American lecture trip was a remunerative way to celebrate fame. W.C. Brownwell, an American critic writing for *The Galaxy* in 1875, analysed the fashion for the American lecture tour as follows:

> There seems to be an idea in England, which prevails with earnestness and enthusiasm throughout the length and breadth of the island, that the United States are the Atlantis of lecturers; and that when any one has earned or acquired a modest portion of fame or notoriety, there remains for him but a tour through American cities lecturing upon American platforms. It is probably not expected that a third-rate novelist, for example, will be acknowledged as a first-rate novelist after his return and by reason of his absence. But it is beyond all question expected that his exchequer will be replenished, and that lodgings and clubs will be attainable thereafter, which had been only sighed for theretofore.[8]

Charles Dickens had successfully toured America as a young author in 1841, and although he came away disillusioned about American morality—he harshly criticized the absence of the application of international copyright in the United States—twenty-five years later he was tempted by James T. Fields to a second visit when the amount of money to be earned in the mid-sixties came home to the author: "My worldly circumstances are very good. I don't want money [. . .] Still, at the age of fifty-five or fifty-six, the idea of making a very great addition to one's capital in half a year is immense."[9] Thomas Henry Huxley too had in 1874 "an *awfully* tempting offer to go to Yankee-land [. . . which was] not to be sneezed at by a *père de famille*,"[10] and a reluctant Matthew Arnold admitted to Charles Eliot Norton that a voyage to the United States was "tolerable to me only in view of making a certain sum of money to enable me to take my small pension and retire."[11]

Although Kingsley ostentatiously went to America to relax, the country had financially much to offer. The rectory at Eversley had

---

[8] W.C. Brownell, "English Lecturers in America," *The Galaxy*, 20(1) 1875, 62.

[9] Una Pope-Hennessy, *Charles Dickens* (Harmondsworth: Penguin, 1970), p. 577.

[10] Adrian Desmond, *Huxley: Evolution's High Priest* (London: Michael Joseph, 1997) 59.

[11] Nicholas Murray, *A Life of Matthew Arnold* (London: Hodder & Stoughton, 1996) 310.

always been a drain on Kingsley's resources, and the additional houses in Westminster and Harrow demanded more money for "painting and repairs"[12] than was available. Kingsley even borrowed from his old school friend Richard Cowley Powles, and his son Maurice had marriage plans but no money. Moreover, thoughts of settling down in old age were becoming recurrent motives in Kingsley's letters. It is difficult, therefore, not to see part of the attraction of America in the promise to earn a bit to realize this settling down in old age. His first letters written to his wife during his stay are full with details of remuneration for lecturing, most of which was carefully removed from the letters when his wife prepared them for publication in *Letters and Memories*. These letters read like a ledger rather than as an account of a visit to a new country. One just needs to compare these letters to the ones written during his visit to the West Indies five years before to notice a certain weariness that had started to transpire in his writings. Already in his first letter home he writes that George William Curteis, a veteran traveller and lecturer with whom he was staying upon his arrival, had given him "most valuable information as to the methods of lecture bureaus, & the prices I ought to stand out for." In the same letter he also writes triumphantly that James Redpath, who had also worked for Wilkie Collins as a lecture agent in America, had engaged him for lecturing in Salem, Boston and Philadelphia, having promised $350 for Philadelphia. Curtis had told him that he "ought to make $8–900 (dollars) by those three lectures, and never lecture under $250." Most promisingly, Kingsley adds in his letter that the East—"the beginning of the season having been so bad—leaves me an open field, & that in the West I can command my own prices."[13] That these high hopes were not that easily realized becomes clear from his second letter home, dated 19 February, when he jots down: "Salem—$150, Boston $200, & Amherst $100 = $450 = £90 so I have saved a little," but still full of hope he adds "I lecture again at Boston on Monday—& if that does, 3 times more, which ought to make $800 more, & at Philadelphia March 4 for $350—& have offers at Montreal for $950 for the 5—so I shall earn a little more, even round here."[14] Moreover, Kingsley was hopeful about the west coast. On 8 March

---

[12] Chitty (1974) 285.
[13] CK to FK, 12/2/1874, MP-C0171–36915.
[14] CK to FK, 19/2/1874, MP-C0171–36915.

he repeats that "at San Frisco & Sacramento I can have all I ask—as the lecture season goes on all the year. So I have a fair chance of making £1500 in all—or more."[15] With the same saving spirit he regularly comments on the hospitality of the Americans, which saved him a lot of money.

III

Kingsley's career had been followed with interest by educated Americans from the early 1850s onward. The first American edition of his works appeared in 1850 when Harper and Brothers published *Alton Locke*. The novel immediately drew the attention of the American reading public and puzzled reviewers described it upon its appearance as the work of a "communist,"[16] a book whose contents is "so far from socialistic, that the reverse is the fact,"[17] a novel which "had quite a run."[18] It "seems to have excited a greater sensation in the world of letters, than any thing since Jane Eyre,"[19] but in its "wild eloquence"[20] still was "a most readable book,"[21] "one of the most readable productions of the day."[22] *Alton Locke* soon became the property of the writers for the *Southern Literary Messenger* who referred to the fictional characters in the novel in all kinds of articles, and a doctor of medicine felt inspired by the tailor-poet who had never seen fresh green grass in his life and composed a poem entitled "Alton Locke" for *The Ladies' Repository*.[23] The author fell in the shadow of his own character and became known as "the author of Alton Locke."

Part of the success of *Alton Locke* in America depended on the way the novel was appropriated by the Southern writers of apologia for slavery in trying to counter the increasing pressure from the

---

[15] CK to FK, 8/3/1874, MP-C0171–36915.

[16] [-], "Critical Notices", *Southern Quarterly Review*, 3(5) 1851, 289.

[17] *Revue des Deux Mondes* quoted in "Editor's table", *Southern Literary Messenger*, 17(6) 1851, 389.

[18] [-], "Editorial and Literary Department", *Debow's Review*, 11(3) 1851, 345.

[19] John Reuben Tompson, "Notices of New Works", *Southern Literary Messenger*, 16(12) 1850, 764.

[20] [-], "Editor's table", *Southern Literary Messenger*, 17(5) 1851, 322.

[21] [-], "Editorial and Literary Department", *Debow's Review*, 10(2) 1851, 240.

[22] [-], "Editorial and Literary Department", *Debow's Review*, 11(3) 1851, 345.

[23] G.M. Kellogg, *Ladies' Repository*, 15(3) 1855, 138.

Anti-Slavery Society, which was British in origin. Although in England slavery had been forbidden by law since Elizabethan times, and, thanks to William Wilberforce's efforts, the slave trade was abolished in the British colonies in 1807 (and slavery itself in 1838), the apologists found in Kingsley's novel evidence that slavery still existed in England, and, moreover, that it was worse than anything existing in the Southern States of America. In 1851 *The Southern Quarterly Review* printed a long review of Kingsley's novel with the significant title: "Negro and White Slavery—Wherein Do They Differ?" in which its writer uses the descriptions of the conditions of the London poor to show that "the white slave of England—great, proud, glorious England—has sunk far lower"[24] than the southern slave-labourer, who, the writer maintains, is dutifully looked after by his masters in times of disease and old age. Full of indignation he adds: "Great God! and in this very town of London there are men who turn from such scenes, to preach a crusade against negro slavery!"[25] *Alton Locke* was also used in an article in the New Orleans-based *Debow's Review* entitled "British Philanthropy and American Slavery," where its female writer, carefully laying emphasis on her words, warned the philanthropist to "Beware how *you* chant the *"Marseillaise!"* and explained that she believed that "Alton Locke [. . .] must show that our system is not the one *monstrum horrendum, informe, ingens, cui lumen ademptum.*"[26] "*Our* poor," she reiterates, "cannot be shoved into garrets and cellars."[27] Again, David Brown, author of *The Planter: or, Thirteen Years in the South*, refers to Kingsley's novel when he formulates in ranting style the following question: "Is it indeed *true*, that BRITANNIA that VICTORIA herself, even, is a *slaveholder?*"[28] An honest man can only answer in the affirmative, he concludes. *The Southern Literary Messenger* in an article on "The Failure of Free Societies" echoes the same sentiment five years later in 1855, still referring to *Alton Locke*

---

[24] L.S.M., "Negro and White Slavery—Wherein Do They Differ?", *The Southern Quarterly Review*, 4(7) 1851, 120–21.

[25] L.S.M., "Negro and White Slavery—Wherein Do They Differ?", *The Southern Quarterly Review*, 4(7) 1851, 128.

[26] [-], "British Philanthropy and American Slavery", *Debow's Review*, 14(3) 1853, 278.

[27] [-], "British Philanthropy and American Slavery", *Debow's Review*, 14(3) 1853, 279.

[28] David Brown, *The Planter: or, Thirteen Years in the South* (Philadelphia: H. Hooker, 1853), 147–48.

"as a much more legitimate object of European Sympathy and consideration than American Slavery."[29] What is clear in these examples is that Kingsley's condition-of-England novel had become a powerful argument for the southern slaveholders in countering the English and the northern abolitionists. Another book which shared a similar fate was Henry Mayhew's *London Labour and the London Poor*.

After the success of *Alton Locke* in America other works followed: while *Hypatia* went through three American editions in one year (1854–5) by Crosby, Nichols and Co., Ticknor and Fields successfully marketed *Westward Ho!* and *Glaucus* in 1855, and in 1856 they brought out a volume of his poems. Especially his Christian Socialism had attracted attention and was closely followed on the other side of the Atlantic. Kingsley's socialism was examined in a review of *Alton Locke* in 1851 in *The Princeton Review* and the following issue the same year noted that its author had "lately delivered at London, a long lecture on the application of Christian Socialism to the relations of landed property."[30] In its review of *Hypatia* in 1855, however, it doubted Kingsley's religious teachings and used the opening line of the novel against its own author: where Kingsley warns the reader that much of the fifth-century life in his novel "will be painful to any reader, and which the young and innocent will do well to leave altogether unread," the reviewer concludes that he "is of the same opinion, at least so far as this book is concerned."[31] *The Southern Messenger* was less hostile to Kingsley's 'gifted pen'[32] and his (and his brother Henry's) muscular approach to religion, where "curates are soldiers of the church militant, with mighty wills and arms, who 'go in' with a rush."[33] In 1851 the more religious-minded *Ladies' Repository* mentions that "Mr. Charles Kingsley, the sketch-writer and sermonizer of Yorkshire [*sic*]"[34] had been favourably reviewed in *The North British Review* for August of that year, and it published his sermon "Religion not Godliness" in the same issue. The following issue (December) also printed the sermon "Life and Death." Both sermons

---

[29] [-], "The Failure of Free Societies", *The Southern Literary Messenger*, 21(3) 1855, 136.
[30] [-], "Literary Intelligence", 23(3) 1851, 564.
[31] [-], "Short Notices", *The Princeton Review*, 27(2) 1855, 366.
[32] Helen, "The Books of Six Months Ago", *The Southern Literary Messenger*, 23(3) 1856, 179.
[33] [-], *The Southern Literary Messenger*, 29(1) 1859, 80.
[34] [-], "New Books", *Ladies' Repository*, 11(11) 1851, 437.

had been published in England by John W. Parker in *Twenty-Five Village Sermons* in 1849, and there is no evidence that *The Ladies' Repository* had paid royalties for either of the sermons. His poems had not gone unnoticed by the *Repository* either. Following Ticknor's publication of his songs, "The Merry, Merry Lark" was printed in full and "The World Goes Up" was discussed in the 'Notes and Queries' section in 1856.[35] By the 1870s, Kingsley's poems were widely anthologized in America.

When Charles Dickens visited the United States in 1842, he had little reason to speak well of the American publishing world. The absence of international copyright made English intellectual property the easy prey of American entrepreneurs who, Dickens maintained, were, "for the most part, men of very low attainment and of more than indifferent reputation."[36] This judgment was no doubt far too coarse, and Dickens overreacted at the very moment America, and its book trade, was going through one of its most profound economic crises of the century. Still, Dickens, and other English writers, had reason to complain. American publishing houses were legally free to reprint the works of popular British authors without remuneration, and although the picture was not as bleak as this, it is true that authors often had to depend on the "bargaining, goodwill, and trade custom"[37] of the American publishing firms.

Kingsley, who was always trying to implement his inadequate income by writing, is not known to have complained about the American practices of piracy. Very likely his relationship with American publishers was more satisfactory than Dickens's. When he emerged as a writer in the early 1850s, the American book trade had become stable again and amicable agreements were made with British authors and publishers.[38] Moreover, a kind of "courtesy of the trade," the prior claim of a publisher to a work for which payment was remitted, had re-emerged, and, at least till 1857, much of the wild piracy and cut-throat competition was avoided. Thus it is likely that Kingsley's American publications of *Alton Locke* and *Yeast* with Harper and

---

[35] [-], 'Notes and Queries', *Ladies' Repository*, 16(11) 1856, 701.

[36] Barnes, James, J., *Authors, Publishers and Politicians; The Quest for an Anglo-American Copyright Agreement 1815–1854* (London: Routledge & Kegan Paul, 1974), 28.

[37] Winship, 133.

[38] Barnes, James, J., *Authors, Publishers and Politicians; The Quest for an Anglo-American Copyright Agreement 1815–1854* (London: Routledge & Kegan Paul, 1974), 29.

Brothers and *Hypatia* with Crosby, Nichols and Co. did not go altogether without remuneration. And by the time depression hit the book trade again in 1857, Kingsley had become one of Ticknor and Fields's regular authors.

Ticknor and Fields had a good reputation with English authors, and paid during the 1850s for more than half of their new foreign publications. For example, they purchased early sheets (advance sheets of first printing) of Kingsley's *Poems* and of *The Heroes* in 1856, and paid £20 for the first and £40 for the latter, after which royalties were paid for each copy sold.[39] Kingsley had become one of the firm's important novelists (together with Walter Scott and Charles Reade). *The Heroes* was worth commissioning the craftsman John Andrew to make illustrations, and *Poems* sold well—the 2,100 sold copies rendered the firm almost $1,000, which was almost double what they earned with 1,900 sold copies of John G. Whittier's *The Panorama*.[40]

By the time of Kingsley's visit in 1874, however, his own publishing house, Macmillan, was fully represented on the American market. In 1867 Alexander Macmillan had gone to America to gauge the market and decided to establish an American branch. He installed an agent in New York, and in 1869 the imprint "London and New York" appeared in their books. Kingsley's works were thus powerfully present on the American market in the 1870s. Macmillan's presence assured the firm's advantage over other publishing houses when bringing out new titles, although, of course, until international copyright was enforced in 1891, it did not impede pirated versions.

IV

Kingsley's literary fame in America had steadily grown over the years and his arrival was announced in the press. He was invited at the Lotos Club in New York where a welcome dinner was held in his honour. The club had been founded a couple of years before by a group of young journalists and critics, who were most eager to intercept newly arrived English men of letters and invite them as dinner

---

[39] Winship 136.
[40] Winship 69; 165–8.

guests. Thus Kingsley was addressed by representatives of the club while still steaming into New York. "But, gentlemen," he answered to the committee, "I am trying to view the approaches to New York. I cannot make any engagements now."[41] Kingsley consented, however, and was officially welcomed and asked to speak on 14 February. The gala was reported in the *New York Daily Tribune* two days later. A number of prominent guests were present, such as Chauncey Depew, but contrary to reports, amongst these of the Lotos Club itself, Bret Harte was not. A previously unknown letter to Anne Botta, now in private hands, discloses that the American writer was prevented from coming. The letter shows, however, that Harte, who was then at the height of his fame, was very much interested in speaking to Kingsley and planned to meet him later on 3 March at the Bottas, notwithstanding the fact that "the baby has been ailing lately, and as she is the centre of our Solar System I may find it hard to get Mrs Harte out of the regular orbit." Meeting Kingsley, although awaited with pleasant anticipation, was above all dictated by "a sense of duty," Harte admits. Similarly eager to meet the Canon was Henry Ward Beecher, who was invited but unable to come, and wrote that "were not Saturday an impossible night for him, he would undergo even a reception and a dinner for the sake of meeting Charles Kingsley."[42]

The reception at the Lotos Club delighted Kingsley, who "enjoyed the wine and company" and spoke freely and humourously of his growing old. But the welcome to America did not end with the Lotos Club dinner: later the same evening he was escorted to the Century Club, just a few blocks away, where he was welcomed by its president, William Cullen Bryant.

The first public appearance in America was in Mechanic Hall in Salem where he lectured on 16 February to a large and cultivated audience. This was followed by a reception and banquet during which Kingsley was welcomed to Salem by Mr Coggswell, Mayor of Salem.

Both the lecture and the reception were given much space in the papers. It got a full two-column, 8000-word review in *The Boston*

---

[41] Elderkin, John, *A Brief History of the Lotos Club* (New York: The Lotos Club, 1895) 13.
[42] Elderkin, John, *A Brief History of the Lotos Club* (New York: The Lotos Club, 1895) 31.

Daily Globe, which included the text of the lecture on Westminster Abbey itself. The two-week sea-voyage to America must have done Kingsley's health much good, as he appeared to his Salem audience a fit representative of muscular Christianity: "his form is erect and handsome, and every indication is given of the possession of a sound mind and body" and the *Boston Globe* even went as far as to state that "his face has the flush of genuine health." Kingsley spoke for an hour and thirty-five minutes, which the writer thought was rather long and therefore a "dangerous experiment with a strange audience," especially as his way of delivery was "very peculiar, being a strange combination of slow and rapid utterances, monotone and nervous exclamation." Nevertheless, the speaker conquered the "entire, undivided attention of the audience" and retained it till the end.[43]

The review must have been disconcerting to Kingsley when he saw it the next day in the *Boston Globe*. A feeling of unease with his American audience transpired in his after-dinner speech at the meeting of the Massachusetts Press Association in the afternoon, where he was accompanied by Mark Twain. After the Salem experience, he seemed less confident about his way of intoning which had been attributed to his cathedral experience: "there grows upon me an increasing fear of addressing an American audience [because I had found that Americans had] remarkable power of public speaking" and that during a week's sojourn he had already heard "half a dozen better speeches rolled off than I should have heard in England in twelve months."[44] Even apologies for the subject of his lecture were presented in the evening in Boston, blaming it playfully upon Mark Twain, who had suggested the subject to him, and a trace of chagrin underlies his mentioning the fact that the text of his lecture had been fully printed the very morning of the day he was to present it in Tremont Temple.[45] Maybe as a result of this, and because he had already met the literary figures of Boston in the afternoon, The Temple was only slightly filled: the audience sat mainly in the floor

---

[43] [-], "Charles Kingsley: His First Public Appearance in America", *Boston Daily Globe*, 17/2/1874, 4.

[44] [-], "Massachusetts Press Association—Annual Meeting—Business Meeting and Banquet—After Dinner Remarks by Rev. Charles Kingsley, Mark Twain and Others", *Boston Evening Journal*, 18/2/1874, 1.

[45] [-], "Charles Kingsley: His First Appearance in Boston—Lecture on the "Westminster Abbey" in Tremont Temple—Introductory Remarks by 'Mark Twain'", *Boston Daily Globe*, 18/2/1874, 8.

while there was only a 'sprinkling' in the balconies and the platform remained vacant. Mark Twain introduced the speaker in his usual humorous and engaging way, but the religious audience, "though not unappreciative," sat through Kingsley's hour and a half in "painful silence." It was not the "ordinary lyceum audience which one would expect to meet at Charles Dickens's or Wilkie Collins's readings," *The Daily Globe* commented.[46] Although Curteis had told Kingsley upon his arrival never to lecture under $250, the lecture in Tremont Temple rendered only $200 while Salem a mere $150. Kingsley came to detest his Westminster Abbey lecture and he is reported to have often suffered from the temptation to stop after a quarter of an hour and "ask his audience if they would prefer to go home."[47]

In Boston the Kingsleys stayed with J.T. Fields, the head of the publishing firm Ticknor and Fields, for a week. In the evenings they played "The Three Fishers" on the piano. The Fieldses were famed for welcoming writers to their house in Charles Street. Dickens had become one of their close friends in 1861. Mrs Field and Rose took to each other immediately while Kingsley was to her a man of genius, modest and honest. In her diary Annie Fields noted that Kingsley's unrest reminded her of Dickens, but that he was the "fuller man", "quick and witty in speech, kindly and modest in behaviour and independent in his expression of thought." But she also found him

> full of hastily made opinion [. . .] which may frequently be quite wrong and unjust to his own higher judgment, but to which he clings with a sudden tenacity quite appalling to one who may wish to persuade him to the contrary. But he is a great and good man and to those who understand him well not difficult to get on with. He is his own greatest discomfort, being excessively nervous, ceaselessly in motion, and apt to get into sudden little storms of temper which he appears to work at in a corner by himself, bringing no harm to any one.[48]

She remarked on his stuttering, which was frightful at times in private, but absent in public, and added that he was a "great eater and drinker." Although Mrs Fields mentions that he was an overworked man, often "tired and sleepless," who found rest in this

---

[46] [-], "Charles Kingsley: His First Appearance in Boston—Lecture on the 'Westminster Abbey' in Tremont Temple—Introductory Remarks by 'Mark Twain'", *Boston Daily Globe*, 18/2/1874, 8.
[47] Adrian 97.
[48] Adrian 96–7.

change of scene, there are no hints of Kingsley's weak health, so that we might safely assume with the newspaper descriptions that he had indeed much recovered.

While Kingsley was staying in Boston with the Fieldses, John Greenleaf Whittier paid him a visit. Whittier, a deeply religious Quaker with interest in social questions, had much in common with Kingsley, and they had "a most like-minded talk"[49] about theology and its social implications. Kingsley thought Whittier "*a[n] old saint*" while what struck the 67-year-old poet was that Kingsley while talking to him was "unobservant of the strange city whose streets he was treading for the first time, and engaged only with 'thoughts that wander through eternity'."[50] He is reported to have asked a friend: "Did thee meet Kingsley? I like him hugely; he is a manly man,"[51] and he wrote to Mrs Kingsley in 1876 that in her husband he had met "a noble nature [. . .] one of the manliest of man."[52] The morning of 19 February Kingsley spent with the naturalist Asa Gray "& his plants" and Henry Wadsworth Longfellow sought him out and invited him to dinner later that day.

On 9 March, the Speaker of the House of Representatives asked Kingsley to open the Session with a prayer on Bill Day. The event was reported in the *Daily National Republican*, and transcribed in *The Times* in England eighteen days later.[53] The journalist describes in detail a lively gallery and floor, while *The Baltimore American* specifies that Kingsley's presence at the House of Representatives had attracted a great number of unfamiliar faces, "the fair sex predominating," including the presence of Washington's literary celebrities Harriet Prescott Spofford and Mary Clemmer Ames.[54] At 12 o'clock Kingsley ascended with Speaker James Gillespie Blaine, later Republican candidate for the presidency in 1884, and the Chaplain of the House to open Congress with a set of prayers from the Episcopal Church Service and he finished with the Lord's Prayer. Next he was submitted to an elaborate process of hand-shaking during the "shower

---

[49] CK to FK, 1/3/1874, MP-C0171–36915.
[50] John Whittier to FK, 30/8/1876, *LML* ii.446.
[51] Samuel T. Pickard, *Life and Letters of John Greenleaf Whittier* (Boston and New York, 1894), ii.595.
[52] John Whittier to FK, 30/8/1876, *LML* ii.446.
[53] *The Times*, 27/3/1874, 4.
[54] [-], "Canon Kingsley", *Baltimore American*, 10/3/1874, 2.

of Bills," which, no doubt, the writer argues, would feature in Kingsley's future "American Notes".

Again, Kingsley seemed to have looked much better than when he left England a month before. Although he seemed to the writer of the *Daily National Republican* a "clerical Howadji, who has outlived his man-of-the-world look," he adds that "one sees in that face—strong, clear, and ruddy—the visible result of a lifetime of luscious beef, good cheer, good digestion, of which the finest intellectual thoughts, the purest poetry, are ever begotten."[55] It is of interest to add here that the journalist writing for *The Baltimore American* on the same event, although not contradicting Kingsley's good cheer, thought that the slender and erect man, dressed in regular English clerical coat, was about 65 years of age, being a full ten years wrong.[56]

The tone of this newspaper report in *The Daily National Republican* is indicative of the esteem the Americans felt for Kingsley, which was vested in his being the author of *Alton Locke* and *Hypatia* rather than his being Canon of Westminster. With this the writer concludes:

> To all lovers of the highest and purest, as well as the sweetest and truest, in literature and thought, to all lovers of humanity, for humanity's sake, the man who wrote *Alton Locke* and *Hypatia* is infinitely nearer and dearer than the Canon of Westminster, honoured though he is, can ever be.

Mrs Kingsley's opinion of the general reception and attitude of esteem of her husband's genius in the United States of America is reflected in a letter written after his death to Mrs Botta. It contrasted painfully, she writes, with her late husband's reception in England: "You gave him and my Rose such a home and such a home-feeling in the great New World—a world I shall always love for its appreciation of him and his works at a time when he was not so responded to in his own country."[57] This comment seems to stem from impressions of kindness, esteem and appreciation of the Americans which her husband, or her daughter, communicated to her back in England, shortly before his death, as such sentiments are not voiced in his letters

---

[55] *Daily National Republican*, reported in [-], [-], "Canon Kingsley at Washington", *The Times*, 27/3/1874, 4.

[56] [-], "Canon Kingsley", *Baltimore American*, 10/3/1874, 2.

[57] Anne C. Lynch Botta, *Memoirs of Anne C.L. Botta* (New York: J.S. Tait & Sons, 1894), 179.

home. In the later editions of her biography Mrs Kingsley softened such expressions of British hostility to her late husband.

The day following the opening of the House of Representatives, Kingsley visited the Senate House where he was introduced to anti-slavery senator Charles Sumner. In the early sixties, when Sumner had become chairman of the Senate Committee on Foreign Relations, Kingsley had corresponded with him,[58] but the two men had become estranged when Kingsley in the mid-sixties made his pro-southern views known. "But the moment the two came face to face all mis-trust vanished, as each instinctively recognized the manly honesty of the other, and they had a long and friendly talk."[59] Sumner, how-ever, had been suffering from a weak heart for some time, and doc-tors had advised him to abandon his Senate work. An hour after his interview with Kingsley, Sumner had a stroke, collapsed, and he died the following day. "Sumner's death has been an awful blow here," Kingsley writes home, "I do not wonder, for with all his faults, he was a magnificent man."[60]

Apart from some of the individuals he met, Kingsley was not very much impressed by America and the Americans at first. The houses, the gardens, the luxuries, he observed, were "like the people—[. . .] all English *with a difference*."[61] Admittedly, Englishness was a positive quality to Kingsley, and he does add later in the same letter that "it is a glorious country, & I dont wonder at the people being proud of it," but the New England winter had little to charm even the "minute philosopher." "New England is—in winter at least—the sad-dest country. All brown grass, ice polished rocks, cedar scrub, low swampy shores—an iron land, which only iron people could have settled in."[62] And again in another letter: "New England is hideous, doleful barren. Like the worst of our commons & fir woods with ice flawed rocks sticking up through the coppices."[63] Such comments belie the 1858 statements in "My Winter-Garden" that "in any life, in any state, however simple or humble, there will be always sufficient to occupy a Minute Philosopher."[64] It shows to what extent 15 years

---

[58] Martin (1958) 32n.
[59] Rose Kingsley's diary, *LML* ii.426.
[60] CK to FK, 23/3/1874, MP-C0171–36915.
[61] CK to FK, 12/2/1874, MP-C0171–36915.
[62] CK to FK, 19/2/1874, MP-C0171–36915.
[63] CK to FK, 1/3/1874, MP-C0171–36915.
[64] "My Winter-Garden" *PI* 140.

of active life had drained energy from Kingsley. He admits on 8 March that he is feeling homesick at times "—& would give a finger to be one hour with you & Grenville & Mary."[65] His health seemed to be improving, however, and he wrote home by 1 March that the winter was doing him good: "I am suddenly quite well. All those sucking craving feelings gone, & my old complaint so utterly vanished, that I am rather in the opposite trouble at times. I never want medicine or tonic, & very little stimulant."[66]

His financial troubles at home and the uncertain future of his children, however, kept disturbing Kingsley during his tour. Although he writes almost triumphantly by the end of March from Boston that he had saved enough money to send both Fanny and Maurice £100 each and that he would soon be able to pay his £200 debt to Powles, in April he read in one of Fanny's letters that: "a little of the money you are so labouriously earning will come in a wonderful help. The £100 came and is gone nearly in bills. And if you can let me have a little more before June, I shall be very thankful."[67] The pressure of lecturing for money started to tire Kingsley, and he was looking forward to having a bit of peace around Easter. At the same time a certain despair of making ends meet set in when the financial success of his tour was not as bright as he had hoped. "The lectures please the cultivated & political beyond what I ever dreamed of, yet the masses have done their lectures for the year."[68] At the beginning of May he admitted that "I have not made much money,"[69] and at the end of the month, very likely after another complaining letter from home, he wrote "I am much vexed that you have been hard up for money. But it will soon be over, please God, & you & I shall settle down into a quiet old age."[70] Quietly settling down in old age had become a major theme in Kingsley's head. Struggling for more money in June—"I cannot make anything, hardly at this time of year"—he realized he would send home only about half of what hoped for at the beginning of the tour. After a life-long struggle to earn enough to satisfy the wants of wife and children,

---

[65] CK to FK, 8/3/1874, MP-C0171–36915.
[66] CK to FK, 1/3/1874, MP-C0171–36915.
[67] Chitty (1974) 285.
[68] CK to FK, 23/3/1874, MP-C0171–36915.
[69] CK to FK, 4/5/1874, MP-C0171–36915.
[70] CK to FK, 31/5/1874, MP-C0171–36915.

he hoped that God would "give me time to reconsider myself, & sit quietly with you, preaching & working—And writing no more—oh how I pray for that—for my childrens' [*sic*] bread."[71] Fanny's demand for more money did not help much to cheer his mood, and worries about Maurice's uncertain future and Grenville's problems at Harrow increased his worries. Maurice needed money and a job to set up a house with his newly wedded wife, Marie Yorke. Grenville in the meantime was not doing well at school, and Kingsley had to send a telegram to tell them to take the 16-year-old boy away from school: "If you ever see that prognathous, drooping look, about the outside of G's upper lips," he hastens to write to Fanny, "he should have idleness & food & fresh air at once, & nothing else."[72] Kingsley found it at times difficult to muster enough energy to keep the interest in the country he was visiting alive.

Still, his interest in North America seemed to revive with the improvement of his health. He was impressed by the grand scenery of Lake Champlain and the Saint Lawrence River and its mountains. They crossed frozen surfaces by tandem sledge and Rose went on toboggan parties. They drove out to the Montmorency Falls with Colonel Thomas Bland Strange and the spectacular ice formations of frozen cascades did not fail to charm. For the first time true enthusiasm came through in his letter home: "the most awful & beautiful thing I ever saw—the fall 260 feet high, fringed with icicles—50ft long, roaring into a horrible gulf of ice, under an exquisite white ice cave 100 feet high formed of its own spray:"[73] The colonel later wrote to Mrs Kingsley that he left her husband "to commune with the Nature he loved so well" and that Kingsley thanked him afterwards for his reserve because "I would as soon a fellow talked and shouted to me in church as in that present." The very day of their visit Strange received a telegram to say that his mother had died, and he was struck that Kingsley spoke not only brave words upon his mother's death but also about his own readiness to go to "his own place."[74]

After Montreal and Quebec, Kingsley stayed for Easter at Ottawa with the Earl of Dufferin, governor-general of Canada. With his

---

[71] CK to FK, 19/6/1874, MP-C0171–36915.
[72] CK to FK, 29/6/1874, MP-C0171–36915.
[73] CK to FK, 1/4/1874, MP-C0171–36915.
[74] Thomas Bland Strange to FK, undated, *LMLM* 333–34.

return to Washington in the middle of April to lecture there and at Baltimore, his more worldly concerns also returned with the wish that "I cannot but hope that there is 'a time of rest & refreshing' for us after I return—for both of us—."[75] They stayed with Clarkson Nott Potter and on 10 March were invited to dine with President Grant. Niagara a week later recaptured his admiration and produced two letters in two days, the normal rhythm seeming to have been a letter every week.

Father and daughter stayed on the East coast all through March and April before they started moving west. They reached St Louis 3 May, which Kingsley thought a marvellous example of progress. But the melancholy tone sets in again. It is not simply writing "ah, that you were here" to the wife at home in England, but in the midst of the marvel it is: "Only I wish already that our heads were turned homeward, & that we had done the great tour."[76] The next stop was Omaha on 9 May where Kingsley did not appear in public—Kingsley and his daughter "arrived in Omaha Saturday evening, and stopped at the Grand Hotel. They will leave to-day for the west," ran the complete text of the article in the *Omaha Daily Bee*— and from there they moved on to Salt Lake City in Cyrus Field's private Pullman car, botanizing on the way. The scenery enraptured Kingsley—"the flowers [. . .] make one long to jump off the train every 5 minutes—while the Geology makes me stand aghast— Geologizing in England (except perhaps Wales) is child's play to this."

V

Kingsley was often during his American tour impressed by the progress of civilization made in barren regions. Upon entering Omaha he had delighted in the idea that the town had grown in five years to a town of 20,000 souls out of the "palavering ground of trappers & Indians" of his boyhood dreams.[77] One would have expected similar expressions of esteem about Salt Lake City. In fact, in his American

---

[75] CK to FK, 9/4/1874, MP-C0171–36915.
[76] CK to FK, 4/5/1874, MP-C0171–36915.
[77] CK to FK, 11/5/1874, MP-C0171–36915.

lecture, "Cyrus, The Servant of the Lord," prepared during his residence at Westminster, he expostulates on the romance of history.
He writes that the growth of civilization is brought about by the
great historic movements which originate in the 'wild freedom' of
the demoniac element, the ministering spirit of genius (the daimon)
which underlies all nature. This he found exemplified in Mormon
history:

> Nay, is not the history of your own Mormons, and their exodus into
> the far west, one of the most startling instances which the world has
> seen for several centuries, of the unexpected and incalculable forces
> which lie hid in man? Believe me, man's passions, heated to igniting
> point, rather than his prudence cooled down to freezing point, are *the
> normal causes of all great human movement.*[78]

The results of such passionate genius in the Mormons were clear in
the irrigation of desert land, the foundation of Salt Lake City out
of nothing, and Mormon economic communitarianism and general
welfare. Kingsley must have known of the role of the founder of
Salt Lake City, Brigham Young, in all this. Of course, it was Young's
contracting the Union Pacific Railway which made the transconti-
nental railway, which took Kingsley "through 1000 miles of desert,
plain & mountain, treeless, waterless almost," possible.[79]

But once on the spot, the foundation of Salt Lake City seems to
have lost its romantic aura to Kingsley. Brigham Young was after
all a character his moral conscience could not accept, and his general veneration of pioneers turned into intolerance. He condemned
the autocratic powers of Young as President of the Mormon Church,
and the private militia which only a few years before had been seen
as a serious threat to the American nation. And above all, Young
had publicly endorsed his doctrine of polygamy in 1852. This led
to a breach with US government and federal troops were stationed
in Utah from 1857 on. Kingsley abhorred polygamy with all his
heart and wrote to Fanny: "It is all very dreadful. Thank God we
at least know what love & purity mean."[80] On the east coast he
must have heard people discussing Ann Eliza Young, Brigham Young's
divorced 19th wife who lectured on the horrors of polygamy—her

[78] "Cyrus, The Servant of the Lord" *HLE* 276; my italics.
[79] CK to FK, 17/5/1874, MP-C0171–36915.
[80] CK to FK, 17/5/1874, MP-C0171–36915.

lecture was part of the same series Kingsley lectured in. He must have discussed Mormonism in the East with his hosts and, subsequently, in Salt Lake City, he had "a most interesting & painful talk with a man who has been *U.S.* governor here." As a result he became more than prejudiced against the polygamist's achievements. He started to resent Mormonite history and its heroic deeds. He writes ponderously upon approaching Salt Lake City:

> Yesterday we were rising through great snow drifts at 5–7000 feet above the sea (we are 5,000 here) & all along by our side *the* old trail—where every mile is fat with Mormon bones. Sadness & astonishment overpower me at it all. The "City" is thriving enough [. . .] But ah! What horrors this place has seen.[81]

Contemplating the horrors of polygamy he could finally see Young only as "the tyrant [who . . .] must soon go to his account—& what an awful one."[82] Thus, when Young offered him the recently-built Tabernacle to preach or lecture in, Kingsley took no notice. Instead, he showed interested in the new Episcopal bishop, Daniel Sylvester Tuttle, for whom he preached in the new Episcopal Church—he arrived one day too late for its consecration—to a crowded congregation of both Gentiles and Mormons.

Kingsley's hostility was also fuelled by the tone adopted by the Salt Lake City papers in reporting his arrival. A bitter polemical tone followed the announcement in the Mormon *Deseret Evening News*, which exulted in the fact that "the celebrated English Divine and literary genius" had arrived in the city. It reported that he and Cyrus Field were welcomed by a committee of prominent citizens who extended the courtesies due to illustrious strangers, and that Brigham Young proffered the use of the Utah Southern railroad, and his private car. It concluded that "they went to Provo to-day for the purpose of visiting President Young, as they desired an interview with him."[83] The next day the *Salt Lake Tribune*, a paper much devoted to diatribes against the Mormons and their *Deseret News*, lashed out sarcastically:

---

[81] CK to FK, 17/5/1874, MP-C0171–36915.
[82] CK to FK, 11/5/1874, MP-C0171–36915.
[83] [-], [announcement arrival Kingsley in Salt Lake City], *Deseret Evening News*, 16/5/1874, 3.

The distinguished party at present visiting Salt Lake, stated yesterday that they had been tendered a special train to visit the President at Provo. We were not aware the President was in Utah. Perhaps the gentlemen have missed their reckoning. The President resides in Washington. There is a polygamous old law-breaker here who sets at defiance human and divine laws, and runs the biggest harem of any man outside Turkey. His name is Young—Brigham Young—Is it possible they call that old scoundrel President?[84]

Another journalist writing in the same column was equally outraged by the *Deseret* report and took it upon him to deny the possibility that Kingsley had gone to Provo "to pay court to Brigham Young" as "Mr. Kingsley was not out of town yesterday," while a journalist of the *Salt Lake Herald* reported on the very same day that the party had just returned to the city from a "flying visit to Provo, and [had] called upon President Brigham Young." However, the *Herald*, generally sharing the *Tribune*'s viewpoints, did not voice any party comment on the supposed visit. The account of events in Rose Kingsley's diary seems to exclude the possibility of a meeting between Kingsley and Young. She stresses that Bishop Tuttle approved of her father's decision.

Although the supposed visit to Provo found space in all the valley papers, Kingsley's evening service at St Mark's Cathedral went almost unnoticed. It was announced in a bare three lines in *The Salt Lake Daily Tribune* of 17 May, and no further report followed on the next day. Rose, however, notes that her father attracted such a huge public that evening in St Mark's "that there was not standing room in the little building and numbers had to go away. The steps outside, and even the pavement, being crowded with listeners."[85] Judging from all this it might seem that Kingsley's stay was 'politically' important for the citizens of Salt Lake City, although it remains difficult to gauge the ultimate importance of the visit. For example, one might have expected that a service preached by the Canon of Westminster just after the consecration of the cathedral would have been relevant in the religious controversy between Episcopalians and Mormons. Yet all polemics in the papers suddenly stop after 17 May and the visit is not referred to anymore, nor is there any report of the success of the service at St Mark's. Not even the *Salt Lake Semi-Weekly*

---

[84] [-], "City Jottings", *Salt Lake Tribune*, 17/5/1874, 3.
[85] Rose Kingsley's diary, *LML* ii.434.

Herald of 20 May refers to the service, while it does feature a long article on the consecration of the cathedral. And in writing his memoirs years later, bishop Tuttle describes his struggles to set up an episcopal community during these year in Salt Lake City, but neither Kingsley's presence nor the success of his service are mentioned.

VI

The party went next from Salt Lake City to Sacramento. Then to Yosemite, and finally to San Francisco. Time was divided between botanizing and preaching, and something of the former Kingsley came back to him. He was the whole day in the saddle, collecting flowers everywhere, chatted with the guides, climbed mountains, forded rivers and said "he felt a boy again."[86] Kingsley's health seemed to have improved with his boyish enthusiasm. Notwithstanding Grenville's school problems, and his frustration at not being able to earn money, Kingsley could not hide his exuberant enthusiasm at this point of his tour. He preached on Whit-Sunday, but was back in the saddle the 25 May. "All is more beautiful & wonderful than I expected, & California the finest country in the world—& oh the flowers."[87] They visited Mariposa Grove of Sequoias the following day, which struck him with awe.

Californian civilization too was full of promise to Kingsley, "the new world beyond the new world." If on the one hand his opinion of the West was tinged by Bret Harte's rugged and romantic representation of it in his fiction, on the other he had had some foretaste of the more religious-minded in the pious San Francisco-based *Overland Monthly*. During the dreary hours of residence at Westminster in the autumn of 1873, Kingsley had killed part of his time reading the *Overland*. In one of its issues the magazine featured an essay on "Our Indian Policy."[88] It is a rather complacent account of the glory reached by the American settlers and argues that treating the Indian tribes with separate sovereignty went against Christian principles. Starting from the premises that "It is blasphemously profane

---

[86] Rose Kingsley's diary, *LML* ii.436.
[87] CK to FK, 31/5/1874, MP-C0171–36915.
[88] [-], "Our Indian Policy", *Overland Monthly and Out west Magazine*, 11(3), 201–214.

to allege that man, created in the image of God, was a savage [. . .]
The savage is the fallen, degraded, disfranchised, human brute."[89]

As a champion of all what the progress of English Christian civilisation stood for, it is not difficult to imagine that Kingsley espoused
the view in "Our Indian Policy." While often glorifying in the purely
physical and heroic because history showed it led to higher states of
civilization, he revolted at what he saw as essentially reasonless and
ideal-less in the brutishness of primitive man, which, as he argued
in *The Water-Babies*, was to him the outward manifestation of inward
moral degradation. Already in *Yeast*, writing of the labourers in
Southern England, he felt disgusted with their "hoggishness" and in
Ireland in 1860 he felt uncomfortable in the presence of the peasants. The descriptions of the American Indians his daughter Rose
had met in Colorado in 1871–72 had confirmed such a view. "Nothing
has ever given me an idea of more thorough degradation than the
way those Indian women clawed bits of bone and skin,"[90] she wrote
in a book that her father edited. Such a view, of course, implied a
duty on the part of the Christian to convert the brute. "Our Indian
Policy" continues that, as "human society is a moral person, [. . .]
not a mob of savages of half-tamed gorillas," it has a duty to exert
itself in elevating the brutes to the "place of citizenship." Indians
should in all respects be seen as equals of the white settlers, with all
their rights and duties. By analogy to the plan of nature, the Indian
had surfeited any claim on independence and had to submit to the
rules of American citizenship, just as the Mormons, the Germans or
any group of immigrants, had to submit to the rulings of Congress.
The moral basis of "Our Indian Policy" was to Kingsley's taste and
he wrote to the editor to say so. The editorial of the February issue
proudly reports that the Canon of Westminster endorsed the views
expressed on the natives and had written, "warmly commending the
magazine," to announce his intention of visiting California the following summer.

Kingsley arrived in California, having left the pernicious practices
of the Mormons behind. He lectured on "The First Discovery of
America" again, the most romantic and least bloody part of which

---

[89] [-], "Our Indian Policy", *Overland Monthly and Out west Magazine*, 11(3), 206.
[90] [Kingsley, Rose Georgiana], *South by West; or, Winter in the Rocky Mountains and
Spring in Mexico*, (London: W. Isbister, 1874), 161.

was printed by the *Overland*,[91] and was invited to address the students of Berkeley University on the subject of culture. He started with the impressive fact that the college bore the name of the most instructive philosopher after Plato in history and then talked of the future, probably unconsciously echoing the conclusion of "Our Indian Policy": "My heart throbs with exultation as I contemplate the possibilities of the future glories of America, a continent in which God has sown the seeds of such various greatness from all the races of the earth, united under a republican government, bestowing upon each the fullest liberty of exercise his God-given powers."[92] Kingsley's way of speaking deeply impressed the President of the University who wrote that he was "so invigorating, and yet so simple [that it] will long be remembered. [...] The man was inspired, and felt every word he spoke."[93] Not surprisingly, Kingsley's reception at San Francisco was more than positive. When he left, the *Overland*, exasperated with "a class of literary tourists who were constantly re-discovering America and writing us up as a naturalist would a new genus or species," praised Kingsley for his lectures ("which have been in grateful contrast to much of the 'popular lecture' business, so called") and his appreciation of civilization in the West:

> Doubtless he has corrected by observation on the spot some of the general misapprehensions concerning California, which have been confirmed, if not partly created, by the partial views of Bret Harte [...] As a result of such correction, we may hope to hear from Mr. Kingsley, after his return to England, not fulsome praise, but juster criticism than has often reached us from returned tourists.[94]

Little could the writer think that Kingsley never lived to write his "American Notes." The damp San Francisco climate did not do his lungs any good and he fell severely ill. Doctors advised him to leave the west coast immediately. At the beginning of June he moved east to Denver, where he happened to meet his younger brother George, who was bear hunting in the Rocky Mountains. He diagnosed his brother's illness as pleurisy.

---

[91] Charles Kingsley, "Our Norse Forefathers", *Overland Monthly and Out west Magazine*, 13(1) 1874, 88–90.

[92] [-], "Our Indian Policy", *Overland Monthly and Out west Magazine*, 11(3) 214.

[93] D.C. Gilman to FK, undated, *LMLM* ii.324.

[94] Charles Kingsley, "Our Norse Forefathers", *Overland Monthly and Out west Magazine*, 13(1) 1874, 90–91.

CHAPTER TWENTY-SIX

NO MORE FIGHTING (1874–1875)

In June 1874 Kingsley and his daughter Rose went south through the Rocky Mountains to Colorado Springs via the narrow gauge track of the Denver and Rio Grande Railway. Colorado Springs had been founded four years before by General William J. Palmer, president of the aforesaid railway. The site was chosen for its stupendous views of Pikes Peak and was thought to make a nice location for a stop on the railroad as a fashionable and genteel resort in the style of Newport (Rhodes Island). Palmer bought land on which he laid out the ground plan of the new town and gave out patches for cultural purposes and promoted his ideal town in a newspaper he started, *Out West* (later *The Colorado Springs Gazette*), which described Kingsley's movements during his stay. Its editor, J.E. Liller, who had emigrated only two years before from Chester, had special interest in the canon of his former home town.

In its first years the influx of English immigrants had turned Colorado Springs into a kind of "Little London" (tea was served at five o'clock, and in the eighties it had police officers who were known and dressed as 'bobbies'). It seemed a natural destination for Kingsley, whose illness made him feel ever less at ease in the far-away country: he had started grumbling about the food—"[which] is to me more & more disgusting"—and about the "everlasting yang-twang of the Natives."[1] The Englishness of Colorado Springs thus made it "a delicious place" to Kingsley. But going to Colorado Springs was like going home in more than one sense. The Kingsleys were closely linked to the founding of this Rocky Mountain town.[2]

General Palmer had come to know the Rocky Mountain area well while surveying for the Kansas Pacific Railway a route west from Kansas to San Francisco. When his advice of building over the Raton Pass and through New Mexico was not followed up and the Kansas

---

[1] CK to FK, 18/6/1874, MP-C0171–36915.
[2] For the Kingsleys and Colorado Springs, see also Sprague, Marshall, *Newport in the Rockies; The Life and Good Times of Colorado Springs*, (Chicago: Sage Books, 1971), ch. 1–5.

Pacific was built into Denver, he started planning his own railway south from Denver to the Rio Grande. While on a trip surveying for this southern railway he convinced himself he had found the ideal place to build his own town and castle for his future wife Queen Mellen. He fell in love with the beautiful scenery, the lakes, the soda springs, the green valleys, and the imposing Garden of the Gods, "a cathedral park" of huge red stones. Palmer married in November and on their honeymoon in England the Palmers were the guests of the Kingsleys for a couple of days. Kingsley and Palmer talked a lot about the new colony, and Kingsley proposed "Monument Dells" as a name for it, which, however, was not adopted. Queen enjoyed English fashionable life and desired to have a house built similar to Eversley Rectory when they returned to the Rocky Mountains. Kingsley, in turn, must have been enchanted with the idea of a pioneer in the Far West. His boyhood dreams had often taken that direction, and, notwithstanding his nationalistic pride, in later life he often felt tired with England. Mrs Kingsley wrote to W.H. Calcott as late as March 1871 that "we sometimes talk all of going off to Colorado in the Rocky Mountains [. . .] to get a rest from Civilization, Polemics &c!!"[3] Moreover, in Palmer's enthusiastic account of his plans for the new colony, Kingsley discerned a possibility of a start in life for his eldest son Maurice, by now 23 and as yet without a profession. As a result, Maurice went out with Palmer to America in 1871 to survey sites for roads, railway tracks and ditches for irrigation, as well as to act as the General's representative for the Denver and Rio Grande Railway in the new settlement under Pikes Peak to sell memberships of what was then still called Fountain Colony.

Rose too played her part in the history of the early months of the new colony. She went out to visit her brother in November 1871, and reached the town just a few days after Palmer's wife Queen had come to reside. She describes in her fascinating travel book *South by West* that, when she arrived at Colorado Springs, the streets and blocks were marked out for construction, and only "twelve houses and shanties are inhabited."[4] Only two months later she wrote

---

[3] Unpublished letter copied into a pamphlet offered by Mrs Kingsley to Calcott; reproduced with courtesy of the Denver Public Library.

[4] [Kingsley, Rose Georgiana], *South by West; or, Winter in the Rocky Mountains and Spring in Mexico*, (London: W. Isbister, 1874) 48.

that it "is growing prodigiously. I find it quite difficult to keep pace
with all the new arrivals, or the new buildings which spring up as
if by magic."[5] Her account also reports how Mrs Palmer exerted
herself in setting up social life in the colony, and how Rose assidu-
ously seconded her. A school was set up, and Queen did the teaching. She stood the undisciplined pupils of different ages for five weeks
before Rose took over. Rose was even less successful and fled after
only two days. On Kingsley's recommendation, J. Elsom Liller had
come over from Chester to edit the local newspaper for Palmer, and
Mrs Liller took it upon her to do the teaching at Queen's school
for the rest of the term. Rose, who often went off on her own rambling along the rocks and pastures on the slopes around the colony,
now proposed a reading room for her newly founded Fountain Society
of Natural Science, and Queen launched the idea of raising funds
for it by means of a concert where she herself would sing as prima
donna in pieces of Verdi. Rose helped rehearsing and played the
piano. The concert was a success and Queen's (local) fame as opera
singer went into the annals of the colony. Maurice sang "The Fox
went out on a Moonlight Night" and "Men of Harlich", "after which
loud cries for M. began; he was obliged to sing again."[6] Rose also
helped rehearsing for the first church service, held on 13 January
1872. She left in March when Maurice resigned from his job in the
colony to become part of Palmer's surveying crew in Mexico, but
"the four months I have spent here [...] have proved to me [...]
that in no country on earth can one find better and truer friends."[7]
Colorado Springs acknowledges its debt to this early pioneer in having called Mount Rosa, south-west of the city, after her.

   Thus going in 1874 with her ailing father to Colorado Springs
was in a sense going "home." In his American lectures Kingsley
often stresses the special link between England and America which
he describes as the relationship between a father and a son. This
sentiment perhaps applied above all to Colorado Springs. When
Kingsley sent Liller out to be editor of Palmer's paper in the colony,

   [5] [Kingsley, Rose Georgiana], *South by West; or, Winter in the Rocky Mountains and Spring in Mexico*, (London: W. Isbister, 1874) 119.
   [6] [Kingsley, Rose Georgiana], *South by West; or, Winter in the Rocky Mountains and Spring in Mexico*, (London: W. Isbister, 1874) 123–24.
   [7] [Kingsley, Rose Georgiana], *South by West; or, Winter in the Rocky Mountains and Spring in Mexico*, (London: W. Isbister, 1874) 136.

he promised to write a series of articles for him. His first contribution came out on 23 March 1872 but was written in December 1871. The opening paragraph, stressing the relationship between the two countries, provides us with a glimpse of his feelings about an approaching Christmas with his own son far away from home:

> Happy shall I be, if my letters form one more link of cordiality and mutual understanding between two Peoples who are one in race, one in genius, and—as I fully believe—one at heart, and whose differences have been only those which so often arise between a father and a son, when both are full of high spirit and original energy. How often, as the son rises into manhood, rivalries and misunderstandings, arise and how often, too, do we see those rivalries and misunderstandings die out, as father and son learn, by experience, to trust and admire each other, and to let each other go, either his own way. The son of twenty and the father of five-and-forty did not know each other's relative position, relative value.[8]

When Kingsley was writing thus of the respective attitudes of the two countries, he had his own son Maurice in mind. He knew Maurice would read the letter in the paper when it came out. But the irony of destiny was that Maurice had just resigned from his job and had left with Palmer.

When Kingsley arrived at Colorado Springs, William A. Bell, another early Rocky Mountain pioneer and director of the Denver and Rio Grande Railway who had become close friends of both Maurice and Rose during the winter of 1871–72, kindly offered to host the Kingsleys at his Manitou house, a few miles west of Colorado Springs, built in perfectly English style. The climate at the base of Pikes Peak was just what Kingsley needed, a climate which, in almost prophetic words in Rose's book is described as "bracing and so dry, that, [. . .] for invalids suffering from asthma or consumption, if the latter disease is not too far advanced, the air works wonders."[9]

Bell used the presence of the Canon of Westminster well. An Irish physician, Bell did much to promote the Englishness of the colony. He and his wife were the leading people in its social life and they set a tone of high standards in an otherwise rugged colony community. During Kingsley's stay he published extensively in the English

---

[8] William Baker (1971) 92.
[9] [Kingsley, Rose Georgiana], *South by West; or, Winter in the Rocky Mountains and Spring in Mexico*, (London: W. Isbister, 1874) 143.

papers (mentioning the Canon's permanence) on the advantages the colony had to offer to young farmers for whom there was no space and work in Britain anymore.

Kingsley's health, carefully looked after by Dr Bell and Dr Gatchell, returned but gradually, and towards the end of June, in search of cooler air, he was taken up to Bell's mountain ranch at Bergen's Park, then a long narrow grassy valley scattered with huge blocks of red sandstone sloping up to pine woods on both sides with south a most beautiful view of Pikes Peak. "To the botanist and geologist there is an endless field of interest," Rose had commented in her book.[10] Here Kingsley passed his time reading and botanizing with the plants that were collected and brought in for him. All this was kept a secret to Fanny, but in one or two passages in his letters one can read of Kingsley's lack of energy: notwithstanding the cooler mountain air he still grumbled that there were "lots of trout here, but it is too hot to catch them." It was here that Kingsley wrote his last poem, that rhythmical ballad "Lorraine, Lorraine, Lorrèe," expressing some of his own fatalistic feelings at that time.

On 5 July Kingsley had recovered enough to read a short service at the ranch, and the following week he moved to Glen Eyrie near Colorado Springs where he stayed at General Palmer's house, which over the years had grown into an eccentric castle, built close to the mouth of a canyon on the slope of a hill "dotted with tall pines and fantastic rocks of every colour."[11] The exceptional beauty of the spot briefly fired Kingsley's admiration, but general tiredness of the tour and the New World was making itself felt. In his last letter home he wrote: "thank God that I am an Englishman, & not an—well, it is not the fault of the dear generous people, but of their ancestors & ours."[12] He felt obliged to deliver a sermon in public in the new and crowded Episcopal Church, and a few days later, just before leaving, to deliver his Westminster Abbey lecture in aid of its Building Fund. The *Gazette* reported that the sermon was characteristically "full of vigorous thought, but eminently plain and practical," while the lecture, notwithstanding "its length considerably exceeded that

---

[10] [Kingsley, Rose Georgiana], *South by West; or, Winter in the Rocky Mountains and Spring in Mexico*, (London: W. Isbister, 1874) 143.

[11] [Kingsley, Rose Georgiana], *South by West; or, Winter in the Rocky Mountains and Spring in Mexico*, (London: W. Isbister, 1874) 126.

[12] CK to FK, 14/7/1874, MP-C0171–36915.

of ordinary lectures [. . .,] it must suffice to say that it afforded our citizens a rare treat."[13] These were Kingsley's last public appearances in Colorado Springs. Liller, like his colleague in the San Francisco *Overland*, rejoiced in Kingsley's favourable impressions of, and hearty interest in the colony, "for there are few men living who could more thoroughly and justly appreciate the peculiar characteristics of both [the people and the country], and who could do us better service with the pen."[14] This was not to be, and Kingsley lives on in the history of Colorado Springs, as an indifferent visitor who despised Americans and was not much impressed by the brand-new pioneer town.

II

On 17 July Kingsley left for Denver, where he lectured for the last time in America. On 24 September 1873 Denver's *Daily Central City Register* had announced the proposed visit of "Bishop Kingsley, the brilliant and popular English author [who] does not come to make money as a lecturer, but to visit a daughter at Colorado Springs, and spend a few months in 'seeing with his own eyes' our wonderful country." The poor writer was immediately corrected by Liller, who, after all, *was* English. He snobbishly corrected the *City Register's* report as follows:

> the brilliant and popular English author is not a Bishop but a Canon— a Canon being one of the "chapter," or governing clergy, of an English cathedral. Canon Kingsley's cathedral is Westminster Abbey. Secondly, Miss Kingsley is not in Colorado Springs, having left here fully eighteen months ago.

As it turned out, in Denver Kingsley had only time to lecture on Westminster Abbey before returning east. The *Rocky Mountain News* reported the lecture at the Guard's Hall, where Kingsley was introduced by Bishop Spalding.[15] The last impression he made on an American audience was captured in the following words: "He speaks with an accent so strong as sometimes to be almost unintelligible,

---

[13] [-], [report of Kingsley's sermon at the Episcopal Church at Colorado Springs], *Colorado Springs Gazette*, 18/7/1874, 2.
[14] [-], *Colorado Springs Gazette*, 18/7/1874, 2.
[15] [-], "Canon Kingsley's Lecture", *Denver Rocky Mountain News*, 18/7/1874, 4.

and while speaking he often puts his arms akimbo, and is continually rolling up his sleeves as if spoiling for a fight." Before starting on the lecture proper, he began by praising Denver and its audience "in what his English friends would consider a remote and out of the way place." But Denver would soon turn into one of the most important cities of America thanks to its strategic position on the "greatest travel route in the world," he prophesied. When he turned his mind to Westminster Abbey and came to the passage of praise of Washington Irving's most elegant *English* prose, applause issued. "I am glad to hear that," he added, "I heard no such recognition of his name in California." Irving had had enormous success as a writer in England just for the fine quality of his language which sounded thoroughly English both in style and in subject. Kingsley's appreciation could thus easily be seen as criticism of American as spoken by his audience in California—indeed he never hid his contempt of American pronunciation. The Denver audience, however, was endeared to Irving because of his accounts and studies of the Far West written in the mid-thirties, and particularly to the exploration of the Rocky Mountains in *The Adventures of Captain Bonneville*. Kingsley most likely mistook the applause for appreciation of his observation on Irving's style.

Kingsley concluded his lecture tour with words that could easily apply to all Americans: "So I wish God to bless you, for I shall never see you again." From Denver he returned to New York to cross the Atlantic once more. He sailed, disillusioned, on 25 July.

III

After Kingsley's return from America in August 1874 hard work awaited him. There was "much sickness and a great mortality in his parish," and, his curate being away on holiday, Kingsley did most of the visiting of the parishioners himself, even if he had not yet fully regained his strength after his illness in Colorado. When, in September, he went up to Westminster he suffered an attack of congestion of the liver which was so severe that it prevented him from preaching. "This attack," Mrs Kingsley writes, "shook him terribly" and he seemed "altered and emaciated."[16] An unnamed correspondent,

---

[16] *LML* ii.449.

who saw Kingsley preach in Westminster Abbey that autumn, remarked on his "bent back and shrunken figure" and felt grieved "to see one who had carried himself so nobly, broken down by illness."[17] When he came to the end of his term of residence in a state of complete exhaustion, he caught a cold in the damp cloister and coughed all night. It was the beginning of the end. During the journey home to Eversley Fanny fell seriously ill. There was concern for her life, and Kingsley was forced to cancel his appointment to preach for the Queen at Windsor. Doctors told him there was very little hope and the children were called home. It was during this period of despair that Kingsley became careless of his own health, and, "reckless of cold and snow," his cough became first bronchitic and then turned into pneumonia. On 28 December he took to his bed and was administrated opium and had wonderful dreams of the West Indies and the Rocky Mountains. On 18 January 1875 *The Times* carried a notice to inform the public that the Canon of Westminster's life was feared for. The Prince of Wales sent his physician, Sir William Gull, down to Eversley, but haemorrhage occurred. During the night he was heard whispering "No more fighting—no more fighting."[18] Not having heard news about Fanny for days, he concluded contentedly that they were dying together. On 23 January Kingsley passed away at the age of 55.

When the news of Kingsley's death reached Westminster Abbey, his friend Dean Arthur Stanley expressed his wish to render the last honours, and telegraphed that "the Abbey is open to the Canon and the Poet."[19] But Kingsley had always wanted to be buried in Eversley, and around the spot he had chosen himself for his grave "a large sad throng" of friends gathered on 28 January. Reactions of mourning came in from all quarters, the bells of Westminster Abbey and Chester Cathedral were tolled, and at Eversley the road from the rectory to the church was blocked by the carriages of all those that came to pay their respect at his funeral. In Birmingham an aged John Henry Newman was shocked to hear of Kingsley's early death and said Mass for him. Afterwards he recorded about Kingsley that he had long "wished to shake hands with him when living, and

---

[17] *LML* ii.450.
[18] *LML* ii.259.
[19] A.P. Stanley to FK, undated, *LML* ii.462.

Illustration 9. The late Rev. Charles Kingsley, Canon of Westminster (engraving in Extra Supplement to *The London Illustrated News*, 30 January 1875)

towards whose memory I have much tenderness."[20] Among the numerous letters that reached the Eversley rectory, the one from Matthew Arnold is an interesting comment on Kingsley's last years and seems the most appropriate to conclude with here. Arnold had followed the accounts of Kingsley's illness, and "feared the worst." He explained: "It has seemed of late years as if he had not fortune on his side as when he was young." But, Arnold predicted, "the injustice, which he and they [his literary works] had in some quarters to experience, will no longer busy."[21] A small emblematic incident might prove that Arnold was too optimistic. Although Kingsley was buried in Eversley, a committee was set up for a small marble bust to be placed in Westminster Abbey. It was executed by Thomas Woolner, and placed on an obscure wall in the baptistery, which the dean had designated as "a new poets' corner." This it never became.

---

[20] *The Letters and Diaries of John Henry Newman* ed. C.S. Dessain *et al.* (London/Oxford: 1961–) xxix.388.
[21] Matthew Arnold to Rose Kingsley, undated, *LML* ii.471.

CONCLUSION

After Kingsley's death, assessments of his importance varied. Many people remembered his endeavours to improve the social conditions of the English working classes—"how wide was his sympathy for human suffering and ignorance in all shapes, and how earnest were his efforts to relieve and enlighten them"[1]—and his capacity to communicate his ideas to aristocrat and peasant alike. Many idolized "that true-hearted man, who did noble work among the poor, unmindful of sneers, opposition, and pecuniary loss, whose intense nature might sometimes lead into mistakes, but whose heart was always in the right place; whose earnest teaching, free from all conventionality of thought or expression, were listened to by the Queen and her family as eagerly as by the humblest peasant. There was nothing of the pale-faced saint or martyr in this healthy, happy, muscular Englishman."[2] These qualities, "added to a true and varied endowment of genius, constituted Charles Kingsley a rare man."[3] What impressed people, when looking back at Kingsley's life, were the many fields on which he had concentrated, "a man who was at once poet, novelist, preacher, professor, ecclesiastic, and scientist, and who was second-rate in nothing which he did [. . .] if not himself a leader in the highest sense, he was certainly the leader of the multitude as the exponent of their thought."[4] "He was not one of those to whom you can refuse a hearing," *The Times* wrote two days after his death.[5] However, Kingsley's leadership and genius was debatable and the more critical could not conceal a sense of contradiction in everything Kingsley had said and done, that he "was not only many-sided, but full of contradictions:"[6]

> Upon the social side he attained, if not to an adequate expression, at least to a coherent doctrine [. . .] which he symbolized under the name democracy [. . .] The course of his political thought made Kingsley

[1] *Scribner's Monthly* 13 (4) February 1877, p. 572.
[2] *The Galaxy* 24 (2) Augustus 1877, p. 282.
[3] *Scribner's Monthly* 14 (1) May 1877, p. 118.
[4] *The North American Review* 124 (256) May 1877, p. 511.
[5] "Death of Charles Kingsley", *The Times* 25 January, p. 9e.
[6] *Scribner's Monthly* 14 (1) May 1877, p. 117.

more conservative and less eager; the course of his religious thought made him more conservative and less confident; his trinitarian speculations faded away, though his trinitarian creed remained. As he grew older he preached positivism in observation, and optimism in feeling, more and more in an arbitrary way, with less and less pretence that the combination supplied a reasonable explanation of fact.[7]

As to Kingsley's reputation as a man of letters critics were divided too. Some did not distinguish between his qualities and found him "a man of rare mental and physical power [. . .] a man who had the capacities of a reformer, of an orator, of a pamphleteer, of a novelist, of a poet."[8] Others thought that "Kingsley's lasting fame will not be that of a divine, or a naturalist, or a *Tendenz*-romancer, however deeply he was himself stirred by questions of theology, science, and social reform, but that as a poet,"[9] while yet others followed the obituary in *The Times* "that it is as a novelist that he will live in English literature,"[10] that "as a poet, it appears, he took himself too seriously."[11]

One hundred and thirty years of criticism have reassessed Kingsley's place in English literature mainly as a novelist. Admittedly, a few of his lyrics have earned a place in English verse and are still anthologized today, but his fame today rests mainly on his fiction, and much of his reputation rests on being the author of one of the greatest classics in English children's literature.

In the history of nineteenth-century England Kingsley has taken a place as an eminent Victorian. His is an important voice in the intellectual debates of the age and very few modern books on (aspects of) the period fail to mention him. As a thinker of non-mainstream ideas, his courageous synthesis of sexuality and Christianity and his delighted participation in God's creation have fascinated modern critics. Although his importance as a divine in the Anglican Church has turned out to be negligible, he remains significant in its history. He has never been taken very seriously as a historian, but modern historiography has shown some renewed interest in his ideas about

---

[7] G.A. Simcox, "Charles Kingsley" *Littell's Living Age* 132 (1704) February 1877, p. 354; originally published in *The Fortnightly Review*.
[8] *Harper's New Monthly Magazine* 55 (326) July 1877, p. 305.
[9] *Atlantic Monthly* 39 (236) June 1877, p. 752.
[10] "Death of Charles Kingsley", *The Times* 25 January, p. 9e.
[11] G.A. Simcox, "Charles Kingsley" *Littell's Living Age* 132 (1704) February 1877, p. 354; originally published in *The Fortnightly Review*.

history. Kingsley's roles as a social reformer and as a naturalist had a considerable impact on his time. He was an impressive populariser of controversial issues and he did much to bring them to the attention of the public. Taking Kingsley as a whole, one cannot but agree with Professor John Maynard when he summed up in 1993 that "his representativeness and wide influence give his copious works an importance beyond the talent they display, which is nonetheless not inconsiderable, titanic in energy and output if not Olympian in control and formal artistry."[12]

What most late Victorian critics agreed upon in their assessment of Kingsley was that "whatever faults may have been charged upon his books or himself, dullness was never one of them."[13] Modern readers will find no difficulty in subscribing to this.

---

[12] Maynard, p. 1.
[13] *Scribner's Monthly* 14 (1) May 1877, p. 117.

BIBLIOGRAPHY

A vast amount of criticism on Kingsley has been published over the last two centuries. For reasons of space, only a selected list of regularly quoted works can be given here. Full references to other publications which have been cited (including numerous anonymous articles) are included in the footnotes to the main text. For a comprehensive list of Kingsley criticism, the following two annotated bibliographies are recommended:

– Harris, Styron, *Charles Kingsley, A Reference Guide*, (Boston: G.K. Hall, 1981)
– Rapple, Brendan, *Charles Kingsley: The 20th Century Critical Heritage* (http://www2. bc.edu/~rappleb/kingsley/kingsleyhome.html)

Adrian, Arthur A., "Charles Kingsley Visits Boston", *The Huntingdon Library Quarterly*, 20 (1956), pp. 94–97
Alderson, Brian, "Introduction to *The Water-Babies*", in Charles Kingsley, *The Water-Babies*, (Oxford: Oxford University Press, 1995), pp. ix–xxxvi
[Aytoun, W.E.], "Alton Locke, Tailor and Poet: An Autobiography", *Blackwood's Edinburgh Magazine*, 68 (1850), pp. 592–610
[———], "The Rev. Charles Kingsley", *Blackwood's Edinburgh Magazine*, 77 (1855), pp. 625–643
Backstrom, Philip N., *Christian Socialism and Cooperation in Victorian England; Edward Vansittart Neale and the Co-operative Movement*, (London: Croom Helm, 1974)
Baker, Joseph Ellis, *The Novel and the Oxford Movement*, (New York: Russell & Russell, 1932)
Baker, William J., "Victorian Chapter in Anglo-American Understanding: Three Letters from Charles Kingsley to 'Little London', Colorado", *Notes & Queries*, 216 (1971), pp. 91–97
———, "Charles Kingsley in Little London", *The Colorado Magazine*, 45 (1968), pp. 187–203
Baldwin, Stanley Everett, *Charles Kingsley*, (London: Oxford University Press, 1934)
Banton, Michael, "Kingsley's Racial Philosophy", *Theology*, 78 (1975), pp. 22–30
Barker, E.E., "The Kingsley Pedigree", *Notes & Queries*, 12 (1916), p. 174
Beer, Gillian, *Darwin's Plots; Evolutionary Narrative in Darwin, George Eliot and Nineteenth Century Fiction*, (London, Boston, Melbourne, Henley: Routledge & Kegan Paul, 1983)
[Beesly, E.S.], "Mr. Kingsley on the Study of History", *The Westminster Review*, 19 (1861), pp. 305–336
Blinderman, C.S., "Huxley and Kingsley", *Victorian Newsletter*, 20 (1961), pp. 25–8
Bloomfield, Anne, "Muscular Christian or Mystic? Charles Kingsley Reappraised", *International Journal of the History of Sport*, 11 (1994), pp. 172–90
Brandenstein, Claudia, "Imperial Positions in Charles Kingsley's *At Last: A Christmas in the West Indies*", *SPAN*, 46 (1998), pp. 4–18
Brock, W.H., "*Glaucus*: Kingsley and the Seaside Naturalists", *Cahiers d'Études et de Recherches Victoriennes et Edouardiennes*, 3 (1976), pp. 25–36
Brose, Olive J., *Frederick Denison Maurice: Rebellious Conformist*, (n.p.: Ohio University Press, 1971)
Brown, William Henry, *Charles Kingsley; The Work and Influence of Parson Lot*, (Norwood, Pa.: Norwood Editions, 1924)
Bryant, Chris, *Possible Dreams; A Personal History of the British Christian Socialists*, (London: Hodder & Stoughton, 1996)

Buckton, Oliver S., *Secret Selves: Confession and Same-Sex Desire in Victorian Autobiography*, (Chapel Hill and London: University of North Carolina Press, 1998)

Cazamian, Louis, *Kingsley et Thomas Cooper; Étude sur une source d'Alton Locke*, (Paris: Société Nouvelle de Librairie et d'edition, 1903)

Chadwick, Owen, *The Victorian Church*, (London: SCM Press, 1987)

——, "Charles Kingsley at Cambridge", *The Historical Journal*, 18 (1975), pp. 303–325

——, "Kingsley's Chair", *Theology*, 78 (1975), pp. 2–8

Chapman, Raymond, "Charles Kingsley and the Lavington Curse", *Notes & Queries*, 216 (1971), p. 91

Chitty, Susan, *The Beast and the Monk; A Life of Charles Kingsley*, (London: Hodder and Stoughton, 1974)

——, *Charles Kingsley's Landscape*, (Newton Abbot, London: David & Charles, 1976)

Christensen, Torben, *Origin and History of Christian Socialism 1848–54*, Acta Theologica Danica (Aarhus: Universitetsforlaget, 1962)

Coleman, Dorothy, "Rabelais and *The Water-Babies*", *Modern Language Review*, 66 (1971), pp. 511–521

[Coleridge, John Duke], [Review of *Yeast*], *The Guradian*, (7 May 1851), pp. 331–2

Colloms, Brenda, *Charles Kingsley; The Lion of Eversley*, (London: Constable, 1975)

[Conington, John], "Kingsley's Saint's Tragedy", *Fraser's Magazine*, 37 (1848), pp. 328–337

[Cox, W.], "Dr. Newman and Mr. Kingsley", *The Westminster Review*, (1864), pp. 137–151

Cripps, Elizabeth A., "Introduction to *Alton Locke*", in Charles Kingsley, *Alton Locke*, (Oxford: Oxford University Press, 1983), pp. vii–xxviii

[Croker, J. Wilson], "Revolutionary Literature", *The Quarterly Review*, 89 (1851), pp. 491–543

Cunningham, Valentine, "Soiled Fairy: *The Water-Babies* in its Time," *Essays in Criticism*, 35 (1985), pp. 121–48

[Dixon, William Hepworth], [Review of *Glaucus*], *The Athenaeum*, 1446 (1855), p. 813

Dorman, Susann, "*Hypatia* and *Callista*: The Initial Skirmish between Kingsley and Newman", *Nineteenth Century Fiction*, 34 (1979), pp. 173–93

Downes, David A., *The Temper of Victorian Belief; Studies in the Religious Novels of Pater, Kingsley and Newman*, (New York: Twayne Publishers, 1972)

Dunn, Waldo Hilary, *James Anthony Froude: A Biography 1818–1894*, 2 vols. (Oxford: Clarendon Press, 1961, 1963)

Egner, G., *Apologia pro Charles Kingsley*, (London: Sheed and Ward, 1969)

[Eliot, George], "Belles Lettres", *The Westminster Review*, 8 (1855), pp. 288–294

Ellis, S.M., *Henry Kingsley 1830–1876; Towards a Vindication*, (London: Grant Richards, 1931)

Fasick, Laura, "Charles Kingsley's Scientific Treatment of Gender", in *Muscular Christianity: Embodying the Victorian Age*, ed. by Hall, Donald E.(Cambridge: Cambridge University Press, 1994), pp. 91–113

Gallagher, Catherine, *The Industrial Reformation of English Fiction; Social Discourse and Narrative Form 1832–1867*, (London: The University of Chicago Press, 1985)

Gikandi, Simon, "Englishness, Travel and Theory: Writing the West Indies in the Nineteenth Century", *Nineteenth-Century Contexts*, 18 (1994), pp. 49–70

Gottlieb, Evan M., "Charles Kingsley, the Romantic Legacy, and the Unmaking of the Working-Class Intellectual", *Victorian Literature and Culture*, 29 (2001), pp. 51–65

Greg, W.R., *Essays on Political and Social Science, Contributed Chiefly to 'The Edinburgh Review'* vol. 1, (London: Longmans, 1853), pp. 458–504

[Greg, Willam Rathbone], "Mr. Kingsley's Literary Excesses", *The National Review*, 10 (1860), pp. 1–24

Grylls, Rosalie Glynn, *Queen's College 1848–1948; Founded by Frederick Denison Maurice*, (London: George Routledge & Sons, 1948)

Haley, Bruce, *The Healthy Body and Victorian Culture*, (London, Cambridge, Mass.: Harvard University Press, 1978)

Hall, Donald E., "On the Making and Unmaking of Monsters: Christian Socialism, Muscular Christianity, and the Metamorphazation of Class Conflict", in *Muscular Christianity: Embodying the Victorian Age*, ed. by Hall, Donald E. (Cambridge: Cambridge University Press, 1994), pp. 45–65

[Hamley, E.B.], "Kingsley's Andromeda", *Blackwood's Edinburgh Magazine*, 84 (1858), pp. 217–225

Hanawalt, Mary Wheat, "Charles Kingsley and Science", *Studies in Philology*, 34 (1937), pp. 589–611

Harrington, Henry R., "Charles Kingsley's Fallen Athlete", *Victorian Studies*, 21 (1977), pp. 73–86

Harris, Styron, "The 'Muscular Novel': Medium of a Victorian Ideal", *Tennessee Philological Bulletin*, 27 (1990), pp. 6–13

Hartley, Allen J., *The Novels of Charles Kingsley; A Christian Social Interpretation*, (Folkestone: Hour-Glass Press, 1977)

Hawley, John C., "Charles Kingsley and Literary Theory of the 1850s", *Victorian Literature and Culture*, 19 (1991), pp. 167–88

——, "Responses to Charles Kingsley's Attack on Political Economy", *Victorian Periodicals Review*, 19 (1986), pp. 131–36

——, "Charles Kingsley and the Via Media", *Thought*, 67 (1992), pp. 287–301

——, "Charles Kingsley and the Book of Nature", *Anglican and Episcopal History*, 61 (1991), pp. 461–79

Haynes, R.D., "The Multiple Functions of *Alton Locke*'s Dreamland", *Cahiers Victoriens et Edouardiens*, 25 (1987), pp. 29–37

Helps, Arthur, "Charles Kingsley", *The Eclectic Magazine*, 21 (1875), pp. 477–78

Hertz, Alan, "The Broad Church Militant and Newman's Humiliation of Charles Kingsley", *Victorian Periodicals Review*, 19 (1986), pp. 141–149

Hughes, Thomas, 'Prefatory Memoir', in *Alton Locke*, ed. by (London: Macmillan, 1876)

Huxley, Leonard, *Life and Letters of Thomas Henry Huxley*, 2 vols. (London: Macmillan, 1900)

[Huxley, Thomas Henry], "Contemporary Literature—Science", *The Westminster Review*, 8 (1855), pp. 246–253

[Jewsbury, Geraldine Endsor], "Yeast. A Problem", *The Athenæum*, 1225 (1851), pp. 428

Johnston, Arthur, "*The Water-Babies*: Kingsley's Debt to Darwin", *English*, 12 (1958–9), pp. 215–19

Kaufmann, M., *Charles Kingsley, Christain Socialist and Reformer*, (London: Methuen, 1892)

Kaye, Richard A., "'Determined Raptures': St. Sebastian and the Victorian Discourse of Decadence", *Victorian Literature and Culture*, 27 (1999), pp. 269–303

Kendall, Guy, *Charles Kingsley and his Ideas*, (London: Hutchinson, [1946?])

King, Richard John, "Charles Kingsley", *Fraser's Magazine*, 11 (1875), pp. 393–406

Klaver, Jan Marten Ivo, "Charles Kingsley and the Limits of Humanity", *Dutch Review of Church History*, 81 (2001), pp. 115–41

Klaver, Jan Marten Ivo, "Jean Paul, Carlyle and Kingsley: The Romantic Tradition in *Alton Locke*'s Dreamland", *Linguæ &*, (2003), 3 (1), pp. 37–44.

Lankewish, Vincent A., "Love Among the Ruins: The Catacombs, the Closet and the Victorian 'Early Christian' Novel", *Victorian Literature and Culture*, 28 (2000), pp. 239–273

Ludlow, J.M., "Some of the Christian Socialists of 1848 and the Following Years", *Economic Review*, 4 (1894), pp. 24–42

——, "Some of the Christian Socialists of 1848 and the Following Years", *Economic Review*, 3 (1893), pp. 486–500

——, *The Autobiography of a Christian Socialist*, (London: Frank Cass, 1981)

Mack, Edward C. and Armytage, W.H.G., *Thomas Hughes: The Life of the Author of Tom Brown's Schooldays*, (London: Ernest Benn, 1952)

Manlove, Colin N., *Modern Fantasy; Five Studies*, (Cambridge: Cambridge University Press, 1975)

Martin, R[obert] B[ernard], *An Edition of the Correspondence and Private Papers of Charles Kingsley, 1819–1856*, (Unpublished B. Litt. Dissertation: New College, Oxford, 1950)

——, *The Dust of Combat; A Life of Charles Kingsley*, (London: Faber and Faber, 1959)

Martineau, Violet, John Martineau, *The Pupil of Kingsley*, (London: Edward Arnold, 1921)

Masterman, N.C., *John Malcolm Ludlow; The Builder of Christian Socialism*, (Cambridge: Cambridge University Press, 1963)

Maurice, Frederick, *The Life of Frederick Denison Maurice, Chiefly Told in His Own Letters*, vols 2 (London: Macmillan, 1884)

Maynard, John, *Victorian Discourses on Sexuality and Religion*, (Cambridge: Cambridge University Press, 1993)

McCarthy, Justin, "The Reverend Charles Kingsley", *The Galaxy*, 14 (1872), pp. 181–191

Meadows, A.J., "Kingsley's Attitude to Science", *Theology*, 78 (1975), pp. 15–22

[Meredith, George], "Belle Lettres", *The Westminster Review*, 11 (1857), pp. 609–611

Menke, Richard, "Cultural Capital and the Scene of Rioting: Male Working-Class Authorship in *Alton Locke*", *Victorian Literature and Culture*, 28 (2000), pp. 87–108

Morgan, Charles, *The House of Macmillan (1843–1943)*, (London: Macmillan, 1943)

Munich, Adrienne Auslander, *Andromeda's Chains; Gender and Interpretation in Victorian Literature and Art*, (New York: Columbia University Press, 1989)

Newman, John Henry, *Apologia pro vita sua*, ed. by William Oddie (London: J.M. Dent, 1993)

Nowell-Smith, Simon, ed., *Letters to Macmillan*, (London: Macmillan, 1967)

[Oliphant, Margaret], "Modern Novelists—Great and Small", *Blackwood's Edinburgh Magazine*, 77 (1855), pp. 554–568

[——], "Modern Light Literature—Science", *Blackwood's Edinburgh Magazine*, 78 (1855), pp. 215–30

[——], "Modern Light Literature—Travellers' Tales", *Blackwood's Edinburgh Magazine*, 78 (1855), pp. 586–599

Page, Frederick, "Froude, Kingsley, and Arnold, on Newman", *Notes & Queries*, 184 (1943), pp. 220–221

Paul, Herbert, *The Life of Froude*, (London: Sir Isaac Pitman & Sons, 1905)

Pink, W.D., "Kingsley of Sarratt, Canterbury, and London", *The Genealogist*, 30 (1914), pp. 35–38; 86–94

——, "Kingsley of Sarratt, Canterbury, and London", *The Genealogist*, 29 (1913), pp. 212–224

Pope-Hennessy, Una, *Canon Charles Kingsley; A Biography*, (London: Chatto & Windus, 1948)

Prickett, Stephen, *Victorian Fantasy*, (Hassocks, Sussex: John Spiers—The Harvester Press, 1979)

Rapple, Brendon, "The Motif of Water in Charles Kingsley's *Water-Babies*", *University of Mississippi Studies in English*, (1993–1995), pp. 259–71

Rauch, Alan, "The Tailor Transformed: Kingsley's *Alton Locke* and the Notion of Change", *Studies in the Novel*, 25 (1993), pp. 196–213

Raven, Charles E., *Christian Socialism 1848–1854*, (London: Macmillan, 1920)

Reboul, Marc, *Charles Kingsley; La formation d'une personnalità et son affirmation litteraire (1819–1850)*, Publications de l'Univers (Paris: Presses Universitaires de France, 1973)

[Rigg, J.H.], "Rationalism in the Church of England", *The London Quarterly Review*, 7 (1856), pp. 1–51

[——], "The Writings of Charles Kingsley", *The London Quarterly Review*, 8 (1857), pp. 1–49

——, *Modern Anglican Theology; Chapters on Coleridge, Hare, Maurice, Kingsley and Jowett, and on the Doctrine of Sacrifice and Atonement*, (London: n.p., 1859)

[——], "Mr. Kingsley and Dr. Newman", *The London Quarterly Review*, 23 (1864), pp. 115–153

Robertson, Thomas L., "The Kingsley-Newman Controversy and the Apologia", *Modern Language Notes*, 69 (1954), pp. 564–69

[Roscoe, W.C.], "Mr. Kingsley's Poems", *The National Review*, 7 (1858), pp. 124–137

Rosen, David, "The Volcano and the Cathedral: Muscular Christianity and the Origins of Primal Manliness", in *Muscular Christianity: Embodying the Victorian Age*, ed. by Hall, Donald E. (Cambridge: Cambridge University Press, 1994), pp. 17–44

Row, Prescott, "Charles Kingsley: 'Vanity Fair' Caricature", *Notes & Queries*, 12 (1922), p. 226

[Sandars, Thomas Collett], "Two Years Ago", *The Saturday Review*, (21 February 1857), pp. 176–7

Savorey, Jerold, "Charles Kingsley and *Vanity Fair* and *Once a Week*", *Victorian Periodicals Review*, 19 (1986 (4)), pp. 137–140

Scott, P.G. and Uffelman, Larry K., "Kingsley's Serial Novels: *Yeast*", *Victorian Periodicals Newsletter*, 9 (1976), pp. 111–19

Scott, P.G., "Kingsley as Novelist", *Theology*, 78 (1975), pp. 8–15

Simcox, G.A., "Charles Kingsley", *The Eclectic Magazine*, 25 (1877), pp. 296–310

[Skelton, John], "Poems from Eversley, By the Rector. A Spring-Tide Study", *Fraser's Magazine*, 57 (1858), pp. 736–747

Smith, S.M., *The Other Nation; The Poor in English Novels of the 1840s and 1850s*, (Oxford: Clarendon Press, 1980)

[Stephen, Fitzjames], "Tom Brown's Schooldays", *The Edinburgh Review*, 107 (1858), pp. 172–93

[St. John, Horace Stebbing Roscoe], [Review of *Two Years Ago*], *The Athenaeum*, (14 February 1857), p. 212

Stubbs, Charles William, *Charles Kingsley and the Christian Social Movement*, (London: Blackie & Son, 1899)

Sutherland, J.A., *Victorian Novelists and Publishers*, (Chicago: Chicago University Press, 1978)

Thorp, Margaret F., *Charles Kingsley, 1819–1875*, (Princeton: Princeton University Press, 1937)

Uffelman, Larry, "Kingsley's *Hereward the Wake*. From Serial to Book", *Victorians Institute Journal*, 14 (1986), pp. 147–156

Uffelman, Larry & Patrick Scott, "Kingsley's Serial Novels II: *The Water Babies*", *Victorian Periodicals Review*, 19 (1986), pp. 122–31

Uffelman, Larry K., *Charles Kingsley*, (Boston: Twayne, 1979)

Vance, Norman, "Kingsley's Christian Manliness", *Theology*, 78 (1975), pp. 30–38

——, *The Sinews of the Spirit; The Ideal of Christian Manliness in Victorian Literature and Religious Thought*, (Cambridge: Cambridge University Press, 1985)

[Vaughan, R.A.], "Hypatia.-or New Foes With an Old Face", *The British Quarterly Review*, 18 (1853), pp. 123–170

Vulliamy, C.E., *Charles Kingsley and Christian Socialism*, (London: Fabian Society Publications, 1914)

Waller, John O., "Charles Kingsley and the American Civil War", *Studies in Philology*, 60 (1963), pp. 554–68

[Whyte-Melville, George], "Westward Ho!", *Fraser's Magazine*, 51 (1855), pp. 506–517

[Wilberforce, Edward], [Review of *At Last*], *The Athenaeum*, (10 June 1871), pp. 711–712

[Wilberforce, Samuel], [Review of Kingsley-Newman controversy], *The Quarterly Review*, 116 (1864), pp. 528–573

Winship, Michael, *American Literary Publishing in the Mid-Nineteenth Century: The Business of Ticknor and Fields*, (Cambridge: Cambridge University Press, 1995)

[Wise, J.R.], "Belle Lettres", *The Westminster Review*, 30 (1866), pp. 268–9

Wolff, Robert Lee, *Gains and Losses; Novels of Faith and Doubt in Victorian England*, (London: John Murray, 1977)

Wood, Naomi, "A (Sea) Green Victorian: Charles Kingsley and *The Water-Babies*," *The Lion and the Unicorn*, 19 (1995), pp. 233–252

Wright, C.J., "'My Darling Baby': Charles Kingsley's Letters to his Wife", *The British Library Journal*, 10 (1984), pp. 147–157

Young, Michael, "History as Myth: Charles Kingsley's *Hereward the Wake*", *Studies in the Novel*, 17 (1985), pp. 174–188

INDEX

BRILL'S STUDIES IN INTELLECTUAL HISTORY

Edited by A.J. Vanderjagt

1. POPKIN, R.H. *Isaac la Peyrère (1596-1676)*. His Life, Work and Influence. 1987. ISBN 90 04 08157 7
2. THOMSON, A. *Barbary and Enlightenment*. European Attitudes towards the Maghreb in the 18th Century. 1987. ISBN 90 04 08273 5
3. DUHEM, P. *Prémices Philosophiques*. With an Introduction in English by S.L. Jaki. 1987. ISBN 90 04 08117 8
4. OUDEMANS, TH.C.W. & A.P.M.H. LARDINOIS. *Tragic Ambiguity*. Anthropology, Philosophy and Sophocles' *Antigone*. 1987. ISBN 90 04 08417 7
5. FRIEDMAN, J.B. (ed.). *John de Foxton's Liber Cosmographiae (1408)*. An Edition and Codicological Study. 1988. ISBN 90 04 08528 9
6. AKKERMAN, F. & A. J. VANDERJAGT (eds.). *Rodolphus Agricola Phrisius, 1444-1485*. Proceedings of the International Conference at the University of Groningen, 28-30 October 1985. 1988. ISBN 90 04 08599 8
7. CRAIG, W.L. *The Problem of Divine Foreknowledge and Future Contingents from Aristotle to Suarez*. 1988. ISBN 90 04 08516 5
8. STROLL, M. *The Jewish Pope*. Ideology and Politics in the Papal Schism of 1130. 1987. ISBN 90 04 08590 4
9. STANESCO, M. *Jeux d'errance du chevalier médiéval*. Aspects ludiques de la fonction guerrière dans la littérature du Moyen Age flamboyant. 1988. ISBN 90 04 08684 6
10. KATZ, D. *Sabbath and Sectarianism in Seventeenth-Century England*. 1988. ISBN 90 04 08754 0
11. LERMOND, L. *The Form of Man*. Human Essence in Spinoza's *Ethic*. 1988. ISBN 90 04 08829 6
12. JONG, M. DE. *In Samuel's Image*. Child Oblation in the Early Medieval West. 1996. ISBN 90 04 10483 6
13. PYENSON, L. *Empire of Reason*. Exact Sciences in Indonesia, 1840-1940. 1989. ISBN 90 04 08984 5
14. CURLEY, E. & P.-F. MOREAU (eds.). *Spinoza. Issues and Directions*. The Proceedings of the Chicago Spinoza Conference. 1990. ISBN 90 04 09334 6
15. KAPLAN, Y., H. MÉCHOULAN & R.H. POPKIN (eds.). *Menasseh Ben Israel and His World*. 1989. ISBN 90 04 09114 9
16. BOS, A.P. *Cosmic and Meta-Cosmic Theology in Aristotle's Lost Dialogues*. 1989. ISBN 90 04 09155 6
17. KATZ, D.S. & J.I. ISRAEL (eds.). *Sceptics, Millenarians and Jews*. 1990. ISBN 90 04 09160 2
18. DALES, R.C. *Medieval Discussions of the Eternity of the World*. 1990. ISBN 90 04 09215 3
19. CRAIG, W.L. *Divine Foreknowledge and Human Freedom*. The Coherence of Theism: Omniscience. 1991. ISBN 90 04 09250 1
20. OTTEN, W. *The Anthropology of Johannes Scottus Eriugena*. 1991. ISBN 90 04 09302 8
21. ÅKERMAN, S. *Queen Christina of Sweden and Her Circle*. The Transformation of a Seventeenth-Century Philosophical Libertine. 1991. ISBN 90 04 09310 9
22. POPKIN, R.H. *The Third Force in Seventeenth-Century Thought*. 1992. ISBN 90 04 09324 9
23. DALES, R.C & O. ARGERAMI (eds.). *Medieval Latin Texts on the Eternity of the World*. 1990. ISBN 90 04 09376 1

24. STROLL, M. *Symbols as Power*. The Papacy Following the Investiture Contest. 1991. ISBN 90 04 09374 5
25. FARAGO, C.J. *Leonardo da Vinci's 'Paragone'*. A Critical Interpretation with a New Edition of the Text in the *Codex Urbinas*. 1992. ISBN 90 04 09415 6
26. JONES, R. *Learning Arabic in Renaissance Europe*. Forthcoming. ISBN 90 04 09451 2
27. DRIJVERS, J.W. *Helena Augusta*. The Mother of Constantine the Great and the Legend of Her Finding of the True Cross. 1992. ISBN 90 04 09435 0
28. BOUCHER, W.I. *Spinoza in English*. A Bibliography from the Seventeenth-Century to the Present. 1991. ISBN 90 04 09499 7
29. McINTOSH, C. *The Rose Cross and the Age of Reason*. Eighteenth-Century Rosicrucianism in Central Europe and its Relationship to the Enlightenment. 1992. ISBN 90 04 09502 0
30. CRAVEN, K. *Jonathan Swift and the Millennium of Madness*. The Information Age in Swift's *A Tale of a Tub*. 1992. ISBN 90 04 09524 1
31. BERKVENS-STEVELINCK, C., H. BOTS, P.G. HOFTIJZER & O.S. LANK-HORST (eds.). *Le Magasin de l'Univers. The Dutch Republic as the Centre of the European Book Trade*. Papers Presented at the International Colloquium, held at Wassenaar, 5-7 July 1990. 1992. ISBN 90 04 09493 8
32. GRIFFIN, JR., M.I.J. *Latitudinarianism in the Seventeenth-Century Church of England*. Annotated by R.H. Popkin. Edited by L. Freedman. 1992. ISBN 90 04 09653 1
33. WES, M.A. *Classics in Russia 1700-1855*. Between two Bronze Horsemen. 1992. ISBN 90 04 09664 7
34. BULHOF, I.N. *The Language of Science*. A Study in the Relationship between Literature and Science in the Perspective of a Hermeneutical Ontology. With a Case Study in Darwin's *The Origin of Species*. 1992. ISBN 90 04 09644 2
35. LAURSEN, J.C. *The Politics of Skepticism in the Ancients, Montaigne, Hume and Kant*. 1992. ISBN 90 04 09459 8
36. COHEN, E. *The Crossroads of Justice*. Law and Culture in Late Medieval France. 1993. ISBN 90 04 09569 1
37. POPKIN, R.H. & A.J. VANDERJAGT (eds.). *Scepticism and Irreligion in the Seventeenth and Eighteenth Centuries*. 1993. ISBN 90 04 09596 9
38. MAZZOCCO, A. *Linguistic Theories in Dante and the Humanists*. Studies of Language and Intellectual History in Late Medieval and Early Renaissance Italy. 1993. ISBN 90 04 09702 3
39. KROOK, D. *John Sergeant and His Circle*. A Study of Three Seventeenth-Century English Aristotelians. Edited with an Introduction by B.C. Southgate. 1993. ISBN 90 04 09756 2
40. AKKERMAN, F., G.C. HUISMAN & A.J. VANDERJAGT (eds.). *Wessel Gansfort (1419-1489) and Northern Humanism*. 1993. ISBN 90 04 09857 7
41. COLISH, M.L. *Peter Lombard*. 2 volumes. 1994. ISBN 90 04 09859 3 (Vol. 1), ISBN 90 04 09860 7 (Vol. 2), ISBN 90 04 09861 5 (Set)
42. VAN STRIEN, C.D. *British Travellers in Holland During the Stuart Period*. Edward Browne and John Locke as Tourists in the United Provinces. 1993. ISBN 90 04 09482 2
43. MACK, P. *Renaissance Argument*. Valla and Agricola in the Traditions of Rhetoric and Dialectic. 1993. ISBN 90 04 09879 8
44. DA COSTA, U. *Examination of Pharisaic Traditions*. Supplemented by SEMUEL DA SILVA's *Treatise on the Immortality of the Soul*. Tratado da immortalidade da alma. Translation, Notes and Introduction by H.P. Salomon & I.S.D. Sassoon. 1993. ISBN 90 04 09923 9
45. MANNS, J.W. *Reid and His French Disciples*. Aesthetics and Metaphysics. 1994. ISBN 90 04 09942 5
46. SPRUNGER, K.L. *Trumpets from the Tower*. English Puritan Printing in the Netherlands, 1600-1640. 1994. ISBN 90 04 09935 2
47. RUSSELL, G.A. (ed.). *The 'Arabick' Interest of the Natural Philosophers in Seventeenth-Century England*. 1994. ISBN 90 04 09888 7
48. SPRUIT, L. Species intelligibilis: *From Perception to Knowledge*. Volume I: Classical Roots and Medieval Discussions. 1994. ISBN 90 04 09883 6

49. SPRUIT, L. *Species intelligibilis: From Perception to Knowledge*. Volume II: Renaissance Controversies, Later Scholasticism, and the Elimination of the Intelligible Species in Modern Philosophy. 1995. ISBN 90 04 10396 1

50. HYATTE, R. *The Arts of Friendship*. The Idealization of Friendship in Medieval and Early Renaissance Literature. 1994. ISBN 90 04 10018 0

51. CARRÉ, J. (ed.). *The Crisis of Courtesy*. Studies in the Conduct-Book in Britain, 1600-1900. 1994. ISBN 90 04 10005 9

52. BURMAN, T.E. *Religious Polemic and the Intellectual History of the Mozarabs, 1050-1200*. 1994. ISBN 90 04 09910 7

53. HORLICK, A.S. *Patricians, Professors, and Public Schools*. The Origins of Modern Educational Thought in America. 1994. ISBN 90 04 10054 7

54. MacDONALD, A.A., M. LYNCH & I.B. COWAN (eds.). *The Renaissance in Scotland*. Studies in Literature, Religion, History and Culture Offered to John Durkan. 1994. ISBN 90 04 10097 0

55. VON MARTELS, Z. (ed.). *Travel Fact and Travel Fiction*. Studies on Fiction, Literary Tradition, Scholarly Discovery and Observation in Travel Writing. 1994. ISBN 90 04 10112 8

56. PRANGER, M.B. *Bernard of Clairvaux and the Shape of Monastic Thought*. Broken Dreams. 1994. ISBN 90 04 10055 5

57. VAN DEUSEN, N. *Theology and Music at the Early University*. The Case of Robert Grosseteste and Anonymous IV. 1994. ISBN 90 04 10059 8

58. WARNEKE, S. *Images of the Educational Traveller in Early Modern England*. 1994. ISBN 90 04 10126 8

59. BIETENHOLZ, P.G. *Historia and Fabula*. Myths and Legends in Historical Thought from Antiquity to the Modern Age. 1994. ISBN 90 04 10063 6

60. LAURSEN, J.C. (ed.). *New Essays on the Political Thought of the Huguenots of the* Refuge. 1995. ISBN 90 04 09986 7

61. DRIJVERS, J.W. & A.A. MacDONALD (eds.). *Centres of Learning*. Learning and Location in Pre-Modern Europe and the Near East. 1995. ISBN 90 04 10193 4

62. JAUMANN, H. *Critica*. Untersuchungen zur Geschichte der Literaturkritik zwischen Quintilian und Thomasius. 1995. ISBN 90 04 10276 0

63. HEYD, M. *"Be Sober and Reasonable."* The Critique of Enthusiasm in the Seven-teenth and Early Eighteenth Centuries. 1995. ISBN 90 04 10118 7

64. OKENFUSS, M.J. *The Rise and Fall of Latin Humanism in Early-Modern Russia*. Pagan Authors, Ukrainians, and the Resiliency of Muscovy. 1995. ISBN 90 04 10331 7

65. DALES, R.C. *The Problem of the Rational Soul in the Thirteenth Century*. 1995. ISBN 90 04 10296 5

66. VAN RULER, J.A. *The Crisis of Causality*. Voetius and Descartes on God, Nature and Change. 1995. ISBN 90 04 10371 6

67. SHEHADI, F. *Philosophies of Music in Medieval Islam*. 1995. ISBN 90 04 10128 4

68. GROSS-DIAZ, T. *The Psalms Commentary of Gilbert of Poitiers*. From *Lectio Divina* to the Lecture Room. 1996. ISBN 90 04 10211 6

69. VAN BUNGE, W. & W. KLEVER (eds.). *Disguised and Overt Spinozism around 1700*. 1996. ISBN 90 04 10307 4

70. FLORIDI, L. *Scepticism and the Foundation of Epistemology*. A Study in the Meta-logical Fallacies. 1996. ISBN 90 04 10533 6

71. FOUKE, D. *The Enthusiastical Concerns of Dr. Henry More*. Religious Meaning and the Psychology of Delusion. 1997. ISBN 90 04 10600 6

72. RAMELOW, T. *Gott, Freiheit, Weltenwahl*. Der Ursprung des Begriffes der besten aller möglichen Welten in der Metaphysik der Willensfreiheit zwischen Antonio Perez S.J. (1599-1649) und G.W. Leibniz (1646-1716). 1997. ISBN 90 04 10641 3

73. STONE, H.S. *Vico's Cultural History*. The Production and Transmission of Ideas in Naples, 1685-1750. 1997. ISBN 90 04 10650 2

74. STROLL, M. *The Medieval Abbey of Farfa*. Target of Papal and Imperial Ambitions. 1997. ISBN 90 04 10704 5

75. HYATTE, R. *The Prophet of Islam in Old French:* The Romance of Muhammad *(1258) and* The Book of Muhammad's Ladder *(1264)*. English Translations, With an Introduction. 1997. ISBN 90 04 10709 2

76. JESTICE, P.G. *Wayward Monks and the Religious Revolution of the Eleventh Century.* 1997. ISBN 90 04 10722 3
77. VAN DER POEL, M. *Cornelius Agrippa, The Humanist Theologian and His Declamations.* 1997. ISBN 90 04 10756 8
78. SYLLA, E. & M. McVAUGH (eds.). *Texts and Contexts in Ancient and Medieval Science.* Studies on the Occasion of John E. Murdoch's Seventieth Birthday. 1997.
ISBN 90 04 10823 8
79. BINKLEY, P. (ed.). *Pre-Modern Encyclopaedic Texts.* 1997. ISBN 90 04 10830 0
80. KLAVER, J.M.I. *Geology and Religious Sentiment.* The Effect of Geological Discoveries on English Society and Literature between 1829 and 1859. 1997.
ISBN 90 04 10882 3
81. INGLIS, J. *Spheres of Philosophical Inquiry and the Historiography of Medieval Philosophy.* 1998. ISBN 90 04 10843 2
82. McCALLA, A. *A Romantic Historiosophy.* The Philosophy of History of Pierre-Simon Ballanche. 1998. ISBN 90 04 10967 6
83. VEENSTRA, J.R. *Magic and Divination at the Courts of Burgundy and France.* Text and Context of Laurens Pignon's *Contre les devineurs* (1411). 1998. ISBN 90 04 10925 0
84. WESTERMAN, P.C. *The Disintegration of Natural Law Theory.* Aquinas to Finnis. 1998. ISBN 90 04 10999 4
85. GOUWENS, K. *Remembering the Renaissance.* Humanist Narratives of the Sack of Rome. 1998. ISBN 90 04 10969 2
86. SCHOTT, H. & J. ZINGUER (Hrsg.). *Paracelsus und seine internationale Rezeption in der frühen Neuzeit.* Beiträge zur Geschichte des Paracelsismus. 1998.
ISBN 90 04 10974 9
87. ÅKERMAN, S. *Rose Cross over the Baltic.* The Spread of Rosicrucianism in Northern Europe. 1998. ISBN 90 04 11030 5
88. DICKSON, D.R. *The Tessera of Antilia.* Utopian Brotherhoods & Secret Societies in the Early Seventeenth Century. 1998. ISBN 90 04 11032 1
89. NOUHUYS, T. VAN. *The Two-Faced Janus.* The Comets of 1577 and 1618 and the Decline of the Aristotelian World View in the Netherlands. 1998.
ISBN 90 04 11204 9
90. MUESSIG, C. (ed.). *Medieval Monastic Preaching.* 1998. ISBN 90 04 10883 1
91. FORCE, J.E. & D.S. KATZ (eds.). *"Everything Connects": In Conference with Richard H. Popkin.* Essays in His Honor. 1999. ISBN 90 04 110984
92. DEKKER, K. *The Origins of Old Germanic Studies in the Low Countries.* 1999.
ISBN 90 04 11031 3
93. ROUHI, L. *Mediation and Love.* A Study of the Medieval Go-Between in Key Romance and Near-Eastern Texts. 1999. ISBN 90 04 11268 5
94. AKKERMAN, F., A. VANDERJAGT & A. VAN DER LAAN (eds.). *Northern Humanism between 1469 and 1625.* 1999. ISBN 90 04 11314 2
95. TRUMAN, R.W. *Spanish Treatises on Government, Society and Religion in the Time of Philip II.* The 'de regimine principum' and Associated Traditions. 1999.
ISBN 90 04 11379 7
96. NAUTA, L. & A. VANDERJAGT (eds.) *Demonstration and Imagination.* Essays in the History of Science and Philosophy Presented to John D. North. 1999.
ISBN 90 04 11468 8
97. BRYSON, D. *Queen Jeanne and the Promised Land.* Dynasty, Homeland, Religion and Violence in Sixteenth-Century France. 1999. ISBN 90 04 11378 9
98. GOUDRIAAN, A. *Philosophische Gotteserkenntnis bei Suárez und Descartes im Zusammenhang mit der niederländischen reformierten Theologie und Philosophie des 17. Jahrhunderts.* 1999. ISBN 90 04 11627 3
99. HEITSCH, D.B. *Practising Reform in Montaigne's Essais.* 2000.
ISBN 90 04 11630 3
100. KARDAUN, M. & J. SPRUYT (eds.). *The Winged Chariot.* Collected Essays on Plato and Platonism in Honour of L.M. de Rijk. 2000. ISBN 90 04 11480 7

101. WHITMAN, J. (ed.), *Interpretation and Allegory:* Antiquity to the Modern Period. 2000. ISBN 90 04 11039 9

102. JACQUETTE, D., *David Hume's Critique of Infinity.* 2000. ISBN 90 04 11649 4

103. BUNGE, W. VAN. *From Stevin to Spinoza.* An Essay on Philosophy in the Seventeenth-Century Dutch Republic. 2001. ISBN 90 04 12217 6

104. GIANOTTI, T., *Al-Ghazālī's Unspeakable Doctrine of the Soul.* Unveiling the Esoteric Psychology and Eschatology of the Ihyā. 2001. ISBN 90 04 12083 1

105. SAYGIN, S., *Humphrey, Duke of Gloucester (1390-1447) and the Italian Humanists.* 2002. ISBN 90 04 12015 7

106. BEJCZY, I., *Erasmus and the Middle Ages.* The Historical Consciousness of a Christian Humanist. 2001. ISBN 90 04 12218 4

107. BRANN, N.L. *The Debate over the Origin of Genius during the Italian Renaissance.* The Theories of Supernatural Frenzy and Natural Melancholy in Accord and in Conflict on the Threshold of the Scientific Revolution. 2002. ISBN 90 04 12362 8

108. ALLEN, M.J.B. & V. REES with M. DAVIES. (eds.), *Marsilio Ficino: His Theology, His Philosophy, His Legacy.* 2002. ISBN 90 04 11855 1

109. SANDY, G., *The Classical Heritage in France.* 2002. ISBN 90 04 11916 7

110. SCHUCHARD, M.K., *Restoring the Temple of Vision.* Cabalistic Freemasonry and Stuart Culture. 2002. ISBN 90 04 12489 6

111. EIJNATTEN, J. VAN. *Liberty and Concord in the United Provinces.* Religious Toleration and the Public in the Eighteenth-Century Netherlands. 2003. ISBN 90 04 12843 3

112. BOS, A.P. *The Soul and Its Instrumental Body.* A Reinterpretation of Aristotle's Philosophy of Living Nature. 2003. ISBN 90 04 13016 0

113. LAURSEN, J.C. & J. VAN DER ZANDE (eds.). *Early French and German Defenses of Liberty of the Press.* Elie Luzac's *Essay on Freedom of Expression* (1749) and Carl Friedrich Bahrdt's *On Liberty of the Press and its Limits* (1787) *in English Translation.* 2003. ISBN 90 04 13017 9

114. POTT, S., M. MULSOW & L. DANNEBERG (eds.). *The Berlin Refuge 1680-1780.* Learning and Science in European Context. 2003. ISBN 90 04 12561 2

115. GERSH, S. & B. ROEST (eds.). *Medieval and Renaissance Humanism.* Rhetoric, Repre-sentation and Reform. 2003. ISBN 90 04 13274 0

116. LENNON, T.M. (ed.). *Cartesian Views.* Papers presented to Richard A. Watson. 2003. ISBN 90 04 13299 6

117. VON MARTELS, Z. & A. VANDERJAGT (eds.). *Pius II – 'El Più Expeditivo Pontefice'.* Selected Studies on Aeneas Silvius Piccolomini (1405-1464). 2003. ISBN 90 04 13190 6

118. GOSMAN, M., A. MACDONALD & A. VANDERJAGT (eds.). *Princes and Princely Culture 1450–1650.* Volume One. 2003. ISBN 90 04 13572 3

119. LEHRICH, C.I. *The Language of Demons and Angels.* Cornelius Agrippa's Occult Philosophy. 2003. ISBN 90 04 13574 X

120. BUNGE, W. VAN (ed.). *The Early Enlightenment in the Dutch Republic, 1650–1750.* Selected Papers of a Conference held at the Herzog August Bibliothek, Wolfen-büttel 22–23 March 2001. 2003. ISBN 90 04 13587 1

121. ROMBURGH, S. VAN, *"For My Worthy Freind Mr Franciscus Junius."* An Edition of the Correspondence of Francis Junius F.F. (1591-1677). 2004. ISBN 90 04 12880 8

122. MULSOW, M. & R.H. POPKIN (eds.). *Secret Conversions to Judaism in Early Modern Europe.* 2004. ISBN 90 04 12883 2

123. GOUDRIAAN, K., J. VAN MOOLENBROEK & A. TERVOORT (eds.). *Educa-tion and Learning in the Netherlands, 1400-1600.* 2004. ISBN 90 04 13644 4

124. PETRINA, A. *Cultural Politics in Fifteenth-Century England: The Case of Humphrey, Duke of Gloucester.* 2004. ISBN 90 04 13713 0

125. SCHUURMAN, P. *Ideas, Mental Faculties and Method.* The Logic of Ideas of Descartes and Locke and Its Reception in the Dutch Republic, 1630–1750. 2004. ISBN 90 04 13716 5

126. BOCKEN, I. *Conflict and Reconciliation: Perspectives on Nicholas of Cusa.* 2004. ISBN 90 04 13826 9
127. OTTEN, W. *From Paradise to Paradigm.* A Study of Twelfth-Century Humanism. 2004. ISBN 90 04 14061 1
128. VISSER, A.S.Q. *Joannes Sambucus and the Learned Image.* The Use of the Emblem in Late-Renaissance Humanism. 2005. ISBN 90 04 13866 8
129. MOOIJ, J.J.A. *Time and Mind.* History of a Philosophical Problem. 2005. ISBN 90 04 14152 9
130. BEJCZY, I.P. & R.G. NEWHAUSER (eds.). *Virtue and Ethics in the Twelfth Century.* 2005. ISBN 90 04 14327 0
131. FISHER, S. *Pierre Gassendi's Philosophy and Science.* Atomism for Empiricists. 2005. ISBN 90 04 11996 5
132. WILSON, S.A. *Virtue Reformed.* Rereading Jonathan Edwards's Ethics. 2005. ISBN 90 04 14300 9
133. KIRCHER, T. *The Poet's Wisdom.* The Humanists, the Church, and the Formation of Philosophy in the Early Renaissance. 2005. ISBN 90 04 14637 7
134. MULSOW, M. & J. ROHLS (eds.). *Socinianism and Arminianism.* Antitrinitarians, Calvinists and Cultural Exchange in Seventeenth-Century Europe. 2005. ISBN 90 04 14715 2
135. RIETBERGEN, P. *Power and Religion in Baroque Rome.* Barberini Cultural Policies. 2006. ISBN 90 04 14893 0
136. CELENZA, C. & K. GOUWENS (eds.). *Humanism and Creativity in the Renaissance.* Essays in Honor of Ronald G. Witt. 2006. ISBN 90 04 14907 4
137. AKKERMAN, F. & P. STEENBAKKERS (eds.). *Spinoza to the Letter.* Studies in Words, Texts and Books. 2005. ISBN 90 04 14946 5
138. FINKELSTEIN, A. *The Grammar of Profit: The Price Revolution in Intellectual Context.* 2006. ISBN 90 04 14958 9
139. ITTERSUM, M.J. VAN. *Profit and Principle.* Hugo Grotius, Natural Rights Theories and the Rise of Dutch Power in the East Indies, 1595-1615. 2006. ISBN 90 04 14979 1
140. KLAVER, J.M.I. *The Apostle of the Flesh: A Critical Life of Charles Kingsley.* 2006. ISBN-13: 978-90-04-15128-4 , ISBN-10: 90-04-15128-1
141. HIRVONEN, V., T.J. HOLOPAINEN & M. TUOMINEN (eds.). *Mind and Modality.* Studies in the History of Philosophy in Honour of Simo Knuuttila. 2006. ISBN-13: 978-90-04-15144-4, ISBN-10: 90-04-15144-3
142. DAVENPORT, A. *Descartes's Theory of Action.* 2006. ISBN-13: 978-90-04-15205-2, ISBN-10: 90-04-15205-9